Native North Americans

an Ethnohistorical Approach

edited by

Daniel L. Boxberger

Western Washington University

KENDALL/HUNT PUBLISHING COMPANY

2460 Kerper Boulevard P.O. Box 539 Dubuque, Iowa 52004-0539

Cover drawing by Linda Robins Clark.
Johnson Reprint Source of Curtis North
American Indian photographs.

Contents

Preface

This book grew out of my need for a text for my course on Native North Americans that I teach to approximately 150 students each quarter at Western Washington University. While there are numerous texts available for such a course, and most of them very good, I nonetheless was unable to find one that suited all of my needs. First of all, most texts I have used tended to gloss over or ignore completely the Great Basin and Plateau areas. Since I have a special interest in these two areas I was annoyed that few texts even dealt with these groups at all. Secondly, my course takes a strong ethnohistorical focus and therefore I wished for a text that would take a similar approach. Too often North Americanists tend to get caught in the mode of attempting to reconstruct the "traditional" culture. In my view this is misguided and we must face the fact directly that Native North Americans are dynamic changing cultures and need to be looked at not in the context of their "pristine" existence but in the context of their relationships with the dominant societies in North America. To ignore the fact that Native people are a part of the overall complex whole of North American culture is to do them a disservice. Last of all, I tend to rearrange my courses every term and I find that textbooks are rarely organized in such a manner that accommodates this. Rarely, if ever, do I organize my course in the same way a text is organized anyway. Therefore this text was designed so that each chapter can stand alone. They can be read in any order and therefore the instructor can begin or end with any area they choose.

When Mariel Damaskin of Kendall/Hunt approached me with the idea of doing a textbook on Native North America I was hesitant. Although I discuss each of the ten culture areas in my course I did not feel confident that I could write a chapter on each that would pass the scrutiny of experts in those areas. Therefore we thought that an approach that would work best would be one that incorporated works from specialists in each of the culture areas. Contributors were sought that were outstanding scholars in their area and that have demonstrated an interest in the ethnohistorical approach to understanding Native North American societies. We believe that the result is a text that is both useful as a teaching tool and as a statement of the anthropological approach to the history of Native North Americans.

The authors would like to acknowledge some of the people who helped put this book together. They include Samuel Proctor, Steven Morin, Eugene R. Anderson, Jr., Sylvia M. Broadbent, Mark Q. Sutton, R. E. Taylor, Philip J. Wilke, Donald R. Tuohy, Richard O. Clemmer-Smith, Maria Billings and Janice Harper.

Introduction

This textbook is designed to accompany a general course on the Native cultures of North America. We must bear in mind, however, that the North American continent was (and is) inhabited by a wide variety of indigenous cultures. When Columbus sailed into the Caribbean some five hundred years ago he encountered societies the likes of which Europeans had never imagined. Here were cultures that in many ways were more sophisticated then the European culture that "discovered" them. Here were cultures that had domesticated dozens of useful plants that were totally unknown to Europeans, Asians and Africans. Here were cultures that developed civilizations independent of Old World influence. Columbus called them "Indios" and the appellation has stuck. But they all had names for themselves. They were the Inuit, the Lakota, the Tohono O'odham, the Dene, and the Seneca, just to name a few. While the general public may consider them all "Indians," they are as different from one another as the British and Chinese. In order to be able to talk about such a large and diverse group of people anthropologists have developed the concept of "culture area" and have classified the Native people of North America (north of Mexico) into ten groups.

A culture area is simply a geographical area occupied by a number of people whose lifestyles show a significant degree of similarity with one another and at the same time show a significant degree of dissimilarity with the lifestyles of people of other such areas. In theory the recognition of a culture area must be based on a representative sample of all aspects of the cultures considered—ultimately it is a statistical problem—but usually working definitions are based on other means—primarily intuition.

The concept of culture area has changed over the years. The anthropologist Clark Wissler in his 1917 book *The American Indian* lumped different tribes together based on their dominant food source. So Native cultures along the Northwest Coast and the Columbia Plateau were subsumed under the "Salmon Area"; and the people of the Northeast and Southeast were the "Eastern Maize Area". While this was a useful concept for understanding the relationship between human cultures and their subsistence base, it ignored some important differences between groups within the areas.

In his 1939 book *Cultural and Natural Areas of Native North America*, the anthropologist Alfred L. Kroeber noted that there was a striking correspondence between the physiographic regions of the geographer and the cultural regions of the anthropologist. Kroeber refined the concept of culture area and divided North America into the culture areas that are still generally in use by North Americanists today. While the concept of culture area has been explored since (for example Harold Driver in his 1961 book *Indians of North America*) the areas outlined by Kroeber have withstood the test of time. The ten culture areas that are explored in this book roughly correspond to the culture areas of Kroeber

Culture Areas of North America

and the culture area boundaries in use by the Smithsonian Institution in their ongoing project the *Handbook of North American Indians.*

The concept of culture area was perhaps best defined by Kroeber when he said that it is a "region which has a relatively similar way of living common to its component socio-economic systems and cultures." Culture area is a useful devise for classification and discussion. It allows us to talk about a large number of distinct groups in general terms. We must not lose sight of the fact though that there is considerable variation within culture areas as well as between culture areas. Even though we may lump several groups together for purposes of discussion we have to remember that each Native American culture is unique, with its own language, its own traditions and its own territory. The ten areas we will explore in this book are the Arctic; the Subarctic; the Northeast; the Southeast; the Plains: the Southwest; the California; the Great Basin; the Plateau; and the Northwest Coast. In addition chapters that discuss the prehistory of North America and the contemporary issues that are of concern to Native communities are included.

This text takes an ethnohistorical approach to the study of the Native people of North America. The term "ethnohistory" usually refers to the use of historical data to conduct anthropological research. We believe that in order to understand the situation of contemporary Native people we must first understand the historical factors that have shaped their societies. The ethnohistorical approach allows us to carry out our anthropological research in a manner that is historically informed. Therefore we must not only consider aspects of traditional ethnography but we must also consider the impact of the dominant society on Native people and the particular circumstances that have had an effect on their lives. For all too long anthropologists have been overly concerned with the attempt to recreate the Native cultures as they existed prior to White contact. While this approach has its use, it ignores much of the change Native societies have experienced and many of the factors of social dynamics that can be observed in any society. Hopefully, what we will do in this text is make the student aware that simply because Native people no longer live a lifestyle like that of their ancestors it does not make them any less interesting to those of us who study human behavior.

Each of the ten chapters that discusses a particular culture area is accompanied by a map which places some of the groups mentioned in the text in geographical context. We feel it is important to know where Native groups are located as well as something about them.

Both the chapter on prehistory (Chapter 1) and the chapter on contemporary issues (Chapter 12) discuss Native Americans in more general terms. The prehistory chapter gives us an overview of how archaeologists have reconstructed the history of North America before there were written records. The contemporary issues chapter outlines some of the issues of general concern to Native people in Canada and the Untied States as we all prepare to enter the twenty-first century.

Chapter 1

North American Prehistory

Molly Raymond Mignon
Western Washington University

Archaeological knowledge of the prehistory of North America has increased at an almost exponential rate during recent years. Yet, with the exception of a few well-studied areas, the prehistory of North America remains largely unknown. This seeming paradox becomes less puzzling when we consider the size of the North American continent in relation to the proportion of it explored by archaeologists up to the present time.

This chapter will review and broadly summarize current knowledge concerning North American prehistory, from the first migrations into a vast, unpopulated continent during the epoch of major glacial advances, to the first recorded contacts between the original migrants' descendants and European settlers many millenia later. In addition, a brief account will be given of the development of American archaeology, and of some major archaeological discoveries contributing to current tentative reconstructions of the manner in which this monumental journey may have taken place; the likely homeland of those who accomplished it; and its permanent consequences for members of the human species, both past and present.

Migrations: Theories, Routes and Time Frames

Ever since Columbus's discoveries, the origins of America's earliest inhabitants has been a subject of interest and conjecture, both to scholars and to the general public. A variety of imaginative theories have attempted to account for the origins of the American Indians since the early sixteenth century. Some of these have traced their homeland to the ''Lost Continent of Atlantis''; others have identified them as survivors of the lost tribes of Israel (Wauchope 1962). A more rational suggestion, first offered by Father Jose de Acosta in 1590, is that the Amerindians' ancestors reached America by migrating from Europe or Asia, via land bridges that may have existed in the past (Beals 1957). The one point of agreement shared by all such theories is that the New World's first inhabitants arrived as the result of migration from some Old World location.

In the twentieth century, studies carried out by archaeologists, geologists and anthropologists have provided some support for Father Acosta's idea, pointing to Asia as the original homeland of native Americans and Bering Strait as the location of the principal land bridge. Geologists have determined that a broad expanse of land connecting Siberia and North America indeed existed periodically in the past, when sea levels dropped as Pleistocene ice sheets trapped much of the oceans' volume in glacial ice sheets. The resulting isthmus of 'Beringia', more than a thousand miles wide at its maximum, would have afforded a natural route for early migrants of all species, including man.

Establishing a time-frame for the earliest migrations into North America has proved to be a more difficult problem. Until quite recently, the earliest accepted date for man in the New World was 12,500 years ago, the approximate date assigned to the earliest Clovis points. While this is now widely regarded as being too late, the matter is far from resolved. The fact that all early human remains found in the Americas are those of modern man (*Homo sapiens sapiens*) indicates a period of migration no earlier than about 50,000 years ago. This date is consistent with the presence of Asian characteristics in all early human remains so far discovered in the New World. Since such ethnic differences between human groups are believed to have originated roughly 70,000–50,000 year ago, the appearance of "Asian" traits would correspond with the earliest known human migrations out of Southeast Asia that led to the peopling of Australia and the Pacific islands at about this time. The earliest populations movements into the Americas may also have taken place within this time span (Shutler 1985:121). While some migration models place humans in North America as early as 250,000 years ago, there is currently no firm evidence to support such an early date.

Other questions concerning the North Americans' origins center on the routes and transportation methods employed in their long journey. Some investigators have postulated that an ice-free corridor existed during much of the Pleistocene, a narrow unglaciated strip of land along the eastern slope of the Canadian Rockies between the advancing Cordilleran (western) and Laurentide (eastern) ice sheets. Those who hold this view maintain that humans could have migrated southward into the North American interior after crossing from Asia via the Beringian land bridge, and subsequently occupied much of the area north of Mexico throughout the Pleistocene, even during glacial maxima. Archaeological evidence of human hunters in North America during the Pleistocene, who appear to have stalked the now-extinct Pleistocene big game fauna that included the woolly mammoth, has been recovered in the form of fluted projectile points. Presumably these were manufactured for making spears used in hunting these large mammals.

Knut Fladmark (Fladmark 1979, 1983) has argued from paleoenvironmental evidence that an ice-free corridor, if it indeed existed, would have presented a harsh, frigid environment, often flooded, and devoid of biological resources needed for food. Fladmark suggests an alternative marine-oriented migration scheme, with early Asians migrating along the coastlines of northeastern Asia, Beringia, and finally North America in a series of relatively short voyages, perhaps separated by fairly long periods of occupation of intervening coastal and island areas. Fladmark notes that a maritime people could have accomplished this, using only small, technologically simple watercraft, similar to those employed by Asian migrants to the Pacific Islands at roughly the same time. Such people would have readily adapted to coastline and island environments. The unglaciated refugia these offered would have been a far more hospitable home for humans during glacial maxima than the putative ice-free corridor. Although the logic of this argument is indisputable, there is unfortunately no archaeological evidence to document such a coastal migration. The dramatic rise in sea level following the melting of the glacial ice flooded the Pleistocene coastline of North America, inundating any remaining evidence of early migrant occupations that may lie beneath the sea on the continental shelf.

Some other models seeking to account for the initial human occupation of North America are based upon linguistic evidence. Lexicostatistical methods developed by Maurice Swadesh have been applied in attempts to date the linguistic divergence of native American populations from earlier parent-language groups (Swadesh 1962, 1964). Such models are based on the assumption that basic vocabularies change through time at a fixed, predictable rate. While such studies have been useful in reconstructing possible migration routes followed by early settlers, as well as suggesting a sequence of several major waves of migration, their principal underlying assumption of a constant rate of linguistic change has not been satisfactorily demonstrated, making conclusions based upon this method somewhat speculative (Ehret 1976; Kinkade and Powell 1976).

Physical anthropologists have attempted to document early migrations through the comparative study of certain human biological traits, in both living populations and in skeletal remains of early North Americans. Such studies consider morphological characteristics of skeletal structures, as well as dental traits and blood group frequencies. It is assumed that statistical frequencies of such traits will, given a sufficiently large sample, permit investigators to determine the degree of genetic relatedness between living population groups, such as those of North America and Asia, as well as their relative genetic distance from earlier groups that may have been ancestral to both (Turner 1983). However, rates of change in gene frequencies reflected in variations of gross physical traits have not been sufficiently well established to provide data supporting migration patterns (Szathmary 1979). Another factor complicating such studies as these is the considerable degree of ethnic mixing that has occurred in New World populations since the time of European contact.

Other studies have attempted to trace the Old World affiliations of native Americans by measuring frequencies of various kinds of skeletal pathology (Stewart 1979). These, however, have been limited by the absence of comparative skeletal data from Asia. In addition, they share with genetic distance studies the handicap of an insufficient data base from which to make valid generalizations.

In all, the evidence documenting the most important migration in human history is extremely tenuous. Drawing firm conclusions about its beginnings, as well as obtaining satisfactory answers to questions concerning its duration, major and secondary routes followed during its course, alternative methods of transportation that may have been used, and the adaptive patterns of early migrants must await the accumulation of more evidence—anthropological, archaeological, and linguistic—than is currently available.

Many theoretical schemes seeking to explain the initial appearance of humans in the New World have treated this phenomenon as an "event", a one-time, discrete, isolated occurrence in time; however, it is now becoming clear to researchers that the journey from Asia to North America was most likely a continuous process, comprising a series of population movements that took place over a vast period of time. Documenting such an extended phenomenon will, of course, require a great deal more evidence than would a single event. Accumulating the evidence needed to reconstruct this epochal journey remains a major goal of North American archaeologists and prehistorians.

The Paleoindians: Were There Humans in North America During the Pleistocene?

The earliest remains of human presence in North America have been characterized by archaeologists as belonging to the Paleoindian Period of cultural development, which includes cultures dating from the earliest period of human occupation up to the time that big-game hunting ceased to be the principal North American economic activity. The decline of big-game hunting is usually attributed to climatic and environmental changes occurring at the end of the Pleistocene, when the ice sheets that had formerly occupied the northern latitudes of North America melted away, sea levels rose, and the landscape began to take on its present form. These extensive environmental changes would also bring about some sweeping changes in human lifeways.

The time span of the Paleoindian era varied in different parts of the New World. Archaeological evidence appears to indicate that it ended sometime between 6000 and 7500 B.C. in most parts of North America, after the big game species on which the Paleoindians may have relied as a principal food source became extinct, requiring the adoption of the new subsistence pattern characteristic of the Archaic Period.

The characteristic artifact produced by Paleoindians was the fluted Clovis projectile point. Mounted at the head of a wooden spear, such points provided efficient weapons for killing the kinds of game that abounded in Pleistocene times. In archaeological sites, points of this type are frequently found in association with other tools that were used for processing meat, hides and bone; these include stone knives and scrapers, as well as spear points and needles made of animal bone; the latter were probably used for sewing clothing fashioned from the hides of animals whose meat was used for food.

The Paleoindian tool kit supports the supposition of a lifeway dominated by hunting. This is further reinforced by the presence of kill sites where early hunters left the butchered remains of their prey, sometimes accompanied by tools used in the butchering process. Species hunted by the Paleoindians included the mammoth, mastodon, moose-elk, and giant bison. The hunting of these animals was very likely a group effort, carried out by small bands of hunters whose cooperation permitted them to procure sufficient food for their families.

Paleoindian populations appear to have been small, mobile groups, each consisting of about 20 closely related persons, who pursued a nomadic life patterned on the migration habits of their primary prey. Certainly smaller animals were also hunted; however, it is usually assumed that large game, when available, will be pursued first, since these provide the highest nutritional return for time and effort invested in hunting. There is also evidence that the Paleoindian diet included some wild plant foods. At the Meadowcroft Rockshelter

4

site in Pennsylvania, remains of hickory nuts, acorns, cherries and other nuts and fruits were recovered from levels radiocarbon dated to between 17,000 and 10,000 B.C. Since these remains were accompanied principally by small blade tools rather than fluted projectile points, they have been considered as possible evidence for a "pre-Clovis" occupation, representing a more generalized adaptation than that displayed by the manufacturers of Clovis points (Fiedel 1987:67).

The question of pre-Clovis habitation in North America remains a matter of controversy. Evidence of this exists in a number of localities, including the Pacific Northwest, where small microblade tools resembling those produced by the Diuktai culture of Northeast Asia frequently occur in early artifact assemblages. Although very little is known about the social organization or religious beliefs of these early Americans, we can infer that these were similar to those of more recent nomadic hunting societies. Such societies are characteristically egalitarian; their religious beliefs are typically dominated by animal deities, and rituals are designed to promote good hunting and an abundance of game.

Although early remains of human activity have been reported from many locations throughout the North American continent, firmly dated material from primary, undisturbed archaeological deposits is quite rare. Skeletal remains of early North Americans are even more scarce; to date, no well-dated human physical remains older than ca. 10,000 years B.P. have been recovered. Cultural remains believed to be somewhat older than this have been found at a number of locations, although their dates have frequently been disputed.

Dating of remains from the Paleoindian period, the earliest cultural period on the American continents, remains a major problem in the study of early man in North America. Other problems include the general lack of cultural material from primary, stratified deposits, and the presence of purported "artifacts" that are often of doubtful human manufacture (MacNeish 1982). A further impediment to identifying and interpreting evidence of early human occupation is that of small sample sizes. This is a consequence of the scarcity of early cultural materials, which often occur in assemblages too small to permit meaningful statistical analysis.

It was long believed by American archaeologists that the first North Americans appeared on the scene approximately 12,000 years ago, and supported themselves by hunting the woolly mammoth, giant bison and other large Pleistocene animals now extinct. The archaeologist Paul Martin proposed a model to account for the rather abrupt disappearance of this Pleistocene megafauna, in which he attributed its extinction to "overkill" resulting from the activities of early human hunters (Martin 1982). According to this view, human populations killed more animals than could be replaced at a normal rate of reproduction for undomesticated species. This view has been criticized on a number of grounds, including the likelihood that human populations of the Pleistocene epoch could not have been sufficiently large to produce an impact of this magnitude on game resources; nor have kill sites been discovered in numbers that would support such a view. In general, archaeologists have attributed post-Pleistocene faunal extinctions to paleoenvironmental changes, which occurred as a result of the disappearance of the continental ice sheets.

The earliest well-dated human skeletal remains found in North America include a skull believed to be that of a woman, from Midland, Texas. Although radiocarbon and uranium dates placing this skull as early as 20,000 years ago have been obtained, these are contradicted by dates some 7,000 years more recent, obtained from deposits underlying the skull. A "best guess" would place the age of the Midland skull at between 9,000 and 10,000 years ago, an estimate supported by overlying deposits that included Folsom-style artifacts. The skull itself displays Asian Mongoloid characteristics (Fiedel 1987:43).

A second well-dated group of human remains was discovered in the 1960s at the Marmes Rockshelter site, located near the confluence of the Snake and Palouse rivers in southeastern Washington State. The skeletal remains were found in association with tools, including leaf-shaped points, scrapers and choppers, that suggest a typical Paleoindian hunting adaptation based upon the semi-nomadic pursuit of large game. Similar tool assemblages dating to the Paleoindian period have been recovered from several other sites in the Northwestern Plateau region near the Marmes Rockshelter, including Windust Cave and Lind Coulee. The human skeletons representing "Marmes Man" have been roughly dated in the 8700–10,000 year range B.P. (Fiedel 1987; Kirk and Daugherty 1978), placing them in the latter part of the Paleoindian period.

The earliest evidence yet found for human hunting of Pleistocene fauna in North America comes from the Manis mastodon site near Sequim, Washington. At this site, the remains of a mastodon butchered about 12,000 years ago contained a bone projectile point, embedded in a healed wound in one of the animal's ribs. This has been regarded as unquestionable evidence of human hunters in the northwestern United States as early as twelve millenia ago (Kirk and Daugherty 1978). The only lithic tool recovered at the Manis site was a cobble spall, although other chipped and broken cobbles may have been utilized as tools (Gustafson et al. 1979). What is perhaps most significant about this site is that the bone point apparently failed to kill the mastodon, since healing of the bone had occurred around the wound. The animal seems to have died later of natural causes; humans living in the vicinity may subsequently have scavenged the remains. The circumstances, plus the lack of specialized tools at the site, suggest these early North Americans were not the big-game hunters featured in the Paul Martin scenario (Martin 1982, 1984), but may have been more generally adapted, relying on smaller game species, fishing and plant collecting for the bulk of their subsistence. This pattern more closely resembles the typical North American lifeway of the Archaic period.

Other archaeological evidence documenting early human activity in North America comes from a group of sites in the Old Crow basin of the northern Yukon. These sites have yielded a number of items classified as artifacts, all of them made of bone, antler, ivory and teeth; no lithic tools have been discovered. Richard Morlan, who has worked in the Old Crow region for many years, believes that humans occupied the area beginning around 30,000 years ago, and possibly even earlier (Morlan 1984). The Old Crow sites display all of the typical problems encountered by those attempting to document early North American habitation. All the deposits are secondary; there are problems in dating, and there are serious questions about the artifactual nature of the tools recovered (Morlan and

Cinq-Mars 1982; Morlan 1984). The Old Crow material appears to support arguments for a pre-projectile point "stage" of North American cultural evolution since, like many other tool assemblages from the Northwest region, it lacks the Clovis point typical of the Plains hunters (Fiedel 1987:53).

Perhaps the best evidence for man's early presence and activity in north America is that recovered from the Meadowcroft Rockshelter in western Pennsylvania (Adovasio, et al. 1977, 1978, 1980). Although the stratigraphy and dating of this important site remain somewhat problematical, it may well yet turn out to provide the earliest firm evidence for human habitation in North American as early as 17,000 years ago.

Post-Pleistocene Adaptations: The Archaic Cultures of North America

The nature of cultural change is such that its processes are not directly observable. While it is possible to say that a given archaeological assemblage represents a particular cultural phase, period or manifestation, and that this particular entity differs from another that temporally preceded it, documenting the process of change itself is not directly possible from material evidence. Such processes must be inferred, from such evidence as changes in the relative frequencies of particular classes and styles of artifacts in successive assemblages at the same site, or at culturally similar sites within a region. While the process of change is dynamic and continuous, its material remnants "frozen" in the archaeological record are static and discrete. This requires the interpreter of such data to make an intellectual leap in order to fill in the missing data, those concerning the mechanisms of change that brought about the evolution of one culture into another, each of which can be identified from its material remains.

The transition from the Paleo-Indian cultural period in North America to the new cultural adaptation we call the Archaic was a case in point. The transformation of the old hunting culture of the Pleistocene epoch, into the very different and varied cultural manifestations of the Archaic, was doubtless a long, gradual process, comprising countless isolated events whose specific details must remain forever unknown in their particulars. Their summed effects are, of course, discernible to archaeologists, in the form of observable changes in tools, settlement patterns, dwelling remains and other material evidence of past human activity, revealing a changing pattern of adaptation leading to the new lifeway characteristic of the Archaic Period.

Since this transition was a gradual process rather than a discrete event, we cannot attach a precise date to its beginning. Archaeological manifestations of the Archaic Period begin to appear at different times in different parts of North America, and to develop with varying degrees of speed and intensity. What we *can* perceive is a pattern of archaeological features, artifacts, and relationships that mark a significant change in the ways in which humans exploited their physical environment and its resources, a change observable in the appearance of new kinds of residences, new varieties of social and family units who occupied these, new technology for getting a living, and evidence of new ideas that accompanied these sweeping changes.

The North American Archaic is characterized by a particular group of diagnostic traits, which together constitute what some Old World prehistorians have termed the "Neolithic Revolution" (Childe 1951). The most important of these is the appearance of polished stone tools. The new technology of stone grinding and polishing has been regarded as being both culturally and technologically significant everywhere in the world. Not only do these new techniques permit better-made and more efficient tools to be made to perform an expanded set of tasks; their appearance has additional significance, for in many areas this transition marks a shift in subsistence, signalling the beginning of a more intensive use of plant foods than was characteristic of the Paleoindian period. Hunting and fishing were to remain economically important throughout the Archaic, but the primary prey species pursued by Archaic and Paleoindian hunters were very different. By Archaic times, the megafauna of the Pleistocene had become extinct, leading to a greater concentration on deer and on smaller species, such as rabbit and birds. Large smooth polished grindstones, appearing at this time, indicate the use of seeds or grain kernels that require grinding to render them edible and digestible.

Where these distinctive new techniques are found, evidence for other changes is also usually present in the form of semi-permanent or permanent dwelling places, occupied by groups larger than the small family band, which had been the basic human unit of Paleoindian times. These habitation sites range from remains of temporary seasonal camps occupied by several families for a limited time, perhaps only while a particular crop or prey species was being harvested, to small clusters of semi-permanent dwellings representing the earliest hamlets.

Taken together, the complex of techniques and traits indicative of an Archaic lifeway constitute evidence of a broad-spectrum readaptation to the changed environmental conditions of the post-Pleistocene epoch. Such change was of considerable significance, involving the appearance of a new and more temperate climate with increased rainfall, and a fairly rapid rise in sea-level. Marine transgressions flooded the old Pleistocene coastline, inundating the continental shelves on the West and East coasts of North America, creating a new marine biotic zone in the resulting shoals and estuaries. This new marine environment provided a habitat for a variety of shellfish and other marine species, affording a new source of food for human populations. New food resources were of concern at this time, due to another dramatic event of the immediate post-Pleistocene period, namely the relatively sudden extinction of most of the large terrestrial mammalian species, including the mammoth, giant ground sloth, and giant bison who had supplied the mainstay of the North American Pleistocene human diet. The disappearance of these large animals forced innovations in subsistence practice upon former hunting peoples, who were now obliged to look elsewhere for their livelihood.

For all these reasons, the post-Pleistocene human readaptation was marked by an increasing diversification of subsistence activities, prompting innovations in lithic tool technology. Utilizing the resources of a variety of microenvironments, including those of offshore marine habitats and the wild grains and other plant foods occurring further inland, required a larger and more varied toolkit than the one that had served the Pleistocene big game hunters. In addition, the use of different resources scattered over a variety of environmental zones required the seasonal scheduling of specialized procurement activities (Flannery 1968). There is evidence that such activities were often combined, since seasonal encampments of enlarged human groups, who came together periodically to take advantage of ripening crops of wild fruits, nuts or grains, tend to be located where two or more microenvironmental zones intersect. This would allow the harvest of more than one food type during the same time period, promoting greater efficiency in food procurement. Camps could be located near rivers or lakes where fish were plentiful, and in a vicinity where wild tree crops were also available; if deer or other game were also present nearby, or within a day's walk, efficiency was was still further increased.

It is also likely that the larger aggregations of humans that resulted, albeit temporarily, from these seasonal activities were significant in allowing greater opportunities for interaction and exchange of ideas. Such expanded interaction would have helped pave the way for a time when large residential groups would become the norm, and the number and range of face-to-face contacts for all humans would greatly increase. Such large temporary aggregations also provided opportunities for extralocal marriages to take place, and for other kinds of interaction to develop. These probably included the formation of defense alliances and trading relationships, as well as simply increasing the scale of human contacts and broadening the social horizons of early Post-Pleistocene people. No doubt much of this interaction was of a ritualized nature, in the earliest stages, and was modeled on existing behavioral rules for interacting with kin. Relationships based upon foundations other than kinship ties do not usually exist in societies at this level of social development, since they require the definition of other kinds of social interaction that cannot exist until a greater degree of sociocultural complexity has been achieved.

Ultimately, the Archaic revolution in life patterns would result in the creation of permanent settlements, occupied by increasingly large populations whose economy was based upon food production.

A significant technical innovation of the Archaic, one that is often regarded as marking its end and signalling the beginning of the Formative Period, is the invention of pottery-making. This is in fact a whole complex of technical processes, centering around the discovery that clay, when heated to a critical temperature, becomes chemically transformed into a permanently hard, durable substance with many practical and decorative uses. Ceramic wares can also be strengthened by the addition of "temper", additional material worked into the clay before firing while it is still soft and malleable. Most potters soon discovered the advantages of this practice, utilizing a variety of temper materials, from vegetable fibers to the crushed shells of mollusks. Temper materials may provide archaeologists with information valuable for dating pottery, as well as a method of tracing the origins of trade wares from the provenience of organic materials added to the clay at the time of manufacture.

Although much of the earliest American pottery is relatively crude, some "developed" Archaic groups produced remarkably well-made ceramic wares, including figurines and other objects in addition to utilitarian vessels. One notable instance is the precocious Poverty Point culture, represented by a large number of archaeological sites in the Mississippi Valley of the southeastern United States. This culture represents one of the earliest examples of growing complexity of organization, a phenomenon that became increasingly common throughout the Archaic Period, and forms the subject of the following section of this chapter.

The Growth of Cultural Complexity in Prehistoric North America

What is cultural complexity, and why did it develop? How can it be recognized in human populations, past and present? Such questions as these are of considerable importance to anthropologists and archaeologists, and have often been addressed in the literature, but satisfactory, comprehensive answers, applicable worldwide, remain elusive (Wenke 1981).

While it is relatively easy to distinguish between simple hunter-gatherers, or even early village horticultural societies, and the high civilizations that developed in some parts of the New World, defining the time range when cultural processes leading to complexity begin to become visible is a far more subtle problem.

The identification and discussion of incipient cultural complexity requires the use of such terms and concepts as *tribe, chiefdom*, and *state* that have not yet been defined in a universally acceptable manner, much less utilized uniformly by archaeologists and prehistorians. Although such entities as tribes and chiefdoms may have no real objective existence, and are perhaps more accurately conceived as representing certain broad developmental categories along a continuum, these terms are widely used by archaeologists and anthropologists alike, and their meaning is well enough understood to justify their continued use as convenient devices for discussing and classifying social phenomena while at the same time recognizing their artificial nature (Earle 1987; Earle and Brumfiel 1987; Sanders and Webster 1979).

Some of factors that appear to be implicated in the growth of complex cultures include the appearance of larger population groups, exceeding those found among the small, family-based bands typical of hunting and gathering cultures. The growth of such larger population units has been suggested as a factor contributing to complexity, since larger human communities will require new mechanisms beyond those offered by the nuclear family for transmitting cultural information to the next generation. Robert Dunnell has suggested this need may have arisen when the amount of information needed by each individual began to exceed the amount that can most efficiently be transmitted from parent to child (Dunnell 1980). When this occurs, new means have to be developed to insure that essential cultural information is passed on and acquired by each succeeding generation.

Among the cultural entities and mechanisms that may have been developed to serve this educational function are centralized religious systems (White 1949), which can facilitate the transmission and perpetuation of religious concepts and practices through a large, and sometimes physically dispersed, population. Another possible development is that of administrative hierarchies to transmit information of a procedural or organizational nature (Flannery 1972). Nucleation of populations in urban centers will also facilitate communication, as well as concentrating a labor pool for carrying out large-scale civic projects for the benefit of an enlarged community, such as the construction of dams and irrigation works, civic and religious buildings, and roads. Ultimately, of course, formal educational institutions assumed most of this information-transmitting function.

So *size* and *scale* appear to be key factors in the development of cultural complexity: enlarged human populations occupying the same geographic area require new mechanisms for accomplishing and maintaining social integration, as well as new formalized rules for ordering human relationships. Such human relationships themselves may also become reordered and redefined in different ways. Social classes and ranked hierarchies, in which individuals occupy different positions relative to one another according to criteria that may not even exist in egalitarian societies, will come into being.

Enlarged and diversified economic activities foster the emergence of specialized occupations that create other kinds of social divisions, crosscutting those based on class and rank. With the development of government and rulership, an ideological rationale will be needed, both to justify this new organizational system and to define the mechanisms for its perpetuation. Rationales for legitimizing rulership may invoke such ideological principles as primogeniture, or even divine right.

When large groups of human beings can no longer be kept adequately informed of rules, policies and other forms of social information by informal social means, new structures must be developed. Communication specialists, whose job it is to see that necessary information is communicated with enough efficiency to allow the social machinery to function smoothly, will be needed, and an administrative bureaucracy will sometimes develop in response to this need.

When viewed in this manner, cultural complexity becomes an almost inevitable result of population expansion and growth within a limited geographic area. The condition of social and geographic circumscription that can result from this kind of situation has been invoked by Robert Carneiro as an important factor involved in the formation of states (Carneiro 1970). Such circumscription may perhaps be implicated not only in state formation, but may possibly play a causal role in the development of increasingly complex social structures at all levels of political integration we can identify in large, permanently settled human groups.

To return to the second question posed at the beginning of this section, "How do we recognize cultural complexity?", it is first necessary to distinguish between the manner in which this can be done if the subject of observation is a living society, and the options available to us if we are investigating an extinct society through its material remains. The former is relatively simple, since we can apply the criteria we have developed by directly observing the behavior of living people. Reconstructing the characteristics of vanished cultures also becomes relatively simple when contemporaneous written accounts, describing behaviors and social mechanisms, exist in the form of early ethnohistoric records. In their most complete forms, such texts can constitute a true ethnography or anthropology of the past.

Such records as these are available for limited parts of North America, in the eyewitness reports of the earliest explorers describing initial encounters with the American Indians. A notable example are the various extant accounts of the expedition of the Spanish explorer Hernando De Soto, who in 1539 began an exploratory journey through what is now the southeastern United States that spanned several years. Although De Soto died enroute, and did not leave his own account, several members of his company kept written records, some of which have come down to us. The following example provides an illustration of the degree of cultural complexity that existed among some southeastern North American Indian groups in the early sixteenth century, as well as of the value of ethnohistoric accounts of this period.

> The Governor [Hernando De Soto] . . . set out for Cutifachiqui, capturing three Indians . . . who stated that the mistress of that country had already information of the Christians, and was waiting for them. . . . After a little time the Cacica came out of the town, seated in a chair, which some principal men having borne to the bank, she entered a canoe. Over the stern was spread an awning, and in the bottom lay extended a mat where were two cushions . . . upon which she sat; and she was accompanied by her chief men, in other canoes. . . . The Cacica presented much clothing . . . and drawing from over her head a large string of pearls, she threw them about his [De Soto's] neck, exchanging with him many gracious words of friendship and courtesy. She directed that canoes should come . . . whence the Governor and his people passed to the opposite side of the river. So soon as he was lodged . . . a great many turkeys were sent to him . . . [there] were large quantities of clothing, shawls of thread, made from the bark of trees, and others of feathers, white, gray, vermilion, and yellow, rich and proper for winter . . . also many well-dressed dear-skins, of colors drawn over with designs, of which had been made shoes, stockings and hose. The Cacica, observing that the Christians valued the pearls, told the Governor that, if he should order some sepulchres . . . in the town to be searched, he would find many. . . . They examined those in the town, and found three hundred and fifty pounds weight of pearls, and figures of babies and birds made of them. (The Narrative of the Expedition of Hernando De Soto by the Gentleman of Elvas, ed. by Theodore H. Lewis; in Spanish Explorers in the Southern United States, 1528–1543, J. Franklin Jameson, ed. Charles Scribner's Sons, 1907, pp. 172–174).

This account of a first encounter by a Spanish explorer with an American Indian chieftainess, who has been identified as the Creek ruler of a chiefdom (Cotifachequi) located most probably in what is now North Carolina or possibly Georgia, gives us a significant amount of information indicative of cultural complexity. The first pertinent fact is that the group in question was headed by a ruler who was recognized as legitimate, and who was served by "principal men" who obeyed her instructions without question. She was accorded special treatment and privileges, such as being carried in a litter and transported in a cushioned boat with a protective canopy. In addition, she wore pearls, and indicated that these were commonly placed in burials (presumably of persons sharing her high status), and possessed sufficient wealth to make make generous and elaborate gifts to her visitor. This implies the likely existence of specialists (e.g., the manufacturers of the shoes and elaborate clothing mentioned, as well as creators of the works of art found in the burials). Trade with some coastal location is indicated by the pearls possessed in such great numbers. Such data further imply the presence of a high degree of organization for coordinating all these activities, of a type commonly found in developed chiefdoms. In this instance, the presence and degree of complexity are easily recognizable by direct observation and reporting of particular behaviors and material data.

Determining the presence and degree of cultural complexity from archaeological evidence alone is far more difficult, since we are confined to examining the material remains (artifacts, site features, settlement data, architectural remains, and relationships among these), which may constitute neither an accurate reflection nor an adequate data sample of the extinct society for reconstructing its characteristics. Furthermore, the archaeologist cannot determine how much of the information necessary for such reconstruction has actually been preserved in the archaeological record, relative to that which has been lost; so the picture emerging from the analysis of archaeological remains may be seriously distorted by the differential preservation of materials, as well as by unknown past behaviors involved in discarding material items, either of which may significantly affect such patterns as are perceptible in the archaeological record. Various methods of modeling alternative interpretations of archaeological data are now available, permitting the testing of hypotheses against such data, with results that have permitted development of some generalizations about the factors and processes affecting the growth of complexity.

The requirements of size and scale that seem to be pertinent to the growth of complexity have already been mentioned. In addition to certain minimum population and site sizes, cultural complexity appears to produce hierarchies, which may be observable from studying settlement patterns.

Another characteristic of complex societies is extensive trade, particularly in "luxury" goods associated with elites. Others include warfare; social differentiation, including differential access to wealth and resources; and an elaborate religious ideology, which may also function as a method of rationalizing the political and social structure. Materially this is often expressed in the production and use of significant numbers of nonutilitarian artifacts, whose chief functions may be symbolic ones that provide clues to the nature of ideology and sociopolitical interaction. These may include public architecture of monumental scale—e.g., the temple and effigy mounds built by early North American Indian populations; and ceremonial artifacts deposited in elaborate burials that reflect ascribed rather than achieved status. The rich burial given a twelve-year-old child at the site of L'Anse Amour on Belle Isle, southern Labroador, by a coastal maritime Archaic population some 7,500 years ago may be an example of the latter phenomenon (Tuck 1976). Other evidence of social differences may include settlement data documenting physical space reserved for the occupancy of elites, or of specialized occupational groups, such as potters or flintknappers.

Still other indicators of complexity that have been recovered by archaeologists include the presence of standardized systems of symbolic communication that fall short of writing. These may serve for record-keeping, or for transferring social information regarded as important through artwork, including sculptures, effigies, emblems or other abstract designs associated with particular lineages, clan groups or ruling families. It is likely that much of the symbolic information encoded in North American Indian rock art is of this nature. Rock carvings have recorded rare astronomical events. Significant repetitive events of this kind—e.g., the positions of rising or setting of planets on dates such as the spring equinox or summer solstice—are often marked by the intentional placement of public buildings in locations where sunrise or sunset on significant dates will illuminate the facade or some distinctive building feature. Such buildings may be present at the Poverty Point site in northeastern Louisiana, and at Chaco Canyon in Arizona (Brecher and Haag 1983; Cordell 1984). At Chaco Canyon, the use of architecture for calendric purposes has been regarded by some scholars as indicative of influences from Mesoamerica, where calendrics and astronomy appear to have been more highly developed than was true in most of prehistoric North America. Special-purpose structures whose primary function is to serve as calendar markers have also been observed. One such structure is the circular "woodhenge" discovered at the Mississippian capital of Cahokia, Illinois.

All these different kinds of evidence have been observed in varying degrees by archaeologists at many different North American locations, within a time frame that includes the late Archaic Period and the Formative Period that followed it. The presence of cultural complexity in North America has been documented well back into the second millenium B.C. at Poverty Point, and throughout the ensuing two thousand years, from the monumental constructions and figurine sculptures of the Poverty Point people, to the elaborate mortuary cults and long-distance trading networks of the Hopewell and Adena cultures, and the complex Northwest Coast and Mississippian chiefdoms, possibly reaching a state level of organization in the Chacoan culture of the southwestern United States (Gibson 1985; Webb 1968, 1982). Although little is yet known of the complex prehistoric societies of North America, the work of archaeologists and ethnohistorians is steadily increasing our knowledge of the accomplishments and lifeways of these early peoples and their achievements.

The Development of North American Archaeology

Archaeology as a discipline had its origins in European antiquarianism, an approach to the past rooted in historic and humanistic studies that began in the early Renaissance. To the antiquarian, the primary focus of interest is the collection of relics of the past. This interest centers upon the archaeological object, or artifact, in isolation, without reference to its original cultural context. Antiquarians in Europe amassed significant private collections of artifacts, acquired through the plundering of ancient tombs and archaeological sites, an activity that, unfortunately, still persists despite legislative efforts designed to put an end to it. The antiquarian interests of early European archaeologists reflected the largely humanistic and historic orientation European archaeology has maintained up to the present (Willey and Sabloff 1980).

Early speculations concerning the origins of native Americans are also traceable to the humanistic-antiquarian tradition. The speculative reasoning upon which such ideas were based constituted a chief method of inquiry in early New World archaeological endeavors; a significant "artifact" of this approach was the Moundbuilder theory, which attributed the construction of pyramidal and effigy mounds in the central and eastern United States to the prehistoric presence in America of an unknown civilized foreign race, presumably of Old World affiliation. Structures of the scale and complexity of the North American mounds were believed to be beyond the abilities of the "primitive" American Indians, a view that had obvious political overtones, whose influence was apparent in the Indian policies of the American government in the latter part of the nineteenth century.

In the nineteenth century, such field investigations as were conducted by American archaeologists were often motivated by the antiquarian desire to acquire ancient and beautiful objects for collections, and secondarily to produce evidence to support existing speculations about the American past. However, archaeology in North America has since its earliest beginnings displayed a more empirical emphasis than its contemporary European counterpart, and even the earliest American archaeologists began to describe and attempt to classify archaelogical finds, and to excavate in a systematic manner.

A notable early example of this characteristically American approach may be seen in the work of Thomas Jefferson, who is credited with the earliest scientific archaeological studies in North America, consisting of controlled stratigraphic excavations in an Indian mound located on his own plantation in Virginia. Although Jefferson has been called the "father of American archaeology" (Willey and Sabloff 1974:38), this title is somewhat misleading, since Jefferson's accomplishments were an isolated case that was not emulated in America for over a century after his death. His work remains, however, as the first example of an empirical field investigation in North American archaeology.

Early classificatory and descriptive efforts of American archaeologists were focused on the mounds, which continued to fascinate investigators. A study by Squier and Davis in the 1840s, combining survey data accumulated by a number of investigators, was motivated in part by a desire to record available information about these prehistoric structures before they were destroyed by development—a concern that is still very much a part of the aims of American archaeologists. Squier and Davis continued to accept the theory of a vanished "Moundbuilder Race", which was finally laid to rest by the excavations carried out by the U.S. Bureau of American Ethnology under Cyrus Thomas in the early 1890s, and reported in the Bureau's Twelfth Annual Report in 1894.

Up to the beginning of the twentieth century, American archeological investigations were primarily focused on the spatial distribution of early cultures rather than upon placing them within a time-frame. Only with the development of relative dating, based on stratigraphic excavation techniques that became standard in the second and third decades of the twentieth century, did American archaeology begin to acquire its present time depth. By the later nineteenth century, American archaeologists such as Cyrus Thomas had begun to used the "direct historical approach". This technique employs the principal of analogy to extrapolate backwards in time, using the material culture of contemporary peoples to

15

reconstruct some of the lifeway of their ancestors who manufactured similar artifacts and occupied the same geographic area. This method has remained an important one in American archaeology up to the present time.

Important developments in the past five decades of the present century include the beginnings of settlement pattern research, pioneered by Julian Steward and Gordon Willey; the development of American archaeology's first theoretical framework in Steward's cultural ecology; and the discovery of absolute dating methods. In the 1960s, important theoretical and methodological innovations introduced by Lewis Binford contributed to what came to be called the "new archaeology".

Another important development in American archaeology during the past several decades has been the introduction of legislation at the national level implementing the protection and preservation of culturally significant archaeological sites, and mandating archaeological investigation of all sites slated for development. An important aim of recent legislation has been to discourage the looting and destruction of prehistoric sites by treasure-hunters, by making such activities a criminal offense and providing penalties for those who continue them. While such laws are a step in the right direction, their systematic implementation and enforcement remains a goal rather than a reality.

North American Indians at European Contact

When the first Europeans arrived in North America in the early decades of the sixteenth century, they found a vast and well-populated continent whose native cultures displayed considerable diversity. Before this diversity could be fully observed and recorded, however, it had largely disappeared, as the result of decimation of the native American population by European diseases to which they had not previously been exposed, and had therefore acquired no resistance. The native cultures disappeared one by one, along with the people who had created them, in what may have been the most massive genocidal episode in human history prior to our own century.

What we know of the state of some North American cultures at the time of European contact has come down to us from the pens of contemporary historians. Although the majority of these early works are monuments of ethnocentric bias, there are exceptional instances of eyewitness accounts that are relatively unbiased, complete, and even rich in detail. Among these are the previously quoted record of the Gentleman of Elvas (see above), describing the events of the De Soto expedition. Similar accounts of other expeditions conducted at about the same time, e.g., those of the travels of Coronado in the Southwest, are far less informative, and tend to follow a typical pattern of describing everything from the conqueror's viewpoint, and to disparage native practices and traditions. Some of these accounts describe acts of incredible treachery and cruelty towards native peoples who, at least in the beginning, were usually friendly, and welcomed the invaders as their honored guests (Jamison 1907).

We know from some of these early accounts that some of the last traditional complex chiefdoms of the Mississippian cultures still remained at the time of contact in some parts

16

of the southeastern United States. One such was the chiefdom described by Elvas; others documented by the De Soto Expedition included the chiefdom of Coosa, whose capital of the same name was visited by De Soto and his party, and whose dominion appears to have included portions of several modern states (Swanton 1985). Other chiefdoms along the Atlantic seaboard from the Carolinas northward to New England are described in Captain John Smith's histories of his voyages during the late sixteenth and early seventeenth centuries, including his account of the ill-fated colony at Jamestown, in which he included a brief native vocabulary (Smith 1624, repr. 1965).

In addition to these literary accounts, the artists Jacques Le Moyne and John White have left us a pictorial record of the sixteenth century chiefdoms of the East Coast, as well as White's paintings of the flora and fauna of the region (Lorant 1965). Although the artists' observations and renderings were colored by their European training and biases, some of these drawings, such as that of a fortified town of the sixteenth century (fig. 1.1), and of mortuary rites conducted for a chief or priest (fig. 1.2), constitute a true ethnographic record of events and places that have long disappeared from the North American continent.

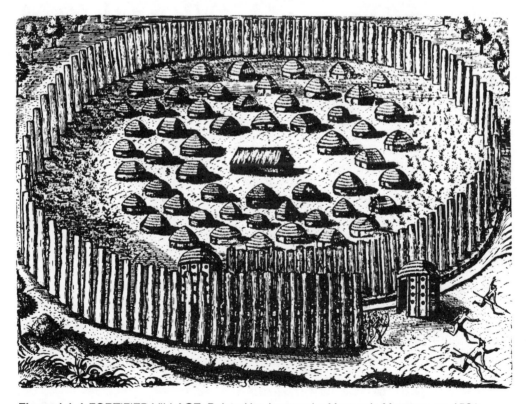

Figure 1.1 A FORTIFIED VILLAGE, Painted by Jacques Le Moyne de Morgues, ca. 1564; engraving by the Flemish artist Theodore De Bry, 1591.

17

Figure 1.2 BURIAL CEREMONIES FOR A CHIEF OR PRIEST. Painted by Jacques Le Moyne de Morgues, ca. 1564; engraving by Theodore De Bry, 1591.

Another important source for the contact period in North America is the *Historia* of Oviedo, compiled from the works of earlier historians that include diaries and eyewitness accounts. Many of these now survive only in such historical works as Oviedo's, since it was the usual practice of the synthesizers of Oviedo's time to discard the original works once they had been incorporated into a general history such as his own (Brain 1985). Although we must lament this practice, which has deprived modern scholars of a great deal of primary source material, we can be grateful for the historical compilations, such as Oviedo's, that have preserved at least portions of these up to the present day.

The ethnohistoric literature of North America, dating to the times of earliest contact in various cultural areas, is a vast library of information whose potential has only recently begun to be tapped. The abundance of this resource for each of the North American culture areas is the subject of succeeding chapters in this book.

REFERENCES

Adovasio, J. M., J. D. Gunn, J. Donahue, and R. Stuckenrath
    1977   Meadowcroft Rockshelter: a 16,000 year chronicle. Annals of the New York Academy of Sciences 288:137–159.
    1978   Meadowcroft Rockshelter, 1977: An overview. American Antiquity 43:632–651.

Beals, Ralph L.
1957   Father Acosta on the first peopling of the New World. American Antiquity 23:182–183.

Brain, Jeffrey P.
1985   Introduction: Update of De Soto Studies since the United States De Soto Expedition Commission Report. In Swanton, John R. Final Report of the United States De Soto Expedition Commission. Smithsonian Institution Press, Washington, D.C. (pp.xi–lxxii)

Carneiro, Robert
1970   A theory of the origin of the state. Science 169: 733–738.

Childe, V. Gordon
1951   Man makes himself. Mentor Books, New York.

Cordell, Linda S.
1984   Prehistory of the Southwest. Academic Press, New York.

Dunnell, Robert
1980   Evolutionary theory and archaeology. Advances in Archaeological Method and Theory 3:35–99.

Earle, Timothy K.
1987   Chiefdoms in archaeological and ethnohistorical perspective. Annual Review of Anthropology 16: 279–308.

Earle, Timothy K. and Elizabeth M. Brumfiel
1987   Specialization, exchange, and complex societies: an introduction. In specialization, exchange, and complex societies, Elizabeth M. Brumfield and Timothy K. Earle, eds. Cambridge University Press. (pp. 1–9)

Ehret, Christopher
1976   Linguistic evidence and its correlation with archaeology. World Archaeology 8(1):5–18.

Fiedel, Stuard J.
1987   Prehistory of the Americas. Cambridge Univ. Press.

Fladmark, Knut R.
1979   Routes: Alternate migration corridors for early man in North America. American Antiquity 44:55–69.
1983   Times and Places: Environmental correlates of Mid-to-Late Wisconsinan human population expansion in North America. In Early Man in the New World, Richard Shutler Jr., ed. Sage Publications. (pp. 13–41).

Flannery, Kent V.
1968   Archaeological systems theory and early Mesoamerica. In Anthropological archaeology of the Americas, B. J. Meggers, ed. Washington, D.C. (pp. 67–87)
1972   The cultural evolution of civilizations. Annual Review of Ecology and Systematics 3:399–426.

Gentleman of Elvas
1907   The Narrative of the expedition of Hernando De Soto by the Gentleman of Elvas, edited by Theodore H. Lewis. In Spanish explorers in the southern United States, 1528–1543, J. Franklin Jameson, ed. Charles Scribner's Sons, New York. (pp. 127–272)

Gibson, Jon L.
1985   Poverty Point: A culture of the Lower Mississippi Valley. Louisiana Archaeological Survey and Antiquities Commission, Anthropological Study No. 7. Baton Rouge, Louisiana.

Greenberg, Joseph H., Christy G. Turner II, and Stephen L. Zegura
1986   The settlement of the Americas: a comparison of the linguistic, dental and genetic evidence. Current Anthropology 27:477–497.

Gustafson, Carl, Richard Daugherty and Delbert Gilbow
1979   The Manis mastodon site: early man on the Olympic Peninsula. Canadian Journal of Archaeology 3:157–164.

Jameson, J. Franklin, ed.
 1907 Original narratives of early American history: Spanish explorers in the southern United States 1528–1543. Charles Scribner's Sons, New York.

Kinkade, M. Dale and J. V. Powell
 1976 Language and the prehistory of North America. World Archaeology 8:83–100.

Kirk, Ruth and Richard D. Daugherty
 1978 Exploring Washington archaeology. University of Washington Press, Seattle.

Lorant, Stefan, editor
 1965 The New World: the first pictures of America. Duell, Sloan and Pearce, New York.

MacNeish, Richard S.
 1982 A late commentary on an early subject. In Peopling of the New World, Jonathan E. Ericson (et al.), eds. Ballena Press. (pp. 311–315)

Martin, Paul S.
 1982 The pattern and meaning of Holocene mammoth extinction. In The Paleoecology of Beringia, D. M. Hopkins (et al.), eds. Academic Press. (pp. 399–408.)

Martin, Paul S., editor
 1984 Quaternary extinctions. University of Arizona Press, Tucson.

Morlan, Richard
 1984 Problems of interpreting modified bones from the Old Crow Basin, Yukon Territory. Paper presented at the First International Conference on Bone Modification, Carson City, Nevada, August 1984.

Morlan, Richard and Jacques Cinq-Mars
 1982 Ancient Beringians: human occupations in the Late Pleistocene of Alaska and the Yukon Territory. In the Paleoecology of Beringia, D. M. Hopkins, J. V. Matthews Jr., C. E. Schweger, and S. B. Young, editors. Academic Press. (pp. 353–381)

Sanders, William T. and David Webster
 1979 Unilinealism, multilinealism and the evolution of complex societies. In Social archaeology: beyond subsistence and dating. Charles L. Redman (et al.), eds. Academic Press, New York. (pp. 249–302)

Shutler, Richard Jr.
 1985 Dating the peopling of North America. In Environments and extinctions: Man in late glacial North America, Jim I. Mead and David J. Meltzer, eds. (pp. 121–124)

Smith, John
 1966 The General Historie of Virginia, New England and the Summer Isles: with the names of the Adventurers, Planters, and Governours from their first beginning Ano 1584 to this present 1624 . . . [facsimile edition]. The World Publishing Company, Cleveland.

Stewart, T. Dale
 1979 Patterning of skeletal pathologies and epidemiology. In The First Americans: Origins, affinities, and adaptations, William S. Laughlin and Albert B. Harper, eds. Gustav Fischer, New York and Stuttgart. (pp. 257–274)

Swadesh, Maurice
 1962 Linguistic relations across Bering Strait. American Anthropologist 64:1262–1291.
 1964 Glottochronology. In a Dictionary of the Social Sciences. Paris, UNESCO. (pp. 289–290)

Swanton, John R.
 1985 Final report of the United States De Soto Expedition Commission. Smithsonian Institution Press, Washington, D.C.

Szathmary, Emoke J. E.
 1979 Blood groups of Siberians, Eskimos, and Subarctic and Northwest Coast Indians: the problem of origins and genetic relationships. In The First Americans: origins, affinities and adaptations, William S. Laughlin and Albert B. Harper, eds. Gustav Fischer, New York and Stuttgart.

Tuck, James A.
  1976   Newfoundland and Labrador prehistory. National Museum of Man/National Museums of Canada, Van Nostrand Reinhold Ltd., Toronto.

Turner, Christy II
  1983   Dental evidence for the peopling of the Americas. In Early man in the New World, Richard Shutler Jr., ed. Sage Foundation. (pp. 147–158)

Wauchope, Robert
  1962   Lost tribes and sunken continents. University of Chicago Press.

Webb, Clarence H.
  1968   The extent and content of Poverty Point Culture. American Antiquity 33(3):297–321.
  1982   The Poverty Point Culture. Second edn., revised. Geoscience and Man, Volume 17. School of Geoscience, Louisiana State University, Baton Rouge.

Wenke, Robert J.
  1981   Explaining the evolution of cultural complexity: a review. Advances in Archaeological Method and Theory vol. 4:79–127.

White, Leslie
  1949   The science of culture. Farrar, Straus and Company, New York.

Willey, Gordon R. and Jeremy Sabloff
  1974   A History of American Archaeology. Thames and Hudson.
  1980   A History of American Archaeology. 2nd edition. Thames and Hudson Ltd., London/W. H. Freeman and Company, San Francisco.

Chapter 2

The Arctic Culture Area[1]

Nelson H. H. Graburn and Molly Lee
University of California, Berkeley

Introduction

The Arctic culture area of native North America is the aboriginal homeland of the Eskimos. Of all native northerners the Eskimos (whose modern self-designation is Inuit, "real people") are the most reknowned, probably because of their unique and exotic way of life. Their vast territory, which extends more than five thousand miles across the circumpolar region, today is embraced by the political boundaries of four nations: the U.S.S.R., the U.S.A., Canada and Denmark. Yet Eskimo lands, despite their extensive size, support a total population of fewer than 110,000. Thinly distributed along the meandering coastline, the people tended to concentrate in small groups at ecologically favorable sites. The Eskimos were largely dependent on the bounty of sea; the land alone could have supported only one-tenth of the population.

The literature on Eskimos, including both scholarly and popular publications, is more extensive than any other on a "primitive" people. This abundance has both advantages and disadvantages, for though we know more about Eskimos, we also hold more stereotypes of them, most of which need modifying. These stereotypes derive from the romantic inclinations of Westerners, who dramatize the exotic, the bizarre, the strange and the remote. This summary can provide only a limited overview of the Eskimos, but its aim is to dispel some of the stereotypes and point the way to further research. The major concentration of this chapter will be on "traditional" Eskimo society, which is to say on what we know about Eskimo society before Western contact and on those aspects of it carried forward into the historic period.

We should mention the problem of verb tense here. There is no absolute date delineating past from present where culture is concerned, and some aspects of traditional Eskimo society persist into the modern day. We have elected therefore to use both the past and present tenses in this section, depending on whether the feature under discussion is still substantially in evidence. The reader should bear in mind, however, that the traditional Eskimo society described in most detail here has largely disappeared and should consult the final pages for an understanding of the extensive modernization of recent decades.

---

1. This chapter, submitted in 1988, is based on "The Eskimos", pp. 137–177 in Nelson H. H. Graburn and B. Stephen Strong, *Circumpolar Peoples: an Anthropological Perspective*. Pacific Palisades, CA: Goodyear Publications, revised by Molly Lee.

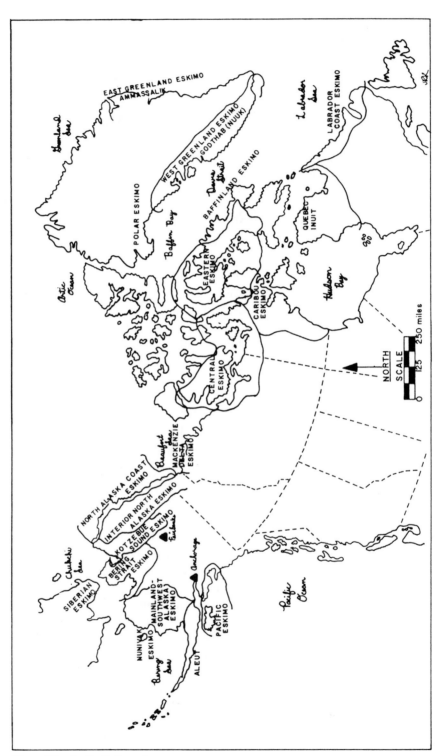

Map of the Arctic Culture Area

The reader should be further reminded that the Aleut people, too, share the Arctic culture area. According to archaeological and linguistic evidence they diverged from Eskimo stock no more than three thousand years ago. Due to limitations of space the Aleut, who most closely resembled the western subarctic Eskimos in adaptation, will be only summarily mentioned here.

Any introduction to the Eskimos must stress both the cultural homogeneity of so far-flung a group and at the same time their considerable range of local adaptation. The Eskimos' cultural homogeneity was the product of two factors, first, successive wave-like migrations from their Bering Strait "hearth" over the past two or three thousand years, and second, the constant inter-area travel and intercultural exchange that has taken place among them since the last major migration (700–1000 B.P.). To summarize, then, from Siberia in the west to Ammassalik in the east, Eskimos shared the same basic culture and reacted in the same fundamental ways to social and ecological pressures.

The extensive local variation characteristic of the Eskimos came about as the result of the extreme technological and demographic flexibility required by the myriad of ecological niches in the Arctic culture area. These in turn led to superficial differences in social and material structures among the subgroups. Fredrik Barth, an anthropologist who has written extensively on ethnicity, explains this phenomenon by pointing out that among human groups the same basic cultural patterns and economic strategies have generated different social forms under different pressures and circumstances. In this chapter we hope to show how the variation among Eskimo sub-populations derived from the basic imperatives of life in the Arctic. Due to space limitations we shall confine ourselves to illustrative examples.

Beginning at different dates in different localities the Eskimos have suffered the incursions of innumerable nations and have fallen prey to the resulting acculturative forces. Owing to the varying dates, rates, and agents of contact, Eskimos as a whole have occasionally shown more cultural variability since contact than before it. As we shall see below, however, with the rapid growth of communications networks in the twentieth century, the groups have since caught up with one another in their knowledge of the outside world and their demands for a significant place in it.

Eskimo Environment: Limitations and Opportunities

Two features distinguish the environment of the Eskimos from those of all other native peoples of North America: residence in the Arctic and dependence on the sea. Most inhabited a typical arctic ecosystem where the rocky land is underlain by a layer of permafrost, limiting the growth of trees and the drainage of water from flat areas in the summer. Long and severe winters contrast with short and only mildly warm summers.

This does not mean, however, that all Eskimos lived in the Arctic or were unable to live elsewhere. For example, the maritime Eskimos of southern Greenland live in a subarctic ecosystem roughly parallel to the Aleuts. Furthermore, with the climatic fluctuations of the last one-to-two thousand years, the boundary between the Arctic and the Subarctic (measured by the presence of *tuvak*, permanent offshore winter ice) has moved north and south along the coast of Greenland. Similarly, at the other end of their aboriginal homeland, the Eskimos of southwestern Alaska as well as the Pacific Eskimo of Kodiak Island, Cook Inlet and Prince William Sound may be categorized as subarctic. It is never as cold in these areas and the sea is never as clogged by ice as elsewhere. Moreover, typically subarctic forests cover the coastline and stretch hundreds of miles inland up the long river valleys. It should be noted that the Eskimo population density in the exceptional subarctic areas was probably ten to fifty times higher than population densities anywhere to the north. Thus we must conclude that Eskimo culture was as positively adaptable to subarctic maritime as arctic environments.

The second major characteristic of Eskimo life was their orientation toward the sea. In broad outline, Eskimo orientation to the land roughly paralleled that of other North American peoples; it was their extreme dependence on marine resources that set them apart. In this they resembled the Aleut (whose culture has since evolved into the most sea-oriented of the Eskimo-related groups), the maritime Chukchi of Siberia, and, perhaps, even the insular Haida Indians of the Northwest Coast.

Two important exceptions must be noted. In large areas of western and southwestern Alaska many Eskimo groups had a riverine, rather than maritime, emphasis. They built their large permanent settlements near the river mouths and inhabited the wooded valleys of large rivers where they depended more on migratory fish than sea mammals. Technologically and ecologically, the riverine Eskimos more closely resembled the neighboring Alaskan Athapaskans.

The other exception is the *Nunamiut* ("people of the land") and Caribou Eskimos. Inhabiting the Brooks Range of interior northern Alaska, the Nunamiut were well adapted to inland hunting. In aboriginal times they probably relied upon economic exchange (principally caribou skins for seal oil) with the people of the coast to the north of them. Similarly the few groups of Eskimos living in the interior of the Ungava Peninsula of northern Quebec depended upon exchanges with coastal peoples, or themselves visited the heads of bays or the tidal portions of rivers for maritime resources.

The most land oriented were the Caribou Eskimos of the Barren Grounds in the central Canadian Arctic, an area of some half million square miles north of the tree line and west of Hudson's Bay. These scattered populations subsisted mainly on vast herds of migratory caribou and fish from lakes and rivers. Although typical Eskimos culturally, the Caribou were economically and technologically the poorest. Limited resources meant they were always on the move. They made shoddier igloos and smaller tents than other groups. Even in recent times they have been subject to drastic periods of starvation. Unlike the nearby Athapaskan and Algonquian Indians, who shared the same caribou herds, they did not enjoy the advantages of living in a wooded area. We may therefore summarize by saying that Eskimo culture and technology was successfully adaptive for arctic and subarctic maritime and riverine environments but less so (in terms of population maintenance) for land-locked arctic environments. It should of course be noted that no other peoples in the world have had to live completely in arctic tundra areas without complementary access to other environmental niches.

Technology and Production Strategies

No Eskimo group depended exclusively on the natural output of precisely that territory it inhabited, for the arctic and subarctic are not closed ecosystems. Maritime Eskimos, for instance, partially subsisted on sea mammals that either spend some of the year in warmer waters or whose food sources migrate from other areas. Migratory fish, which pass a significant part of their immature life in warmer and richer waters, contributed substantially to the diet of most Eskimos. At certain times of year, migratory birds such as geese, ducks, and swans were the staple of all groups. Even the Nunamiut could hunt the caribou only during the summer when they travel north to fawn.

Not all arctic animals are migratory, however. For instance, the caribou herds on the high arctic islands and Greenland are accessible year round, as are some species of fish and a few of birds. Wolves, foxes and owls, though not major food sources, are non-migratory. Some minor food sources such as crustaceans and mollusks, certain plants and seaweeds, are virtually sessile and therefore a permanent part of the local natural habitat.

The land-sea dichotomy can be seen as the linchpin of traditional Eskimo existence, and though more pronounced in the East than West, we may conveniently classify and discuss most aspects of Eskimo culture in terms of it. For the Eskimos generally, this distinction was not only technologically and ecologically apparent, but was also the basis of symbolism and world view. At this deeper level of analysis the same dualism could be mapped onto such aspects of life as aesthetics, mythology, spatial arrangements, household organization, the annual cycle, and religious belief. Although it could be argued that the opposition of complementary halves is fundamental to all cultures because notions of complementarity form the basis of human logic, nowhere, perhaps, was it more graphically manifest than among the Eskimos. We shall return to it often in later sections of this chapter.

To summarize here we might say that the Eskimos were an "edge" people who looked to the land and the sea, the winter and the summer, the appropriate hunting and domestic technologies for both the seasonal and geographical cycles, and who arranged their living and ideological categories in a series of more or less overt oppositions accordingly.

In this section we shall see that the diversity of resources available to the Eskimos was probably greater than that for other northern peoples. The poverty of the Eskimo environment does not lie in the paucity of species or phyla represented but in their uneven and irregular distribution and in the geographical and climatic features that make access to them so difficult. To meet these exigencies, the Eskimos devised sophisticated technologies and strategies that maximized the diverse products of their environment. We shall emphasize the sea and its resources here because it was these adaptations that set apart Eskimo culture.

Sea Mammal Hunting

For the Eskimos living in the true Arctic the sea is not a unified concept, as it is perhaps for us. They conceptualize it in two forms. The summer sea is wet, windy, and relatively full of diverse resources; the winter sea is covered—or nearly covered—with a virtually impenetrable layer of floating ice. At the same time it is possessed of relatively few and almost inaccessible resources. For comparative purposes we may say that the subarctic Eskimos see the sea around them in a "permanent state of summer" compared with the majority.

Winter comes early to the Arctic Eskimos. From September on it is often stormy and soon begins to freeze. The smoother fresh water of lakes and large rivers freezes and melts earlier than the sea. Especially near land, the ocean freezes over gradually; early winter storms continually break up the ice so that practically no hunting can be done until weeks, or even months, have passed. Once the surface was fairly solid, the Eskimos traditionally made use of a special technology to tap the few resources beneath it. Fish were hooked through holes in the ice, kept open with chisels. Ice fishing, however, was not the major food source. The near-shore ice mass (*tuvak*) may grow to ten or twenty feet deep, but two species of seal, the ringed or common seal (*natsiq*) and the bearded or square flipper seal (*ujjuk* or *ugrook*), inhabit the under-ice water. They maintain open breathing holes (*maupuk*) by rising to the surface for air every few minutes and disturbing the newly formed ice. Eskimos used their keen-sniffing dogs or thin probes to find these holes, and, for catching this single most important winter resource, developed a complex technology for which they are justly famous.

The hunter poked a light-weight movement indicator such as a stick through the thin crust of snow above the breathing hole and waited with his harpoon at the ready until the indicator moved or he heard the animal exhale. Then he thrust the harpoon down into the center of the breathing hole, hoping to hit the seal in the head or neck. The harpoon head remained attached to the sealskin line but the handle was discarded. As the powerful seal tried to swim away, the Eskimo quickly made the line fast round his body and arms and braced himself across the hole. Sooner or later the seal tired and the Eskimo cut away the snow around the hole to pull it out. From this position lifting an animal weighing as much as six-or seven hundred pounds onto the ice was no easy task. To accomplish it a man either sought help from nearby hunters or used his dog team.

Another kind of seal hunting was done at the floe edge. Though the *tuvak* might stretch many miles from land, in most areas it has an edge or has long, wide leads of open water. There, the Eskimo could harpoon a seal from the ice or could use the traditional summer technology of boats, harpoons, and floats for walrus or seal hunting. Even this aspect of Eskimo culture had its characteristic "edge", symbolically and technologically dividing winter and summer. As the season progressed and the sea ice thickened, fishing through it became unfeasible. Barring the availability of birds or land resources, late winter was a time of extreme privation.

By April, May, or June, as the days lengthen and solar radiation warms the Arctic, both species of common seal climb through their breathing holes to bask on the ice. (As

Figure 2.1 Kadloo and Idlouk, two Canadian men from Pond Inlet, Baffin Island, N.W.T., examine a seal harpooned through the sea ice. (Courtesy of D. Wilkenson, National Film Board/National Archives of Canada, PA 145172.)

this is the season when they shed their winter hair, their skin occasionally sunburns thus lowering its quality). With the onset of summer another, easier seal hunting technology was employed. At this time of year basking seals stand out like black dots against the flat ice and can be spotted from miles away. A hunter, restraining his dog team, would crawl toward the seal and shoot or harpoon it before it had time to dive down its nearby hole. They often hid behind a small white blind, peering over it now and again to keep an eye on the seal. Or, dressed in sealskin clothing, a man would crawl toward the animal, wiggling and scratching in seal-like imitation until he was close enough (within a few feet in traditional times) to ensure the kill. The hunter used a harpoon (some groups used an unusual long, heavy sliding harpoon made like a sled runner), a bow and arrow or, more recently, a rifle.

Early in summer, fresh water ice either breaks up or becomes too dangerous to walk on. Salt water ice, however, is very tough and, though it may break up in large masses, detached floes float around in the Arctic seas almost all summer. Gradually the massive *tuvak* crumbles and the open sea approaches the shore, which widened the Eskimos' choice of summer hunting techniques. Large migratory bird populations formed an important resource of the Eskimos in spring and summer. These birds were killed with bird spears, bolas, and bows and arrows. Sometimes the Eskimos climbed cliffs to raid the nest of the clouds of *akpa* (guillemot) and raided the nests of water birds such as ducks, geese, swans, gulls, and the numerous species of shore bird. In many areas ptarmigan (Arctic grouse) were an invaluable staple as they never leave the Eskimo area entirely and can be hunted even where the snow is deep. Since they are slow witted, ptarmigan could be downed by a well-aimed stone. Of the permanent populations of birds widely distributed across the Arctic, only the ptarmigan and the arctic owl seem to have been considered "proper food." The ubiquitous sea gull, although fit to eat when in the egg or embryo stage, was considered inedible when adult and was taken only in times of starvation. According to Eskimo mythology sea gulls were the descendants of women who had turned into cannibals and eaten their own children. Likewise, the raven, another permanent resident, was only eaten as a last resort. These comical birds also play an important role in oral tradition, where they are often endowed with human attributes.

In full summer the major maritime hunting emphasis was on seal, walrus, and beluga (white whale) hunting, usually undertaken by kayak. All groups save the most northerly Polar Eskimos used some form of kayak, as did the Aleut. Although this vessel varied considerably in length, breadth, detail, design, and even skin covering, it was basically a one-man, closed-deck hunting canoe. The light frame was made of small pieces of wood (or, occasionally, other materials) lashed together with bones or sinew and covered with a seal or caribou skin sewn with waterproof seams. The man lowered himself in through a tight-fitting hole and sat on the bottom of the craft, slightly aft of the middle. Sometimes he "integrated" himself with the vessel by lashing his waterproof parka to the frame of the opening, thus becoming a single impermeable unit with his craft.

The kayak had no form of rudder and usually was propelled by double-bladed paddles; though swift in smooth water and seaworthy in choppy seas, it had two disadvantages. It was easily blown off course by side winds and was inherently unstable; thus it required constant effort for the kayaker both to remain upright and to steer a straight course. Though superbly adapted to hunting, they were very tiring to navigate, and one can understand why Eskimos everywhere quickly adopted Western boats, both for hunting and long-distance travel.

Kayak hunting was often undertaken collectively, in small groups or large, for companionship, safety, and effectiveness. Eskimos concentrated on the sea mammals (*puiji:* "those that show their noses, come up to breathe"). Successful kayak hunting depended on approaching the quarry close enough to where it would surface so that it could be taken with the three-part harpoon, thrown so that the detachable head would embed securely in its flesh. The hunter therefore approached the animal's last-sighted surfacing place as quickly as possible, calculating from that point the distance and direction it might be expected to swim until the next breath.

The presence of additional hunters facilitated sea mammal hunting. Once having secured the animal the hunter uncoiled the long harpoon line to prevent the kayak from being swamped or damaged by the powerful struggle. When walrus or whale hunting, several hunters attempted to fix their harpoons in the animal. To impede the animal, and mark its progress and direction, a float made of an inflated sealskin (*avatak*) was attached to the line. For the larger sea mammals, a drag (a large circular hoop covered with a skin like a drum) was attached to the line so that it could be pulled along at right angles to the water motion. This debilitated even the most powerful animals. Sooner or later the animal tired and the hunter approached closer, drawing his line and further securing it if necessary. Because most sea mammals were too large to haul on board the kayak (let alone stuff inside it), the hunter, with the animal in tow, made for the nearest land or large block of floating ice where it was beached and butchered immediately.

Eskimo hunting strategy was based on a complex of knowledge far more elaborate than the kayak. It required utilization of as many methods as possible to increase the efficiency and size of the take and a sophisticated and detailed knowledge of the natural environment. Eskimos knew where in their territory sea mammals were apt to congregate; they knew their migration routes within a few miles and their schedules within a few days. They had an ethnotaxonomy for the larger species such as white whales, baleen whales, walruses and harp seals and distinguished individual members by age, sex, and other important features.

Further, it is possible that they employed collective strategies such as driving such animals into shallow bays where they would be stranded. Thereafter entire herds could be dispatched like "shooting fish in a barrel." Large hauls were cached for months to supply the needs of the group during lean times such as late fall and late winter.

Occasionally, opportunities arose for taking large sea mammals in quantity. For example, white whales sometimes become trapped by gradually freezing sea ice. Unlike seals, they are unable to maintain breathing holes and become confined to decreasing patches of open water. By late fall or early winter, thrashing around, gasping for air, half dead from crowding and overexertion, these unlucky creatures were easy targets for Eskimo hunters.

Another species sometimes taken in quantity were walrus who, unlike other sea mammals, like to haul up at favored places in huge herds. This applies to both the Pacific walrus, mainstay of some of the Bering Strait Eskimos, and the slightly smaller Atlantic walrus, found off the coasts of Labrador and southern Baffin Island. As the walrus is such a dangerous and aggressive animal, Eskimo hunters preferred to stalk a herd on land. Approaching unseen, they got as close as possible, then rushed the herd, harpooning the slower animals. The technique was extremely dangerous because the powerful walrus, if even halfway into the water, could drag several men on the other end of the line along with it. Walrus hunting sometimes turned into a tug of war in which an Eskimo could lose as little as his harpoon or as much as his life. From a kayak it was perhaps even more dangerous because in trying to defend the herd aggressive males sometimes attacked the vessel, piercing it with their tusks or charging and sinking it.

Kayaks might also be used for hunting other prey. In many areas water birds were very common and the hunter would use a light, three-pronged bird spear, propelling it with a throwing board, to catch the birds in flight or on the surface of the water. The lightweight kayaks could be carried over the land to lakes and rivers where they might be used for fishing and in some favorite locations for killing caribou where the migrating herds crossed the water. With their killing spears the hunters quickly dispatched as many of the swimming herd as possible.

Sometimes kayaks were used for transportation. In that case gear and, occasionally, people could be stowed in the empty fore and aft sections beneath the decks or lashed to the deck itself.

The main form of water transport was the *umiak*, a large open boat common to maritime and riverine Eskimos everywhere but in the subarctic and the extreme north. The *umiak*, like similar vessels of the Aleut and Chukchi, had a skin cover (usually *ujjuk* or walrus) tightly fitted over its twenty to thirty foot wooden frame. The *umiak* was open decked but even so, was fairly seaworthy even when heavily loaded. In some areas the *umiak* was propelled with a small sail. Usually, though, they were rowed or paddled by women and captained by one of the older men, who gave directions and held the steering oar. It might be noted that the oval shape of the *umiak*, commonly known as the woman's boat, replicates the shape the oil-burning soapstone lamp, the quintessential woman's possession, whereas the sleek, pointed kayak used exclusively by men echoes the shape of the sharp hunting weapons that were quintessentially male. In this division we see an example of the dualism materially and symbolically mapped in Eskimo life. Psychoanalytically minded readers might note (as have the Eskimo themselves) that these fundamentally opposed shapes recall the shapes of male and female genitalia.

In summer, the umiak could transport a whole family, or as many as several households, along the coast to islands, or even far inland up the huge rivers where they might camp near the best hunting places. It could be loaded with as many as forty people, their possessions, tents, dogs, and sometimes sleds. It was sometimes dragged over the ice and snow on a sled in the winter but was usually kept for summer use.

In northwest Alaska the *umiak* had a special purpose retained with some modifications in modern times. Here, it is the supreme hunting vessel used in the hazardous but exciting chase of baleen whales, the leviathans that migrate along the coast in the spring. Though men almost always paddle the *umiak* for whale hunting it is perhaps significant to note that the boat was launched by ritually selected women, who dance and gave gifts to the crew.

For whale hunting, as many as eight to ten *umiaks* and their crews, each led by an experienced *umialik* (boat owner, captain), camp on the floe edge from April to June to await their arrival. The pivotal crew member is the harpooner, whose job it is from his position at the prow to approach the whale as closely as possible (sometimes even climbing on its back) in order to thrust the extra-heavy harpoon deep into its flesh. A long attaching line is released with at least three floats and drags fastened to it. Alarmed, the whale then dives, taking the line and floats with it. When it resurfaces the other *umiaks* position themselves as close as possible. Again and again they impale the animal, slowing it down until it is too winded to struggle. The men then finish it off by thrusting killing spears into its vital parts. The assembled *umiaks* tow the huge animal triumphantly back to shore where it is butchered and distributed throughout the community in a ritually proscribed pattern. With the advent of wooden boats, the *umiak* has disappeared everywhere but in the whaling villages of northwest Alaska.

Land Animals

Before we consider the land animals, we should mention the polar bear. These animals roam throughout the circumpolar regions but are especially concentrated in certain areas of northern Alaska, the central Canadian Arctic, and northern Greenland. Though they hibernate in dens deep in the snow on land, polar bears, who are excellent swimmers, are most often encountered near the shore or on floating sea ice. There, using their enormous but limber paws, they scoop up seals and fish, their major food sources, from the water. Although known by all Eskimo groups, polar bears were not an especially stable resource, first, because they are rarely present in large numbers, secondly because they are an awe-inspiring and dangerous animal and thirdly, perhaps, because of their anomalous position of belonging both to the land and sea. Along with the walrus, the polar bear was regarded as the most awe-inspiring member of the animal world. Their humanoid characteristics and their worthiness as opponents are reflected in Eskimo folklore where human/polar-bear transformations are common. In areas where they are concentrated (such as in the lands of the Polar Eskimos) polar bears are hunted for clothing. Their pelts make excellent garments; therefore they were a good substitute when caribou were not abundant.

Before the advent of rifles, hunting polar bears, either in water or on land, was extremely dangerous. Harpooning these animals from a boat could result in a fatal counterattack. A fast runner and powerful fighter on land, the polar bear could be killed only if the hunter got close enough to hit it with the bow and arrow or spear. In this case, the Eskimos' dogs were his greatest defense; relentlessly attacking the bear, they provided distraction while the hunter moved in for the kill.

Across the Arctic a role reversal commonly took place between the Eskimos and hungry polar bears, who raided houses in search of food. Though they sometimes broke in and terrified the inhabitants, people were only their incidental quarry just as the polar bear was only the occasional prey of the sea-mammal-hunting Eskimos.

Of the land animals, the caribou was by far the most important and was found in nearly all areas inhabited by Eskimos. On the mainland the Eskimos usually encountered large numbers of caribou in spring, summer, and early fall, as the animals came north to drop their fawns and to feed on the young tundra grasses and mosses. In the late summer most Eskimos made a concerted effort to hunt caribou to supply themselves with the best skins for making new sets of clothing for the coming winter. In some areas caribou were also found in smaller or larger numbers in the winter. Although the hair is thick on their skins at this time, it was deemed nonetheless to be of lower quality because long hair breaks off and falls out. Winter furs were commonly used only for bedding. Although caribou meat and back fat were thought to be one of the most desirable foods, sea mammals or fish nonetheless comprised the bulk of the Eskimos' diet. According to the Eskimos, caribou meat is strengthening but is not as good for humans (or for the all-important dog teams) as the fat-rich sea-mammal meat.

Caribou hunting was usually a communal activity. The object was to meet the herds where they were most concentrated, as at important crossing places or in narrow valleys and defiles along the migration routes. Here, the caribou would gather, or would be frightened by "beaters" or *inukshaks,* (stones piled to resemble men) into places where other hunters were lying in wait with their bows and arrows or kayaks and spears. At other times of the year caribou were found in small numbers or as stragglers from the main herd, offering an unforeseen bonus.

Until early in this century when the fads and fashions of the Western world created a demand for fox skins, other land animals were of little importance to the Eskimos. Although occasionally caught, trapped, or shot in the past, foxes provided very little meat. Muskoxen, though they may have been widely distributed prehistorically, have been found in more recent times only in the northernmost regions of the Canadian mainland and on the high Arctic islands. In these places they may once have been an important food source. Muskoxen are also easy to hunt. Rather than fleeing when confronted, the herds draw together and stand their ground, a defense that may have served them well against wolves but turned them into sitting ducks for the Eskimos.

Lemmings are the most plentiful Arctic land animals. These tiny creatures, which live on the plants, roots and seeds of the tundra, burrow along the surface of the ground and under the snow in the winter. The Eskimos rarely ate them (though, young boys practicing their male roles often "hunted" them with stones or bows and arrows). Nevertheless, owing to their enormous numbers, lemmings are the basis of the carnivorous food chain in the far north, supplying the nutritive bulk for foxes, owls, other birds of prey, and probably wolves. Thus they are the prime movers of the processes of nature which convert the weak solar energy of these latitudes to vegetal foodstuffs and thence into the predatory chain.

Fish have always comprised an essential part of the Eskimo diet. The staple species were such anadromous fish as the salmon in easternmost Alaska, and the purely freshwater varieties found in larger lakes throughout the Eskimos' homeland. Though cod and sculpin were abundant most Eskimos lacked the appropriate technology to take large, exclusively marine fish. Only in the far southwest of the Eskimo range did deep-sea fishing occur aboriginally. The huge halibut and cod of the warmer waters of the Pacific Coast were caught at great depths by lines that held a number of hooks.

Eskimo fishing technology was extensive enough to enable fish to be taken at almost any time of the year in fresh or salt water. Traditional fishing assumed three major forms. Hooks (with or without lures) were used for jigging both in fresh and salt water, often through cracks or holes in the ice. This activity was open to even the oldest and weakest among them. The three-pronged fish spear (leister), almost universal among Eskimos, could be used for whitefish, lake trout, salmon and other medium-sized fish all year long. In the winter the leister could be driven down through holes in the ice. The fisherman jigged a lure below the surface of the water with one hand while holding his spear at the ready with the other. The spear was thrust down through the fish which was then hauled up and landed.

At other times Eskimos employed leisters at fish weirs, dams of large boulders they constructed from bank to bank of shallow streams to trap migrating species. In favored locations, men, and sometimes women, waded in and speared the thrashing fish by the hundreds. Along with hook and lure, the leister was also used for taking small fish from the banks of streams and rivers, from kayaks, between ice cracks or from floe edges. The western Alaskan Eskimos, for whom fish comprised the major food source, developed fish traps, more sophisticated techniques, possibly borrowed from their Athapaskan Indian neighbors. Fish traps of varying form direct and catch the large migrating shoals near the shores of the huge rivers.

The antiquity of Eskimo netmaking is debated in the literature. It seems likely that this skill was confined to populations of the western Alaska and eastern Greenland. Interestingly, the distribution of net sealing is negatively correlated with *maupuk* or breathing hole hunting described above. Where nets were found, they were used for fishing and sealing. Seal nets were made of strips of sealskin or braided baleen ("whalebone") and were used in the open water for species migrating in large herds. More often they were placed at restricted areas such as the entrance to bays and rivers. In the subarctic environments use of nets was much more feasible. There, they were made of the same materials and sometimes of braided vegetal matter such as spruce root. In these more temperate marginal areas they were strung in streams, along river edges or the seashore, or even under the ice. Today, indigenous nets have given way to more efficient imported types.

Technology and Materials

One of the most deeply-entrenched stereotypes of Eskimo culture is of a "stone age" technology. This assumption distorts one of the truly remarkable features of Eskimo life: inventive use of such raw materials as were available.

Asen Balikci, a well-known anthropologist of Canadian Eskimos, has usefully divided these raw materials into four distinctive complexes: snow and ice (used for snow houses, ice houses, ice caches and the like); skin (for such indispensibles as clothing, kayaks, *umiaks*, and tents); bone, antler, and ivory (for making the "business ends" of weapons, tools, and needles); and stone (hard: for cutting edges, points, and scrapers; soft: for oil lamps and cooking pots). To these we may add wood, which, though unevenly distributed throughout the Eskimo range, was used when available for tool and weapon handles, tent poles, boat frames, and, where abundant, for house-building. Other locally available indigenous materials include meteoric iron (found and occasionally worked in northern Greenland) and copper (from its occurrence in northwestern Canada the Copper Eskimos, who cold-hammered it, were named). On occasion even frozen meat and fish were utilized as structural materials (as in chinking sled runners, for instance).

Dwellings

Another stereotype connected with Eskimo materials and technology is the association of the igloo (snow house) with Eskimos as a whole. In fact, snow houses were largely confined to the central Eskimo region, where they were the principle—though not the only—winter dwelling. Nor is the igloo thought to be a particularly ancient house form. Even as recently as the early historic period the Central Arctic Eskimos, like their forebears, made turf-covered houses with supports of whales' bones. By the mid-nineteenth century, however, most Central Eskimos had adopted the snow house. Only occasionally did western and Greenlandic Eskimos construct snow houses for temporary shelter. Igloo-building, despite its limited distribution, is one of the unique technological features of Eskimo culture, and therefore will be described here in some detail.

The first step in building a snow house was to inscribe a circle for the perimeter with a sharp bone or antler snow knife. Ideally, the construction required two men, one to cut the blocks, the other to position them. The cutter worked inside the circle, removing the snow in trapezoidal sections from the floor. This had the added advantage of lowering the floor below ground to conserve heat. The builder worked outside, spiraling the blocks upward, positioning them at an increasingly-inward slant, and locking them in place with sharp blows. The points where the blocks did not touch were chinked by the women with loose snow chips.

The igloo held its shape primarily because of the properties of the snow blocks and the effect of the building process upon them. Through pressure, each blow of the knife instantaneously melted the ice crystals at the point of contact. The momentarily-created water immediately refroze cementing the adjoining blocks together. Thus the entire structure became physically integrated; as it aged the upper inside walls constantly melted (due to rising heat) then refroze, forming a layer of ice that further strengthened it.

The passageway to the outside, built after the dwelling itself, sloped downward through the snow so that the lowest point of the igloo was the floor at the entrance. The advantage (and this applied to all the various types of winter dwellings found among the Eskimos) was that the cold air that would otherwise flow in at the lowest level was trapped, and the heat rose to warm the upper part. Excessive smoke and dirty air escaped through a small ventilating "nose" (qignaq) cut into the top of the igloo. Light was provided by a block of freshwater ice inserted into the south-facing wall. As the weather warmed, the sun and wind eventually caved in the roofs. When this occurred the dwellings were covered with skins. This modified structure (a variant was also used in autumn) was known as the qarmat.

One additional feature of snow house construction that should be mentioned here is its structural flexibility. With respect to settlement pattern, a single dwelling constituted a minimal unit capable of almost infinite replication. Among the igloo-building Central Eskimos, winter was the time of optimal sociability. As the season progressed and the group expanded, by merely cutting through a wall, snowhouses could be clustered together to form communities of as many as fifteen to twenty contiguous living spaces. This had the additional advantage of maximizing heat potential. Conversely, if a dwelling were abandoned, heat loss could be minimized by walling it off, a modification that required little effort.

Eskimo winter dwellings, regardless of material, shared the same basic floor plan. A permanent winter igloo was as much as ten or fifteen feet across and could be occupied by six to ten people. The principle living space, a raised bench called the sleeping platform, occupied the rear of the dwelling opposite the entrance. Raised above the floor level, the sleeping platform was covered with a cushioning layer of willow twigs or baleen strips, then insulated with skins and clothing. Directly in front of the platform next to the wall was the oil-burning, soapstone lamp (*qullik*). Over it were suspended the cooking pot or a net-like frame for drying clothes. The *qullik* was the keystone of Eskimo culture. Providing the only dependable source of light and heat, the lamp required continuous tending, and the women, whose job it was, occupied the space next to—or near—the outside wall of the sleeping platform. On the floor opposite, just inside the doorway, could be found the meat, spare skins, tools, and, in extremely cold weather, the dogs.

The more permanently settled Eskimos on the west coast of Alaska lived in square or oblong semisubterranean houses with wooden frames and sod-covered roofs. Inhabited for as many as ten months a year, these dwellings were built following the same thermodynamic principle as the snow house. A long, sloping passage was dug down from the surface and under the walls of the house such that the entrance was at the lowest point in the floor. Only in the southwestern subarctic did the houses have direct entrances through the roof from the outside, for in these areas there was no need for a "cold trap."

In Greenland, at the other end of the Eskimos' range, most populations built their winter houses of stone (sometimes also utilizing whales' bones and sod). In floor plan and elevation these resembled the semisubterranean structures of western Alaska. Particularly in southwest Greenland the milder climate and abundant resources permitted more permanent settlements.

Additionally, ceremonial meeting houses, or "men's houses" (*kashgi, karigi,* or *qaggi*) were found everywhere in the Eskimos' homeland. Replicating the dwelling on a larger scale, they were built according to local technology. Among the igloo-building Eskimos, the ceremonial house (*qaggi*) consisted of an oversize version of the dwelling. Sometimes an entire cluster of ten or more dwellings was domed over to create a vast space where the entire community of a hundred or more people could congregate, demonstrating once again the structural adaptability of the igloo.

More invariant still was the Eskimos' summer shelter, the *tupik,* or skin tent, which dotted the Arctic from the Bering Sea to Ammassalik from late spring to early autumn when these semi-nomadic people moved from place to place to take advantage of the season's bounty. The *tupik* generally consisted of a wood or bone frame with a skin cover. Most were more or less rectangular, and approximated the floor plan of the winter dwelling, although conical tents were used by some central and northern Alaskan Eskimos, and a dome-shaped type by the nearby Nunamiut.

Figure 2.2 Elderly Canadian Inuit couple in their winter igloo: note the abundance of imported materials, typical of the "trapping period" of the 1920s–1950s. (Courtesy of Bud Glunz, National Film Board/National Archives of Canada, PA145171.)

Division of Labor

In the use of materials and technology, the sexual division of labor was quite distinct. As a general rule, women were responsible for activities and implements relating to the inside of the house. These included, for example, maintaining the lamp, cooking, clothes making, boot sewing, food gathering from the land and the final apportionment of animal products. Their principle tools of hard materials—the ivory needle, the semicircular stone *ulu* ("woman's knife") and the stone skin scraper—were made for them by men.

Conversely, the men's material world comprised tools and instruments of the outside, the sea, those concerned with hunting, production and manufacture, movement, and the ice, snow, bone-horn-antler, stone, and wood complexes. Thus we might pursue our dualistic analysis of Eskimo society by generalizing that men were concerned with the hard, pointed, cutting and thrusting materials of the outside mobile world, whereas women were responsible for the softer, pliable, enclosing materials of the inside world. Men built kayak and *umiak* frames whereas women made their skin covers. Men built the main structure of the igloo and the women chinked it airtight. Men made and erected the tent poles; women made and installed their skin covers. Men made and used the quintessential stone-tipped harpoons, spears, and arrows, and the long-bladed knife; with the semi-lunar *ulu* the women apportioned and made the final distribution of the game.

The very dwelling space itself was conceptually divided into the soft-covered sleeping platform, primarily the domain of women, and the colder floor and storage area, the province of males. The metaphor can be extended almost indefinitely to suggest that virtually every aspect of traditional Eskimo society could be mapped as a symbolic microcosm of complementary halves.

Socioeconomic Organization

In general we may conceptualize Eskimo social organization as a set of nested units of decreasing size. With the possible exception of the Alaskan population, Eskimos lack "tribes" in the conventional sense of territorially fixed and politically unified groups. Instead, they identify themselves and others with features associated with the region where they live, adding the suffix-*muit* ("the people of") to a geographical name.

The largest political and social unit the Eskimos recognized was the people of the entire area in which they lived. They considered themselves related through actual kinship at the most, and annual co-residence at the least. This social unit is most accurately described as a "band". It usually consisted of anywhere from sixty people (as, for example, in central Canada at times of the year when these groups were smallest) to three hundred (in the more-or-less permanent villages in western Alaska and Greenland, for instance, or the seasonal social and trading encampments in northern Alaska). Bands reckoned their relationship bilaterally (that is, through both parents). Sometimes the band was clustered around a core kin group consisting of a powerful family and their less powerful relations who occupied the same dwelling or one nearby. At the season when group size swelled, other families with less significant economic ties to the core group also might join the band. (These units will be discussed further on in this chapter).

The camp or settlement, the next smallest social group, was even more flexible. At some seasons, the camp was composed of several households, at others it could shrink to a single household.

The smallest unit of Eskimo social organization was the household. The household was also flexible in number. Usually, it consisted of an extended family: a nuclear family (parents and their offspring) around which were gathered other relatives such as grandparents, newly married children and their spouses and children, and, sometimes, more distant relatives of unfortunates without families. Rarely did people live by themselves, and if they did it was usually temporary. Eskimo social organization, like the material

Figure 2.3 AN ESKIMO NUCLEAR FAMILY: Kenojuak and her husband Johnniebo, famous Canadian Inuit graphic artists, in their summer tent at Cape Dorset, N. W. T., early 1960s. (Courtesy of B. Korda, National Film Board/National Archives of Canada, PA145170.)

and technological aspects of their culture, was based on the division of labor. This in turn required a minimal economic unit of at least two persons, one adult male and one adult female. Within their own domains adult men and women made decisions autonomously, and in this sense the unit could be considered a partnership. Nevertheless, men were responsible for the more life-and death decisions over group movement and economic strategies, and it would be a distortion to present the situation any other way.

Camps and settlements usually had a *de facto* leader, who, owing to experience and seniority, was sought out for his advice. The *umialiks* of Alaska mentioned above are one example of such *de facto* leaders. Rarely, though, was it obligatory to follow his advice, for though some people obviously were more successful than others there was little formal differentiation between rich and poor. In the more permanent villages of western Alaska the role of such leaders sometimes more closely approximated chieftainship; their authority over social, ritual and economic affairs was more institutionalized and permanent, and, in extreme cases, might be passed on to the next generation.

The shaman, (*angakuk*), or religious specialist, present in many settlements and bands, also exercised a leadership function in Eskimo society. This role (discussed more fully in the section on religion and ceremony below) was usually assumed by men, but sometimes by women. The shaman's power over the community, however, was negative. Stemming from access to the supernatural and control over it, this fear-inspiring power could put the community in his, or her, debt. Shamans may have been disliked, but they were always important social forces, exerting control over the lives of every individual in their realm. Occasionally, secular leaders and shamans belonged to the same extended family. More rarely, the same individual assumed both roles. In this case the family or individual could muster even greater "political" control. Sometimes this led to the development of incipient class differences. In ordinary situations the secular leader and the shaman shared such socioeconomic authority as there was, including, for example, the apportionment of big game, the organization of cooperative hunts, the arbitration of quarrels, and the relationship between men, animals and the supernatural.

The Annual Cycle

It has long been acknowledged that in times past the major organizing principle of Eskimo social life was the annual cycle of movement between camps. Along with this went the fairly regular shrinking and swelling of group size throughout the year. Although it is important to remember that environmental factors limit—but do not necessarily determine—cultural features such as group composition, this cycle of fluctuating socioeconomic organization certainly correlated with the nature and location of resources at different times. Moreover, the annual cycle, though characterized by oscillating group size in general, differed in local expression according to ecological circumstances, resultant specialization, and, to some extent, choice. For example, the Central Canadian Eskimos, whose resources were poor and scattered, were the most nomadic, moving six or more times a year. In contrast, the Bering Sea Eskimos of richer and more temperate climes were far more sedentary, passing nine or ten months annually in one settlement.

Let us examine two local variations of Eskimo socioeconomic organization and annual cycle. Each was typical within its area but neither should be taken as prototypical of the entire cultural area.

Taking the best-known Eskimos, the igloo-living peoples of the seacoast of the central Canadian Arctic, we may start with the winter phase. At a location near expanses of *tuvak* where seal breathing holes were numerous, large aggregations (up to a hundred people) lived together in clustered snowhouses for several months. From there, the men commuted to the economically productive areas, returning with their catches of sea mammals. During March and April, as the days grew longer and the weather improved, these large camps splintered, most often into extended families, who built smaller igloo villages at seasonally strategic points along the coast. From there they continued to hunt seals through the ice and, as it got warmer, basking seals on the surface. Until June or July, as the *tuvak* contracted and eventually broke up, hunters from several households cooperatively engaged in walrus hunting from boats in the open sea. In the same period large numbers of migrating caribou began to approach the area. The more active men sometimes went together to hunt them over the inland snows, dragging the caribou back to the coastal camps.

By early summer, even the transitional *qarmat* was uninhabitable, and welcoming the end of the long winter, the Eskimos gladly abandoned their snow houses for portable sealskin tents, erecting them on patches of land bare of snow. Rivers began to run fast and salmon and char began their annual migrations. This was the season for fishing, both at weirs and in other localities. The size of coastal camps often dwindled further as families wandered along the coast or up rivers and to the lakes for fishing, hunting, and egg gathering. Dog sleds were put on blocks until the next winter and the dogs were fitted with backpacks to help move the family belongings. "Richer" men refurbished their *umiaks* in preparation for transporting their households to more productive sites. From there, they engaged in open water kayak hunting for seals, relatively abundant at this season.

At summer's end families left the coast, moving inland with their tents and paraphernalia to fish and undertake the most important caribou hunting of the year. From these large cooperative hunts, which felled the animals on their southward migration, came the meat to be cached for the coming winter, but even more important were the skins (in prime condition at this time of the year) for winter clothing. Caribou hunting continued as long as the herds were present. The Eskimos were loathe to return to the coast until the autumnal storms had abated and the new sea ice was once again strong enough for *maupuk* hunting.

Thus in early winter the larger settlements reaggregated and social and ceremonial life began anew. And despite the stereotype of improvidence we sedentary agriculturalists have of this largely nomadic people, the Eskimos were only too aware of the threat of impending starvation that the approach of winter could mean and took such steps as they could accordingly. Dog sleds were refurbished, dogs were fattened and nourished to strengthen them for their winter tasks, and the women worked ceaselessly, cutting and sewing new sets of boots and garments for their families. It was during the late autumn that socio-psychological conflicts and illnesses were most prevalent, probably from the unvoiced apprehensions about the deprivations the oncoming winter could bring.

By contrast, Pacific Eskimos of subarctic Alaska illustrate a second type of social organization and annual cycle. The following reconstruction is more tentative, however, because less is known of their aboriginal lifeways owing to the earlier date when they were contacted.

Since little sea ice and no *tuvak* occurred in this area, sea mammals could be hunted from kayaks nearly year round. Especially in the spring and early summer, the men hunted sea otters, fur seals, from one- and often two-holed kayaks. Whale hunting was also practiced though only by the most skilled hunters thoroughly versed in the appropriate rituals. In summer the men fished in the deep-sea for halibut and cod, but some families migrated with tents up the large rivers to net and trap the abundant migratory salmon. Throughout the year, but especially in the fall, women harvested the plant foods more readily available in this area: berries, tubers, roots, and even some kelp and seaweed. A great variety of shellfish available along the coast could be gathered, especially in the winter when other resources decreased, or stormy weather discouraged sea hunting. Land animals, though less important, were also taken throughout the year. These included bear, mountain goat, and smaller species such as mink and marten, virtually unknown in other areas.

Among the subarctic Eskimos, social organization, like the area's settlement pattern, was more permanent. The alternating wax and wane of group size was less of a factor there than elsewhere. The constant interaction of these larger populations was characterized by more formalized social relationships. The Pacific Eskimos are thought to have had hereditary chiefs (or near-chiefs) who, along with their extended families, sometimes occupied larger houses. These houses often served as ceremonial centers for the more elaborate ritual life of winter. As mentioned earlier, most Alaskan Eskimo villages had a ceremonial or "men's house" that constituted the ritual and social center of the settlement, in addition to serving as a sleeping place for men.

Characteristic of this area also was hereditary, hierarchical ranking by which people were assigned positions of power or, at the other end of the scale, servitude. Servants or slaves (often captives of the warfare common there) performed the menial tasks, their lives considered very cheap by their "owners". Thus we can see that in many ways the annual cycle and social organization of these peoples resembles their not-too-distant relations, the Aleut, and also is reminiscent of the neighboring Northwest Coast Indians.

Kinship and Social Structure

Classic Eskimo-type social organization closely parallels our own Euro-American kinship structure in many features. According to George P. Murdock, an anthropologist knowledgeable about kinship worldwide, Eskimo-type social organization is characteristic of all societies having Eskimo cousin terminology and lacking exogamous unilinear kin groups. It is further distinguished by monogamy, independent nuclear families, lineal terms

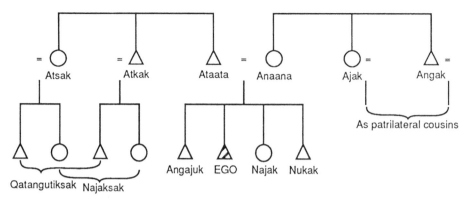

Figure A Bilateral kinship terminology (the Eskimo type) which differentiates siblings from cousins, and uncles and aunts from parents and from each other.

for aunts and nieces, the bilateral extension of incest taboos and the common presence of bilateral kin groups such as kindred and demes (though these are often unreported). The variations in this basic structure, Murdock goes on to say, may come about through rules of postmarital residence other than the normal neolocal one: by polygyny, by extended families, and so on. The heart of "the Eskimo type" system, as represented by the bilateral kinship terminology, differentiates siblings from cousins, and uncles and aunts from parents and from each other (Figure A). Murdock's description is based on the excellent early ethnographies of the Central Eskimos. Since in many areas the fundamentals of the traditional kinship system survive (and because other societies reckon their kinship similarly), we shall employ the present tense in the following discussion.

The Eskimo system would lead us to expect equal reckoning of degrees of relationship on either side, that is, bilaterally: through both mother and father and perhaps statistically equal choices of residence and alliance with either the mother's group or the father's group. Bilaterally organized societies are said to be most amenable to flexible social structure, which is necessary for—and found throughout—most Eskimo groups.

Recent comparative evidence, however, has shown us that such a simple basis by no means accounts for the majority of Eskimo social organizations, and that strict bilateralism, even in the central area, usually occurs to a lesser extent than the tendency toward emphasizing kinship relationships on the father's side. This trend occurs not only in the kinship terminology system but also in a general tendency toward patrilocal residence and kinship groups composed of fathers and their married sons or sibling groups of brothers.

Not surprisingly, the greatest degree of variation and deviance from the bilateral norm has been found among the more densely populated and permanently settled peoples of western Alaska. A well-documented example is the social organization of the St. Lawrence Island Eskimos. These Eskimos do not have the familiar bilateral cousin terminology; although they usually differentiate between siblings and cousins, they lump cross-cousins together and use different set of terms for maternal and paternal parallel cousins. In fact, paternal cousins are often called by the same terms as siblings, deemphasizing the closeness of the male/male link through the father (Figure B).

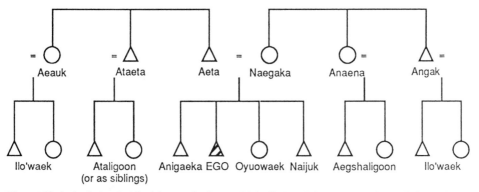

Figure B A deviation in kinship terminology which distinguishes paternal parallel cousins and emphasizes the male/male link through the father.

Under conditions of stability all Eskimo groups would probably tend to emphasize patrilineal kinship and to establish patrilocal residences because the cooperative productive group is based on the number of males, and in a kin-based world this generally means groups of brothers. Furthermore, it is more advantageous for men to live permanently in one area during their lives, for a man raised in an area knows its ecologically productive possibilities better, whereas a stranger faces great disadvantage when outside his own territory.

Thus there appears to be more variety in Eskimo kinship patterns than has been acknowledged. Nevertheless in areas such as northwestern Alaska, the differences in kinship terminology and in kinship relationships can be correlated with the local ecological imperatives and the consequent need for certain kinds of cooperation. Similarly anthropologists have also shown that Eskimo kinship terminology among the various subregions of the "typical" Central Eskimos is not altogether homogeneous. There, major deviations result from overriding the distinction between siblings and cousins, differentiating matrilateral from parallel cousins, and, often, from emphasizing the patrilateral consanguineal kin group. Perhaps we might conclude that one cannot explain all variations on the basis of functional-adaptive correlations; some may be the result of historical accident or microdiffusion.

Let us now demonstrate, in one case of "typical" Central Eskimo social organization, how the kinship terminology and social relationships are functionally adaptive for the kind of existence that requires constant splitting and aggregation of groups and dependence upon a flexible set of ties to other bands and camps outside one's own area, whom one may have to visit or depend upon in times of local privation. At the same time, minor variations from the strictly bilateral system are quite relevant to a patrilateral-patrilocal bias where any degree of stability may hold.

In this social organization, diagrammed in Figure C, postmarital residence is Pacific Eskimo matri-patrilocal. Thereby the man goes to live in or near the household of his new bride and hunts with his father-in-law for a year or more, at least until the first baby is born. Thus he will be incorporated into his father-in-law's camp and areas for a relatively short period of his life, during which he is ill-at-ease and in a subordinate position while he

45

Generation	Own (Father's) Camp		Other Camps	
	Male	Female	Male	Female
+2 GrParents	Ataatacia	Aanak	Ataatacia	Anaanacia

	Own Household Male	Own Household Female	Other House Male	Other House Female	FaSi Camp Male	FaSi Camp Female	MoSi Camp Male	MoSi Camp Female	MoBr Camp Male	MoBr Camp Female
+1 Parents	Ataata	Anaana	Atkak	Arngnajuk	Ningauk	Atsak	Ningauk	Ajak	Angak	Ukuak

	Own Household		Male	Female
Older	Angajuk	Najak	Male	Female
+0 Younger	Nukak		Qatangutiksak	Najaksak

Figure C Kinship terminology and residential alignments of Ego, an unmarried male (using terms presented in Figure 12.2). Note that the patrilocal, patrilateral bias of the special terms for females aanak and arngnajuk (indicated by asterisks), who are found only in Ego's (father's) camp, is also reflected in the affinal kinship terminology used by married men and women. (After Graburn, Taqagmiut Eskimo Kinship terminology, 1964, Fig. 6, p. 84.)

proves himself. Ideally and in fact, the young couple move back to the husband's father's territory or camp for the rest of their lives, returning presumably to an area familiar to the man. Since most of the essential tasks of women do not depend upon location, they can be performed equally well in anybody's camp. Given such a residence rule, a man will have in his own camp his father (if alive), his brother and his family and their descendants, and most probably his father's brother and his wife and children. His father's sister will live in another camp, having moved there fairly soon after her marriage; his mother's brother will live in yet another camp with his own brother and father and children; and his mother's sister, if she has been married for more than a few years, will be living in another camp with her husband and his family.

Thus, apart from the members of their own household, children raised in any given camp are likely to know best their father's brother and his wife and children. And perhaps for short periods of time when they are younger, they will know well their father's sister and her husband, and occasionally their mother's sister if she is unmarried or newly married, and their mother's brother and/or father who remain at the camp that their mother originally came from. Siblings living in the household are terminologically distinguished from cousins living in another household, for extended family residence is rarely permanent. Among all the cousins, father's brothers' children are most likely to be coresident in the camp, at least during certain times of the year, and in many areas this is reflected by their terminological differentiation from all other cousins who may live in nearby camps and who may visit or be visited by the household in which Ego lives. Thus a person grows up having a series of graduated consanguineal ties within his own camp and with camps in adjacent areas.

As he goes through his life cycle the individual develops further ties. For instance, when a man's sister marries, her new husband will join them for a time before returning with her and their children to his original camp; the man's brother may go to live in another camp with his new bride and then return later with his young family to his patrilocal camp; and later, of course, a man's children marry and form further links to other camps.

The rule of exogamy is not well demarcated in Eskimo culture. Although Eskimos usually distinguish siblings from cousins terminologically, this perhaps reflects the nature of the residence groups rather than the allowability of sexual access. Most Eskimo groups permit sexual access to first cousins, but discourage it. Marriages, frequently arranged by parents during their children's youth, often reflect the preference of creating or cementing ties with more distant families through marriage with distant relatives. Endogamy does occur but the majority of the population frowns upon it. On the other hand, although it might be advantageous to have alliances through marriage with very distant groups, the Eskimos' great fear of strangers and the risks they might incur usually prevent such arrangements. Thus marriages most often take place between distant relatives or not-too-distant nonrelatives.

Partnerships

A major characteristic of Eskimo social organization, the partnership, enabled Eskimos to extend their ties and to create trustworthy relationships through alliances outside the circle of *ilagit* ("bilaterally reckoned kinsmen"). In the range of Eskimo groups various forms of partnership received more or less formal or ritual recognition. In wife exchange, the best known (and most frequently misunderstood) form, two friends, almost always nonkinsmen, agreed to swap wives for a period of time, sometimes to emphasize their friendship but often because of a practical necessity such as the inability of a pregnant woman to travel. Any children that were the issue of an exchange relationship were considered full siblings, thus extending the number of people these individuals would later be able to count as close relatives.

Other forms of non-kin-based partnerships were found throughout the Arctic but varied in concept and function from place to place. Quite commonly, partnerships were based on friendship and economic cooperation, and the formal social recognition of two men as partners served to bind an already existing relationship. Often such men became partners for life, and were required to help each other, generously share their goods, and even practice wife exchange, though this last was not the main purpose. Partners may have had to defend each other and even avenge the other's death. Such economically based partnerships might extend across local and even tribal boundaries, especially in the western Arctic where long-distance trade occurred more frequently. Men inherited or created trading partnerships with other men who had access to different ecological resources. Whenever the two groups met, which might be at annually-specified times, each man sought out his trading partner to exchange, for instance, products of the land for products of the sea, without haggling or hostility, even though each individual might be hostile to or suspicious of other members of the out-group. In some places in western and southwestern Alaska such trading partnerships extended even to non-Eskimos (as for example with Indians along the Kobuk River in northern Alaska) where interrelations were not overly hostile.

Partnerships functioned in other ways too. For example, "joking relationships" were extremely common, and these might or might not be combined with partnerships of the kinds already described. Such men—who may have formed friendships from their fathers, as was obligatory between children of half-cross-cousins on Nunivak Island (Alaska)—were expected to insult each other continually. They often composed songs and rhymes to disparage each other and sang or recited them in public without fear of retaliation. This type of joking relationship has often been termed "song (contest) partnership". In the central Arctic such pairs were known as *illurit* (see also the following section on "Social Control").

A further means of extending friendly and more or less permanent relationships to non-kinsmen is illustrated by the extremely prevalent "namesake" system found among the Eskimos. Two people with the same name call each other *saunik* (bone) or *atitsiak* (good name) and have a special relationship based on the ancient belief that one of the souls governing the personality is attached to the name; thus two people with the same name are in a way spiritually identical. If an Eskimo entered a new and distant village and felt uneasy in a social group, he struck up a special relationship with a namesake, thus creating an ally. More important, he could then put himself in this person's place in the local kinship system and call upon his namesake's relatives for aid and comfort in the same way as a real relative would. This led to a wide network of often incongruous relationships, for names are not sex-specific. Even today one occasionally hears an old woman call a young boy "my mother" because he shares her deceased mother's name.

Though the kinship system formed the continuing basis of traditional Eskimo social organization, social and ecological imperatives often disrupted the stable group making outside alliances a crucial determinant of life or death. The uncertainties of economic resources and the relatively weak social control in these groups (see below) often created circumstances wherein the normal social ties and the first line of economic co-operation broke down. In such a case the person with secondary or tertiary relationships to fall back on was the person who survived.

Leadership and Social Control

The annual cycle and unforeseen ecological circumstances were major influences on the oscillations of Eskimo groups. Except in northern Alaska, even groups that reunited regularly were not "territorial"—that is, there were no inherited or permanent rights to the resources of the land and sea. Thus the Eskimos lacked a territorially based political system, and the groups they lived in had relatively little continuity or rigid organization. As the reader will perceive, these statements apply only partly to the more densely and permanently inhabited subarctic areas at the eastern and western extremes of the Eskimos' homeland.

Aside from kinship, there were few statuses in traditional Eskimo society, and none were primarily political or legal in nature. Secular leaders were leaders primarily because they could bestow economic benefits upon their followers. They were normally "rich" or skillful men who could organize hunts, advise on seasonal movements, and oversee the important and equitable distribution of game products. As senior males they usually wielded authority in their own nuclear or extended families, but their influence over others was voluntary. Their social-control functions, primarily in the economic sphere, usually took the form of advice, which might or might not be heeded. All senior men and women, however, did have authority over—and commanded the respect of—the young, irrespective of kin ties. More specific social controls were exercised by the shaman and the taboos on which his authority rested. Though these taboos regulated social intercourse to some extent, they were more apt to be concerned with the control of ecological imperatives and the uncertain, dangerous forces of the supernatural.

At the best of times traditional Eskimo life was peaceful, co-operative and joyous, embracing much that Westerners romanticize as the "simple, natural life of the close-to-nature primitive". As we have seen, however, the best of times were the ideal, and the worst of times frequently intervened. The three main recurring sources of anxieties were starvation and (for the men especially) mate selection and fertility. These themes often intertwined because the successful hunter was the best provider and hence could support the greatest number of wives and offspring.

In every family or household, physical skill and personality allowed for the emergence of the *de facto* leaders described above. But those who dominated could also instill fear and jealousy. Thus others in the prestige competition were constantly attempting to overthrow them. If they were unsuccessful their choices were to accept defeat for the sake of economic security, or alternatively, to leave and join another group where their chances of success were greater. Women also competed for desirable men and for the status reaped from numerous healthy (and preferable male) offspring.

At the other end of the scale were the incompetents unable to perform successfully in either sphere. Regardless of sex they were a burden to the community. These deadweights were the butt of jokes and were sometimes conscripted into servitude by stronger group members. If they could not bear their lot, they could abandon the group or, under extreme circumstances, commit suicide.

In times past the Eskimos condoned various forms of what to us would be unacceptable violence. This included infanticide—particularly of female children or the weaker of twins—gerontocide (the usually passive killing-by-abandonment of old people unable to look after themselves), suicide, and cannibalism (under the extreme duress of starvation). Those who committed such deeds were not punished. Acts of violence perceived as a threat to individual or group unity, however, were subject to reprisal. For example, stealing might be excused in cases of need, but wife stealing—or the threat of unsanctioned seduction—was cause for action. Most violence developed from the competition for women. Often men tried to take the wives of other men. Some killed to do it, others merely snatched them. Before or after the fact, the offended man might try, with least personal risk, to kill his rival. Sometimes a notorious philanderer would be killed by the other men in the group, all acting to protect themselves.

Killings ("justified" or otherwise) incurred further violence, for usually the partners, close relatives or offspring of the dead sought vengeance. This resulted in long-term feuds that sometimes ended the lives of the most productive and essential group members—the young and able men. In many populations it was the rare man who had not been involved in a killing at some time or another. This fact of Eskimo life probably represented as great a threat to the perpetuation of viable social groups as the many environmental hazards. Thus we can see the necessity of forging and maintaining alliances and relationships in the widest possible circle.

In periods of starvation the rule was everyone for him- or herself. The living ate the dead, those with food hid it from their closest kin, and the fit and mobile abandoned the weak. Marriages and families could break up never to reconcile. The mother-child bond was probably the strongest, but during the worst times the youngest were among the first to die or be killed and eaten by the more able. The elderly committed suicide or were killed. In the end, even the fit adults waited for each other to die so they might eat. And sometimes they did not wait. In circumstances of extreme privation women were apt to outlive men, either because of metabolic differences or because in the course of life they made less taxing physical efforts overall. Thus small groups of women sometimes found themselves eating their husbands, to be found later in the final stages of starvation themselves.

The pervasive threat of violence that could escalate into killing led to other less dire social controls. The mildest was avoidance. We have already mentioned that the unsuccessful or unpopular left the group. The reverse occurred when the group avoided or abandoned the offender. Another result, however, was the pretense that the problem did not exist by merely protecting one's property or wife when the offender is present. In some cases the shaman was called in to deal with the social deviant (see the section on religion and the supernatural below).

Another form of conflict resolution was the joking relationship already discussed. To relieve tension, the two parties in disagreement would be encouraged to engage in public song duels; the community then selected the winner. Boxing competitions were another form of social control, the victory and prestige going to the last man left standing. Another common means was the scolding of the young by older more prestigious family members; sometimes this method succeeded and at other times it led to flight or suicide. An even more common mechanism was the constant gossip so much a part of group living everywhere; additionally gossip had the more benign purpose of reinforcing group values.

Thus Eskimo social life, despite its idyllic moments, was more often rife with competition and strife, perhaps less so in the more rigidly organized subarctic regions. However, warfare, feuding and other more organized forms of violence was prevalent among these groups.

Religious Ideology and Organization

What we would call the supernatural played a prominent role in the traditional life of the Eskimos. The distinction between natural and supernatural, however, was nowhere near as sharply defined as in our ideology. Furthermore, control over both domains was far more tenuous. The shaman alone exerted positive influence over the supernatural. For the remainder of the population the only access was the negative adherence to taboos; infractions against them could engender severe repercussions to the individual and possibly the entire group.

As with other aspects of Eskimo society there were many local and regional variations in religious practice, belief and beings, but ultimately they all clustered about two major components, shamanism (the special status of one who has greater access to and control over the supernatural) and animism (the belief that people, animals, inanimate objects and the world in general are possessed of spirits or souls that can affect the lives of all). The names, appearance and numbers of these spirits differed according to locality, as did the particular conception of the human soul and the practices and status of shamans, their acquisition of power and degree of influence. Throughout the Eskimo area, however, the fundamental nature of these concepts was the same.

Soul Spirits

Every individual was conceived of as a relatively unimportant physical entity inhabited by numerous soul spirits. The most important was the *turngak* (in the eastern Arctic dialect), whose loss was a major cause of disease or death. The soul spirit did not determine the individual's personality, but his or her existence; after death this soul resided in an extra-territorial afterworld, the nature of which usually depended on the individual's behavior during the lifetime. Thus these afterworlds were conceived of as a hierarchy from bad to good. Though the concepts varied regionally, these nether worlds were usually located in the heavens, near the earth's surface, deep within it, or at the bottom of the sea. The individual's *atirk* (name) represented the social aspects of the soul, for as mentioned already, the name was a major determinant of the social personality and characteristics. These characteristics were associated with the name and were reincarnated along with it through the generations. Thus when an individual died the *atirk* was freed into the atmosphere where it was a potentially dangerous force. About the time of birth, the mother or someone close to her chose an *atirk* for the newborn from this reservoir; thereby the child was invested with the associated attributes of its name.

In the past, if individuals' lives were unhappy they might change their names to acquire a more beneficial social personality. Another type of soul spirit was the breath-soul, which left the body at death and disappeared without harm or destination; thus for both animals and human beings we might interpret the breath soul as "life". In addition to these individual soul spirits, parts of the body, particularly the joints, were said to be inhabited by *inua*, a concept literally translating as "its person". *Inua* were locationally fixed and resided not only in humans but also animals and important inanimate objects in the surrounding world. The loss or angering of an *inua* could lead to illness or disaster.

Supernatural Beings

In actuality we should not classify such phenomena as "supernatural", because, existing as they did within (*ilu*) a person, animal, or inanimate object, they in fact constituted the "nature" of things. Their presence was the norm, their loss a divergence from it. At a more general level, the entire physical world was conceived of as encompassing free-roaming spirits of the outside (*sila*), many of whom were also called *turngak* (or the equivalent). As a class *turngaks* had contradictory attributes: they could be good or bad, large or small, and could assume many appearances natural, unnatural, or awesome. The acquisition of personal *turngaks* was the major avenue to shamanhood, for such acquisition led to access, and this in turn led to control, of supernatural beings and ultimately, the world they inhabited.

Other *turngaks* were not personally acquired but were harmful if encountered. One might repel them with magic or by wearing amulets. Since *turngaks* often assumed animal form, one could not always be certain whether one was seeing a "natural" or supernatural being (here we see an illustration of the gray area between these categories). Much of the inexplicable was attributed to *turngaks* and in a few places an extremely powerful manifestation was elevated to the status of deity, controlling such aspects of the world as weather and animal migration. Finally, *turngaks* occasionally assumed human form; social deviants were sometimes said to have married them and borne them children.

The Eskimo acknowledged numerous other classes of beings we would call supernatural. For instance, *ijuruk* were humanoid manifestations of the souls of the dead whereas *inuragulligak* were perfectly formed miniatures of Eskimo people, both benevolent, and malevolent, and endowed with powerful physical and supernatural attributes. Eskimo mythology is populated by such "extra-terrestrials" as misshapen humanoids and races of giants, exceptionally strong but rather witless man/animal beings who inhabit an area called *tunit*.

In Eskimo society, taboos constituted the major means to avoid angering the souls of the all-important animals or the spirits that controlled them. Therefore personal and community disasters were believed to be the result of transgressions against them. In nearly all groups the supreme power, particularly over the sea and sea mammals, resided with an angry old women who, according to myth, had been outcast when young and now lived in the deep. This deity is often called *Sedna* in the literature, although it is unlikely that the Eskimos ever called her by this name. *Sedna* is probably a corruption of a term meaning "in the bottom of the sea". the Eskimo name for her changes from place to place, the most common being *Nuliajuk* ("the one who is a wife/fornicates"). Belief in an undersea female deity was prevalent from northern Alaska to Greenland, but entirely absent in western Alaska and among the Caribou Eskimos. More variable was the belief in another powerful spirit *Sila,* who controlled the weather and sometimes land animals. This force, more important than *Nuliajuk* had less direct concern with individuals, but where anthropomorphized, was conceptualized as male and resided in the sky above.

Shamanism

The personality of Eskimo shamans and acquisition of shamanic power have been subject to debate, but contrary to popular opinion there is no overriding evidence that such individuals possessed the "psychopathic" personalities that have been alleged for Siberian shamans. Certainly, shamans had powerful identities, were extremely perceptive, and though not necessarily likable, were capable of exerting considerable influence over others. The Eskimo attitude toward shamans was ambivalent. Their unique powers were at once feared and welcomed.

There was no one road to becoming a shaman, and the art was practiced by both sexes. In some areas young people consciously sought to acquire a familiar *turngak,* the only absolute prerequisite. This spirit quest, similar to others among other North American natives, required a solitary journey of some duration. The individual hunted or meditated, waiting for a dream, vision or sign indicating the procurement of extraordinary supernatural power. Equally common among Eskimos, however, was the unintentional obtainment of such power through a happenstance such as starvation, isolation, accident, or illness. Frequently, a shaman had had a parent who also controlled the supernatural and thus may have been predisposed to acquire spirit power.

Becoming a shaman required a long apprenticeship and the acquisition of a vast body of knowledge and an intricate complex of skills and practices. It required not only a special relationship with the supernatural world but also the ability to perform awe-inspiring feats before the social group. Practitioners needed the powers to benefit both individuals and community. They were called upon to cure the individual illnesses thought to be incurred by infringements against taboo. This was sometimes ascertained through lifting the person, whose lightness or heaviness was interpreted as negative or positive indication of offense. Sometimes the resulting illness was cured by sucking out the offending substance or spirit; at others the shaman dispatched his spirit to the nether world to repossess the soul of the ailing person.

The shaman also functioned on behalf of individuals in the instigation of "black" or "white" magic, to harm an enemy for example, or conversely, to positively dispose a potential sexual partner or ensure fertility. Services on behalf of individual or community were paid the shaman in material goods.

One reason shamans engendered mistrust was their frequent abuse of power. They sometimes dispatched their familiars for self-benefit. Moreover, though they might not be successful community members themselves they often formed alliances with those who were.

More critical to shamans' success was their performance on behalf of the well-being of the community as a whole. If disaster struck in the form of inclement weather or absence of game, for example, the shaman's job was to determine whether one or more persons had broken an important taboo, for example, a woman hiding a miscarriage or a man who had used the same weapons for hunting sea and land mammals. Even when he could diagnose the cause, the shaman usually had to dispatch his soul to visit *Nuliajuk* on the ocean floor. Though entertainment was one function of the shaman, such journeys were undertaken to appease the deity and convince her to calm the seas, or return the animals to the hunting grounds. Dangerous and sometimes unsuccessful, these soul flights required intensive preparation, psychic energy and co-operation from the group. In areas lacking such deities the shamanic performances required a deep trance and the projection of the soul for appeasement of less anthropomorphized controlling forces.

In the more densely populated regions of Alaska the social organization of religion was more complex. There the annual cycle was punctuated by communal feasts which were partly religious in nature. These festivities often included dance performances in which masked figures impersonated the *inua* of animals or the natural world. These performances were dedicated to appeasing the spirits and expressing the proper relationship with them. For instance, for the Bladder Feast enacted in communities around the Bering Sea, residents inflated animal bladders (thought to contain the souls of dead animals), displayed them during performances in the ceremonial men's house, then, to renew their relationship with the spirits controlling them, returned them to the sea. Typical of the same area were elaborate feasts commemorating spirits of the dead which at once comforted the bereaved and assisted the departing spirits on their journey to the other world. In the central Arctic the highlight of the ceremonial social season was the *gitingirk* (midwinter feast) when people from the whole region gathered to share food, competitive games, watch shamanic performances and exchange wives in the ritual of "putting out the lamps".

In sum, Eskimo religion functioned to restore balance when outside forces threatened, to relieve anxiety, and to reduce interpersonal tensions. Though technologically sophisticated, the Eskimos were nonetheless subject to extreme environmental pressures and prey to overpowering and unpredictable circumstances. Their belief system did not assure them of complete control over the world around them and the Eskimo individual was virtually powerless to combat these forces save by observing taboos. Supernatural power was channeled through the shaman, who mediated between the community and the usually malevolent spirits. Eskimo mythology and folklore explained the relationships between all things, but only superficially. In the main, this rich body of oral tradition operated to provoke the raucous humor that the Eskimos welcomed as their main defense against the inevitable and imponderable forces of the world.

History, Acculturation and Modernization

In this section we discuss the history of Eskimo colonization and the major changes that have occurred in Eskimo culture and society as a result of the intrusions of Westerners. There have been four major colonizers of the Eskimos: Denmark, Canada, the United States and the U.S.S.R., affecting Greenland, the Canadian Arctic, Alaska, and Siberia respectively. We here limit ourselves to consideration of the three North American Eskimo populations.

Greenland

The Vikings inhabited Greenland for hundreds of years (ca. 1000–1600 A.D.), but as far as we can determine they little influenced recent history. The Danes "rediscovered" Greenland in the sixteenth century but did not undertake full-scale colonization until after 1721, when Protestant missionaries established a permanent settlement in West Greenland. The Eskimos were co-operative owing in part to the missionaries' serious study of the language and relatively non-exploitive attitudes. Thus the West Greenlanders were the first of their race to be subject to permanent agencies of European culture.

The Church acted as an official arm of the Danish Crown, and the missionaries therefore governed on behalf of God and Country. Consequently the Greenlanders, unlike the other Eskimos, were administered by intruders who came, not to exploit both the people and their natural resources, but who, while unavoidably paternalistic, were at least humane.

Owing to racial admixture, the Eskimos became known as Greenlanders (much as the Labrador Eskimos have become "settlers" or "livyers"). From 1774 until the 1950s, the missionary settlers, purportedly for the benefit of the Eskimos, operated trading stores under government monopoly. These stores stocked only goods that they judged beneficial to Eskimo life; luxuries were in short supply and very expensive. Tobacco and alcohol, for example, have come on the market only in the past few decades, and, until very recently, spirits were subject to prohibitively strict controls. At first the stores only took in trade Eskimo products not deemed essential to their life and health, prohibiting, for instance, the potentially lucrative trade in whale blubber. To prevent disruption of the scattered aboriginal settlement pattern, "post living" (a common result of colonization in the Canadian and Alaskan North) was discouraged and the stores dispersed among the best hunting areas.

At the same time, the missionaries stressed education, both for spiritual purposes and to foster continuance of local self-government. The major emphasis was on literacy, and for this purpose a written version of the Eskimo language (based on Latin orthography) was devised and disseminated. For the past century and more, local councils have administered law and welfare. The Eskimos have been represented in these bodies, though control has rested mainly in the hands of Danes, or Danish-speaking Greenlanders.

We have already mentioned the relatively mild climate of West Greenland. In the past two hundred years the warming trend has driven away the seals and brought in vast shoals of Atlantic fish, thus effecting changes in the local and commercial economies. At the same time European whaling fleets have virtually eliminated the baleen whale and other smaller species that were the Eskimos' mainstays. The introduction of firearms in the last century led to the near-extinction of native caribou, another local and commercial resource. Nevertheless, the West Greenlandic Eskimo population, estimated at approximately 5,000 in the last eighteenth century, had doubled a hundred years later due to availability of medical services and increased material security. The introduction of animal husbandry—hardy sheep and cattle—did little for the economy. With no significant minerals for extraction, commercial fishing became the principle occupation.

As the result of these changes, wooden boats and fishing lines soon replaced the kayak hunting culture in West Greenland. Unfortunately, until recently, their commercial operations could not compete against the more technologically advanced fleets of Western nations; nonetheless, the lives of the people increasingly resembled those of European peasant fishermen. By the turn of the century, the government-owned stores began stocking lumber and tools and household equipment of metal, and the Eskimos soon abandoned their stone and sod houses and oil lamps for the coal-heated rectangular wood structures typical of coastal villages in Scandinavia.

During the twentieth century, even as advancing technology has led to ever-larger fish catches, the Danish Government's investment in the health, education, welfare and administration of Greenland has far outweighed the income they receive from there. This imbalance in favor of a colonized people is virtually unique worldwide.

The history of the Polar Eskimos and East Greenlanders is markedly unlike that of the west coast. The Polar Eskimos, also known as the Thule Eskimos, whose aboriginal population is estimated at 200, were not contacted until 1818 and continued to lead an almost undisturbed hunting existence until well into the present. Their earliest extended contact with Westerners was between 1891 and 1909, when members of this remarkable group were the backbone of Peary's North Pole Expeditions. Shortly thereafter, the explorer Knud Rasmussen, a West Greenlander of mixed parentage, established a store in their territory. The profits were used to finance the famous Fifth Thule Expedition Rasmussen led across arctic America between 1921 and 1924. During World War II, when Denmark was occupied by the Nazis, the United States administered Greenland, and at that time an Air Force base (and, later, other military installations) were established at Thule. Until recently, however, contact between the Eskimos and the military was banned. The few hundred Thule Eskimos live in scattered hunting and trapping villages near government-operated stores and schools.

The East Greenlandic Eskimos (about 400 in number at the turn of the century), whose territory centered around Ammassalik, were first contacted in 1884. By this time the east coast had been nearly depopulated by ecological pressures, and by the drift of inhabitants to the more hospitable west coast. This trend was halted by the construction of schools and stores, and with the subsequent increase in food supply and decrease in infanticide, the population increased steadily. Shark fishing was introduced, but the demands of the burgeoning population soon exceeded the supply. Resultingly, new settlements have been established to the north and south of Ammassalik. By 1970, owing to education, political reorganization, and direct government efforts, the two thousand or more East Greenlanders had approximated the level of acculturation prevalent in the west.

In 1946, when Denmark resumed control of the subcontinent, the local population became increasingly insistent on a greater degree of self-determination. In 1950 a Provincial Council for the entire country was inaugurated at Godthab (now known as Nuuk) and shortly thereafter, in response to Greenlanders' demands for greater equality, Danish was substituted for Greenlandic in the schools. Meantime it had become a common practice for students to finish their secondary school education in Denmark. In 1953 the country was incorporated as a county of Denmark and thereafter Greenlanders have been permitted two elected representatives to the Parliament at Copenhagen. Denmark continued its hefty subsidies during the following decades, modernizing the fishing fleet, erecting modern apartment blocks, houses, schools and hospitals in the major population centers. These policies negatively impacted the smaller communities, however, as many were deprived of local services and then closed down.

In the 1970s, the young Denmark-educated politicians began making demands for autonomy as opposed to assimilation. Running successfully for election to the Godthab Council, they organized political parties aimed at attaining Home Rule. Eventually they achieved a majority and Denmark was forced to negotiate. In 1978–79 the Council drew up plans, and Home Rule was implemented in May 1979. Among the provisions and consequences of the change are:

1) Denmark retains authority over foreign relations, defense, and the financial system (although the Home Rule government successfully challenged this policy when they voted to withdraw from the European Common Market in the interest of their fishing industry).

2) Control over expenditure of the continuing Danish subsidy now rests in local hands. In 1980 this amount exceeded 300 million Kroener ($4 million) for a population of 40,000 Greenlanders.

3) Denmark has agreed to continue supplying technical and administrative expertise. Although needed, this has led to the presence of an ever-increasing population of Danes (more than 10,000 in 1986).

4) The Home Rule government has jurisdiction over domestic policy. For example, in 1984 the party in power attempted to curry favor for the upcoming election by abolishing liquor rationing (a holdover from colonial rule). Unfortunately this has led to an escalating crime rate.

In the 1980s, after centuries of benevolent subjugation and consequent losses to their language and culture, the approximately 40,000 Greenlanders turn increasingly to the appreciation of their past. One result has been the establishment of an institution in Nuuk whose purpose is to disseminate information about the traditional culture and foster pride among modern Greenlanders in the marvelously adapted lifeway of their forbears.

Canada

We can usefully divide the history of the changes leading to Canadian Eskimo modernization into three stages as demarcated by the nature of the external influences and their effects on Eskimo culture and society.

In some areas of northern Canada traditional life as described above continued until well into the twentieth century despite temporary modifications from the incursion of traders and explorers over several centuries. The first stage of contact might therefore be described as "modified-traditional", beginning almost four hundred years ago on Baffin Island and the coast of Labrador, nearly there hundred years ago around Hudson Bay, and as little as fifty years ago in the lands between and beyond. During this time large parties of whites explored the Eskimo homeland for economic purposes: to establish shorter routes to Asia and to commercially exploit sea resources such as whales and walrus and, occasionally, minerals. During this early and sporadic trade the Eskimos exchanged skins, meat, and, occasionally, women for metal and metal products. These interactions had little permanent effect on Eskimo life save the greater efficiency that metal tools allowed them and the introduction of diseases that were eventually to prove so disastrous.

The second stage was the fundamental revolution caused by the introduction of commercial fox trapping. Until the past century, trading posts among the Eskimos were few. In the first three decades of the twentieth century, however, with the rise in popularity of White Fox fur, the Hudson's Bay Company (HBC) and other competitors established permanent trading posts at thirty or more advantageous sites in the eastern and central Arctic. In all but the most isolated groups the effects were immediate. In autumn, the companies extended credit to the Eskimos so that in the spring hunters would bring them the valuable white skins to pay off their debts.

Introduction of the credit system brought about profound and far reaching changes to the traditional patterns of Eskimo life. Running lucrative trap lines necessitated prolonged journeys inland; these demanded a greater concentration on provisioning both dog teams and people alike and correspondingly more intensive summer hunting, with rifles and ammunition (bought on credit) and, more recently, wooden boats. Winter hunting was also altered by the greater time allotted to trapping and the correspondingly shorter time available for sea mammal hunting. Combined with the cyclical decline in caribou, the Eskimos thus came to depend ever more increasingly on imported food purchased on credit at the trading post.

Among the irreversible consequences of finding themselves ensnared in the credit system was that the Eskimos' well-being now depended on the caprice of the outside market, a force even further beyond their control than the anxiety-producing whims of weather and animal migration that earlier had plagued them. Furthermore, the annual cycle was disrupted by the new emphasis on inland exploitation in winter and coastal exploitation in summer. These changes, in combination with the appeal of handouts and occasional wage labor, encouraged the trend in "post living" mentioned above.

The history of Eskimo contact in Canada assumed the classic colonial pattern in which flag follows commerce and God follows the flag. Among the earliest government agencies to arrive after the trading posts was the Royal Canadian Mounted Police (RCMP), dispatched to "keep order", but also to serve as a visible reminder of Canada's claim to the far North. The RCMP took on such additional functions as handing out relief payments, census-taking and fostering respect for the Crown and Canadian sovereignty among these hitherto autonomous peoples. Soon thereafter the missionaries arrived. In the east, the Anglican Church moved in from neighboring Indian territory, establishing missions and introducing literacy in the form of syllabics. In the Central Arctic the Roman Catholics established permanent outposts and in the far west both Anglicans and Catholics set up missions, schools, and hostels.

Not all effects of early twentieth century acculturation were detrimental. For example, the HBC, the missionaries and the RCMP co-operated successfully to reduce violence among the Eskimos. It was to the Company's advantage to have the people spend their time trapping, not fighting; the Christian gospel substantially relieved the Eskimos' fears of the supernatural and the shaman's malevolent powers, and the authority of the police to punish offenders was an added deterrent to brutality.

During the Great Depression and World War II the price of fox skins plummeted. Between shrinking credit and an ever-growing dependence on imported goods, the effect on the Eskimos was devastating. In some places trading posts closed down altogether, causing near starvation and forcing migrations to the increasingly populated localities where they still operated.

The situation was ameliorated somewhat by the arrival of the military. As the Americans entered World War II, supply bases, air strips and meteorological stations mushroomed up across the Arctic. These installations proved a windfall for the Eskimos. In addition to medical services and handouts, the waste materials discarded by such huge operations supplied the basic necessities not only for the local populations but in many cases for growing numbers of refugees from less fortunate areas. For the first time wage labor was common. On the negative side, however, this human invasion encouraged the spread of infectious diseases to which the Eskimos had no immunity.

Fur prices rose again toward the end of the war and have remained high ever since. With the radical changes of these years, however, trapping never again reached its former level. Soon thereafter, the Canadian Government extended the family allowance system to the Eskimos. Administered through the HBC or RCMP, payments from this program, which are based on the number of children in a family, have often been substantial among the prolific Eskimo.

During the two following decades the Canadian Government became increasingly aware of their responsibilities for the Fourth World peoples living within their boundaries. One of the most profound instruments of change was the establishment of federal day schools. Compulsory attendance further encouraged the trend toward sedentary living, and the mandatory use of English and southern-oriented curricula caused added social disruption. Thus the schools accomplished little beyond delaying acquisition of the skills imperative to Arctic living. The nursing stations established across the Eskimos' homeland were more beneficial, prolonging life and encouraging a significant population increase.

Since the 1950s, as the result of the many factors described above, the majority of Canadian Eskimos have lived in relatively permanent settlements. Here, they engage in numerous occupations, assisting in the administration, education construction and maintenance of their communities. Only in more isolated areas has sea-mammal hunting continued as the major source of livelihood. Seal meat is still a prized food, but the expense of firearms, ammunition, snow machines, and fuel makes hunting prohibitive without the subsidy of other income. Moreover, the seal populations, due to noise and, possibly, pollution, have moved further away from human habitation. Some fox trapping is undertaken on snowmobiles, but only in areas of great abundance does the cost make it viable. At this point, in many settlements only men with dependable wage labor jobs can afford to hunt.

In recent decades, Eskimos in the central and eastern Canadian Arctic have increasingly availed themselves to an alternative source of income: arts and crafts. Though their sale to military personnel brought in occasional money during the war years, it was not until the early 1950s that this practice became widespread. Since then HBC traders and government agents have encouraged Eskimo men to make soapstone and ivory carvings (formerly used as toys) for sale. In the intervening years the total income from soapstone carvings alone has grown from a few thousand to hundreds of thousands annually. Thus carving now occupies most unemployed Eskimo men. The small sculptures are sold through local stores, many of them now reorganized as co-operatives, or are marketed in

Figure 2.4 Inuki Arkulukjuk stencilling graphic prints in the cooperative print shop at Pangnirtung, N. W. T. Sale of their commercial arts has been one of the main sources of livelihood for the Canadian Inuit since the 1950s. (Courtesy of Nelson Graburn, 1986.)

the south and elsewhere through government subsidized distribution channels. In the late 1950s printmaking was introduced, first at Cape Dorset (Baffin Island) and later in at least four other settlements. By 1972 the sale of prints earned the Eskimos a total income of over half a million dollars, and carving more than two million. By 1986 these figures had probably more than doubled.

The Eskimos do not find artmaking enjoyable: the older Eskimos prefer to be out hunting, the younger prefer wage labor. Nevertheless, soapstone carving and printmaking have been the saviors of local economies. A man may subsidize a hunting expedition from the sale of carvings, hence permitting the more traditional life he prefers. Often, when Eskimos ask for welfare, carving is suggested as an alternative. Store managers also encourage this occupation as it puts money in the pockets of their clientele.

Sociologically, there are positive aspects to carving. It does not make full-time demands on the Eskimos, imposes no time schedule, and allows them independence. Given that carvers do not pay income tax on the profits, it is also lucrative. Furthermore, carving fits in well with Eskimo concepts of work and manliness and has become a competitive activity, requiring skill and encouraging pride through its high degree of ethnic identifiability. Finally, it is on carving and printmaking (in which women also participate) that the new cooperatives depend. At a time when only a few Eskimos have the security of wage employment the sale of carvings reduces the gap between the haves and have nots. In a few cases, men with permanent employment have left their jobs and taken up carving so that they may be freer to hunt; some have even made a larger income.

Recently, the 25,000 Canadian Inuit (as they prefer to be called), like the Greenlanders, have assumed a more active political role. In 1970, the younger educated generation formed the Committee of Original Peoples Entitlement (COPE) to press for land claims. In 1971 they organized Inuit Tapirisat of Canada (ITC), a second arm, to oversee cultural and political matters. Since then, the negotiations for land, language retention and education rights have been carried out separately in the various geographical regions.

Mackenzie Region

It was not long before COPE and ITC reached an impasse over policy decisions. One difference of opinion was whether the organization should conduct business in *Inuktitut,* the eastern Canadian language still predominantly in use today. Most western Canadian Eskimos, descendants of the largely English-speaking Alaskan Eskimos, speak neither *Inuktitut* nor *Inupiag,* the north Alaskan language. This and other disagreements eventually led the organizations to split off. Today, COPE and the Canadian Government are in the final stages of negotiation over a land claim settlement patterned after the Alaska Native Claims Settlement Act (ANCSA).

Northwest Territories—Nunavut

ITC also took on another land claims issue farther east. Between 1977 and 1979 they worked out and put forward a proposal to form a separate territory (and later province) out of the Eskimo-occupied part of the Northwest Territories (NWT). Located north of the treeline, the new territory was to be called Nunavut ("Our Land"). Despite federal reluctance a plebiscite was held in 1982, and received a majority of the NWT electorate's vote. Although the Federal Government of Canada has agreed to cooperate, implementation is still a long way into the future.

Northern Quebec

Also known as Arctic Quebec and Nouveau Quebec, Northern Quebec was originally designated as a part of the NWT. In 1912 the region was ceded to the province of Quebec. It soon was clear, however, that the provincial government was interested in the land, not the Northern Quebec Inuit. Since jurisdiction over Indians is in the hands of the federal government, Quebec, to avoid assuming responsibility for the Inuit, pressured Ottawa to have them legally declared "Indians." After Quebec's "Quiet Revolution" of the 1960s and the subsequent emergence of Quebec nationalism or separatism, the French-Canadians set up provincial schools, administrative centers and police in Northern Quebec, largely replacing federal agencies. The 4,000 Inuit, who identified the French-Canadians with the Catholic Missionaries of previous generations, at first were dismayed by the change. They had learned English and had established an allegiance to Ottawa. What is more they had developed a strong system of Inuit owned co-operative stores, a venture that had made them politically astute. By the 1980s the Inuit have become more adjusted to Quebec rule, some even electing to have their children learn French, not English, as a second language in school.

In the late 1960s, the political evolution of Northern Quebec Inuit was accelerated by the instigation of the massive James Bay Project. Slated to affect both Indian and Inuit aboriginal lands, the purpose of the Project was to dam rivers, erect power stations and sell electricity to the State of New York. The Inuit began legal protests which were eventually defeated, forcing them to negotiate cessation of their lands. In 1973 the Inuit, Indians and Quebecois signed the James Bay Treaty. Again modeled after ANCSA, the treaty extinguished aboriginal rights in exchange for $90 million (Canadian), outright retention of 5,000 sq. mi. of land, and retention of the hunting and fishing rights on an additional 60,000 sq. mi. Three Inuit settlements refused to sign the treaty, and at present, have no land rights and no monetary settlement. The dissidents, unlike the signers, saw that the provisions of the treaty are unfair. Like the NWT Inuit, they hope to negotiate for better terms and greater autonomy. Unfortunately this courageous refusal has set them at odds with the complying Inuit communities.

Labrador

The history of the Labrador Inuit more closely parallels the Greenland case than the rest of Canada. From 1763 to 1949 Labrador was part of the colony of Newfoundland. The Inuit inhabitants, who numbered fewer than 2,000, were intensively missionized by Protestants, mainly Moravians, who gathered them into settlements centered around monopoly trading posts. However, the numerous white fishermen ("Livyers", "live here's") had also settled along the coast. The Livyers and Inuit, whose standard of living is roughly parallel, have intermarried to a considerable extent. Political and ethnic consciousness came late to this marginal area but in 1978, to press for land claims, the Labrador Inuit Association was formed. The white settlers objected until they, too, were declared "native people" and included in the negotiations.

Alaska

As stated above, the Eskimos of Alaska include the nomadic inland hunters of the North, the whale hunters of the Arctic Ocean, and the more settled and stratified hunters and fishermen of the Southwest. Two major Eskimo language groups are found in Alaska: Inupiaq in the North and Yupik (also spoken by the Siberian Eskimos) around the Bering Sea and the Pacific Coast. The related Aleut, whose population now is about 2,000, inhabit the Aleutian Islands and the tip of the Alaska Peninsula.

The southwestern Eskimos first met Europeans after Russian colonization of Alaska began in 1742. The Russians, interested only in Alaska's rich stocks of sea otter and fur seal, drastically exploited the native peoples and converted them to Orthodox Christianity. In 1867, the fur stocks depleted and the prices plummeting, the Czar sold Russian-America (Alaska) to the United States for $7 million.

Even earlier (1848), Yankee whalers, who had been pushing ever northward in pursuit of the lucrative baleen whales, sailed through Bering Strait into the Arctic Ocean, bringing with them disease, liquor and trade items to the Eskimos of northern Alaska. After 1910, the near extinction of the whales meant disaster for this group who, like the Canadian Eskimos, had become dependent on trade and credit. Fox trapping brought some relief but was never as lucrative as in Canada. The earliest wholesale invasion of the Bering Sea region occurred during and after the Nome and Klondike Gold Rush years of the 1890s. Later the canneries established along the Alaskan coast provided some employment to the native peoples including Eskimos. Shortly before the turn of the century the U.S. Government established boarding schools for rural Alaskans severely disrupting the family unit so intrinsic a part of Eskimo society. In the 1970s this policy was reversed and most rural villages now have primary and secondary schools.

As in Canada, World War II was the watershed in the history of contact between Eskimos and the outside world. Government installations in the Alaskan Arctic provided wage labor, but employment opportunities nonetheless were limited for a population now dependent on Western goods and commerce. Resultingly the people have gravitated increasingly toward the urban centers of Anchorage and Fairbanks, where the major concentration of Alaska's 4,000 Eskimos is found.

Native Alaskans including Eskimos have been the pioneers in aboriginal land claims disputes. In 1958, as part of the ratification of Statehood, Congress ceded significant federal holdings to Alaska. In the 1960s as a result of the discovery of oil on the North Slope, educated native Alaskans began to pressure the state and federal governments for sovereignty over their homelands and resources. In 1967, Eskimo, Aleut and Indian leaders formed the Alaska Federation of Natives, and through this organization pressed their claim for 370 of Alaska's 375 million acres of land.

Under pressure to construct the 1,200 mile Alaska Pipeline, the government began negotiations with the native people, and in 1971, the Alaska Native Claims Settlement Act (ANCSA) was signed. In extinction of aboriginal rights to the rest of Alaska ANCSA gave the native people (41,000 of whom are Eskimos) ownership of 44 million acres and $962 million. Ten percent went directly to individuals ($300–$5,000 per capita), and the remainder was invested in profit making ventures through thirteen regional corporations of which eight are primarily Eskimo and/or Aleut.

ANCSA provisions have created some major problems. The profit making arms of the regional corporations have met with varying degrees of success. Moreover, shareholders are restricted to those born before 1971, and although shares can be inherited, future generations are not automatically accorded membership status in the corporations. Furthermore as the 1971 Act was written, shareholders were to be free to sell their shares after 1991. In 1988 Congress amended ANCSA with a provision that the regional corporations could hold elections to enable shareholders to decide as a body whether to give individuals the right to sell their stock in 1991. To date, the other shortcomings have not been legally addressed.

SUGGESTED READINGS

Birket-Smith, Kaj
    1959   The Eskimos, W. E. Calvert, trans. [1936] Rev. ed. London: Methuen.

Boas, Franz
    1964   The Central Eskimo [1888]. Lincoln: University of Nebraska Press.

Briggs, Jean L.
    1970   Never in Anger: Portrait of an Eskimo Family. Cambridge: Harvard University Press.

Burch, Ernest S., Jr.
    1988   The Eskimos. Norman: University of Oklahoma Press.

Creery, Ian
    1984   The Inuit (Eskimo) of Canada. *Minority Rights Group Report,* 60. London.

Damas, David, ed.
    1984   The Arctic. *Handbook of North American Indians,* 5. Washington, DC: Smithsonian Institution.

Dumond, Don
    1977   The Eskimos and Aleuts. London: Thames and Hudson.

Lantis, Margaret
    1970   The Aleut Social System, 1750–1810, from Early Historical Sources. Pp. 139–.301 in Ethnohistory in Southwest Alaska and the Southern Yukon. Margaret Lantis, ed. Lexington: University of Kentucky Press.

Nelson, Edward W.
    1984   The Eskimo about Bering Strait [1899]. Washington: Smithsonian Institution.

Oswalt, Wendell
    1979   Eskimos and Explorers. San Francisco: Chandler and Sharp.

Senungetuk, Joseph E.
    1971   Give or Take a Century: an Eskimo Chronicle. San Francisco: The Indian Historian Press.

Spencer, Robert F.
    1964   The North Alaskan Eskimo: a Study in Ecology and Society [1958]. *Bulletin of American Ethnology 171.* Washington.

Weyer, Edward M., Jr.
    1962   The Eskimos: their Environment and Folkways [1932]. Hamden, CT: Archon Books.

Chapter 3

The Subarctic Culture Area

Shepard Krech III

Brown University

The Subarctic, which spans more than 100 degrees of longitude from the Labrador Sea to within sight of the Bering Sea, is a land of physiographic and seasonal climatic extremes. Home for thousands of years to Indians whose descendants speak Athapaskan or Algonquian languages or in recent years, English or French, this land has provided its inhabitants with sustenance and, endowed by them with meaning, has been transformed in countless cultural ways. The Subarctic has also been generally regarded as an uninviting and unforgiving land by non-native explorers, traders and other entrepreneurs, missionaries, and governmental workers who have travelled through it and lived there, sometimes for decades, in the process altering the aboriginal inhabitants and the land in both predictable and unforeseen ways. These outsiders have sought various goals, but their most constant desires have been to claim the land as their own, to extract its resources and to "civilize" or "humanize"—from their perspective—the aboriginal inhabitants. Today, the Subarctic extends across six Canadian Provinces and two Territories as well as much of Alaska.

Environment, Climate, and Biome

As a culture area, the Subarctic is bounded on the north by the Arctic, on the west by the Northwest Coast, and on the south by the Plateau, Plains, and Northeast. By no means uniform, the vast space—6000 km west to east, up to 1,800 km north to south in the Cordillera—can be subdivided into four separate physiographic regions: the Canadian shield, including the lowlands around Hudson Bay and the Mackenzie River; the Cordillera west of the Shield, that complex mountainous extension of the northern Rocky Mountains except for the westernmost flanks; the Interior Plateau, centered mainly on the drainages of the Yukon, Tanana and Kuskokwim Rivers in Alaska; and the Alaska Coast, a region of steep mountain ranges and coastal fringes in Cook Inlet and along the Copper River.

Except for the Alaska Coast, where temperatures are more moderate and precipitation greater, and some western sections of the Cordillera where snowfall is substantial, the Subarctic is characterized by long, exceedingly cold winters; short, surprisingly warm summers; and low precipitation, which falls mostly in the form of snow and which, because of cold, darkness, and permafrost, covers the ground for 5–7 months each year.

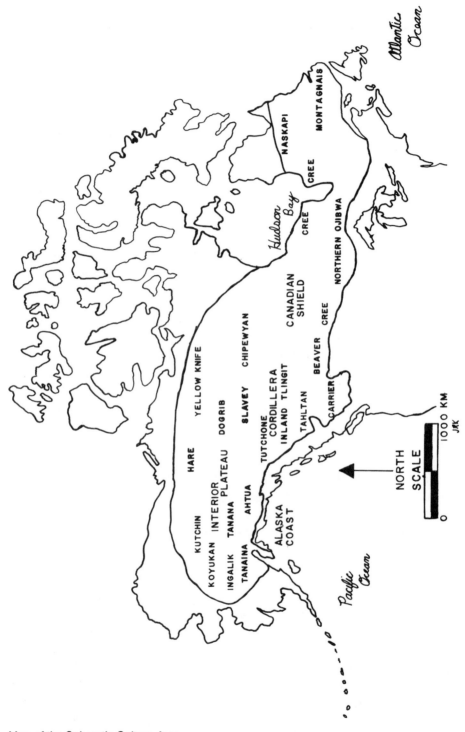

Map of the Subarctic Culture Area

All Subarctic plant communities are affected by permafrost, which is discontinuous throughout all but the northern borders of the Subarctic; by soils, most of which are acidic and marked by slow rates of organic decomposition; and by low moisture and temperatures. Conifers of four genera—spruce, pine, fir, tamarack—dominate; of deciduous trees, four species of birch and aspen-poplar are widespread; willows are extremely common shrubs. The farther north in the Subarctic, the greater the predominance of spruce; the farther south, the greater the admixture of deciduous species, which are plentiful and varied in the southeastern parts of the region, and the more significant become mosses. The northernmost parts of the Subarctic are marked by a transitional forest-tundra zone of stunted spruce, a lichen-covered open woodland. In the mountainous sections of the Cordillera and Alaska coast, except for river borders and protected declivities, alpine tundra typically occurs. Berries are common throughout the area.

The Subarctic biome is marked by few species but large populations of each; many species undergo still poorly understood population fluctuations and cycles. The harvest of culturally important species depends ultimately on temperature and precipitation; on the availability of lichens, willows and other shrubs, and aquatic plants for grazing and foraging, access to which is often determined by fire and sometimes by toxicity; on epidemiological variables; on clouds of mosquitos, blackflies and other insects; and on accessibility of prey and pressure from predators, including man.

The ecosystemic web as a whole is quite complex. The faunal trophic pyramid ranges, with local variations, from a plethora of mice, voles, shrews, and insectivorous birds; the snowshoe hare, squirrel, hoary marmot, several species of grouse and ptarmigan, and numerous migratory ducks and geese; the muskrat, beaver, and porcupine; the moose, two varieties of caribou and buffalo, the mountain goat, elk, musk-ox, and mountain sheep; and several species of whitefish and five of salmon, the sucker, pike, burbot, sheefish, grayling and other anadromous and freshwater fish; to ermine, marten, mink, lynx, river otter, fisher, wolf, wolverine, black bear, grizzly bear, and hawks and owls; several species of seals and the beluga; and man.

The Subarctic: Corridor and Home

Long before people of recent European extraction developed designs on the Subarctic with their mercantilistic, hegemonic or proselytical agendas, native Americans passed through it; later, still long before the beginning of the era of non-native influences, other native people settled there, where their descendants were "discovered" by white explorers.

When discovered, native people had culturally constructed pasts in which they explained their origin in a number of different ways; the Kutchin, for example, account for the genesis of land, the sun, and man and woman in a cycle of tales involving raven, who is represented as a trickster, transformer, and creator. An ethnohistory of the Kutchin or any other Subarctic people would be incomplete if it did not deal seriously with tales of this sort—with native eschatology, history, and myth. But any history of the people of the Subarctic must also encompass evidence of another kind concerning origins, gathered by glaciologists, archaeologists, physical anthropologists, linguists, and others. The cumulative weight of this evidence concerning the peopling of the Subarctic and rest of the New World is substantial. At several recent points in the Pleistocene, which ended 10,000 years ago, water locked up in icecaps caused sea levels to fall, and as waters receded in Bering Strait, the wide land mass known as Beringia, which was a complex ecosystem encompassing both plains and canopy forest, appeared. There is compelling evidence that humans, following animals across Beringia, were in the New World 12,000 years ago; arguments for much earlier occupations are less firm, contestable, and susceptible to revisionism. An ice-free corridor through Alaska to the east side of the Cordillera led to rich faunal resources beyond, and in the hundreds of years that followed, man spread throughout the New World at the same time that climate warmed, biotic communities became more homogeneous, and many large animals became extinct mostly, it seems, because of climate change although pressure from new efficiently armed predators may also have played some role.

The first inhabitants of the Subarctic were probably transient, or their descendants were, en route unintentionally southward. It is difficult to be certain about either this early period or the thousands of years that came after (but before the records of literate non-natives) because the Subarctic archaeological record is fragmentary. The continuity between native people non-natives encountered and the distant past is less clear-cut here than elsewhere in North America due to the primitive state of archaeological work in the Subarctic, the transient and non-acquisitive nature of most hunter-fisher band societies, and the difficulties of work in the Subarctic itself. Nevertheless, it seems clear that a succession of big-game hunters and fishers have lived in the Subarctic for the last 7,000 to 9,000 years.

Where archaeological work has been extensive, some major ancestral traditions can be traced: for the Athapaskan Yellowknife and Chipewyan, for example, there is a time-depth of 2,500 years, and for the Kutchin, one of 1,000 years. There are other certain archaeological traditions, but many more gaps, uncertainties, and evidence of importation into the region of non-Subarctic ideas about technology. Furthermore, several controversies over the connections between archaeological and ''historical'' cultures exist; without doubt, these will be clarified as archaeology in the Subarctic matures.

The People and Their Languages

Ethnographic maps and official band or tribe lists record some 30 names for Subarctic people. East to west, they are the Algonquian-speaking Montagnais, Naskapi, Cree (East, West, and Western Woods), Northern Ojibwa, Saulteaux (of Lake Winnipeg); the Athapaskan-speaking Chipewyan, Yellowknife, Beaver, Slavey, Bearlake Indians, Mountain Indians, and Hare, all Canadian Shield dwellers; the Chilcotin, Carrier, Sekani, Tsetsaut, Tahltan, Kaska, Inland Tlingit, Tagish, Tutchone, Han, and Kutchin (in Alaska; Loucheux in Canada), all Athapaskan-speakers living in the mountainous Cordillera; the Tanana,

Koyukon, Ingalik, and Kolchan, who are Interior Plateau Athapaskans; and the Athapaskan-speaking Alaska Coast Tanaina and Ahtna.

In most cases these names bear little relationship to traditional native self-designations. Examples are legion: Naskapi, a term borrowed from Montagnais, came to designate the most "primitive" natives of the Quebec-Labrador Peninsula, while the "Naskapi" themselves in this century preferred Cree as their ethnonym; Cree, a name the Ojibwa borrowed from elsewhere, perhaps from an obscure itinerant band that used something like it for themselves; Montagnais or "mountaineers," which is a term of French origin; Slave (Slavery), a translation of a Cree term for captive or slave, which was early applied to Athapaskans other than the ones who accept that term today as their name; Nahani, until recently on the ethnographic map, a term Athapaskans widely used for other Athapaskan-speakers who usually lived at a distance and were considered untrustworthy or malevolent; Loucheux, which was applied beginning in the late-eighteenth century to eastern bands of Kutchin (who continue to use it today), and which is a French translation of a Chipewyan word that means 'squint' or 'sharp' eyes; and Ingalik, a name borrowed by Russian trader-explorers from the Yupik term for Indians—*iŋqiliq,* 'having many nits.'

The traditional names that Subarctic Indians used, and may still use, for themselves are rarely preserved on maps or official lists. The Ingalik call themselves (in translation) 'people from here.' The Kutchin distinguish the names of nine or ten bands in which 'Gwich'in' is always appended as 'people of,' as 'people among the lakes' for Crow Flats Kutchin; in English, Canadian Kutchin today refer to themselves as Loucheux. The self-designation of Slavey today is Slave or Slavey; in the past they had no name for the collectivity except *dene* 'people,' and distinguished different regional bands: 'people of the forks [the conjunction of the Liard and Mackenzie Rivers],' for example, was one. The West Main Cree's self-designation was *ininiw* 'person, (Indian' or *omǎ skéków* 'muskeg person, swamp person'; they distinguished each specific regional group—like 'groundhog lake people')—from others. Subarctic Indians referred to themselves by terms that translated 'person,' 'human being,' or its equivalent; they often distinguished among small local bands as well as among larger regional bands using terms that translated 'people of [place-name]'; and they seldom had terms for the collectivities perceived and recorded in the "tribal" names that persist today, by the non-natives at whose trading and mission posts they aggregated.

All Subarctic Indians spoke an Algonquian or Athapaskan language. Linguistic affiliation has been identified in the list above: natives east of the 90th meridian spoke one of the seventeen varieties of Cree and Ojibwa, two major branches of the Algonquian language family; those west of the 115th spoke one of twenty-three varieties of the Athapaskan language family; and between the two meridians were the Algonquian Western Woods Cree and athapaskan Chipewyan. Whether these "varieties," which in most cases, for neighbors, are to a substantial degree mutually intelligible, are to be best regarded as many languages or as dialects in continuums of fewer languages, is a matter of some debate; in most instances, evidence and definitions currently favor the latter.

Missionaries who first provided accounts of many Subarctic languages also translated religious materials and published grammars and dictionaries. In one notable instance, literacy was promoted beyond a narrow religious context: "Cree syllabics," which was developed by Rev. J. Evans, has been used by Cree and Ojibwa for many purposes. The system is based on altering the orientation of a consonant when the vowel following the consonant changes (the orthography does not distinguish either long from short vowels or preconsonantal *h*-): *he,* ▽; *hi,* △; *hoo,*▷ ; *pe* ∨; *pi,* ∧; *te,* ∪; *to,* ⊃; etc.

One nearly constant trend in the years following contact with Europeans is native language loss and the substitution of English (widely) and French. Native languages survive where Subarctic people have been most isolated. In most communities today, there exist noticeable generational differences between the oldest generation (some members of which are monolingual in the native tongue), the middle generations (which contain the greatest number of bilingual speakers) and the youngest generation (of which most are monolingual in English (French) and have a high passive knowledge of their native tongue but poor, and perhaps no, speaking ability). In this century, formal education has hastened language loss, although in the most recent 20 years, greater native control over schools, radio and television, and educational programs, together with work by linguists, has resulted in the development of Roman orthographies and teaching materials. Still, the picture is not bright: for example, in 1980, of 27 Subarctic Northern Athapaskan languages or dialects, one was extinct, one nearly extinct, thirteen moribund, two precarious, and ten viable.

The Traditional Subarctic

Detailed, accurate reconstructions of aboriginal (pre-European-contact) Subarctic societies and cultures are problematic, because in certain sections of the Subarctic first contact with Europeans occurred four centuries before in-depth, reliable ethnographic observations. Nevertheless, the judicious use of both the observations and data of ethnographers and ethnohistorians permits, on the most general level, the reconstruction of demographic, economic, social, and religious patterns. Changes that resulted from contact with the European world are discussed in the section following this one.

Demography

There are scant data and few estimates on prehistoric demography in the Subarctic. Compared to many other regions of North America, both Subarctic population and density were low: 1.7 persons per 100 km^2 for the Kutchin, for example, or one person per 100 km^2 for the entire Cordillera. In general, the lowest population density was on the Shield, the highest among Alaska Coast and Interior Plateau Athapaskans. While population size and density may have been related principally to ecological and climatic factors, there is strong evidence that female infanticide skewed some sex ratios, damping the size of some populations. Aboriginal Subarctic demographic patterns were probably produced by cultural and ecological-environmental-climatic variables combined.

70

Economy

The emphasis Subarctic Indians placed on maintaining deeply respectful relations with the animistic world was a reflection of their intimate relationship with—indeed, their dependence on—animals, fish, and to a lesser extent plants. Northern Algonquians and Athapaskans were opportunistic fishers and hunters for whom to have focussed attention exclusively on a single preferred source of food increased the risk of starvation. This danger probably became greater after the coming of whites, whose mercantilistic appetites caused faunal population depletions and whose diseases left surviving Subarctic natives more vulnerable than ever before.

For most Subarctic Indians, fish were of singular importance for subsistence: eels for the St. Lawrence Montagnais, whitefish for the West Main Cree and Slavey, salmon for the Carrier and Tanaina, salmon, whitefish, and burbot for the Ingalik, and so on. Fish were everywhere important, even if secondarily, and were often preserved by smoking or drying, or both, and stored for later consumption. Consequently, an elaborate technological complex devoted to fishing existed in the Subarctic as a whole: hooks, spears, gaffs, leisters, weirs, funnel and box traps, gill nets and dip nets. Fish products were regionally important for containers and clothing.

Although most Subarctic Indians devoted a significant proportion of their time to hunting caribou, moose, and other big-game, and whereas these animals have always been culturally important, Indians often preferring to think of themselves as hunters of caribou or other big-game, their significance to Subarctic subsistence should not be overstated or overgeneralized. This is not to deny their importance for subsistence or clothing for many Subarctic Indians, in particular the Caribou-Eater Chipewyan and some Interior Plateau Athapaskans. For many, the major caribou hunt took place in autumn, when caribou skins were at their prime for clothing. With the aid of caribou fences or barriers, lakes into which the animals were driven, snares, spears, bows and arrows, and a technology adapted also to transportation, including a variety of remarkably finely woven snowshoes and bark canoes, hunters killed many large animals and, as with fish, sometimes stored meat for the future. Supplementing the diet (and rising to seasonal significance) were many types of small mammals caught in snares, deadfalls, traps, and nets, or speared; birds shot with bow and arrow or snared; and berries and roots.

There were quite marked regional variations in subsistence. St. Lawrence Montagnais ate a remarkable variety of animals and fish, ranging from moose, caribou, seals, many small animals, a dozen species of fish, many types of fowl, and berries, roots and maple sap. In fall, they caught large numbers of eels and dried and took them to the interior. They hunted moose in winter, when snow was deep, and hibernating bears in early spring. At any time hares, porcupines, beavers, and other animals were the prey. The West Main Cree depended upon fish, which they supplemented with caribou, bears, geese and ducks, beavers, and other large and small animals. The Beaver Indians ate moose, bison, woodland caribou, and beavers and hares; for them, fish were unimportant. Koyukon subsistence ranged from a dependence upon salmon in summer supplemented by small animals, to caribou in fall and winter supplemented by fish, to muskrats, beavers, and waterfowl in spring. The Tanaina depended upon salmon; caribou, moose, bears, seals, belugas, and waterfowl supplemented their diet.

Subarctic Indians used the skins and bones of mammals and birds, the skins of fish, as well as stone, wood, vegetal materials, antler, sinew, etc.—in all, a relatively narrow range of raw materials—for their material possessions. Compared with Indians in adjacent regions, Subarctic Indians had few possessions, befitting a more mobile lifestyle; exceptions occurred among certain more sedentary Cordilleran, Interior Plateau, and Alaska Coast Athapaskans, but even for these, material culture was neither extensive nor complex. As with their cultural and social patterns, in material culture Indians living in different parts of the Subarctic reflected propinquity to their neighbors, coming to resemble them in some respects—Cordilleran Athapaskans to Northwest Coast Indians, Interior Plateau Athapaskans to Southwest Alaska Eskimos, etc. For Subarctic Athapaskans, structures ranged from substantial plank hoses or semi-subterranean log, earth and moss dwellings, to skin-covered dome-shaped or conical structures, to more temporary shelters; clothing was of the skins of caribou, moose, beavers, hares, or other animals; snowshoes were made of willow or some other wood and babiche netting; vessels and containers were constructed of bark, skins of animals or fish, or roots; canoes and boats were made of birch or spruce bark, moose hide, or dugout cottonwood; and hunting and trapping equipment and fishing tackle—bows (in some instances, sinew-backed), arrows, spears, barriers, nets, snares and deadfalls nets, weirs, traps, and hooks—were made of wood, stone, sinew and other products. Subarctic Indians decorated clothing and other items of material culture in various ways: they painted hide clothing (Naskapi), dyed porcupine quill belts and fringes (Canadian Shield and Cordilleran Athapaskans), carved designs on birchbark containers (Attikamek, Carrier), and ochred seams and sewed seeds on tunics (Cordilleran Athapaskans), for instance. The human body was also decorated in a number of ways, and hair style, nose and ear ornamentation, and the application of pigment to the face were all subject to varying cultural expression.

In production and consumption, the local group, which often consisted of individuals connected to each other by ties of kinship or affinity, or both, and which seasonally might be small, was in principle independent and self-sufficient. There was no economic specialization, only differing degrees of individual competence and motivation. Division of labor was gender- and age-based. Males and females, after attaining the appropriate age, performed predictable tasks connected, respectively, to procuring large animals and mobility and to child-birth and training, although in Subarctic cultures the divisions of responsibility were neither persistently rigid nor inflexible.

Economic distribution in Subarctic societies was according to principles of reciprocity. Sharing and generosity were highly valued. Despite food accumulations and storage in many societies, redistribution and hoarding were rare, the sole widespread exception being, among many Cordilleran and Interior Plateau Athapaskans, the potlatch, which was strongly influenced by Northwest Coast practices. The Tanaina also present an exception: for them, redistribution was of great importance. In most Subarctic Indian societies, when large numbers of people were gathered to collectively drive caribou into a barrier or fish at a weir, a large group of people benefitted from principles of generalized reciprocity; most often, however, the group was much smaller, consisting of families linked to each other by affinal or consanguineal ties.

Society

Subarctic Indians spent much of their lives in groups small in size—they consisted of several families linked through close consanguineal or affinal ties—that often joined with like groups to become seasonally quite large. Principles of kinship, marriage, post-marital residence, and descent varied greatly; in these domains as in no other, debate over what might have constituted aboriginal rules, or what might have resulted from the incorporation of native people in the expanding economies of world-system mercantilists, has been sharp.

Although the centuries of European intrusion make aboriginal patterns uncertain, the enculturation of Subarctic children probably stressed self-reliance, independence, autonomy, practical resourcefulness, patience, passivity, deference, hospitality, generosity, cooperation, emotional suppression, and good humor; a set of partly contradictory values that would also present choice in the uncertainty of circumstances surrounding European influences. Both men and women internalized these cultural values. Women were almost everywhere isolated at puberty and subject throughout their lives to menstrual taboos; nevertheless, they possessed considerable autonomy in many Subarctic societies, and in several wielded both authority and power.

Marriage patterns varied greatly, both at any specific moment in a particular society and through the life cycle of individuals. Polygyny was everywhere possible although in practice only the most successful hunters and shamans—men of wealth and power—had more than one wife. Monogamy prevailed everywhere. Sororal polygyny was a preferred form in some societies and in others, at least in the post-European-contact period, young men, frequently brothers, might share for a temporary period the sexual and economics services of one woman in a polyandrous fashion. Cross-cousin marriage was preferred in a number of societies. Marriages were often arranged.

Although demographic, epidemiological, and environmental circumstances placed an emphasis on expediency, Subarctic Indians seem to have preferred what might be termed matriorganization as a principle of post-marital residence. A period of bride service, which was widespread, might be followed by matrilocality. In some Cordilleran and Interior Plateau societies, avunculocality expressed an emphasis on male ties. In other societies, patrilocality was either the rule or followed in practice. No matter what the rules might have been, however, demographic and other factors probably caused bilocal choices to be most frequently made. It is difficult to be certain.

Principles of descent are even more difficult to reconstruct because of the fragmentary nature of the evidence. Nevertheless, it appears that in almost all societies in the Cordillera, Interior Plateau, and Alaska Coast, descent was matrilineal; in Canadian Shield cultures, descent principles probably varied from an emphasis on matrilineality (Montagnais)

73

to patrilineality (Saulteaux, Northern Ojibwa) to bilaterality (others). Regardless of the precise rule, what should be emphasized is the unclear nature of evidence, the seeming unimportance of unilineal descent in the Shield, and the probability that both environmental and social (and historical) circumstances modified expression of formal principles of descent.

There were predictable associations among these principles of social organization. Among the Montagnais, for example, women were quite autonomous, divorce was easy, residence was matrilocal, and inheritance was from a man to his sister's sons—all rules, not consistently followed in practice. For the Saulteaux, post-marital residence was matripatrilocal, cross-cousin marriage was preferred, and individuals belonged to non-residential totemic clans. For the Hare Indians and other Mackenzie Drainage Athapaskans, bilocality (following initial matrilocality) and bilateral descent were typical in the post-European-contact period, as they might also have been before that time. Ahtna social organization (and that of most other Alaska Coast, Interior Plateau, and Cordilleran Athapaskans) stressed initial matrilocality, matrilineal descent (and the existence of moieties or sibs), bifurcate merging terminology, and preferred bilateral cross-cousin marriage.

Polity

The group effectively responsible for joint political, economic, and social decisions was neither large nor consistently stable, In much of the Subarctic, a distinction can be drawn between the local band of from 10 to 75 people—the building blocks are extended families—and the regional band of approximately 100 to 500 people. In many instances, a leader was a man of hunting skill, generosity, diplomacy, authority, rhetorical skill, consensus-attaining abilities, and perhaps supernaturalistic knowledge; but he led only to the extent that people chose to follow. While a leader did not necessarily seek his position he filled it usually by achievement, not ascription; in some cases, a leaders' status influenced a son's chance of succession. In the Shield, territories were recognized and exploited but their resources were evidently not exclusively possessed, nor were their boundaries inhibiting to non-members. Membership in a particular local or regional band, or in a band that formed for purposes of a specific task, was nonbinding and flexible. The "nation" was the smaller regional band, or sometimes the local band, not each unit to which Europeans assigned a "tribal" name.

Territoriality, interband solidarity, and ascribed leadership seem all to have been stronger in the Cordillera and Interior Plateau, and on the Alaska Coast than on the Shield. For example, despite the diffuse nature of leadership and absence of collective activities, the Cordilleran Chilcotin were able to respond effectively to external threat. The Cordilleran Tahltan—this system might have emerged in the post-European-contact period from a more nebulous band organization—had matrilineal clan leaders who attained their positions in part through birth into the aristocratic class and matrilineal succession, in part through the diligent, aggressive exercise of rights in connection with redistribution and reacting in the potlatch. The Tanaina comprised three quite sedentary societies, in each of which a number of matrilineal clans were represented. In each Tanaina society, a man of wealth who functioned as the leader did so because his male relatives co-residing avunculocally numerically strengthened the size of a supportive uterine faction. The leader of each ranked society was a generous "rich man" skilled in the chase and war, who was a redistributor offering leadership, care, and protection in return for assistance in subsistence, trade, and trapping. Rich men were polygnists who maintained their positions through the production of their wives, through potlatching in order to successfully validate their claim to status, and by continuing to display leadership qualities. They also served as leaders of intersocietal wars and kept captives as slaves.

For Alaska Coast Athapaskans, reciprocity was an important means of exchange and the ability to change band membership was a freedom, as it was elsewhere in the Subarctic. However, in contrast to many other Subarctic societies, in particular on the Shield, in Alaska Coast Athapaskan societies rank, ascribed status, stratification, and warfare were concretely and elaborately present.

The causes of aboriginal hostilities, feuds, and warfare are obscure. It is quite possible that hostilities everywhere were due to quarrels over women, or to the need of revenge following aggression against trespassing strangers whose motives were always suspect, or following murder or abduction. Warfare and feuding were most prevalent and the technology of warfare—armor, caribou antler pick-clubs soaked in grease or oil to make them heavy, voluted knives hafted on spears—more developed among Cordilleran and Alaska Coast Athapaskans than elsewhere. For them, however, as for other Subarctic Indians, the unit of warfare was the band, rarely a large collectivity.

Religious Beliefs and Practices

An elaborate mythology; the belief in a trickster-transformer-creator, in an abstract impersonal power, in spiritual power or soul in humans, animals, plants, geographic features, man-made objects, in personal supernaturalistic beings; the fear of "bushmen" and other malevolent superhuman beings; the belief in reincarnation; the belief in the efficacy or predictability of dreams or visions, or visions in dreams; the development of a special relationship between an individual and certain animal; the belief that one must show respect for animals and their souls; pervasive systems of taboos connected with the life cycle, with the biological and physiological states of women, and with hunting; the vision or guardian spirit quest; the belief that sickness is caused by soul loss, shamanism, witchcraft or sorcery, or the infraction of a taboo; shamanism; and divination: these collectively constituted Subarctic Indian religion; many specific traits were widespread. If there is any uncertainty, it is because of the incomplete and biased nature of the historical record; however, some contemporary decidedly non-Christian beliefs can reasonably be projected to the past where patterns of social, economic, and political behavior cannot.

The diversity, as well as common elements, in Subarctic religion are revealed in a closer examination of three groups: Montagnais-Naskapi, Kaska, and Ingalik. Montagnais-

Naskapi mythology focused on the transformative abilities of a creator-trickster, a "cosmic champion," and the tales of his exploits served to explain the physical features of the universe and natural characteristics of animals. A number of other-than-human beings inhabited the Montagnais-Naskapi world, including "little people" and "underwater man"; especially malevolent was the cannibal Windigo, sometimes perceived as a human insanely transformed by eating human flesh.

The winds, seasons, sudden meteorological events, physiographic features, celestial objects, animals and plants, man-made articles, human beings: each contained a spirit, and a certain category of beings (e.g., animals of a particular species) might have a spirit that is that category's owner or master. Maintaining a respectful, healthy, and productive relationship with the spirit world was the single most important feature of Montagnais-Naskapi religion. Developing such a relationship was within reach of any individual who observed taboos so as to prevent misfortune, and learned magical techniques in order to exert control. Animals—and animal remains—were reverentially and respectfully treated. Both scapulimancy—divination by interpreting burn marks on a shoulder blade—and the shaking tent rite—in which a shaman goes inside a small tent which begins to sway when spirits arrive—were used as techniques of divination to sift information and report on possible events beyond immediate knowledge. Men and women most adept at developing powerful relations with the spirit world might become shamans and predict events, translate the sacred realm, cure the sick and, as sorcerers, kill.

In Kaska cosmology, the current world was regarded as the second or third created. In the first (or the first two) there existed initially only animals, then animals and humans, the latter threatened by monsters; each of these worlds, if there were two, ended with a flood. Raven or Loon was responsible for the re-emergence of the world, and culture heros helped the Kaska learn what they needed in order to survive. The Kaska world included other-than-human beings: dwarfs, a cannibalistic big man, a mild-mannered bald man, and others.

In adolescence, a Kaska youth spent a period in isolation in the bush, where he ate and drank little and hoped to dream of animals that would come to him offering their power. This was the sign of a successful vision quest. The ability to cure and prophesy—to perform shamanistic acts—was within reach of all Kaska men and women, but only a few gained renown as shamans. In curing illness brought on by the infraction of one of a large number of taboos—those connected with several powerful animals like mink, otter, and wolf were especially important to observe—by sorcery, or by some other cause, or in divining future events, a shaman relied upon his animal helper as his principal source of power. Often, songs acquired from an animal helper were sung in order to ensure a successful hunt. The Kaska also practiced scapulimancy.

For the Ingalik, the four-layered universe was inhabited by a number of supernatural essences, among them a vague, distant creator; a powerful spirit or spirit-complex that causes death; spirits of the water, sun, moon, wind, cold, and stars, both helpful and malevolent; dangerous bushmen; various monsters; a thunderbird; salmon, berry, mountain people; and pygmies and giants.

Fundamental to Ingalik religious thought was the notion that all distinct things have a spirit, and much of Ingalik ritual was directed at ensuring a proper relationship between human beings and the spiritual world. Shamans were needed especially to divine the causes of misfortune and prescribe remedies, if any. Individuals sought, in their behavior, to avoid attracting the spirit(-complex) that was believed to seek human bodies for nourishment as humans do the bodies of animals. The Ingalik sought the aid of animal spirits, some of which were very powerful, and shamans who had more powerful connections through their dreams than other people were crucial in community well-being. Shamans were regarded with ambivalence because they killed as sorcerers as well as cured as physicians and psychiatrists. Amulets and charms were commonly worn or carried. Animal songs—magical spells—were used to bring about various ends: to obtain animals, to cure, to succeed in trade, to heal one's eyes, to bring someone temporarily back to life, etc.

The Ingalik, influenced in part by their Yupik-speaking Eskimo neighbors, and unlike the Subarctic Montagnais-Naskapi and Kaska, observed seven major ceremonies each year. One was principally social: the partner's potlatch. The others, though multidimensional—all were social amusements and some functioned to increase prestige—had principally religious goals: to increase the number of animals (mask dance, animal's ceremony, bladder ceremony, hot dance), to know the dead (potlatch for the dead), and to prognosticate (doll ceremony). Five of the seven ceremonies involved invitations to another village; one of the "increase" ceremonies, at which respect was shown to animals over a 14–21 day period, was the most important moment of the ceremonial year and emphasized, in a more formal way than elsewhere in the Subarctic, this most important of Subarctic religious attitudes.

Whitemen and Subarctic Indians: Change and Continuity

Subarctic Indian history did not begin when whitemen came, although it often is assumed that it did. Subarctic Indian societies, cultures, and adaptations were not static before the coming of whitemen and did not automatically or equally change after, although they are often made to seem as if they were and did. What follows is a historical sketch of native-white contact. It is by no means a full Subarctic Indian ethnohistory, which would draw upon native cultural conceptions of time, narrative, the past, and events. One problem with the latter is that one group's ethnohistory is not another's. This survey is of the effects of contact between whitemen and Indians in the Subarctic as a whole. It employs a four-stage temporal framework—a heuristic scheme that reflects the different attempts by whitemen to push their cultural agendas in the Subarctic: Stage 1, the era of exploration and mercantilism; Stage 2, the era of mercantilism and missionization; Stage 3, the era of mercantilism, missionization, enhanced transportation, mineral exploitation, and governmental interest; and Stage 4, the modern post-World War II era that has been marked by intense national interest in resources of the north.

The timing of each stage differs from one section of the Subarctic to the next. Stage 1 began in easternmost portions of the Canadian Shield by 1500, among the easternmost

Athapaskans by 1680, among the northernmost (Kutchin) and westernmost (Tanaina) Athapaskans by 1780, and in the interior Cordillera by 1820. Stage 2 began in the easternmost Subarctic by 1610, in much of the rest of the Shield in the period 1825–1860, and elsewhere from 1850–1900. In Stage 3, which began in the 1890s, substantial new impulses came from the outside: new methods of transporting trade goods, goldrushers, governmental agents whose aims were to obtain native lands and civilize native people, and others. After World War II (Stage 4), the involvement of government increased significantly in all arenas of Subarctic native life.

The lives of Subarctic natives altered as a result of the penetration of whitemen. Each new wave pushed a separate cultural agenda. Fur traders were principally interested in weaning natives from subsistence pursuits that conflicted with trapping and exchanging pelts and skins. Missionaries wished to civilize natives and ban pursuits in conflict with Christianity: female infanticide, polygyny, shamanism, warfare, the potlatch. Governmental agents acted both out of paternalistic concern for the welfare of native peoples and as a result of the desire to obtain title to Indian lands, on and underneath which were potentially lucrative resources.

The focus in the discussion that follows is on neither agents of change nor the temporal framework—because a particular change sometimes resulted from more than one class of agent and spanned more than one stage—but on some of the domains in which more obvious alterations occurred: ecology, demography, material culture, economy, society and polity, and religious belief and practice.

Ecology

Prior to the coming of whitemen, the major impact of Subarctic Indians on the environment was through fire: many, but not all, Northern Algonquians and Athapaskans probably practiced controlled burning, producing thereby new econiches, a different succession of forest type, and richer environments for a multitude of species.

After whitemen came, the response to the demand for furs and skins (in Stages 1–2) was sufficient to cause locally severe depletions of animals. Beaver, caribou, moose, and bison were the species most affected. The decline in their populations affected both nutrition and comfort; the skins or pelts of all were useful for clothing and bedding as well as covers for shelter.

Historical records contain numerous references to faunal depletions across the Subarctic. Fur-bearers of all types fluctuated periodically in numbers; many observers sensed a broad decline in a number of species, of which the beaver was most noticeable. Beaver conservation measures became necessary because the demand for pelts by European fur traders did not encourage Subarctic natives to develop conservation practices. Iroquois and other Indians were employed by the North West Company in, for example, the Lake Athabasca region, where they obliterated beaver populations in the early nineteenth century; resident Chipewyans and Beaver Indians adopted some of the techniques of the Iroquois, further damaging beaver populations. The steel trap efficiently reduced beaver populations in many areas.

It is clear that declining numbers of some big-game species were related to naturally-occurring and man-made fires—declining numbers of moose and caribou in some regions of the Interior Plateau in the late-nineteenth century, for example, resulted in part from fire, in part from firearms. But elsewhere, pressure from the trade in skins or meat was clearly responsible. This was particularly the case with moose, caribou and bison in the territory of the Beaver Indians and with caribou east of the Mackenzie River in the Arctic Drainage Lowlands. Intense pressure for pemmican to feed transportation crews, for tongues to satisfy alimentary tastes, and for skins for the trade led to the slaughter.

One result of faunal depletions was an eventual, forced reliance on other species for food and other sources for clothing. All nineteenth-century observers of Subarctic Indian life noted that starvation was a recurrent problem. Although what was meant by "starvation" is not always clear—in some instances, "starving" Indians were not always in that state—it is evident that on a number of occasions Indians starved to death and survivors owed their lives to cannibalism. The reasons for food shortages and starvation are extremely complex. They include population cycles in hares and other animals, climatic conditions, diseases that left Subarctic Indians in a weakened state, focussing one's attention on furs for trade not fish or animals for subsistence, and interethnic hostilities that led natives to flee to unfamiliar territory. One variable in this systemic web was faunal depletion. Fewer animals made the lives of Subarctic natives less secure.

Since 1950, the major changes to ecology have resulted from the interest in fossil fuel reserves or hydroelectric power in the north. These are discussed in the final section of this essay.

Demography

Major demographic trends in the post-European-contact period are due to epidemic diseases and the demographic transition. The former wrought havoc during Stages 1–2, the latter has been characteristic of Stage 4.

Epidemic diseases of exogenous origin periodically struck Subarctic Indians both in advance of whitemen, transmitted by native middlemen, and after contact. When these diseases reached populations with no previous exposure, they caused great mortality. So-called virgin-soil epidemics, they constituted the most traumatic post-European-contact events for native people. The diseases were various: measles, scarlet fever, smallpox, influenza, cold, whooping cough, dysentery. They were commonly introduced with annual shipments of trade goods, spread rapidly, affected both sexes of all ages, killed many, left survivors weakened, and complicated the subsistence quest.

Few populations in the Subarctic were exempt from at least one devastating epidemic; most experienced more than several. For example, in the nineteenth century some bands of Kutchin were battered by an unknown contagion in 1825, influenza in 1834, whooping cough in 1843, some disease in 1851, scarlet fever in 1862 and 1865, diphtheria in the early 1880s, and scarlet fever in 1897. All were most serious; entire bands were obliterated. While no one doubts that each epidemic produced deaths and extraordinary suffering, the exact mortality is difficult to ascertain, in part because census data are not extensive. The Kutchin might have numbered 5400 in the late-eighteenth century and lost four-fifths of their population in seventy years. Tuberculosis and venereal disease also afflicted Subarctic Indians.

The nutritional consequences of the post-European-contact era include, in Stages 1–2, less readily available food because of faunal depletions due to overhunting and overtrapping and the inability of hunters, because of debilitating epidemics, to effectively hunt prey; and in Stage 4, the incorporation into the diet of store-purchased food (which began far earlier in some areas, everywhere by Stage 3). White flour, refined sugar, tea, oatmeal and an increasing range of store foods have been added to the diet. One of the most noticeable consequences to health during Stage 4 is advanced dental decay at an early age.

Female infanticide, a characteristic of some Subarctic populations in the years following contact by Europeans, was practiced by some during the initial historical period; in Stage 2, however, missionaries made systematic, ultimately successful calls for its cessation, and the population subsequently rose during Stages 3–4.

Population processes in Stage 4 have been marked by constantly moderate rates of emigration and exogamy (some Subarctic Indians move "outside" to southern Canada or the lower 48 states and some, women especially, marry non-natives, with the result that a portion of the population undergoes a "metisization" or "creolization" process); by a high birth rate, to which bottle-feeding may contribute; and by a decline in mortality but an increase to disproportion of fatalities due to drownings, accidents, suicides, and violence, in which alcohol abuse is often implicated; alcohol, when available, has long been consumed to excess in the Subarctic, as elsewhere, and its use defies simplistic explanations.

Material Culture

Over its long sweep of time, the post-European-contact period has been marked by losses in many cultural domains, not least in knowledge of traditional (aboriginal) processes whereby objects were made and assigned meaning. At the same time as objects were discarded, techniques lost, and knowledge evaporated, new items were substituted. Typically introduced and subsequently adopted in Stages 1–2, especially in conjunction with the fur trade, were metal files, kettles, knives, and axes; fish hooks and cotton twine, guns, powder, shot and ball; chisels and steel traps, blankets, clothing, and canvas; and tobacco and beads. Replacement technology steadily accumulated: metal for bone, stone, hide, and bark; cloth of European manufacture for furs and skins; log cabins for a range of traditional dwelling structures; repeating rifles and fish wheels for caribou barriers or fences and dipping platforms. While it is difficult to generalize about the timing of replacements in material culture for the Subatrctic as a whole, by the end of Stage 3 much aboriginal knowledge had been lost everywhere, and for some natives, that loss had occurred long before.

In one domain, that associated with dog-traction, there was an efflorescence and then a loss of material culture. The use of dogs and associated technology expanded or was introduced during Stages 1–3, but in Stage 4 the snowmobile has taken their place universally.

Both new materials, decorative techniques, and structural features altered the appearance of Subarctic Indian clothing, which in the post-contact period was embroidered with beads alongside the traditional use of porcupine quills, dentalium shells, ocher, seeds, and fringes; was embroidered with silk floral patterns, edged with ribbon appliqué, and decorated with wool tassels; and was cut in patterns that were definitely new, as with the open-at-the-front, hoodless Subarctic jacket, or probably new, as with the Naskapi coat. Another type of material culture replacement took place among the Cordilleran Tagish in the nineteenth century: they increasingly adopted the ceremonial clothing of the Tlingit, whose relationship to them was that of an aggressive middleman-trader to an unequal partner.

Economy

From the outset of the fur trade, most Subarctic Indians were interested in the goods that traders offered for pelts. The traders—the Hudson's Bay, North West and Russian-American Companies are best known—in most instances were making a healthy profit, sometimes by giving short, not "good" or full measures of cloth, powder, shot, brandy, tobacco and other items measured or weighed at the time of trade. But native people themselves also viewed the exchange as to their benefit, at times thinking that European traders had as little sense giving them valuable trade goods for ordinary furs as the traders thought they, the Indians, had.

Misunderstandings in the trade abounded. Subarctic natives reacted to changing trade tariffs in unexpected ways: sometimes, when the price (demand) offered for fur increased, usually because a monopoly had not yet been instituted or was breaking up, the number of furs brought by native trappers (supply) actually decreased—the so-called backward sloping supply curve, produced by limited transportation capacities, limited desires, gift-giving which partly satisfied desires for goods, lack of accumulation of material things, and the conversion by natives, through gifts, of goods into prestige. Subarctic Indians are surprising in retrospect, because their behavior went against received wisdom: they were not passive recipients of trade goods, passive respondents in an exchange over which Europeans held total sway. To the contrary, Subarctic natives were often aggressive traders themselves, were savvy manipulators of the exchange sometimes, for example, refusing to trade furs unless the goods were to their liking, and were quick to take advantage of non-monopoly competitive conditions. They were, in other words, active makers of their post-European-contact history, itself one of a general incorporation into the expanding economics and polities of nation-states.

Sometimes, trade goods were interpreted in cultural terms not understood at all by European traders. For example, in the early-nineteenth century, the Kutchin craved blue and white beads, which delighted the Hudson's Bay Company up to a point because what it considered to be low-cost, easy to transport "baubles" brought handsome profits. Company traders could see clearly that the Kutchin attached beads to their tunics and moccasin-leggings, their quivers and their hairbands. They did not immediately understand so clearly the other uses of beads: to distinguish men of wealth from the poor; to pay a shaman for his prognostication, cure, or other services, or to pay for the furs and skins of Indians living farther from the trading post (beads functioned as a general purpose money for the Kutchin); to settle a feud as a form of blood-money; to destroy if a man were sick, in the hope that he would be cured; and to destroy following a death or to distribute in a potlatch. The desire for beads did not represent a radical cultural departure for the Kutchin; before whitemen came, they probably used porcupine quill and seed decoration on clothing and dentalium shells as septum ornaments and signs of wealth. But these aboriginal cultural understandings became more elaborate as a result of the trade, as the number of economic, social, and religious occasions for their use expanded, and as the epidemiological frontier, which guaranteed the destruction of beads, heightened the demand. Despite the ignorance of traders, the Kutchin desire for beads was intensely rational: with beads, they could advertise social standing and success as hunters, trappers, and traders; with beads, some could proclaim their potential as leaders; with beads, they could—by giving them away—convert property to prestige; with beads, they could assert their ability to provide for more than one wife; with beads, they could pay a shaman for his cure or prognostication; and with beads, they could discharge their obligations to members of other matrilineal decent categories.

Through time, the exchange of furs for European and trade goods promoted the growth of individualism and mercantilism. Through time, reciprocity, one of the cardinal values of Subarctic Indian culture eroded. Through time, Subarctic Indians became dependent. Individualism, mercantilism, dependence: none developed quickly, with the exception of mercantilism, and reciprocity did not erode rapidly. A number of Subarctic Indians quickly seized upon their new positions as middlemen to exploit Indians living farther from posts than they, and through strength and firearms kept others at bay. This happened often—the Yellowknife, for example, controlled the trade around Great Slave Lake for decades, and some bands of Kutchin held tight reins on access to posts on the Mackenzie and Peel Rivers, keeping other Kutchin, Han, and Inuvialuit (Mackenzie Eskimos) at a distance.

The development of dependence was not an inevitably quick process in the Subarctic. In fact, in instances during Stage 1, European traders depended on natives. For example, in the 1840s–50s, Hudson's Bay Company traders were dependent on Kutchin hunters and fisherman, without whom they might have starved; in addition to provisioning the traders, the Kutchin were interpreters, laborers and, of course, trappers.

All but a few Subarctic Indians were very interested in the exchange of furs, skins, provisions, and services for European trade goods. Many travelled long distances for trade goods. Many jealously guarded middleman networks and exorbitantly marked up European goods they had obtained at the trading post and would trade to more distant Indians. Many craved tobacco. Many used cotton twine and guns and ammunition. But dependence—reliance on unsubstitutable productive technology and food for the fulfillment of one's needs—was neither an automatic nor rapid process. It is important not to lose sight of regional, even sub-regional variations in economic change. In many instances, long periods of interdependence—European traders and Subarctic natives on each other—were characteristic. In others, as with the so-called Home Guard of Cree coasters who lived on James and Hudson Bays, there was a marked dependence by the mid-nineteenth century on the post for guns, kettles, twine, blankets, cloth, oatmeal, geese, and fish, and a concurrent precipitous decline in numbers of caribou. In still other cases, as with the Cree uplanders or inlanders, or some bands of Montagnais in southeast Labrador, or Caribou-Eater Chipewyan, Indians were quite disinterested in the trade and its goods, preferring instead the traditional subsistence round.

An intensification of processes of dependence took place widely at the turn of the twentieth century—the beginning of Stage 3—with new methods of transportation, greater quantities of foods being shipped north, and more effective responses to the paternalistic welfare urges of traders, missionaries, and nascent governmental enterprises. More natives swelled the ranks of the non-traditional labor force at posts, in transportation, near mining endeavors, etc., the creolization of one segment of the population continued, and more Subarctic Indians than ever before threw their lot in with posts, increasing by degrees their dependence on post-supplied goods. In Stage 4, this process again intensified, but still there remain today counter-tendencies, and it may be most accurate to think of the existence of two separate spheres of exchange and modes of production in the Subarctic—one focused on the bush and marked by exchange according to traditional values, one focused on town and marked by capitalist understandings. Even today, dependence in the north takes a "peculiar" form, at least for some Crees, in that they exploit the bush with technology obtained principally with cash obtained primarily from furs, and it (the bush) provides one-half the amount of calories they consume. For other Crees, however, who are reliant on wage work and transfer payments, the bush provides only one-quarter the total caloric consumption and the links to the capitalist sphere of the economy are far stronger. In many Subarctic communities today, bush foods remain important for subsistence, and both the penetration of the culture of merchant capitalism and dependence are incomplete.

Society and Polity

Several of the more fundamental changes in band organization, movement, leadership, and interband relations were: the formation of large, trading-post or regional aggregations; a splintering of moderately sized bands into smaller, fragmented groups; an increase in time spent near trading/mission posts; formalization of leadership in the institution of the trading chief; heightened interethnic tensions as a result of the demand for furs and skins, then a rapid decline in the open hostility of feuding or warfare.

Some of these changes seem contradictory. At the same time that large band assemblages occurred and trading and mission posts became magnets to which some individuals were attracted for lengthening periods of time, the ecology of trapping and the mercantilistic ties that linked native people to whitemen encouraged individualism and production for exchange.

The entire post-European-contact era has been marked by a progressive orientation away from the bush and toward the settlement of whitemen and Métis or Creoles. The process was gradual and uneven. In almost all cases, bands that might not have been in contact with each other aggregated near a post, waiting for the arrival of trade goods. Later, the celebration of Christian rituals brought more Subarctic Indians to posts. Bands formerly (and still) tied to particular localities—local bands—began to sense that connections with other bands in a region were also meaningful, and members of one of these larger aggregations, the regional band, could renew ties with each other as well as, through time, with other regional bands, at a post. Leadership, always ephemeral, was expressed formally in the office of trading chief, a misnomer because the chief lacked power, although he might possess authority in trade as well as in hunting, shamanism, or warfare, or he might, as in Cordilleran and Interior Plateau cases, have prestige either because of his redistribution and non-accumulation of material assets or because he was in fact more wealthy. The Europeans who needed to deal with individual leaders, often appointed as chiefs men who already seemed to possess such authority. Later on, leaders of bands defined by the Canadian government following the signing of treaties between 1871 and 1921, in which aboriginal rights in land were exchanged for certain entitlements and promises, were not necessarily also leaders in traditional internal affairs, where discussions and consensus-building, not unilateral decision-making, have always been important.

One expression of the growing importance of sedentary animals whose "management" affected a trapper's income was the family hunting territory, which by the beginning of Stage 3 was widespread among Northern Algonquians. There has been considerable, continuing debate over whether or not the so-called family hunting territory, which variously embodies in its resources (land fur-bearers, big-game animals) ideas of usufruct, ownership, and inheritance by a group or individual, is aboriginal. Regardless of the outcome of this debate, hunting territories seem not to have existed in some areas until the fur trade had become well-established, and the development (or elaboration) of these territories represented one of the numerous changes in social and political organization that resulted from the fur trade. In contrast, in other areas of the eastern subarctic, hunting territories seem to have been well-established at the inception of the trade.

Where territoriality was strongest, trespass produced the most tension. In the post-European-contact era, tensions on the interband or interethnic level were stimulated by mercantilism and cases are legion in which one group possessing European goods and arms became muscular middlemen in the trade, or went beyond their own territory, which they had stripped of furs, to the lands of their neighbors, where they attempted to do the same. Only the steady geographical spread of white traders themselves, changing demographic balances, and missionaries put an end to these heightened hostilities.

These changes in band organization, leadership, and territoriality began in Stage 1. Missionaries, whose entrance into the Subarctic initiated Stage 2, engineered changes in kinship, marriage, descent, and ceremonies that had secular as well as sacred content. As with so much else that has been depicted here, generalization to the entire Subarctic is difficult. Nevertheless, in all societies the following cultural rules, practices, or institutions eroded (in societies in which they had been present aboriginally), and in many they disappeared completely during the post-European-contact stages: polygyny, the sororate, the levirate, cross-cousin marriage, wife-exchange, arranged marriage, female puberty seclusion, traditional forms of gambling, exogamy, moiety and phratry influence, matrilineal clans. Despite formal missionary and governmental disapproval, the potlatch was enhanced and elaborated in many societies because of the influx of new wealth (and influence of Northwest Coast societies). Missionaries were largely responsible for the social structural and organizational alterations, and formal education, about which more will be said in the concluding section of this essay, was one of the primary means of change.

Religious Belief and Practice

Throughout the Subarctic, missionaries of different persuasions—Anglican, Oblate, Jesuit, Episcopalian, Methodist, Presbyterian, Russian Orthodox, and others—assaulted traditional religious beliefs and practices and attacked what they considered to be pagan sentiment and ritual. At the same time, they competed against each other in the contest for souls. Some missionaries were genuinely interested in native culture; some married native Subarctic women; some trained native catechists; some developed native orthographies and translated religious texts. Regardless of the variations, all sought to convert natives to Christianity, to baptize them into their own faith and, through various means, to "civilize" them.

Aided by epidemic disease to which they possessed some immunity (unlike natives), by faunal depletions, by their control over goods which they might exchange to converts, and by the absence of a formal, highly structured religious system in Subarctic culture, missionaries had a pervasive impact. Many natives became converts. Through time, there were vast erosions in traditional culture, not simply in social domains mentioned above but in religion itself: the sharp decline and, through time, the virtual end of sorcery, shamanism, shaking-tent divination, traditional medicine, the vision quest, the Midewiwin, burial customs like cremation, puberty seclusion, part of the repertoire of myths and legends, and so forth.

Despite these changes, selected aspects of the traditional religion continued to exist alongside Christianity: the guardian-spirit complex, shamanistic curing, scapulimancy and other techniques of divination, the belief in malevolent beings, belief in reincarnation, etc.

Because of the evidence for the persistence of non-Christian beliefs, there is much debate over the degree to which conversions to Christianity, in the Subarctic and elsewhere, were genuine or nominal and over whether or not the separate belief systems—Christian and aboriginal—became fused in novel, syncretic ways or co-existed alongside each other. These are not simple questions to answer unequivocally, nor can one generalize with ease in response. The following is certain: whereas some Subarctic Indians resisted baptism, and others saw nothing contradictory in accepting tangible economic benefits of

85

conversion, when they were offered, still others were noted for their rapid and seemingly genuine conversion to Christianity and they and their descendants became devout Christians; many Subarctic natives adhere to old, fundamentally non-Christian, beliefs which embody their relationship to animals and to animal spirits; and in some areas, both during moments of acute stress and at other times, revitalization movements combining elements of the old and new religions flared briefly. In other words, in the Subarctic as a whole, some natives became devout Christians, others held tenaciously to some traditional beliefs, some did both, and some followed new syncretic beliefs for a short time.

The Subarctic Today

For the past forty years, native people in the Subarctic have undergone great changes, many of which have been discussed in the preceding section. In Canada and Alaska, both federal and territorial or state governments have taken an increased interest in natives' lives. Concurrently (and not coincidentally), multinational oil and gas companies have consistently pressed for favorable conditions for the extraction and transportation to southern markets of hydrocarbons. Throughout the Subarctic, the agenda of these multinationals has been in direct conflict with the fulfillment of native political rights.

Since 1950, the population of Subarctic natives has been growing steadily. Population processes, discussed earlier, have been marked by a higher birth rate, steady emigration, and a disproportionate number of deaths caused by drunkenness, violence, and suicide.

Since 1960, almost ala subarctic children have spent their adolescence in school. There may be no more significant cause of social and cultural changes in the Subarctic (and elsewhere) than formal education. In Canada, school attendance in the 1950s was linked to the monthly "family allowance" payment that mothers received. The threat of withholding payments in cases where children remained in the bush with their parents loomed large in the minds of some parents who chose classroom over traditional bush education for their children. At the same time, some parents began to evaluate more highly than ever before whiteman's education, and their children in turn desired the jobs that whitemen (and women) held, to which however, until the most recent years, access has been denied. The potential for frustration, so clearly evident in these circumstances, was manifest in a number of ways.

As the number of non-natives with interests in natives—missionaries, traders, teachers, governmental officials, entrepreneurs, in-marrying outsiders—increased, so did the settlement orientation of natives. While there is variation in this as in other aspects of Subarctic native life, since 1950, natives almost everywhere have spent greater amounts of time in the settlement, and lesser amounts in the bush. The social centers have shifted from traditional bush camps to log cabins and prefabricated houses in town. Mechanized transport—the ubiquitous outboard motor-driven scow and the snowmobile—has paradoxically shortened the distance from traditional camps to town, although the need for fuel has heightened the dependence on a cash economy.

The importance of the bush has declined along with traditional knowledge of how to speak about it and exploit its resources. Where traditional languages have been lost, inevitably, traditional interactions that individuals, as persons, have had with the culturally-constructed environment have altered greatly.

Throughout the Subarctic, the purchasing power of furs has declined, as have the values of some pelts. Traditional subsistence species have remained important, but for most natives, these have long been significantly supplemented in the diet by store-purchased foods. Nevertheless, traditional foods like moose, caribou and fish often, but not always, circulate according to traditional canons of reciprocity, while store foods are treated otherwise.

By the 1980s, many Subarctic natives had become dependent on government support programs. Welfare was everywhere important. Many had lost much of their old self-sufficiency. The old bush ethic might remain strong and the desired state of affairs, but in many instances, the lure of town was too great, at least at most seasons of the year.

Counteracting these tendencies has been an emergent, strong political consciousness borne from adversity. In the mid-1970s, the native people of Quebec signed the James Bay and Northern Quebec Agreement. Their land rights were extinguished and the massive James Bay hydroelectric project began. Implementation of the agreement has been a constant frustration, and the Crees face more massive inundation of their traditional lands, but have nevertheless gained significant control over their political and educational lives and a new political unity in the face of external adversity.

In the western Canadian Subarctic, the comparable event enhancing political consciousness and leading to political unity was the mid-1970s Mackenzie Valley Pipeline Inquiry, which resulted in the imposition of a caveat on an energy corridor along the Mackenzie River and on land use and development in the Northwest Territories. Mackenzie drainage Athapaskans visibly organized themselves as the Dene Nation, declared that certain of their fundamental understandings in early 20th century treaty signings had not been recorded, and successfully combatted energy projects. For the last 20 years, they have sought increased control over territorial and local decisions that affect their economy, government, and education.

In Alaska, the discovery of oil at Prudhoe Bay set the stage for the Alaska Native Claims Settlement Act of 1971, in which all Alaska natives gave up their aboriginal rights for 40 million acres of land and $962 million in cash. They also, however, accepted that access to the Act's rights would be through native local and regional corporations, organizations fractured by one controversy after another.

In all cases—Alaska, Quebec, the Northwest Territories—native people have given up something substantial (in Alaska and Quebec, their aboriginal title) in the face of pressure from companies seeking to extract energy resources. In return, aside from monetary or territorial considerations, they gained far more political authority as well as actual control over the development or preservation, or both, of their remaining resources and their lives than they ever possessed before.

It is in these political movements, led by natives who have a firm understanding, through formal education, of the whiteman's world, as well as a deep respect for the opinions of their elders and their traditional cultures, that one can find hope for the future of Subarctic natives.

SUGGESTED READINGS

Bailey, A. G.
   1969   The Conflict of European and Eastern Algonquian Cultures 1504–1700; A Study in Canadian Civilization. 2nd ed. Toronto: University of Toronto Press.

Bishop, C.
   1974   The Northern Ojibwa and the Fur Trade: An Historical and Ecological Study. Toronto: Holt Rinehart & Winston of Canada.

Brody, H.
   1982   Maps and Dreams. New York: Pantheon.

Clark, A. M., ed.
   1975   Proceedings: Northern Athapaskan Conference, 1971, 2 vols. National Museum of Man Mercury Series. Canadian Ethnology Service Paper 27. Ottawa: National Museums of Canada.

Francis, D. and T. Morantz
   1983   Partners in Furs: A History of the Fur Trade in Eastern James Bay 1600–1870. Kingston & Montreal: McGill-Queens University Press.

Fumoleau, R.
   1975   As Long as This Land Shall Last. Toronto: McClelland and Stewart.

Helm, J.
   1976   The Indians of the Subarctic: A Critical Bibliography. Bloomington and London: Indiana University Press.

Helm, J. ed.
   1981   Handbook of North American Indians. Vol 6: Subarctic. Washington: Smithsonian Institution.

Honigmann, J. J.
   1949   Culture and Ethos of Kaska Society. Yale University Publications in Anthropology 40. New Haven.

Krech, S. III
   1984   Ethnohistory and Ethnography in the Subarctic. American Anthropologist 86: 80–86.
   1984   (Ed.) The Subarctic Fur Trade. Vancouver: University of British Columbia Press.
   1986   Native Canadian Anthropology and History: A Selected Bibliography. Winnipeg: Ruperts Land Research Centre.

Leacock, E.
   1954   The Montagnais "Hunting Territory" and the Fur Trade. American Anthropologist 56 (5), Memoir 78.

McClellan, C.
   1976   My Old People Say: An Ethnographic Survey of Southern Yukon Territory. National Museum of Man, Publications in Ethnology Ottawa: National Museums of Canada.

Nelson, R. K.
   1973   Hunters of the Northern Forest: Designs for Survival Among the Alaskan Kutchin. Chicago: University of Chicago Press.
   1983   Make Prayers to the Raven. Chicago: University of Chicago Press.

Osgood, C.
   1936   Contributions to the Ethnography of the Kutchin. Yale University Publications in Anthropology 14. New Haven.

1940   Ingalik Material Culture Yale University Publications in Anthropology 14. New Haven.
1958   Ingalaik Social Culture. Yale University Publications in Anthropology 53. New Haven.
1959   Ingalik Mental Culture. Yale University Publications in Anthropology 56. New Haven.

Ray, A. J. and D. Freeman
1978   "Give Us Good Measure": An Economic Analysis of Relations Between the Indians and the Hudson's Bay Company Before 1763. Toronto: University of Toronto Press.

Ridington, R.
1989   Trail to Heaven. Iowa City: University of Iowa Press.

Shkilnyk, A. M.
1985   A Poison Stronger Than Love: The Destruction of an Ojibwa Community. New Haven: Yale University Press.

Speck, F.
1977   Naskapi: The Savage Hunters of the Labrador Peninsula. Norman: University of Oklahoma Press.

Tanner, A.
1979   Bringing Home Animals: Religious Ideology and Mode of Production of the Mistassini Cree Hunters. New York: St. Martins Press.

VanStone, J. W.
1974   Athapaskan Adaptations: Hunters and Fishermen of the Subarctic Forests. Chicago: Aldine.
1979   Ingalik Contact Ecology: An Ethnohistory of the Lower-Middle Yukon 1790–1935. Chicago: Field Museum of Natural History.

Watkins, M. ed.
1977   Dene Nation: The Colony Within. Toronto: University of Toronto Press.

Chapter 4

The Northeast Culture Area

Kathleen J. Bragdon

Colonial Williamsburg Foundation

Introduction

As the scene of long-term interaction between native peoples representing many cultures and Europeans with differing preconceptions and goals, the Northeast is a region best studied from an ethnohistorical perspective. Peoples of the northern coastal regions may have been in contact with Norsemen circa 1000 A.D. (McGhee 1984) while other contacts with Europeans began by at least 1498 (Brasser 1978a:79; Quinn 1977). Many descriptions of the natives of the northeast dating from the time of the Norse sagas through the present day have been written, providing a rich resource for the ethnohistorian. Ethnographic fieldnotes, folklore studies, and linguistic materials, in the form of translations of religious works, contemporary grammars and modern tape recordings, and in some cases native vernacular texts, are also abundant for the northeast, providing some insight into the native experience of contact and sustained interaction with non-natives in their own words. As the indigenous people of the northern hemisphere longest in contact with Europeans, the northeastern hunters and horticulturalists have in many cases experienced extraordinary disruption, which can often be documented in the historical sources as well. In many ways however, the native northeast is poorly understood, and what has been written about it is only now being reassessed.

Aboriginally, the northeast was a region of great cultural diversity, and its designation as a culture area is largely a matter of anthropological and archaeological tradition. Trigger (1978a:1) defines the northeast in terms of ecological, linguistic, economic, and culture-historical features. Northern boundaries coincide with the lower edge of the boreal forests that extend from Alaska to eastern Canada. The western border marks the line between the Woodlands horticulturalists, and the mounted hunting groups of the Prairies. To the south, all Algonquian- and Iroquoian-speaking peoples except the Cherokee are traditionally included (See Map 4.1). With some exceptions, it can be argued that the cultures of the Northeast shared an orientation towards horticulture and/or maritime/lacustrine pursuits which distinguished them from the boreal and prairie hunting bands to the north and west, with whom they shared other features.

Within this vast area, regions defined by distinctive linguistic and ecological characteristics can also be identified: the Coastal region, including the Beothuk of Newfoundland,

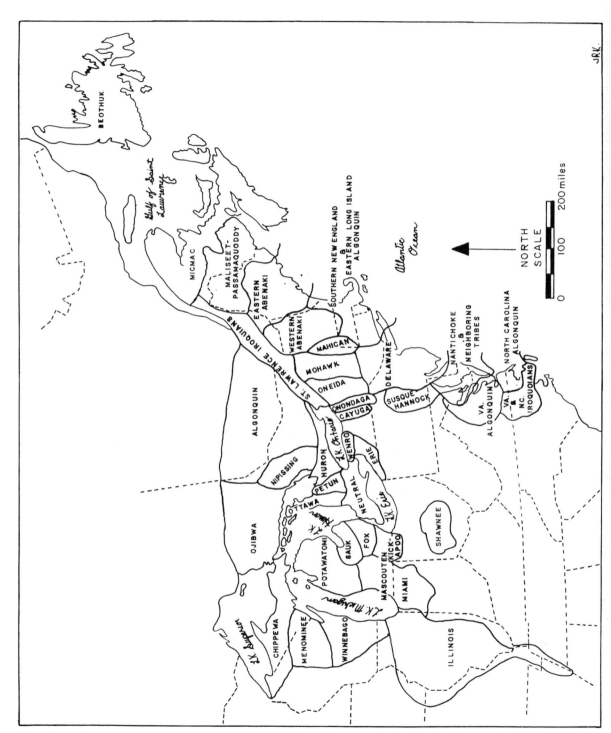

Map of the Northeast Culture Area

and the Algonquian- and Iroquoian- speaking natives of the north and mid-Atlantic regions; the area of the St. Lawrence lowlands, including all Iroquoian-speaking groups except those of Virginia and North Carolina; and the Great Lakes-Riverine region, inhabited by speakers of Siouan and Central Algonquian languages (Trigger 1978a:1-3). Dean Snow (1980:1-6) would further isolate a distinctive New England culture area, extending from the St. John River valley to Long Island, and west to the Mohawk river drainage; while Helen Hornbeck Tanner includes in the Great Lakes region three groups: original residents (Iroquoian, Algonquian, and Siouan speakers), refugees from the Atlantic seaboard (Algonquian and Iroquoian), and later allies and opponents from south and west of the Great Lakes (Muskogean and Siouan) (1987:2).

As in other areas of the New World, population estimates for the northeast have ranged from the conservative (e.g. Mooney 1928; Kroeber 1939) to the generous (Dobyns 1983; (but see Henige 1986)). For the New England and southeastern New York region, Cook estimates a population of 71,900 in 1610 (1970:84) while Snow and Lanphear argue for an early seventeenth-century population there of 156,200 (including Mohawk and Munsee) (1988:24). For the mid-Atlantic coastal areas Feest (1978a:242; 1978b:256; 1978c:272) gives late sixteenth- to early seventeenth-century figures of 31,000 to 40,000. Early reports estimated Huron population to have been about 30,000 spread among eighteen villages (Heidenreich 1978:369). Bruce Trigger suggests that the preepidemic population of the Five Nations was equal to that of the Huron (1985:236). Populations of other Northern Iroquoian groups such as the Petun, Wyandot and Erie were poorly recorded, but Garrad and Heidenreich estimate the protohistoric Petun population to have been about 8000 (1978:395). The southern Iroquoian-speaking Nottaway and Meherrin could muster 140 fighting men in 1669, and the nearby Tuscarora 1200 in 1709 (Boyce 1978:287-288). Marquette and Jolliet found 8000 Illinois living on the Iowa river in 1673 (Bauxar 1978:594).

Protohistoric population density in the Northeast varied with specific ecological conditions; northern New England, Nova Scotia, Newfoundland and the colder regions of the Great Lakes-Riverine area were sparsely settled, while the southern New England and mid-Atlantic regions supported a larger population. For example, Snow (1980:34) suggests population densities for northern New England of 12–29 people per 100 square kilometers, and for southern New England of 193 per 100 square kilometers. Preepidemic Huron population was relatively large, reaching nearly 2,400 people per 100 square kilometers (Heidenreich 1978:369). Protohistoric populations are difficult to assess with accuracy, however, and since the sixteenth century, native population in the Northeast has varied greatly due to the effects of various European-introduced epidemics and/or endemic diseases, the depredations of war, and the relocation of some peoples following intensive European settlement (Ubelaker 1976).

Languages

The native peoples of the Northeast spoke a large number of different languages, falling into three major language families; Algonquian, Iroquoian, and Siouan. Algonquian speakers of the Great Lakes-Riverine area spoke languages of the Central Algonquian group, while those in the east spoke languages of the Eastern Algonquian group as defined by Goddard (1965;1978a). Iroquoian languages were spoken in the St. Lawrence lowlands, the Great Lakes region, and in western Virginia and North Carolina. The Siouan-speaking Winnebago also lived in the Great Lakes-Riverine region, and there may have been Siouan speakers in western Virginia and North Carolina as well (Alexander 1971:307). While speakers of related languages shared many cultural traits, the influence of neighboring tribes (as in the case of the Delaware and the Iroquois) was often equally important in determining the character of a particular group.

Subsistence and Technology

In the protohistoric period in the Northeast, three different subsistence patterns prevailed: a hunting/collecting pattern, a mixed hunting/horticultural pattern, and the horticultural pattern of the northern Iroquois. Each was associated with different ecological and culture-historical conditions (Flannery 1939, 1946; Trigger 1978 a,b). All were characterized by specialized technologies and were associated with varying social and belief systems (to be discussed in Sections IV and V).

The Hunting/Collecting Pattern

The hunting and collecting pattern is one of great antiquity in the Northeast. Archaeological studies suggest that by 10,000 B.P. Archaic hunter-gatherers were settled throughout the region, with technologies well-adapted to their local environments (Snow 1980:159,170–171; Trigger 1978b:798). In the protohistoric period, Algonquian-speaking peoples of the northern interior and coastal regions continued to subsist on game, fish, and wild plants, according to their seasonal availability. Some coastal groups also exploited sea mammals and marine resources as a specialized form of hunting/collecting as well (Nash and Miller 1987).

These groups spent the winter in scattered single- or extended-family dwellings, hunting large game with stone-tipped spears and arrows, and other mammals with snares and deadfalls (e.g., Lescarbot 1606:269). Some, including the Micmac, Ojibwa, and Abenaki, stalked game with snowshoes, and the Eastern Abenaki used a toboggan as well (Snow 1978:139). The Micmac and Abenaki also used dogs for hunting, as did some of the horticulturalists to the south and west. The Nipissing, Ottawa, and Algonquin of the St. Lawrence River region, although practicing limited farming, depended heavily on fowl and game, which they hunted with bow and arrow and snares. These groups, like those to the east, also made extensive use of fish, sometimes caught in winter with nets through holes in the ice (Day 1978b:788; Feest and Feest 1978:781; Day and Trigger 1978:795).

In spring, the hunting groups of the northern regions moved into larger settlements, generally located near rich fishing spots. Here they caught and smoked the abundant fish of rivers and ocean, in particular codfish, herring, alewives, shad, eel, salmon and sturgeon (Champlain 1907 [1604]:39–41). Many groups used sugar maple sap collected in the spring as a sweetener (e.g. Ritzenthaler 1978:747). Bruce Bourque has argued that natives of northern New England spent late winter and spring near the coast, fishing and collecting shellfish, and moved inland during the summer months (Bourque 1973). Elsewhere, summer witnessed continued emphasis on fishing, as well as the collecting of berries, roots, and nuts, some of which were dried and formed into cakes. In autumn, hunting again took on greater importance, along with the harvesting of wild nuts, seeds, and berries. In the northern Great-Lakes Riverine region, the Menominee (who also farmed) and Southwestern Chippewa spent several weeks in fall gathering wild rice, which was collected by knocking the grains into a canoe as it passed through the fields (Ritzenthaler 1978:747; Spindler 1978:708).

The Micmac, and to a lesser extent, the Eastern Abenaki, in addition to their reliance on deer, bear and smaller game, also made use of sea mammals and other marine resources (Nash and Miller 1987:46). Among the Micmac, seal were hunted with harpoons in January (Biard in Thwaites 1959 [1616]:79–81). Native men used fishhooks and nets for cod, trout, salmon, and smelt, and weirs for communal fishing. The Micmac sometimes employed decoys and disguises in hunting sea mammals, which they then killed with clubs or harpoons (Bock 1978:112). Most northern New England people fished for salmon by attracting them with torchlight and spearing them with barbed fish spears (Gyles 1936 [1736]:27). The Eastern Abenaki took harbour seal, porpoise and water fowl in the warm months (Snow 1978:139), and the Maliseet-Passamaquoddy sometimes hunted whale in shallow waters (Erikson 1978:127). Like their southern coastal neighbors, the hunter/collectors of the St. Lawrence lowlands and northern coastal areas gathered shellfish as well.

The hunting peoples of the Northeast made extensive use of bark canoes for fishing and travel. The seventeenth-century Jesuit missionary Biard described the Micmac or Eastern Abenaki canoe as "a large hollow cradle . . . so capacious that a single one of them will hold an entire household of five or six persons, with all their dogs, sacks, skins, kettles, and other heavy baggage" (Thwaites 1959: 3:83). A model of a birchbark canoe found in a young Beothuk boy's grave in 1886 has each gunwale peaked in the center and rising again to a peak at each end (Reynolds 1978:104 (illustration)). The Maliseet-Passamaquoddy and Eastern Abenaki also made moosehide canoes. Other more southerly and western groups, including the Western Abenaki, Massachusett and Menominee used a bark canoe as well as a dugout type (Spindler 1978:710). As a light and maneuverable craft the bark canoe made the mobile way of life of the northern hunters practical, and enabled peoples spread over an extensive area to maintain consistent contact, through use of the myriad natural waterways of the Northeast.

Housing among the hunter/collectors of the Northeast was also well suited to mobility. Winter dwellings were oval- circular- or pyramidal-shaped wigwams or lodges framed with saplings and covered with overlapping strips of bark, woven mats, or skins.

These dwellings were large enough to house a single- or extended-family group, but generally contained only a single hearth, located in the center (Bock 1978:112). The Eastern Abenaki house had a central post, and two doors, shielded with skin flaps (Snow 1978:140). By 1605, these people, along with the Ottawa and the Algonquin to the west, constructed Iroquoian-like barrel-shaped longhouses with bark coverings (Snow 1980:62; Feest and Feest 1978:781; Day and Trigger 1978:796), as well as conical tents for temporary use (Feest and Feest 1978:781). The dirt floors of the dwellings were covered with brush. Sleeping skins were arranged around the perimeter, and other belongings and utensils were hung from the framing poles. All these house types were relatively easy to construct and dismantle, and could be adapted to all weather conditions.

The hunters of the Northeast wore clothing constructed of animal skins, including belted robes or coats with detachable sleeves, leggings, and moccasins. In 1524, Verrazzano saw clothing made of bear, lynx, and sea-wolf furs among the Eastern Abenaki (Wroth 1970:140–141). Most men, like the Micmac, wore tanned skin loincloths under their robes in winter (Bock 1978:113), while the Eastern Abenaki wore a kilt-like garment (Snow 1978:141). Western Abenaki women wore leggings, moccasins, a knee-length skirt, and a long skin shirt (Day 1978a:154). Women of the southwestern Chippewa wore a two-sided skin dress, over a woven fiber skirt (Ritzenthaler 1978:747). Garments used by both sexes probably included skin breechclouts and aprons (Feest and Feest 1978:775).

Champlain said of the Western Abenaki "these savages shave off the hair far up on the head, and wear what remains very long, which they comb and twist behind in various ways very neatly, intertwined with feathers which they attach to the head" (Champlain 1907 [1605]:61–63). Some people wore caps ornamented with feathers or fur (Day 1978a:154). The roach, a bushy crest of deer or moose hair, sometimes dyed red and ornamented with porcupine quills, and worn down the center of the head, was affected by many groups (Ritzenthaler 1978:747). Oil and grease or marrow were applied to the body and hair, and tattooing and body painting were common forms of personal ornamentation (Champlain 1907 [1605]:61–63). Like the Micmac, many hunting people habitually wore "chains, gewgaws, and such finery" (Biard in Thwaites 1959:3:72–83).

Basketry, woven mats, and bags were made by all the northern hunter/collectors. Mats were sometimes used to cover the exterior of wigwams, and perhaps to line the interior of dwellings as well. Soft baskets and carrying bags of hemp, rush or sweetgrass were woven in geometric designs (King 1982:27–29). Some groups made skin and basswood bags, and possibly some type of sturdier basket (Bock 1978:112; Day and Trigger 1978:796). Many northern people used birchbark containers of varying sizes, which were often decorated with incising, scraped designs, or quillwork embroidery (Gyles 1936 [1736]:29). Fishing lines, nets, and temporary tumplines woven from fibers and sinew and thongs were used for webbing snowshoes and sewing canoe covers (King 1982:25–29;75–77).

Other domestic utensils included ceramic containers, soapstone dishes, and wood bowls, cups, and spoons. Women's tools included needles, skin-processing equipment such as stone scrapers, cooking implements, and mortars and pestles. Men used hunting equipment, fishing gear, and wood-working tools such as axes, and adzes, as well as the well-known northern "crooked knife" (Snow 1980:58).

Mixed Hunting/Horticulture

The practice of horticulture came relatively late to the Northeast (See Chapter One) and most of the farmers of that region continued to follow the ancient hunting/collecting cycle as well. In both the east and west, the range of the hunting/horticulture pattern extended to the northernmost area where the minimum of 120–140 frost-free days required for successful harvesting of aboriginal maize regularly occured. In the marginal areas, groups such as the Nippissing, Ottawa, Algonquin and Southwestern Chippewa to the west, and the Maliseet-Passamaquoddy and Eastern Abenaki to the east, cultivated crops in mild years, but depended most heavily on traditional wild food sources. Upper Great Lakes-Riverine groups practiced agriculture, hunting, collecting, and fishing (Tanner 1987:19–23).

Like the hunter/collectors, the horticulturalists of the central and mid-Atlantic coasts and interior gathered, hunted, and planted according to the seasonal availability of resources. Winters were spent in single-family dwellings near hunting grounds, where deer, moose (in northern areas), bear, and smaller game were stalked with bow and arrow and spear, or caught in snares and deadfalls. Some groups used snowshoes for stalking game, and others hunted with dogs. Late winter was occasionally a time of scarcity, as dried and smoked food supplies were low, and hunting became increasingly difficult through the thawing snow.

In spring, larger groups came together near rivers, streams and falls, to take advantage of the spawning fish, and the flocks of migratory birds. Men, working singly and in groups, fished with hooks, lines, scoops and nets, and many groups constructed wiers (See Figure 4.1 Champlain map of 1605). Some groups fished from canoes, using spears (Keesing 1939:20). Removal to the spring fishing camp was followed by the return to the summer planting grounds, in river bottoms, or in coastal areas near the seashore.

The summer villages in coastal regions were loosely grouped single- or multiple-family dwellings, located next to planting fields. Of the river-dwelling Powhatan, Strachey wrote "Their houses are not manie in one towne, and those that are stand. . . scattered, without forme of a street, far and wide asunder" (1953 [1612]:79). In some areas, summer villages were palisaded, and consisted of up to two dozen houses. The swidden-type of horticulture practised in the Northeast required moving the planting field every eight to ten years, and new planting grounds were prepared by burning the large trees and undergrowth, and removing stumps and brush with stone axes and hoes. The Fox, Kickapoo, Mascouten and Potawatomi of the western Great Lakes Riverine area, having access to prairie lands, hunted bison during the summer as well (Tanner 1987:Map 4; Callender 1978c:637; Callender et.al.1978:658: Goddard 1978c:670; Clifton 1978:729).

Most of the horticulturist/collectors of the Northeast planted a highly nutritious combination of three basic crops; maize, beans, and squash. Men (or sometimes groups of men and women) did the heavy work of clearing and breaking up the fields, but women were

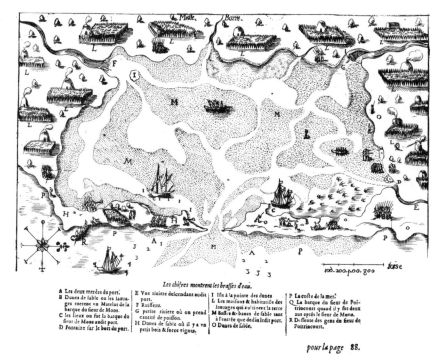

Les chiffres montrent les braſſes d'eau.

A Les deux entrées du port.
B Dunes de ſable ou les ſauuages ruerent vn Matelot de la
  barque du ſieur de Mons.
C les lieux ou fut la barque du
  ſieur de Mons audit port.
D Fontaine ſur le bort du port.

E Vne riuiere deſcendant audit
  port.
F Ruiſſeau.
G petite riuiere où on prend
  cantité de poiſſon.
H Dunes de ſable où il y a vn
  petit bois & force vignes.

I Iſle à la pointe des dunes
L Les maiſons & habitatiõs des
  ſauuages qui cultinent la terre
M Baſſes & bancs de ſable tant
  à l'entrée que dedãs ledit port.
O Dunes de ſable.

P La coſte de la mer.
Q La barque du ſieur de Poi-
  trincourt quand il y fut deux
  aus aprés le ſieur de Mons.
R Deſſente des gens du ſieur de
  Poittrincourt.

pour la page 88.

Figure 4.1 Champlain map of 1605: Map of Malle Bar. (Courtesy of Library of Congress.)

responsible for the bulk of the planting, weeding, and harvesting tasks (Williams 1936:99). The corn was generally planted in hills with several kernals to each. Beans of several varieties were planted in the hills as well and allowed to grow up the corn stalk. Squash was interplanted among the hills. Such planting methods conserved moisture, prevented weed growth, and resulted in a high yield per acre (Cronon 1983:44). After the seed was planted, and throughout the summer, children or adult look-outs camping on sheltered platforms prevented birds from disturbing the crop. In coastal areas, successive corn crops were planted (Champlain 1907:82; Barlow 1981 [1954]:447). Tobacco was also cultivated among all groups, and unlike other crops, was sometimes the responsibility of the men (Williams 1936:99).

During the planting season, people in coastal areas caught eel and other fish, and collected shellfish, including quohog, clams, mussels and lobster. Men stalked seals sunning on rocks nears shore, and larger fish were speared and netted from boats. Some villages constructed large wiers of stone and brush, or large conical nets at the mouths of streams (See Figure 4.1: Champlain [1605]:Map of Malle Bar). Even during this season of abundance, deer and other animals were hunted, and archaeological as well as documentary evidence for coastal areas indicates a heavy dependence of game (Bennett 1955; Ceci

1982). After harvest, communal hunting drives were held, in which deer were forced into V-shaped fenced areas, and dispatched with spears and arrows. Late autumn signalled the return to winter hunting grounds.

Housing among the horticultural groups was similar to that of their more northerly neighbors. Champlain's 1605 map of Malle Bar harbour (Figure 4.1) shows summer dwellings of dome- or barrel-shaped houses, which were framed of saplings, and covered with woven mats or bark strips. Woven mats of geometric design were used to cover the interior walls and floor as well. Sleeping platforms covered with skins were constructed around the perimeter of the house, and a central hearth was positioned beneath a smoke hole in the roof, which could be closed with a flap. These dwellings usually had two doors, which could be adjusted to different openings. Further west, groups such as the Sauk, Fox, and Shawnee built bark-covered lodges resembling those of the Iroquois (Callender 1978b; 1978c). Summer villages of western groups such as the Illinois were very large, and those of the Sauk were also unusual in their size and their orderly arrangement into "streets" (Callender 1978d; 1978c).

Winter dwellings were similar in design and materials to summer houses, but generally smaller. By the tight construction of the mats, made of a variety of rush resistant to decay, and/or layering of bark strips, and the careful arrangement of doors and smoke holes, these dwellings were warm and waterproof yet well-ventilated in the coldest weather. Temporary brush and frame structures were erected at hunting and fishing stations, and separate sweat lodges were built near streams and rivers. In the Great Lakes Riverine area, groups such as the Shawnee and Illinois built large wooden structures for rituals and council meetings in the center of each semi-permanent summer village (Callender 1978b:625; 1978e:674) which sometimes included over thirty lodges.

Transportation was primarily by canoe, of which there were two types in use: the birch or spruce bark canoe, and the log dugout. Some groups had skin-covered canoes as well (Barlow 1981 [1584]:449). The wooden dugout was well-suited to ocean-travel, and could carry up to 40 people (Williams 1936:107). The lighter bark canoes were favored for river travel.

The coastal horticulturalists were renowned for their twine and textile work. Baskets of grass, roots, and bark, and bags of hemp and basswood were woven and twined. Most were decorated with geometric designs executed in dyed fibers. Western groups such as the Siouan-speaking Winnebago twined elaborately decorated storage bags of basswood and (later) wool (Lurie 1978:698). All groups used birch bark containers of several sizes, which were decorated with paint and incising. Rope and twine of many thickness as well as netting and cord were made from hemp, bark, and thong. All groups made use of woven tumplines, which likewise were decorated with geometric designs (Bragdon 1988).

Ceramic vessels with incised, cord-marked, and other decorations were used for cooking, serving, and storage. Soapstone containers (Snow 1980:82), and bowls made of wood were also manufactured. Wooden spoons and cups were finely carved from burl wood, and often carried by a thong from the belt of a traveller (King 1982:30).

Clothing styles were similar to those of further north as well. Winter cloaks with detachable sleeves were painted or embroidered with shell beads. Men wore breechclouts with front and back flaps held by belts. Winter moccasins reached above the ankle. Both men and women wore leggings, attached to the belt with thongs. Women wore knee-length skirts or aprons. Hair styles were elaborate among the horticultural people, and distinctive styles were sometimes indicative of status (Williamson 1979). Feather and fur strips were used as ornaments, and headbands of woven checker-work wampum were also worn [See Figure 4.2, (Ninigret)]. Animal grease was applied to the body and hair, and paint and tattooing were common. For some groups, such as the Menominee, body paint color and designs may have had ceremonial importance (Spindler 1978:710). Earrings, pendants, collars, and necklaces of shell, copper and stone were worn by people of all ages. George Hammell has suggested that much of this ornamentation was "symbolically charged," with various colors, including white, azure, and red, having associations with fertility and good fortune (1987:63–87).

Women's tools included farming implements such as clamshell and stone hoes and digging sticks, skin-processing tools such as scrapers, cooking and sewing implements and mortars and pestles. Women also manufactured pottery and wove mats and baskets. A man's tool kit would include stone and wooden hunting equipment, woodworking tools such as axes, adzes, chisels and burins, and fishing equipment (King 1982:12–21).

The Northern Iroquois

The Northern Iroquois, a label usually reserved for the historic Five (and later Six) Nations of the lower Geat Lakes region, including Seneca, Cayuga, Onondaga, Oneida, Mohawk, and Tuscarora, were a distinctive group of people who were primarily dependent on agriculture, and who lived for the most part in quasi-permanent, often palisaded villages. As with all other Northeastern peoples, the Iroquois way of life was one of adaptation to a seasonal cycle. Although most dependent on agriculture of all groups in the area, they too were hunters, fishers, and collectors, and each season of the year was devoted to making greatest use of abundant and varied natural resources.

A large portion of each year was spent in villages, located near the planting fields, and most often by a major body of water. These villages were stockaded, and enclosed a number of multi-family dwellings known as longhouses. Spring and summer months were devoted to clearing, planting, cultivating, and harvesting crops, especially the fabled "three sisters" maize, squash, and beans. The fields were burned and roughly cleared by men, but women were responsible for tilling, planting, and harvesting. Summer months were also spent gathering, drying and storing berries and nuts, and collecting fresh greens, as well as fishing and hunting (Fenton 1978:301).

Autumn was a time of communal deer hunts, and witnessed the removal of parties made up of men and some women from the villages to stations in hunting territories, where game was both hunted and processed for future use. Midwinter saw the dispersal of these groups to the village, from which occasional hunting trips continued to be launched until

Figure 4.2 Portrait of Ninigret II. (Courtesy of Museum of Art, Rhode Island School of Design; gift of Mr. Robert Winthrop.)

early spring. At that time, people removed to sugar maple groves to collect sap, and to fishing camps near the river, seeking the swarming fish and flocks of migratory fowl, which they caught with nets (ibid.).

The distinctive dwellings of the Iroquois were vaulted structures up to 200 feet in length. These longhouses were constructed of a curved sapling frame, covered with thick pieces of bark. The interior of the longhouse was divided into a number of two-room sections each with its own hearth, around which resided a single family. The sections were separated from one another by storage bins filled with dried grains. Some longhouses housed up to 25 people, members of a maternal lineage. Iroquois villages were made up of a number of these structures "in rows like streets" (Harmen Meyndertsz van den Bogaert 1909 [1634]:140). Other structures included the sweatlodge, and temporary shelters used at hunting and fishing stations. The Delaware and the Mahican, Algonquian-speakers to the east, also had longhouse-like dwellings, and palisaded villages have also been recorded among the Western Abenaki (Thomas 1985:136). The Iroquois longhouse villages were moved approximately once every twelve years, or as fresh planting fields were required (Engelbrecht 1985:164).

Means of transportation varied in different environments. To the north, the Huron, Petun, and Erie made use of a birch bark canoe, and travelled extensively on the rivers and lakes of the northern Great Lakes region. The northern Iroquois had a rather heavy and unmaneuverable craft of spruce bark, not suited for rapid or rough river travel. The Iroquois of the Five Nations were primarily forest travellers, and renowned for the speed of their movements on foot (Fenton 1978:303).

The Iroquois were skillful weavers of baskets, straps, and matting. They used a variety of materials including corn husks and rush, basswood fibers and hemp, and splines of spruce. Twine was fashioned by rolling hemp or other fiber between palm and thigh (King 1982:27,50)

Costume in protohistoric times was undoubtedly like that described for the Huron: belted winter robes worn over breechclouts and leggings by men, and skirts and leggings by women, Winter and summer moccasins were worn, and some peoples wore woven hemp shoes in summer. Iroquois men were tattooed, and used body paint as well. Hairstyles were elaborate and clothing was painted and embroidered (Sagard-Theodat 1939:143–147).

Social Organization

The forms of social life were varied and complex among Northeastern groups. All were nevertheless united in serving to organize daily life, the ritual year, and relationships with outsiders. Each reflected at several levels, native theories of their own creation, and of their relationship to beings both human and "other than human."

The Hunter/Collectors

The oldest and most widespread of adaptations, the hunting/collecting pattern of the Northeast, was associated with a band type of social organization, which consisted in general of a several households, or sometimes a larger cluster of local groups. Such groupings were not tribes, in the modern legal sense, but rather loose confederations, recognizing similarities of language and custom. Nor were such groupings necessarily associated with specific drainage systems as Snow (1980) has argued. Particularly in northern New

England, river valleys were often occupied by several ethnically or linguistically distinct communities (Prins and Bourque 1987:140).

Each band or group of bands was led by a chief who in northern New England was called sagamore (Bock 1978:116). The sagamore's power was derived from consensus within the community, and although he was often a member of a privileged lineage, his status was generally maintained through personal qualities of courage, hunting prowess, and oratorical skill.

Some bands, including those of the Maliseet-Passamaquoddy were bilateral, that is, they reckoned descent from both parents (Erikson 1978:130), while others, such as the Western Abenaki, were patrilineal (Day 1978a:156). Even those groups with bilateral descent systems had a strong patrilineal bias often expressed in the inheritance office, or (later) in the inheritance of specific hunting territories through the male line. Based on the kinship terminology of Algonquian-speaking peoples such as the Western Abenaki (Day 1978a:156), it appears that at some point in their history, cross-cousin marriage was the norm.

Many of the northern hunting peoples recognized larger kin groupings, usually called clans, or totemic descent groups, members of which were thought to be descended from a common ancestor. Such clans were often linked to specific animal totems, for which they were named. The clans were often in turn divided into two groups, called moieties, which took opposite sides in athletic competitions, and in council discussions (Day 1978a:156). In the western region, groups such as the Southwestern Chippewa were patrilineal and belonged to totemic clans named for certain animals (Ritzenthaler 1978:753). Unlike other Algonquian groups however, the Southwestern Chippewa were organized into a number of phratries, or groupings of clans. Clans in some groups were exogamous, so that a member of one was required to seek a marriage partner in another (Day 1978a:156). Dean Snow argues that such totemic clans were evident in the historic period in northern New England, but may have been relatively late developments there (1980:49).

All kin were associated with specific sets of rights and obligations, which formed the basis for all social interaction, within the community itself, and in its relationships with outsiders. The nuclear family, consisting of husband, wife, and their offspring, all of whom shared a dwelling, was generally the primary kin unit. Sustenance, clothing, shelter, and the nurturing and education of children were all basic needs fulfilled by the nuclear family group. In fall and winter, single or extended families often operated independently of others, in solitary hunting camps or trapping stations.

In spring and summer, larger social units such as clans, phratries or moieties were operative in the practice of rituals and ceremonies, in the planning of warfare, and in cooperative efforts such as communal game drives, fishing, and whaling. The band itself also acted as a corporate group, laying claim to certain territories and making joint decisions in council.

There were often several specialized roles found among hunting/collecting groups, among them that of war-chief, those known as "camp police" and religious practitioners and curers, often called shamans. These roles were associated with special ability, or in the case of the shaman, a particularly powerful relationship with the supernatural (to be discussed in more detail below). In the early historic period, some sagamores combined political skill and shamanistic powers to remarkable effect, achieving true "big man" status, and enormous personal influence (Snow 1980:62; Burton and Lowenthal 1974).

The Hunter/Horticulturalists

While the band-type of social organization remained in force among the mixed economies of the Northeast, several innovations possibly associated with the adoption of horticulture also appear among these groups. Primary among them were increased social stratification and the development of hereditary leadership in several areas, particularly southern New England and Virginia.

The bands of the hunter/horticulturalists were named groups associated with specific geographic localities, who lived for part of the year in villages near the coast or the major rivers of the region. The bands were led by chiefs, whose positions, especially in southern New England, were inherited by virtue of their membership within privileged lineages. These leaders, called sachems or sagamores in New England, and werowances in Virginia, were usually men whose hereditary right to rule was necessarily reinforced by personal courage, generosity, and skill at speechmaking, and still depended on the support and consensus of the community. Some groups, such as the Narragansett, apparently had two leaders, one whose responsibilities were civil and domestic, and another who was concerned with war (Wroth 1970 [1524]:138–139; Williams 1936:140). This dual political organization was more overt in western hunting/horticultural groups, who often had parallel organizations for peace and war, each having a separate chief (Callender 1978a:610).

For the central Algonquian-speaking people, Callender (1978a) has recognized two basic patterns of sociopolitical organization. One, associated with the Omaha type of kinship nomenclature, is characterized by its inclusiveness, classifying a number of people as nuclear family members. Fox terms for example, class all men called by ego's father "brother" as "father" (Tax 1955). Similarly, the husbands of all ego's mother's sisters are also called "father." All those ego's mother calls "sister" are called "mother." People using this nomenclature are also usually characterized by patrilineal lineages, with bilateral tendencies, and a system of exogamous totemic clans (Callender 1978a:610).

Groups of the second type, thought to be the older of the two, including the Ottawa and Chippewa-Ojibwa, were patrilineal, and had terminological systems usually called Iroquoian, with separate terms for cross- and parallel-aunts and uncles, and in which the children of same-sex aunts and uncles were called siblings, and those of cross-aunt and uncles were termed cross-cousins (ibid.).

For eastern hunting/horticultural groups, kinship systems are more difficult to reconstruct. The Western Abenaki were patrilineal, with totemic clans whose members were thought to descend from a common male ancestor (Day 1978a:156). Southern New England Algonquian kinship terminologies shared a number of features with Western Abenaki (Bragdon 1981:81–82), although there is some evidence to suggest that the Narragansett, like the Mahican, were matrilineal (Simmons and Aubin 1975; Brasser 1978b:200).

As horticultural people, the mixed hunting/farming groups of the Northeast were organized in part around the use of land, of which each group controlled a recognized portion. Members of each group had usufruct rights to the land belonging to their band. Among the Massachusett, individual parcels were allotted by the sachem, in exchange for tribute paid to him in the form of a share of the harvest. Choice portions of game, and wild resources such as shellfish, berries, and beached whales, were also given in tribute (Winslow 1910 [1624]:57; Wood 1977 [1634]:97). The sachem was expected to redistribute this surplus generously, if informally, for the benefit of the community as a whole.

In southern New England, the sachem and his advisors were responsible for making decisions concerning warfare, and for distributing land. In other areas, chiefs representing the various clans made joint decisions in council. Evidence from the Powhatan of Virginia and the Massachusett and Narragansett of southeastern New England indicates that in the protohistoric period, some chiefs had attained the status of "paramount" ruler, and had dominion over lesser sachems, who owed him tribute, and who may have been related to the paramount ruler by blood or marriage (Bragdon 1981:129; Turner 1985). In spite of their many privileges however, the rulers of these groups were still dependent for their authority upon acceptance by their followers.

The Northern Iroquois

The sociopolitical organization of the Iroquois of the St. Lawrence lowlands area was distinct from the hunting and mixed economies to the east and north in a number of ways. The Iroquois organized themselves into kin groups determined by descent through the female line. For the Iroquois, the most important social unit was this matrilineal lineage, which often resided within a single longhouse and was headed by a matron, the eldest female (Fenton 1978:312). The lineage was responsible for certain religious obligations, and exercised a moral influence over the appointment of new chiefs. The lineages were further grouped into clans, which Elisabeth Tooker has defined as "groups in which membership was ascribed at birth" (1984:111), usually on the basis on membership within a particular lineage. Each Iroquois village had several clans represented there, and was further divided into moieties, consisting of one or more clans each. These moieties were responsible for conducting certain ceremonies, and took opposite sides in athletic competitions (Tooker 1984:111; Fenton 1978:310). Iroquoian kinship terminology, first described by Lewis Henry Morgan (1871) is distinctive in ignoring the distinction between lineal and collateral relatives. Such an inclusive system allows each member of the social group, in Morgan's words, a "greater assurance of safety," (cited in Tooker 1984:118).

Archaeologists have identified fifteenth- and sixteenth-century Iroquois sites that seem to indicate increasing consolidation of large native populations into tribes (Trigger 1985:101; Englebrecht 1985:170–173). Clan groupings, which may have dated back to the

Middle Woodland period, probably contributed to this consolidation. Other special groupings, particularly phratries and moieties also served as models and vehicles for cooperation between groups, further solidifying the Iroquois into tribes (Trigger 1985:102–103).

The Iroquoian tendency to treat and think of others in terms of kin relationships, and their strongly held belief in the principle of reciprocity, contributed directly to the origin and growth of their most significant sociopolitical institution, the League of the Iroquois. Developed some time in the early 1600's, the League was instituted to promote peace among the five Iroquois tribes, Seneca, Oneida, Cayuga, Onondaga, and Mohawk, and to further their mutual advantage in the developing fur trade with the French and English (Tooker 1978b:418). Archaeological evidence in support of this view includes indications of increased intermarriage among tribes in the protohistoric period in the form of shared ceramic decorative motifs, and increasing numbers of European trade items found on sixteenth and seventeenth century sites (Englebrecht 1985:178–179).

While accounts of the history of the League differ, most agree that the founder was Deganawida, who carried the message of Peace to the leaders of each of the five nations, convincing all, including the powerful Thadodaho of the Onondaga, to join together. Thenceforth, the Onondaga became "firekeepers" of the League and Great Council meetings were held there. The first chief of the League, who is named for the original chief, Thadodaho, is always chosen from an Onondaga clan (Tooker 1978b:422; Morgan 1851).

A traditionally determined number of chiefs from all member nations were sent to council. Chiefs were chosen by the senior women of the clan, and given the name of the position inherited by the clan (Tooker 1984:112). The chiefs of the council were divided into moieties, based on the perceived similarities of their eponymous totems. When a chief of one moiety died, it was the responsibility of the opposite moiety to conduct the Condolence ritual, and to raise up a new chief.

All decisions of the council were expected to be unanimous. If agreement could not be reached, the council fire was "covered," and the decision put off. If consensus was reached, the council of the League was able to determine trade policy, alliances, and internal affairs. Its role became increasingly significant during the decades preceding the Revolutionary War, when the League was able to play off the English, French, and American forces to the mutual benefit of all its members (Jennings et al. 1985).

For the Iroquois, the theme of kinship was naturally extended to encompass social relations with non-League and non-Iroquoian groups as well. Thus the Delaware became one of the group of "Younger Brothers" of the Iroquois, and the "Elder Brothers" to the Delaware, implying reciprocal rights and responsibilities similar to those owed by true siblings (Fenton 1978:311). Rituals associated with League activities stressed these relationships, as well as sacred beliefs and moral principles. Thus from the highest levels of League activity, to the most commonplace experiences of the fireside family, the same principles of reciprocity obtained, forming a highly integrated framework for behavior and experience.

Religion and World View

Although several aspects of Northeastern aboriginal life have so far been treated separately, each is closely bound to all others, and from the native perspective, all part of a single continuum. This is particularly true of religious beliefs and world view. Beliefs about the world, and the place of human beings with respect to it were fundamental to all aspects of native life in the Northeast and none can be explained without reference to these beliefs.

To the native peoples of the Northeast, the world was inhabited by a number of "persons-other-than-human," beings with many of the qualities of humanness, i.e. self-awareness, understanding, the ability to communicate, and occasional irrationality, treachery, and hostility (Hallowell 1960:43). These beings are sometimes called *manitou* (Tooker 1979:28). For the Winnebago, Paul Radin explained:

> the world is peopled by an indefinite number of spirits who manifest their existence in many ways, being either visible, audible, felt emotionally, or manifesting themselves by some sign or result. From a certain point of view, all the spirits demonstrate their existence by the result, by the fact that the blessings they bestow upon man enable him to be successful, and this holds just as much for the spirit who manifests himself in the most intangible, emotional manner as for that one who is visible to man (1923:283–284).

The world was one in which both human persons, and persons-other-than-human could change shape while their essence remained unchanged (Tooker 1978:27). The human soul, which communicated through dreams, was capable in native belief, of leaving the body and assuming another shape as well (Hallowell 1960:41). Dreaming experiences were "real," as were the events chronicalled by sacred stories. Thus the distinction between the natural and the supernatural could not be easily made in native thought, for each impinged upon the other.

The Hunter/Collectors

The cosmology of the northern hunting peoples was founded on the belief that the world was formed by a creator, called by various names, who was sometimes associated with the sun (Bock 1978:117). Many northern groups also have tales about giant culture hero/transformers, such as the Micmac Gluskap, a mythic warrior of enormous power. To him are attributed feats that created visible landscape features, and explain the presence and appearance of certain animals and plants. Other spirits populated the world, some benign, others capricious or evil. Native tales tell of tricksters, such as the Western Abenaki *azuban*, the Racoon, whose actions in mythic times are said to explain certain natural phenomena, the origin of native social institutions and of religious ritual. Such trickster tales also provide contemporary commentary on the follies and failings of human beings.

Underlying such beliefs was a coherent world view including an emphasis on moderation, equality, and a willingness to believe that things are not what they seem. Also characteristic of hunting groups was the fatalistic acceptance of hardship, and accompanying feelings of helplessness against the forces of nature (Hallowell 1960). Such fatalism was

107

counterbalanced by a belief in and search for personal power through sacrifice, fasting, and dreams (Tooker 1979:93). Principles of dualism, expressed in art and myth, were also reflected in the value placed on reciprocity among all northern people.

The religious practitioners of the northern hunters were shamans, who were also responsible for curing. Powerful shamans sought the aid of numerous spirit helpers in curing rituals in which the illness was sucked or blown out of the victim's body. With spirit help the shamans were also able to predict the location of game. Shamans acquired their spirit helpers through training or dreams, or were born to their powers by virtue of special status as a younger twin, or a seventh son (Erikson 1978:132).

The Hunter/Horticulturalists

The world of the hunting/farming people of the northeast was populated by a number of spirit beings, the most important of which was often the creator, known among the Narragansett as Cautantowwit. Cautantowwit, a benevolent god, lived in the southwest, and it was to his house that the human soul travelled after death (Williams 1936:130, 137). For some groups, benign spirits shared the cosmos with a frightening, evil spirit, such as the Powhatan Okewis, to whom the people made sacrifices, and whose temple was tended by priests (Smith 1986 [1624]; Hariot 1588).

Among the western Algonquian-speaking people of the Northeast was a belief in a supreme spiritual being often associated with the sun. The Shawnee recognized a supreme creator being known as Our Grandmother, and her grandson, Cloudy Boy. She was "witnessed" by intermediaries such as tobacco, fire, water, and eagles.(Callender 1978b:628). Many, including the Menominee, conceived of the universe as divided into two tiers, an upper and lower, each inhabited by supernatural beings, good and evil, respectively. Each tier was in turn divided into four levels, occupied by beings of different status. Below the sun/creator lived the Thunderbirds, gods of war, and Morning Star; on the next level were the war eagles and swans. Below them lived the Great White Bear, the Great Underground Panther, and the Horned Serpent, who inhabited the streams and lakes (Spindler 1978:711).

Like the hunters to the north, the hunter/farmers had a number of mythic culture heroes, including the giant/transformer, called Moshup by the Massachusett. Moshup was said to be responsible for the physical appearance of many landscape features in southern New England, and for the presence and appearance of certain animals as well. Stories of animal tricksters such as Rabbit have also been collected in all regions.

Religious practitioners or shamans, (see Figure 4.3) were able to summon helper spirits, which often took the forms of animals. These spirits were invoked to aid in curing ceremonies, and to forecast the outcome of war. Witches and shamans sometimes used the power of their guardian spirits to harm their victims as well. Puberty rituals for all males (and probably females) in the coastal region included isolation, fasting, and sacrifice, with the goal of recognizing one's personal guardian spirit, for whom one might then be named. Many people believed in the separate life of the soul, which could leave the body at night,

The flyer.

Figure 4.3 The flyer. Reproduced by Courtesy of the Trustees of The British Museum.

and often took on another form. The Massachusett, among others, believed that dreams provided messages for the living (Simmons 1976).

Some groups, including the Kickapoo, Shawnee, and Potawatomi made ritual use of sacred packs or bundles, which were owned by clans, and which contained "medicines" invested with powers which could be invoked through specific ceremonies. (Spindler 1978:712; Callender, Pope, and Pope 1978:661). Other important rituals included the Delaware Big House Ceremonial, performed in a specialized structure, called a Big House, the form of which was dictated in a dream at the time the ceremony originated (Tooker 1979:104).

Although everyday objects and occurences were permeated with the sacred, the locus of morality among all Northeastern people was not the spirit world, but rather the living community. Behavior was judged in terms of its benefit or harm to the social group, and people were expected to conform to norms of conduct that included loyalty to the community, generosity, bravery, stoicism, and moderation (Tooker 1979:69). Sacred tales and culture-hero stories emphasized these positive values, and taught the consequences of their betrayal. Landscape features described in these stories were visible to all, and served as a daily reminder of good conduct, while reinforcing native identification with the land they inhabited and made use of (Simmons 1986).

The Northern Iroquois

The Iroquoian people of the protohistoric period believed in the existence of a supreme creator, Sky Woman, who in falling from the heavens, was brought to rest on earth collected by animal divers from the sea bottom and placed on Turtle's back. Her daughter gave birth to twin sons Tharonhiawagon "He who grasps the sky" or "Sapling," and his evil brother. The Good Twin was responsible for the creation of the earth as it exists today (Tooker 1979:33–34; Fenton 1978:319).

The Iroquois believed that after death, the soul travels through a series of trials to the place in the west where the sky allows entry into the land of the dead. During life, the soul communicates its wishes and desires through dreams, and the Huron believed that such desires should be realized if the dreamer was to remain healthy and happy (Wallace 1958).

Among other rituals, the Iroquois performed the ceremony of Midwinter and (formerly) the Feast of the Dead (Tooker 1970). Several societies such as the False Face Society, and the Little Water Medicine Society are responsible for certain rites of curing and of strengthening of medicines and provide services and goods to the poor and elderly. Modern Iroquois ritual is performed according to seasonal agricultural and hunting cycles, and features of all rituals are shared among all Iroquois groups (Sturtevant 1984). Since the eighteenth century, many of the traditional beliefs and practices of the Iroquois have been perpetuated as part of the Longhouse religion founded by the Seneca prophet Handsome Lake (Tooker 1970:3).

Much of Iroquois belief and ritual is concerned with celebration of life, the remembrance of ancestors, loyalty to the community, and reaffirmation of sacred teachings. The principle of duality in nature is explicitly recognized in social groupings such as moieties, and underlies the importance of reciprocity among Iroquois people. Reference to these beliefs and principles is necessary to understand another significant aspect of traditional Iroquoian culture; warfare and the capture and torture of prisoners. Warfare was conducted in revenge for the killing of a community member, to acquire territory, goods, and captives, and as a means of demonstrating honour and courage (Trigger 1985:98). War parties were sent out in autumn, at the instigation of eager young men, or after council determined their objectives. Rituals were performed before their departure, and at their return (Fenton 1978:315).

Male prisoners captured during raids were often tortured, usually on a platform in view of the sun, where their hearts were cut from their bodies. Parts of the victims were cooked and eaten, and the entire ritual was endowed with sacred significance. Prisoner torture, and its association with sun sacrifice, are evidently traits which diffused northwards from Mesoamerica, taking different forms among many Northeastern groups (Trigger 1985:97).

If spared, adopted prisoners served both to replace community members, whose numbers dwindled during the height of Iroquoian warfare in the seventeenth and eighteenth centuries, and as a symbol of renewal for the tribe. Both torture and adoption rituals were cathartic as well as unifying, reaffirming positive cultural values and the solidarity of the group (Heidenreich 1978:386).

Historical Overview

The previous sections have presented native cultures of the Northeast using the time-honored device of the "ethnographic present," describing each group synchronically, as it appeared in earliest accounts, or as it has been reconstructed through "memory ethnography." Although this convention is useful in providing an introduction to the diverse cultures of the Northeast, it is now widely recognized by scholars that such a static portrayal distorts the creativity of native cultural institutions, and devalues the effects of interaction with other natives before and during the contact period. Further, since many descriptions of natives were written by naive or biased non-Indians, the information they contain must be used with caution. Finally, many accounts and ethnographies describe a time relatively late in the contact period, and do not necessarily reflect a "pristine" cultural states but rather various adaptations to the new conditions of contact (Wolf 1982).

Viewing the natives of the Northeast as creative participants in their own destiny, and attempting to account for their institutions and actions both in terms of cultural premises and as pragmatic solutions to individual and group problems has opened up many fascinating lines of inquiry for ethnohistorians of the Northeast. Among these are the role that native groups played in the unfolding drama of the northeastern fur trade (Trigger 1976; 1986), as well as the rise of rich and powerful native traders, "strong men" who skillfully manipulated the flow of goods between natives and Europeans (Fitzhugh 1985). Other post-contact phenomena of great interest are the various native responses to Christianity and the florescence of nativistic religions among many groups. Changing subsistence, residence and descent patterns, and the development of new institutions such as the controversial patrilineal hunting territories described for the nineteenth century, are all seen as creative responses to new conditions, proceeding from traditional premises. European institutions and material goods brought to the Northeast with the traders and settlers took on new roles and significance in native societies, consistent with traditional beliefs and practices as well.

While some generalizations can be made about native history in the Northeast since contact, it is important to emphasize that the experiences and responses of each group were different, depending on their geographic location, their traditional economy and sociopolitical organization, the period in which they were significantly disrupted, and the expectations and goals of the Europeans with whom they interacted. Archaeological and ethnohistorical studies have shown that native societies have always been dynamic, yet the persistence of native cultural institutions during the past several centuries is evidence of their effectiveness as ways of ordering daily life.

History of the Natives of New Brunswick and Northern New England since 1524.

The line between the contact and precontact period in northeasternmost regions of the northeast is particularly blurred. Norse sagas describe contact with peoples of Newfoundland and perhaps New England as early as A.D. 1000, and the natives of this region were certainly trading with eastern Arctic cultures with connections to Norse Greenland in subsequent centuries as well (Fitzhugh 1985:28–29). Norse goods were apparently sought after, and obtained through established coastal trade routes as far south as Maine.

The period of sustained interaction between the natives of Nova Scotia and Maine and Europeans began at least by the time of the voyages of Giovanni de Verrazano in 1524 (Quinn 1977). By 1602, when Bartholemew Gosnold visited southern coastal Maine, natives there were wearing copper ornaments manufactured from trade kettles and articles of European clothing. These items and others had apparently reached them via Micmac and Maliseet middlemen, trading along the coast in wooden shallops, with goods obtained from Basque and French traders and fishermen in the Gulf of St. Lawrence (Borque and Whitehead 1985). Like the Labradoran Inuit to the north (Kaplan 1985:61–62), the Micmac and Maliseet took advantage of their geographical position along the coastal trade route, and became "brokers" to more southerly groups. In this way, already powerful sagamores such as the Eastern Abenaki "big man" Bashabes and the Micmac shaman/leader Membertou gained additional influence through their control over goods and trade routes.

Thus it was that when European settlers arrived, they met native groups with long-established and far-flung trade relations, who were familiar with European technology, and who were furthermore undergoing social and political changes in response to the introduction of new and "symbolically charged" items into their local systems (Hammell 1987; Bradley 1987). Local strong men, traditional leaders who had acquired additional power and prestige through their control of trade mediated much of the early interaction between natives and European settlers.

While the casual exchange of goods between fishermen and the natives was the source of original native-European trade, the focus of the new economic interaction soon came to be centered on furs. By the late 1500's, the importance of fur in European markets was stimulating rivalry between the French and English in northern New England and the St. Lawrence lowlands, and drawing more natives into the trade. Winter was increasingly devoted to trapping fur bearing animals, with the result that some Indians became dependent on alternate sources of food and clothing. As the fur trade developed, some natives devoted themselves (and their families) entirely to the trapping and processing of furs, further disrupting the traditional subsistence cycle.

At the same time, attempts by the natives to control the trade, and protect their favored position as middlemen, led to an increase in inter-tribal warfare. By 1600, the Micmac had ousted the Iroquois from the Gaspé Peninsula in order to control the regional trade. Easter Abenaki groups joined into a confederacy to protect their position in the interior as well (Brasser 1978:85).

Rivalry for access to trading centers, along with competition for rich trapping areas led to the development of more rigidly defined tribal boundaries, and to individually owned hunting territories as well. Inheritance of these territories, associated with male activities, emphasized still further the patrilineal tendencies of northern hunting societies, while putting pressure on traditional relationships of reciprocity, sharing, and communal access to tribal lands (Leacock 1954). Additionally, the importance of particular individuals in the fur trade sometimes led to the increased influence of some lineages over others, in contrast to the marked egalitarianism of traditional social relations.

On the other hand there is little evidence to suggest, as Calvin Martin has done, that the excesses of the fur trade were entirely disruptive to native life, or that natives began to wage "war" on animals in revenge against the their spirit protectors for lack of protection from European diseases (Martin 1978). Many peoples involved in the fur trade emerged from the devastation of the seventeenth century with their religious beliefs intact, and with a continued although attenuated dependence on traditional subsistence sources (Trigger 1985:242–251; Krech 1981).

As Bruce Trigger has argued, more devastating to the natives of the Northeast than the depletion of the beaver population or threat to native worldview, were the terrible epidemic diseases of the seventeenth century, which had permanent and far-reaching effects on economic and political organization (1985:242–251). Snow and Lanphear estimate that between 1616 and 1639, native populations in the Northeast were reduced as much as 86%, and in some areas, as much as 95% (1988:28). Subsequent epidemics introduced by European settlers reduced the native population still more (Crosby 1986). Traditional methods of organizing society, based on kinship relationships, and the dominance of certain lineages, were necessarily disrupted by the loss of personnel, particularly older people. It is this fact which leads ethnohistorians to question whether most of even the earliest of

European descriptions of natives of the Northeast reflect what were truly "precontact" cultures.

New Brunswick, northern Maine, and Nova Scotia were controlled by the French from the sixteenth to the mid-eighteenth century (McGee 1974:31–67). During that period, natives including the Micmac, Maliseet-Passamaquoddy, Eastern Abenaki, and Western Abenaki were primarily influenced by their contact with fur traders and Jesuit missionaries. Some converted to Catholicism, and adopted elements of European material culture. This began a period of great creativity in native dress, and in other crafts such as quill- and bead-work, birchbark etching, and basketry. Women adopted the peaked woolen cap and embroidered overdress often shown in later illustrations of the Micmac and Maliseet, and men wore a variety of clothing styles, both native and European. All wore ornaments made from glass beads and silver. [See Figure 4.4 Denny Sockabasin.]

More significantly, the natives came into contact, however superficial, with European ideas about the supernatural, and with the European tradition of literacy. Religious works were translated into most languages, and the missionary Chretien Le Clercq invented a system of "hieroglyphs" to be used by the natives as mnemonic devices for memorizing prayers. Although these early symbols have gone out of use, the Micmac secretly developed their own phonemic writing system in the eighteenth and early nineteenth centuries. This system, with some modifications, is still in use in some areas. (Bock 1978:109, note by Ives Goddard).

At the close of the French period in 1760, many Indian groups in the northern regions began to experience land-pressure from white settlers. After several decades of depredations, the British government established a number of reserves in New Brunswick for the Micmac and Maliseet. These reserves provided the Indians with a marginal living, being largely trapped-out, but subsistence practices continued to focus on hunting, fishing, and collecting throughout the eighteenth and nineteenth centuries. Leadership remained in the hands of the sagamores, chosen by consensus or inheriting their position through the male line. Election of Maliseet-Passamaquoddy tribal chiefs began in the late nineteenth century (Erickson 1978:131).

Further south, the Eastern Abenaki shared many experiences with their northern hunting neighbors. Maintaining for a time a pivotal position in the fur trade, the Eastern Abenaki were ultimately defeated by raiding Tarrentines (Micmac) in 1615. European-introduced diseases caused sever population loss in the early years of the seventeenth century, and further loss of life resulted from wars and skirmishes between the French and English in their territories throughout the seventeenth and early eighteenth centuries.

The Eastern Abenaki maintained a limited trade in furs with the English of Plymouth and Massachusetts Bay colonies throughout the seventeenth century. In exchange for pelts, the Abenaki desired wampum, metal tools, and corn. Settlement pattern and social organization remained traditional, with an increase in horticultural activities. The Abenaki successfully ousted encroaching English coastal settlers during King Philip's war of 1676, but were later forced further inland (Snow 1978:143; Speck 1940).

Figure 4.4 Denny Sockabasin. (Courtesy of Smithsonian Institution.)

Their central position between the French and English allowed the Eastern Abenaki to exercise diplomatic influence on both. Officials from all three groups met in councils which followed traditional etiquette, and involved the use of elaborate oratory (ibid:143). Hostilities between the rival European powers ultimately affected Abenaki hegemony in the region, however, culminating in the abandonment and sacking of the fortified village at Norridgewock in 1724 (Prins and Bourque 1987). Although many of the Eastern Abenaki moved north to Canada, part of their nation, known as the Penobscot, maintained their diplomatic power and independence throughout the early eighteenth century, when they became spokesmen for all the Algonquian-speaking "Wabanaki" of New England (Snow 1978:144).

After the Revolution, in which the Penobscot sided with the Americans, their lands were restricted by treaty to two coastal islands, and the lands running north from their main village at Old Town (near Orono, Maine). Later treaties further limited the Penobscot to four townships, which were sold to the state of Maine in 1833. These townships were still ruled by sagamores chosen from the forest animal moiety, but a split occured along moiety lines in 1838 (ibid:145). After 1866, leaders from alternating moieties were elected annually.

While all Algonquian-speaking peoples discussed thus far remained for the most part in their original homeland, the Western Abenaki of the Saco, Merrimack, and Connecticut river valleys responded to the pressures of contact by abandoning much of their traditional territory. In the early seventeenth century, Western Abenaki were encountered by French missionaries who called them Loup (Day 1975). As early as 1636, Abenaki living in the Connecticut river valley entered into trade relations with English entrepreneur William Pynchon at Agawam, now Springfield Massachusetts. In succeeding decades, English settlement expanded northward towards principle Abenaki settlements at Pocumtuck (Deerfield) and Squakheag (Northfield). Until 1650, relations were amicable, with Indians trading maize and pelts for European manufactured goods such as tools, metal pots, wampum, and cloth.

At the same time, Mohawks raiding east were threatening Abenaki settlements, leading to the abandonment of the main Squakheag village at Fort Hill in 1664 and the destruction of Pocumtuck in 1665 (Thomas 1985:145). Fluctuations in the fur trade, and the frequent destruction of crops due to warfare led the Abenaki to trade land in an attempt to maintain their favored position with English traders or to pay off debts incurred with them (ibid. 149). Excavations at Fort Hill indicated that traditional native subsistence patterns were maintained, but that the community was experiencing stress, and depending more heavily than formerly on small game and seed corn (ibid).

In 1651, the missionary Gabriel Druillettes persuaded the Western Abenaki to join with the Mahicans and possibly the Algonquin in resisting the Iroquois (Day 1978a:150). In the early 1660's, however, Iroquois depredations and increasing land pressure led to the abandonment of their southern range by the Western Abenaki, some of whom moved northward to the St. Lawrence River, others west to the Hudson river settlement of Schaghticoke. After King Philip's War in 1676, some Abenaki moved to the Montreal and

Trois Rivieres region, and others to Missisquoi. Some intermarried with Algonquin and Nipissing women, and others became mercenaries for the French.

By the mid-eighteenth century, Western Abenakis living at Schaghticoke and Missisquoi withdrew northwards, and after the Revolution, settled permanently at St. Francis at Odanak, and Becancour on the St. Lawrence. There and in lands to the north, they continued to hunt, trap and fish (Day 1978a:152; 1984).

History of the Coastal Algonquians from 1524

Peoples of the Atlantic coastal regions from the Saco River to the Pamlico Sound were among the natives of the Northeast most heavily impacted by contact. In addition to the effects of disease, and of the fur trade, which reached deep into their country, these natives experienced enormous, and ultimately irresistible land pressure from increasing English colonization.

The first recorded contacts between the coastal natives and Europeans occured in 1524 in southern New England, and 1560 in North Carolina and Virginia. Verrazano, the first explorer known to have dropped anchor in Cape Cod harbour, found summer coastal villages surrounded by cornfields, and natives already familiar with European goods (Wroth 1970). When Gosnold arrived in 1602, he found some natives speaking English. These fragmentary pieces of evidence, plus that from sixteenth century maps of the New World, indicates that sporadic contact between Europeans and the coastal natives was occuring throughout the sixteenth century. Natives learned of Europe through such direct contact, and indirectly through goods flowing down traditional coastal and inland trade routes running ultimately to the Gulf of St. Lawrence (Bourque and Whitehead 1985).

At the time of contact European technology, with the exception of guns and seafaring equipment, was little superior to that of the Indians. Further, the Indians were much more highly skilled at hunting, trapping, fishing, and woodworking. As residents of the coastal regions for many centuries, they were well-adapted to local conditions, and knowledgeable about local resources. Their garden plots, although not large, often produced a surplus, and were adequate to support their relatively dense populations. Their skills and agricultural produce kept many European settlements from starvation in the first several decades of colonization. (Jennings 1975).

Native strength, skill, and knowledge of the local environment were often outweighed however, by their vulnerability to infectious diseases introduced by traders and settlers. In the years between 1616 and 1619, it is estimated that the coastal people of southern Massachusetts Bay lost up to 95% of their population (Snow and Lanphear 1988). Figures were equally high in other parts of the mid-Atlantic region as well.

In the decades following the establishment of the English colonies along the Atlantic seaboard, natives pursued a limited number of options for survival. Many, particularly in southeastern Massachusetts, became converted to Christianity, through the efforts of Protestant missionaries such as John Eliot of Roxbury, and Thomas Mayhew of Martha's Vineyard. Eliot was particularly concerned that the natives fully comprehend the Christian

117

scriptural message, and developed a practical orthography for Massachusett, the language spoken in southeastern Massachusetts, Cape Cod and the islands of Martha's Vineyard and Nantucket (Goddard and Bragdon 1988). Through his efforts and the remarkable energies of the Indians themselves, approximately 30% of the Massachusett people were literate in their own language by 1698. The Christian natives of Massachusetts Bay were settled into permanent communities called "Praying Towns" or plantations, where they governed themselves in a manner which combined new and traditional methods. Some of these communities, most notably Gay Head on Martha's Vineyard, and Mashpee, on upper Cape Cod, are still largely native communities today (Bragdon n.d.).

Natives of Rhode Island and Connecticut, although not unscathed, survived the early sixteenth century epidemics with fewer casualties than did the Massachusett (Robinson, et al. 1985; Kelly, et al. 1987). The Narragansett also retained some autonomy throughout the seventeenth century by virtue of their control over wampum manufacture. However they, and unconverted Abenakis and Pokanokets, who were later called Wampanoag, were ultimately defeated by the English in King Philip's War of 1676. In the eighteenth century, the Narragansett were confined to a reservation in Charlestown, Rhode Island, where their descendants remain today (Simmons 1978).

In Connecticut, the most powerful of the coastal groups were the Pequot, who were closely allied to the Narragansett, and who controlled access to the Connecticut river, and the early upriver fur trade with the interior. They were defeated by English forces in the earliest of the seventeenth century Indian wars, and dispersed to related groups in 1637. Other Connecticut natives including the Mohegan remained in traditional lands along the Thames River until 1765, when the Christian Mohegan leader Samson Occom persuaded the majority to remove the Brothertown, New York (Belknap and Morse 1955). There they settled along with some Montauks, Shinnecocks, and Oneidas (Conkey, Boissevain, and Goddard 1978:182,184). These people, along with members of the refugee communities at New Stockbridge, New York, eventually migrated to Wisconsin. Groups remaining in Connecticut included some Mohegan, Pequot, Western Niantic, Quiripi and others, who lived in a migratory fashion, or settled in mixed communities such as at Schaghticoke, Connecticut, or in reservations established in the 18th century at Turkey Hill, Coram Hill, and Golden Hill (ibid. 183–184).

English explorers visited the southern coast, but the most significant early contacts there were with Spanish adventurers and missionaries. French and Spanish exploratory voyages dating to the early decades of the sixteenth century surely reached as far as Virginia (Quinn 1977:189–191), and in 1576, a short-lived mission station was established in Powhatan country on the banks of the York river (Lewis and Loomie 1953). The abortive English colony at Roanoke Island, now North Carolina, established in 1585, was soon succeeded by a permanent settlement at Jamestown, Virginia, established in 1607. From the early decades of the seventeenth century, this region was increasingly settled by the English.

European contacts with the Delaware and Nanticoke of the mid-Atlantic region were early but poorly recorded. Verrazano's descriptions of natives at New York harbour in

1524 indicate native familiarity with Europeans by that date (Goddard 1978b:220). Henry Hudson's hostile encounter with the Staten Island natives in 1609 was a foretaste of future Indian-Dutch relations in New York. His explorations were succeeded by colonization efforts by the Dutch in New Netherlands, and the English in New Jersey, Pennsylvania, Maryland, and Delaware. As the coastal regions enjoyed mild climatic conditions, good soil, and accessible ports and waterways, they were of primary interest to colonizers, who in general were unsympathetic to Indian claims to the same land.

The Delaware and Nanticoke retained their independence while fur-bearing animals remained within their lands, but their depletion, and increasing pressure for settlers led to a series of conflicts after the mid-sixteenth century. Delawares and Long Island natives withdrew westwards, consolidating themselves into communities, where a relatively traditional seasonal round was conducted. Ultimately, however, through the combined efforts of the government of Pennsylvania, and the Six Nations, many Delawares were displaced still further west to the Susquehanna and Ohio Vallies, and ultimately to Ontario (Zeisberger 1885). Other Delaware, settled for a time on the White River in Indiana, moved to Missouri and to Kansas. A further move brought some of the Kansas Delaware to south-central Oklahoma. Most of the remaining Kansas Delaware settled in northeastern Oklahoma after 1867, forming both progressive and traditional communities (ibid:224).

The experience of the Indians in Maryland and Virginia differed as a result of their contrasting relations with the respective colonial governments (Fausz 1985). Hostility between the Powhatan and Jamestown settlers increased throughout the early part of the sixteenth century. In 1622, the Powhatan rose against the English, killing nearly half of them. Relations worsened after the war, leading to another native uprising in 1644. The death of powerful Powhatan leaders, and the enormous increase in English population after 1640 forced the Powhatan to withdraw west and north. The surviving natives were eventually settled on reservations on the Pamunkey and Mattaponi rivers, while others, most notably the Chickahominy, lived nearby on unreserved land. In the eighteenth and nineteenth centuries, these isolated communities, like those of North Carolina, lived a relatively traditional way of life, supplementing their crops with game and fish (Mooney 1890).

Hostilities between the Jamestown settlers and the Powhatan diverted the fur trade north to Maryland, where English authorities developed peaceful trading ties with local natives. These relations continued into the eighteenth century, when most Nanticoke were settled on reservations established by treaty. Pressure on these lands by English settlers led to the ultimate establishment of reserves in isolated areas of northern Maryland and the Eastern Shore (Feest 1978a:243). In 1743 a large body of Nanticoke moved north to Pennsylvania, and were "adopted" by the Cayuga of the Six Nations in 1753. Other Nanticoke travelled west with the Delawares (ibid. 246).

Iroquois History from 1534

Iroquois-French interaction began inauspiciously in 1534 with the capture of two of the sons of chief Donnacona, a St. Lawrence Iroquoian then fishing at the Baie de Gaspé

(Trigger 1978c; 1985c:130). In subsequent years returning French expeditions penetrated the St. Lawrence, and French settlements were established near Quebec in 1541 and later at Tadoussac. For many years, the St. Lawrence Iroquoians were successful in preventing significant settlement along the river, but changing intertribal relations resulting from fur trade competition led ultimately to their destruction or disappearance (ibid.:346). Warfare increased throughout the sixteenth century, as the Iroquois to the south of the St. Lawrence attempted to break the hold of the Montagnais and their allies the Algonquins over the trade centered at Tadoussac.

The desire for European goods, which were clearly valued for reasons other than technological (Hammell 1987), increased among Iroquois peoples living to the west and south of the St. Lawrence. Some scholars have seen the unification of the Huron and their alliance with the Algonquin, and perhaps the development of the League of the Iroquois itself, as part of the concerted efforts of these inlanders to acquire trade goods.

The Huron alliance retained control of the trade until 1642. During this period, the French sent traders and missionaries into the interior, and the rich descriptions of Huron life contained in the Jesuit Relations date from this time. The Relations tell of changes in Huron society as the desire for trade goods continued, and as other groups, particularly the Mohawk, skirmished over their borders and disrupted established trade routes. Warfare among all Iroquois peoples increased in subsequent decades, which, with the additional effects of epidemic disease, reduced Iroquoian populations including that of the Huron, by as much as one half (Trigger 1985:234).

Although scholars debate the exact date of the League's origin, it is certain that by the mid sixteenth-century it was playing a decisive role in regional politics as the League chiefs sought their mutual advantage in the fur trade, while pitting the English against the French, and both against native rivals. Mohawk raids against the Huron increased in intensity after 1642, and by 1649, the Huron region had been overrun, and its people captured, dispersed, or killed. For the next century and a half, the League played a decisive role in Anglo-French relations.

The American Revolution brought dissention to the League, whose members could reach no unanimous decision in choosing allies. After efforts to maintain neutrality failed, most sided with the British against the Americans, and withdrew from their homelands northwards. At the close of the war, the Iroquois found their position with respect to the new American government precarious, and some groups removed permanently to Canada. The remaining Iroquois settled in small communities and later reserves in various parts of upper New York State (Tanner 1987; Wallace 1978:443).

While the Six Nations continued to exercise influence during the early nineteenth century, particularly during the war of 1812, they gradually became isolated as western expansion continued. Dissolution and decline were halted, however, by the assistance given them by the Society of Friends (Tanner 1987:100–101), and more importantly, by the remarkable influence of the Seneca Prophet Handsome Lake (Wallace 1969;1978). In 1799 Handsome Lake began preaching a message of revival and hope to the Iroquois, based on a series of visions he had experienced that same year. In these visions, Handsome Lake was instructed concerning new rituals, and given a series of commandments which he passed on to his followers. His teaching, most of which advocated socially beneficial behavior, and reverence for traditional ways (Wallace 1978), were codified after his death, primarily by his grandson, Jimmy Johnson, and were finally recorded in 1845 by Ely S. Parker (Tooker 1978:452). These codes are now the basis for the Iroquois Longhouse Religion, and the source of much of the conservatism and vitality of modern Iroquois culture (ibid. 454).

Great Lakes-Riverine History Since 1640

The history of the natives of the southern and western portions of the Great Lakes regions was closely tied to the fur trade, as well as to the western expansion of white settlement in the eighteenth and nineteenth centuries. Groups such as the Sauk, Fox, Kickapoo, Illinois and others experienced pressure from this expansion both directly in terms of competition with white settlers for land in the newly opened Northwest Territory, and indirectly in the form of encounters with other native groups who were being displaced westward.

After the destruction of Huronia in 1642, the fur trade shifted west, bringing peoples such as the Ojibwa and Nipissing into increasing conflict with Fox and Dakota. In the meantime, refugee groups from southern New England began to arrive in the Great Lakes region causing further disruption (Tanner 1987:29). The Iroquois continued to wage war to the west and north until 1680, when the French began to establish forts on the Illinois River, in order to protect their native allies there (Tanner 1987:31). In 1701, peace between the Iroquois and the French (with their native allies) was concluded at Montreal and thereafter, the Five Nations adopted a position of relative neutrality between the French and the English based at Albany (Tanner 1987:34).

Native occupation of the Great Lakes-Riverine region varied throughout the eighteenth and early nineteenth centuries, as a result of continued French- and British rivalry, and the effects of the American Revolution. Conflict between the Mesquakie (Fox) and their allies, and the French-supported Indian nations such as the Illinois, continued until 1740, when the surviving Sauk and Fox resettled on the Mississippi and Wisconsin rivers (Tanner 1987:42). Western moving Ojibwa came into contact with the Minnesota Dakota in the 1730's, resulting in hostilities between the two groups that lasted into the nineteenth century. The French dominance over the fur trade continued until circa 1761, when the British defeated French forces at Montreal, and occupied most French forts in the Great Lakes region.

Conflicts did not end with the establishment of British forces in the area of former French control, however. Native protests against European presence and interference led to uprisings such as that of the Ottawa chief Pontiac, in 1763. Although the treaty of Fort Stanwix, concluded in 1768, established the line of westward white settlement at the Ohio River, the natives of the Great Lakes region soon found themselves threatened by a new menace, the newly formed United States of America.

Land pressure from the Americans, following the opening of the Northwest Territory, became increasingly burdensome. Native military chiefs, such as the Miami leader Little

Turtle (Carter 1987), led several successful attacks against American forces, but united native resistance failed to stop the new nation's encroachments. In 1795, with the treaty of Greenville, two-thirds native-held Ohio territory was ceded to the United States.

By the beginning of the nineteenth century, indigenous people of many cultures, including Iroquois, Delaware, Ojibwa, Ottawa, Iowa, and Potawatomi were resident in the Great Lakes region. Some, especially the Potawatomi and Ojibwa, expanded their territories into depopulated areas. Others, like the Sauk and Fox, moved west and north, adopting an increasingly Prairie-oriented lifeway. Beginning in 1784, a number of reserves were established for these people in the United States and Canada. The natives resident in southern Michigan, northern Indiana and western Ohio were evacuated between 1837 and 1840, and were later moved west of the Mississippi. Isolated pockets of people remained, including the Winnebago in western Wisconsin, the Potawatomi in Michigan, and the Ojibwa, Ottawa and Menominee in Michigan, Wisconsin and Minnesota. Ultimately, their lands were designated reserves and were protected by treaty (Tanner 1987:166–168).

Since the early nineteenth century, natives of the Great Lakes region have developed a distinctive adaptation loosely termed "Upper Great Lakes Indian Culture" (Quimby 1960:147–157). All groups share an emphasis on hunting and collecting, and a distinctive style of clothing, ornamentation, and material culture. Although some groups, most notably the Ojibwa, took up farming by 1830 (Rogers 1978:764), most of the natives of the Great Lakes region continued to practice a relatively traditional seasonal round until the late nineteenth century, when the fur trade ceased to provide an adequate living. Native religion remained strong, revitalized by nativistic elements such as the Medicine Dances of the Midewiwin in the late eighteenth century (Hickerson 1970; Vastokas 1984). Leadership continued to be by chiefs selected from appropriate lineages, and most decisions were made in councils (Rogers 1978:763–765), or by elected officials acting as a council (Gearing 1970:91).

The Northeast Culture Area Today

While some groups within the Northeast culture area have been well studied by ethnographers, public interest in the native peoples of the Northeast declined throughout the nineteenth centuries as settlement moved increasingly westwards and remaining groups struggled to subsist on marginal reservations. Many non-Indians were unaware of native presence in their area. Native people who managed to remain in place were discouraged by insensitive governmental policies, which often robbed them of control over their own affairs (Gearing 1970:104–105).

Nationwide concern for the American Indian was rekindled during the late 1960's and 1970's, as non-Indians rediscovered the traditions many natives had kept alive within their communities. Natives in many areas took advantage of this new awareness to draw national attention to the hardships of their economic conditions. At the same time, Indians living in what had been marginal or inaccessible areas suddenly found their lands threatened by developers and vacationers.

Two related themes of modern Northeastern native life have been an increased public expression of Indianness, in the form of heightened ceremonialism, and the development of a number of programs designed to conserve and promote native cultural practices, including native language programs, literacy programs, and craft cooperatives. These have been accompanied by strenuous efforts through legal channels to secure better living conditions for Indian people. Most of the latter have taken the form of land claims and tribal recognition petitions, made both to state and federal agencies. Although some claims have been successfully concluded, a number are still pending, and governmental policies concerning the claims of Northeastern groups, many of whom do not have reservation status, are still unformulated (Campisi 1984).

A number of reservation communities have also developed successful industries and tourist attractions, the income from which is devoted to raising the community standard of living, and improving schools, housing, and medical care for reservation residents. While there are numerous administrative and/or legal problems with these endeavors, they represent an important move toward self-determination for many Indian people (Porter 1987).

The artistic traditions of the native Northeast are undergoing a revival as well. Public appreciation for native crafts and improved channels for its sale have resulted in the strengthening of a number of traditional skills, including basket- and bag making, canoe and snowshoe manufacture, quill and bead work, leather working, birchbark etching, and carving (Coe 1986).

While many natives of the Northeast find employment in white- and blue-collar jobs, and live off their reservation or away from their Indian communities for some or all of the year, they remain distinctively Indian. In spite of difficult economic conditions and governmental interference, a surprisingly large number of native groups in the Northeast retain large portions of their mythology, knowledge of native language, familiarity with traditional subsistence methods, and adherence to indigenous patterns of thought and action. The native tradition, a force in the Northeast for the past eight thousand years, although altered in form, continues to be a strong one.

SUGGESTED READINGS

The following readings are only a limited selection from the vast literature on the Northeast culture area. Emphasis has been placed on general works, recent theoretical contributions, and primary sources.

Brumble, H. David III
1981   An Annotated Bibliography of American Indian and Eskimo Autobiographies. Lincoln, University of Nebraska Press.

Coe, Ralph T.
1986   Lost and Found Traditions: Native American Art 1965–1985. American Federation of Art.

Hakluyt, Richard
1965   The Principall Navigations, Voiages and Discoveries of the English Nation.[1589]. David B. Quinn and Raleigh A. Skelton, eds. 2 vols. Cambridge, England: University Press.

Fitzhugh, William W., ed
  1985   Cultures in Contact: The European Impact on Native Cultural Institutions in Eastern North America A.D. 1000–1800. Washington D.C. Smithsonian Institution Press.

Foster, Michael K., Jack Campisi, and Marianne Mithun, eds.
  1984   *Extending the Rafters: Interdisciplinary Approaches to Iroquoian Studies.* Albany: State University of New York Press.

Purchas, Samuel
  1625   Hakluytus Posthumus or Purchas, His Pilgrimes. 4 Volumes. Longon: Printed by W. Stansby for Henry Fetherstone. (Reprinted : J. MacLehose and Sons, Glasgow, 1905–1907).

Quinn, David
  1977   North America from Earliest Discovery to First Settlements: The Norse Voyages to 1612. New York: Harper and Row.

Smith, John
  1986   The Complete Works of John Smith. Philip Barbour ed. Chapel Hill: University of North Carolina Press for the Institute of Early American History and Culture.

Tanner, Helen Hornbeck, ed.
  1987   Atlas of Great Lakes Indian History. Norman: University of Oklahoma Press.

Thwaites, Reuben G. ed.
  1896–   The Jesuit Relations and Allied Documents: Travel and Explorations of the Jesuit Missionaries in
  1901   New France, 1610–1791; the Original French, Latin, and Italian Texts, with English Translations and Notes. 73 Vols. Cleveland: Burrows Brothers. (Reprinted: Pageant, New York, 1959).

Tooker, Elisabeth
  1979   Native North American Spirituality of the Eastern Woodlands. New York: Paulist Press.

Trigger, Bruce C.
  1978   *Handbook of North American Indians.* William Sturtevant Gen. Ed. Volume 15. *The Northeast.* Washington D.C. Government Printing Office. pp. 344–356.

Williams, Roger
  1936   A Key into the Language of America [1643]. 5th ed. Providence: The Rhode Island and Providence Plantations Tercentenary Commission.

REFERENCES

Alexander, Edward P.
  1971   An Indian Vocabulary from Fort Christanna, 1716. *Virginia Magazine of History and Biography* 79:3:303–313.

Axtell, James
  1985   The Invasion Within:The Contest of Cultures in Colonial North American. New York: Oxford University Press.

Barlow, Arthur
  1981   The First Voyage made to the coasts of America, with two barks. . .in David, Richard ed. *Hakluyt's*
  [1584] *Voyages.* Boston: Houghton Mifflin. pp. 445–453.

Bauxer, J. Joseph
  1978   History of the Illinois Area. in Trigger, Bruce Ed. *Handbook of North American Indians.* William Sturtevant Gen. Ed. Volume 15. *The Northeast.* Washington D.C. Government Printing Office. pp. 594–601.

Belknap, Jeremy, and Jedidiah Morse
  1955   Report on the Oneida, Stockbridge and Brotherton Indians [1796]. *Museum of the American Indian, Heye Foundation. Indian Notes and Monographs.* 54:5–39.

Bennett, M. K.
  1955   The Food Economy of the New England Indians 1605–75. *The Journal of Political Economy.* 63:360–396.

Bock, Phillip
  1978   Micmac. In Trigger, Bruce Ed. *Handbook of North American Indians.* William Sturtevant Gen. Ed. Volume 15. *The Northeast.* Washington D.C. Government Printing Office. pp. 109–122.

Borque, Bruce J.
  1973   Aboriginal settlement and subsistence on the Maine coast. *Man in the Northeast* 6:3–20.

Bourque, Bruce J., and Ruth H. Whitehead
  1985   Tarrantines and the Introduction of European Trade Goods in the Gulf of Maine. *Ethnohistory.* 32:327–41.

Boyce, Douglas W.
  1978   Iroquoian Tribes of the Virginia-North Carolina Coastal Plain. In Trigger, Bruce, Ed. Handbook of North American Indians. William Sturtevant, Gen. Ed., Vol. 15. The Northeast. Washington, D.C.: Government Printing Office. pp. 282–289.

Bradley, Jim
  1987   Native Exchange and European Trade: Cross-Cultural Dynamics in the Sixteenth Century. *Man in the Northeast.* 33:31–46.

Bragdon, Kathleen J.
  1981   Another Tongue Brought In: An Ethnohistorical Study of Native Writings in Massachusett. Ph.D. Thesis. Brown University.
  1988   The Material Culture of the Christian Indians of Massachusetts. In Beaudry, Mary ed. *Documentary Archaeology.* Boston:Cambridge University Press.
  n. d.   Literacy, Christianity, and Cultural Distinctiveness among the Massachusett. Papers of the 1983 Wilfrid Laurier Conference on Ethnohistory. In Preparation.

Brasser, T. J.
  1978a   Early Indian-European Contacts. in Trigger, Bruce Ed. *Handbook of North American Indians.* Williams Sturtevant Gen. Ed. Volume 15. *The Northeast.* Washington D.C. Government Printing Office. pp. 78–88.
  1978b   Mahican. in Trigger, Bruce Ed. *Handbook of North American Indians.* William Sturtevant Gen. Ed. Volume 15. *The Northeast.* Washington D.C. Government Printing Office. pp. 198–212.

Burton, William and Richard Lowenthal
  1974   The First of the Mohegans. *American Ethnologist* 1:589–599.

Callender, Charles
  1978a   Great Lakes-Riverine Sociopolitical Organization. in Trigger, Bruce Ed. *Handbook of North American Indians.* William Sturtevant Gen. Ed. Volume 15. *The Northeast.* Washington D.C. Government Printing Office. pp. 610–621.
  1978b   Shawnee. in Trigger, Bruce Ed. *Handbook of North American Indians.* William Sturtevant Gen. Ed. Volume 15. *The Northeast.* Washington D.C. Government Printing Office. pp. 622–635.
  1978c   Fox. in Trigger, Bruce Ed. *Handbook of North American Indians.* William Sturtevant Gen. Ed. Volume 15. *The Northeast.* Washington D.C. Government Printing Office. pp. 636–647.
  1978d   Sauk. in Trigger, Bruce Ed. *Handbook of North American Indians.* William Sturtevant Gen. Ed. Volume 15. *The Northeast.* Washington D.C. Government Printing Office. pp. 648–655.
  1978e   Illinois. in Trigger, Bruce Ed. *Handbook of North American Indians.* William Sturtevant Gen. Ed. Volume 15. *The Northeast.* Washington D.C. Government Printing Office. pp. 673–680.

Callender, Charles, Richard K. Pope and Susan M. Pope
  1978   Kickapoo. in Trigger, Bruce Ed. *Handbook of North American Indians.* William Sturtevant Gen. Ed. Volume 15. *The Northeast.* Washington D.C. Government Printing Office. pp. 656–667.

Campisi, Jack
 1984   National Policy, States' Rights, and Indian Sovereignty: The Case of the New York Iroquois. in Foster, Michael K., Jack Campisi, and Marianne Mithun eds. *Extending the Rafters: Interdisciplinary Approaches to Iroquoian Studies.* Albany: State University of New York Press. pp. 95–108.

Carter, Harvey
 1987   The Life and Times of Little Turtle, First Sagamore of the Wabash. Urbana and Chicago: The University of Illinois Press.

Ceci, Lynn
 1982   Method and Theory in Coastal New York Archaeology: Paradigms of Settlement Pattern. *North American Archaeologist.* 3:5–36.

Champlain, Samuel de
 1907   Voyages of Samuel de Champlain, 1604–1618. (Original Narratives of Early American History.) W. L. Grant, ed. New York: C. Scribner's Sons.

Clifton, James
 1978   Potawatomi. in Trigger, Bruce Ed. *Handbook of North American Indians.* William Sturtevant Gen. Ed. Volume 15. *The Northeast.* Washington D.C. Government Printing Office. pp. 725–742.

Coe, Ralph T.
 1986   Lost and Found Traditions: Native American Art 1965–1985. American Federation of Art.

Conkey, Laura, Ethel Boissevain, and Ives Goddard
 1978   Indians of Southern New England and Long Island: Late Period. in Trigger, Bruce Ed. *Handbook of North American Indians.* William Sturtevant Gen. Ed. Volume 15. *The Northeast.* Washington D.C. Government Printing Office. pp. 177–189.

Cook, S. F.
 1970   The Indian Population of New England in the Seventeenth Century. Berkeley: University of California Press.

Cronon, William
 1983   Changes in the Land: Indians, Colonists, and the Ecology of New England. New York: Hill and Wang.

Crosby, A. W.
 1986   Ecological Imperialism:The Biological Expansion of Europe, 900–1900. New York: Cambridge University Press.

Day, Gordon M.
 1975   The *Mots Loup* of Father Mathevet. *National Museum of Man, Publications in Ethnology 8.* Ottawa.
 1978a   Western Abenaki. in Trigger, Bruce Ed. *Handbook of North American Indians.* William Sturtevant Gen. Ed. Volume 15. *The Northeast.* Washington D.C. Government Printing Office. pp. 148–159.
 1978b   Nipissing. in Trigger, Bruce Ed. *Handbook of North American Indians.* William Sturtevant Gen. Ed. Volume 15. *The Northeast.* Washington D.C. Government Printing Office. pp. 787–791.
 1984   The Ouragie War: A Case History in Iroquois-New England Indian Relations. in Foster, Michael K., Jack Campisi, and Marianne Mithun eds. *Extending the Rafters: Interdisciplinary Approaches to Iroquoian Studies.* Albany: State University of New York Press. pp. 35–50.

Day, Gordon M. and Bruce G. Trigger
 1978   Algonquin. in Trigger, Bruce Ed. *Handbook of North American Indians.* William Sturtevant Gen. Ed. Volume 15. *The Northeast.* Washington D.C. Government Printing Office. pp. 792–797.

Dobyns, H. F.
 1983   Their Number Become Thinned: Native American Population Dynamics in Eastern North America. Knoxville: University of Tennessee Press.

Englebrecht, William
   1985   New York Iroquois Political Development. in Fitzhugh, William, Ed. Cultures in Contact: The Impact of European Contacts on Native American Cultural Institutions A.D. 1000–1800. Smithsonian Institution Press. pp. 163–186.

Erikson, Vincent O.
   1978   Maliseet-Passamaquoddy. in Trigger, Bruce Ed. *Handbook of North American Indians.* William Sturtevant Gen. Ed. Volume 15. *The Northeast.* Washington D.C. Government Printing Office. pp. 123–136.

Fausz, Frederick J.
   1985   Patterns of Anglo-Indian Aggression and Accommodation along the Mid-Atlantic Coast, 1584–1634. in Fitzhugh, William W. ed. *Cultures in Contact: The European Impact on Native Cultural Institutions in Eastern North America* A.D 1000–1800. Washington D.C.Smithsonian Institution Press. pp. 225–270.

Feest, Christian F.
   1978a   Nanticoke and Neighboring Tribes. in Trigger, Bruce Ed. *Handbook of North American Indians.* William Sturtevant Gen. Ed. Volume 15. *The Northeast.* Washington D.C. Government Printing Office. pp. 240–252.
   1978b   Virginia Algonquians. in Trigger, Bruce Ed. *Handbook of North American Indians.* William Sturtevant Gen. Ed. Volume 15. *The Northeast.* Washington D.C. Government Printing Office. pp. 253–270.
   1978c   North Carolina Algonquians. in Trigger, Bruce Ed. *Handbook of North American Indians.* William Sturtevant Gen. Ed. Volume 15. *The Northeast.* Washington D.C. Government Printing Office. pp. 271–281.

Feest, Christian F. and Johanna E. Feest
   1978   Ottawa. in Trigger, Bruce Ed. *Handbook of North American Indians.* William Sturtevant Gen. Ed. Volume 15. *The Northeast.* Washington D.C. Government Printing Office. pp. 772–786.

Fenton, William N.
   1978   Northern Iroquoian Culture Patterns. in Trigger, Bruce Ed. *Handbook of North American Indians.* William Sturtevant Gen. Ed. Volume 15. *The Northeast.* Washington D.C. Government Printing Office. pp. 296–321.

Fenton, William N. and Elisabeth Tooker
   1978   Mohawk. in Trigger, Bruce Ed. *Handbook of North American Indians.* William Sturtevant Gen. Ed. Volume 15. *The Northeast.* Washington D.C. Government Printing Office. pp. 466–480.

Flannery, Regina
   1939   An Analysis of Coastal Algonquian Culture. *Catholic University of American, Anthropological Series 7.* Washington.
   1946   The Culture of the Northeastern Indian Hunters: A Descriptive Survey. in Frederick Johnson, ed. *Papers of the Robert S. Peabody Foundation for Archaeology* 3. Andover, Massachusetts.

Fitzhugh, William W., ed.
   1985   Cultures in Contact: The European Impact on Native Cultural Institutions in Eastern North America A.D. 1000–1800. Washington D.C.Smithsonian Institution Press.

Foster, Michael
   1984   On Who Spoke First at Iroquois-White Councils: An Exercise in the Method of Upstreaming. in Foster, Michael K., Jack Campisi, and Marianne Mithun eds. *Extending the Rafters: Interdisciplinary Approaches to Iroquoian Studies.* Albany: State University of New York Press. pp. 183–208.

Garrad, Charles and Conrad E. Heidenreich
   1978   Khionontateronon (Petun). in Trigger, Bruce, Ed. Handbook of North American Indians. William Sturtevant, Gen. Ed. Vol. 15. The Northeast. Washington, D.C., Government Printing Office. pp. 394–397.

Gearing, Frederick O.
1970   The Face of the Fox. Chicago: Aldine Press.

Goddard, Ives
1965   The Eastern Algonquian Intrusive Nasal. *International Journal of American Linguistics.* 31:3:206–220.
1978a   Eastern Algonquian Languages. in Trigger, Bruce Ed. *Handbook of North American Indians.* William Sturtevant Gen. Ed. Volume 15. *The Northeast.* Washington D.C. Government Printing Office. pp. 70–77.
1978b   Delaware. in Trigger, Bruce Ed. *Handbook of North American Indians.* William Sturtevant Gen. Ed. Volume 15. *The Northeast.* Washington D.C. Government Printing Office. pp. 213–239.

Goddard, Ives and Kathleen J. Bragdon
1988   Native Writings in Massachusett. American Philosophical Society, Memoir Series. 185. In Press.

Gyles, John
1936   Memoirs of Odd Adventures, Strange Deliverances, etc., in the Captivity of John Gyles, Esq., Writ-
[1736] ten by Himself [1736]. Facsimile Reproduction. Photostat Americana. Second Series.

Hakluyt, Richard
1965   The Principall Navigations, Voiages and Discoveries of the English Nation.[1589]. David B. Quinn and Raleigh A. Skelton, eds. 2 vols. Cambridge, England: University Press.

Hallowell, A. Irving
1960   Ojibway Ontology, Behavior, and World View,'' in Stanley Diamond ed. *Culture in History: Essays in Honor of Paul Radin.* New York: Columbia University Press. pp. 19–52.

Hammell, George R.
1987   Mythical Realities and European Contact in the Northeast During the Sixteenth and Seventeenth Centuries. *Man in the Northeast.* 33:63–87.

Hariot, Thomas
1588   A Briefe and True Report of the New Found Land of Virginia. London. Reprinted in Quinn, David B. ed. The Roanoke Voyages, 1584–1590. Cambridge University Press for the Hakluyt Society.

Heidenreich, Conrad
1978   Huron. in Trigger, Bruce Ed. *Handbook of North American Indians.* William Sturtevant Gen. Ed. Volume 15. *The Northeast.* Washington D.C. Government Printing Office. pp. 368–387.

Henige, David
1986   Primary Source by Primary Source? On the Role of Epidemics in New World Depopulation. *Ethnohistory* 33:293–312.

Hickerson, Harold
1970   The Chippewa and Their Neighbors: A Study in Ethnohistory. New York: Holt, Rinehart and Winston.

Hutkrantz, Ake
1982   Religion and Experience of Native North American Hunting People. *Trönso Museum Shrifter.* 18:163–186.

Jennings, Francis
1975   The Invasion of America: Indians, Colonialism, and the Cant of Conquest. Chapel Hill: University of North Carolina Press.
1978   Susquehannock. in Trigger, Bruce Ed. *Handbook of North American Indians.* William Sturtevant Gen. Ed. Volume 15. *The Northeast.* Washington D.C. Government Printing Office. pp. 362–367.

Jennings, Francis, William Fenton, and Mary Druke eds.
1985   The History and Culture of Iroquois Diplomacy: An Interdisciplinary Guide to the Treaties of the Six Nations and their League. Syracuse: Syracuse University Press.

Kaplan, Susan
    1985   European Goods and Socio-Economic Change in Early Labrador Inuit Society. in Cultures in Contact: The European Impact on Native Cultural Institutions in Eastern North America A.D. 1000–1800. Washington D.C. Smithsonian Institution Press. pp. 45–70.

Keesing, Felix M.
    1939   The Menomimi Indians of Wisconsin. Philadelphia. American Philosophical Society.

Kelly, Marc A., Paul Sledzik, and Jean P. Murphy
    1987   Health, Demographics and Physical Constitution in Seventeenth-Century Rhode Island Indians. *Man in the Northeast.* 34:1–25.

King, J. C. H.
    1982   Thunderbird and Lightning: Indian Life in Northeastern North America 1600–1900. London: British Museum Publications.

Krech, Shepard III. ed.
    1981   Indians, Animals, and the Fur Trade: a Critique of Keepers of the Game. Athens: The University of Georgia Press.

Kroeber, Alfred.
    1939   Cultural and natural areas of native North America. *University of California Publications in American Archaeology and Ethnology* 38.

Leacock, Eleanor B.
    1954   The Montagnais "Hunting Territory" and the Fur Trade *Memoirs of the American Anthropological Association* 78. Menasha, Wisconsin.

Lescarbot, Marc
    1928   Nova Francia, a description of Acadia. New York: Harper and Row.
    [1606]

Lewis, C. M., and J. J. Loomie
    1953   The Spanish Jesuit Mission in Virginia, 1570–1572. Chapel Hill: Virginia Historical Society.

Lurie, Nancy O.
    1978   Winnebago. in Trigger, Bruce Ed. *Handbook of North American Indians.* William Sturtevant Gen. Ed. Volume 15. *The Northeast.* Washington D.C. Government Printing Office. pp. 690–707.

Martin, Calvin
    1978   Keepers of the Game: Indian-Animal Relationships and the Fur Trade. Berkeley: University of California Press.

McGee, Harold Franklin
    1974   Ethnic Boundaries and Strategies of Ethnic Interaction: A History of Micmac-White Relations in Nova Scotia. Ph.D. Thesis. Southern Illinois University.

McGhee, Robert
    1984   Contact Between Native North Americans and the Medieval Norse. *American Antiquity* 49:1:4–26.

Mooney, James
    1890   The Powhatan Confederacy, Past and Present. *American Anthropologist* n.s. 9;1:129–152.
    1928   The aboriginal population of America north of Mexico. *Smithsonian Miscellaneous Collections* 80(7):1–40.

Morgan, Lewis H.
    1851   League of the Ho-de-no-sau-nee or Iroquois. Rochester, N.Y.: Sage; New York: (Reprinted as League of the Iroquois. Corinth Books, New York: 1962.)
    1871   Systems of Consanguinity and Affinity of the Human Family. *Smithsonian Contributions to Knowledge* 17. Washington.

Nash, Ronald J. and Virginia P. Miller
    1987   Model Building and the Case of the Micmac Economy. *Man in the Northeast.* 33:41–56.

Porter, Frank III ed.
  1987   Strategies for Survival:American Indians in the Eastern United States. New York: Greenwood Press.

Prins, Harald and Bruce Bourque
  1987   Norridgewock: Village Translocation on the New-England-Acadian Frontier. *Man in the Northeast.* 33:137–158.

Purchas, Samuel
  1625   Hakluytus Posthumus or Purchas, His Pilgrimes. 4 Volumes. London: Printed by W. Stansby for Henry Fetherstone. (Reprinted : J. MacLehose and Sons, Glasglow, 1905–1907).

Quimby, George
  1960   Indian Life in the upper Great Lakes, 11,000 B.C. to A.D. 1800. Chicago: University of Chicago Press.

Quinn, David
  1977   North America from Earliest Discovery to First Settlements: The Norse Voyages to 1612. New York: Harper and Row.

Radin, Paul
  1923   The Winnebago Tribe. Annual Report of the Bureau of American Ethnology. 37.

Reynolds, Barrie
  1978   Beothuk. in Trigger, Bruce Ed. *Handbook of North American Indians.* William Sturtevant Gen. Ed. Volume 15. *The Northeast.* Washington D.C. Government Printing Office. pp. 101–108.

Ritzenthaler, Robert E.
  1978   Southwestern Chippewa. in Trigger, Bruce Ed. *Handbook of North American Indians.* William Sturtevant Gen. Ed. Volume 15. *The Northeast.* Washington D.C. Government Printing Office. pp. 743–759.

Robinson, Paul, Marc Kelley, and Patricia Rubertone
  1985   Preliminary Biocultural Interpretations from a Seventeenth Century Narragansett Indian Cemetery in Rhode Island in Fitzhugh, William ed. *Cultures in Contact: The European Impact on Native Cultural Institutions in Eastern North America* A.D. 1000–1800. Washington D.C.Smithsonian Institution Press. pp. 107–130.

Rogers, E. S.
  1978   Southeastern Ojibwa. in Trigger, Bruce Ed. *Handbook of North American Indians.* William Sturtevant Gen. Ed. Volume 15. *The Northeast.* Washington D.C. Government Printing Office. pp. 760–771.

Sagard-Theodat, Gabriel
  1939   Father Gabriel Sagard: The Long Island Journey to the Country of the Hurons [1632]. George M. Wrong, ed Toronto: The Champlain Society.

Salwen, Bert
  1978   Indians of Southern New England and Long Island: Early Period in Trigger, Bruce Ed. *Handbook of North American Indians.* William Sturtevant Gen. Ed. Volume 15. *The Northeast.* Washington D.C. Government Printing Office. pp. 160–176.

Simmons, William S.
  1970   Cautantowwit's House: An Indian Burial Ground on the Island of Conanicut in Narragansett Bay. Providence. R.I. Brown University Press.
  1976   Southern New England Shamanism: An Ethnographc Reconstruction. William Cowan ed. *Papers of the Seventh Algonquian Conference.* Ottawa. pp. 217–256.
  1978   Narragansett. in Trigger, Bruce Ed. *Handbook of North American Indians.* William Sturtevant Gen. Ed. Volume 15. *The Northeast.* Washington D.C. Government Printing Office. pp. 190–197.
  1979   Conversion from Indian to Puritan. *New England Quarterly.* 52:2:197–218.
  1986   The Spirit of the New England Tribes. University Press of New England.

Simmons, William S. and George F. Aubin
   1975   Narragansett Kinship. Man in the Northeast 9:21–31.

Smith, John
   1986   The Complete Works of John Smith. Phillip Barbour ed. Chapel Hill: University of North Carolina Press for the Institute of Early American History and Culture.

Snow, Dean R.
   1978   Eastern Abenaki. in Trigger, Bruce Ed. *Handbook of North American Indians.* William Sturtevant Gen. Ed. Volume 15. *The Northeast.* Washington D.C. Government Printing Office. pp. 137–147.
   1980   The Archaeology of New England. New York. Academic Press.

Snow, Dean R. and Kim M. Lanphear
   1988   European Contact and Indian Depopulation in the Northeast: The Timing of the First Epidemics. *Ethnohistory* 35:1:15–33.

Speck, Frank
   1915   The Family Hunting Band as the Basis of Algonkian Social Organization. *American Anthropologist* 17:2:289–305.
   1928   Territorial Subdivisions and Boundaries of the Wampanoag, Massachusett, and Nauset Indians. *Museum of the American Indian, Heye Foundation. Indian Notes* 5:2:167–173.
   1940   Penobscot Man: The Life History of a Forest Tribe in Maine. University of Pennsylvania Press.

Spindler, George and Louis Spindler
   1971   Dreamers without Power: The Menomini Indians. New York: Holt, Rinehart, and Winston. Case Studies in Cultural Anthropology.

Spindler, Louise S.
   1978   Menominee. in Trigger, Bruce Ed. *Handbook of North American Indians.* William Sturtevant Gen. Ed. Volume 15. *The Northeast.* Washington D.C. Government Printing Office. pp. 708–724.

Strachey, William
   1953   The Historie of Travell into Virginia Britania. Hakluyt Society, 2nd Series, no. 103. Louis B. Wright and Virginia Freund, eds. London: Cambridge University Press.

Sturtevant, Williams
   1984   A Structural Sketch of Iroquois Ritual in Foster, Michael K., Jack Campisi, and Marianne Mithun eds. *Extending the Rafters: Interdisciplinary Approaches to Iroquoian Studies.* Albany: State University of New York Press.

Tanner, Helen Hornbeck ed.
   1987   Atlas of Great Lakes Indian History. Norman: University of Oklahoma Press.

Tax, Sol
   1955   The Social Organization of the Fox Indians. in Eggan, Fred ed. *Social Anthropology of North American Indian Tribes. Chicago:University Chicago Press. pp. 243–282.*

Thomas, Peter
   1985   Cultural Change on the Southern New England Frontier, 1630–1665. in Fitzhugh, William, Ed. Cultures in Contact: The European Impact on Native Cultural Institutions in Eastern North America A.D. 1000–1800. Washington D.C.Smithsonian Institution Press. pp. 131–162.

Thwaites, Reuben G. ed.
   1959   The Jesuit Relations and Allied Documents: Travel and Explorations of the Jesuit Missionaries in New France, 1610–1791; the Original French. Latin, and Italian Texts, with English Translations and Notes. 73 Vols. Cleveland: Burrows Brothers. (Repeated: Pageant, New York, 1959.)

Tooker, Elisabeth
   1970   The Iroquois Ceremonial of Midwinter. Syracuse: Syracuse University Press.
   1978   The League of the Iroquois: Its History, Politics, and Ritual. in Trigger, Bruce Ed. *Handbook of North American Indians.* William Sturtevant Gen. Ed. Volume 15. *The Northeast.* Washington D.C. Government Printing Office. pp. 418–441.

1979   Native North American Spirituality of the Eastern Woodlands. New York: Paulist Press.

1984   Iroquois Women. in Foster, Michael K., Jack Campisi, and Marianne Mithun eds. *Extending the Rafters: Interdisciplinary Approaches to Iroquoian Studies.* Albany: State University of New York Press. pp. 109–124.

Trigger, Bruce G.

1976   Children of Aataentsic: A History of the Huron People to 1660. 2 vols. Montreal: McGill-Queen's University Press.

1978a   Introduction. in Trigger, Bruce Ed. *Handbook of North American Indians.* William Sturtevant Gen. Ed. Volume 15. *The Northeast.* Washington D.C. Government Printing Office. pp. 1–3.

1978b   Cultural Unity and Diversity. in Trigger, Bruce Ed. *Handbook of North American Indians.* William Sturtevant Gen. Ed. Volume 15. *The Northeast.* Washington D.C. Government Printing Office. pp. 798–804.

1978c   Early Iroquoian Contacts with Europeans. in Trigger, Bruce Ed. *Handbook of North American Indians.* William Sturtevant Gen. Ed. Volume 15. *The Northeast.* Washington D.C. Government Printing Office. pp. 344–356.

1985   Natives and Newcomers: Canada's "Heroic Age" Reconsidered. Montreal: McGill-Queen's University Press.

Trigger, Bruce G. and James F. Pendergast

1978   Saint Lawrence Iroquoians. in Trigger, Bruce Ed. *Handbook of North American Indians.* William Sturtevant Gen. Ed. Volume 15. *The Northeast.* Washington D.C. Government Printing Office. pp. 357–361.

Turnbaugh, William

1984   The Sociocultural Significance of Grave Goods from a 17th Century Narragansett Cemetery. Paper presented at the 49th Annual Meeting of Society for American Archaeology, Portland.

Turner, E. Randolph

1985   Socio-Political Organization within the Powhatan Chiefdom and the Effects of European Contact, A.D. 1607–1646. in Fitzhugh, William Ed. *Cultures in Contact: The European Impact on Native Cultural Institutions in Eastern North America* A.D. 1000–1800. Washington D.C.Smithsonian Institution Press. pp.

Ubelaker, Douglas

1976   Prehistoric New World population size: Historical review and current appraisal of North American estimates. *American Journal of Physical Anthropology* 45(3):661.

Van den Bogaert, Harmen Meyndertsz

1909   Narrative of a Journey into the Mohawk and Oneida country, 1634–1635. in Jameson, J. Franklin ed. *Narratives of New Netherland, 1609–1664.* pp. 135–162. New York: Charles Scribner's Sons.

Vastokas, Joan M.

1984   Interpreting Birch Bark Scrolls. in Cowan, William ed. *Papers of the Fifteenth Algonquian Conference.* Ottawa: Carleton University. pp. 425–437.

Wallace, Anthony

1958   Dreams and Wishes of the Soul: A Type of Psychoanalytic Theory Among The Seventeenth Century Iroquois. American Anhropologist 60 (2):234–248.

1969   The Death and Rebirth of the Seneca. New York: Alfred A. Knopf.

1978   Origins of The Longhouse Religion. in Bruce Trigger, Ed. Handbook of North American Indians, William Sturtevant, Gen. Ed. Vol. 15, The Northeast. Washington, D.C.: Government Printing Office pp. 442–448.

Williams, Roger

1936   A Key into the Language of America [1643]. 5th ed. Providence: The Rhode Island and Providence Plantations Tercentenary Commission.

Williamson, Margaret Holmes

1979   Powhatan Hair. *Man* n.s. 14:392–413

Winslow, Edward
    1910   Winslow's Relation [1624]. in John Masefield, ed Chronicles of the Pilgrim Fathers. New York E. P. Dutton.

Wolf, Eric R.
    1982   Europe and the People Without History. Berkeley: University of California Press.

Wood, William
    1977   New England's Prospect. Alden Vaughan ed. Amherst: University of Massachusetts Press.

Wroth, L. C.
    1970   The Voyages of Giovanni da Verrazzano: 1524–1528. Yale University Press.

Zeisberger, David
    1885   Diary of David Zeisberger, a Moravian Missionary Among the Indians of Ohio, 1781–1798. Eugene F. Bliss, ed., and trans. 2 vols. Cincinnati: Robert Clarke.

Chapter 5

The Southeast Culture Area

Brent R. Weisman

Florida Bureau of Archaeological Research

Introduction

The southeastern United States was the setting for some of the most complex and dramatic cultural developments in aboriginal North America. From the subtropical Gulf shores of southwestern Florida to the rich, alluvial plains of the Mississippi River drainage, native societies in the Southeast were able to flourish for more than 10,000 years before the coming of the Europeans. While no true cities developed anywhere in the Eastern Woodlands, with the possible exception of the site of Cahokia located on the outskirts of present-day St. Louis, in the Southeast there did occur a splendid elaboration of native politics, art, ritual, and ideology that has long fascinated students of the American Indian and continues to be the subject of anthropological inquiry.

The Southeastern Culture Area includes the modern states of Florida, Georgia, Alabama, Mississippi, Louisiana, Kentucky, Tennessee, and South Carolina, and portions of North Carolina, Virginia, Oklahoma, Missouri, and Indiana. This area contains four broad physiographic regions. The first of these is dominated by the Appalachian Mountains, stretching from northeastern Alabama in the south to the southwestern corner of Virginia, then north to New England. While much of the Appalachians is rugged terrain, it is also threaded by numerous stream valleys and plateaus that were favored for aboriginal settlement. In historic times, the Cherokee Indians were associated with the Appalachian highlands, and were often noted by early chroniclers for their successful mixed hunting-farming adaptation to this region.

The second region is the piedmont, or fall line, an area of rolling uplands, heavy forests, and broad river valleys between the Appalachian Mountains and the extensive coastal plain of the Atlantic Ocean and Gulf of Mexico. Piedmont forests contain a bountiful supply of plant and animal species that were integral to human subsistence, plus the soils of its river valleys were able to sustain the productive cultivation of corn, beans, and squash, the "American trilogy." The Creek Indians of the historic period are particularly known for their adaptations to the Southeastern piedmont, and at the time of European contact were living in large, fortified mound centers governed by a chief or priest. These centers, some containing up to 300 acres, also included a plaza where the populace would assemble, large rotundas or council houses used for ceremonies and public assembly in the

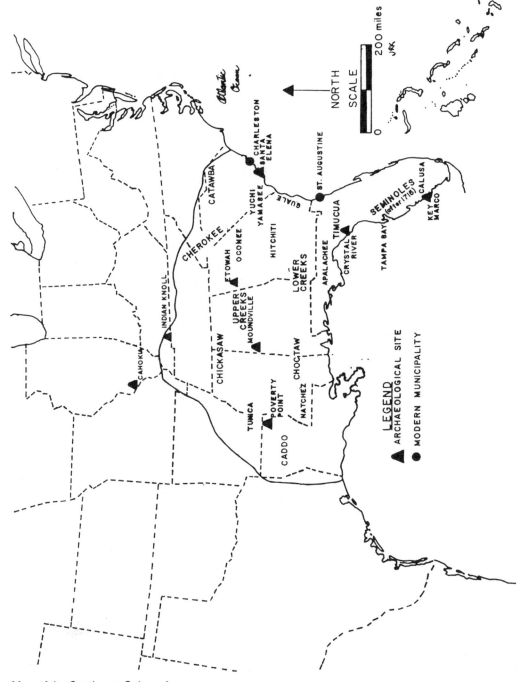

Map of the Southeast Culture Area

winter months, and burial mounds for the interment of chiefs and other high-ranking individuals.

A third physiographic region is the vast coastal plain bordering the Atlantic Ocean and the Gulf of Mexico. Despite the generally mild climate, flat terrain, and ample rainfall, most of the coastal plain did not support a large aboriginal population because plant and animal foods in the coastal pine forests were relatively scarce and lacked dietary variety. However, the biologically productive salt marshes of the lower Atlantic and northern Gulf coasts were especially suited for aboriginal lifeways, as many species of fish, shellfish, birds, and mammals could be seasonally harvested during an annual round of activities. Jesuit missionaries in the 1560s blamed their failure to Christianize the local Guale Indians of the Georgia Sea Islands on the seasonal movements of these people to procure abundances of resources. On the Gulf coast of Florida and Alabama the ample supply of estuarine resources made for a relatively long and stable aboriginal existence, to judge from the numerous wetland shell middens that date from about 1000 B.C. up to the early historic period.

The fourth physiographic region is south Florida, from the area around Lake Okeechobee south to the Florida Keys and including the Atlantic and Gulf coasts from Palm Beach around to Charlotte Harbor. Unlike the rest of the temperate Southeast, south Florida has a truly subtropical climate. Wet, grassy prairies occur over most of the area, popularly known as the Everglades. Thick cypress swamps also are found in the interior, while heavy mangrove forests grow along the coasts. Small "islands" of hardwood trees, or "hammocks," occur infrequently in the otherwise low-lying terrain, and it is here that the Seminoles of the recent past made their camps of pole-and-thatch dwellings, called "chickees" after the Seminole word for house.

Long before the Seminoles inhabited the south Florida glades, prehistoric people constructed large geometric earthworks of sand and shell, built large burial mounds to prepare and entomb the dead (Sears 1982), and carve in intricate detail wooden effigies of the eagle, owl, bobcat, panther, and many other species to serve perhaps as guardian spirits for the dead. From the Key Marco site (Cushing 1896) on the Gulf coast near the present city of Naples, a number of human and animal masks were recovered from the muck, some of which still were marked with their original paint. Other wooden artifacts from this remarkable site include a small catamaran, perhaps used as a toy, a painted deer head with detachable ears, a collection of large plaques carved with representations of spiders and felines, and one board bearing a very graceful and realistic depiction of a leaping dolphin. (Gilliland 1975).

When the explorer Juan Ponce de Leon brought the first Spaniards to the southwest Florida coast in 1513, the region was ruled by the powerful and numerous Calusa Indians, so named after their ruler that the Spanish called Carlos. Carlos and the Calusa were very hostile towards the Spaniards, twice driving Juan Ponce from their shores and finally inflicting him with a mortal would. The Calusa were unique in the Southeast because their chiefdom level of political organization was supported by a fishing-gathering-hunting subsistence rather than the corn-based agriculture typical of other New World chiefdoms (Marquardt 1986).

These four physiographic regions are useful in providing a broad outline of the Southeastern Culture Area, but the most important developments in southeastern prehistory occurred in the Atlantic or Gulf coast estuaries or in the valleys of the major rivers. Important rivers in the Southeast include the Mississippi and the Tennessee, the Green River in Kentucky, the Tallapoosa and Coosa rivers in Alabama, the Savannah River and the Chattahoochee River in Georgia, and the St. Johns River in Florida. The many shell middens, burial mounds, and temple mound-village complexes along the rivers and coasts of the Southeast attest to the early and sustained attractiveness of these areas to the southeastern Indians. Early archaeologists working in the Southeast were able to readily determine that these archaeological sites were not the products of some mythic race of extinct moundbuilders, but were created by the ancestors of the native Americans first encountered by sixteenth century European explorers (Thomas 1894; Willoughby 1932).

Estimating the numbers of people that lived in the aboriginal Southeast is difficult because the populations recorded by the early chroniclers already had been seriously decimated by introduced European diseases. Documents aside, there is no simple or agreed-upon formula for deriving population estimates from the archaeological record. The gap between historical and archaeological estimates is often disparagingly wide—in Florida, for instance, population figures are given at 100,000 (Milanich and Fairbanks 1980:18) and up to one million (Dobyns 1983). However, in order to appreciate the magnitude of the demise and displacement of the southeastern Indians in the historic period, it is necessary to gain some idea of their numbers in the years just before contact.

The south Florida Calusa probably numbered between 20,000 and 30,000 in the first decade of the 1500s before the first explorers touched their shores. Slave raiding from Caribbean ports probably began soon after contact, and was accompanied in its effects by great turbulence and intrigue as native ruling dynasties sought to maintain their power in the face of the ever increasing European presence. In the seventeenth century, the Spanish colonial government of Florida alternately courted and avoided these Indians depending on circumstances of the moment (Lewis 1978), and was not effective in blocking relentless slave raiding originating to the north in the British Carolinas. When Florida was ceded by Spain to Great Britain in 1763, only 80 families of the once-powerful Calusa Indians survived, and they quickly set sail for Cuba (Sturtevant 1978).

The same story can be told for the Timucua Indians of north Florida. Numerous small Timucua chiefdoms were encountered in 1539 by the Spanish conquistador Hernando de Soto in his northward trek through the peninsula in search of gold. While none of these groups were ultimately able to repel attacks by mounted Spanish swordsmen, crossbowmen, or men armed with matchlock firearms, the Spaniards were impressed by the tenacity of the Indian resistance and the numbers of warriors that could be brought to battle. In a pitched fight with the Timucuans Indians near present-day Lake City, Florida, Soto's force of about 600 faced and defeated a foe two or three times stronger in number. When the French were attempting to establish a colony among the Timucua in 1564, chiefs accompanied by up to 1500 warriors would visit their settlement for diplomatic talks (Lorant 1946:42).

The Timucua area still held fairly numerous aboriginal populations early in the 1600s when Franciscan missionaries worked their way west into interior Florida from their base at St. Augustine on the Atlantic coast. The coming of the missions to the Timucuans of north Florida sounded the death knell for native society, as a series of epidemics swept the missions while British and Indian raiding intensified from the north. Organized assaults on the missions in 1702 and 1704 brought about their final destruction, and the few surviving Timucuans sought out the relative security provided by the Spanish capital at St. Augustine (Milanich 1978). By the 1740s, the north Florida Timucua, once with an estimated population of at least 40,000 individuals at the time of European contact, had been reduced to extinction (Milanich and Fairbanks 1980:227).

The situation perhaps was even worse on the Atlantic coast of Georgia and the Carolinas. Here the nations of Great Britain, France, and Spain, engaged in a fierce and ruthless rivalry for colonial control soon after the era of initial discovery, with the decimation of native peoples as the predictable result. The Guale of the Georgia coast appear to have been particularly hard hit by the cultural consequences of the European presence, perhaps because they were already experiencing some biological and cultural stress resulting from their relatively recent adoption of maize horticulture (Thomas 1987:63). The Guale made several strikes against the Spanish missions established among them on the Georgia coast (Larson, 1978), but by 1680 they too looked to St. Augustine as a safe haven from the British and Indian raiders of the Carolinas. San Marcos pottery types associated with the Guale begin to appear with some frequency in archaeological deposits in St. Augustine dating to this time. The remaining Guale in and around St. Augustine removed to Spanish Cuba in 1763 when Florida came under official British control, and thus ceased to be a factor in the colonial history of the Southeast.

European diseases were carried to the Creeks and Cherokees of the interior by the expeditions of Soto in 1539 and Juan Pardo in 1567. The restructuring of native society and politics following the depopulation of these peoples was an important shaping event in the formation of the historic Indian tribes with which the various colonial governments had to interact (M. Smith 1987). It is difficult to estimate the numbers of the Creeks and Cherokees, in part because documented population figures, when mentioned, speak of individual towns or settlements and not of these groups as a whole. It is not out of the question that the Cherokees numbered as many as 50,000 when reached by the Pardo expedition. By 1729 it is recorded that there were 20,000 Cherokee, and by 1761 this figure had decreased dramatically to an estimate of 2,590 individuals (Swanton 1946:114). By 1840 most of the remaining Cherokees had been forcibly removed to the present states of Oklahoma and Texas in an epic trek known as the "Trail of Tears." While some Cherokees live today in North Carolina and Georgia, most reside on federal reservations in Oklahoma.

This same basic scenario tells the story of the Choctaws and Chickasaws, living in what is now Mississippi and Tennessee, and the Caddo, Tunica, and other tribes of Louisiana and Arkansas. All suffered the effects of depopulation and social disruption following sixteenth century European contact. All eventually accommodated the European presence in their homeland, and some, like the Tunicas and Seminoles, became particularly successful as traders and entrepreneurs in the commercial economy of the colonial Southeast. None were effectively able to withstand the relentless pressure of United States expansionism following the War of Independence, and today it is the mounds and middens of the southeastern Indians that most strongly attest to their former presence in this region of the American South.

Languages of the Southeastern Indians

Many diverse languages were spoken by the southeastern Indians. Much of this diversity no longer exists, as many tribal languages have gone to extinction with barely a trace. Language history is of interest to Southeastern prehistorians because linguistics offers another means of evaluating the evidence for migrations and other population movements into and throughout the Southeast. The interest is particularly keen because several important Indian legends recount epics of tribal migrations from the west, southwest, and north (Gatschet 1884, Swanton 1946:21–33).

Early in the historic period, languages belonging to four distinct families were in use by the southeastern Indians (Haas 1971:50). The first of these Muskogean, included the languages of the Choctaws, Chickasaws, Creeks, and the Apalachees of the Florida panhandle. The Creek Indians spoke several different but related languages, and the Florida Seminoles today speak Mikasuki, related to the extinct Hitchiti tongue, and Muskogee or "Creek," the language spoken by the Creeks living in what is now Alabama.

The second language family is called Algonkian, and included the languages spoken by Indians of coastal Virginia and North Carolina. Also in the Algonkian family is the language of the Shawnee Indians, a highly mobile tribe that appears to have made fragmentary moves into the interior Southeast from the Ohio River drainage in the mid seventeenth century. A third language family, Iroquoian, like Algonkian ultimately of northern origin, contained languages spoken by the Cherokees of North Carolina and other tribes of the Atlantic coast of North Carolina and Virginia.

The fourth family is called Siouan, and included the languages of peoples living in South Carolina and along the Gulf coast of Louisiana and Mississippi.

While the geographical location of these four language families early in the historic period does suggest that a wedge of Muskogean speakers drove into the Southeast from a general northwesterly location as told in the Creek migration legend (Gatschet 1884), the situation is really to complex to allow for ready generalization. For one thing, detailed local archaeological sequences in many areas occupied by Muskogeans in historic times show no material signs of migration, at least within the several hundred year immediately preceding European contact (B. Smith 1984). Another problem is that the Muskogean family appears to have little if any historical relationship with any other language family outside of the Southeast, which tends to argue against long distance movements of Muskogeans from other regions of the continent.

140

Finally, there are many aboriginal languages in the Southeast that cannot be grouped within the four major families and show no strong affiliation with language families elsewhere in North America. One such language is Timucua, spoken by many Indians of peninsular Florida. Despite our having a relatively good knowledge of seventeenth-century Timucua thanks to the writings of the Franciscan priest Francisco Pareja (Milanich and Sturtevant 1972), it is not possible to place Timucua within the four major language stocks of the Southeastern Indians. There have been suggestions that Timucua is related to languages of Caribbean peoples or tribes in the Orinoco River delta of northern South America (Granberry 1971; Milanich 1978:62). These ideas are plausible based on the location of Florida within the circum-Caribbean area, but lack the supporting evidence of archaeology or strong ethnographic parallels in material culture or social organization that cannot also be accounted for by cultural adaptation to similar environments.

It is tempting to equate the linguistic divisions of the southeastern Indians with the political and tribal factions that developed in the eighteenth and nineteenth centuries. The lack of unity in the so-called Creek Confederacy, for example, is said to have been caused by the frictions between Muskogee-speaking and non-Muskogee speaking Creeks. Likewise, the tribal divisions that now exist among the Florida Seminoles are thought by some to have resulted from that fact that some of these Indians speak Mikasuki while others speaks Muskogee or "Creek." Although members of one of the tribes do speak Mikasuki as their first language, the other tribe contains both Muskogee and Mikasuki speakers. Many Indians are fluent in more than one native language, and in the historic period several trade languages developed to ease communication between people of far-flung tribes. While the geographical distribution of the southeastern language families during the contact period no doubt reflect the paths of migration of peoples into and around the southeastern region, the linguistic diversity of the southeastern Indians was only one of many historical and political reasons behind the development of the rival tribes that existed on the colonial frontier.

Subsistence and Technology

From the time of the earliest big game hunters some 10,000 to 12,000 years ago to the historic period farmers and herdsmen, subsistence practices of the southeastern Indians depended upon a detailed understanding of the availability of wild plant and animal foods and the local circumstances in which they occurred. The agricultural way of life did not appear in the Southeast until about A.D. 900 or later, and never entirely replaced the seasonal round of hunting, fishing, and gathering activities, even among those societies that were most reliant upon the cultivation of corn, beans, and squash. The changes in subsistence practices through time in the Southeast do not reflect a general evolutionary trend towards the selection of specific dietary complexes and the abandonment of others, but perhaps are better thought of as additions to a relatively stable pattern of food procurement.

Subsistence practices of the southeastern Indians were supported by a technology based solely on the energy of human labor. The power of wind and water was not harnessed in the aboriginal Southeast, nor were there any animals available for draught until very late in the historic period. Bronze and iron metallurgy did not develop. Human muscle power fueled the harvesting and production of all food resources, aided by a stone, bone, and wood technology very similar to Paleolithic and Mesolithic Europe.

The fundamental economic unit in the Southeast was the nuclear family. All other forms of labor organization were superimposed upon the basic family group. Although individuals at times owed various obligations of service, labor, or production to the larger social units of clan or chiefdom, it is likely that the nuclear family was the most enduring and unvarying form of human organization in the entire span of southeastern prehistory. Chiefdoms did arise from time to time late in the prehistoric Southeast, but one gets the feeling from early historic accounts that they were fundamentally unstable and never able to successfully usurp domestic control over labor and production activities.

Families did not exist in isolation from a broader network of social interaction. In fact, many archaeologists interpret the archaeological record to indicate that for most of southeastern prehistory groups of related families were aggregated into bands. Band societies generally lack strong centralized leadership, but instead depend on the voluntary association of individuals to accomplish short-term tasks. Members of a band share the same geographical territory, and there is a corresponding emphasis in band societies on sharing resources that occur there. Two types of archaeological sites are thought to correlate with band societies—small, single-family campsites scattered throughout the band territory often at some distance from one another, and large midden or refuse sites in places where the entire band had gathered together.

The many rivers of the Southeast were favored locations for such sites. One of the best known is the site of Indian Knoll, on the Green River in west-central Kentucky, with beginning occupation about 3,000 to 4,000 B.C. (Winters 1974). The Indian Knoll midden is about 1.5 meters high, and contains large quantities of riverine mussel shells, deer and turkey bones, the remains of fish and reptiles, and evidence for the processing of hickory nuts, acorns, and other seeds (Webb 1974). Some 55,000 artifacts have been collected in systematic excavations at the site, and are abundant testimony to the diversified but specialized nature of Indian Knoll technology. Among the artifacts are chisels, awls, pins, projectile points and fish hooks made from sharpened deer and bird bones, atlatl (spear thrower) handles and chisels made from antler, ground stone axes, mauls, hammerstones, pestles and nutting stones for grinding seeds and nuts, and thousands of chipped stone scrapers, drills, and spear points. Many artifacts and food bones were found in and around cooking hearths, marked by concentrations of burned and cracked rock found throughout the strata of the midden. No pottery was found in the Indian Knoll excavations, and archaeologists place this and similar sites in the Archaic period, beginning about 6,000 B.C. and ending about 700 B.C. in most areas of the Southeast.

Besides having little or no pottery, the Archaic period was a time when virtually all of the Southeast was inhabited by peoples quite skilled at making a living from their local surroundings. Many of the basic lifeways that first developed in the Archaic period persisted

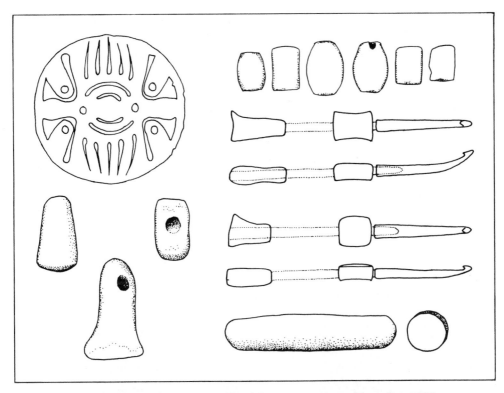

Figure 5.1 Southeastern Indian Artifacts. Top left, copper earspool from Crystal River; bottom left and right, hammerstones and pestles from Indian knoll; top right, atlatl weights ad reconstructed atlatls from Indian Knoll. Not to scale (Drawing by Merald Clark.)

until historic times, despite the fact that pottery, the bow and arrow, and the cultivation of corn all came to the southeastern Indians after Archaic adaptations were already in place.

In 1947, archaeologist Joseph Caldwell introduced the concept of primary forest efficiency to account for the development of stable, semi-sedentary communities among the southeastern Indians before the introduction of agriculture (Caldwell 1958). In Caldwell's view, the natural productivity of the Eastern Woodlands was so great that little incentive existed to adopt farming as a way of life, despite the fact that corn and other domesticates already formed the dietary staples of the Mesoamerican cultures. The food surpluses provided by the natural abundances of game, nuts, and shellfish, according to Caldwell, underwrote the first real floresence of aboriginal religion in the East, in the cultural phenomenon known as Adena-Hopewell.

Particularly along the Gulf coasts of Florida and the lower Southeast, fish and shellfish assumed a primary role in providing subsistence for burgeoning levels of population in post-Archaic times. Harvesting these resources did not require the organization of a specialized labor force. Fish were taken in traps, nets, and weirs, and, rarely, by hook and line and harpoon. Shellfish were probably gathered by hand. Most of these activities were probably performed by members of a nuclear family, and the gathering of fish, turtles, and other wildlife from traps and nets could even have been done by children. Indeed, the questions of how and why chieftains in some areas of the Southeast were able to gain some degree of control over this domestic mode of production still remain largely unanswered by southeastern prehistorians.

Perhaps the two artifacts that best represent the broad spectrum adaptations of the early southeastern Indians are the spear thrower, or atlatl, and the grinding stone. Both were essential components of the southeastern tool kit from Archaic times if not before, and both persisted in some form into the historic period.

The atlatl is a composite tool, made by inserting a short wooden shaft into a small hook made of bone and antler. A spear, often tipped with a sharpened stone point, is fitted into the hook, and the shaft of the spear and the shaft of the atlatl are held together in one hand. When an appropriate target is sighted, the arm is cocked back and the spear is hurled through the air, with the thrower holding on to the shaft of the atlatl and using its extra length as leverage greater than what could be achieved by the arm alone. Armed with the atlatl, southeastern Indians stalked their favorite prey, the white-tailed deer, and must have been quite successful in the hunt.

Figure 5.2 A Florida Seminole skinning an alligator in the Everglades, 1936. (Courtesy of Oral History Project, University of Florida.)

The drilled stone weights mounted on the shaft and other atlatl parts are found in numerous archaeological sites throughout the Southeast, and in some cases appear to have been intentionally broken and placed in with burials as grave offerings (Webb 1974:328). There has even been the suggestion that the stem of the famous calumet, or pipe of peace, of the historic Plains and Southeastern Indians was the symbolic representation of the atlatl, weapon of war (Hall 1977). In this view, the ritual display and handling of the calumet encouraged an atmosphere of peace and harmony, in the way that a handshake in our culture symbolizes that neither person has any hostile intent to conceal.

Grinding stones, or mortars, are also found on many southeastern sites from Archaic through historic times. These are often flat slabs of limestone, sandstone, or igneous rock that have a hollowed out portion on the center where seeds and nuts could be placed for grinding. Pestle stones, polished cylindrical stones held in the hand to do the actual grinding, are also found at many sites. In Florida and probably elsewhere in the Southeast where sources of stone were limited, mortars and pestles were made of wood. Key Marco on the Gulf coast of southwest Florida is one site where wooden mortars and pestles were preserved, in muck deposits perhaps 800 or 900 years old (Cushing 1896).

These implements were used to grind a variety of seeds and nuts, but throughout the Southeast the favored plant food seems to have been the hickory nut. A traveler's account from a visit to the Creek Indians in 1774 recounts the technology associated with processing the nuts from the shell-barked hickory:

> I have seen above an hundred bushels of these nuts belonging to one family. They pound them to pieces, and then cast them into boiling water, which, after passing through fine strainers, preserves the most oily part of the liquid: this they call by a name which signifies hiccory milk; it is as sweet and rich as fresh cream, and is an ingredient in most of their cookery, especially homony and corn cakes (Bartram 1955:57).

The use of domesticated plants by the southeastern Indians has a long but uneven history. Even the three plants that eventually came to have the most significance in the southeastern diet—corn, beans, and squash—complemented rather than replaced the role of gathered foods. Among the native plants domesticated in the Southeast between 3000 and 4000 years ago are sumpweed, sunflower, and chenopodium or goosefoot (Smith and Cowan 1987). While a limited sedentary lifestyle was probably necessary to cultivate and harvest these plants, there are no indications in the archaeological record that this type of horticulture triggered any dramatic changes in the social, political or technological spheres of southeastern culture.

The role of corn, or maize (*Zea mays*), in southeastern prehistory is also difficult to evaluate. Maize was first introduced into the southeast from the Midwest between A.D. 100 and A.D. 300 (Chapman and Crites 1987). Judging from the archaeological contexts from which this early maize has been recovered, it served as an ordinary foodstuff and was not restricted to strictly ceremonial use. However, there appears to have been no immediate reordering of society following the introduction of maize, and it is likely that its cultivation was integrated into the existing seasonal round of the southeastern Indians.

By A.D. 900 or so, the situation was quite different. For reasons that are not well understood, maize cultivation had intensified among some southeastern societies, particularly those located in the floodplains of the major rivers. These societies also developed more centralized economies, based on the redistribution of stored foods and other items by the village chief. Of all the plant foods exploited by the Southeastern Indians, maize perhaps had the best agricultural potential. It lends itself well to the production of a food surplus, as we know in our own society, can be stored very easily with relatively little loss, and can be converted into a number of food uses, from *sofki,* or corn soup, to corn cakes and bread.

These advantages cannot be taken as sufficient justification for the increased role of maize in the southeastern diet, because they do not explain the basic transformation of labor that must have occurred when families stopped producing only for themselves and began directing some of their efforts towards the creation of a communal surplus. This surplus resulted from the cultivation of large fields shared by the whole town, described as follows for the Florida Seminoles in 1770s:

> This plantation is one common enclosure, and is worked and tended by the whole community; yet every family has its particular part, according to its own appointment, marked off when planted; and this portion receives the common labour and assistance until ripe, when each family gathers and deposits in its granary its own proper share, setting apart a small gift of contribution for the public granary, which stands in the centre of the community (Bartram 1955:170).

While in the anthropological sense the increased emphasis on maize agriculture by the southeastern Indians can be viewed as having led to more complex forms of political and social organization, it should not be thought that the average southeastern Indian enjoyed a substantially better life as the result of an agricultural lifestyle. For one thing, there are a number of nutritional deficiences that can result from an over reliance on corn in the diet. Malnutrition, anemia, and increased occurrence of infectious disease are all evident on the bones and teeth of aboriginal burials belonging to agricultural population of A.D. 950 and later (Goodman and Armelagos 1985). Second, it is probable that farming peoples of the southeast experienced greater population densities than were present in hunting and gathering societies, thus there may have been a feeling of overcrowding in some of the larger communities.

There are other perils associated with an agricultural lifestyle. Agriculture is a way of life more fraught with risk than living off the land, because the investments of time and labor involved with cultivation often require that less time be spent in broader and more diversified subsistence activities. Should the crop fail due to irregularities of weather or numerous other natural causes, it may be too late to hunt or gather sufficient wild foodstuffs to make up for the shortfall.

Finally, there are costs involved for the individual living in the chiefdom type of society often associated with maize farming. Organized warfare becomes more prevalent as the territorial investment in land becomes higher. People may find themselves called upon either to attack a neighboring settlement or to defend their community and its storehouses from marauders. Rivalries and political factions within the chiefdoms themselves may have added to the tension of everyday living.

By about A.D. 1200 the bean (*Phaseolus vulgaris*) had been added to the southeastern diet, and was grown in the fields with maize and several species of squash. These three crops formed the backbone of the southeastern domesticated food complex, and were being grown by the Indians at the time of first European contact and well into the historic period.

Long term trends in the development of southeastern subsistence and technology are marked by conservatism and persistence of traditional forms. In only a few instances were the basic lifeways adopted during the Archaic period totally abandoned during the historic period. Southeastern Indians of the last several centuries continued to hunt, fish, and procure a wide variety of plant and animal foods from their surroundings. Tools and weapons continued to be made of wood and stone using techniques known to the Indians for more than a millenium. Even pottery, which made its first appearance in the Southeast some 4,000 years ago, was still being manufactured past the turn of this century by the Creeks and other reservation Indians (Quimby and Spoehr 1950).

This is not to say that there were no changes in subsistence practices or technology in all of southeastern prehistory. It is, however, very difficult to establish the direction of causation from technology and subsistence to changing forms of social organization or new developments in religion and ideology. This is often because there is a basic disagreement among archaeologists about seemingly simple archaeological points of fact. For instance, the introduction of the bow and arrow into the Eastern Woodlands around A.D. 500 is said by some to have been responsible for the dramatic changes in native society and ceremony that occurred at about this time (Ford 1974), while others argue that no correlation exists because the bow and arrow did not appear until A.D. 900 (Griffin 1967). Likewise, the archaeological literature often gives the impression that maize-based agriculture permitted the development of chiefdom level societies in the Southeast (referred to as "Mississippian" chiefdoms), while in fact the intensification of maize farming that had occurred in some societies by A.D. 1000 may have been an effect and not a cause of more complex forms of social and political organization. There is still much about the relationship between subsistence and technology and the organization of society and religion that remains to be understood in southeastern prehistory, but it seems relatively certain that as long as the means of production and distribution of food, status items, and other critical resources stayed under domestic control there was little potential for new developments in technology, society, or politics.

Social Systems of the Southeastern Indians

One of the most intriguing questions in the study of southeastern prehistory is what factor or factors were responsible for the development of forms of social organization above that of the nuclear family. Many tribes of the historic Southeast were organized into matrilineal clans, with certain clans providing the war leaders, other clans providing the peace leaders, and others the medicine men. The clans themselves in any given community were grouped into two opposing moieties of red clans and the white clans, and held together in a system of checks and balances that discouraged the centralization of power.

Matrilineal clans seem to be associated with agricultural societies the world over (Schneider and Gough 1961), thus their presence in the historic Southeast does little to inform us about the kinds of social systems that existed in pre-agricultural times, that is, for most of southeastern prehistory. The question is, did lineages emerge before the coming of intensive agriculture, and if so, when, and for what reason?

Long distance trade is the factor most consistently advocated by archaeologists to explain why social ties were strengthened and maintained by a group of related families (a lineage) above the level of the nuclear family. There is good evidence that southeastern Indians as early as 2000 B.C. to 3000 B.C. were circulating a variety of stone, clay, and shell items throughout the region and into areas of the Midwest and Northeast. Between about 200 B.C. and A.D. 200 these networks of exchange were operating at their peak, in what archaeologists have called the Hopewell Interaction Sphere (Caldwell 1964). Some archaeologists believe that the goods that were the objects of exchange—large conch shells from the Gulf of Mexico moving north into the Appalachian piedmont and all the way to the Great Lakes, quartz crystals, greenstone, copper, and meteoric iron moving from north to south—were passed down the line among members of the same lineage, exchanged to members of another lineage and passed further along until the network was complete.

For the most part, the actual exchange of goods took place on the local level, between people related through lineage ties. One way in which such a system may have worked is evidenced at the site of Crystal River, on the central Florida Gulf coast. Crystal River was a ceremonial mound center for a number of outlying sites on the estuaries and small islands that dot this portion of the coast. The primary object of trade among these people appears to have been finely decorated pottery, manufactured further south along the coast and further north along the Florida panhandle, but not in the immediate vicinity of Crystal River. Upon death, when the deceased was taken to the Crystal River mound for interment, this valued pottery was also included as a burial offering (Bullen 1966), which accounts for these types being nearly absent from the domestic refuse of the Crystal River site itself.

Other Florida sites in the years between A.D. 350 and A.D. 500 give suggestions that wealth, in the terms of the day, was being accumulated by some groups more than others, and that these groups tended to perpetuate themselves through time. Good evidence for the emergence of a social elite comes from the archaeology of the Weeden Island culture of south Georgia and north Florida, whose burial-ceremonial mounds contain the remains of likely religious specialists or priests who may have exerted at least limited political and economic control over the local populace. The Weeden Island mound builders were not the first or last culture in the Southeast to build mounds or earthworks. Impressive site complexes exist at Poverty Point, Louisiana, Fort Center, Florida, in the Lake Okeechobee drainage, at Crystal River, and at numerous other locations bordering the Gulf of Mexico. With Weeden Island, however, one gets the impression of a society just on the verge of allowing the concentration of wealth and privilege in the hands of the favored few, resulting in a stratified society of chiefs and priests at the top, commoners in the middle, and perhaps an underclass of slaves, retainers, or war captives.

This is just the kind of society that emerged in many places throughout the Southeast between about A.D. 900 and the mid sixteenth century. However, the relationship between these Mississippian chiefdoms and Weeden Island and other preceding cultures is anything but clear. In the Weeden Island area, no specific developmental sequence has yet been demonstrated to link the Weeden Island priests and the Mississippian chiefs. In fact, it seems as if Weeden Island and other near-chiefdoms in the Southeast did not give spontaneous rise to the chiefdoms of late prehistoric times, but instead chiefdoms developed in areas where specialized developments had not previously occurred. This phenomenon has probably helped give rise to the many theories attempting to derive Mississippian chiefdoms via direct migration from mesoamerican sources.

Whatever their cause (or causes, as is more likely), and their ultimate source of origin, chiefdoms made life for the natives in the aboriginal Southeast much different than what had been experienced by their ancestors. For one thing, tribute in the form of food and labor was owed to the chief, who resided in a large palisaded village where he presided over an increasingly complex array of civil and ceremonial functions. The large temple mounds at such sites, for example the 300 acre site of Moundville in western Alabama, were constructed using citizen labor, perhaps willingly contributed in service to the community.

The chief lived in a wooden building constructed atop one of the large, flat-topped mounds, while other nobles lived within the palisade on smaller mounds arranged around a central plaza. These elites enjoyed a diet rich in meat, and possessed the finest in clothing, jewelry, and weapons, to judge from burial analysis conducted by archaeologists at several sites (Larson 1971, Peebles and Schoeniger 1980). Most of the population of a chiefdom lived beyond the palisade walls, in small hamlets or farmsteads. In these outlying locations, fields for maize, beans, and squash were cleared using slash and burn techniques, and forest and stream were utilized for hunting, gathering, and fishing.

It is probable that these small communities were organized into matrilineages, and it is almost certain that the elite group made up of the chief and nobles were also kin-related through matrilineal descent. One of the best examples of this is furnished by the Natchez Indians of the lower Mississippi, whose highly structured chiefdom organization was still intact in the early decades of the 1700s. At the apex of Natchez society was the Great Sun, descended from a line of Suns ultimately traced back to the Sun itself. The Great Sun experienced tremendous power and deferential treatment from his subjects while alive, even being carried from place to place by eight men hoisting a specially designed litter made of cedar and painted deerskins (Swanton 1946:600). The death of the Great Sun was a time for great mourning and was frequently accompanied by the suicide of his most devoted followers. Members of the Sun's family and close advisors were expected to take their own lives and follow the Sun to his grave (Hudson 1976:328) which in most cases they did willingly. The new Sun was the son of the deceased man's sister, and was therefore a member of the same matrilineage.

The political importance of the chief's office among the southeastern Indians waxed and waned due to changing cultural and historical circumstances. The fundamental instability of chiefdoms in general acted to prevent the prolonged dynastic succession that characterizes kingdoms and non-industrial states. The one constant in the social organization of the aboriginal Southeast in late prehistoric times and throughout the historic period is the importance of the clan. By the nineteenth century, the clan had become the primary economic, political, and residential unit of the Creeks, Seminoles, and other southeastern tribes, and continues to this day to be an important determinant in the selection of medicine men, tribal chairmen, and other positions in contemporary society.

Clans were often named after animals—Panther, Bird, Snake, Deer, and Bear were particular favorites—natural forces, such as the influential Wind Clan of the Creeks and Seminoles, or, more rarely, place names such as Talahasee signifying in Creek "old town," and Talwalako, a Mikasuki word for "big town" (Spoehr 1941:14,15). Women of a single clan often would set up households near one another, creating small communities linked together through matrilineal descent. Among the Creeks, these communities were known as *huti*. Because a man would be a member of his mother's clan and not the clan of his wife, his *huti* was not this actual residence but the residence of his mother and other members of his maternal clan (Swanton 1928:171). The clan camps, or *istihapo*, of the Florida Seminoles of this century are distinct geographical expressions of matriliny, where related women set up distinct but communal households, sharing in cooking, child rearing, and other duties of camp life (Spoehr 1941).

Figure 5.3 Seminole Camp scene, Florida Everglades, 1936. (Courtesy of Oral History Archives, University of Florida.)

There is some indication, at least among the Creeks and Seminoles, that clan bonds were weakening in the late eighteenth and early nineteenth centuries during a time when many of these Indians were engaged in a fairly prosperous trade economy with the European colonists. The nuclear family was the center of social and economic activities, as it is contemporary American society. Clan bonds were again strengthened during the war years between 1814 and 1842, when the United States government forcibly attempted the removal of the Creeks and Seminoles from the Southeast. It is probable that the native resistance to the American presence was organized along kin lines, as broader ties beyond the nuclear family became a matter of necessity. The social structure of this period—nuclear families loosely aggregated into clans, and clans loosely aggregated into tribes—is essentially the system that prevailed among the southeastern Indians until very recent times.

Figure 5.4 A Florida Seminole family, 1936. (Courtesy of Oral History Project, University of Florida.)

Belief Systems of the Southeastern Indians

As is the case in all of prehistory, the belief systems of the very early inhabitants of the Southeast are difficult to determine. Reconstruction relies primarily on archaeology, aided somewhat by the very careful use of ethnographic analogy. Still, the emphasis is on the interpretation of artifacts, mainly items recovered as grave goods or personal adornments of the dead.

Belief systems of course do not exist in a cultural void. Culturally-determined beliefs about the world (cosmology), the views of an individual about his or her place in society and the cosmos (world view), the ritualized expression of these behaviors (religion) and their practical expression (ideology), all influence and are influenced by the ways in which society, politics, and the economy are organized. Southeastern belief systems can be grouped into two broad categories, one belonging to peoples of the agricultural chiefdoms after about A.D. 900, and the other belonging to the hunting and gathering societies of earlier prehistory and those societies in which this lifestyle persisted until the historic era.

Two themes capture the essence of the belief systems of the southeastern hunter-gatherers. The first of these involves the ritual concern for the dead, first expressed in the careful, intentional interment of individuals with their accumulated possessions, as in the shell middens on the Green River in Kentucky. Burials in the Indian Knoll midden contained quantities of the mineral red ochre, probably having been sprinkled over the corpse, and included such items as atlatls, turtle shell rattles, necklaces of shell beads, copper and pendants and bone hairpins (Webb 1974). Slightly later, perhaps by 400–500 B.C., earthen burial mounds were being constructed for the purpose of housing the dead. Archaeology suggests that many of these mounds were built over log or earthen tombs, containing the remains of one or several individuals who must have had special religious significance while alive.

Antler headdresses, quartz crystals, cooper pendants and ear spools, sheet mica and copper cut into human and animal shapes, and other exotic artifacts associated with these interments suggest the burial of shamans with their religious paraphernalia. Shamanism, the second major theme in the belief systems of these nonagricultural societies, has as its core concern the relationship between human beings and the forces of the natural world. While in a state of trance, the shaman communicates directly with these vital and potentially dangerous forces, and thus possesses powers of curing and divination. Consequently, the shaman is looked upon both with fear and awe by other members of society.

Unlike their fellows, shamans are perceived to have the ability to assume more than one form, often taking the form of a particularly revered animal. It is possible that the antlered headdresses associated with burials in Hopewell-period mounds were meant to represent the transformation from human to animal, especially given the fact that antlers themselves periodically shed and then regrow. Curiously, antlered frogs and other antlered and horned beings continued to figure in southeastern myth and ritual until recent times (Capron 1953; Sturtevant 1954:40). Shamans have very little real political or economic authority, and exercise at best only situational leadership.

While religion and politics are never completely independent of one another, it is not until the development of chiefdoms that the two become inextricably intertwined. Thus, it is with the emergence of chiefdoms in southeastern prehistory that we see the first conflation of religious and political power. Along with the growing complexity of politics and economy that occurs in chiefdoms, belief systems also become correspondingly complex as the ritual behaviors associated with different sectors of society become fused into one shared religion. Part of the complexity arises from the fact—evident in the Southeast—that belief systems in chiefdoms tend to accommodate rather than reject earlier rites and practices, and thus embody virtually all variations of religious belief that ever existed in a particular culture. Religion in chiefdoms becomes institutionalized, that is, there exist relatively fixed sets of beliefs and practices that are officiated by a relatively fixed set of practitioners, or specialists.

Three complementary cults are thought to have coexistence in the religion of the late prehistoric southeastern chiefdoms between A.D. 1000 and A.D. 1550 (Brown 1985, Knight 1986). The terms Southern Cult or Southeastern Ceremonial Complex are often used to refer to a rather standardized set of artifact styles and motifs that appear at this time, which include circle and cross designs, elaborately garbed figures of dancing warriors or priests ("eagle warriors"), and depictions of composite animal beings or "monsters."

The first cult emphasized the rites and rituals of warfare, and probably involved the successive rewarding of warriors with increased status ranking as they accomplished themselves with acts of bravery and courage. Associated symbolism of the warrior cult included the stylized war axes, arrowheads, and maces that appear on pottery, shell, and a variety of media, and the dancing warrior figures mentioned previously. Some of these figures appear to be brandishing severed heads or wearing them in belts around the waist, perhaps as trophies of successful combat. Rituals of the warrior cult may have been staged for public viewing, but it is likely that they were exclusive events shrouded in esoterica.

The second cult revolved around the practice of building the large flat-topped substructure or "platform" mounds found in the ceremonial centers of the late prehistoric chiefdoms. These mounds served as the stages for much of the Southern Cult ritual, and it was here that the temples of the priests and chiefs stood. Temple mounds were not constructed haphazardly or all at once, but probably grew in regular stages using labor coordinated by the chief. It is possible that the control exerted by a chief in the act of moundbuilding was one means of reinforcing the legitimacy of his office, and it is also probable that the people gave their labor more or less voluntarily, as such activities were probably strongly associated with the well-being of the community. Building the large earthen platforms was a communal activity, participated in by both the chief and his people. Further, as recent scholars have come to argue (Knight 1986), moundbuilding was a very tangible expression of the core metaphor of southeastern Indian thought, the triumph of purity and order over pollution and disorder. This is because the construction of a mound involved placing layers of clean, white sand (the color associated with purity and order) over a layer of red clay (associated with disorder). After a period of use, when the surface of the mound had become polluted by human activity, its purity was restored by adding a new mantle of white sand. Sacred fires were also lit as part of the renewal ceremonies.

The third aspect of the ceremonial complex involved a cult of the ancestors, probably very similar in practice to the ancestral cults of agricultural peoples around the world. In the Southeast, the central figures of these cults were the temple figurines of stone, clay, and wood embodying the spirits of the ancestors. One of the functions of the priest was to guard

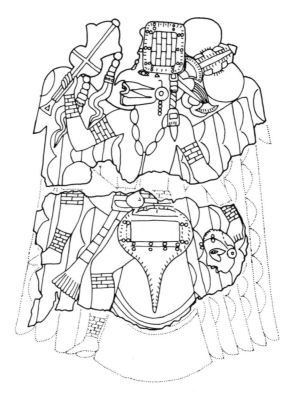

Figure 5.5 An eagle warrior on an embossed copper plate from the Etowah site. (Drawing by Merald Clark based on Willoughby 1932: fig. 14.)

these figures and carry appeals to them from the populace and perhaps even the chief. Many of these figurines exist today in museum collections, for example the famous pair of marble male and female figures from the Etowah mound in Georgia (Larson 1971).

No European ever witnessed the rites of the Southeastern ceremonial complex in their entirety. Many cultures in the region had abandoned the more elaborate rituals before the time of first contact, during a time when many of the chiefdoms were disintegrating. However, the southeastern Indian never relinquished their core beliefs about the world and how it operated, even under intense pressure from Christian missionaries beginning in the sixteenth century. In the Green Corn Dance of the historic centuries, these same themes of purity, balance, and order again are given full play, in forms that must be very closely derived from the cult ceremonies of late prehistory.

Historical Overview

The historic period ushered in many changes in the lifeways of the southeastern Indians, but was also a time marked by a persistence of traditional cultural patterns and the

154

emergence of new elements in native society, religion, and politics. The historic period can be divided into three eras, defined on the basis of broad shifts in attitudes held by the native Americans and the Spanish, French, British, and finally, American, settlers with respect to one another.

The first era, the time of first contact, begins with the arrival of Christopher Columbus in the Caribbean in 1492 and ends with the 1567 expedition of Juan Pardo from the site of Santa Elena on the Atlantic coast of present-day South Carolina westward into the Tennessee Valley. In the intervening 75 years between these two explorations of discovery, Europeans had for the first time penetrated much of the Southeast, and in so doing exposed the peoples known to history as the Creeks, Cherokees, Choctaws, Natchez, and others to new repertoires of cultural values based on the ethics of commercial enterprise and a technology based on harnessing the forces of the natural world. In the bargain, native peoples played host to a variety of imported European diseases, including smallpox, typhus, and influenza.

The Taino and Carib societies of Caribbean were the first and hardest hit by initial European contact. Archaeological and documentary sources confirm massive depopulation on Hispaniola and neighboring islands by 1520 (Deagan 1988) due to disease and attempts at enslavement. What direct influence these early depredations had on the people of Florida is not known, but when Juan Ponce de Leon first made landfall on the southwest Florida coast in 1519 he met with a very hostile reception and was twice prevented from establishing a base camp on shore.

Further Spanish explorations north along the Florida Gulf coast also met with little success. In 1528, Panfilo de Narvaez and a force of 400 men landed near the mouth of Tampa Bay to begin an overland journey that would inadvertently last eight years and claim all but four lives. The fabulous account of Cabeza de Vaca, one of the survivors, furnishes the first European glimpse of the southeastern Indians, and contains hints of untold riches of gold hidden somewhere deep in the interior (Nunez Cabeza de Vaca 1905).

By the mid 1530s Spanish conquistadores had successfully toppled the great Aztec empire of central Mexico and the Inca empire of Andean Peru, and had done so against overwhelming odds. By 1539 Hernando De Soto, a veteran of the Inca campaign and already a wealthy man, had mounted a similar campaign to plunder the troves of southeastern riches, perhaps spurred on by the tales of Cabeza de Vaca. Sailing from Havana, Cuba on May 18, 1539, Soto and over 600 men of the best equipped New World expedition yet assembled, made landfall on a spit on land just south of present-day Tampa Bay.

Archaeologists and anthropologists continue to be fascinated with the Soto expedition, in part because the several first-hand chronicles of the journey record the native inhabitants and geography in sufficient detail to allow for archaeological identification, and in part because these same documents, however flawed, describe customs, beliefs, and material cultures of societies about to share their world with the Europeans for the first time. Some of the first encounters were hostile. Besides a near-constant sniping of the Spanish force by concealed Indian archers, pitched battles broke out at several locations in Florida and Alabama. On most occasions however, the Indians attempted to move the

Spaniards through their territory as quickly as possible, telling them that the proverbial pot of gold could be found in the lands of the next tribe just over the hill. Almost from the day of landing Soto's force was in need of provisions, and the Spaniards would from time to time camp at a particularly well-stocked Indian village—like the Apalachee town of Iniahica in what is now Tallahassee—causing the natives to flee or at best seek an uneasy truce with the explorers. Soto and his men crossed seven southeastern states, from the Gulf coast of Florida north to the Appalachian Mountains and west to the Mississippi River, in search of the gold and other riches like had been found in Mexico and Peru (Swanton 1939). By 1542, three years after their landing, their numbers and their expectations much reduced, the Spaniards felt lucky enough to find food. Soto himself died of illness on May 21, and his body was quietly disposed of in the middle of the Mississippi River so as not to alert the Indians.

The effect of the Soto entrada on the native southeastern societies is a hot topic of debate, particularly as a number of newly-discovered archaeological sites attributable to that period have provided new lines of inquiry into the nature of contact between Spaniard and Indian. Some post-1539 sites contain evidence of mass burial (Mitchem and Hutchinson 1987), as might be expected in the wake of disease epidemics brought on by the Europeans. Massive depopulation would result in a weakening of virtually every aspect of society and politics in the kin-based southeastern cultures, and movements of peoples from one place to another seem to reflect the general unstable conditions that set in by the late sixteenth century (M. Smith 1987).

However, despite this damaging evidence, it is too simplistic to say that Soto and his men destroyed the southeastern Indians. While the Indians did value the glass beads and iron implements of the explorers, they seem for the most part to have invested these exotic objects with traditional values and meanings. Glass beads were strung in necklaces like aboriginal shell and bone beads. Iron tools and weapons, even pieces of armor, either were reworked to conform to traditional forms, or were substituted in place of their aboriginal counterparts as part of one's personal possessions.

To complicate matters further, the role of the Spanish explorers in bringing about the demise of the southeastern chiefdoms is now being called into question, as archaeologists are becoming increasingly aware that native societies were experiencing dramatic social and political instability during the several centuries prior to the voyage of Columbus. It is difficult to evaluate the impact of European contact on native societies until all the indigenous processes of culture change are understood, but there still remains much in southeastern prehistory that is unknown.

By 1565, after several fitful starts, Spain made a concentrated effort to colonize what they referred to as *La Florida*, in their meaning virtually the entire Atlantic coast of North America. The Spanish desire for colonization perhaps had been heightened by recent (and contested) French interest in settling *La Florida*, and Pedro Menendez de Aviles sailed off to the Americas to settle the French question and establish a Spanish port to protect the shipping lanes that extended from Mexico, South America, and the Caribbean back to Europe. In September 1565, Menendez founded the settlement of St. Augustine on the north coast of the present State of Florida, which is today hailed as the oldest continuously occupied city in the United States. It was Menendez who in 1567 ordered Juan Pardo and 120 soldiers to march inland to the Appalachian Mountains in search of a westward passage to Mexico, and it is the presence of Menendez in the southeast that brings in the second era of the historic period. This, the era of Acculturation, begins with Menendez and ends with the consolidation of American control in the region by 1821.

The two and a half centuries of acculturation saw the frequent contact between the southeastern Indians and the Spanish, French, and British colonists, and was a time when all societies, however reluctantly, adapted to coexist with one another. It was also an era of tremendous factionalism. The Spanish, French, and British never presented a unified European front with respect to the Indians, with each power continually vying for ascendancy over the others. For their part, the natives never mounted a unified policy with respect to the European presence. Had they done so, it has been argued, the course of American history may have been greatly different than that which in fact came to pass.

The principal agents of acculturation were the priest and the trader. Jesuit priests working under Menendez's initiative established a chain of missions along the Atlantic coast from the Chesapeake south to Florida and around the Gulf of Mexico to Tampa Bay. These efforts largely resulted in the martyrdom of a number of priests at the hands of the Indians, and the Jesuit missions proved to be short-lived. Franciscan priests, again based in St. Augustine, were responsible for a second wave of missionary activity, founding over 100 missions from St. Augustine west through the Florida panhandle between 1597 and the early 1700s.

The real wealth in the Southeast, as Spain and the other colonial powers had come to realize, lay not in mineral resources but in human beings. Thus, while many of the priests were undoubtedly earnest in their desire to bring Christianity to the Indians, the missions themselves were expected to be self-sufficient agricultural communities, with land and labor provided by the Indians. Many of the southeastern Indians were by this time at least part-time agriculturists in their own right, but the concept of permanently residing in or near one fixed location was not easily accepted. The outbreaks of epidemics in many of the missions early in the 17th century suggest the wisdom of the Indian settlement pattern and also indicate the overwhelming negative consequences the mission experience was to have on native lifeways.

It is clear from the surviving documents of this period that, at least at first, the negative consequences were unintended. However, the priests, and the soldiers that were sent to garrison the larger interior missions, found themselves in a position of having to trade with the Indians to survive. This was not at all what had been originally envisioned in the plan to convert the natives for the service of God and King. But, due to Spain's inadequate provisioning of the Florida colony, the realities of life there made such lofty goals virtually unobtainable. Thus was born the southeastern deer skin trade. At first, it was nothing more than a few loads of skins being passed on by the priests to the port at St. Augustine. But within one hundred years, by the middle of the 1700s, an immense export business rested on the deerskin trade to a Europe that had itself eliminated its native fauna in the desire for skins and furs. By the time of the American Revolution, Charleston, South Carolina, and other southeastern ports shipped up to 306,000 pounds of skins annually to Europe (Wright 1987:59), mostly obtained by Creek Indians hunting the interior forests.

The deerskin trade, and with it trade in other fur-bearing animals, agricultural produce, honey, wax, and other natural items, essentially transformed the southeastern Indians into commercial hunter-gatherers. This intensive harvesting of the natural Southeast had obvious ecological consequences, but it also meant that the Indians were drawn into a net of mercantilism that was cast far beyond the southeastern shores. Gone were the chiefs of the temple mounds. In their place was a new breed of leader—like Alexander McGillivray of the Creeks who were skilled at reading the still unresolved political rivalries that existed between the French, British, and Spanish and then maneuvering in the Indians' best interest.

Gone too were the palisaded temple mound villages, replaced by smaller towns arranged around a central public square, but with most of the populace living out on family farmsteads. Instead of clothing made of skins or Spanish moss, the Indians now proudly wore shirts made of European calico and breechclouts cut from red stroud cloth. Eventually, the deer too had vanished, so the Creeks, Seminoles, and other southeastern Indians turned to herding escaped Spanish cattle as a source for meat and skins.

Again, population movements occurred, this time in part as a response to better trading opportunities available in specific locales. Archaeologists have chronicled the movements of the Natchez and Tunica peoples of the lower Mississippi valley, continually realigning themselves as suppliers and middlemen in the horse trade with the French (Brain 1977; I. Brown 1985). Likewise, the resettlement of the Florida peninsula, emptied of its native population by relentless British and Creek raiding of the mission towns, by the peoples that came to be known as Seminoles (derived from the Spanish *cimarrone,* meaning wild ones or runaways) occurred as Spanish, then British, ports of trade opened up (Weisman 1989). In all of this, many individual Indians were quite successful as traders, and proved themselves time and again to be shrewd businessmen. Collectively, however, the territory of the southeastern Indians grew smaller and smaller, as numerous land cession agreements ratified by small and disparate groups of Indians for a variety of purposes gave more land over to European control. Once lost, these lands were not regained, except in some small measure by the federal reservations of this century.

The final era in the historic period, from about 1812 to the present time can be characterized as the era of Conflict. Although the trends had been evident for some time that would make the outbreak of hostilities seem inevitable, the immediate catalyst for conflict came with the American attempts following the Revolutionary War to gain control of the Southeast. This had to be done by ousting the Spanish and British, accomplished with amazing directness by Andrew Jackson in several bold military sweeps, then by containing the Indians for eventual removal to Indian Territory west of the Mississippi.

The result of the American policy was a series of wars with the Creeks and Florida Seminoles and the removal of the Cherokees and others in the infamous Trail of Tears. Meanwhile, official Indian Agents had been dispatched to the southeastern tribes, in a last

Figure 5.6 Long Warrior, a Seminole leader of the 1770s. (Drawing by Merald Clark, after Bartram 1955.)

ditch effort to introduce the technology of the plow and loom. Indeed, in outward appearance, many Indians of the 19th century bore little resemblance to their forebearers of just three centuries previous. However, in at least one important respect, the southeastern Indians of this era and even of today carry on with the traditions of their ancestors. This is in the area of religion, given full expression in the ceremony of the Green Corn Dance.

The Green Corn Dance is descended from the religious cults of the late prehistoric southeastern moundbuilders, and many of its individual elements are traceable to customs and motifs of that time. Its existence in the 17th and 18th centuries is not known with any certainty, but the ceremony appears full-blown in the 1800s when it was described in some detail by several observers. The Green Corn Dance continues to be practiced in recent times, by the Seminoles on the south Florida reservations and by the Creeks, Seminoles, and others living on reservations in Oklahoma.

The Green Corn Dance rites stress the Indian desire for purity, balance, and an ordered world. Typically, the ceremony lasts four days, although both longer and shorter versions are known. Men and women are kept carefully separated, and in some cases women are not allowed until the end to enter the dance ground itself. Meanwhile, while the dance ground and the sacred fire are being prepared with fresh earth and logs by the medicine man and his helpers, the men must fast, not eating until the medicine man cooks the green corn on the sacred fire and prepares several herb teas, or "black drinks." The teas are imbibed to induce vomiting, and thus bring about a state of purity.

One day of the ceremony is set aside as Court Day (Capron 1953, Sturtevant 1954) when an individual is permitted to atone for his wrongdoings against his clan or community. Early in this century, the Florida Seminoles were known to execute repeat offenders who gave no sign of repentance, and reportedly, the condemned met final punishment with stoic acceptance (Capron 1953). Other features of the Green Corn ceremony include a variety of symbolic and "stomp" or recreational dances, and a ball game in which teams attempt to score by striking a wooden ball post with a hard, deerskin ball. The ceremony concludes with the Green Corn Dance itself, with men and women mingling on the circular dance ground of clean, white sand. While Christianity again has made inroads into the southeastern Indian culture, it has not replaced the traditional importance of the Green Corn Dance and the basic values it expresses.

The Southeastern Culture Area Today

The contemporary situation for the remaining southeastern Indians can only be described as one of near-constant adversity with the federal government and the state and local jurisdictions in which they reside. There are many reasons for this, not the least of which is the fact that the extremely complex culture histories of the southeastern tribes defy easy understanding. The lack of understanding has been exacerbated by the Indians themselves, who, not unexpectedly, have often been extremely reticent in their interactions with non-Indian society.

The federal government, while seemingly well-intentioned in many instances, has repeatedly taken legislative actions that leave a wake of unintended consequences. Beginning in the 1930s, the few remaining Indians in the Southeast were encouraged to organize into federally-recognized tribes, with a political structure modelled after the constitutional government in Washington, D.C. Once tribal organization (or, in the words of the legislation, "reorganization") was accomplished, then the tribes could come before the Indian Claims section of the U.S. Department of Justice to formally petition for compensation for lands lost in the American period. This was a move perhaps taken to head off a potential perpetual tangle of individually-filed claims, but it resulted in the formation of tribal polities where previously none had existed. These contemporary tribes, like the Seminoles and Miccosukees of Florida and the Seminole Tribe of Oklahoma, as might be expected from the historical record of Indian factionalism in the Southeast, were to agree on virtually nothing, and have themselves battled bitterly over the distribution of court-awarded judgements.

Other factors promoting the continuing antagonism between the Indian and the government concern native fishing and hunting rights, land use rights, and what restrictions, if any, apply to business enterprises operated on reservation lands. Various state and federal agencies themselves seem not to have reached any common agreement about their own spheres of judicial and legislative influence. The Florida reservations, for example, while administered by the U.S. Department of the Interior, are also subject to certain state and local laws. In 1987, Seminole Tribal Chairman James E. Billie was charged by the U.S. Justice Department for the 1983 killing of a Florida panther, an animal protected by the Endangered Species Act. Previously, Billie had been charged with essentially the same crime by the State of Florida, although the charges were subsequently dropped. The justice Department pursued conviction on misdemeanor charges, claiming that none of the several treaties between the Seminoles and the United States granted the Indians special rights to hunt and fish on the reservation. Billie and his attorneys held that the Indians had the right to hunt and fish in the traditional manner, and that Billie's freedom of religion had been violated because the claws and skin of the panther were important parts of Seminole medicinal rites. The case, several years in the making, ended in mistrial and failed to establish the needed precedent in the area of native hunting and fishing rights.

Daily life on the Seminole reservations takes place without much interaction with contemporary white society, except for the occasional tourist and those who come for high-stakes bingo and tax-free cigarettes. The reservations have their own governing boards of elected officials, their own police, fire, and medical services, and their own schools through the primary grades. Cattle ranching was introduced some decades ago through a program of government assistance, and in addition to land leases, the commercial construction of the pole and thatch ''chickee'' or traditional Seminole house, and profits from bingo, form the backbone of contemporary Seminole economy. The Green Corn Dance is still danced on occasion, and Seminole interests are gaining increasing attention in the Florida legislature.

Reservation life poses only one set of challenges confronting native and contemporary American society. There are a number of native southeastern Indians who do not live on reservations, many descended from the ''friendlies'' who were not forced to emigrate in the Indian diaspora of the 1830s and 1840s. A major problem for these Indians, most of whom are not members of federally-recognized tribes, has been forming bonds of ethnic identity. Once this has been accomplished, activism on the part of a few individuals has brought about the increased recognition of Indian needs (Paredes 1980). However, until very recent years the trend has been for both reservation and non-reservation Indians to leave their homes seeking work in the urban areas of the south and mid-Atlantic states.

These urban Indian communities, in Baltimore and elsewhere, have not tended to fare well in cities packed with competing minority populations. There is even talk among the Indian leadership, like James Billie of the Seminoles, that the time is drawing near when even the strongest of the southeastern tribes will no longer exist as independent entities. Indeed, there appears to be no consensus among either Indian or white about what the future does, or should, hold for the southeastern Indians.

SUGGESTED READINGS

Adair, James
  1986   *The History of the American Indians,* edited by Samuel Cole Williams. Promontory Press, New York. Originally published 1775, London.

Bartram, William
  1955   *The Travels of William Bartram,* edited by Mark van Doren. Dover Publishing, Inc., New York. Originally published 1791, Philadelphia.

Howard, James H.
  1968   *The Southeastern Ceremonial Complex and its Interpretation.* Missouri Archaeological Society Memoir No. 6, Columbia.

Hudson, Charles
  1976   *The Southeastern Indians.* University of Tennessee Press, Knoxville.

Hudson, Charles, (editor)
  1986   *Ethnology of the Southeastern Indians: A Sourcebook.* Garland Publishing, Inc., New York.

Lewis, Thomas M.N., and Madeline Kneberg
  1958   *Tribes That Slumber: Indians in the Tennessee Region.* University of Tennessee Press, Knoxville.

Sturtevant, William C. (editor)
  1987   *A Seminole Source Book.* Garland Publishing, Inc., New York.
  1987   *A Creek Source Book.* Garland Publishing, Inc., New York.

Swanton, John R.
  1931   *Source Material for the Social and Ceremonial Life of the Choctaw Indians.* Bureau Of American Ethnology Bulletin 103, Washington, D.C.
  1939   *Final Report of the United States De Soto Commission.* United States Government Printing Office, Washington, D.C. (reprinted 1985 by Smithsonian Institution Press, Washington, D.C.)
  1946   *The Indians of the Southeastern United States.* Bureau of American Ethnology Bulletin 137, Washington, D.C.

Williams, Stephen (editor)
  1968   *The Waring Papers.* Papers of the Peabody Museum of Archaeology and Ethnology, Volume 58, Cambridge, Mass.

REFERENCES

Bartram, William
  1955   *Travels of William Bartram,* edited by Mark Van Doren. Dover Publications, Inc., New York.

Brain, Jeffrey P.
  1977   *On The Tunica Trail.* Louisiana Archaeological Survey and Antiquities Commission, Anthropological Study No. 1, Baton Rouge.

Brown, Ian
  1985   *Natchez Archaeology.* Mississippi Department of Archives and History, Archaeological Report No. 15, Jackson.

Brown, James A.
  1985   The Misissippian Period. In *Ancient Art of the American Woodland Indians*, edited by David S. Brose, James A. Brown, and David W. Penney, pp. 93–146. Harry N. Abrams, New York.

Bullen, Ripley P.
  1966   *Burtine Island, Citrus County, Florida*. Contributions of the Florida State Museum, Social Sciences, No. 14, Gainesville.

Caldwell, Joseph H.
  1958   *Trend and Tradition in the Prehistory of the Eastern United States*. American Anthropological Association, Memoir No. 88.
  1964   Interaction Spheres in Prehistory. In *Hopewellian Studies*, edited by J. R. Caldwell and R. L. Hall, pp. 133–143. Illinois State Museum Scientific Papers No. 12, Springfield.

Capron, Louis
  1953   The Medicine Bundles of the Florida Seminole and the Green Corn Dance. *Bureau of American Ethnology Bulletin 151, Anthropological Paper* No. 35, pp. 155–210.

Chapman, Jefferson, and Gary D. Crites
  1987   Evidence for Early Maize (*Zea mays*) from the Icehouse Bottom Site, Tennessee. *American Antiquity* 52:352–354.

Cushing, Frank Hamilton
  1897   Exploration of Ancient Key-Dweller Remains on the Gulf Coast of Florida. *Proceeding of the American Philosophical Society* 25:329–448.

Deagan, Kathleen
  1988   The Archaeology of the Spanish Contact Period in the Caribbean. *Journal of World Prehistory* 2:187–233.

Dobyns, Henry
  1983   *Their Numbers Become Thinned: Native American Population Dynamics in Eastern North America*. University of Tennessee Press, Knoxville.

Ford, Richard
  1974   Northeastern Archaeology: Past and Future Directions. *Annual Review of Anthropology* 3:384–413.

Gatschet, Albert S.
  1884   *A Migration Legend of the Creek Indians with a Linguistic History, and Ethnographic Introduction*. Daniel G. Brinton, Philadelphia.

Gilliland, Marion S.
  1975   *The Material Culture of Key Marco, Florida*. University Presses of Florida, Gainesville.

Goodman, Alan H., and George J. Armelagos
  1985   Death and Disease at Dr. Dickson's Mounds. *Natural History* 94(9):12–18.

Granberry, Julian
  1971   Final Collation of Texts, Vocabulary Lists, Grammar, of Timucua for Publication. *American Philosophical Society, Yearbook 1970*, pp. 606–607.

Griffin, James B.
  1967   Eastern North American Archaeology: A Summary. *Science* 156 (3772):175–191.

Haas, Mary R.
  1971   Southeastern Indian Linguistics. *Red, White, and Black*, edited by Charles Hudson. Southern Anthropological Proceedings No. 5 Athens, Georgia.

Hall, Robert L.
  1977   An Anthropocentric Perspective for Eastern United States Prehistory. *American Antiquity* 42:499–518.

Hudson, Charles
  1976   *The Southeastern Indians*. University of Tennessee Press, Knoxville.

Knight, Vernon J., Jr.
1986 The Institutional Organization of Mississippian Religion. *American Antiquity* 51:675–687.

Larson, Lewis H., Jr.
1971 Archaeological Implications of Social Stratification at the Etowah Site, Georgia. In *Approaches to the Social Dimensions of Mortuary Practices,* edited by James A. Brown. *Society for American Archaeology Memoir* 25, pp. 58–67.
1978 Historic Guale Indians of the Georgia Coast and the Impact of the Spanish Mission Effort. In *Tacachale: Essays on the Indian of Florida and southeastern Georgia During the Historic period,* edited by J. T. Milanich and S. Proctor pp. 120–140. University Presses of Florida, Gainesville.

Lewis, Clifford M.
1978 The Calusa. In *Tacachale; Essays on the Indians of Florida and Southeastern Georgia During the Historic Period,* edited by J. T. Milanich and S. Proctor, pp.; 19–49. University Presses of Florida, gainesville.

Lorant, Stefan
1946 *The New World.* Duell, Sloan, and Pearce, New York.

Marquardt, William H.
1986 Politics and Production Among the Calusa of South Florida. Paper delivered at the Fourth International Congress on Hunting and Gathering Societies London School of Economics and Political Science, Sept. 8–13, 1986.

Milanich, Jerald T.
1978 The Western Timucua: Patterns of Acculturation and Change. In *Tacachale: Essays on the Indians of Florida and Southeastern Georgia During the Historic Period,* edited by J. T. milanich and S. Proctor, pp. 59–88. University Presses of Florida, Gainesville.

Milanich, Jerald T., and Charles H. Fairbanks
1980 *Florida Archaeology.* Academic Press, New York.

Milanich, Jerald T., and William Sturtevant
1972 *Francisco Pareja's 1613 Confessionario: A Documentary Source for Timucuan Ethnography.* Florida Department of State Division of Archives, History, and Records Management, Tallahassee.

Mitchem, Jeffrey M., and Dale L. Hutchinson
1987 *Interim Report on Archaeological Research at the Tatham Mound, Citrus County, Florida, Season III.* Florida State Museum, Department of Anthropology, Miscellaneous Project Report Series No. 30, Gainesville.

Nunez Cabeza de Vaca, Alvar
1905 *The Journey of Alvar Nunez Cabeza de Vaca.* Translated by Fanny Bandelier. Allerton Book Co., New York.

Paredes, J. Anthony
1980 Kinship and Descent in the Ethnic Reassertion of the Eastern Creek Indians. In *the Versatility of Kinship: Essays Presented to Harry W. Basehart,* edited by L. S. Cordell and S. Beckerman, pp. 165–194. Academic Press, New York.

Quimby, George I., and Alexander Spoehr
1950 Historic Creek Pottery From Oklahoma. *American Antiquity* 15:249–251.

Schneider, David M., and Kathleen Gough, editors
1961 Matrilineal Kinship. University of California Press, Berkeley.

Sears, William H.
1982 *Fort Center: An Archaeological Site in the Lake Okeechobee Basin.* University Presses of Florida, Gainesville.

Smith, Bruce D.
1984 Mississippian Expansion: Tracing the Historical Development of an Explanatory Model. *Southeastern Archaeology* 3:13–32.

Smith, Bruce D., and C. Wesley Cowart
  1987   Domesticated Chenopodium in Prehistoric Eastern North America: New Accelerator Dates from Eastern Kentucky. *American Antiquity* 52:355–357.

Smith, Marvin T.
  1987   *Archaeology of Aboriginal Culture Change in the Interior Southeast: Depopulation During the Historic Period.* University Presses of Florida, Gainesville.

Spoehr, Alexander
  1941   Camp, Clan, and Kin Among the Cow Creek Seminole of Florida. *Field Museum of Natural History Anthropological Series* 22:1–27.

Sturtevant, William C.
  1954   The Medicine Bundles and Busks of the Florida Seminole. *The Florida Anthropologist* 15:31–70.
  1978   The Last of the South Florida Aborigines. In *Tacachale: Essays on the Indians of Florida and Southeastern Georgia During the Historic Period,* edited by J. T. Milanich and S. Proctor, pp. 141–162. University Presses of Florida, Gainesville.

Swanton, John R.
  1928   Social Organization and Social Usages of the Indians of the Creek Confederacy. *Bureau of American Ethnology Annual Report* No. 42, pp. 23–472.
  1939   *Final Report of the United States De Soto Commission.* U.S. Government Printing Office, Washington, D.C.
  1946   *Indians of the Southeastern United States.* Bureau of American Ethnology Bulletin 137, Washington, D.C.

Thomas, Cyrus
  1894   *Report on the Mound Exploration of the Bureau of American Ethnology Annual Report No. 12, Washington, D.C.*

Thomas, David Hurst
  1987   *The Archaeology of Mission Santa Catalina De Guale: 1. Search and Discovery.* Anthropological Papers of the American Museum of Natural History, Volume 63, New York.

Webb, William S.
  1946   *The Indian Knoll, Site Oh 2, Ohio County, Kentucky.* University of Kentucky Reports in Anthropology and Archaeology No. 4.

Weisman, Brent R.
  1989   *Like Beads On A String: A Culture History of the Seminole Indians in North Peninsular Florida.* University of Alabama Press, Tuscaloosa.

Willoughby, Charles C.
  1932   History and Symbolism of the Muskhogeans. Reprinted from *Exploration of the Etowah Site in Georgia,* by Warren K. Moorehead, Yale University Press, New Haven.

Winters, Howard
  1974   Introduction to the New Edition. In *Indian Knoll,* by Williams S. Webb, pp. v–xxvii. University of Tennessee Press, Knoxville.

Wright, J. Leitch, Jr.
  1986   *Creeks and Seminoles.* University of Nebraska Press, Lincoln.

Chapter 6

The Plains Culture Area

Elizabeth S. Grobsmith
University of Nebraska

Introduction

The plains region generally connotes the vast, flat, semiarid grasslands, sometimes called the North American grasslands, that stretches from the Mississippi-Missouri Valley on the East and the Rocky Mountains on the West, from the coniferous forests of the Saskatchewan River Basin in Canada on the North, to the Rio Grande River in Central Texas to the South (Wedel:1961). This expanse of plains and prairie, with its unique physiographic and climatological features, forms a unique ecological zone which supported a wide variety of hunting and gathering as well as farming tribes long before the historic era. Zebulon Pike, after a two-year exploration of the plains, wrote in 1808 that he considered it a Great American Desert, "incapable of cultivation" and rightfully left to the "wandering and uncivilized aborigines" (Wedel 1961:278). An early anthropologist and student of the American Indian, Lewis Henry Morgan believed that the plains was a barren wasteland, "not congenial to the Indian, and . . . only made tolerable to him by possession of the horse and the rifle" (White, in Wedel 1961:279). Even Alfred Kroeber, whose "Cultural and Natural Areas of Native North America" in 1939 revolutionized our thinking about the plains even believed that the plains had been prehistorically "only sparsely or intermittently inhabited" and held no inducement to men without horses or even farmers without the plow (Wedel 1961:299). At that time, archaeologists had not found evidence of inhabitants other than present day, and current thought was that man had not existed on the plains until a century or two before the arrival of the white man. The notion was that there was no prehistoric occupation of the plains, and only during the early horse days did Indians come out onto the plains. We know now this is untrue—that it is no longer a question of whether the plains was inhabited—it is only a question of when and for how long. One thing is certain: while the plains may have been prehistorically scantily populated, there is evidence for occupation of the plains for more than 11,000 years!

Plains Geography

This vast plains region, which spans 1500 miles from north to south and about a 1000 miles from east to west, is a unique and variable expanse whose landscape is

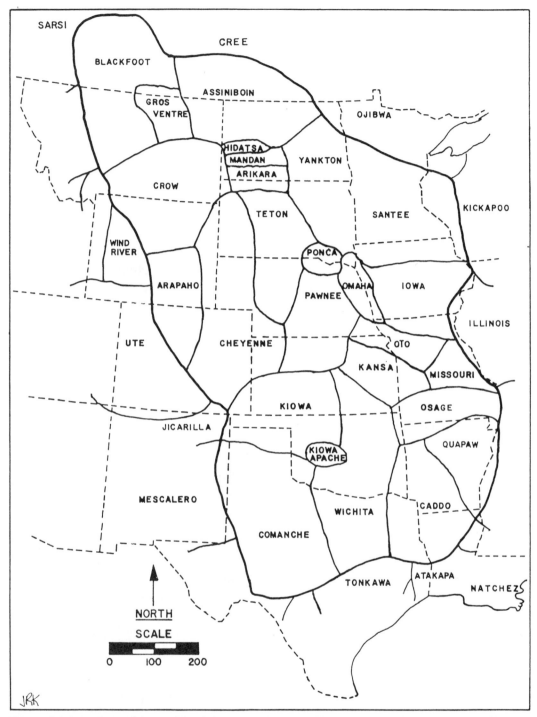

Figure 6.1 Location and distribution of plains tribes at contact. (Reprinted from the Ethnographic Bibliography of North America, 4th edition, by George P. Murdock and Timothy J. O'Leary, Human Relations Area Files, HRAF Press, New Haven, 1975.)

predominantly characterized by flatness and only moderate relief. This comparatively level surface is a grassland supporting different kinds of vegetation depending on such factors as rainfall, temperatures, aridity and humidity levels. Wooded areas are intermittent and generally follow water courses. A constellation of environmental forces helps shape the plains into what it is: a) generally the climate is considered semiarid to subhumid, meaning rainfall is insufficient for the sort of agriculture practiced in humid lands b) the summers tend to be very hot and the winters dry and cold c) the temperature is predictably variable from year to year and even season to season, as is the precipitation d) droughts tend to be cyclical and e) there is a large amount of evaporation, especially in winter when there is scanty precipitation to begin with. As the treeless prairie permits ruthless winter winds to blow snow around, the soil loses its ability to store moisture. No wonder the plains seemed uninhabitable! Today, living in the plains requires a healthy attitude and tolerance for this variable weather—people say "if you don't like the weather, just wait a minute and it will change".

Although we think of the plains as a relatively uniform expanse, in fact it is readily distinguished into two subregions, the eastern and western plains. This division is important because it reflects two different types of prehistoric adaptations. The eastern plains is a more humid region, with tall-grass prairies of such deep-rooted plants as the six foot tall bluestem, wheat grass, and other bunch grasses. Rainfall averages between 20 and 40 inches annually. In the north(east) plains, farming is precarious, because even though rainfall is greater, the number of frost-free days in which to achieve a harvestable crop is limited to about 100. In the south, 140 to 200 frost-free days permit greater dependence on crops, but this area, like the north, is still subject to variability in precipitation and high evaporation by wind. The crops grown prehistorically in the plains were sensitive to frost as well as these other limitations (Wedel 1961:34).

On the west, the gentle rolling prairies give way to drier expanses of short-grass prairies, sometimes called "steppe", as it is somewhat higher in elevation. This area belting the front of the Rocky Mountains is characterized by grasses like blue grama and buffalo grass which are shallow-rooted to utilize the sparse rainfall more efficiently, and have a higher nutritive value for wildlife (Wedel 1961). Here rainfall is half of what it is in the eastern portions, only 10–20 inches, and that too is highly irregular.

The abundance of game animals supported by the varied grasses permitted an adaptation to the plains based largely on hunting, although the degree of dependence on hunted foods depended on the geographic location of the group and the relative security of their harvest. Bison, in particular, flourished in abundance and had an overwhelming influence on native cultures. Other animals in varying supply were mule and white-tailed deer, elk, pronghorn antelope, bighorn sheep, grizzly and black bear, cougar, wildcat, beaver, otter, mink, racoon, wolf, fox and jackrabbit, burrowing animals such as the prairie dog and badger and an abundant variety of birdlife (Wedel 1961).

Despite the impressive variability in plains adaptations, it was the western part of the plains which came to typify plains cultures, creating in people's minds the stereotypic image of a nomadic mounted warrior, wielding lance and shield, and becoming almost a

Figure 6.2 A herd of antelope graze in this typically western plains environment. (Courtesy of Elizabeth Grobsmith.)

T.V. caricature. Unfortunately, anthropologists helped to foster this inaccurate view by referring, in their theoretical approaches, to the western plains tribes as the "typical" ones, thereby permitting our inference that nomadic hunters were typical to the area whereas farming tribes were located on the "periphery" and were considered "marginal" in their scheme. In point of fact, while the prehistoric plains hunters were unquestionably the oldest residents of the plains, at the time of contact, the number of sedentary village tribes exceeded the number of nomadic ones, and so farmers were indeed more "typical" of aboriginal subsistence.

Plains Prehistory

Archaeologists designate the Paleo-Indian period (12,000 B.C.–5500 B.C.) as the early subsistence pattern on the plains, during which time hunters sought large game. In the southern and central plains, Pleistocene hunters hunted large fauna such as camels, bison (antiquus), native horses, and mammoth. In the plains, their adaptation was to these large fauna which roamed the grasslands following the last major glacial advance in America.

Although there is no evidence for structural remains, no patterns of food storage, and no hearths indicating prolonged use, we know these Paleo-Indian hunters returned irregularly to their campsites, and left evidence of their tools in association with these extinct fauna. The earlier Clovis tradition revealed the manufacture of a fluted projectile or knife and other flint tools found in association primarily with extinct mammoth bones. The later Folsom archeological tradition reflected finer techniques of projectile manufacture, and an extensive tool kit with points finer and smaller than the Clovis ones. As this period drew to a close, bison became the animal these tribes depended on with greatest regularity. As climatological shifts occurred and the plains became hotter and drier, less aridity meant less vegetal cover, and the large game which had been plentiful to Paleo-Indian hunters became extinct.

The Archaic period (5500 B.C.–0 B.C./A.D.) showed an adaptation to a wider range of foods, a mixed economy with greater dependence on small game rather than large bison, and the supplementing of the diet with gathered foods (Wedel 1986). During the Archaic, regional adaptations became the norm, and it was during this period that the eastern and western plains began to reflect truly distinct adaptations and subsistence. In the west, dependence on big game hunting was still common, but in the east, plains life shifted to a foraging economy with heavier dependence on small game such as deer, rabbits and collecting of roots, nuts and seeds, ground into flour with milling stones. There is clear evidence of fishing during this period as well. The shifts in this foraging period then show a clear division into eastern and western plains tribes, the western ones drifting toward the mountain valleys and shifting from nomadic hunting and gathering to more fixed base hunting, and the eastern tribes turning to a mixed economy with far more dependence on vegetal foods than before.

The Plains Woodland prehistoric period (0–1000 A.D.) was definitely influenced by the development of the eastern Woodlands cultures and shows an emergent cultural lifestyle which "set the stage" for the sedentary horticulturalist tradition which existed at the time of contact. Early on, this period was characterized by a mix of simple gardening with creek-valley hunting and gathering, but the adoption of cultigens change this lifestyle from that of simple food collectors to true food producers. During this period tribes established firmer occupancy of the land. It was during this period that "three major innovations" appeared in the plains area: the burial of the dead in or under earthmounds; the manufacture of pottery, with vessel style influenced by the Woodland pottery of the Mississippian and Ohio valley peoples such as the Adena and Hopewell; and true cultivation of corn and beans (Wedel 1986:81).

The final period is called the Plains Village Period (1000 A.D.–1850 A.D.) which, itself, is divided into earlier and later phases. During the early phase, multi-family habitations of semi-subterranean earth lodges with covered entryways were constructed. These substantial structures were grouped into fixed villages. Food was stored underground. The ceramic tradition beginning during the Woodland period continued and became well-developed and a far greater range of artifacts appeared, made of stone, bone, horn and shell as well. The most distinguishing artifact and indeed the hallmark of this entire period is a bone hoe made of a bison scapula and used for cultivating. Fishing activities greatly increased, as indicated by remains of curved bone fish hooks and bones, nonexistent during the prior period. In the early part of this period, villages were small and widely scattered, with square or rectangular earth lodges. During the latter part of this period, earth lodges became circular and these early small settlements were abandoned in favor of fewer but more consolidated settlements. These fewer settlements were fortified for defense purposed with ditches and stockades, reflecting the incursions of newcomers into the territory. This greater concentration of the population and consolidation of villages into a smaller number of towns (as opposed to earlier villages where lodges were strung along lesser streams with ample water and habitat for hunting) may have meant greater stability for the residents, and a fluorescence of their culture. The rich and elaborate culture of these plains farmers was as its height as fur traders and trappers began to make their way up the Missouri River, turning these aboriginal centers into major trading posts. The tribes found at the time of contact were the direct predecessors of modern plains peoples—the Mandan, Hidatsa, Arikara, Pawnee, Wichita, the Omaha, Oto, Ponca and Kansa. But it also reflected a new era which was to bring drastic social and cultural change, devastating political and economic consequences, and an end to an exclusively aboriginal way of life in the plains.

Early Inhabitants

We can identify three major types of groups who are identified as plains tribes. Symmes Oliver classifies the first group as "True Plains Tribes of Hunting and Gathering Origin" representing those tribes who lived as pedestrian (on foot) hunters who roamed the plains hunting buffalo and whose cultures and social organization represented the loose, flexible societies of nomads (1962:20). These tribes, such as the Blackfoot, Plains Cree, Sarsi and Assiniboine show no evidence of ever having been horticultural, show no evidence of sedentism and, while they survived without the horse, quickly incorporated it and became the full-blown equestrian nomads we think of today as the "typical plains" hunters.

Next came the "True Plains Tribes of Farming Origin" by which Oliver means tribes whose origins were those of sedentary farmers, but who adopted a nomadic way of life as they pushed westward out onto the central plains. (Isn't the use of the word "true plains" tribes still reminiscent of earlier attitudes about who was a real or true plains resident?) Probably the most well-known of these are the Teton-Dakota or "Sioux" and perhaps the Cheyenne. In one century, these tribes shifted their lifestyle and came to resemble the purely hunting tribes and their political presence on the plains was indeed formidable, for as they acquired horses, their need for increased hunting territory threatened farmers and displaced smaller, weaker tribes. Many of these tribes underwent a radical cultural transition, giving up their clan structure, system of government and reckoning authority and permanently altered their economic activities.

Oliver's third category "Peripheral Farming Tribes" reflects his view of these groups as marginal to the plains area when, in fact, their presence on the plains certainly predates

172

the "true plains tribes" discussed above. These ancient horticulturalists, such as the Mandan, Hidatsa and Arikara as well as the Iowa, Oto and Missouria, were villagers with elaborate cultures, complex social structures (some even had classes of individuals), elected leaders and rich ceremonial activities (Holder 1970, Wedel 1986). For a thousand years prior to the coming of the white man, these native peoples of the plains were not "typical" nomads, but sedentary villagers who lived in semi-permanent villages. The extent to which hunting played a significant role in meeting their dietary requirements brings scholars into serious debate. These aboriginal farmers, whose earth lodge villages dotted the tributaries of the Missouri River, farmed the river bottoms and, while they did leave their villages to hunt, they returned to a fixed village where crops were tended, mostly by women, and harvests protected. Their staple crops were the famous triumvirate, corn, beans and squash, supplemented by melons, sunflower seeds, and pumpkins. In addition to farming, they gathered wild turnips, groundnuts, and berries like choke and buffalo, to supplement their otherwise inadequate diet of harvested vegetal foods. Archeological evidence points to their return to their villages year after year, so we know their occupation was continuous. Probably their food supply was dependable enough to permit them to become truly sedentary, and they developed sophisticated techniques of drying and storing their food. Alan Osborn, an archeologist with a more controversial view, questions whether sedentary villagers could have survived with such a heavy dependence on farming. Because of the climatological condition, he believes they were really "sedentary hunters" who hunted but came back to a fixed base. Osborn believes that these individuals depended primarily on meat and not plant resources due to the cost effectiveness of hunting (1980). Because of the limited number of frost-free days, especially in the north, it is likely that hunting activities were an essential "addition" (if not the staple food item) of these villagers' diets.

The ecological origins of tribes such as the Kiowa and Kiowa-Apache are less certain; still other tribes such as the Northern Shoshone and Kutenai are regarded as "peripheral (western) hunting and gathering tribes" (Oliver 1962:370).

Tribes of the Plains: Language and Culture

Who were the tribes that inhabited this vast region of North America? Using Oliver's scheme for convenience, we will group all the tribes by ecological adaptation and linguistic affiliation. We can drop the "true plains" characterization since it is not very meaningful, but for convenience, we will separate the groups into western (originally hunter-gatherers or farmers, but appearing at contact as nomadic tribes) and the more eastern sedentary villagers.

The nomadic or western plains tribes who roamed on foot following the bison left an archeological legacy providing us with clear indications of populations which, for thousands of years, followed traditional methods of hunting and gathering which enabled them to survive. Bison kill and butchering sites indicate where these tribes lived, the size of their groups, the number of animals obtained in a single hunt, butchering techniques, and seasonal information. These tribes as well as those who shifted from farming groups into nomadic plains hunters, and their neighbors on the northwest periphery of the plains are generally grouped into the following language families:

Nomadic or Western Plains Tribes

Language family	Tribe

Algonkian	Cheyenne
	    Northern
	    Southern
	Sutai
	Arapahoe
	Gros Ventres (Atsina)
	Blackfoot
	    N. Blackfoot
	    Piegan
	    Blood
	Plains Cree
	Plains Ojibwa

Siouan	"Sioux"
	    Teton
	    Santee
	    Yankton
	Assiniboine
	Crow

Athapaskan	Sarsi Kiowa-Apache

Uto-Aztecan	Shoshone
	    Wind River
	    Northern
	Comanche

Kiowan	Kiowa

All the tribes within one language family spoke related languages which were structurally similar to each other but were by no means mutually intelligible. Sub-tribes or bands within tribes, however, such as the Teton and Santee Sioux, spoke dialectical variations which were comprehensible to each other.

The farming tribes whose ancient roots in the plains were at least contemporaneous with, if not earlier than the pedestrian hunters, lived in villages along tributaries of the Missouri River and were members of either the Siouan or Caddoan language families:

Sedentary or Eastern Plains Tribes

Language Family	Tribe
Siouan	Mandan
	Hidatsa
	Iowa
	Otoe
	Missouria
	Kansa
	Winnebago
	Omaha
	Ponca
	Osage
	Quapaw
Caddoan	Arikara
	Pawnee
	Wichita
	Kitsai

Subsistence, Technology and Social Systems

Aboriginal tribes of the plains, as we have already suggested, fit into one of two different basic adaptations: either they were pedestrian or equestrian nomads and made their living through hunting and gathering, or they were primarily sedentary horticulturalists, making their living by farming fertile river bottoms adjacent to their villages, and supplementing their diet with hunted and gathered foods. We will take a closer look now at each pattern and provide detailed descriptions of samples of each. Following Oliver's model set forth earlier in this chapter, tribes will be considered according to their adaptations before and upon contact.

Aboriginal Hunters of the Plains

The pedestrian hunters of the plains who roamed on foot in search of bison include tribes such as the Algonkian Blackfoot and Plains Cree, the Shoshonean Comanche, the Athapaskan tribe known as the Sarsi, and the Siouan Assiniboine. What did these tribes have in common, and how, together, do they come to typify one kind of adaptation to the plains?

Certain characteristics appear in these hunting and gathering societies which helps us group them into a single "type". First, these tribes possessed a band type of social organization which, by definition, permitted them a kind of flexibility in size and structure. When resources were abundant, these bands might have several hundred individuals who camped together and hunted collectively. Their fluid, mobile structure permitted them to disband into smaller, autonomous groups so that when resources became scarce they might go their separate ways, and then perhaps reunite for the annual communal buffalo hunt at summer's end. The band was the only real social and economic unit. A group of related families might reside together, offering assistance to each other in hunting. No supra-family structures such as those found among farmers existed, for their livelihood required constant movement, and large kin-groups did not form. Politically, tribes were controlled by a headman or band leader whose authority was earned by his demonstration of superior hunting and leadership skills, the ability to organize people and make decisions his followers regarded favorably. He was not in any way a "chief" as we think of it. If he failed in his duties, he simply stopped doing them and was soon replaced by a more able leader. The tribal leader had little real authority, and governed his people more through his charismatic personality and personal influence. While political organization among nomadic peoples was generally weak, tribes such as the Blackfoot, Comanche and Sarsi did have military or medicine societies which unrelated men might join. Status was achieved for skill in hunting and warfare, and war honors were bestowed upon those who had skillfully accomplished such feats. Let us "zoom in" and take a close look at one such tribe—the Blackfoot.

The Blackfoot

Although the Blackfoot are considered a single tribe, in fact they are comprised of three autonomous bands, the Piegan (or Pikuni), the Northern Blackfoot proper (or Siksika) and the Blood. The band was the basic economic and social unit for the Blackfoot. The Blackfoot probably inhabited the Western Great Lakes region and entered the plains on foot, having been pushed out onto the plains from the east by other Algonkian groups whose populations were expanding (Ewers 1958). Before they acquired the horse around 1730, they hunted the buffalo on foot, driving the buffalo into a corral of upturned travois (Ewers 1958:11–12). This period of their prehistory is referred to as the "dog days" for they used the dog as a beast of burden to transport their belongings on a travois. Their adoption of the horse was rapid and complete, as they called the horse *ponokamita* or "big dog" and quickly assimilated it into their culture. They became one of the most famous equestrian tribes and transformed their culture as a result of this acquisition. As with other nomadic hunters, acquisition of the horse enabled them to over-harvest the buffalo, the excess of which was often traded for European goods (Ewers 1958). The horse totally revolutionized Blackfoot culture. Systems of ranking based on horse wealth emerged in this originally egalitarian society. Raiding for horses became a dominant activity, and aggressive, intertribal hostile acts generated an increase in warfare:

> "A horse raid directed against a tribe previously at peace with that of the raiders was recognized as a legitimate cause for retaliation in kind or in force against the aggressors' tribe . . . horse raiding in the intertribal warfare of the late 18th and early 19th century . . . suggests that the Indians' needs for horses to use in hunting buffalo and transporting food and domestic articles furnished a major motive for that early warfare" (Ewers 1955:174).

By making buffalo much easier to kill, the Blackfoot probably engaged in greater squandering of this vital resource, hastening the extermination of the buffalo and so contributing to the overall breakdown of the traditional culture (Ewers 1955).

Before the adoption of the horse, each Blackfoot band probably contained 20–30 families or up to 200 individuals (Oliver 1962), a group large enough to encircle the buffalo and defend themselves, but small enough to survive when resources became scarce. The Blackfoot share their ancient residence on the plains with the Arapahoe and Gros Ventres (Atsina), who became politically allied with them during the historic period. The territory inhabited by the Blackfoot at contact, in north and western Montana, is the same they inhabit today, just east of the Rockies and bordering Canada. Their aboriginal dependence on the buffalo was complete: they depended on it for food, clothing, shelter and ornamentation. Following the migratory buffalo herds, bands set up encampments, sometimes for the duration of the winter (Ewers 1958). Meat was dried and jerked and made into pemmican, a food which could be stored and transported easily. Other food resources on which the Blackfoot depended included roots and berries, harvested in the fall and early summer.

The Blackfoot, as did most band level peoples, lived in nuclear-extended families, a group which had to be a self-sufficient economic unit. Descent was usually bilateral (traced through both mother's and father's sides) or ambilateral (traced through either side), and because the preference was to marry outside of one's own band, a woman generally joined her husband's band upon marriage.

Unlike other smaller hunting and gathering societies, the Blackfoot had a rather elaborate set of seven age-graded men's organizations known collectively as the All-Comrades to which individuals could belong (Oliver 1962). These included the warrior societies of the Mosquitos, Pigeons, Braves, Buffalo Bulls and All Crazy Dogs, religious societies and the less formal dance societies. These societies also known as sodalities, were comprised of members of different bands and really only functioned when the whole tribe came together, such as for the annual buffalo hunt and Sun Dance (Oliver 1962:21). Religious societies were primarily responsible for healing and curing. Religious activities, as with most nomadic peoples, tended not to be elaborate. Religious worship was largely an individual matter, and men sought guardian spirit helpers by seeking a supernatural vision. Fasting alone on a hill, men received dreams in which an animal, bird or power of nature appeared to him. The spirit instructed an individual in special songs or prayers he might call upon, and also showed him how to prepare and use special sacred objects. These objects could be manipulated to afford protection and success in ventures undertaken (Ewers 1958:163). Following supernatural instruction, the individual would fashion a medicine bundle which afforded him supernatural aid and protection in both hunting and warfare throughout his life.

The adoption of the Sun Dance by the Blackfoot did not occur until the historic period. They probably learned it from the Arapahoes or their allies the Gros Ventres (Ewers 1958:174). As with other plains tribes, it has become the singlemost important modern ritual and serves both as an expression of individual prayer and commitment as well as a revitalization of modern Indian identity.

Hunters with Farming Origins

Tribes which had once had farming origins but changed their way of life upon their arrival on the plains are exemplified by such well-known Algonkian groups as the Cheyenne, Arapahoe, and Gros Ventres, and the Siouan Teton-Dakota (Sioux) and Crow. These tribes had far more elaborate social structures and religions because of their legacy of once having been settled, farming villagers. While they may have shifted their lifestyle once they came out onto the plains in pursuit of bison, their social complexity often was retained. Coming predominantly from the northeast, these tribes had all the characteristic features of sedentary farmers. Although they appeared as band-level societies during the early historic period, a closer look shows their recent clan groupings and the more complex social structure emanating from it. The transition from farmer to hunter was indeed rapid: the Cheyenne, living in earth lodges in the early 1700's, had acquired the horse by 1760, and although some Cheyenne villages still clung to horticultural life until after 1790, they had undergone a dramatic change to the "typical plains nomad" by 1830, only a century later (Ewers 1955). The Siouan Crow had ceased being farmers but retained their thirteen matrilineal exogamous clans. They have a special reason for not abandoning their clans when they came out onto the plains—namely, their continued association with their relatives the Hidatsa, from whom they had split earlier. Most of these tribes, unlike the "pure hunters" we just discussed, reflected descent and residence groupings reminiscent of a sedentary people—namely, possessing a tendency toward unilineal descent systems and unilocal, as opposed to bilocal (or multilocal) patterns of post-marital residence. Band leaders were informally chosen as with the pure hunting tribes in most cases, but the Cheyenne, for example, had a formally selected group of leaders representing each of their 10 bands. Leaders' status was in fact partly hereditary or "ascribed" and they sat on a council of chiefs who determined policy. Like the aboriginal hunters of the plains, these cultures supported large numbers of men's societies whose functions were both military and religious. Discipline at the annual communal fall hunt was enforced by groups of "police" who saw to it that no infractions of regulations occurred. Status was achieved largely through war exploits, and as the horse became incorporated into the fabric of life, one's skill in hunting and warfare necessarily had to include excellent horsemanship.

The Lakota (Sioux)

The largest of these aboriginally-farming-turned hunting tribes was the Teton-Dakota or Sioux whose western divisions had begun to wander out onto the plains from their Minnesota homeland in pursuit of the buffalo by 1660 and across the Missouri River by 1750. A decade later they had acquired horses, and began revolutionary change in their way of life. Coming from the eastern woodlands, this large group came out onto the plains as a "nation" or political grouping called the Seven Council Fires, consisting of three separate sub-tribes or divisions: the western or Teton Sioux groups whose dialect was Lakota, the eastern or Santee division who spoke Dakota, and the northern or Yankton division who spoke either the Nakota or Dakota dialects. Termed "Nadoweisiw-eg" by their enemies the Chippewa (meaning "lesser adders"), this powerful tribe underwent a dramatic social and cultural transformation. Clan structure and elected chieftainships gave way to band groupings consisting of *"tiyospaye"* or communities of bilateral extended families. Any trace of unilineal descent disappeared as they underwent a shift to the bilaterality common to nomadic hunters. The chiefs of earlier days lost their influence and skilled warriors now enjoyed leadership roles. As early as 1730, Sioux chiefs had been divested of their authority and were now merely heads of kin groups (Oliver 1962).

Political Structure of the Sioux Nation

Seven Council Fires		
Western/Teton Lakota	Eastern/Santee Dakota	Northern/Yankton Nakota
(1)	(2, 3, 4, 5)	(6, 7,)
Oglala	Sisseton	Yankton
Sicangu (Brule)	Mdewakanton	Yanktonai
Miniconjou	Wahpeton	
Itazipčo (Sans Arcs)	Wakpekute	
O'ohenonpa (Two Kettles)		
Sihasapa (Blackfeet)		
Hunkpapa		

As with the Blackfoot, horses totally revolutionized the Lakota way of life (Grobsmith 1981). They were transformed from a loose aggregate of small bands to "an organized and powerful society" (1981:9). Like the Blackfoot, the horse, *šunka wakan* ("big dog") replaced the dog as the beast of burden, gave them greater mobility to cover much more territory, enhancing the depletion of the very resources on which they were so dependent. This left them especially vulnerable during the late trade period, when, lacking a viable economy, they suffered military defeat and, as so many contemporary plains artists depict, became the vision of the defeated "warrior without weapons" (Macgregor 1946).

The way of life of the Lakota, like the Blackfoot, was largely dependent on buffalo and so was quite nomadic. The location of their settlements was determined by the location of the herds (Hassrick 1964). Winter camps were generally chosen which offered stable supplies of wood and water, as well as good grazing for horses, and security from the winter elements and enemies. Women gathered and dried meat to offset the difficulties of winter. To insure themselves a winter's supply of food, a communal hunt or buffalo drive was arranged. This group activity, "formalized by religious and political jurisdiction", was "by far the most spectacular and . . . most efficient method of securing game in quantity" (Hassrick 1964:198). The surround or running buffalo over the edge of a cliff were effective ways to procure great quantities of meat. Claiming the kills bearing his arrows, each hunter retrieved, butchered and distributed his meat. Conflicts over rightful ownership might be settled by the Akičita, the policing society which governed the rules of the hunt. Animals with tendencies to herd, like antelope, were also hunted in collective drives.

The dependence on the buffalo was so complete that nearly every part of the animal was used in daily life: the hide for tipi covers and robes, the stomach or paunch as a cooking container used for stone-boiling the meat, the sinew for thread and rope, the skull as an altar of worship. Deer meat was also greatly desired, as were the hides for clothing. Men hunted individually and in family groups, or communally. All manner of game were sought—antelope, bears, small fur-bearing animals, badgers, wolves, coyotes, skunks and muskrats, raccoons, prairies chickens and birds. Eggs, turtles and tortoises as well as fish were important additions to the diet. Gathered tubers such as *timpsila* or wild turnips, buffalo and gooseberries, choke cherries, wild onions, teas and medicinal plants were readily harvested and supplemented a diet of boiled or dried and jerked meat, and pemmican, which the Lakota termed *wasna,* was taken along on the hunt and used for ceremonial purposes.

Hunted and gathered resources were shared, recognizing that those whose efforts had not been rewarded would receive their share and be expected to reciprocate at another time. This value of sharing was imperative to survival on the plains, and was embraced as one of the four Lakota virtues: bravery, generosity fortitude and fidelity.

Religious development was more elaborate for this large "nation" of tribes than for the Blackfoot. Their religious expression centered largely on the Sacred Pipe brought to them in a sacred legend by a figure in their cosmology known as the White Buffalo Calf Pipe Woman. Seven Sacred Rites were given to the people by this powerful woman: the *Inipi* or Sweatlodge, the *Hunka* ceremony or Making of Relatives, *Hanblečeya* or Vision Quest, a Girls' Puberty Ritual called *Išnati alowanpi,* the Throwing of the Ball or *Tapa wankayeyapi,* the Keeping of the Ghost ceremony, *Wakičagapi,* and the Sun Dance, *Wiwanyang wačipi,* the most important of all Lakota rituals. While the Sweatlodge was the oldest and most basic purification ritual, the Sun Dance was the largest and most impressive. After the annual communal buffalo hunt, all of the tribes would gather for a single Sun Dance, each taking their special place in the great camp circle. A more in-depth discussion of the Sun Dance follows later in the chapter under the heading "Belief Systems".

Farmers with Farming Origins

Arikara and Mandan

The third and last type of ecological adaptation on the plains is represented by village farmers, Siouan and Caddoan tribes such as the Mandan and Arikara (respectively) who share a deeply-rooted prehistory as aboriginal horticulturalists, (or "sedentery hunters", as the case may be), originating perhaps as long ago as fifteen hundred years (Holder 1970:24). Living in relatively permanent consolidated villages, these diverse groups farmed the fertile river bottoms of tributaries of the Missouri River. "The general impression from archeological remains is that ancestral Arikara populations were widespread and dominant along the reaches of the Missouri River in late prehistoric and protohistoric times, and the same can be said for the Pawnees, Wichitas, and Caddos to the south (Holder 1970:30). Villages sprang up where a supply of arable land and wood fostered a stable, secure existence. Men were primarily hunters and warriors and sought bison, elk, deer and smaller mammals to supplement the diet. Men also provided protection of the communities, while women were charged with the production of staple vegetable foods, as well as processing skins and furs from which they made clothing (Holder 1970). Gardens were prepared by felling trees which, when burned, enriched the soil for planting. Bottomlands afforded crops protection from hot, dessicating winds during the summer and early killing frosts in the fall. Maize, adapted to the short growing season, was the primary staple crop and was supplemented with sunflowers, squash, beans and tobacco (Spencer and Jennings 1977). Fish were trapped with the aid of willow weirs set into the river (Spencer and Jennings 1977).

Because women owned the garden plots, they were in charge of the distribution of their harvests to the families in their households. As with most sedentary farmers, descent was traced unilineally (through one side) and in Arikara society, as with Mandan and Hidatsa traditions, inheritance was matrilineal, or through the female line. Residence after marriage was similarly matrilocal. "This matrilineal extended family was the functioning economic unit, as the women of the household cooperated in working the cultivated fields and the men hunted together" (Spencer and Jennings 1977:323). Several nuclear families related through women shared an earth lodge which could hold as many as 40 people.

Unlike the nomadic tribes, sedentary villagers possessed far more elaborate social and ceremonial organizations. Rather than achieving high status only through war deeds, prestige was afforded relative to one's "class", whether "nobles" or "commoners" (Holder 1970). Village leaders were not merely capable headmen, but actually inherited chiefly status. "High rank had to be validated by lavish giving and personal achievement, but members of the truly hereditary leading families seem not to have lost status completely even in the absence of validation . . . (however) the most lavish gift giving and striking personal exploits seem *not* (emphasis mine) to have allowed a commoner family to rise to the position of hereditary leader family" (Holder 1970:37). Age-graded societies and ranked social clubs united non-relatives for dancing, curing or hunting.

Figure 6.3 The Slant Village Site near Bismarck, North Dakota, is an earth lodge village based on archaeologists' reconstructions. (Courtesy of Elizabeth Grobsmith.)

The basic unit of village life was the extended family, consisting of approximately 20 people who shared an earth lodge. Both Mandan and Arikara societies traced descent matrilineally and were grouped into matrilineal exogamous clans, a sharp contrast to the bilateral nomads of the plains. A sharp division of labor in which men hunted and provided military protection to the household and women performed gardening tasks, assigned the care of the young to grandparents, who were largely responsible for bringing up the children. Women also cared for the lodge, processed the meat, skins and furs, the manufactured clothing, baskets and pottery as well (Holder 1970). Being largely responsible for day-to-day survival, women enjoyed important and influential roles.

This reverence for women's contribution is clearly reflected in Arikara (and Mandan) ceremonial life. Sacred bundles were called ''Mother'', and symbolized the emphasis on fertility and crop productivity. Ritual activity revolved largely around ownership of ''bundles'', small envelopes containing symbols to be used in religious worship. Bundles were owned by specific individuals (men) who cared for and guarded them, and handed them down to their lineal descendants. The entire village's welfare was affected by the power of the bundle: villagers believed that ''the loss or 'death' of the bundle would mean the death of the people'' (Holder 1970:46). In contrast to the Arikara, the Mandan practiced an elaborate communal ritual which perhaps foreshadowed the Sun Dance of the nomadic tribes. The Okipa Ceremony was an annual ritual of sacrifice and entailed the physical torture and piercing of men's chests in a ritual enactment of their cosmology.

Changes in Aboriginal Subsistence

Trade and Its Impact on the Plains

Because of the nature of diversity among the plains tribes, a natural pattern of trade emerged and was well-established long before the coming of Europeans or their technology. Prior to the time of Lewis and Clark a system of aboriginal trade had been in place which provided a ready mechanism for the dissemination of items of European manufacture. This early trade period was a system of barter between nomadic and sedentary tribes (Ewers 1968). This "direct exchange between producer and consumer" involved primarily perishable goods, such as food and skins (Ewers 1968:21). Nomadic tribes traded proficiently dressed buffalo and deer skins, lodge covers and clothing such as skin shirts, leggings and moccasins for items of produce such as corn and pumpkins as well as the much desired tobacco plant. Tribes like the Crow, who had split earlier from their relatives, the sedentary Hidatsa, still had a taste for corn, and enjoyed this trade relationship. Intertribal trade also included items that did not even come from that vicinity—for example, Pacific dentalium shell, desired for clothing ornamentation, steatite (soapstone) for carving from Montana, Yellowstone obsidian, shells from the Gulf Coast and Great Lakes copper, all reflecting tremendous borrowing and trading throughout the continent. The trade of perishable items reinforced the separation between nomad and villager by intensifying the way of life each led (Ewers 1968).

Two primary aboriginal trade centers had been well-established by the time French fur traders noted them in their journals and diaries. To the north, in the southern part of what is now North Dakota, were located the Mandan villages on the Knife River. To this center came the more northerly tribes—the Assiniboine, Plains Cree, and Crow as well as the Cheyenne, Arapahoe, Kiowa and Kiowa-Apache from the south (Ewers 1968:17). The other major center was that of the Arikara, whose villages were just north of the mouth of the Grand River in what is now South Dakota. To this center came the Cheyenne, Arapahoe, Kiowa, Kiowa-Apache and Comanche (although they also frequented the Mandan center). The western or Teton bands of Sioux such as the Oglala, Brule and Miniconjou also came here (Ewers 1968:17).

During the early 1700's, seventy years before Lewis and Clark's voyage up the Missouri River to the Pacific, French fur traders began to visit the Upper Missouri tribes in search of trading partners. Pierre La Verendrye, a French fur trader, learned from the Assiniboine near Lake Winnipeg of Indians living in villages from whom that tribe obtained its corn. In 1738, he and an Assiniboine trading party observed six large fortified earth lodge villages belonging to the Mandan. They observed that an ongoing system of in-

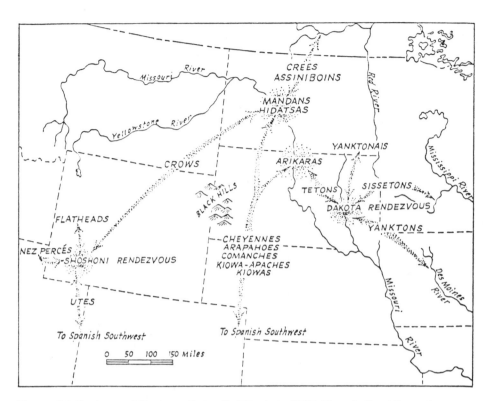

Figure 6.4 Routes and Centers of Intertribal Trade in 1805. From *Indian Life on the Upper Missouri*, by John C. Ewers. Copyright © 1968 by the University of Oklahoma Press.

digenous trade was well in place, where products of the chase were being exchanged for products of cultivation. Grains, beans and corn were traded for skins that had been beautifully quilled or painted. La Verendrye noted something else—that the Mandan already had guns which they had obtained from their neighbors to the North, the Assiniboine. Not only did they have guns, but they already owned and were trading horses. Although they kept relatively few horses for themselves, they kept them for trading (Ewers 1968).

The Algonkian and Siouan tribes, once formerly sedentary, were being pushed south and west by better-armed tribes to the north and east. This unique set of historic circumstances caused the convergence on the plains of two items of foreign technology which forever changed the pattern of existence among aboriginal Americans. One was the gun, and the other the horse and they became equivalent in value. The early gun was inefficient and so its acceptance was neither rapid nor immediate.

During Coronado's 1540 exploration of the Southwest, horses, owned by the Spaniards, were cared for by native tribes, particularly the Pueblos (Haines 1938). There is considerable controversy over the diffusion of horses from the southwest to the plains, but one thing is clear: horses were traded (and probably smuggled, stolen and bred) to plains tribes who were being pushed out of their homelands by northeast tribes whose early acquisition of the European gun enabled them to displace residents of desired hunting territory. Two routes are generally recognized as the main ones through which the horse spread—"the more direct and probably the older route was through Arapahoe, Cheyenne, Kiowa, Kiowa-Apache and Comanche nomadic intermediaries via the western high plains. The other route was through the Shoshonean tribes west of the Rockies and the Flatheads

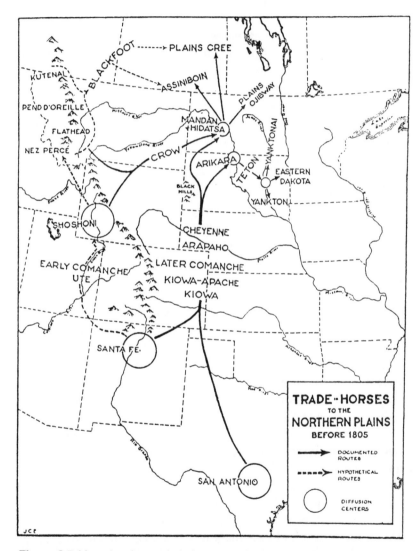

Figure 6.5 Map showing trade in horses to the northern plains before 1805. By permission of the Smithsonian Institution Press. From "The Horse in Blackfoot Indian Culture, with Comparative Material from Other Western Tribes," by John C. Ewers, *Bulletin of American Ethnology* No. 159. Smithsonian Institution, Washington, D.C., 1955.

and Nez Perce . . . and thence through the Crows who obtained horses at the Shoshone rendezvous'' (Ewers 1968:25). While the sedentary tribes did not adopt the horse wholeheartedly and abandon their village way of life, they kept horses for trading. ''There is no indication that the Mandans, Hidatsas or Arikaras were rich in horses at any time in buffalo days'' (Ewers 1968:27).

The phase of trading characterized by the exchange of items of European manufacture, in the absence of direct intensive trading with whites, is referred to as the ''protohistoric'' trade period—just before contact (Ewers 1968:23). Native trade routes opened up the plains for exchange of items of European manufacture which came to replace those of native manufacture. Although the horse and gun were the two most important items, demand grew for such items as axes, knives, firesteels, kettles, awles, mules, riding gear, gunpowder, bullets, brass and iron tools and decorative items—all manner of weapons and tools were traded, as well as household utensils, articles of clothing and adornment, buttons and trade cloth. The focus of trade had grown considerably away from the perishable goods characteristic of the aboriginal trade period. Now the pressure was to obtain imperishable items.

Fur traders, although present during this period, were more or less observers of intertribal trade, even though the items exchanged were European. They did, however, point out the valuable potential of furs as well as suggesting good sites for trading posts which might establish direct trade networks with the older centers on the Upper Missouri. By 1830, new trading posts were springing up—Fort Union, at the mouth of the Yellowstone River, and Fort Piegan, at the mouth of the Marias River, to serve the trade interests of the Crow and Blackfoot respectively.

The union of the horse and the gun had tremendous implications for native habitation on the plains: combined on the hunt, a hunter could kill far more animals and drive them greater distances; he could cover a much wider range of territory and threaten the hunting and territorial boundaries of other tribes with whom he had formerly not come into conflict; and of course a group lacking guns and horses were at a far greater disadvantage than one that possessed them. Mounted tribes south and west of the Missouri began to have an increasing demand for guns to maintain the control over the new territory they had acquired.

The flourishing trade network began to take on a different dimension when fur traders began to be true participants—rather than mere observers—of trade. While their role in the early 1730's was that of interested bystander, and while their dependence on native peoples ingratiated them to their hosts, the ''historic'' trade period saw a turn to the fur trader and not the Indian as producer of trade goods. Two patterns of trade characterized this period: the western or Rocky Mountain trade pattern, and the Upper Missouri system. To the west, fur trappers sought skins and pelts such as beaver, muskrat, ermine, otter, fox and mink to satisfy the tastes of Europeans and easterners in the United States. Western plains tribes, rather than becoming the producers of these furs, played a passive role in permitting (or not permitting) trappers from entering their region to obtain pelts. On the Upper Missouri, on the other hand, buffalo robes and small furs were in the greatest demand. In this pattern of trade, Indian people were directly involved as producers and obtained, traded and sold furs

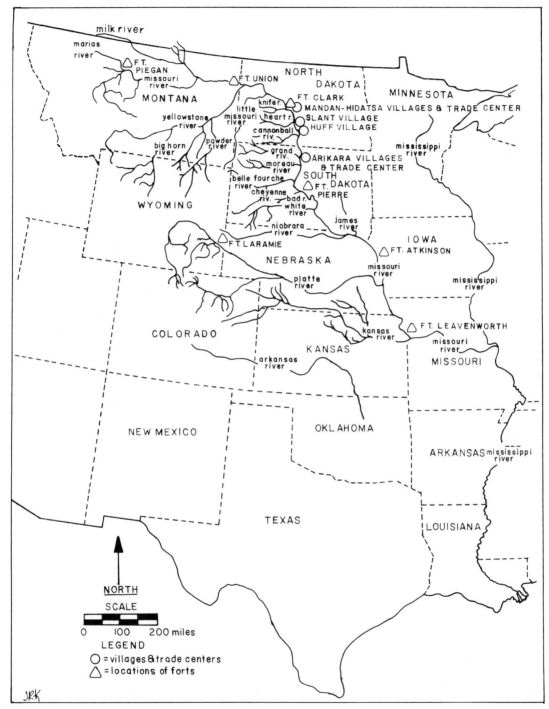

Figure 6.6 Location of fur trade posts on the Upper Missouri. (Courtesy of Elizabeth Grobsmith).

187

to traders who were in business for particular trading companies. Subsistence items were not considered important trade items any longer—rather, money was needed to obtain other trade goods. The Upper Missouri system was far more stable and secure than the Rocky Mountain trade due to the dependability of steamboat transport down to St. Louis and on to eastern cities like New York—and across the Atlantic. Fur trading was a thriving business. Fur companies entered into bitter rivalry and competition to control the centers and traders offered better prices to keep their place. The American Fur Company came to monopolize fur trading on the river. The posts, which were ever-expanding, were oases for whites, providing little centers of "civilization" with gardens, tailors, gunsmiths, blacksmiths, gardens and even boatyards. Many were stockaded with bastions to withstand war parties. These posts also became the target for military occupation as skirmishes between frontiersmen and Indians increased following the 1849 gold rush.

Fur trading was a thriving business until its collapse in the 1870's. But the decline in the market for furs was inevitable, and in its wake came the demise of a century of aboriginal existence. Fur traders believed themselves to be benefactors and bringers of civilization to the Indian. Despite the government's efforts to legally control liquor trafficking, fur traders plied Indians with whiskey and fostered a dependence on alcohol that still plagues these tribes today. The trading posts were devastated by smallpox—one outbreak in 1738 and a major one at Fort Clark, the Mandan center in 1837—which spread throughout Indian communities, particularly sedentary villages where population concentration was higher. Fort Union was abandoned in 1867; others sold out to the government. White hunters roamed the plains slaughtering remaining buffalo herds which, by 1884, had nearly been destroyed. With the virtual annihilation of the bison herds, the fur trade ceased to be an important and vital industry. But its impact on the native tribes was permanent. Indian populations were decimated by disease, their cultures and social systems in shambles from the devastating population loss. Their native style of subsistence—hunting and gathering or farming—was gone, with nothing to take its place. The economy on which they depended for hundreds or even thousands of years was defunct, wild resources had been trapped or hunted out, they suffered high rates of alcohol addiction, and many had been displaced. Diseases to which they had no resistance—measles, influenza as well as smallpox—had decimated them.

The Reservation Period

The incursion of whites into the plains in the mid 1850's had forced the United States Congress to create a policy for handling the "Indian problem". A century of vacillation in policy concerning "what to do with the Indians" began—from exterminating them, or hoping they would go away, to assimilating them.

As with other areas of the country, reservations were created in the plains between 1850 and 1871, by any one of three different means: by an Executive Order, by Congressional Proclamation or as a result of a treaty. Because of the loss of subsistence, government agents distributed rations and, hoping to effect the assimilation of native tribesmen, offered agricultural instruction and technological assistance. Teachers and missionaries also flocked to the reservations and, by the late 1870's, were vying for control over the newly-established schools. This period of forced assimilation culminated in the passage of the Dawes Allotment or Severalty Act of 1887, a piece of legislation so devastating that it dealt the final blow to tribal integrity. Under this law, newly-created reservations were divided into allotments of generally 160 acres per family or 80 acres per individual. The government believed that by forcing individuals to assume responsibility for their own land, they would adopt the American ethic of "rugged individualism" and would better assimilate into the mainstream. While in some areas like the southwest, people accepted allotments on paper but never physically divided up tribal land, in the plains, allotments were issued and tribes had to accept them. Each allotment was to be protected for a period of 25 years by the government's retaining the title until the individual had proven himself worthy of receiving it. Then, Indians who had earned the respect of agents received their allotments "in fee simple" (meaning they received the title to the land), and sometimes even received U.S. citizenship. Once the individuals received title to their allotment, they were expected to pay the taxes on it! Many could not, and a period began in which individuals "sold out", leaving the reservation vulnerable to sale to non-Indians. The consequence of this was called "checkerboarding" and it reflected the mixed ownership of Indian land. It was not a coincidence that the government regained an enormous portion of allotted reservation land. Throughout the United States, 91,000,000 acres of reservation land was declared "surplus" and was consequently opened up for sale to non-Indians. The consequences of this act were and are devastating to native people, and although the 1934 Indian Reorganization Act ended further allotment forever, the damage this act caused has permanently impacted native tribes. Native systems of inheritance had been undermined; individuals who died "intestate" (without a will) had their land taken over by the state and disposed of; individuals who had family herds or hunted and farmed collectively had to split up their lands and livelihoods; and worst of all, tribal autonomy was destroyed. It is no wonder that this last century of Indian policy has become notorious as the "century of dishonor" (Jackson 1881).

Politically, the plains was in turmoil in the last half of the 19th century. The establishment of reservations (and their subsequent allotment), the influx of missionaries, the policy of compulsory education, and finally military defeat resulted in the total upheaval of a native way of life, and an end to tribal domination of the plains.

In 1889, word spread throughout the plains about a new Messiah named Wovoka, whose vision it was that the injustice suffered by tribes would be punished by the disappearance of whites from the earth, the regeneration of Indians' ancestors, return of the buffalo, and restoration of the supremacy of the aboriginal race. By performing a special dance called the Ghost Dance and singing special songs, the miracle would be achieved. The regeneration was anticipated durig the spring of 1890 The regeneration was anticipated during the spring of 1890. News of this new faith spread throughout the plains and there was great excitement, particularly among Sioux tribes. Although the Ghost Dance did not uniformly depend on visions obtained in a trance state, and although its performance was not violent, U.S. military response to the dance was one of alarm. Troops were called in to exert control over the tribes. A band of Sioux under Big Foot's leadership were returning from the Badlands and were camped at Wounded Knee Creek on the Pine Ridge Reservation. Major Whitside of the 7th Calvary demanded the unconditional surrender of the tribes and had set up 4 Hotchkiss guns in preparation for trouble. The Indians were ordered to surrender; a military search for guns in the Indians' tipis resulted in a skirmish between a soldier and an Indian—a handful of dust being thrown into the air and precipitating rifle fire—and a hand-to-hand struggle ensued, quickly escalating to the use of revolvers, knives and warclubs. The troops opened fire, pouring explosive shells into the camp, mowing down everything alive. During the panic, survivors flew in panic to the shelter of the ravine, and the Hotchkiss guns opened fire on those fleeing, massacring not only Indian men, but women and children as well. Promises that the Ghost shirts worn by men were impervious to the white man's bullets were destroyed, as over 300—perhaps as many as 370—lay dead and dying. Bodies lay strewn and frozen as, days later, they were gathered for burial in a mass grave (Mooney 1973). Today, the memorial at Wounded Knee stands as a bitter memory of the massacre of native peoples by the U.S. government and—as we shall see—continues to serve as a symbol of the native struggle for survival among modern plains tribes. The so-called "Battle of Wounded Knee", the massacre of hundreds of innocent men, women and children, dealt the final blow to plains societies, and has left a legacy of poverty, unemployment and paternalistic government structures empowered to resolve the problems.

Belief Systems

People of the plains resemble all other Native North Americans in several basic but important ways. One fundamental belief which underlay all ritual activity was the adoption of a guardian spirit, usually an animal, whose images appeared to an individual during a solitary vision-seeking encounter, or in a dream or prayer. These guardian spirits empowered the dreamer with special songs, prayers and symbols the individual could draw upon in a time of crisis or great need, and would afford protection from evil or death. The emphasis on spirit helpers was an important part of vision-seeking, a ritual widespread among nomadic plains tribes, in which a person ventured out alone on a hill and, through fasting and prayer, received supernatural instruction about guardian spirit helpers. The importance of vision seeking or "migration" (transcendence) into the spirit world was so great that "the everyday world was often subordinated to and shaped by the vision experience" (Harrod 1987:25). Visions could be obtained either in a dream state or in a waking-vision, and could be transferred ritually to others. It was greatly desirable to obtain a vision, and vision-seeking was widely practiced throughout the plains by Crow, Blackfoot, Arapahoe, Gros Ventres, Sioux and Cheyenne, among others. Women as well as men sought visions; neither were these activities confined to higher ranked segments of society.

Figure 6.7 The Mass Grave at Wounded Knee stands as a bitter reminder of the U.S. government's slaughter of hundreds of Sioux in the Wounded Knee Massacre. (Courtesy of Elizabeth Grobsmith.)

Visions formed the underpinnings for the interpretation of supernatural beliefs and cosmology, and great symbolic weight was assigned to the interpretations of these visions. Medicine men or shamans assisted in their interpretation, assigning premonitions and explanations abut the universe and its order to the tribe. Harrod (1987) tells how beliefs and their interpretation provided critical understanding of the paradoxes which occurred in daily life, and assisted in their resolution. Stories and legends which form the basis for ritual, provided the mechanism by which plains peoples resolved their ambivalent relationship with animals which they revered but had to kill for their own sustenance, with human frailty, and with death.

The emphasis on individuality and the individual's interpretations of supernatural signs was another characteristic feature of plains ideology. Medicine men were not only interpreters of the supernatural, but healers and curers as well. Their own spirit helpers assisting them, they were sought to provide spiritual guidance, protection in war, relief from economic and social stress, doctoring, and even location of lost objects or individuals. Among the Lakota, the *yuwipi* ('to wrap him up') was—and still is—an important ceremony whose purpose was to recover lost objects, effect a cure, or insure a particular outcome to an event. Today, it would not be uncommon for a family to sponsor a *yuwipi* meeting as a prayer for someone's recovery from alcoholism.

Although medicine men were not full-time specialists and so had to provide their own livelihood, gifts for services rendered helped to support both a practitioner's family as well as his status as religious leader in the community, and reinforced the value of reciprocity and sharing.

The Sun Dance

The cosmology of plains tribes reflects their adaptation to this challenging, mysteriously beautiful, and vast terrain. One of the most widespread and significant rituals on the plains is the Sun Dance, exhibiting considerable variability between tribes. It was practiced by nearly all of the nomadic tribes. While farming tribes had similar rituals (such as the Mandan Okipa), they did not formally practice this annual rite. For all the nomadic peoples, however, it occurred at summer's end at the time the tribes had gathered for the annual communal buffalo hunt.

Sun Dancing brought together and embodied many of the plains values: individuality, vision-seeking and use of supernatural spirit helpers, sacrifice, and recognition of bravery and fortitude, values essential to survival in the harsh plains environment. It is difficult to pinpoint the exact time of the Sun Dance's origins on the plains, however, it is believed that the complex was not fully developed until the horse forever altered plains subsistence, for it was the rich subsistence from buffalo hunting that permitted large aggregates of people to form for summer communal ceremonial activities (Liberty 1980). It wasn't much more than a century following its fluorescence that the Sun Dance became outlawed by the U.S. federal government, and for many tribes, the ritual either went underground or became fully extinct. Its recent revival has been part of a conscious attempt on the part of plains peoples to revitalize their indigenous rituals in hopes of returning to a healthier and stronger cultural position than they have enjoyed since they were forced onto reservations. As we have noted, for the Lakota, arrival onto the plains was marked by the bestowing on the people of the Sacred Pipe by the White Buffalo Calf Woman who brought with her ritual knowledge and instructions. Her gift of the Seven Sacred Rites became the foundation and structure of Lakota belief and practice. Of the Seven Sacred Rites, the Sun Dance became the most spectacular ritual, a ceremony in which all aspects of their cosmology were interwoven. *Wakan Tanka*, The Great Spirit, sometimes equated with the Judeo-Christian concept of God, was the head of a pantheon of sixteen gods, each of whom represented an important force of nature. Earth, Sky, Wind and Sun were all part of the Creator, and were revered in prayer, ritual offerings and sacrifice. The number four was especially sacred, representing the quartering of the sacred hoop of the universe into the four cardinal directions, the pantheon of gods (four multiples of four), and even the four "hills" or stages of life—infancy, childhood, adulthood and old age.

The purpose and focus of the Sun Dance varied from tribe to tribe: for some it was an earth-renewal ceremony; for others, a dance of vengeance for death, and for yet others, a prayer for fertility (Liberty 1980). For the Sioux, the Sun Dance was the enactment of a bond between the individual and the universe; its performance brought benefits to the individual as well as unification to the nation (Hassrick 1964). Early documentation of the Sun Dance reflected the perception of this ceremony as a dramatization of the capture, torture and release of the enemy (Walker 1917). Every aspect of the ritual, from the felling of the sacred pole to the piercing of men's chests, was said to be symbolic of this dramatic enactment. Today, few Lakota draw upon these early symbolic meanings. Originally the Sun Dance lasted for twelve days: the first four were devoted to general preparation of the campsite; the second four were spent giving instruction to the candidate; and the last four were the "Holy Days" in which the dancing proper occurred (Hassrick 1964). Today, the ceremony is a four-day ritual, with extra preparation time preceding the four day ceremony.

Regardless of the number of days, every Sun Dance is preceded by two things: the offering of a Sacred Pipe to one's spiritual mentor or medicine man, the acceptance of which symbolizes the beginnings of an important relationship between the two in which the candidate receives religious and moral instruction; and vision-seeking, normally done prior to the actual Sun Dance. An individual who has decided to participate in the Sun Dance generally does so in fulfillment of a vow he has made with the Great Spirit. Vows may be prayers of well-being for friends or relatives, sacrifices in hopes of achieving a cure for someone's illness, a prayer for the safe return of a soldier, or a general sacrifice for the well-being of the Lakota people. When these early requirements have been fulfilled, the Sun Dancers begin the preparation of the site, and go in search of the sacred tree to be placed in the center of the arbor. The tree must be a tall, straight cottonwood, the leaves of which represent the heart and pulse of human life, and it is ritually felled and carried back to the site. Its placement is accompanied by special songs and prayers and the lowering of ritual items such as buffalo fat, *wasna* (pemmican), a ceremonial food, or tobacco into the hole. Special items which have been prepared are placed in the tree before it is raised—a nest of sixteen chokecherry sticks or branches to symbolize the eagle's nest; a rawhide effigy of a man on a horse, a picket pin for securing a captured horse, a rawhide buffalo which symbolizes the essence of life and survival, and cloth banners of red, black, white and yellow, the colors of the four cardinal directions. The decorated tree, fastened with the ropes each Sun Dancer will use to attach himself to the sacred pole, is hoisted into the hole by the dancers.

The Sun Dance was performed in one of four ways: gazing at the sun while being pierced on the front or back; gazing at the sun while staked to four posts; gazing at the sun while suspended; and dragging the buffalo skull. Today, Sun Dancers pierce both on their chests or backs, on one side or two, and may drag four or five buffalo skulls until they tear free; gazing at the sun while staked is not practiced any more, and the form in which the individual is suspended is rarely practiced. Because of the tremendous variability in medicine man style, some Sun Dances have the dancers all pierce on the same day, usually the fourth. Other medicine men instruct the dancers to pierce on the day which is symbolically appropriate for them: piercing on the first day represents a sacrifice for the Sacred Pipe, the

Figure 6.8 The sacred Sun Dance tree at Pine Ridge, 1972, fully decorated, at dawn. (Courtesy of Elizabeth Grobsmith.)

way of the people; piercing on the second day is for a memorial; the third day is reserved for prayers of healing; and the fourth is for the warrior (Laravie 1987, personal communication). While most individuals make a commitment to Sun Dance for four consecutive years, the sequence of participation is up to the individual and his vow.

Although the nomadic tribes and their annual calendrical activities largely revolved around the summer Sun Dance and buffalo hunt, these beliefs and practices were not held by the sedentary villagers. Siouan tribes like the Mandan, Hidatsa, Oto, Omaha and Winnebago had clan and sometimes moiety structures where responsibility for ceremonial activities was placed in the hands of clan chiefs. Summer and Winter moieties, divisions of tribes representing one-half the society, assigned specific rituals regarding warfare, the hunt or the harvest to the specific clan in charge of those affairs. Secret societies were common. But because these societies were smaller and their populations more adversely affected by disease brought about by contact, their religious were more vulnerable and, unfortunately, many traditions were lost.

Figure 6.9 A Sun Dancer prepares himself to be pierced as the medicine men straighten the ropes and attend to him. (Courtesy of Elizabeth Grobsmith.)

The Native American Church

The turn of the century was a very critical period for religious change and had important consequences for all plains peoples, but because of population density in sedentary villages, the plains farmers suffered great population loss, breakdown of native family and clan structures and inability to carry on much of their traditional religious activity. And so they were especially receptive to new religions and ideologies, one of which was the peyote cult, now called the Native American Church. Southwestern tribes like the Lipan and Mescalero Apache and plains tribes like the Comanche, Caddo, Wichita and Kiowa had learned of peyote from their Mexican tribal neighbors to the south, such as the Tarahumara and Huichol. The peyote cult quickly diffused from the southern plains to the north, as individual members of tribes, while visiting with southern peyote-using tribes, experienced cures from ingesting the sacramental plant, peyote, and took news of this panacea back with them to their tribes. The use of peyote became widespread in the plains, and a new syncretic religion developed modeled on a blend of Christianity and indigenous elements. Members of this ''cult'' attested to the significant changes the use of peyote brought to their people: peyotists were strongly anti-alcohol, against gambling, and discouraged sexual license. They stressed the importance of self-reliance, brotherly love, assuming responsibility for one's family and regaining control over one's life. More important than anything else, peyotists believe that, during the times of stress they were enduring, they needed to find a way to return order and control to their lives. Peyotism offered them just that: a religion deeply rooted in native culture, yet incorporating basic elements of Christianity, to which they had become accustomed, and an emphasis on accommodation to the present circumstances they encountered, rather than an escape from the. Above all, peyote use encouraged and reinforced sobriety for native people at a time when the devastating effects of acculturation were deeply felt. Different branches of peyotists emerged, some of which were more Christian than others.

The ritual use of peyote involves the ingestion—usually in a mashed form or, for women or sick individuals a tea—of a dried cactus bud known pharmacologically as *Lophophora Williamsii Lemaire.* Although non-Indians feared it as an hallucinogenic drug, it is considered neither habit-forming nor dangerous. Ritual ingestion generally produces profound sensory experiences, such as intensity of color and sound. Ceremonies are normally held all night long on a week-end, ending in a Sunday morning feast. Like all Indian ritual, the reasons for sponsoring a ceremony may vary, but regularly include doctoring, commemoration of a death, prayers for welfare and health, and thanksgiving.

A Native American Church service must have both special items and individuals for its proper performance. The four elements of life—earth, water, fire and air—are used, and tobacco, cedar and sage are used for purification, prayer and offerings. As people pass the peyote, singing and drumming accompany quiet meditation and prayer. The "Road Chief" is the official leader of the ceremony, and has the authority to run it in his own style. Other important participants are the "Fire-Chief", "Cedar-Chief" and "Drummer". Despite efforts by the federal government to ban the use of peyote, its legal use was upheld and by 1934 the Native American Church of North America had been formed and was fully incorporated. Today, peyotism continues to be an important religious force among plains tribes.

Historical Overview

Legal policy in the plains

More than any other culture area, the plains underwent radical transformation even before the period of forced assimilation because of its geographic, environmental and social situation. The convergence of the horse and the gun on the plains "set the stage" for a series of historical events that was to forever change native subsistence. Early (aboriginal) and protohistoric trade, as we have seen, brought non-natives heavily into contact with native peoples resulting, finally, in the forced abandonment of a native lifestyle and a replacement, following the demise of the fur trade, with a new era of forced assimilation. U.S. military victory ensured the federal government control over policy, and the "Indian problem" was something the government attempted—in many unsuccessful and unfruitful ways—to "solve".

From 1850 to 1871, the government created federal reservations which, by 1877, had been alloted into individual holdings. Surplus land was opened up for sale to non-Indians, resulting in a "checkerboarding" of the land causing small, fractionated allotments. With the demise of the buffalo herds and the absence of a real economic alternative, plains people fell into a new century of dependence, economic instability and helplessness. Today, tribes continue their struggle to extract themselves from this powerlessness, and as more tribes resume control over their own affairs and exercise the right of "self-determination", the more dignity and self-sufficiency they experience.

At precisely the time of maximum vulnerability, Christian missionaries appeared throughout plains reservations. At first, each reservation was assigned to a particular denomination, and responsibility for educating Indians was overseen by the Church. Grant's 1870 Peace Policy "divided up the pie", assigning some reservations to the Catholics, others to the Episcopals or Methodists. But by 1878, President Hayes re-instituted political rather than religious control over reservation Indians, and by 1881, reservations were opened up to the competitive missionization of the churches. This period is referred to as the era of "forced assimilation" and the federal government used the churches to assist in their program of turning Indians into white ranchers and farmers. This period of heavy missionization had multi-faceted effects on the tribes. First, conversion to Christianity was tremendous. Missionaries recorded native languages and printed books and bibles in the native tongues; the offered boarding school facilities (support) which many Indian families depended on, for they were frequently too poor to feed, house and clothe their children; and they severely criticized native religious practice, condemning rituals like the Sun Dance as heathen and barbaric. While many converted to Christianity with little conflict with their native ideologies, many others deeply resented the inroads made by the church, and either went underground with their native ceremonials or simply lived in a state of resentment and hatred toward them. Today, the majority of Native Americans are Christian to a degree—that is, they attend church, and depend on ministers and priests to help them in the performing of marriage and funeral ceremonies—however, this new involvement has not precluded a continuing ideological and spiritual tie to native religions which, in the last few decades, has undergone a tremendous revitalization.

The policy of forced assimilation not only was carried out by missionaries and agricultural advisors, but was aided by the policy of deliberate removal of Indian children from their homes. Children, attending boarding schools for nine months of the year, became increasingly alienated from their parents, losing touch with the roots of their traditions—their language, ceremonies and familial ties. During the summer, rather then permit the "regression back to the blanket", girls were forced into positions as domestic helpers, and were further kept from renewing their tribal ties. This policy of "legalized kidnapping", as it became known, was terribly destructive in successfully alienating many plains people from their traditions, and even today, the after-effects, namely the rejection of native culture by elders, is not uncommon. Some of these elders find it absurd that the young are now struggling to regain knowledge of their ancient languages and cultures, which they were told by missionaries were intrinsically inferior. Beaten into compliance with the policy of forced assimilation, these individuals—the few elders that remain—are a strong assimilitive presence on the plains.

During the decades following allotment, serious concern over the depressed economic and social conditions of Indians resulted in an investigation of Indian Affairs. This study, the Merriam Report, blasted the allotment system, criticized previous policy and recommended a series of reforms. As a result, the Indian Re-Organization Act (or Wheeler-Howard Act, as it is sometimes called) was passed which reversed much of the damaging policy. No further allotment of Indian land was allowed, and individuals were authorized to swap allotments to consolidate land holdings for improved economic opportunities. A credit fund was established which permitted tribes to borrow money for economic development. Probably the policy having the most impact on plains tribes was the provision which allowed tribes to set up ''IRA'' governments, adopting a constitution and by-laws based on a model of representative democracy. Tribes voted whether to adopt this form of government or not, and in the plains, most tribes agreed to it. The beginning of these new tribal government structures had an impressive impact on tribes, but scholars disagree as to whether this impact has been positive or negative. Because of the adoption of a new government structure, some Native Americans believe that this dealt the final blow to native political structures and systems of leadership. Others believe that without IRA governments, tribes could not function on a government-to-government basis with the U.S. government. Today, tribal governments receive revenue from the federal government to run reservation programs and meet the needs of the residents. However, policy concerning Native Americans is overseen by the Bureau of Indian Affairs, an agency accused of great paternalism and inefficiency and one that is perceived by many Native Americans as being as much a part of the ''problem'' as it is a solution.

Probably the most devastating piece of legislation to impact American Indians since the Dawes Act was the Termination policy of the Eisenhower-Nixon administration in the early 1950s. Passing Public Law #280 and House Concurrent Resolution #108, states desiring could bring under their jurisdiction tribal groups contained within their borders. Rather than remaining under the albeit paternalistic arm of the federal government and its legal jurisdiction over ''major'' crimes, certain states—in the plains area, Nebraska—became ''Public Law 280'' states and began an era of maintaining jurisdiction on federal reservation ''trust'' property. State police and court systems, accused by Native Americans as being racist and discriminatory, came into tremendous conflict with tribal governments and police, resulting today in the retrocession—the withdrawal from state control—of two of the three Nebraska Indian tribes, the Omaha and Winnebago, returning criminal jurisdiction to federal authorities instead.

The 1950s saw another policy which permanently impacted the course of Native American affairs—the policy of relocation. Because of economic depression on many reservations in the plains (as well as in other areas), a new federal policy of removing people from their reservation environments and relocating them in urban centers to seek employment, became common policy. In the plains, Indians were sent to Chicago and Denver and later to Omaha, Tulsa and Minneapolis. Because of a lack of economic opportunity on the reservation, it was thought that employment opportunities, particularly in blue-collar wage work, would be readily available. Rather than enjoying economic advantages, they found themselves isolated into urban ghettos, too poor to afford getting established in a new residence, lonely and alienated. In addition, urban relocation meant giving up free health care to which they were entitled on the reservation, and so their condition worsened rather than improved. As a result of this policy, over one-half of today's Indian population is urban.

Recent Indian Policy

During the 1960s and 1970s, the policy of the termination era gave way to a period of self-determination, culminating in a gradual reawakening of tribal identity and autonomy (Prucha 1984). Some critical legislative acts were passed which have aided in steering the course of Indian history more toward revitalization of Native American rights and restoration of rights previously denied. Ironically, it was Nixon (whose administration authored the Termination bill) who, in 1970, was largely responsible for urging Congress to pass the 1968 Indian Self-Determination and Education Assistance Act, Public Law 93–638. This law symbolized an end to BIA paternalism by encouraging tribes to take over control of services being administered to them, such as health care, child welfare, and education. Indian tribes could apply "to 638" a program, meaning to place it under local control, permitting community input, structure and decision-making. While this program appears to be enjoying tremendous success, some tribes fear that the federal government may use it as an excuse to withdraw their financial support of these agencies. This is precisely what has occurred during the Reagan administration. Tribes are being pushed into finding funding from "the private sector" for their programs, and this reawakens fear of termination—the withdrawal of federal support—for their programs.

Two very significant legislative acts were passed in 1978 which have restored certain basic tribal rights. The 1978 American Indian Religious Freedom Act has returned to tribes the right to practice in full their native religions, including the religious use of feathers of birds of protected species such as the eagle. While some non-Indians are critical of this bill, Indian people rightfully point out that they were not the ones responsible for the over-exploitation and endangering of the species; and that their hunting strategies and religious needs were in harmony with, rather than in violation of, nature. The federal court has upheld this right, and only Native Americans with special permits may retain feathers of these birds. The other important piece of legislation was the American Indian Child Welfare Act, drawn up by the Association on American Indian Affairs, who, in response to tribal concern over the alienation of Indian youth from the family, helped return control of Indian children to the tribes from which they came. Under this new law, a child whose custody was removed from his parents was not permitted to be placed either in foster care or for adoption in the home of a non-Native American unless no Indian family could be found. Prior to this time, Indian children removed from their families by state courts could easily end up in a non-Indian home, losing their bonds to their family, language and traditions. Although tribes complain that violations of this law frequently occur, at least it is no longer routine that Indian children are raised by well-intentioned but culturally insensitive whites.

Changes in the Plains

The changes brought about by historical events and the policy generated to deal with those left the plains a deeply scarred region. Subsistence and economy, political and social structure, ritual and ideology—all were transformed as tribes entered the 20th century. While government policy was characterized by vascillation from forced assimilation in the last quarter of the 19th century to cultural pluralism and ethnic pride a century later, one thing became clear in the modern era: Indians were neither going to be exterminated nor assimilated; rather they were here to stay, their cultures and languages thriving, and their economic and political struggles continuing. A century after the 1890 Massacre of Wounded Knee, symbolically the death knell for an aboriginal way of life in the plains, the American Indian Movement (AIM) had raised the consciousness of middle America concerning the plight of its first inhabitants. Originating in 1968 in Minneapolis by a group of

Figure 6.10 A poignant lesson in history is told in this picture of the church at Wounded Knee, burned down during the 1973 AIM occupation, in front of which stands an old decaying Sun Dance arbor. (Courtesy of Elizabeth Grobsmith.)

urban Indians, this organization of young activists brought media attention to the impoverished living conditions and economic depression experienced both by urban and reservation Indians. While many plains residents found AIM's tactics to be too violent, their takeover of Wounded Knee in 1973 did successfully focus national attention on government irresponsibility in meeting its commitment to Indian tribes and encouraging Indian organizations to lobby in Washington for rights to which they were entitled by virtue of the "trust" relationship.

Today Native Americans are the only ethnic group for whom an entire bureaucracy exists in Washington to oversee their needs. While this has its problems, federal responsibility to tribes is met through the new political structure set up by Indian Reorganization in the 1930s, i.e. "government to government" relations from federal authorities to tribal councils. Democratic, representative government typifies current tribal organization.

The Plains Culture Area Today

Economic Development

Both reservation and urban plains residents today exhibit the full range of variability with regard to their hold on their traditional cultures. It would not be inaccurate to say that many have assimilated; but neither would it be inaccurate to say that many still live a largely traditional life style. For the majority, life is lived in two worlds.

Economic development has been a high priority for all plains tribes, but the successful programs are few and far between. Since funding for employment has to come either from the federal government such as the Economic Development Agency or from the private sector, job opportunities in reservation areas remain inadequate. Many Indians live far below the poverty level, depending on small sums of income from leased land or, in some areas, mineral leases. Where jobs are available, labor is generally unskilled, as in construction, operation of heavy equipment and factory work. Government work funds the majority of reservation workers, ranging from 50–60% in North Dakota (Schneider 1986) to 80–90% in South Dakota (Grobsmith 1981). Attracting large manufacturing firms to reservations is difficult, resulting frequently in tribes obtaining only temporary manufacturing contracts. At Fort Berthold, the Three Tribes (Mandan-Hidatsa-Arikara) Stoneware plant exemplifies the problem—lacking the ability to develop marketing capacity, the business shut down (Schneider 1986). On the Rosebud Sioux Reservation in South Dakota, a contract to produce desk tops for the U.S. Postal Service ended, leaving all its employees without steady income. Inconsistencies resulting from changes in tribal governments prevents long-range tribal planning in some instances, and so contracts awarded to tribes to complete jobs are temporary, and unemployment rates throughout the plains are extremely high, sometimes 85% (Grobsmith 1981). Difficulties sustaining industry on reservations are attributed to "insufficient capital and inexperienced management" as well as problems of establishing markets and transporting finished products to markets (Schneider 1986:158):

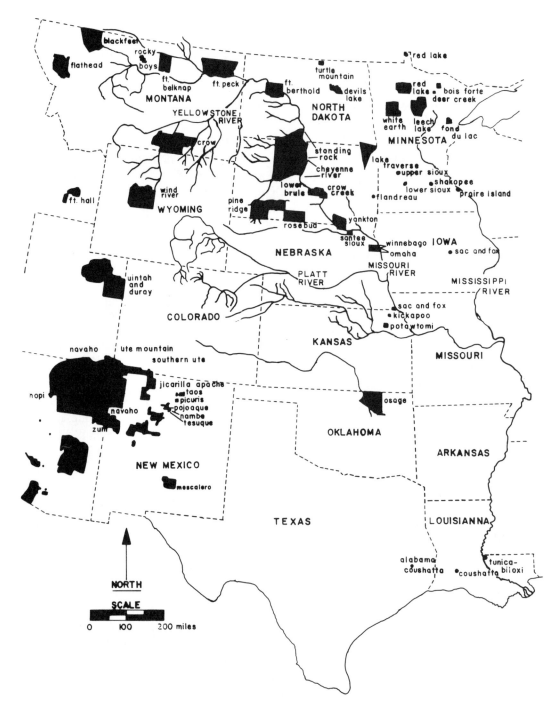

Figure 6.11 Contemporary reservations in the plains. (Adopted from Indian Land Areas map produced by Bureau of Indian Affairs, Department of the Interior, Washington, 1987.)

Location of Plains Tribes by Reservation and State

Montana

Reservation	Tribe
Blackfeet	Blackfoot
Rocky Boy	Blackfoot
Fort Belknap	Assiniboine, Gros Ventres
Fort Peck	Sioux, Assiniboine
Crow	Crow
Northern Cheyenne	Northern Cheyenne

North Dakota

Reservation	Tribe
Turtle Mountain	Chippewa, Cree
Fort Berthold	Mandan, Hidatsa, Arikara
Devils Lake	Sioux (Sisseton, Wahpeton)
Standing Rock	Sioux (Hunkpapa)

South Dakota

Reservation	Tribe
Standing Rock	Sioux (Hunkpapa)
Cheyenne River	Sioux (Hunkpapa, Itazipčo, Miniconjou, Sihasapa)
Lake Traverse	Sioux (Sisseton, Wahpeton)
Lower Brule	Sioux (Sičangu/ Brule & O'ohenonpa/Two Kettle)
Crow Creek	Sioux (Hunkpapa)
Pine Ridge	Sioux (Oglala
Rosebud	Sioux (Sičangu/Brule)
Yankton	Sioux (Yankton, Yanktonai)

Nebraska

Reservation	Tribe
Omaha	Omaha
Winnebago	Winnebago
Santee	Sioux (Santee)

Kansas

Reservation	Tribe
Kickapoo	Kickapoo
Potawatomi	Potawatomi

Iowa

Reservation	Tribe
Iowa	Iowa
Sac and Fox	Sac and Fox

Oklahoma*

Reservation	Tribe
Osage	Osage

*Numerous tribes are federally recognized but have no reservation as a result of having been "removed" there from the southeast: Cheyenne, Arapahoe, Kickapoo, Kiowa, Caddo, Kaw, Ponca, Tonkawa, and Otoe-Missouri

"The main factor prohibiting industrial development on reservations is the lack of capital. Despite the millions of dollars which have been set aside for Indian needs, Indian tribes have little or no funds to invest in industrial development" (Schneider 1986:160).

But many tribes are succeeding in generating long-term employment opportunities, reflecting long-range goals. Nebraska's Winnebago tribe, for example, striving for economic self-sufficiency, works with a private Indian-owned business which manufactures mobile homes (Prichard 1984). The Omaha produce kit cars, have a dairy farm, and a barge grain-shipping enterprise. The Santee Sioux produce medical supplies in its Becton-Dickinson plant. In South Dakota, Pine Ridge, the nation's second largest reservation, has a well-known moccasin factory. North Dakota tribes such as the Turtle Mountain Chippewa are somewhat more prosperous than the South Dakota tribes, where a wheelbearing plant supports numerous residents. The Devil's Lake Sioux have a small manufacturing plant where non-destructive armaments such as camouflage nets are produced (Schneider 1986); at Standing Rock, many run cattle or lease land to ranching firms in Texas (Ahler 1987, personal communication). The Crow Tribe of Montana operates a large visitor center and motel complex.

The key issues for plains employment are long range goal planning, management training for Native Americans, and firm commitments of federal support. Without these, income levels and the standard of living will continue to be insecure for tribal peoples.

Contemporary Social Life

Despite the economic pressures of modern plains residents, a social life rich in cultural heritage and pride in ethnic identity provides community cohesion and personal satisfaction. While many non-Indians don't see why Indians don't leave the reservation in search of better employment opportunities, reservation life offers many important rewards: proximity to one's kin, strong bonds to the land, comfort, particularly for older Native Americans, in the freedom to use their native tongue, rich community social life, and deep attachments to religion and ritual.

While not restricted to the plains area, social occasions like pow-wows and Giveaways have come to exemplify the continuity of life in the plains, as people travel around on the "pow-wow circuit" during the summer, dancing, feasting and visiting relatives on nearby reservations. Pow-wows occur locally, within individual communities on the reservations, or are reservation-wide, and summer's end always brings the great intertribal celebrations like the Rosebud or Crow Fair.

Like the phenomenon of the plains pow-wow, Giveaways are contemporary socioreligious events which bring together family and community. Ceremonial gift-giving has long been an important part of plains life. For the Lakota, Giveaways originated int he feast held to release the spirit following its being ritually held during the Keeping of the Soul ceremony, one of the seven Sacred Rites. When the spirit went on its path to the afterlife, the family distributed all their goods, frequently leaving themselves totally impoverished. The community would reintegrate them by giving them the minimal necessities of life.

Figure 6.12 Tipis and horses are reminiscent of traditional scenes at this modern inter-tribal pow-wow, Crow Fair, in Montana. (Courtesy of Elizabeth Grobsmith.)

Today, Lakota Giveaways, *wopila,* are still held largely to commemorate the anniversary of a death; but they are also held to thank the community, to celebrate a birth or graduation, or to honor a political candidate (Grobsmith 1979). While Giveaways are considered largely as social events, they contain important ritual elements and reflect deeply held moral convictions concerning mutual aid and support. Values of reciprocal sharing and generosity are foremost in plains tribal cultures, for dependence on the family was—and still is—the only insurance one had to be taken care of if ill, enfeebled or infirm. Today, Native Americans say that the values inherent in the Giveaway are a reflection of a philosophy of live—"what goes around comes back around", meaning that if you live a generous existence, others will treat you similarly. Giveaways exemplify this philosophy for they are the public, ceremonial and social expression of reciprocal thanks given to friends in the community. No matter what the reason is that a Giveaway is held, reciprocal giving cements social ties and binds the community into a web essential to survival in the plains.

The evolution of music and dance styles, preparation of traditional costumes, the sale of quilled and beaded crafts, and large inter-tribal fairs all bring together people who celebrate the plains existence, a unique and strong culture unto itself. Children who may

Figure 6.13 A hoop dancer dazzles the public at Crow Fair in Montana. (Courtesy of Elizabeth Grobsmith.)

Figure 6.14 An elaborate memorial Giveaway is held on the Rosebud Sioux Reservation in South Dakota, to honor the passing of an important member of the community. (Courtesy of Elizabeth Grobsmith.)

lack familiarity with their native languages now take Indian Studies in school, and enjoy a renewed sense of pride in their Indianness as they learn crafts, history, music, language and stories told by the elders.

One area in which a great amount of revitalization has occurred is in religious expression. Despite missionary criticism, federal prohibitions and forced assimilation of many Indian people, native ritual enjoys tremendous popularity among young and old and seems to have given many a renewed sense of purpose in life. The most visible revitalization in the plains is, of course, the Sun Dance, described earlier. What the Sun Dance offers is not only an individual and collective prayer for well-being, but an assertion of the right to be Indian in a predominantly non-Indian world. A Native American may work from nine to five, send his children to public school, and do his banking and shopping locally, but his religious life is as likely to be traditional as it is to be Christian or part of the Native American Church.

Figure 6.15 An indoor memorial Giveaway at Rosebud honors the death of two members of this family. (Courtesy of Elizabeth Grobsmith.)

One of the reasons for the terrific popularity and revitalization of Indian religion is its effectiveness in helping alleviate one of the major crises facing plains tribal peoples—alcoholism. The high rates of alcohol and drug addiction which originated following the fur trade period have, unfortunately, not waned; rather, with poverty and unemployment, they have soared. Many Indian youth are turning to their native traditions to reinstill pride so necessary to recover. Today, recreational programs for youth, alcohol treatment and prevention programs, and community adult education are all increasingly geared toward resolving the most devastating killer of Native Americans—alcohol-related accidents, homicides and suicides, and cirrhosis. The eradication of alcoholism aims at restoring the integrity of the family, the basic building block of plains (and all) cultures.

Not only is there a revitalization of traditional belief among plains tribes, but a renewed sense of political awareness has made these groups a force to be reckoned with. The famous Black Hills land claims is a case in point. Despite the federal government's 1984 offer of $11.15 million (now grown to about $192 million) in compensation for sacred land unlawfully taken, the Sioux have refused a cash settlement, and are continuing their litigation to resume control of their land. A proposal by the Honeywell Corporation to construct a munitions testing facility in Hell's Canyon in the southern Black Hills was

Figure 6.16 A traditional feed is an important part of all contemporary Indian social events. (Courtesy of Elizabeth Grobsmith.)

fought by the Oglala Sioux, who succeeded in getting Honeywell to withdraw their plans. While the establishment of Camp Yellow Thunder in the Black Hills was highly controversial and the occupation finally ended, the demands for sovereign rights continues to alert the federal government of their continuing obligation to fulfill their treaty obligations.

SUGGESTED READINGS

Brown, Joseph Epes
    1971   *The Sacred Pipe,* Black Elk's Account of the Seven Rites of the Oglala Sioux, Penguin Books, Baltimore.

Ewers, John C.
    1958   *The Blackfeet, Raiders on the Northwestern Plains,* University of Oklahoma Press, Norman.
    1968   *Indian Life on the Upper Missouri,* University Oklahoma Press, Norman.

Grobsmith, Elizabeth S.
    1981   *Lakota of the Rosebud, A Contemporary Ethnography* Holt, Rinehart and Winston, New York.

Harrod, Howard L.
    1987   *Renewing the World, Plains Indian Religion and Morality,* University of Arizona Press, Tucson.

Hoebel, E. Adamson
    1960   *The Cheyennes, Indians of the Great Plains,* Holt, Rinehart and Winston, New York.

Holder, Preston
    1970   *The Hoe and the Horse on the Plains, A Study of Cultural Development among North American Indians,* University of Nebraska Press, Lincoln.

Hassrick, Royal B.
    1964   *The Sioux, Life and Customs of a Warrior Society,* University of Oklahoma Press, Norman.

Lowie, Robert H.
    1963   *Indians of the Plains,* American Museum Science Books published for the American Museum of Natural History, Natural History Press, Garden City, N.Y.

Powers, William K.
    1975   *Oglala Religion,* University of Nebraska Press, Lincoln.
    1982   *Yuwipi, Vision and Experience in Oglala Ritual,* University of Nebraska Press, Lincoln.

Powers, Marla N.
    1986   *Oglala Women, Myth, Ritual and Reality,* University of Chicago Press, Chicago.

Schneider, Mary Jane
    1986   *North Dakota Indians, An Introduction,* Kendall/Hunt Publishing Company, Dubuque, Iowa.

Stewart, Omer C.
    1987   *Peyote Religion, A History,* University of Oklahoma Press, Norman.

Wood, W. Raymond and Margot Liberty, eds.
    1980   *Anthropology on the Great Plains,* University Nebraska Press, Lincoln.

REFERENCES

Ahler, Janet
1987   Visiting lecture on Native American tribes in North Dakota, University of Nebraska, Lincoln.

Ewers, John C.
1968   *Indian Life on the Upper Missouri,* University of Oklahoma Press, Norman.
1958   *The Blackfeet, Raiders on the Northwest Plains,* University of Oklahoma Press, Norman.
1955   *The Horse in Blackfoot Indian Culture,* Bureau of American Ethnology, Bulletin 159, Smithsonian Institution, Washington.

Grobsmith, Elizabeth S.
1981   *Lakota of the Rosebud, A Contemporary Ethnography,* Holt, Rinehart and Winston, New York.
1979   "The Lakhota Giveaway: A System of Social Reciprocity", *Plains Anthropologist,* Vol. 24, May.

Haines, Francis
1938   "The Northward Spread of Horses Among the Plains Indians" *American Anthropologist* n.s. Vol. 40, No. 3, pp 429–437.

Harrod, Howard L.
1987   *Renewing the World, Plains Indian Religion and Morality,* University of Arizona Press, Tuscon.

Hassrick, Royal B.
1964   *The Sioux, Life and Customs of a Warrior Society,* University of Oklahoma Press, Norman.

Holder, Preston
1970   *The Hoe and the Horse on the Plains, A Study of Cultural Development among North American Indians,* University of Nebraska Press, Lincoln.

Jackson, Helen Hunt
1881   *A Century of Dishonor: A Sketch of the United States Government's Dealings with Some of the Indian Tribes,* Harper and Row, New York.

Kroeber, A. L.
1939   *Cultural and Natural Areas of Native North America,* University of California Press, Berkeley and Los Angeles.

Laravie, Tony
1987   Presentation to Plains Ethnology class on the Sun Dance, University of Nebraska, Lincoln.

Liberty, Margot
1980   "The Sun Dance", IN: *Anthropology on the Great Plains,* edited by Raymond Wood and Margot Liberty, University of Nebraska Press, Lincoln.

Macgregor, Gordon
1946   *Warriors Without Weapons,* University of Chicago Press, Chicago.

Mooney, James
1973   *The Ghost-Dance Religion and Wounded Knee,* Dover Publications, Inc., New York (originally published in 1896 as 14th Annual Report/Part 2 of the Bureau of American Ethnology, Smithsonian Institution).

Oliver, Symmes C.
1962   *Ecology and Cultural Continuity as Contributing Factors in the Social Organization of the Plains,* University of California Press, Berkeley and Los Angeles.

Osborn, Alan J.
1980   "Cache Pits, Scapula Hoes, and Antler Rakes Do Not a Village Farmer Make: Sedentary Bison Hunters of the Eastern Great Plains", unpublished manuscript, paper presented to 38th Annual Plains Conference, Iowa City, Iowa.

Prichard, Marshall
1984   "The People Today, Economic Development", *Nebraskaland Magazine,* Vol. 62, No. 1, January–February.

Prucha, Francis Paul
   1984   *The Great Father,* The United States Government and the American Indian, University of Nebraska
           Press, Lincoln.

Schneider, Mary Jane
   1986   *North Dakota Indians, An Introduction,* Kendall/Hunt Publishing Co., Dubuque, Iowa.

Spencer, Robert F. and Jesse D. Jennings, et al.
   1977   *The Native Americans* 2nd edition., Harper and Row, New York.

Walker, J. R.
   1917   "The Sun Dance and Other Ceremonies of the Oglala Division of the Teton-Dakota", *Anthropologi-
           cal Papers of the American Museum of Natural History,* Vol. 16, Part 2, New York.

Wedel, Waldo
   1986   *Central Plains Prehistory, Holocene Environments and Culture Change in the Republican River
           Basin,* University of Nebraska Press, Lincoln.
   1961   *Prehistoric Man on the Great Plains,* University of Oklahoma Press, Norman.

Chapter 7

The Greater Southwest Culture Area "Diverse Lifeways in a Varied Environment"

John F. Martin

Arizona State University

T. L. McCarty

University of Arizona

Introduction

"A piece of land is like a book. A wise person can look at the stones and mountains and read stories older than the first living thing . . . and since the first people made homes on the land, many people and many tribes have come and gone. The land still remembers them, however, and keeps . . . the things they left behind" (Sam and Janet Bingham, *Between Sacred Mountains,* 1984, p. 1).

Land and People

Only six or seven generations have passed since the people indigenous to Southwestern North America gave up most of their territory in the face of Anglo-American expansion and conquest. The Treaty of Guadalupe Hidalgo, signed in 1848, ceded much of what is now New Mexico and Arizona to the United States. Within six years, American boundaries grew to embrace all of modern Arizona south to Sonora, Mexico.

But the land and the native peoples that came to be governed by the United States and Mexico already possessed traditions extending back centuries and millennia. Though highly diverse, those traditions were unified by a connection to Mesoamerica that preceded Christianity and was manifested in agriculture, pottery making, trade, and in social and religious systems.

The events of the 19th century led to tremendous reductions in tribal land and population, and this in turn impacted tribal cultures and languages. Yet what distinguishes modern Southwestern tribes from those in some parts of North American is their retention of portions of their original lands. This accounts in great measure for the tenacity of native

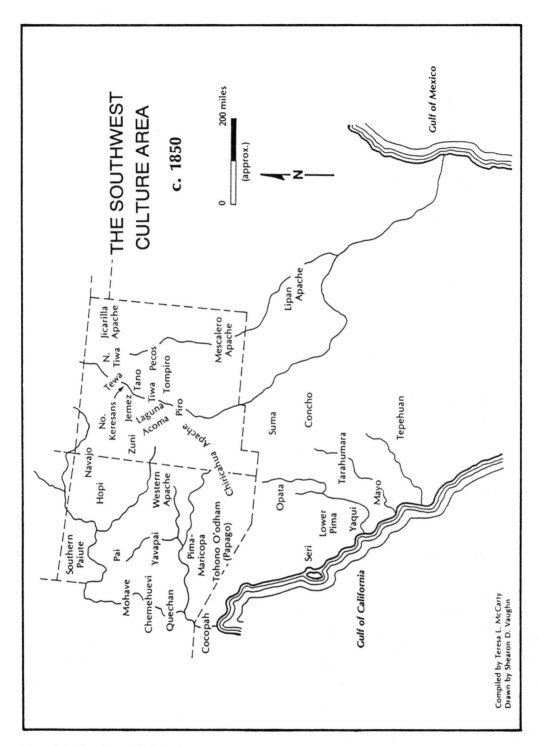

Map of the Southwest Culture Area

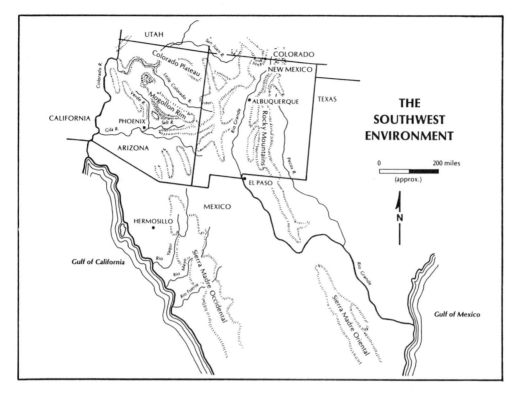

Figure 7.1 The Southwest Environment. (Compiled by T. L. McCarty. Drawn by Shearon D. Vaughn.)

Southwestern traditions despite overwhelming changes that occurred within a few generations. Today, we see striking evidence of those traditions, even as tribes vigorously pursue modern developments in housing, transportation, education, health and their economies.

The Southwest Environment

For the anthropologist, the Greater Southwest is a vast region extending southward from what is now Colorado and Utah well into Mexico, and reaching from the Colorado River and the Sea of Cortez on the west, eastward to the edge of the Great Plains and the Gulf of Mexico. The people of this region felt the impact of European conquest well before most of them saw a European. Old World crops, European material cultural artifacts, livestock and disease spread faster than did the Europeans and their sociopolitical systems. Thus, prior to European conquest diseases led to the decline of native populations, and their connections with central Mexico, which provided the region with some cultural unity, began to atrophy. With the conquest of Mexico and later, the political separation of the Southwest into Mexico and the United States, the Greater Southwest as a cultural entity began to lose its integrity.

This withering away of the central Mexican connection even before modern boundaries divided the land has imbued the region's environmental diversity with great importance. For while the distribution of languages and of important elements in art, religion and material culture remains as testimony to earlier links between the people of the region, much of what anthropologists and other recent observers report reflects the Southwest's great environmental variety and the distinct historical experiences of its native peoples. To understand these peoples, we must take stock of both their lands and their tribal histories. We begin by sketching the Southwest as a human environment.

One passage into this environment is from the south, where the Sierra Madre Occidentales loom upward behind the coastal plain of the Sea of Cortez and the Pacific. Winds laden with moisture from the sea drop precipitation on the higher reaches of this range. Much of this then drains off into a series of short rivers that flow westward back into the sea. These streams and the short valleys they water make portions of the coastal plain potentially rich agricultural environments—environments that were used productively by Indian people.

But while runoff from the mountain rains watered the coastal plains and valleys, sustaining large Indian populations there, little water dropped on the eastern slopes. Hence, to the east of the Sierra Madre Occidentales is a trough consisting of desert valleys and ranges extending northwest into Arizona. Here, populations were much more dispersed.

Still further east of this trough in Mexico lie the Sierra Madre Orientales, which emerge to the north as the Rocky Mountains. Falling off to the east, the Rockies gradually give way to the plains that sweep across west Texas to the Gulf Coast. On the west, the Rockies break up into smaller ranges, including those that cut diagonally from south-central New Mexico to central Arizona. Within Arizona these formations end abruptly at the Mogollon Rim, a rugged chain of mountains reaching 8,000 feet and supporting dense coniferous forests. North of the Rim elevations fall off to the still high Colorado Plateau, where spiraling sandstone columns and multihued canyons punctuate wide stretches of desert sage and grassland.

Below the Rim to the west elevations drop off sharply, first to embrace shrubby desert foothills, then falling to the Sonoran desert and riverine lowlands. In Arizona this low, hot region consists of desert valleys and intervening mountain ranges. In the valleys temperature extremes can vary as much as 50 degrees in a day, rising to a searing 120 degrees in summer and plummeting well below freezing in winter.

Within the Southwest, then, human cultural adaptations responded to four ecological zones: the high mountains, the desert ranges and valleys, the riverine valleys and the high plateau. All share one feature characteristic of the Southwest—aridity. Most precipitation occurs in the mountains, supporting extensive coniferous forests and mountain meadows. But much of this precipitation, especially the winter snow melt, drains off into a series of rivers. In the northeast the Pecos and Rio Grande drain eastward from the Rockies, eventually emptying into the Gulf of Mexico. Across the Continental Divide the Colorado, San Juan and Little Colorado River system drains the northwestern Rockies, while the Gila and Salt drain the southwestern reaches. Joining just west of Phoenix, the Gila and Salt continue as the Gila, winding through desert valleys to join the Colorado River. After flowing westward across the Colorado Plateau through the chasm of the Grand Canyon, the Colorado turns south to follow a broad valley to its delta at the head of the Gulf of California. Most of these rivers are longer than the rivers of western Mexico but as we shall see, the Mexican rivers historically supported the largest populations.

Beyond the major river valleys and below the highest elevations, water is scarce. Small seeps and springs at the base of desert mountains, some sustaining small perennial streams, and runoff from seasonal rains provide water in small amounts. More rain falls on the Colorado Plateau and in the desert ranges, but much of it comes in torrential summer downpours and occasional winter snows that either run off, evaporate or sink to water-bearing rock well below the plateau surface. Surface water is therefore limited, and most common at the bases of surrounding mountains and in the canyons carving deep enough into the plateau to reach the aquifer.

Wild resources follow the distribution of water. Big game—deer, elk, and bighorn sheep—are most common in the mountains and their lower slopes. Many, in particular elk and deer, move from higher to lower elevations in the winter months. This and the presence of plant foods maturing at different seasons makes regions with marked variations in elevation within a short distance attractive to hunter-gatherers. For instance, along the crest of the Mogollon Rim, a long but narrow ponderosa forest stretches from southern New Mexico to north-central Arizona. Deer and elk dwell in those forests, moving northward into the juniper-pinyon country of the Colorado Plateau and southwestward into the mountain breaks in the colder months. The same region supports a wide variety of useful wild plants, many of which mature at different seasons. In the spring, agave and young green plants are available on the lower slopes. As the weather warms, mesquite beans, pigweed and saguaro fruit become available farther out into the desert foothills. Later the fruit of prickly pear ripens, first at lower elevations, then in higher places. Eventually seed-bearing plants such as shooting star are ready to harvest in the higher regions, as are acorns and juniper berries. In the fall pinyon nuts make the higher elevations especially attractive.

The Colorado Plateau lying between the Mogollon Rim to the southwest and the Rockies to the east supports similar resources at higher elevations, as well as major streams where water and valleys afford horticultural resources. But until the introduction of live-stock, which can transform the grass on these high deserts into meat and fiber, much of the plateau was of little use to Indians. Outside the river valleys and a few oases there, native population densities remained low through much of this region.

The river valleys in Mexico, the Salt-Gila and the Colorado in Arizona, and the Rio Grande and Pecos in New Mexico offered Indians the richest resources. Bounded by flood plains thick in mesquite, the Salt-Gila and the Colorado also abutted foothills where many rich, lower Sonoran flora were plentiful. The rivers themselves offered not only fish, but water for horticulture. This conjunction of water, long riverine plains, and in Arizona and along the Mexican rivers, a long, hot growing season, made the low desert valleys well suited to horticulture. Indians living along the Pecos and Rio Grande faced more problems as the growing season was shorter in those higher valleys, but they too provided rich horticultural resources. Horticulture was possible in other areas as well, but throughout the mountains growing seasons are short and elsewhere water is not in good supply.

Given all this, it is not surprising that when we examine the pre-conquest distribution of Indian peoples, we find the largest populations and those most dependent on horticulture in the major desert river valleys of Mexico, southern and western Arizona, and along the Rio Grande. Along the Mogollon Rim and in the mountain ranges of New Mexico and Mexico, populations were thinner, relying more on hunting and gathering than on horticulture. The lower and drier desert valleys and ranges supported even smaller populations of hunter-gatherers who did some supplemental horticulture. Until Navajos obtained livestock and entered the Colorado Plateau, that region, too, had very low population densities, with settlements restricted to the river drainages and isolated oases.

The Emergence of Historic Southwest Tribes

People lived in the Greater Southwest well before the region exhibited the cultural similarities that gave rise to its identification as a culture area. From about 10,000 B.C. until 9000 B.C., the Southwest was home to big game hunters. In those times the climate was wetter and cooler, and much of the Southwest was in fact environmentally and culturally an extension of the plains. As the climate warmed and dried out, the culture of the early Paleo-Indians gave way to Archaic traditions. These responded to local variations in environment, but they shared an emphasis on the opportunistic use of many types of flora and fauna in arid environments. Archaic mixed hunting-gathering traditions distinguished the entire Southwest after about 8000 B.C. and until the peoples of the region began to be drawn into contact with the peoples of Mesoamerica.

This contact began first in the south, with the introduction of cultigens, bottle gourds, squash, corn and beans. By the time of Christ squash were in use, and by A.D. 500 people used corn and beans in the farthest reaches of the Greater Southwest. Ceramics, irrigation and village life followed, as did trade in exotic goods such as copper bells, marine shells, parrot feathers, and in religious ideas centering on Quetzalcoatl, the plumed water serpent, and Huitzilopochtli, the Aztec sun god. In return the inhabitants of the Southwest sent turquoise, peyote and other products southward.

As the fortunes of the various central Mexican civilizations waxed and waned, so did their contacts with the Southwest and by extension, so did the Southwest cultures that grew in response to Mesoamerican stimuli. Some hundreds of years before the Spanish arrived in the Southwest, this contact atrophied. The diseases introduced by the Spanish also preceded them into the Southwest and as a result, indigenous populations were shrinking and moving in many areas for some time before the Spanish arrived.

In what is now Chihuahua, Mexico the trading center at *Casas Grandes* collapsed in the middle 1300s, though descendants of the Casas Grandes people appear to have survived to Spanish times as the Jova and Jocomes. Farther south in Durango, the *Chalchihuite* culture, established by migrants from the south, grew up after A.D. 600. Characterized by large towns, roads, ball courts, pyramids and a complex, class-structured society, this culture also collapsed by the middle 1300s, leaving behind a people we now call the Tepehuan.

Though less intense, Mesoamerican influences in Arizona and New Mexico critically influenced development there. In these regions, four major archaeological traditions either grew out of the Archaic desert cultures in response to the introduction of corn, beans, squash, and irrigation from the south, or were introduced directly by migrants from the south.

In the desert river valleys of southern Arizona, the *Hohokam* emerged after 300 B.C. Modern observers disagree as to whether the Hohokam migrated into the area from the south or emerged from the indigenous Desert Archaic tradition. Whatever the answer, it is clear that the Hohokam—so named by their putatative descendants, the Pimas, as "Those Who Have Gone Before"—represent a northern outlier of Mesoamerica. Relying on irrigation horticulture, the Hohokam eventually built extensive irrigation systems and large villages and towns in the Gila and Salt River Valleys, engaging in vigorous trade with people to the north and south. Their irrigation works remain the foundation for the canals serving modern Phoenix.

For unclear reasons, the Hohokam disappeared by about 1450 A.D., abandoning their villages and towns. Some lay the Hohokam collapse to their dependence on the civilizations of central Mexico; when those collapsed so did the trade that stimulated residential concentration and the Hohokam's intense production. Others argue that constant irrigation of their farmlands caused salts to build up and eventually destroy the Hohokam horticultural system.

Whatever the causes, the Hohokam were gone by A.D. 1450. In Spanish times, Piman-speaking people occupied this region. The Tohono O'odham or Desert People lived in the desert mountains and valleys west and south of the Gila, the Sobaipuri occupied the San Pedro and Santa Cruz River Valleys south and east of modern Tucson, and the people we call today the Pimas lived in the Gila River Valley.

East of the Hohokam, in the mountains along the Arizona-New Mexico line, the *Mogollon* tradition grew up, again in response to new cultigens and technologies introduced from the south. Beginning about 500 B.C. the Mogollon slowly evolved from simple hunter-gatherers living in small pit-house villages—settlements of pole and brush structures built over earthen pits—to intensive horticulturalists who constructed "apartment-style" villages of up to 500 rooms. Ceremonial chambers called *kivas* grew in size and importance as trade brought the Mogollon copper bells, turquoise, shellwork and other valuables and paraphernalia.

After about A.D. 1250, the Mogollon tradition lost much of its distinctiveness, blending with influences from the *Anasazi* peoples to the north. The Navajos, modern inhabitants of this land, use the term Anasazi to refer to the "Ancient Ones" who, like the Mogollon, began as hunter-gatherers in small, scattered pit-house settlements but eventually aggregated in large apartment-style villages along major river valleys. Many of these impressive villages, with their great ceremonial kivas and plazas, remain intact or nearly so today,

Figure 7.2 Taos Pueblo, 1985. (Courtesy of T. L. McCarty.)

testimony to the unique, integrated social and economic systems of the ancestors of modern Pueblo Indians.

Finally, in the western desert valleys and ranges and along the lower Colorado River, another archaeological culture called the *Hakataya* developed. The people bearing this culture probably came from California about the time of Christ. By historic times their descendants had organized into a series of tribes of 3,000 or more people, who together controlled the Colorado River from its mouth to the Great Bend near what is now Boulder Dam. Other manifestations of the Hakataya pushed up the tributaries of the lower Colorado River and by A.D. 1300 a northern, upland extension of this tradition dominated the desert valleys and ranges of western and central Arizona, even reaching into the plateau to the northeast. The historic peoples who carried these traditions were the ancestors of the modern Havasupai, Hualapai, and Yavapai Indians.

All of these peoples grew out of traditions of considerable antiquity in the Southwest. But by about 1500 A.D., the northern and eastern reaches of the Southwest environment became home to newly arrived Apacheans who probably came from the north. One Apachean branch, the ancestors of modern Navajos, arrived in what is now the Four Corners area of Arizona, New Mexico, Colorado and Utah. Others, the ancestors of modern Western and Chiricahua Apaches, moved into the mountains below the Little Colorado between present-day Arizona and New Mexico, while still other Apache groups moved eastward, to the plains.

In the 19th century the Chemehuevis, Southern Paiutes like the Kaibab band living north of the Grand Canyon, moved from the southern California desert to the Colorado River Valley, establishing themselves between two of the largest Colorado River tribes, the Mohaves and the Quechan. Incessant warfare there had by then decimated the Halchidhoma, Halyikwamai and Kahuan native to the area. The survivors from these groups eventually settled among the related Cocomaricopas and the Pimas, where they came to be known as the Maricopas.

222

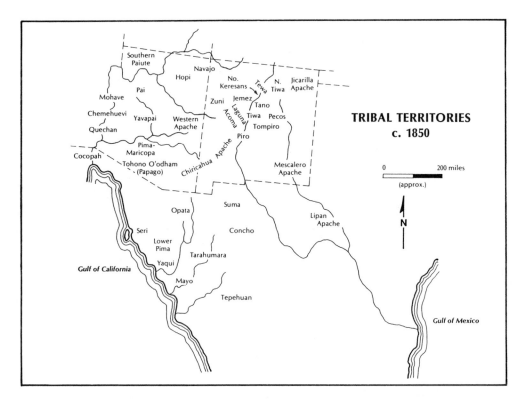

Figure 7.3 Tribal Territories c. 1950. (Compiled by T. L. McCarty. Drawn by Shearon D. Vaughn.)

This, then, was the human configuration in the Southwest by about 1850 A.D. (see Fig. 7.3). In the following sections we explore the cultural and linguistic connections between these peoples, and the similarities and differences in their uses of the environment.

Land, People and Languages

Some observers liken native North America to an "American Babel" (Spencer, Jennings et al. 1965:100). Certainly this description fits the Southwest, where at least 26 tribal languages are still spoken, many as different as are Mandarin and English. Within language groups, people often speak distinct dialects, some so different they merit being treated as separate languages. Figure 7.4 shows the major language families in the Southwest at about 1600 A.D. Within each there are smaller, closely related branches or subgroups. Table 7.1 outlines those groups, showing their origins and where their speakers live today.

As the map shows, Uto-Aztecan speakers dominate the northwestern and southwestern reaches of the region: the Kaibab Paiutes, Chemehuevis and Hopis to the north and west, the Pimans, Opatas and Tepehuanes in the southern deserts, and the Mayos, Yaquis

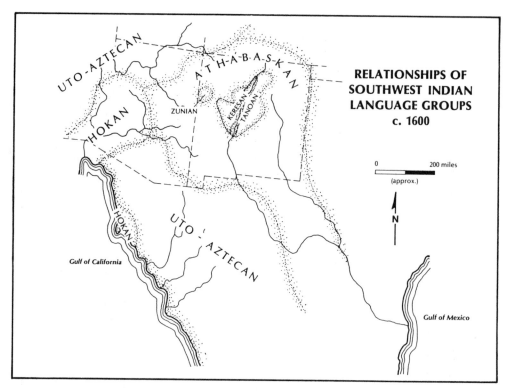

Figure 7.4 Relationships of Southwest Indian Language Groups c. 1600. (Adapted from E.H. Spicer 1962: 10–12. Drawn by Shearon D. Vaughn.)

and Tarahumaras in the river valleys and mountains of western Mexico. Altogether some 100,000 Uto-Aztecan speakers live in the Southwest today.

Between the northern and southern Uto-Aztecans are the Hokan-speaking River Yumans—the Mohaves, Quechan, Cocopahs and Maricopas—living along the lower Gila River and Colorado River Valleys. To the northeast, the closely related Upland Yuman Hualapais, Havasupais and Yavapais occupy north-central Arizona. A third Hokan branch, the Serians, still live in coastal mainland Mexico opposite Tiburon Island. Today there are perhaps 3,300 speakers of these Hokan languages in the Southwest.

Athabaskans live throughout the northeastern Southwest. These groups include the Navajos, with over 150,000 speakers, and the closely related Western Apaches with 12,000 speakers. Another 1,700 people speak Mescalero Apache, and about 800 speak Jicarilla Apache, for a total of at least 164,500 Athabaskan speakers in the Southwest. When we add to these the speakers of Keresan, the Tanoan dialects and Zunian, the number of speakers of native languages in the Greater Southwest exceeds 270,000.

No simple connections exist, however, between language affiliations, culture and lifestyle. The Uto-Aztecans, for example, include puebloan horticulturalists (the Hopis), riverine-village horticulturalists (the Pimas and Yaquis), hunter-gatherers (the Southern

TABLE 7.1

Indigenous Southwest Language Groups and Location of Speakers, 1600 to the Present

Language Group	Location of Speakers 1600	1850	1989
Southern Athabaskan			
Navajo	New Mexico, Arizona, Utah	→	Navajo Reservation
Western Apache	Eastern Arizona, Western New Mexico	→	San Carlos Reservation Fort Apache Reservation
Mescalero	Central New Mexico	→	Mescalero Reservation
Jicarilla	Eastern New Mexico	→	Jicarilla Reservation
Lipan	Southeast New Mexico, Southwest Texas	→	Language extinct; descendants of speakers at Mescalero Reservation
Hokan			
River Yuman			
Mohave	Mohave Valley of Colorado River	→	Fort Mohave and Colorado River Reservation
Quechan	Junction of Gila and Colorado Rivers	→	Fort Yuma Reservation
Maricopa	Gila River, junction of Salt River, and Gila River to Gila Bend	Gila River, near St. Johns, AZ	Gila River and Salt River Reservations
Kaveltcadom	Lower Gila River	With Maricopas	→
Halchidhoma	Colorado River, between Quechan and Mohave	With Maricopas	→

Language Group	Location of Speakers 1600	1850	1989
Cocopah	Delta of Colorado River	→	Cocopah Reservation, Northern Sonora, Baja del Norte
Kahuan	Between Cocopah and Quechan	With Maricopas	Language extinct; descendants of speakers are Maricopa
Upland Yuman			
Hualapai*	Northwestern Arizona south of Grand Canyon	→	Hualapai Reservation
Havasupai*	Northwestern Arizona south of Grand Canyon and east of Hualapai bands	→	Havasupai Reservation
Yavapai*	Western Arizona north of Gila and Salt Rivers, south of Pai bands	→	Fort McDowell, Prescott, Camp Verde and Payson Tonto-Apache Reservations
Serian			
Seri	Tiburon Island, Sonoran coast opposite the island	→	Sonora coast
Keresan			
Keres (7 dialects)			
Western Acoma* and Laguna*	Acoma Pueblo; Laguna	→	Acoma Pueblo,* Laguna Pueblo

*Dialect difference

Language Group	Location of Speakers		
	1600	*1850*	*1989*
Rio Grande Keresans*	7 villages along Rio Grande	→	Zia, Santa Ana, San Felipe, Santo Domingo, Cochiti
Tanoan			
Northern Tiwa	Taos, Picuris,	→	Taos, Picuris
Southern Tiwa	Sandia* (20 villages), Isleta*	Sandia, Isleta, Tigua	Sandia, Isleta, Tigua (Tigua dialect extinct)
Piro	6 villages along Rio Grande	→	Language extinct; descendants of speakers at Isleta del Sur
Southern Tano (Tewa)*	4 villages in Galisteo Basin, New Mexico	Hano village, Hopi Mesas	Hopi Reservation
Northern Tano (Tewa)*	7 villages along Rio Grande	→	Santa Clara, San Juan, San Ildefonso, Nambe, Tesuque, Pajoaque
Towa	Jemez (11 villages) and Pecos	→	Jemez
Uto-Aztecan			
Shoshonean			
Southern Paiute	Kaibab Plateau	→	Kaibab Paiute Reservation
Chemehuevi	Southern California deserts	Colorado River	Chemehuevi Reservation; Colorado River Reservation

*Dialect difference

Language Group

	Location of Speakers		
	1600	*1850*	*1989*
Hopi	Hopi Mesas	→	Hopi Reservation
Southern Uto-Aztecan			
Upper Piman (Pima and Tohono O'odham*)	South-central Arizona; Sonora, Mexico	→	Pimas: Salt and Gila River Reservations; Tohono O'odham: San Xavier, Ak Chin, Gila Bend and "Main" Tohono O'odham Reservations
Lower Piman	Chihuahua and Sonora, Mexico	→	
Northern Tepehuan	Chihuahua, Mexico	→	
Southern Tepehuan	Durango, Mexico	→	
Tarahumara	Chihuahua, Mexico	→	
Guarijío	Chihuahua, Mexico	→	
Mayo* and Yaqui*	Sonora and Sinaloa, Mexico	→	Guadalupe, Arizona; Yaqui Reservation, Tucson; Yaqui and Mayo River Valleys in Mexico
Zunian			
Zuni	Zuni	→	Zuni Reservation

*Dialect difference

Paiutes) and pastoralists (the Tarahumaras). Similarly, Hokan speakers represent many distinct traditional lifestyles, including riverine horticulturalists (the Mohaves, Quechan and Maricopas), hunter-gatherers who also did a little farming (the Upland Yumans), and the Seris, who relied heavily on marine resources. In many respects the traditional lifestyle of the Athabaskan Western Apaches was much more closely aligned with that of the Upland Yumans who shared a similar environment, than it was with the linguistically related Navajos or Jicarilla Apaches.

Hence, variations in lifestyle cut across language families. These were not random variations, for they reflected differing cultural and social environments. We turn now to those influences and their interrelationships.

Subsistence

When we consider traditional Southwestern subsistence patterns—the ways people made their living—we see a mix of environmental and historical influences. The principle ecological zones—the desert riverine lowlands, the high mountains, the desert ranges and basins, and the plateau—provided potentialities and imposed limits. Within these life zones the particular sequence of historical events, including trade with more developed centers in Mesoamerica, the movements of people northward from central Mexico and subsequent expansions by Athabaskans and intrusions by Anglo-Europeans, further defined and redefined these potentialities. What elements and resources—human and material—were present in particular environments, and how did people use these in their daily lives? We begin by looking at life in the lowlands.

Riverine Farmers

The river valleys of what is now Western Mexico and of Arizona and New Mexico sustained large populations. In immediate pre-Spanish times, for instance, about 30,000 Yaquis lived along the flood plain of the Yaqui River. Strung out in perhaps 80 loosely organized settlements of circular, thatch-covered domed houses, rectangular wattle-and-daub houses, and *ramadas* or shade houses, the Yaquis raised the classic Southwestern crops: corn, beans and squash. In these basic patterns they resembled the closely related Opatas in the neighboring valleys and the tribes of the lower Colorado River.

The Pimas shared a similar subsistence and settlement pattern, residing in six dispersed villages or *rancherias* between modern Gila Bend and Coolidge, Arizona. To the south and west, near Picacho Peak, they occupied another rancheria along the Santa Cruz River. People the Spanish called Sóbaipuris lived in similar settlements in the Santa Cruz and San Pedro River Valleys.

The Colorado sustained a chain of tribes, from north to south: the Mohaves, Halchidhomas, Quechan, Halyikwamais, Kahuan and Cocopahs. Each numbered in the thousands, and all depended on the annual floods to wet and fertilize their lands. When the spring floods receded, leaving behind their moisture and load of silts, the Indians planted their gardens, again of corn, beans, pumpkins and for the Mohaves especially, sunflowers. These foods, along with mesquite beans and river resources, afforded a rich diet in years when the floods came.

But one year in four, the floods failed and starvation ruled. Some argue that this environmental volatility led to the warfare endemic to this region—warfare so thoroughly institutionalized that the causes probably transcended any ecological bases and came to be rooted in feud, revenge, political rivalries and definitions of manliness invoking prowess in battle. Warfare ranged from short, quick raids involving as few as eight or 10 men, to pre-arranged, massed battles with hundreds on each side. Armed with clubs made of ironwood that resembled World War II German grenades (potato mashers), warriors aimed to seize the enemy's hair and smash his face with an upward blow.

Like the Yaquis and other Mexican riverine people, the Colorado River Yumans lived in rancherias strung out along the river. These had no obvious boundaries, and one would have difficulty identifying when one village had been passed and another entered. In the summer months people sought shelter from the sun under shades or ramadas near their fields. In the cooler, non-farming months they moved back from the river to high ground where they built shades, dome-shaped houses of arrowweed over a frame of bent poles, and more substantial, sometimes semi-subterranean earth-covered structures based on a four-post frame of cottonwood logs.

Upland Hunters and Gatherers

West and south of the Gila River were a people Anglos called Papagos, and who call themselves the Tohono O'odham or Desert People. Tohono O'odham territory is one of the most diverse provinces of the Sonoran Desert: here, elevation ranges from below sea level to desert peaks of nearly 7,000 feet. To optimize the varied resources in this area, the Tohono O'odham moved back and forth between summer and winter villages. In summer, they gardened at the mouths of washes, planting corn and beans where flood waters fanned out on the valley floors. While their crops matured and even after the harvest, they continued to rely on wild foods, especially mesquite beans and cactus fruits. In the fall, the summer field villages broke up and people dispersed to winter "well villages" near springs in the mountains. From there the men hunted javelina, deer and rabbits, while the women continued to gather.

Water was harder to find in the lowlands to the west, and the 500 or so Tohono O'odham who lived in that harsh environment, called the Sand Papagos, hunted and gathered all year long. Their constant search for wild foods made a sedentary life impossible.

To the north of the Gila and east of the Colorado River, a series of desert valleys and ranges run on a southeast-northwest axis. Rising in elevation from west to east, they culminate at the Mogollon Rim. On the north this desert basin and range province is terminated by the Grand Canyon. This country sustained the Pai, ancestors of the Hualapais and Havasupais, and the closely related but hostile Yavapais. The distribution of these

Figure 7.5 Tohono O'odham women carry water in clay *ollas* from a well, c. 1900. (Courtesy of The Heard Museum, Fred Harvey Collection No. H202, Phoenix, Arizona.)

peoples reflected the distribution of water and other resources. In the west, the lower, drier mountains contain fewer resources and the valleys are generally dry. Not surprisingly population densities were lowest there, increasing from west to east with the most people living around the higher eastern ranges, the spurs projecting off the Mogollon Rim and on the Rim itself.

In spring, family groups moved to garden sites near springs and along stream banks and washes, planting beans, corn and squash. Once the seeds sprouted men and women left their gardens in the care of elderly relatives, moving up and down the desert slopes to harvest wild foods as they came into season. Early fall marked the harvest, a time when people came together at garden sites to collect, dry and store the crops. Later these larger groups broke up into small bands of 10 to 50 people to gather wild seeds, pinyon nuts and acorns, and to hunt deer, antelope, bighorn sheep, rabbits and other game.

Farther north, on the western edges of the plateau, many Yuman-speaking Pai bands faced a much more difficult summer environment. While the plateau nurtured many herbaceous plants, rainfall and surface water were scarce. The scarcity of water led the easternmost Pai to summer in canyons that cut down to the aquifer, where useful flora were more abundant and where springs made irrigation horticulture possible. During this time Pai bands came together at agricultural sites, sometimes forming villages or rancherias reminiscent of those on the Colorado and the Gila, though smaller in scale. But these Pai too were primarily hunter-gatherers who used horticulture to fill out their diet in what would otherwise have been a difficult season.

Still farther east, over the Rim and the White Mountains and other high ranges extending westward from the Rockies, Apaches lived much like the Pai and Yavapais. Indeed, for many years outsiders lumped them together, the Yavapais in particular being confused with the Apaches. There, in higher, wetter country, hunting-gathering supplemented by horticulture and later, by raiding riverine peoples, sustained higher population densities and larger social groups. While this richer ecological zone created differences in size and intensity, the basic patterns of life there were very similar to those farther west.

Thus, both to the north and south of the Salt and Gila, there lived people who were closely related linguistically to the tribes along the rivers. But whereas the river tribes relied primarily on irrigation horticulture supplemented by hunting and gathering, the reverse was true of the Upland Yumans and the Tohono O'odham, and of the Apaches. In keeping with this shift in emphasis, the settlements to the north and south were smaller, and overall these upland populations were smaller, too. While the Riverine Yumans may have included as many as 20,000 people in 1600, the Upland Yumans, who occupied a far vaster territory, probably did not exceed 5,000. In the south the Tohono O'odham, though more numerous than the Upland Yumans, were also but a fraction of the Uto-Aztecan populations living along the rivers in modern Arizona and Mexico.

Other Uto-Aztecan speakers like the Tarahumaras in the Sierra Madre Occidental practiced a mixed economy of hunting, gathering and horticulture much like the mountain Athabaskans and the Upland Yumans. As they obtained Old World crops and livestock, horticulture and animal husbandry expanded in importance for the Tarahumaras. Affected by introduced diseases but shielded by their isolation in the rugged mountains, the Tarahumaras remained numerous, numbering in the tens of thousands in the 1870s.

Plateau and Plains Adaptations

Far to the north and east of these populations, the Eastern Pueblos of the Rio Grande and its tributaries also adopted a riverine lifestyle, diverting water through canals to their fields. Those who lived along smaller streams and the Western Pueblos—the Hopis and Zunis—practiced flood water and rainfall farming. Both the canal irrigators and the rainfall and flood irrigators lived in compact, apartment-style villages. This settlement pattern may reflect their origins; the 30,000 to 40,000 who lived in villages of this type when the Spanish arrived in the early 1500s were probably remnants of still larger populations that earlier occupied such centers as Chaco Canyon, the large abandoned pueblos of the Four Corners region, and the ruined towns in the Little Colorado Valley.

The pueblos east of the Rio Grande had access to the plains, and for some of them—notably Taos and Picuris—hunting deer and even bison may have provided additional resources. But by the early 1500s the advent of Athabaskan-speaking bison hunters on the plains probably led the puebloans to reduce their use of that area, as they were drawn into a symbiotic relationship with their new neighbors, trading agricultural products for meat.

West of the Rio Grande on the Colorado Plateau, population densities were light, and it was not until the Spanish brought livestock into the Rio Grande Valley that this area came to be significantly occupied. As this occurred, puebloans began to use the areas around their pueblos for grazing, and Athabaskans—in particular the Navajos—added live-

Figure 7.6 Historic Navajo site near Monument Valley, Utah, as seen in 1981. (Courtesy of T. L. McCarty.)

stock to their horticultural economy. While the Eastern Puebloans remained tethered to their fields and the river, the Navajos expanded westward, finding a virtually unexploited niche in the great expanses of plateau grassland.

Many Navajos settled in small family groups around canyon washes and in other well watered places during the summer months, moving their sheep and goats to higher elevations during winter. Others kept winter camps in the lower grasslands, returning in summer to cool mountain pastures. At each location they built or repaired their *hogans,* circular or conical mud-and-log dwellings that were quickly erected. In addition to these major seasonal movements, families and their individual members made shorter trips throughout the area to hunt deer, antelope and smaller game, and to harvest ripening plant products such as sumac berries and pinyon nuts. Though they ranged over a huge area, the Navajos were never truly nomadic for in general they returned to the same locales—and often, the same home sites—over the course of a year.

The presence of livestock changed the Navajo economy in yet another way: with the introduction of horses, Navajos mounted raids against pueblo villagers for livestock, food and other goods. A reciprocal pattern of raiding and reprisals took root and by the 1700s, became thoroughly integrated into the Navajo economy.

Like the Navajos, other Athabaskans in the Southwest also expanded territorially and in numbers. The Athabaskan Jicarilla and Lipan Apaches made use of the resources of the western edges of the plains, mixing horse-mounted bison hunting with some horticulture and more generalized hunting and gathering. After obtaining horses these Apacheans, with the Western Apaches, Chiricahuas and Navajos, became involved in raiding the sedentary, riverine village and rancheria peoples. The Western and Chiricahua Apaches in particular continued to expand at the expense of the Pimas, forcing the Sobaipuris from the San Pedro and southern Santa Cruz River Valleys in the 18th and 19th centuries.

In sum, Southwestern patterns of resource use reflected not only the possibilities in given environments, but historical influences and the relationships among indigenous peoples as well. The spread of horticulture and associated technologies from the south transformed the river valleys, making possible large, settled populations and providing a valuable addition to hunting and gathering in the mountains and desert lowlands. The introduction of livestock transformed the Colorado Plateau into a critical resource for grazing. Horses, cattle, and the presence of sedentary horticultural populations made raiding a viable economic activity. By the middle of the 19th century some of the mountain dwellers—the Chiricahua and Western Apaches, for instance—had become raiding horsemen, dependent upon the presence of sedentary populations for livestock and horticultural products. In areas far removed from the village farmers and sources of livestock, people like the Pai used horses little for raiding, eating them instead as they did cattle. In other areas such as the Hopi Mesas, the very early expansion of the Navajos into surrounding grazing areas inhibited the development of pastoralism there.

Social Systems

If Southwestern Indians' economic adaptations reflected ecological variables and the events of history, the organization of their traditional social and political life reflected both history and these economic adaptations. We can see this by looking again at pre-conquest life in distinct environmental zones.

Flexibility in the Uplands and Mountains

We have noted the abundant wild plant and animal resources available in the environmentally varied uplands. This environment also nurtured steams and other limited water resources, making summer farming possible. Social groupings among the peoples who lived here—the Upland Yuman Pai and Yavapais and several Apache groups—allowed them to optimally tap those resources.

Among the Pai, enduring larger groups emerged most significantly in the colder moths when hunting grew in importance. During these times families came together at locales near water, wood and good hunting, coalescing around four to eight men who cooperated in the hunt. These *local groups* or *bands* probably never included more than 55 people, and most averaged about 25.

Generally one of the men in the group came to be recognized as the leader or first among equals. The Pai called them "men who go forward," "good men," "superlatively good men" and simply, "talkers." These descriptions indicate the lack of formal, institutionalized or territorially-based political statuses. For while others respected and valued the opinions of local group leaders, the latter led by strength or character rather than by coercion, articulating conventional wisdom, leading discussion in matters of local concern and speaking for the group. The group's unity depended less on this leadership than on the ad-

Figure 7.7 Havasupai local group headman, called Captain Burro by Anglo-Americans, with water basket, c. 1898. (Photograph by George Wharton James, courtesy of The Heard Museum, Phoenix, Arizona.)

vantages of cooperation in hunting and the overlapping ties of kinship, marriage and friendship among group members.

Because of the groups' small sizes, people, who married non-relatives, generally looked for spouses in other local groups. When a Pai man married he spent some time living with his bride's family, hunting and working for them. Normally the couple returned to live with the groom's family, though in cases where the bride had no brothers or the groom's group was too large, the couple might remain with the bride's natal group. This normal type of residence is called *viripatrilocality,* meaning ''residence at the groom's father's place.''

This preference for viripatrilocal residence after marriage did not restrict the couple's interactions with either of their natal groups. They frequently visited with family members living elsewhere, and children, who obtained rights to hunt and gather by virtue of growing up in a local area, developed rights in both their mother's and father's natal areas. All this meant people had relatives, in-laws and friends—and hunting and gathering rights—in numerous areas. Bounded territorial groups did not exist and individuals, including

Figure 7.8 Havasu Canyon looking north; fields in left foreground, c. 1898. (Photograph by George Wharton James, courtesy of The Heard Museum, Phoenix, Arizona.)

leading men, readily changed local groups. This weakening of local group ties and the strengthening of ties between groups occurred most noticeably during the warmer months when members of different local groups came together around horticultural resources and concentrations of wild plants.

But for most of the year the fundamental unit in Pai society was the *family*. Indeed, during many seasons the family *was* the local group. These were the people who lived and worked together, and who cooperated in daily affairs. Sometimes families included no more than a husband, his wife or wives and their immature children. Less frequently they included a senior couple, a married child and his or her spouse, in addition to their mature children. When a couple had no sons, daughters often remained with their parents, and young married couples without living parents sometimes teamed up with older siblings or older aunts and uncles. Family membership, then, took many forms.

Figure 7.9 Paiute wife of Manakaja, Havasupai regional band leader, with child in burden basket, c. 1898. (Photograph by George Wharton James, courtesy of The Heard Museum, Phoenix, Arizona.)

In early spring, these family groups broke away from other members of the local group, moving to stands of agave and other seasonally available plant foods. By March or April, many found their way to horticultural sites. Havasu Canyon, an arm of the Grand Canyon, was one such place where perhaps 35 households or 200 to 250 people from eight to 10 local groups came together to plant and irrigate gardens in the summer months. During the winter, the ties between groups were reinforced and new ones forged through intergroup marriages.

These interpersonal connections between members of different camp groups afforded the basis for a sense of common interest, and served to channel cooperative efforts when Yavapais and later, Spanish, Mexican and Anglo slave raiders attacked. During those times—in the farming season and when facing outside threats—several leading men emerged to articulate their larger groups' efforts and interests. The Pai recognized these larger groups and named them after geographic features in their domains. In the mid-19th century, 13 such regional bands existed, of which the Hualapai or *Hwala'pay* (Ponderosa

Pine People), and the Havasupai or *Havasuw'apa* (Blue-Green Water People), were but two.

The Pai also recognized still larger groups, though these were even less clearly institutionalized than the local groups and regional bands. The Pai identified these larger "subtribes" by reference to their location, a practice that remains common today.

This propensity and the emergence of common problems with the Anglo-American onslaught after 1850 may account for the development of a supra-regional band organization. It seems difficult, however, for such an organization to have been sustained in pre-contact times given the low population density of the Pai and the difficulty of communication between groups not in direct contact. Thus, while the Pai viewed themselves as a distinct people as against all others (Pai means people), spoke dialects of a common language and formed a continuous marriage network, they lacked any overall tribal organization or formal system of government. In this sense they constituted a cultural rather than a political tribe.

This flexible organization characterized the mountain range and basin peoples. The Pai, Yavapais, Kaibab Paiutes and the Chiricahua, Mescalero and Western Apaches all were similarly organized.

But atop these basic similarities were some differences. Perhaps because they enjoyed richer environments, local groups and regional bands were larger among the mountain-dwelling Apaches than they were among the Upland Yumans and Kaibab Paiutes. In addition, while the latter preferred residence near the groom's parents after marriage but actually lived in a variety of arrangements, the Apaches preferred residence near the bride's parents. Anthropologists call this *matrilocal* residence.

One result of this arrangement was that domestic groups formed around related women and their husbands. As Apache boys matured, married and went to live with their wives' families, women remained the enduring domestic team who lived and worked together on a daily basis. Because they stayed in particular locales over time, women became particularly knowledgeable of and adept at using local resources. This gave them a revered status in Apache society. Among the Western Apaches this was reinforced by a *matrilineal descent* system whereby children at birth became members of the named "line" of their mothers. Members of the same matriline could not marry.

Many of these matrilines were related or believed to be related to others through female ancestresses. Related lineages or *matrilineal clans,* of which there were historically about 60, were named after the place where the clan ancestresses supposedly first made gardens. In this emphasis on kinship through women the Western Apaches resemble the Hopis and the closely related Navajos rather than the Mescalero and Chiricahua Apaches, who trace kinship equally through males and females as do the Pai, the Paiutes and Anglo-Americans.

Whether they have clans or not, Apache men are expected to show great respect for their parents-in-law. Men especially must avoid their mothers-in-law, never being in a room alone with them or speaking directly to them. Today, when traveling in sedans some families hang blankets between the front and back seats to separate sons-in-law from mothers-in-law. In this, too, the Apaches differ from the Upland Yumans.

However large such differences may seem to those who lived and are living them out, the fact remains that in early historic times the social organizations of the Yuman-speaking Pai and Yavapais, the Uto-Aztecan Kaibab Paiutes and the Athabaskan Chiricahua, Mescalero and Western Apaches had much in common. These commonalities grew out of their similar ecological adaptations.

Riverine Village and Rancheria Life

When we shift our attention to the riverine peoples, we see that their social organizations also reflected their fundamental ecological adaptations, for the villages along the river corresponded very directly with the distribution of resources. Like the Pai, the Riverine Yumans preferred post-marital residence with the groom's family. Hence, households were similar to Pai households, most often forming around men and their wives and eventually, sons and their wives and children. But as the Riverine Yumans had more abundant and concentrated resources as well as larger populations, the densities of their populations were higher than those in the uplands. Rancherias numbered in the hundreds, being more or less equivalent to Upland Yuman regional bands in scale.

Within each rancheria, leading men, sometimes called "talkers" or "real men," exercised some political leadership. Like Upland Yuman leaders, their influence was limited. Rancherias had little political significance, and interests within them grew out of kinship, marriage and friendship relations. Land in pre-conquest times was not owned; river channels frequently shifted, formerly valuable tracts became worthless, and valueless tracts became valuable. Further, while starvation occurred when the floods failed and people sought the produce of others, everyone had access to irrigable land. The members of rancherias therefore had no real interests in fixed, scarce resources and rancherias did not focus around land rights or territoriality.

This may not have been true at the tribal level, for the Riverine Yumans transcended their cousins in the uplands in having not only a sense of being one people, but in having tribal-wide leaders. The Mohaves, for example, had a single tribal chief. The Quechan had two, one who served in times of peace and another to whom people looked in times of war. Yet no tribal chiefs were of great influence, and some scholars believe the chiefs emerged only in early historic times in response to intrusions by outsiders.

The River Yumans nonetheless all had other tribal-wide affiliations, most notably a complex world renewal and mourning ceremony in honor of the deaths of leading individuals. Given periodically by groups of families, the ceremonies were attended by the tribal membership and by members of other tribes. Along with tribally organized warfare, these ceremonies reinforced each tribe's sense of nationhood and the authority of its leaders. Further reinforcing this was a system of *patrilineal clans*. At birth, children joined their father's clan, remaining a member until death. Because people married outside their clan, clan relatives were scattered throughout the tribe, enhancing the tribe as a unit of social significance.

The Riverine Pimas lived much as the Colorado River Yumans, in loosely structured rancherias. In historic times at least, all the Gila River Pimas recognized a single tribal chief. Again like the Yumans, the Pimas preferred to live after marriage near the groom's family, and Pima children became members of the father's clan at birth.

The five Gila River Pima clans were organized into two named groups, the Red Ants and the White Ants. Anthropologists call such complementary, paired groups *moieties*. People could marry non-relatives within their clan and moiety. Moieties, then, functioned not to regulate marriage but instead ordered ceremonial life. With the exception of the moieties, early River Pima social life very much resembled that of the River Yumans and for that matter, what we know of pre-Spanish Yaqui organization.

Tohono O'odham life south of the River Pimas was a less intense version of life on the river. In the warmer months people lived in farming rancherias near water and arable land; in the fall and winter they moved to winter hunting and gathering camps near permanent water sources. Tohono O'odham political leadership was less developed than that among the river peoples, with villages or rancherias being the largest political units. In these features the Tohono O'odham were to the River Pimas as the Upland Yumans were to the River Yumans: a less intense, more fluidly organized version of what was basically a flexible lifeway.

Distinctive Lifestyles on the Plateau

Life on the eastern edge of the Southwest, on the plains and the Colorado Plateau, was similarly loosely structured. After obtaining horses, the ancestors of those we call the Jicarilla, Lipan and the easternmost Mescaleros added bison hunting to their mixed economy of hunting, gathering and horticulture. Among these groups, regional bands and political groupings were even less developed than they were among the mountain range and basin peoples.

On the Colorado Plateau the horse and other livestock came to play important roles in defining tribal social life and in the relationships among tribal groups. Sometime after the pueblo abandonment of the Four Corners region in the 14th century, the ancestors of the Navajos began moving into the area. There, in the pinyon-dotted canyonlands Navajos call *Dinétah* or "Navajo Homeland," they developed a complex social system based on farming, hunting, gathering, animal husbandry and trade with the pueblos.

We know little of daily life in Dinétah, but native oral tradition and archaeological evidence place both Navajos and puebloans there in the late 16th and early 17th centuries. As Navajos and puebloans interacted and inter-married, Athabaskan traits fused with pueblo culture. Some argue that the Navajos' matrilineal clans developed at this time. Whatever the origin of the clans, the fortified mud and stone pueblitos in Dinétah, accessible only by wooden ladders and often surrounded by stone walls and towers, suggest a lifestyle frequently threatened by enemy raids. These settlements also suggest a leadership

Figure 7.10 Fortified stone pueblito in Dinétah, as seen in 1981. The fortification housed a spiraling "staircase"-like ladder leading to the pueblito's main rooms. (Courtesy of T. L. McCarty.)

style capable of organizing large numbers of people, both to respond to attacks and to build the massive fortifications.

This time of formation of what we think of as traditional Navajo culture ended in the mid-18th century, when droughts and enemy raids drove the Navajos from Dinétah. Entering the virgin grasslands on the Colorado Plateau, they took up an increasingly pastoral lifestyle. For most of the year families lived in relative isolation, moving from summer to winter camp sites as their needs for grazing and water resources changed. In this context, the fundamental social units were camp groups—those close relatives who traveled together and cooperated in herding sheep, farming, child care, and building and maintaining the hogans.

Women formed the core of these groups. They owned the fields and the sheep, and after marriage, couples tended to live with the bride's family. Descent, too, was traced through women. These ties through women bound people together in a wide network of clan relatives. Since clan relatives could not marry, marriages linked families from different clans and locales, greatly expanding the number of people on whom one could rely for aid and support.

241

Figure 7.11 Navajo homesite, including hogan and shade house, in 1981. (Courtesy of T. L. McCarty.)

The Navajo concept *k'é* embodies the profound significance of this broad kin and clan network. Signifying kinship, "kindness, love, cooperation, thoughtfulness, friendliness, and peacefulness," *k'é* articulates the mutual obligations that sustained balanced, harmonious human relationships in what was often an isolated and volatile environment (Witherspoon 1983: 524–525; cf. Bia et al. 1983:3).

As camp groups grew and evolved from generation to generation, they developed ties with neighboring camps. While these regional groupings or bands did not interact on a daily basis, they cooperated in ceremonies and afforded a basis for mutual aid in times of need. Occasionally, when dealing with outsiders, regional bands in particular locales united under the direction of a regional headman or *naat'áanii*. Typically men of wealth in livestock who were well placed in their kin and affinal networks, the *naat'áanii* led by personal persuasion rather than force. Their following emerged from respect for their oratory, their hunting and raiding abilities, and their ritual knowledge, considered to protect supporters. Coalitions formed under these headmen had short-term aims—raiding or retaliating against a raid—and quickly dissipated once their immediate purpose dissolved.

Some have reported a wider tribal-wide council of Navajo war chiefs and peace chiefs, but the council's organization is difficult to document. The fact that treaties signed by Navajo headmen prior to the reservation period had little force outside the headmen's constituency suggests such tribal-wide structures, if they existed, lacked much authority. Hence, though the members of regional groups considered themselves one people, the *Diné,* sharing a common language and culture, they did not come together as a whole, unite under a single leader, or recognize any overall tribal political authority. Like the Apaches and the Upland Yumans, they represented a cultural rather than a political tribe.

As the Navajos expanded, they came to surround the Uto-Aztecan speaking Hopis, who had lived along the southern extensions of Black Mesa for centuries. Though this area receives only 12 inches of rainfall a year, the Hopis developed a complex social and economic system based on rainfall and flood and spring irrigation horticulture. For Hopis, corn has provided the basis of life, and Hopi women have traditionally controlled this valuable resource. They own the fields, the corn and other crops, as well as the houses. At marriage, men move into their wife's household.

Traditionally, one daughter remained with her mother, inheriting primary rights to her mother's house and gardens. The mother, her primary successor and the daughter's children made up the household's "main line," while other daughters and their families lived near the main household. These daughters stood in reserve, ready to fill in for the favored daughter if she could die or prove less than competent in managing the household property.

Over time this process resulted in villages made up of individuals who shared households or lived in neighboring households headed by women. The natal members of the households formed matrilineages, and households related through women formed matrilineal, named clans. The Hopi themselves recognized the existence of the clans, naming and identifying the head of the central household as the clan mother.

The property of the primary descent line within the clan included not only the house and gardens, but also any paraphernalia controlled by the group and used by a senior man—an uncle, a brother or son—in religious activities. Aimed at sustaining fertility and rainfall, religious activities were the domain of men who performed their duties in the context of religious societies. These included men from other clans and households. The chiefs of these societies, along with a village chief, formed a loosely organized political elite, controlling the ritual cycle as well as the allocation of clan lands among various clan households. They also settled disputes within the village and made policy concerning outsiders. When religious leaders retired or died, a sister's son or another member of the same or a related clan succeeded them.

The Hopis' system of fixed, not easily divided property (houses, prime gardens and ritual offices), and the natural variation in births and deaths between households and clans, sometimes presented problems. Even in times when village populations remained stable, some households waxed and others waned. This led to imbalances in the amount of land versus the number of people, as some lines lacked enough land while others controlled a surfeit. Similarly, the presence of declining clans controlling powerful ritual offices in competition with larger, growing clans controlling few, created problems. In times of population growth when most households had multiple surviving offspring over several generations, these problems increased.

The upshot has been a settlement pattern in which "mother villages"—those controlled by the main-line households—gave rise to outlying settlements established by people who lost out in land inheritance or by men who did not succeed to ritual office. When disease, starvation or warfare threatened, villages were abandoned, the survivors turning to other better situated villages. All this has created variations in the number of Hopi villages

Figure 7.12 Hopi village of Walpi at First Mesa, c. 1880–1900. (Courtesy of The Heard Museum, Phoenix, Arizona.)

even in historic times. Thus, while in 1880 there were only eight villages, by 1987 there were 12. These are organized into groups on each of three mesas, with each mesa having a mother village, a colony village and a guard village. A separate daughter village, Moencopi, began as a farming settlement west of Third Mesa. Two other villages, Polacca and Kyokotsmovi, sit below the mesas.

Along the Zuni River in what is now New Mexico, the Zunis lived a life resembling in its broad outlines that of the Hopis. Still farther east, the Western Keresans at Acoma and Laguna also practiced rainfall and irrigation horticulture, were organized into matrilineal households and clans, and individuals joined a kiva society through the sponsorship of a ceremonial father.

Along the Rio Grande and its tributaries different patterns prevailed. The Keresans—Cochiti, San Felipe, Santa Ana, Santo Domingo and Zia Pueblos—and the Towa-speaking Jemez have matrilineal clans, with individuals marrying outside their clan. Among the Southern Tiwa (Isleta and Sandia Pueblos), people are divided into corn groups significant in ritual activities. Recruitment to these groups at Sandia is matrilineal, but at Isleta they are voluntary associations, being neither matrilineal nor patrilineal. The Northern Tiwa (Taos and Picuris Pueblos), and the Tewa (Nambe, Pojoaque, San Ildefonso, San Juan, Santa Clara and Tesuque), have nothing resembling clans. Whether the overall reduction in the ubiquity of clans in the east dates to pre-Spanish days cannot be determined, but today the pervasiveness of matrilateral organizations clearly declines from west to east.

In the Rio Grande Valley, nuclear families, extended families tracing descent equally through women and men, moieties and religious societies are all important. In addition to these, political offices introduced by the Spanish have become thoroughly integrated into the social fabric of most Eastern Pueblo villages.

244

San Juan Pueblo provides an excellent illustration of this (Ortiz 1969). There, households form around nuclear families and children inherit property through both their mother's and father's lines. Through a series of rites of incorporation, children join one of two moieties, the Winter People or the Summer People. If a woman marries outside her moiety, she joins the moiety of her husband.

As individuals mature they may join up to two separate societies, including religious societies, two clown societies and a society associated with each moiety. The officers of religious and clown societies come from both moieties, while the officers of the moiety societies are moiety-specific. Called the "head," "right arm" and "left arm," the officers of the various societies form the core of the political elite. They plan the ritual cycle and select their successors; since they also select political officers, they control the secular offices as well. The latter include a war chief, five war captains and, of clear Spanish origins, the governor, two lieutenants and the sheriff. All of these individuals represent the ordinary or "Dry Food People," and when they are selected they become *Towa'é*. The war chief and his captains maintain internal political control, basically executing the orders of the officers of the secret societies who collectively are known as *Patowa* or "Made People." The governor, lieutenant and sheriff deal with outsiders. They too are *Towa'é*.

Each year the *Towa'é* are selected from among the Winter People and the Summer People. In one year, the top official of the Winter People chooses the governor from among the members of his moiety, then the Summer Chief chooses the right arm lieutenant from his moiety and so on, until all positions are filled. The following year the Summer Chief chooses first. The Summer and Winter Chiefs similarly alternate control of such activities as chief of the village, the Winter Chief ruling from the autumnal equinox to a month before the vernal, and the Summer Chief for the remainder.

In most Eastern Pueblo villages, the political elite—the officers of the secret societies—exercise great political power. Some lay this to the importance of irrigation and the central control required for construction and maintenance of the irrigation works. Others suggest that a variety of factors account for the power of Eastern Pueblo society chiefs, not the least of which is the impact of the Spaniards and Anglos who settled among the pueblos, usurped their lands and generally made it more difficult for people to escape the dictates of their society chiefs, while simultaneously imbuing these offices with great significance as symbols of pueblo identity and resistance.

Belief Systems

We have seen that those peoples who lived near concentrated resources—water and arable land—tended to have more formal structures organizing their social groups. In the uplands, mountains and plains, and for Navajos on the plateau, social groups on the other hand tended to be more fluid and flexible, changing as people dispersed or coalesced for specific economic and social pursuits.

Traditional Southwest Indian religious systems in many ways paralleled these social-ecological adaptations, manifesting two primary emphases. One, the *shamanistic complex*, characterizes hunting and gathering societies throughout the world, and typified Southwestern rancheria and band peoples. The second, involving an *organized priesthood and communal ritual*, was and is more developed among the village-dwelling pueblos. As we will see, however, these contrasts are really matters of degree, and outsiders and the events of history also played important roles in the belief and ritual systems that developed in the Southwest.

Shamanism

Shamanism is perhaps the most ancient religious complex in the world. At its heart is a view of the world as permeated with power, conceptualized in both personalized terms—in the form of spirit beings and gods—and impersonal terms. Individuals in general and specific individuals with greater intensity live in this world of power, affecting and affected by powerful beings. Personalized powers, usually named and operating much like humans in terms of motives and desires, sometimes possess humans or are appealed to to reveal the causes of sickness, to cure and help in life's endeavors, or are coerced by humans using verbal and material offerings to establish obligation and reciprocity. People manipulate impersonal powers through the proper use of appropriate ritual, again to cure and ensure well being, success and fruitfulness in life.

Those who experience this interaction with the powers most fully are the shamans, religious practitioners who obtain their powers through dreams or visions. Among most Yumans, Pimans and Apaches, shamans receive their special powers through dreams in which their guardian spirit reveals to them the songs, techniques and symbols that give them the power to cure or be especially effective in some other endeavor. Among some Yavapais, shamans obtain power while in a trance, when the individual and the guardian power become one. The spirit possesses the individual when he first obtains power, and in subsequent religious performances, when as a practitioner the shaman divines the cause of misfortune, cures or otherwise makes use of power.

Generally among the hunting-gathering peoples, shamans minister to individuals and small groups, using rituals to divine and cure ill health and other misfortunes, and to ensure longevity and robustness or bring success in specific endeavors such as hunting. Along with the emphasis on curing, the doctrine is that sickness usually results from an imbalance in the powers permeating people and the world around them. Touching, blowing smoke over the patient's body, sucking or stroking with feathers can remove the evil causing and resulting from this imbalance.

Peoples' stories of their origins validate and explain much of this practice and belief. Among the Yumans, the first people of the world are cut from water reeds and instructed in the things that make them Havasupai, Yavapai or whatever by the elder of two brothers. Among the Upland Yumans, Elder Brother then dies from the symbolic cannibalism of his daughters who, having turned into frogs because of their father's incestuous abuse, eat his feces. His corpse, thanks to his daughters' symbolic rather than actual cannibalism, is available for cremation, but the trickster Coyote steals Elder Brother's heart before the fire can completely consume it. Because the sacrifice is incomplete, the Upland Yumans do not receive the same skills and powers in horticulture as do other peoples. After all this, they travel upward through several worlds, finally passing into the world as it was in ethnohistoric times. But the abused daughters, still angry, cause a flood to well up through a hole from which the people emerged. All drown except a small girl who is placed in a log along with the people's cultigens and other important artifacts. The girl survives as the log rides out the flood and lodges in a mountain.

Athabaskans share the flood story, and Havasupais and Yavapais tell a subsequent cycle of related events very similar to the Navajos' account of the birth and education of the Hero Twins. In the Havasupai and Yavapai stories, the surviving female is impregnated by the Sun with dripping water. She gives birth to a daughter, who is also impregnated by the Sun and dripping water. The daughter gives birth to a son, but her incest is avenged when a cannibal Eagle kills the daughter, leaving her son to be raised by his maternal grandmother. The son has many adventures, killing numerous monsters and learning how to live before he finally reunites with his father, the Sun.

Each of these accounts has many episodes that can be told separately, in any order, on winter nights. A source of entertainment, the stories also charter the rationale for a lifeway, providing lessons on how one should live.

The origin stories of the Yumans, Apaches and Pimans are said to be less detailed and rich in symbolic associations than are those of the Navajos and horticultural tribes. That they are less studied may have something to do with this statement, but it does seem clear that the Navajos and horticultural peoples combine other elements with the shamanistic complex almost to the point of totally obscuring it.

These other elements are evident in nascent form among some of the Yumans. The Colorado River tribes, for example, practice a complex communal mourning ceremony. Its inspiration is the cremation of the incestuous brother; following this prototype the ceremony is given periodically to commemorate the recent death or deaths of important mortals. Combining ritual drama, songs, speeches, feasting and gifts, River Yuman mourning ceremonies are very much like the calendrical world renewal and fertility rituals of the more horticultural peoples.

We know little of River Piman religion. However, the Tohono O'odham grafted rituals characteristic of horticultural peoples to a shamanistic complex. These included a series of rituals concerned with rain-making and the growth and harvest of corn, calendrical rituals organized in each village by a prominent leader, called Keeper of the Smoke. Ritual drunkenness, dancing and rain symbolism all emphasized the community's well being. In addition, until very recently the Tohono O'odham put on a world renewal ceremony every four years at two different locations. A complex ritual drama intended to keep the world in order and involving masked dancers, clowns, cloud and rain symbolism, corn and prayer sticks, the ceremony was organized by individuals from a number of villages. In all these characteristics Piman rituals typify horticultural village religious practice. Yet leaders gain access to the supernatural through dreams, a feature distinctive of shamanism.

Pueblo and Navajo Religion

The concern with renewing or keeping the world in order, cloud and rain symbolism, fertility symbols—most notably, corn—prayer sticks and masked dancers also distinguish Pueblo Indian religious activities. The pueblos, however, manifest these elements in a greater number and variety of rituals organized by priests, the religious specialists who act as officers of the religious societies. Pueblo priests differ from Yuman and Apache shamans in that priests gain access to powers by apprenticeship, learning the ritual procedures that bring about the desired ends of fertility, rain, social peace and long, fruitful lives.

Priests control various puebloan rituals, which are conducted by the members of discrete societies. Community well being is nonetheless the rituals' intent, for while different societies divide the community into groups, the members of each group need the ritual services of other groups for their own well being. In keeping with this separation and synthesis, most rituals have both a private or restricted set of activities undertaken in ceremonial chambers (kivas), and more open rites performed in public plazas. In many of the rites masked dancers represent *kachinas,* benevolent but potentially dangerous spirit beings. In an almost shaman-like fashion, dancers are possessed by the spirit of the kachinas, but typical of the priesthood complex, dancers learn or are trained to perform their roles.

Congruent with all this, pueblo religion is characterized by official knowledge graded in terms of who may know it. This contrasts with information about power in less horticultural groups, where it is not so much secret as personalistic, and where accounts of origins, the details of how power affects things and what to do about it vary considerably between individuals. Similarly, as pueblo societies with their many social divisions are more complex, the accounts of the origins of their social orders and the worlds they experience tend to be more complex than are those among the Yumans, Apaches and Tohono O'odham, if only because there is more to describe.

In practice, these contrasts between the shamanistic complex characteristic of hunting-gathering and rancheria peoples, and the priesthoods of horticultural village-dwellers, exist along a continuum or series of continua. The Navajos even more than the Pimans and River Yumans offer an example of a people whose religious practices represent a synthesis of the two extremes.

Curing illness and misfortune is central to Navajo religion. The principle religious practitioners—singers or medicine men and a few medicine women—are shaman-like in that they minister to individuals and small groups (families, households and today, the personnel of tribal and federal offices and programs). Further, like shamans generally they were not, until recently, organized into societies, and they are specialists, controlling the knowledge and having access to the power associated with one or a few disorders. On the other hand, like priests their access to power is through learning. As apprentices they acquire the complex rituals, symbolism and other knowledge that allows them to drive out evil or improper, unnatural forces, and to bring their patients into harmony or union with the powers of the universe.

The cosmology associated with this is also complicated, with a great deal of directional and color symbolism, considerable emphasis on horticulture (corn and rain symbolism), and many pueblo motifs. Navajo accounts of their origins and of the Navajo lifeway also share a good deal with pueblo accounts.

Blends of Native and Alien Traditions

Indigenous Southwestern religions thus exhibit considerable variation. This is enhanced by borrowings from Spanish Catholic practices that occurred early enough in the contact period for them to be reformulated and more or less integrated into tribal life.

The Yaquis, whose origin accounts begin with the formation of the eight sacred towns in the Yaqui River Valley, most clearly evidence this. We know from historical accounts that the Spanish created these towns as instruments in their drive to destroy the Yaquis militarily, reduce them geographically and integrate them politically, economically and religiously into the empire and church. The Spanish failed, but in their efforts Yaqui life was totally reorganized, and a form of folk Catholicism left as a precipitate of those efforts has been a major factor in the maintenance of Yaqui ethnic identity.

In Mexico each of the eight towns that emerged as a result of Spanish rule created its own independent church. The church was in the overall charge of a council consisting of the heads of the female caretakers (*kiyoteim*), the sacristans in charge of church finances and property, and the head of the *machtom*, who controlled ritual. The council advised the church governor (*te opo kopanum*), who coordinated ritual, and the *pihkam* who indoctrinated the children. These individuals, along with the three male and three female societies charged with leading church ceremonies, constituted the "church authority," one of five branches of Yaqui town government. The "fiesta authority"—24 men and women chosen each year to manage the celebrations for the town's patron saint—and the "custom authority"—two men's societies called the Judases and the Horsemen—carried out the church authority's religious activities.

The civil and military authorities maintained internal order and the town's military capabilities. But the military authorities also had religious overtones. Holding Spanish military titles—captains, flagbearers, lieutenants, sergeants, corporals and drummen—the officers served as the core of the military during war and dedicated themselves to the worship and service of the Virgin of Guadalupe. Among other things, this involved carrying her image and performing rites directed toward the sun at sunrise, noon and sunset. These rituals were bound up with the fiesta and custom authorities and three other cults focusing on Jesus, the Virgin and the dead.

The Horsemen and the Judases were dedicated to the service of Jesus, the Horsemen to the Christ child and the Judases to Jesus after the crucifixion. From Ash Wednesday to the Day of Finding the Cross in May, the Horsemen and Judases took increasing control of the town, taking over the roles of the church, civil and military authorities. During Lent and Holy Week their activities peaked in the production of a Yaqui version of the Passion.

Following this season of gravity and restraint, the *matachines* became prominent during the summer and fall ceremonies associated with the Virgin. Under the direction of the *te opo kopanum* or head church governor, the matachines assisted the church authority's control of ritual during these seasons. In addition to all this, the Yaqui deer dancers hosted and performed at most major rituals at a special structure near the sacred structure or altar.

Most of these offices, the rituals and a good deal of the accompanying cosmology are Spanish Catholic in origins, but have been thoroughly revised and integrated into Yaqui culture. Indeed, Yaqui ceremonial organization is the major vehicle for the maintenance of Yaqui ethnic identity, especially in the United States.

The Tohono O'odham were also missionized early and have sustained a folk Catholicism. Many villages support a chapel dedicated to Saint Frances and saints' days, and the Christian ritual calendar and religious rites play important roles in people's lives. The result is that Tohono O'odham religious life involves not only aspects of the shamanistic complex and the priest-corn-fertility-rain complex of village horticulturalists, but a separate folk Catholicism as well.

The Eastern Pueblos, too, have adopted a good deal from Spanish Catholicism. Here it has not displaced the traditional religions, but elements of folk Catholicism, while important in people's lives, remain separate from the traditional activities and offices.

The differing responses of Southwestern Indians to alien religions continues into the 20th century. Missionaries and Indian religions of non-local origins, such as the Native

Figure 7.13 Church at Taos Pueblo in 1985. (Courtesy of T. L. McCarty.)

American Church (the "Peyote Church"), have received decidedly different receptions among the tribes. Generally, the pueblos with their entrenched religious authorities have been the most resistant to subsequent missionizing and to the Peyote Church, although few have been totally successful in keeping out or suppressing other religious practice. Others, such as the Upland Yumans, while more open to missionaries, have not embraced new faiths with much enthusiasm. Still others, such as the Navajos, have been influenced by both Christian missionaries and the Peyote Church. The last in particular is widespread and many Navajos participate simultaneously in traditional Navajo ritual (itself a mixture of ancient shamanistic and Pueblo materials), the Peyote Church, and Catholic or Protestant ritual at the missions.

Indigenous Southwest Peoples after Anglo-European Contact

In previous sections we explored native Southwest societies as they were about 140 years ago, when the United States sent troops into the area. Prior to this time indigenous Southwesterners had already felt the influence of Europeans, who introduced new diseases, cultigens, livestock, social structures and belief systems. The sedentary villagers were perhaps most affected by these influences, as their concentrated settlements not only made them more susceptible to the spread of disease but also made the villagers attractive targets for raiding, horse-mounted Athabaskans and eventually, for the Spanish. The pueblos in particular suffered grievously during the early period of European contact. The Hopi population, for example, declined from as high as 10,000 in 1500 to several thousand by 1850. Zuni declined from as many as 5,000 to 1,300 during the same time, and the population of the Eastern Pueblos was decimated, from perhaps 30,000 in 1500 to about 15,000 by 1750.

Hence, by the time Anglo-Americans entered the area in the 18th and 19th centuries, native populations had already undergone tremendous social, economic and demographic change. For most of them, governance emerged as a natural part of their economies and the social life developed in particular environments. Leadership derived not from any overarching authority, but from the relationships within and between local groups. With the exception of the riverine and pueblo villagers, most groups constituted "tribes" in a cultural rather than a political sense. Moreover, while various groups engaged in trade with one another and formed occasional military alliances, Southwestern peoples did not develop any pan-tribal or regional unity. In this land of highly diverse resources and ecologies, tribal populations and within them, local groups, operated autonomously.

There was thus no natural cohesion, no unified military or political force either within tribal groups or between them, that might have been organized to resist the encroaching Anglo-Americans. Within a few years of the signing of the Treaty of Guadalupe Hidalgo, most tribes faced the forced integration of their people into one of two national cultures. This happened differently for groups north and south of the U.S.-Mexican border.

The Yaquis in Mexico and the U.S.

Just as the Yaquis had resisted Spanish settlements in their valley, Yaquis continued to resist Mexican efforts to integrate them politically and culturally into the national system. Initial successful revolts, such as the one led by Juan Banderas after Mexican Independence, were followed by defeats and increasingly draconian efforts by the Mexican government to break the Yaquis' resistance.

Early on, the Mayos, Lower Pimas and Opatas joined the Yaquis in opposing the government. But the populations of the former groups had all declined significantly, and people and institutions of the national system had entered their area quite early, usurping lands and penetrating native settlements. As a result, these groups all eventually abandoned their alliance with the Yaquis, becoming increasingly assimilated into the Mexican national system.

The Yaquis, however, continued to resist militarily well into the 20th century. As Mexicans settled on Yaqui land and as *hacendados* appropriated it for large estates, some of the Yaqui towns were destroyed. The Yaquis' strenuous opposition to the hacienda system led the Mexican government to initiate a "scorched earth" campaign, driving hundreds of Indians from their towns and selling those suspected of being rebels to plantations in the Yucatan. The ensuing diaspora broke up and scattered Yaqui families. Many fled to the United States.

Those who remained in Mexico found their towns taken over by people of national culture, or ruined by changes in the course of the Yaqui River resulting from floods and a dam. Some towns were rebuilt and new ones constructed, but the Mexican Yaquis lost control of most of their old domain, and subsequently divided into two groups. The *civilistas* have sought to maintain Yaqui political and cultural autonomy. The *militaristas* joined the Mexicans during the Mexican Revolution, and have become integrated into the national political system as supporters of regional political bosses or *caciques*. Modern Yaqui communities in Mexico tend to be dual, with Mexican sections containing the buildings backing Mexican institutions (government offices, army headquarters, schools, bakeries and bars), and a Yaqui section with wandering paths and roads, homesites and the Yaqui church.

Yaquis who came to the U.S. settled around Nogales, Tucson and Phoenix, taking unclaimed lands near places where adults found work in agriculture, on irrigation projects or for the railroads. Others settled on lands owned by their employers. After 1921, 40 acres of land some six miles north of Tucson fell into the hands of a charitable organization, which made the land available for Yaqui settlement. The place has become known as Pascua Village or Old Pascua. To the south of Tucson another area, Barrio Libre, grew up as well, and in 1964 the federal government granted the Yaquis 200 acres southwest of Tucson. This settlement, called New Pascua, received federal recognition in 1978 and New Pascua became the Yaqui Indian Reservation.

Elsewhere in Arizona, Yaqui communities developed at Guadalupe just southeast of Phoenix, and in Scottsdale, a suburb of Phoenix. Some members of these communities are enrolled members of the Yaqui Tribe, but others are not. The community at Guadalupe

Figure 7.14 Modern Indian Reservations in the American Southwest. (Compiled by T. L. McCarty. Drawn by Shearon D. Vaughn.)

maintains a church and the Yaqui ritual cycle, in which residents of the Scottsdale community, called Pénjamo or Eskatél, also participate.

Indian Experiences North of the Border

With the creation of a reservation, the Yaquis became exposed to the federal system that has defined the basic influences on the lives of most Southwestern Indians in the United States. In the Southwest and farther east where the reservation system first developed, its purpose was to restrict Indians to tracts out of the way of Anglo-American development, and to protect or "reserve" some land for Indian use.

Most Southwest tribes resisted this effort, all without success. In 1863, following Kit Carson's scorched earth campaign that left Navajo homesites and herds destroyed, over 8,000 Navajos surrendered at Ft. Defiance near the Arizona-New Mexico border. From there they were forced to trek some 300 miles across wintry plains to a new reservation at Fort Sumner, New Mexico. The journey there on foot is referred to as "The Long Walk," and is still considered a tragic turning point in the tribe's history. Many Navajos died along the way, succumbing to dysentery and the cold. Others, including pregnant women and the elderly who were too weak to walk, died at the hands of the soldiers.

The hardships continued at Fort Sumner, where Navajos were interned with several hundred Apaches in a government experiment designed to train them to become sedentary farmers. Plagued by repeated crop failures, dysentery, syphilis and smallpox, over 2,000 died within a few months. Sometimes at bayonet point, soldiers forced the survivors to put in 12-hour days (Bailey 1978:225).

By 1867, following a Congressional investigation that cited the Fort Sumner Reservation as little more than a concentration camp (Bailey 1978:226), the experiment there was abandoned. A treaty signed the next year gave the Navajos three-and-a-half million acres within their former range—about one-fifth the land they had used prior to their internment. In subsequent expansions the Navajo Reservation came to include over 25,000 square miles, extending over parts of Arizona, New Mexico and Utah (see Figure 7.14).

The Navajo experience following Anglo-American contact was not atypical. Both the Chiricahua and Western Apaches strongly resisted the Anglo-Americans who entered their territory in the 1850s. Uprisings continued with the escape of Geronimo and the Chiricahuas even after the reservation period. The Chiricahuas were confined at Fort Sill, Oklahoma until 1913, when many returned to the Mescalero Apache Reservation in southern New Mexico.

The Upland Yumans faced a similar Long Walk or "Trail of Tears." Some years after their defeat, the western and southern Pai bands, identified as the Hualapai by soldiers, were marched to La Paz on the Colorado River, where they suffered from the heat, disease and the Indian agent's corruption. Later, the Hualapai Reservation was created for the survivors, while the government established a separate reservation in a tributary canyon of the Grand Canyon for the northeastern Pai, most of whom had escaped the La Paz experience, and who Americans called Havasupais. Following a decade of conflict, the Yavapais were also forced in the late 1800s to march to San Carlos, Arizona where they were interned with Apaches for 25 years before being released and given several small parcels of their original territory at Fort McDowell, Camp Verde, Prescott and much later, at the Tonto Apache Reservation in Payson.

Most of the River Yumans had little contact with Anglo-Europeans until the Gold Rush brought visitors and settlers there in the 1850s. Eventually they were settled on several tracts along the Colorado River. Following similar encroachments on their land by miners and ranchers, the Pimas and Tohono O'odham received reservations on the Salt and Gila Rivers, and at Ak Chin, Gila Bend, San Xavier and the "Main" Tohono O'odham Reservation.

In short, by the early part of the 20th century, the Indians who survived the Anglo-American intrusion in the Southwest and their descendents had been settled on reservations. In Arizona there are today 22 reservations and in New Mexico, in addition to the main Navajo Reservation, there are 19 pueblo reservations, two Apache reservations and the Cañoncito, Ramah and Alamo Navajo Reservations. The reservation system reflects and perpetuates the "trust" relationship between tribes and the federal government, likened to that of a ward to his or her guardian. The Bureau of Indian Affairs or BIA is the chief agency responsible for administering and maintaining that trust. This system has colored all of the subsequent experiences of Southwestern Indian peoples, and continues to both constrain and provide opportunities for social, economic and political development among tribes. In the final section of this chapter we examine how this has occurred, and the critical issues facing Southwest tribes today: control of land and resources, economic development and its associated impacts on tribal political organizations, and the role of education in both the survival of native languages and cultures, and in the socioeconomic transformation of Southwest Indian communities.

Southwest Indian Cultures Today

Land and Resources

For many years the federal government did not recognize the Eastern Pueblos as tribes. Because of this, neither they nor their lands were subject to the restrictions and safeguards accompanying trust status. As a result, the Rio Grande pueblos in particular have faced encroachments by outsiders and the alienation of their lands through sale and out-marriage. The Sandoval Decision in 1913, the Pueblo Lands Act of 1924 and the federal acquisition of new lands partially mitigated this situation. In 1970, when President Nixon signed into law a bill transferring 48,000 acres from the Carson National Forest to Taos Pueblo, Taos' sacred Blue Lake and the surrounding area came under the pueblo's control.

Taos' successful efforts and the impact of the lake's religious significance has not been lost on other groups. Among these are the Havasupais. In 1880 the Havasupai band of the Upland Yuman Pai received a reservation in Havasu Canyon. One year later Congress reduced the reservation to 518 acres on the floor of that canyon. While the national forests and eventually Grand Canyon National Park absorbed the northern reaches of the Havasupais' traditional use area along the Grand Canyon's south rim, the tribe managed to maintain a presence on those lands. The Forest Service in particular granted them grazing leases on Forest Service lands, and families who had traditionally maintained camps near Grand Canyon Village found employment with the Park Service and park concessionaires. Havasupais also maintained settlements in the park, and scattered cattle and hunting camps in the forest.

Through the years the Havasupais, often supported by the BIA, sought to gain greater control over some of these lost lands. Their efforts culminated in 1975 when President Ford signed into law an act restoring 185,000 acres to the tribe. In their campaign the Havasupais' arguments frequently referred to the existence of sacred springs and other sites they wished to protect by bringing them and the surrounding areas into the reservation. This argument may have had some effect, though probably less than did the facts that the Havasupais had maintained a presence on these lands through grazing leases and park employment, and their population had grown from 166 to 450 by 1970.

More recently the Havasupais have used both religious and ecological arguments against the development of a uranium mine in an upper drainage of Havasu Canyon. To date they have failed, as have the Hopis and Navajos who used similar arguments to block the expansion of ski facilities on the San Francisco Peaks near Flagstaff.

Arguments invoking sacred sites are also being used by both the Hopis and Navajos in their continuing dispute over lands in northern Arizona. By the 1820s the Navajos enveloped the Hopis, and in 1882, a federal executive order set aside a reservation for Hopis and "other Indians." Large numbers of Navajos, a few Paiutes and the Hopis lived within the boundaries of that reservation. But since 1882, the populations and livestock of both the Hopis and Navajos have grown. Competition over this land has been exacerbated by the presence of vast coal deposits under Black Mesa, of which the Hopi Mesas are the southern extensions.

Since 1936 when the BIA set aside part of the 1882 reservation for the Hopis' exclusive use, a series of administrative, judicial and legislative actions have progressively divided the 1882 reservation, assigning a portion to each tribe. As Navajos live in dispersed camps throughout the area while most Hopis live in more concentrated settlements at the southern edge of Black Mesa, the reservation partition has forced the removal and relocation of thousands of Navajos. The Navajos continue to resist, but by and large their resistance has won them little more than a slowdown in the resettlement process and some small compensatory additions to their reservation. Moreover, the 1974 Act of Congress providing for the partition and relocation also allows the Hopis to sue for Navajo Reservation lands lying outside the 1882 reservation. These lands number in the millions of acres in Arizona, and their loss would bring the Navajos severe economic and social hardship.

At the same time, the Navajo Tribe has purchased a very large private ranch in northern Arizona that takes up the area east of the Hualapai Reservation and south of the expanded Havasupai Reservation. This acquisition has caused consternation among the Havasupais and Hualapais, some of whom see the Navajos as expansionary and destructive of the environment.

Reservation Economics

The Navajos' recent land acquisition is an attempt to expand their resources, for like most tribes in the American Southwest, they face special economic problems. The Navajo Reservation is rich in resources, especially coal used to fuel electric plants. But outside corporations run the plants and mining operations, paying the tribe for the coal. For many years the payments were well below market prices. The mines also afford jobs, as do Navajo tribal enterprises such as a vast agricultural development and timber operations. Most Navajo wage earners nevertheless work for tribal, federal and state agencies and their jobs ultimately depend on appropriated tax monies. As these wax and wane so does unemployment, which often surpasses 75 per cent.

In this respect the Navajo Reservation typifies Southwestern reservations, whose economics remain highly dependent on federal funding. Most of these funds support education, health, tribal administrations, housing and social welfare. On reservations away from urban areas, the federal government often provides the largest single source of reservation earned income. Reservations near urban areas, such as the Gila River and Salt River Reservations, have profited from the development of large industrial parks. Private industries in these parks pay lease money to the tribes and provide jobs for tribal members. Gila and Salt River, like Ak Chin and the Colorado River Reservation, also benefit from large tracts of irrigated farm lands. Except at Ak Chin where the profitable, tribally run farm employs a high percentage of the tribal labor force, these agricultural developments have not offered a great deal of employment. Much of the land is leased to outside agribusinesses that run highly capitalized commercial operations. These generate lease money paid to the tribe or to individuals, but few jobs for tribal members. As a result, most individuals find work off the reservation in metropolitan areas.

A number of other reservations, generally limited in resources but located near or in the midst of developed areas, are from an economic point of view residential enclaves where Indian people live with those of their own culture and more cheaply than they could off-reservation. The Yavapai-Apache Reservation at Camp Verde is one such example, as are the Yavapai-Apache Reservations at Prescott and Payson, the Cocopah and Fort Mohave Reservations, and many of the Eastern Pueblos. Still others, far removed from towns and cities and without substantial resources relative to their populations, face even greater economic difficulties. Hualapai, a reservation of just under a million acres, has extensive grazing lands, but cattle herds are limited by a shortage of surface water and the inability of residents with little other income to withhold consumption and build their herds. The Hualapai Reservation also has a stand of ponderosa pine, but due to low rainfall and the small size of that stand, continuous timber operations cannot be sustained. Havasupai, now over 185,000 acres, is blessed with beautiful Havasu Canyon which draws tens of thousands of tourists each year. But grazing land there is very poor, and federally funded construction projects and social services provide most of the reservation's earned income. San Carlos, a reservation of 1,853,817 acres, is also poor, having some timber and a substantial cattle industry, but little else.

Changing Tribal Political Organizations and the Roots of Factionalism

This poverty and dependence on federal funding have had important political consequences for many reservations. The rancheria and band tribes in particular were ill equipped to cope with the changes brought by their conquests. These peoples had been organized very loosely into families, households, local groups, regional bands, subtribes and cultural tribes. Conquest brought major residential and economic realignments, disrupting the organization of social interests and related political structures. These tribes moved from hunting, gathering, horticulture and a flexible, rancheria and band settlement to welfare, wage labor, cattle raising and in some cases, to village life. Without developed political institutions for dealing with expanding community- and tribal-wide economic and social problems, the definition and resolution of those problems fell easily to the Bureau of Indian Affairs. For many years—indeed, even after most of these groups accepted tribal governments under the 1934 Indian Reorganization Act—the BIA governed the reservations, with tribal members employed by the BIA in largely unskilled jobs executing the agency's decisions.

This situation developed with much greater difficulty among the horticultural pueblos. The Hopis and most of the Eastern Pueblos have been able to maintain their traditional settlement patterns and in many cases, continue to use ancestral lands in a more or less traditional fashion. The political and economic base of village leaders—clan heads and the heads of societies—has not been undermined, and these elites have successfully resisted outside attempts to displace them. In a few places relocation, population decimation and immigration have combined to destroy the indigenous system and facilitated political transformations. At Pojoaque for example, the traditional system based on society and moiety heads and town officials dissolved and has been replaced by a tribal council.

Recent federal legislation has strengthened tribal councils. The IRA provided the legal bases for tribal government but a number of subsequent acts, in particular the 1975 Indian Self Determination and Education Assistance Act, gave tribes the economic means to realize the IRA's potentialities. The Self Determination Act allows federal funds to be channeled through tribal governments for the operation of education, BIA and U.S. Public Health Service programs. This not only has enabled tribes to run their own schools, but has funneled monies directly through tribal governmental offices. Tribal governments are now displacing the BIA as the service providers, the important employer and the agency in charge of development. As this has occurred, tribal governments have built bureaucracies to manage various development and service programs. And while outsiders were initially hired for these new management positions, tribal members increasingly take these opportunities.

As a result of their increased economic significance, tribal governments have assumed increased political significance. Among those tribes where the indigenous political system was destroyed, the rising power of tribal government has been checked by limits in federal appropriations. Among the pueblos these developments have sometimes exacerbated the struggle for power between traditional leaders and those in the new tribal government, who frequently are individuals not well placed in the traditional system.

The struggle at Hopi between the traditionalists and those oriented toward economic growth and tribal government affords one example of such a struggle. At Zuni traditional leaders formerly controlled the tribal council by virtue of their controlling its membership. This has weakened in recent years because as in most pueblos, the number of individuals involved in wage work and off-reservation activities outnumbers more traditional people. Mooveover, formal education, off-reservation experience and connections with people in federal and state bureaucracies have begun to surpass traditional knowledge, inherited property and society membership as the means to a livelihood.

The root of this factionalism is in the simple fact that traditional pueblo economies have been unable to expand sufficiently to provide for their growing populations. Those who have lost out, who failed to obtain sufficient resources, either had to leave their communities altogether or supplement or replace traditional economic activities with wage work and involvement with tribal and federal bureaucracies. As they have done this, traditional leaders have not only lost one of the bases of their power with these people, but they have often found their interests in opposition.

Such factionalism cuts even deeper, affecting life in the family. Households that formerly lived from horticulture or cattle now find their resources will not sustain all households formed by their children. In some places changing values and discontent with traditional lifestyles led to the exodus of young people looking for better lives. In others, struggles have developed within families over the short supply of resources, and the losers have been forced to leave unless they can find employment through the tribe or federal government.

The results have been the development of factions built around those with stable traditional resources such as land, as against those who have lost out, and concomitantly, a steady exodus of young people. They have moved largely to Southwest urban centers—Phoenix, Albuquerque and Tucson—and to smaller cities near reservations such as Gallup, Holbrook, Winslow and Flagstaff. These movements have had significant impacts. While tribal populations continue to grow in the Southwest, those living in off-reservation urban areas are increasing faster than are reservation populations. This growth has brought with it the development of some pan-Indian institutions such as pow-wow organizations, intertribal councils and urban Indian centers. Such developments would probably be greater were it not for the proximity of home reservations to the urban centers. Thus, people main-

Figure 7.15 Pan-tribal pow-wow in the plaza of Taos Pueblo, 1985. (Courtesy of T. L. McCarty.)

Figures 7.16–7.17 Students lined up in from of the school at Supai, Arizona, in 1898, and on the playground of the Rough Rock Demonstration School in 1981. (Havasupai photograph by George Wharton James, courtesy of The Heard Museum, Phoenix, Arizona; and Rough Rock Demonstration School photograph courtesy of T. L. McCarty.)

tain their connections with kin and home communities, visiting, sending money and serving as hosts when relatives come to town. This helps maintain both social connections with reservation communities, and ethnic identities.

Education, Ethnicity and the Transformation of Southwest Indian Communities

As this has occurred and as tribal and individual interests have been pulled into the national system, Southwest Indians have also faced the threat of the extinction of their languages and cultural traditions. In some tribes, especially those situated near large urban areas, this extinction is complete or nearly so, with only a few members of the grandparent generation speaking the language. Intermarriage between members of different tribes has enhanced the value of English as a common language, but the single most significant force in the assimilation process and concomitant loss of tribal languages and traditions has been formal education.

At least since the 1819 Civilization Act gave the federal government primary responsibility for educating Indians, federal Indian policy has had as its goal the annihilation of tribal languages and cultures and the "civilization" of Indian people according to Western standards. In 1910 the Commissioner of Indian Affairs articulated this policy, noting that "the task . . . is to provide the needed development and supply the lacks caused by a faulty environment, so that the Indian child may be brought up to the standard of cleanliness, order, regularity and discipline which the public school presupposes in its white children. *The task is changing a way of living*" (McKinley et al. 1970: 7, emphases added).

Federal boarding schools, established throughout the Southwest by the early 1900s, became the vehicles for operationalizing this policy. Many of these schools were located at the military forts instrumental in the conquest. Reflecting the military emphasis, children recruited to boarding schools were transported in army trucks and wagons, issued cast-off army uniforms and had their hair shorn to meet school standards. Drills and manual labor complemented a curriculum in English, arithmetic and for boys, manual arts, while girls studied homemaking.

Perhaps most importantly, children were forbidden to speak their native language at school. Those who did risked additional punitive labor and corporal punishment, including having their mouth "washed" with lye soap. Witnessing or being subjected to such experiences, many Indian students fled from the schools. Indian agents sent to round up the truants returned them to school, where they were shackled to ensure they did not escape again.

For most students in federal Indian schools, education involved one overriding message: their native languages and cultures were not only great liabilities, but deficits to overcome. One powerful cumulative effect of this has been a general ambivalence about cultural and linguistic identities. The upshot today is that many Indian parents try to avoid similar socially disabling experiences for their children, teaching them English and limiting the use of the tribal language at home.

261

In the wake of the decline of tribal languages resulting from these cumulative experiences, as well as from the economic and political forces already discussed, a growing number of tribal members have begun to advocate bilingual education programs. Their initiatives have been propelled by the reforms of the 1960s and by the passage of the Self Determination Act, the 1968 Bilingual Education Act and the 1972 Indian Education Act, all of which provide funds for bilingual instruction. In the small Navajo community of Rough Rock, Arizona, federal funds in 1966 provided for the first Indian school to have a locally elected Indian governing board. There, the Rough Rock Demonstration School also became the first to use Navajo language and culture in classroom instruction. Today, 60 such community- or tribally-controlled schools exist across the country, many of them in the Southwest.

Other communities have made similar efforts. At Peach Springs on the Hualapai Reservation, the public school has instituted a sequential Hualapai-English curriculum in all subject areas. Much of this curriculum now incorporates computer technology. The program's uniqueness and effectiveness in raising Hualapai students' academic achievement have led the U.S. Department of Education to recognize it as one of a handful of "Programs of Academic Excellence."

On the Tohono O'odham and Pascua Yaqui Reservations, each tribe has developed language and education policies representing similar goals. The policies make the native language the reservation's official language, and require that both the language and culture be meaningfully integrated into children's school experiences. The Tohono O'odham Tribe has also adopted standards specifying skills in all subject areas to include the native language and culture. The tribal education staff, all native speakers, has instituted a training program for both public and federal school personnel to ensure the standards and the language policy are implemented.

Efforts like these have fostered the emergence of a cadre of trained Indian education professionals. The legislation supporting such programs as those at Rough Rock and Peach Springs includes funds for teacher training. Many Indian people, often women who began as teachers' aides, have taken advantage of this, and the number of trained, certified, native-speaking teachers and school administrators has grown tremendously. This has both reinforced the role of native languages and cultures in schools, and led to better integration of schools and communities. In places like Rough Rock, where local residents make up the majority of the school staff, the school is no longer an alien, intrusive element brought in by outsiders, but is a central and highly significant aspect of community social and economic life.

These transformations—the growth of an Indian professional class increasingly in charge of education and other social services, and the revival of native languages and cultures in the schools—act to both maintain and alter Southwest Indian languages, cultures and communities. Indian languages are being spoken in new contexts and committed to writing, and there is a growing native language literature. Southwest Indian cultures, too, have assimilated new elements; literary and other modern artistic productions offer two examples. These new cultural forms, along with elements of traditional cultures, are in many places directly incorporated into children's educational experiences, and have taken on new meaning as representative of ethnic identities. At the same time, the social and economic foundations of Southwest Indian communities have been transformed as education and other social services supplant traditional agriculture and animal husbandry as the major economic base, and as a growing class of formally educated people emerges.

The issues facing Southwest tribes today, then, are complex and derive from the juxtaposition of their institutional dependence on federal support, with the growing ability of individuals to transcend that dependency. Tribal communities remain largely reliant on the federal monies supporting the social service institutions that provide much of their employment. Simultaneously, Indian people emerging through these institutions are developing the skills to operate in the national system, while maintaining their competency in and allegiance to their native languages and cultures.

SUGGESTED READINGS

Basso, Keith
    1970   The Cibecue Apache. Holt, Rinehart and Winston, New York.

Dozier, Edward P.
    1970   The Pueblo Indians of North America. Holt, Rinehart and Winston, New York.

Hinton, Leanne, and Lucille J. Watahomigie (eds.)
    1984   Spirit Mountain—An Anthology of Yuman Story and Song. Sun Tracks and University of Arizona Press, Tucson.

McCarthy, James
    1985   A Papago Traveler—The Memories of James McCarthy. Sun Tracks and University of Arizona Press, Tucson.

Ortiz, Alfonso (vol. ed.)
    1983;   Handbook of North American Indians, Vols. IX and X. W. C. Sturtevant, gen. ed. Smithsonian In-
    1979   stitution, Washington, D.C.

Spicer, Edward H.
    1962   Cycles of Conquest—The Impact of Spain, Mexico and the U.S. on the Indians of the Southwest, 1533–1960. University of Arizona Press, Tucson.
    1980   The Yaquis—A Cultural History. University of Arizona Press, Tucson.

Spier, Leslie
    1928   Havasupai Ethnography. AMS Press, New York.
    1978   Yuman Tribes of the Gila River. Dover Publishers, Inc., New York.

REFERENCES

Bailey, L.R.
    1978   The Long Walk: A History of the Navajo Wars, 1846–68. Westernlore Publications, Pasadena, CA.

Bia, Fred, T. L. McCarty and Regina Lynch
    1983   Of Mother Earth and Father Sky—A Photographic Study of Navajo Culture. Navajo Curriculum Center Press and Northland Press, Flagstaff and Rough Rock, AZ.

Bingham, Sam, and Janet Bingham (eds.)
    1984   Between Sacred Mountains. University of Arizona Press, Tucson.

McKinley, Frances, et al.
    1970   Who Should Control Indian Education? Far West Laboratory for Educational Research and Development, Berkeley.

Ortiz, Alfonso
  1969   The Tewa World—Space, Time, Being and Becoming in a Pueblo Society. University of Chicago Press, Chicago and London.

Spencer, Robert F., Jesse D. Jennings, et al.   ~~Text~~
  1965   The Native Americans. Harper and Row, New York.

Spicer, Edward H.
  1962   Cycles of Conquest—The Impact of Spain, Mexico and the U.S. on the Indians of the Southwest, 1533–1960. University of Arizona Press, Tucson.

Witherspoon, Gary
  1983   Navajo Social Organization. *In* Handbook of North American Indians Vol. X. A. Ortiz, vol. ed. W. C. Sturtevant, gen. ed., pp. 524–535. Smithsonian Institution, Washington, D.C.

RECOMMENDED FILM/VIDEOS

Hopi Songs of the Fourth World (58-min., color). Ferrero Films, 1259-A Folsom St., San Francisco, CA 94103 (415) 626-3456.

A Weave of Time (59-min., color). Ferrero Films, 1259-A Folsom St., San Francisco, CA 94103 (415) 626-3456.

Seasons of a Navajo (57-min., color). KAET-TV, Arizona State University, Tempe 85287 (602) 965-3506.

Chapter 8

California Culture Area

Lowell John Bean and Sylvia Brakke Vane
California State University–Hayward

Introduction

The traditional peoples of California and their present-day descendants represent one of the great challenges to students of American Indian culture and history. There were within the area now known as the state of California examples of the highest socio-cultural development known among the so-called hunting and gathering peoples. Peoples of widely desperate cultural backgrounds, language, and religion lived side by side, sharing much, while keeping their autonomy and identity quite distinct.

Because of ignorance and prejudice and various needs of others to characterize those cultures in ways comfortable to them, California Indians have for a very long time been viewed as simple peoples. Nothing could be further from the truth. Their diversity and highly developed social, economic, artistic, and philosophical skills preclude any facile description of them. This chapter is but a brief introduction to their extraordinary culture and history.

Those who have written about California Indians have defined them either as those whose ancestors occupied what is now the State of California or as those making up the California culture area. A. L. Kroeber, in his *Handbook of the Indians of California* (1925) chose the first course. Kroeber, who took a leading part in defining culture areas within the United States, especially California, pointed out affinities of California peoples with peoples across the various borders of the state (Heizer 1978:2).

In the more recently published *Handbook of North American Indians* (Heizer 1978), on the other hand, the editors chose to include in the California volume (Vol. 8) only the peoples in a more narrowly defined California "culture area". The Shoshone/Paiute peoples east of the southern Sierra Nevada are covered in the Great Basin volume (d'-Azevedo 1986), and the peoples who live along the Colorado River are covered in the volumes dealing with the Southwest (Ortiz 1979, 1983). A small area at the northern edge of the state will be included in the Oregon volume. In this chapter we discuss all the groups that occupied any part of the state.

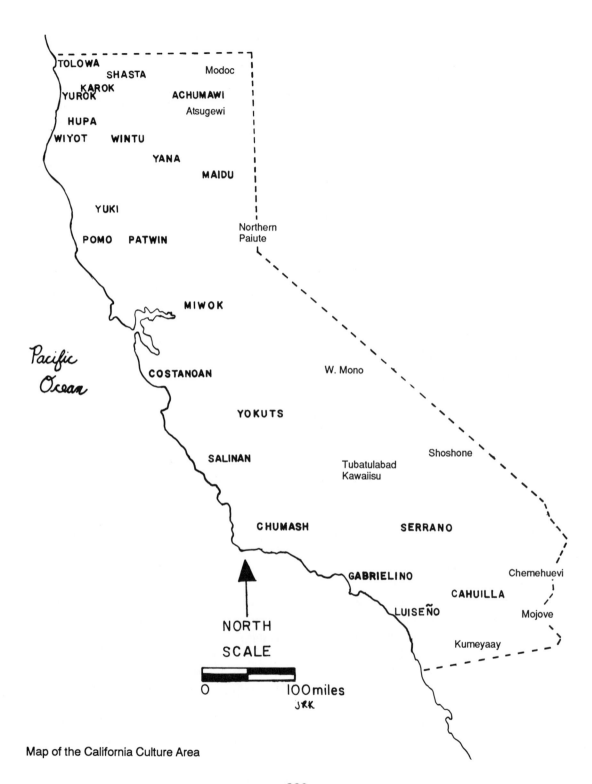

TOLOWA

SHASTA

Modoc

KAROK

YUROK

ACHUMAWI

Atsugewi

HUPA

WIYOT

WINTU

YANA

MAIDU

YUKI

Northern
Paiute

POMO

PATWIN

MIWOK

*Pacific
Ocean*

COSTANOAN

W. Mono

YOKUTS

SALINAN

Shoshone

Tubatulabad
Kawaiisu

CHUMASH

SERRANO

Chemehuevi

GABRIELINO

CAHUILLA

LUISEÑO

Mojove

Kumeyaay

NORTH

SCALE

0   100miles

JRK

Map of the California Culture Area

Geography of California

California is bounded on the west by the Pacific Ocean, and on the east by the Great Basin. The Sierra Nevada is the backbone of the state along the northern two-thirds of its eastern side. The Coastal Range, somewhat less dramatically vertical, and interrupted frequently by large and small valleys, lies inland from the Pacific Ocean. Between the two mountain ranges lies the great Central Valley, flat and relatively arid. The valley is bounded to the south by the Tehachapi Mountains. In Southern California, south of the Sierra Nevada and southeast of the Tehachapis, lies the Mojave Desert, into which runs the Mojave River, a river that rises in the San Bernardino Mountains to the south and sinks into the earth at Soda Lake, or the "Sink of the Mojave." The southernmost part of the state is marked by numerous small mountain ranges separated by valleys. Aridity is greater in the Colorado Desert in the southeastern part of the state, part of the Sonoran Desert that stretches into Mexico.

The mountains and valleys of California, the ocean at its western border, and its rivers and lakes create a rich and varied environment for its peoples. The state today has wealth, population, and accomplishments greater than those of many an independent nation. Before the arrival of Euro-, Afro- and Asian Americans, the state was occupied by a diversity of hunting and gathering peoples. Like their modern counterparts, these had wealth, population, and accomplishments greater than those of hunting and gathering peoples in less favored situations.

Population

Just how many California Indians there were is not known. They were rapidly killed off by the invading Europeans and disease before anyone could count them, but it is estimated that there were between 300,000 and 400,000 of them in some seventy "tribes", and perhaps as many as 1,000,000 (Dobyns 1976).

Language

Many different languages or dialects of languages were spoken in California. Because language is such an important ethnic boundary marker, the various groups have come to be identified in terms of their languages. Language distribution also gives some of the most useful clues to the prehistory of the state, although only a tentative idea about what happened can be put together from these clues.

The distribution of languages and their degree of diversity suggests that peoples speaking Hokan languages were the first to arrive in California, perhaps well before the end of the Pleistocene. Of course, there may have earlier peoples whose languages have long since disappeared.

In the course of time, peoples speaking languages of the Yukian family (found in no place other than California) pushed into the northwestern part of the state, Penutian speakers came in from the northeast, and Uto-Aztecan speakers from the southwest, replacing many of the Hokan speakers in a process that took thousands of years. Algic and Athapascan speaking peoples appear to have arrived in northwestern California during the last two thousand years (Moratto 1984).

The Yukian speakers may have arrived from the north "as early as 9500–9000 B.C." and may be associated with archaeological remains of the "Borax Lake Pattern," which is found in the North Coast Ranges, suggesting they probably occupied, between 4,000 and 2,000 B.C., an area along the north coast of California from just below the present-day Oregon border to San Francisco Bay. In the next several thousand years they lost some of their territory to Penutian speaking peoples who moved into the central part of the state and thence into the areas around San Francisco Bay. They also lost territory to Hokan speakers, ancestors of the Pomo, pushing westward (Moratto 1984:544).

By 1000 A.D., the Pomo had moved all the way to the coast, (from a homeland that may have been in the Clear Lake area) following the Russian River and adjacent valleys, and splitting the Yukians into two groups, one occupying a small area in Napa Valley south of Clear Lake, and a larger group still reaching the coast north of the Pomo area. By now the Algic peoples had moved down from the North to occupy a coastal area to the north of the Yuki area along the Klamath River, probably in two separate waves of migration. Their languages, Wiyot and Yurok, had developed from the same roots as Algonquin languages spoken in eastern North America, separating from Algonquin long before (Moratto 1984:551–552).

About 1200 to 1300 A.D., people speaking Athapascan languages, related to those of the Navajo and Apache in the Southwest, moved into Northwestern California. These were the ancestors of the Tolowa (who were primarily an Oregon group), the peoples speaking the Hupa, Chilula, Whilkut, and Mattole dialects of the Hupa-Chilula language; and those speaking the Nongatl, Sinkyone, and Lassik dialects of the Wailaki language. The Wailaki language spread, so that by the time Euro-Americans arrived, there were two dialects of the Wailaki language that were spoken by peoples whose physical and cultural characteristics were Yukian. The Yukian language by then was spoken only by the peoples of isolated Round Valley and an adjacent area reaching westward to a narrow coastal area (Moratto 1984:564, 570–571).

Inland from the cluster of fairly recently arrived peoples on the north coast were such Hokan-speaking peoples as the Karok, who shared many of the cultural characteristics of their Algic and Athapascan-speaking neighbors, the speakers of Shasta, New River Shasta, Konomihu, and Okwanuchu languages. Still further inland, in the northern Sierra Nevada, were the Achumawi and Atsugewi, sometimes called the Pit River Indians in modern times. Another people speaking Hokan languages, the Washoe, survived in the Lake Tahoe area, surrounded by speakers of Penutian and Uto-Aztecan languages (1984:558–586, 566).

Penutian Speakers

When Europeans arrived in California, the peoples of the Central Valley and bordering areas, those on the central coast from the San Francisco Bay Area south about halfway to the Santa Barbara area, and those in the Klamath and Modoc areas in northern California spoke some 30 to 40 languages in many dialects. These have traditionally been classed by linguists as Penutian languages. Linguists have, however, been unable to confirm the hypothesis that these languages belong in one language superfamily. It appears that Klamath and Modoc make up a language isolate, and that the others instead make up four language families, Wintuan, Maiduan, Yokutsan, and Utian, which are conveniently grouped together as Penutian for the purposes of historical discussion. The speakers of these languages are those that most typify the California culture sphere. Wintuan languages include Wintu, Nomlaki, and Patwin; Maiduan includes Maidu and Nisenan; Utian includes Miwok and Costanoan; and Yokutsan includes the various Yokuts languages of the southern Central Valley (1984:553–557).

The peoples who spoke languages that were the precursors of the Penutian languages are thought to have lived in the upper Columbia River valleys of eastern Washington and Oregon some eight to ten thousand years ago. Between four to six thousand years ago, they had apparently moved southward along the eastern border of what is now California to an area somewhat south of Lake Tahoe, and were beginning to move southwestward. Moratto suggests that shortly after 2000 B.C., they had moved into the eastern Bay Area, where they can be identified as the "Windmiller" people well known to California archaeologists from sites found in San Joaquin Delta and neighboring areas (1984:553).

Archaeological evidence suggests that the Costanoans arrived in the area around San Francisco Bay about 2500 years ago, and merged with an earlier Hokan-speaking population. At about the same time, western Miwok separated from eastern Miwok, and displaced Yukian-speakers and/or Pomo to the north. The Yokuts probably arrived in the San Joaquin Valley about the same era, having more recently come into California from areas further to the north than the Costanoans and Miwok (1984:554–557; 560–564).

Although linguistic evidence suggests that Wintuan speakers came into California at least 2500 years ago, placenames and archaeological data indicate that they arrived between 1000 and 1100 years ago from some place in Oregon, bringing with them "such traits as the bow and arrow, harpoons, flanged stone pipes, and pre-interment grave-pit burning" (Moratto 1984:557, 563).

Uto-Aztecan Speakers

People speaking Uto-Aztecan languages apparently came into California from the east about 5,000 years ago, perhaps shortly before the time that some Uto-Aztecans moved southward to Mexico. Between 2700 and 4000 years ago, the northern subfamilies separated into the Tubatulabal/Numic and the Takic/Hopic speaking groups. Tubatulabalic speakers moved into the southern Sierra Nevada and Kern River areas between 2300 and 3000 years ago, separating from the Numic groups who occupied much of the Great Basin.

The Numic Subfamily split somewhat later into the Western group, which includes speakers of Northern Paiute-Bannock languages, sometimes called Paviotso, to be found along the northeast coast of California and adjacent Idaho areas; the Central group, which includes people in the Bishop, Lone Pine, and Death Valley areas whose language is often called Western or Panamint Shoshone; and the Southern group, which includes Kawaiisu, spoken in the southern Sierra Nevada along the Kern River and an area that included parts of the Mojave Desert, Southern Paiute-Chemehuevi, spoken in the eastern Mojave Desert and into Nevada, as well as a number of languages spoken in the Great Basin to the east, including Ute (1984:559–560; 567–570). The non-Indian invaders of California in the nineteenth century tended to call any of these desert dwelling peoples Paiutes, Pah-utes, or Shoshones, making it very difficult to write ethnographic and ethnohistorical accounts that define exactly the traditional territories of the various groups.

The other Uto-Aztecan subfamily important in California is the Takic. Speakers of Takic languages had separated perhaps about four thousand years ago from their Hopi-speaking relatives in a homeland that was perhaps somewhere in southeastern California or Arizona, and moved westward into California, probably reaching the coast somewhere in the region of Los Angeles about 2,000 years ago. By that time they may have occupied an area as far north as Tulare Lake in the southern San Joaquin Valley. They perhaps shared the Mojave Desert with the Mojave, a Hokan-speaking people whose traditions are that they long had control of the Mojave Desert, though not necessarily exclusive occupancy. On the coast, the Takic speakers replaced an earlier Hokan-speaking people between the Santa Barbara area and the San Diego area (1984:560).

In the Santa Barbara area, the Chumash, whose language belongs to the ancient Hokan stock, developed a rich maritime economy along the coast and on the adjacent Channel Islands. Yuman, another language family belonging to the Hokan stock, probably remained in place from very early times in San Diego County (and adjacent Baja California), along the Colorado River, and in parts of Arizona (1984:551,556).

A map showing California languages at the time Europeans arrived looks like a patchwork quilt, with the largest "patch" representing the area occupied by Uto-Aztecan speaking peoples across most of the southern part of the state. Isolated from this large block were the Northern Paiutes in the northeastern corner of the state.

The next largest "patch" represents the so-called Penutians who occupied the central part of the state, including the Central Valley, the San Francisco and Monterey Bay areas, parts of the central Sierra Nevada and the North Coastal ranges, and a small area in the extreme northern edge of the state.

Just south of the Athapascans on the coast lived the major remnant of Yukian-speakers. The other remnant occupied Napa Valley.

Hokan speakers included a number of rather isolated small groups (Karok, Shastans, Ochamawi, Pit River peoples, etc.) who occupied fairly large areas of mountainous northern California; the Pomo, who occupied the Sonoma, Russian River, and Clear Lake areas; the Chumash in the Santa Barbara-San Luis Obispo areas; the Washo in the vicinity of Lake Tahoe; and the Yumans of extreme southern California (south of the Takic-speakers).

There were also small remnants of Esselen and Salinan peoples who appear to have been survivals of the Hokan speakers who once surrounded San Francisco Bay.

Why should there be such great diversity of language in California? Although the mountainous environment isolated one group from another, this isolation does not appear to be the sole explanation, since other peoples even more isolated speak languages related to those of their neighbors. Rogers has argued that the diversity of languages on the Pacific coast of the North American continent is evidence that this area has been occupied for a much longer time than other parts of the continent. Groups would have moved southward along the ice-free coastal route during the Pleistocene, one group following another over many centuries. He points out that there was very little linguistic diversity in the area glaciated during the Wisconsinan glacial maximum. Even the area where there was an interior ice-free corridor at one point during the Pleistocene was peopled by speakers of languages developed on the west coast (1985).

Subsistence and Technology

Californians were active participants in the care and nurturance of biological resources, whether in an agricultural sense, planting or harvesting, or through techniques such as irrigation, pruning, and the like. Most of the peoples of California, living in a comparatively favorable environment with many resources, hunted, fished, collected and harvested foods. They can be described as proto-agriculturalists (Lawton and Bean 1973). Those along the Colorado River were farming people. Certain others, most notably those around Owens Lake, farmed in the early nineteenth century and probably did so earlier. Coastal peoples where good harbors existed had maritime economies, and, in fact, salmon were a major economic resource along California rivers as far south as the Santa Barbara area. Lacustrine resources such as tule, fish, and water birds dominated the economy of peoples who lived around lakes.

Within the territory of any one group, hundreds of plants and animals were available for the group's care and use. These varied greatly from area to area in terms of specific resources and their abundance, a factor that contributed much to the cultural diversity of California (Beals and Hester 1974).

Plants

A few of the most important and commonly used plants were acorns, buckeye, pinyon nuts, mesquite and screw beans, sage, cacti, grass seeds, berries and other fruit, and the roots of certain plants. These plants are still significant to many Indian people for food and medicine, some of them in ceremonial context. Several accounts of plant usage are available, including Bean and Saubel's TEMELPAKH (1972), which describes the uses of nearly three hundred plants by the Cahuilla Indians. Similar accounts are available for other groups, including works by Chesnut (1902), Barrows (1900), Hudson and Blackburn (1982, 1983, 1985, 1986, and 1987), and Zigmond (1981).

271

Wherever oaks (**Quercus** sp.) grew well, on the foothills and in mountain valleys, acorns were a major staple. They provided a more stable subsistence base than other staples. Groups that had an abundance of oaks within their territories had higher populations, more fixed boundaries, and more wealth than other groups. Acorns were ground and leached before being eaten, in order to remove the tannic acid they contained. It was even more important to grind and leach buckeyes (**Aesculus californica**), a secondary staple important in time of need in part because they were so poisonous that animals did not eat them (Baumhof 1978:17). The deep mortars in which the grinding took place appeared in California as early as 5,000 years ago.

In mountain areas, piñon nuts were important. Mesquite and screw beans, cacti, yucca and agave supplemented these in the deserts of southeastern California. In all areas, staples were supplemented by many other plant products, including berries, pit fruits, seeds, greens, and tubers.

Sage (**Salvia sp.**) seeds, or **chia,** were another important secondary staple. **Chia** was abundant in the South Coast Range and in the deserts to the east. A third secondary staple consisted of the roots of the epos or hampa, **Perideridia sp.,** which could be dug in many parts of northern California and eaten raw or cooked. They were nutritious and easily prepared for eating—a nutritious staple to accompany other foods as potato or rice would in American culture. It was, in part, because California Indians were often observed by early explorers and settlers digging for these tubers that they were known to many by the opprobrius term "diggers." The digging stick they used was a simple and efficient tool.

In addition to staples such as these, California peoples made a use of wide spectrum of the numerous plants that were found in the different environmental niches in their homelands, and the territories of others whose surplus was acquired by gift, trade, or purchase. An extraordinary variety of plants in any given environment were used for food, medicine, clothing, shelter, or tools.

The division of labor was less sexually demarcated than in some areas of North America. Gathering, collecting, and nurturing plant seeds, nuts, and fruits, while usually women's work, was also done by men and children. They especially tended to help with such large seasonal events as the acorn or pinyon nut harvests. These major harvests were an occasion for important ceremonial events such as thanksgiving rituals giving thanks to the deities for successful harvests. These harvest festivals had the additional function of managing and controlling the harvest distribution of foodstuffs so that resources were not over-exploited, and so that they did not end up in the hands of few people.

Animals

As with plants, hundreds of mammals, birds, reptiles, insects, etc. provided food, clothes, tools, and raw material for manufacture. Large game mammals, such as elk (**Cervus canadensis roosevelti** and **Cervus nannodes**), bighorn sheep (**Ovis canadensis**), pronghorn antelope (**Antilocapra americana**), and deer (**Odocoileus hemionus**) were significant important staples in the California diet. These were hunted by men in traditional ways associated with religious belief and special ritual. Both bows and arrows, in recent times, and atlatls in distant times, were used for hunting, in which strategy was often as significant a factor as the weapons. Ritual sweating to remove human odor with herbs characteristic of the area in which the animals lived preceded the hunt. The rituals also were often accompanied by sexual abstinence and fasting in order to prepare the hunter psychologically for his arduous and painstaking task. Deer hunters, for example, were wont to disguise themselves with antlers and deerskin, and to approach their quarry from downwind. With some game, such as antelope, teams of hunters worked together to capture game. Large game animals were especially attractive because of the large amount of meat involved. They were often shared with a large group of close relatives and friends, sometimes with considerable ritual. Meats were roasted and eaten, or dried for preserving. The large game animals also provided valuable hide from which blankets, clothing, and other things could be made. Sinew and bone provided invaluable material for tools of various sorts, such as basket awls, sinews for bows and the like.

The significance of these large game animals was often celebrated in ritual and belief. A guardian spirit of the game, for example, was often an important spiritual entity.

Chumash living on the coast hunted deep sea mammals. They and the neighboring Gabrielino made sea-going plank canoes for hunting, trading, and inter-island travel. Salmon were an important staple for riverine peoples from the northern border of California as far south as the Santa Barbara area.

The hundreds of various small game animals, birds, and fish within the territory of a group made an even greater contribution to subsistence than the large animals, because there were so many of them and because they were relatively easy to capture. Rabbits, for example, were valued not only for their meat, but also for fur, from which were woven rabbit-skin blankets that kept people warm in the cold of winter. In many parts of California it was customary to hold rabbit drives in which a ring of hunters surrounded an area and drove the rabbits in it into the center of a circle, where they could be caught and clubbed. Large nets were often stretched over an area and a controlled fire started to guide the animals and birds into these nets. Such drives had the effect of keeping game animals in ecological balance with their environments.

Men usually made the equipment that was used in hunting and fishing. This included traps, nets, decoys, blinds, bows, arrows (and arrow poisons), quivers, slings, rock throwers, spear throwers, throwing sticks and wrist guards used by hunters; traps, nets, sinkers, hooks, fishlines and reels, fish spears, harpoons, and fish poisons used by fishers; and the canoes, dugouts, paddles, anchors, anchors, bailers and knee pads used by deepsea fishermen. These fishermen, in the Chumash area, had a discoidal compass stone, on which painted lines radiated from a short stick inserted in the center, that they used to calculate both directions and the time of day (Hudson and Blackburn 1982).

Among some groups, the skills necessary for the manufacture of tools and other items was a specialized craft owned by a family or guild. Capital equipment was owned by individuals, sometimes chiefs and other important people.

Technology

Probably the most widely used and comprehensively valuable technology was that of basketry, whose manufacture was carried on primarily by women. California peoples made baskets for gathering, carrying, and storing plant and animal products. They made baskets for winnowing and parching seeds, for draining the water used to leach ground acorns, and for cooking anything that could be boiled or parched with hot stones. They made large burden baskets in which large quantities of meat, acorns, mesquite beans, or pinyon nuts were carried on the back for long distances. They made baskets (granaries) that were mounted on stilts for storing acorns, mesquite beans, pinyon, and other staples that needed to be kept away from rodents and other animal scroungers.

Baskets were either coiled or twined, and were often beautifully decorated. Baskets from various tribes can now be identified by basket experts who know the plants that each group tended to use, the characteristic shapes and sizes, the designs, and the quality of workmanship. Each group's work was distinct, art style being a group specific ethnic marker.

Besides their use as food containers and processing equipment, baskets were used as cradles for infants, for carrying and storing water, as items to trade, and as ceremonial objects.

Stone and lithic materials were used for many useful and religious objects, including containers and equipment. Most important, day in and day out, were the grinding tools: mortars and pestles, and manos and metates. Wherever in California there is bedrock in or near an ecological niche that would have supported oak trees, there are bedrock mortars where in bygone days women ground acorns for their family's meals. Elsewhere portable mortars were used. Granite was a favored stone. These same tools were used for processing other seeds as well. Small mortars were used for grinding medicines and pigments for body and face paint.

Metates, shallower than mortars, have been in use in California for thousands of years. It is assumed that they were used from the first as they were in the "ethnographic present" to grind small seeds and the meat and bones of small animals and thus make them easier to eat. Mortars were introduced between two and three thousand years ago, probably in association with the beginnings of acorn utilization—an advance made possible by the discovery that the tannic acid could be removed by leaching the acorn meal.

It is easy to understand the importance of the grinding stone if one thinks of it as the "food processor" in the Native California home, an aid in the preparation of a wide variety of seeds and nuts, as well as animal foods, and ceremonial necessities. The ceremonial necessities included such things as face and body paint; paint for ritual objects made of red hematite, charcoal, and other pigments; or the hallucinogens that were used in some groups to induce trance.

The utility of the mortar was sometimes increased by the use of a basket hopper attached to the top of the mortar with asphalt or sometimes other adhesive. The basket hopper kept the meal particles from flying out of the mortar.

Another class of stone tools were the various kinds of knives, scrapers, and projectile points that were skillfully fashioned by pressure and percussion flaking; and the pecking tools, adzes, axes, wedges, abrading stones, and so on with which other tools of stone, bone, and wood were made. Some idea of the complexity of California material culture can be gained from the five volume *Material Culture of the Chumash Interaction Sphere* (Hudson and Blackburn 1982, 1983, 1985, 1986, and 1987), and Barrett's *Material Aspects of Pomo Culture* (1952), although one must bear in mind that not all the peoples of California had as complex a material culture, or have been as well studied as those on the southern California coast and the Pomo.

Property and Exchange Systems

Property. Californians in general had definite property rights. Groups laid claim to the territory they occupied, and vigorously defended it against trespass. Within this territory, groups, families, or individuals owned rights to certain hunting, fishing, planting or collecting areas. Property rights also extended to such things as songs, places mentioned in songs, ritual paraphernalia, medical information, and the like.

Exchange. Problems that would have arisen because food supplies varied from season to season and year to year, and because some resources were not available in all areas, or were less from one year to another were ameliorated by a complex of trade and reciprocity systems. In order to acquire goods or tools not available in one's own area, or within one's own group, trade was carried on, not only between individuals and groups, but also by professional traders, who travelled long distances carrying portable items. It was also carried out at "trade fairs" attended by many of the people in a wide area of different political and language groups. There was, for example, a trading center at Cantrel, in the northwestern part of the Mojave Desert, where coastal and Central Valley peoples met regularly to trade with the people of the desert and of the Colorado River, but there were also two trails along the Mojave River, one used by the Chemehuevi/Southern Paiute and another by the Mojave. International trading centers such as the one at Cantrel and alliance exchanges of trading groups existed throughout the state. These conjoined peoples living in different environments with different assets.

Trade, of goods and services, also occurred at ceremonial events. These were, more importantly, the major settings for a system of reciprocity managed by the political and religious leaders of the groups. These gifts could be either foodstuffs, medicinal plants, raw materials, manufactured goods (e.g., blankets), or other necessities if supplies were plentiful, or manufactured goods such as shell beads, baskets, or tools when necessities were scarce. Leaders arranged that people from areas hit by drought or other calamity brought manufactured goods, and went home with necessities. In most parts of the state, marriage rules that forbade marriage with anyone related within three to five generations, and ceremonial rules that made it necessary to invite all relatives to ceremonies assured that this system of reciprocity levelled the significant variations in subsistence levels (Bean 1972). In the absence of a formal system of banking and coinage, this system made it possible to "bank" human energy and time in seasons of scarcity by making manufactured goods that could be converted to food and other necessities (Bean 1972).

Social Organization in Native California

The nature of social organization in Native California has been the subject of research by anthropologists for nearly seventy years. As research has continued through these several decades, a picture of increasing complexity has emerged as one scholar after another has added seminal concepts that provide the necessary understanding for more complex forms. The earlier view that California Indians were rather simple folk has been replaced by a realization that they were complexly organized hunters and gatherers whose social systems were similar to those of peoples with presumably greater technological advantages: e.g., horticulturalists and some agriculturalists. Their extensive socio-economic network apparently permitted a maximal use of resources across ecological ad political boundaries.

Basic Social Units

Kroeber conceptualized the "tribelet" as the basic landowning group in California, pointing out that the "so-called tribes" were usually non-political ethnic nationalities, except on the Colorado River and in the northwestern part of the state. It was usually the largest group over which any one person might have recognized authority and was the largest group that was autonomous, self-governing, and independent.

The non-political ethnic nationality is a cultural unit—a group of people sharing a language, culture, history, and philosophical concepts. It is represented in European socio-cultural conditions. For example, the Germans were a non-political nationality a hundred years ago, but were not yet a nation. They comprised Prussians, Bavarians, Saxons, Hessians, Westphalians, and others. These regional groups, and their particularistic governments, correspond to the Masut, Elem, Yokaia, and other tribelets whose aggregates composed the Pomo nationality (Kroeber 1954:39).

There were several hundred tribelets in California. They ranged between one hundred and three thousand persons per group. Tribelets were composed of family groups—parents, children, collateral relatives, lineal or affinal relatives, and sometimes non-relatives. The average family consisted of seven or eight people.

Tribelets varied in structural form. In south-central and southern California, they were usually composed of patrilineages. Often several lineages were linked into clans. Descent was traced over three to five generations. Women married out shortly after puberty, but usually maintained rights in their natal lineage. Adult women in the tribelets were consequently from various other groups. Lineage exogamy was often the rule.

Population density varied from 0.5 per square mile to as high as ten or more in the Yokuts-Chumash area. The least advantageous environments required more territory for smaller numbers of people. Territories ranged from 50 square miles among the Miwok to as many as 6000 square miles.

Each group appears to have expanded to the greatest extent that the requirement for cohesiveness permitted, lowering subsistence competition and conflict. One model attributes the equilibrium between resources and population to a complex system of socio-economic checks and balances (e.g., ritual reciprocity, exogamy, and trade feasts.)

A central town usually served as a political, ritual, and economic center. Large caches of food, goods, and treasures were maintained there.

Variations of this California pattern were found on the Colorado River and in northwest California. Groups centered around the lower Klamath River (Tolowa, Hupa, Chilula, Wiyot, Karok, and Yurok) shared a cultural tradition that suggests alliances with the northwest coast, and forms of social organization that had not developed the socio-political rigidity and complexity found in central and southern California. The tribelet in the northwestern part of California was a loosely connected set of separate settlements with people of different families clustered in towns or villages. It has been reported that competition rather than cooperation was emphasized as an ideal. Certain ritual safeguards against flagrant individualism, however, were imposed by the religious and legal system.

The Mojave and Quechan along the lower reaches of the Colorado River were unique among California peoples in that they had centralized tribal governments.

Two major forms of organizational style were characteristic of California tribelets. The lineage principles were dominant among groups south of the San Francisco area, whereas in north central California, one or more kin groups, each headed by a chief and generally composed of people related bilaterally, made up each village.

In the Sacramento Valley people were linked patrilaterally, and chiefly succession and inheritance of property tended to be patrilineal. In the northwestern part of the state people favored patrilocal residence. Settlements consisted of one of more residential kin groups led by a wealthy man, his extended family, and various collateral kin and hangers-on.

Political confederations, possibly nations, have been suggested for the Chumash (L. King 1969), Pomo, Miwok, Patwin, Shasta, Gabrielino, Kumeyaay, and Salinan. Trade and ritual and military alliances between groups are noted all over the state. Stable trade and military alliances seem to have involved at least three tribelets, often including different ethnic nationalities, whose ecological potential was mutually useful (e.g., ocean, river, foothill and mountain peoples allied for mutual exchange and protection). These alliance structures correlated with ecological factors, extended to the logical, naturally imposed limits within an area. In northern and north-central California the distances are small—from the coast inland to mountain ranges. In southern California, alliances extended across deserts and mountains, through passes, from the Pacific Coast into Arizona and Nevada. At least three such alliances crossed this broad area. These linked the Kumeyaay with the Yuma, the Gabrieleno with the Cahuilla, Halchidoma, and Coco-Maricopa groups, and the Chumash with the Yokuts and Mojave. There were also north-south alliances on the coast: Gabrielino, Chumash, and Salinan; and Miwok with the Southwestern Pomo.

In addition, there were ritual congregations associated with religion that linked each California tribelet with other tribelets and ethnic nationalities (Bean 1972). Peoples within a radius of fifty to seventy-five miles were usually linked in rituals or trade feasts that brought several hundred to several thousand people together on various occasions. Religious centers for the World Renewal system (where a few centers or towns held the World Renewal rituals for a large area in northwestern California) are a case in point. Among the Yokuts, three thousand people at a single ritual mourning ceremony were observed by an early explorer. Other centers are described for the Chumash (Point Mugu), Gabrielino (Povongna), and Kumeyaay (Pamo). The economic exchange maintained through these network involved communities, two or more nationalities, and several ecological zones (e.g., coast, foothill, riverine-mountain).

Many groups classified their members into two groups, or moieties. Moiety membership defined potential marriage alliances and ritual partnerships. Marriage between members of the same moiety was usually forbidden. This prohibition, along with the forbidding marriage between people related within three to five generations, created very extensive social networks between neighboring groups, since marital partners were necessarily sought from a wide sociological and ecological base.

Totemic associations involved taboo or privileged relationships with animals or birds and often signalled social relationships associated with ritual and economic privileges and responsibilities. A person holding a totemic status was responsible for the proper care and keeping of the totem animal on earth. This system maintained the man-land-animal balance in nature so that totemic guardians would continue to cooperate with man on earth. It further acted as a means of economic redistribution, since lineages, moieties, or families controlled valuable totem-related ritual items, such as eagle feathers, which were extremely valuable economically.

Marriage

Marriage was a closely regulated institution in native California. Young girls were usually married shortly after puberty to young men not much older than themselves. Great difference in age between spouses was rare, but it could occur, especially if the husband was a wealthy man, such as a chief or shaman. The possession of more than one wife indicated the possession of sufficient wealth to support more than one, and a special willingness of families to ally with the man.

People of high rank married into comparable families. Among many peoples, birth determined social rank, and women were part of a complex system of economic and political strategies for the long range benefit of their own families or lineages.

Most men had one wife, but might divorce and remarry several times during their lifetimes. Polygyny was accepted, especially for chiefs, for whom it was proper and necessary to have more than one wife, a reflection of the economics and political needs of their office. Sororal polygyny was commonly practiced. Where multiple wives were permitted, a man often married two sisters, an arrangement the wives sometimes preferred to the alter-

278

native of sharing household responsibilities with complete strangers. Alliances and proper child care were also encouraged by the practice of levirate and sororate rules. The custom of marrying the sister of a deceased wife protected the inter-family relationship and presumably provided for a positive continuity in child rearing. In the opposite case, the wife married the brother or close kin of a deceased husband. This was probably a more common and comfortable form since it did not require the socialization of new personnel, and it more easily protected the inter-family alliance structure and child-rearing aspects or the marriage. In all tribes there were frequent instances of marriage with persons from other ethnic groups. Thus Shastas married Modocs, and Luiseños married Kumeyaays. In the Gabrilino village of Tungva there were marriages with members of thirteen other villages, three of which were in other language families-Chumash, Yokuts, and Kitanemuk (Forbes 1966).

Since marriage was economically so important to families, individual interests were often subordinated to group needs. Divorce disturbed the economic and political alliances set up by marriages. Divorce, however, was possible. A man divorced a woman with greater ease than vice versa, common reasons being sterility, laziness, or sexual infidelity. Cruelty was the principal reason for a woman to leave her husband. An expectation that a wife would be protected from an unfavorable marriage by her own kin served as a safety mechanism for the wife. A woman usually retained some basic right within her own kin group and could return to it if she wished.

Classes

Class distinctions were expressed in behavior and in native terms for statuses, such as "wealthy person," "commoner," "poor person," "drifter," or the like. It appears that a tripartite system of elites or nobility, commoners, and the poor (sometimes slaves and vagabonds, as well) existed in most groups.

High rank and wealth tended to be inherited. Elites controlled distribution systems through control of political and ritual privileges and/or the control of capital resources and surplus. They maintained special religious knowledge and often spoke a special refined language which set them apart from others. They tended to marry among themselves. Their rank was justified in cosmological and normative postulates. Mechanisms for social mobility were available thought the acquisition of supernatural power or wealth derived from special skills in hunting, crafts, etc.

Chiefs

Chiefs were economic administrators, managing the production, distribution, and exchange of goods. They were not usually subordinate to other authority, although they were variously influenced by councils, secret-society officials, shamans, other officials and wealthy men. Since the primary duty of the chiefs was to control the collection, distribution, and exchange of food stores, money, and valuables for the benefit of the group, they needed ties with others. Intermarriage, ritual alliances, gift-giving, and other reciprocal acts guaranteed the agreements that corporate administrators maintained with one another as a means of stabilizing their economies. Such arrangements were essential where every group faced the danger of occasional food stress.

Positions of leadership were generally hereditary, and were associated with wealth. If a man were not conspicuously wealthy before he assumed office, he became wealthy after holding office, having become the economic administrator of the tribelet. A candidate for the chieftainship, however legitimate by hereditary standards, was replaced (usually by a brother or another son of the previous chief) if he were clearly unsuitable in temperament and talent, or unwilling to serve.

He lived in relative luxury in comparison with other men; his house and household was conspicuously large, his clothing more extravagant than that of others, and his possession of regalia and shell bead money, food stores, and treasure goods greater than others. He was often but not always released from ordinary labor, and was generally supported by the community, inasmuch as his many functions required freedom from many ordinary routines.

He was a man of prestige, respected and sometimes feared. His several wives were often from different tribelets, daughters of other chiefly or wealthy families. He thus provided himself and his children with kin among the elite of other communities. Occasionally the role of principal chief extended throughout a confederation of tribelets. The groups in this confederation might, as they did among the Shasta, or might not, constitute the entire membership of an ethnic nationality.

In post-contact times many chiefs used their traditional role to bring together larger numbers of people. They were recognized as major leaders by the invading European authorities, and were able to negotiate with them for political accommodations because their considerable power bases were acknowledged and respected.

Shamans

Shamans were the principal religious functionaries in most groups. They frequently assumed priestly status, and the role was often carried simultaneously with others. Shamans specialized in various activities, and a man might be both a chief and a shaman, engaging in various types of curing, divination, or control of particular guardian spirits, natural phenomena, guardians of game, and the like. They were integral to the political, economic, and legal institutions. Nowhere were they separate from these institutional frames. Gayton's classic discussion of the role of shaman, which describes the close integration of chiefs and shamans in political and economic institutions among the Yokuts and Western Mono, applies generally to the entire state (Gayton 1930).

Shamans ranked second only to chiefs in authority and prestige, but they were more often criticized than chiefs. It was generally assumed that they were both malevolent and good, although some argue that this is a matter of differing philosophies or conceptions of the role between professionals and laymen. Shamans were paid for their services. Their roles tended to be inherited and maintained in family lines, although inheritance was not as rigidly determined as that of chiefs. The position was open to persons in every social rank who had the appropriate talent.

Councils and Managers

A chief was assisted by a managerial or administrative class associated with the ritual or cult systems. These "bureaucrats," usually men over 40, composed the council of "elders" who advised chiefs. Tribelet chiefs together formed councils for larger political entities. Positions on councils were often passed along in family lines.

In council, consensus was an ideal. It was achieved in an informal manner. When conflict was unresolved, higher opinion was brought to bear on the group by calling in higher-level chiefs. A principal duty of these officials was to represent and communicate to the people. They acted as judicial authorities, as masters of ceremonies at ritual events, and as managers of protocol when visitors came to the village.

The assistant or sub-chief acted as a messenger or reporter to the chief. Traveling singers and traders also gathered socio-political data which they reported to their chiefs. There were also clowns, dance managers, other ritualists, peacemakers, and war chiefs. The "clown" or jester made fun of the chief, acted disrespectfully, and sometimes pointed out the chief's foibles to the public. His burlesquing role served to emphasize the usual respect due the chief. The role of ritual manager was important. War chief and peacemaker (negotiator) were usually temporary offices; a skilled warrior would be selected as war chief by the council or the chief.

Specialists and Other Professionals

Occupational specialization created status differentiation and provided economic advantages for many. Degree of specialization varied in direct proportion to ecological advantages and population density. Specialists occurred in all groups (trading, basket-making and clam-shell disk manufacturing). In the more complex societies such as the Chumash, "craft guilds" that controlled an industry were established.

For the Patwin, Nomlaki, and Pomo, "functional families" controlled an activity and an accompanying spiritual guardian. Some craftsmen exchanged their products for other goods and were often completely relieved of other subsistence activities.

In northwestern California, rich men had slaves so they could spend their energy making luxury items. For women, basket-making, midwiving, herbalism, and shamanism were important activities. Specialists stood as a class between the nobles (chiefly families) and commoners. They were somewhat analogous to medieval burghers, clustering in larger towns where their crafts would have more ready markets.

Commoners

Commoners or ordinary persons included people who were not conspicuously important in terms of inherited rank, wealth, talent, or position. They were a "ruled class," intimidated by their social superiors, who controlled spiritual, economic, and religious institutions that commoners supported by donation (taxes), gifts, and various fees.

For the ordinary person there was little opportunity for geographic mobility and control. He might migrate to another village where relatives would support him, or become a vagabond or wanderer.

Commoners were somewhat "provincial" in thought, tied mainly into local social networks. They did not have the protection of high status. Their traditions and values were somewhat different than those of elites. Their knowledge was of the more ordinary rituals, the "folkloric" little traditions, rather than the esoteric great tradition aspects of their culture. They shared a dependence on the people of power, treated them with deference, and recognized their right to rule by tradition and divine right (supernatural power implied by rank).

Lower Class

Most groups in California recognized a "lower class" of individuals. These are described for several groups in northwest California. There is also what Katherine Luomala has described in some detail as vagabonds, "an aggregate of nonconforming individuals who congregated seasonally without organizational identification" (Luomala 1963). These may well have been typical of much of the state.

Slavery

Certain tribes, including the Karok, Hupa, Klamath, Modoc, Mojave, and Quechan institutionalized slavery. Slaves were usually taken from other ethnic groups. Atsugewi were a favorite target for capture by the Modoc, and the Chemehuevi by the Mojave. Slavery was not an hereditary status. Oftentimes slaves were eventually returned to their people as part of a negotiated settlement of conflict. Escape was apparently common.

Special Friends, Trading Partners, and Other Fictive Kin

The roles of trading partner, special friend, or fictive kin extended an individual's social, psychological, economic, and political networks to other areas. Special friends stood in a sociologically primary relationship to each other, a relationship that was cemented by the exchange of valuable gifts.

Trading partner relationships were found throughout the state, sometimes reinforced by intermarriage. The relationship assumed a high level of trust and reciprocity; often the partners operated in a mode that placed a higher value on service to one another than on profit. Thus the advantages of the non-profit, reciprocal economic relationship generally found within the extended family or lineage were extended to a foreign group.

The population density, extensive social scale, and societal complexity that developed in California were not just a consequence of efficient technology and a fortunate environment that provided an extraordinary energy potential; they were also a consequence of specific social institutions that served to increase productive resources and redistributed energy in such a way that the resultant socio-cultural complexity was truly analogous to that customarily found in agricultural societies. These social institutions were as follows:

1. An extension of economic and political alliances by marriage rule (three to five generations) and/or moiety exogamy that meant that all corporate groups (tribelets) had affinal relationships with several other groups with differing economic potentials;

2. Ritual obligations and kinship obligations requiring that whenever a group held a ritual, it would necessarily invite ritualists and relatives from other corporate groups. Obligatory gifting and fee payments occurred in these contexts and they were opportunities for formal trading relationships to develop;

3. Acknowledgement that certain persons had administrative rights to the production and distribution of goods. Such rights might include sanctioned membership in secret societies, or status as a chief, shaman, craft specialist, or the like;

4. A banking procedure implicit in all of these situations, in that subsistence goods could be transformed into treasure goods, money, or craft goods.

Belief Systems

A number of scholars have addressed the issue of how California Indians perceived their universe, and how they ordered their personal behavior as a result of their ideas about correct and incorrect behavior. What follows is a synthesis, a summary of findings on California Indian belief systems and world view by various scholars that apply to California Indians in general (Bean 1976; Blackburn 1977; Kearney 1984; Lee 1950).

Understanding these philosophical issues is important because these concepts defined reality for people. Every culture has an orderly view of its universe that explains its nature, and a set of ideas—values—that guides the individual in his or her day-to-day actions. Without such parameters social chaos would result.

Such concepts are directly applicable to day-to-day living. Although on the surface they may sometimes seem unrelated to real life, even the most esoteric appearing of them often have very practical direct and indirect functions (see Bean 1972; Blackburn 1975; and Bean 1976).

The nature of these concepts is found in part and most explicitly in the oral literature of California Indians, a literature rich in poetic and literary quality. In most groups it was recounted in both sacred and secular contexts, often set to music and accompanied by dance, pantomime, and other theatrical events. All California Indians had some knowledge of their group's oral literature. The ritual specialists, chiefs, and shamans had a more detailed and compete understanding of it than did ordinary people.

Belief systems varied from one region to another. Several major religions (great traditions) were present in the state, each as distinctive as the other great religions of the world. In northwest California there was the World Renewal religion; in central California, Kuksu religions; and in south central and southern California, the Toloache religions in which the hallucinogen **toloache** from "jimsonweed," **Datura meteloides,** was used in certain aspects of religious practice.

World Renewal Religion. The World Renewal rituals in northwest California re-enacted in song and dance the creation of the world, and thus restored the world to a renewed primal state in which humans had an ordered relationship with each other and with the universe. This world of humans, it was assumed, required regeneration because of "pollution," i.e., incorrect behavior on the part of humans over a period of time (Bean and Vane 1978).

Kuksu Religions. The Pomo; the Yuki and Huchnom; the Cahto; the Patwin; the Hill and Valley Maidu; the Valley Nisenan; and the Coast, Lake, and Plains Miwok were associated with the Kuksu religion, a religion in which most males (and occasional females) were formally initiated into one or more secret societies in a ceremony that involved the impersonation of spiritual beings. Initiation into one of these secret societies involved indoctrination into a body of sacred lore kept secret from non-initiates. The initiation ceremonies, however, were public affairs for which participants wore elaborate costumes and enacted spectacular ceremonial dramas. Members constituted an elite group who wielded social, political, and economic as well as sacred power.

In most of the groups within the Kuksu system there were also somewhat lower ranking ghost societies, whose members impersonated the dead. Ghost societies were especially important in rites of passage marking the beginning of adulthood for adolescent boys and girls. In the ceremonies, ghost costumes and behavior were consistent with the idea that the land of the dead was a reverse of this world, with people sleeping in daytime and working at night, for example. Ghost societies did not exist where annual mourning rites were held, and may have filled some of the functions of the latter, mediating between the living and the dead (1978).

Toloache Religions. In southern California, the major religions were characterized by ceremonies in which trance was achieved by some participants by using **toloache** or jimsonweed (**Datura meteloides**). Among the groups who used toloache were the Yokuts, the Chumash, the Takic-peoples, the Kawaiisu, the Tubatulabal, and the Colorado River peoples. Among the Chumash, the ʔAntap religion, in which leaders of the group were symbolically associated with powerful deities, had developed out of the Chumash religion by the ethnographic present.

Among the Luiseño-Juaneño, Kumeyaay, and Gabrielino, a variant of toloache religions, the Chinigchinich religion, had developed, perhaps as recently as the late eighteenth century. It was spreading southward to the Kumeyaay in the nineteenth century.

This religion was characterized by belief in a creator-hero whose avenging spirits (Rattlesnake, Spider, Tarantula, Bear, Raven, etc.) enforced the moral order.

Toloache is a hallucinogen that can be lethal, and was used only after careful ritual preparation, such as fasting and other purification. Among the Serrano, Cahuilla, Luiseño, Gabrielino, Cupeño, and Kumeyaay, **toloache** was given to young men prior to initiation, who were then encouraged to dance until they were in a trance. While in the trance state, they saw visions that were symbolically and emotionally meaningful. They were then taught secret cosmological concepts of their people, and given training in proper adult behavior. Among many groups, only elite youths—sons of chiefs, shamans, or other tribal leaders—were initiated, but in the other groups all young men were initiated (Strong 1929).

Among the Yokuts and Western Mono, the taking of **toloache** depended more on individual decision. Women, as well as boys and men, might decide to take it. It was never taken, however, without careful ritual preparation. Its use was often for medical purposes, i.e., to relieve pain, and brought people the power to identify the sources of trouble or illness, or luck in gambling.

Shamans in these groups took **toloache** in most religious ceremonies, using it to gain access to power, for magical flight, to diagnose and heal the ill, to foretell the future, to ensure success for people in hunting and other ventures, and to perform acts of sorcery.

Power

Underlying the belief systems of California Indians was a perception of supernatural power as the prime mover in the universe. This power was understood as the cause of all things, responsible for the creation of all that is, and a continuing living energy omnipresent in the world. Differences between peoples, individuals, and things could all be explained as differences in kind or degree of power, which was and is present in both animate and seemingly inanimate things. It decreases as the original creation recedes in time, but because individuals have power, they have knowledge and can manage their universe intelligently.

The world as we know it today was created at a magical time in the past. Within the universe there are both human and non-human beings. Together they manage the universe. The Indians interact with some of the non-human beings, who have great powers upon which humans can draw in order to acquire energy, food, ability to diagnose and treat disease, and the like. Priests and shamans have greater knowledge and access to this power than other people.

Humans have more power than most other creatures and are in the midst of a great continuum of power. In effect, they are the beings responsible for the proper management of the world through correct ritual behavior. Rituals are directed toward supernatural beings and certain other non-human beings in this world, as well as toward the plants and animals that provide them subsistence. Rituals are also used to assure good weather, good health, fertility, and the like.

Power is omnipresent and malleable—thus all phenomena are potentially useful because they may contain power. Indians for this reason maintain an empirical attitude toward all things that is essentially scientific. Through the centuries they have experimented with the environment in order to see if it was useful—a fact accounting for the very detailed and precise knowledge they had about plants, animals, astronomy, and the like.

The individual was very much a part of a tightly knit kin group, and his or her ethnic identity was closely identified with the history of the group. The individual was keenly aware that individual actions were important to the well being of all. Children were apprised of this at an early age. They were contributing and responsible members of their societies through productive action as early as possible. Women, for example, were often married and the mother of children by their early teens.

It was almost impossible for the individual to stand apart from his group, and very difficult to change his or her group affiliation. Individuals identified themselves by a group name. If an Indian were asked for a definition of a wealthy man, he or she might reply that a wealthy man was one with many relatives everywhere, since reciprocal relations with them would mean that he had many social, economic, and political resources to call upon when in need.

The individual was an integral part of a larger, powerful universe—a well-defined one. The entire universe was like the person. There was sentient power everywhere. A plant was not just a passive, non-thinking thing. It was a sentient being. It had personality, knowledge, and feelings, and it made decisions as a human did. It was treated accordingly, not unlike the way one would like to be treated oneself. The same was true of animals and other phenomena. While humans might have more power than members of other species, they were still obligated to them as other beings. The other beings, in turn, had obligations to provide home, food, and various resources to humans. If humans did not behave properly, these beings could withdraw their availability.

All beings were, in a sense, alike. In the beginning, they were all created by one set of power relationships or causes. Thus all were one, or alike, but in different ways. Differentiations of being and types of phenomena occurred later in creation when plants, animals, humans, rocks, and astronomical phenomena became differentiated—yet they all continued to have sentience.

These ideas were responsible for a sense of relativity that influenced Indian thought and behavior. One could never be quite sure about what one was dealing with. Things were not always what they seemed on the surface to be. Thus the world was approached cautiously, thoughtfully and with respect. Decision-making in most areas of life was carefully considered in terms of possible indirect and direct impacts. Incorrect or badly chosen behavior could affect others. One's kinfolk—wife or husband, child, parents, or siblings—could be harmed by one's behavior. In a sense, both the individual and his or her group were responsible for the individual's actions and at risk as a result of them.

Indians had not only observed the phenomena of their world carefully, they had classified it. Their categories, though different from those of Europeans, were logically organized according to specific criteria attached to each category.

286

The California Indians' concept of time differed from that of Europeans. Past, present, and future were not as distinctly separate, nor was what we refer to as mythic time or dream time as distinct from "real time." For them, mythic time was and is more a part of day-to-day reality—a time of great power and primal creation that is still with them when rituals are carried out and at sacred places.

The universe is tripartite, with many beings and phenomena within its three levels—upper, middle, and lower. The upper universe is that in which many of the supernatural beings of the dream time still reside and act. It is often the place where the souls of the dead reside.

In this upper universe there resides most of the power and knowledge of the world from the beginning of time. It can be acquired and used for the good or bad, if one knows how to go there. One goes there by magical flight, and returns the same way. It is a trip made by shamans, who must know at least the route they should go, so they can guide souls, after death, to the land of the dead.

The middle universe is this world where people live and die. Humans, animals, plants, and mountains are all a part of that. It is different from the upper and lower universe primarily in that there is less power here. However, beings of the dream time—often characterized as sacred beings—are still here, and interact with humans. Eagle, Coyote, and Bear are names attributed to supernatural beings, each a different type. There were also places within the middle universe where there was residual power left over from the time of creation.

The lower universe is the place of other beings from the dream time—sometimes more malevolent beings than those of the upper world. The lower world is especially associated with amphibians and reptiles; e.g., rattlesnakes, frog, lizard, and the like.

Although power decreases as time goes on, people may return via ritual to the older sacred times and places in order to acquire more power. The older times are viewed as more sacred and their ways more beneficial than those of today. California Indian religions persist to the present day, in large part because their traditional beliefs are still operative.

Space

The cosmological aspects of space described above were common to most California Indians. In other respects, space was defined in different ways by different California groups, especially in respect to the immediate environment. East, west, north, south, and often up and down were recognized by most groups. Upriver and downriver, and toward and away from the coast or mountains were important to groups in environments where such features dominated the environment. For many groups there was a specific direction that was more prominent than others. East was often such a direction, usually because the sun rose there. The world was generally viewed as round, surrounded by water.

Boundaries of areas owned by groups were well defined, often marked by rock art, a mountain top, a river, desert, or other feature. Within each group's territory, space was divided between that which was sacred and usable only by those with the requisite knowledge to use its power safely, the shamans and priests, and other space.

There were some areas that were used in common by the groups that bordered them. These were usually areas that had resources useful to all, such as pinyon, that were erratic in production. Space belonging to a non-political ethnic nationality was divided into space belonging to the nationality as a whole, and that belonging to a tribelet within it. Within the tribelet, groups, families or individuals owned productive resources. These could be living spaces, areas of food production such as oak groves where acorns could be harvested, places where women collected basketry materials, clay for pottery, or hematite for paints.

Ritual

Ritual was used to coordinate religious matters and the redistribution of economic resources, to balance political affairs, and to socialize and resocialize members of groups into the belief and behavior patterns expected of each member of society.

Throughout an individual's life, and, for that matter, throughout the life of the group, ritual guided and marked important happenings. Changes in the status of individuals were celebrated and used as instructional vehicles to mark their entrance into and departure from the life of the community. Birth, a boy's puberty, the occasion of a girl's first menstrual period, marriage, and death, as well as changes in rank were such important times—the occasions for important rites of passage. They were consequently attended by considerable ritual—the gathering together of many people from within and without the group, especially kinfolk. The occasion was carefully managed by ritual officials—priests, shamans, and their assistants.

Other rituals—rituals of intensification—celebrated occasions important to the whole group. These were often connected with the livelihood of the group, and included thanksgiving rituals celebrating the maturation of a new crop, such as acorns or pinyon nuts, or the beginning of the fishing season.

There were also rituals that ensured a human's stable relationship with the supernatural world. In effect, these rituals celebrated the life and death of the group. These were present in all California groups. These included the World Renewal and Kuksu rituals, and the Nukil rituals associated with toloache religion.

At such rituals, people from many communities came together annually or semi-annually to intensify their sense of group identity, to fulfill their international obligations to one another, to exchange goods, to find marital partners, and to join together their assets: ritual knowledge and power, and such economic assets as food, ornaments, tools, and the like.

Recreation

Although making a living was a full time chore for most people in California Indian societies, recreation was important to them. It included storytelling for all, but especially children, and games of various sorts. Girls' and women's games generally emphasized skill. They included jacks, dice games, cat's cradle, and others. Boys' games focused upon skills and manual dexterity important for their later adult male activities, especially hunting. They include dart games, shooting with bows and arrows, running, and hoop and pole games.

Besides these games that were sources of pleasure and training in skills needed in adulthood, there was gambling. The arts and skills of gambling were highly developed. The hand game, for example, was played in all groups. It involved the skillful hiding of objects, and guessing which combination of objects were held in which hand of a player. Considerable wagers were placed on the outcome of these games. The use of power was an integral part of winning or losing. The games were associated with a rich literature of song. Gambling is still a favored activity among California Indians.

Historical Overview

Europeans first reached California in the sixteenth century and the very early seventeenth century, when Spanish explorers reached both the Colorado River area and coastal California, and the English under Sir Francis Drake visited the San Francisco Bay area. While the results of these early contacts are for the most part a matter of conjecture, it is probable that, like later Europeans who came, these early explorers brought devastating epidemic disease in their wake.

The Europeans came to stay in 1769. The invasion began with Spanish missionaries sent out from Mexico—Franciscans who established a chain of missions approximately a day's journey apart along the California coast. The Franciscans were accompanied by small military forces to afford protection and provide coercive power to subdue the Indians, and by farming colonists from Mexico. The avowed purpose of the missionaries was to bring Christianity to the peoples of California, to transform them into Hispanic people. These purposes were achieved with some Indians, mostly coastal people, but with devastating loss of life and culture.

As each mission was founded, peoples near it were brought into the mission system and baptized. Except at Mission San Diego and Mission San Luis Rey, this meant leaving their traditional communities and living at the missions under the direct supervision of the mission fathers. European diseases spread rapidly and were deadly to these populations, who had little or no immunity to them. Birth rates fell, because conditions at the missions were unclean, and foods were less than nutritious. It was particularly hard on girls and women. Despondency and despair affected their will to live and bear children. Some Indians, alert to possibilities for gaining access to new sources of power, did not resist initial baptism, and introduction to new technologies and such novelties as domesticated animals. As time went on, however, most died or deserted. The Spanish took particular umbrage at desertions and often sent military expeditions out to bring back runaways and severely punish them.

As time went on, the mission populations dwindled, and the inhabitants of ever more distant villages were sought to be baptized and to serve as a renewal of the labor force.

Nonetheless, by 1825 to 1830, when fur traders from eastern Canada and the United States began to arrive in California, the missions were thriving agricultural systems. By this time, the Spanish had been overthrown in Mexico and California was a province of Mexico rather than Spain. Mexican ranchers saw the mission lands and herds as comprising too much wealth for the Indians, and pressured the Mexican governor into taking control of the missions from the Franciscans.

There followed a period of disruption during which many of the mission buildings were vandalized and their lands and flocks taken over by Mexican ranchers. Some of the Native Americans who had been inducted into missions were left homeless and bereft. For others, this period was one of opportunity and freedom. They went back to their communities and lived their lives as they chose, weaving into their traditional patterns the new ideas they had learned at the missions. Most Native Californians were outside the mission system and continued their traditional life style. Some profited by new knowledge (a form of power) brought them by missionized Indians and those who had lived and worked in Mexican communities as farmers and craftspeople. To a significant degree, this period was, in fact, the "ethnographic present" that ethnographers would learn about in the late nineteenth and early twentieth century.

In the meantime, more and more non-Indians were entering California from the East. Some came to trade in furs, some to explore, and some to settle as farmers, vaqueros, and ranchers. They were a significant factor in California's separating itself from Mexican rule.

After gold was discovered in 1846, the trickle of invading peoples became a flood, a circumstance leading to California's becoming a territory of the United States, and then a state. Although California's native peoples were at first incorporated into the newly developing social system as a source of labor, they were very shortly shut out. Most of their land and resources were taken from them without acknowledgement of their ownership rights. When they attempted to substitute domestic animals for the game that was disappearing, they were subject to retaliatory measures of great severity. Their attempts to defend their rights militarily reminded the invaders of their numerical disadvantage, and resulted in the appointment of a team of three Indian agents to negotiate a settlement with California's Native Americans. These three agents met with eighteen different groups of Native American leaders throughout the state during 1851 and 1852 to negotiate treaties. In these treaties the United States agreed to set aside large tracts of land as reservations for the Indians, and the latter agreed to United States occupation of the rest of their lands in return for the reservations, and a number of other concessions, such as farm tools and seed, educational opportunities, and supplies of food and clothing. In effect, California Indians "ratified" and conformed with these treaties for some time, whereas the United States never ratified them, and conformed with them only with respect to the few promised payments of food and supplies distributed upon completion of the negotiations.

Some funds were allotted by the U.S. Congress during the 1850s for the relief of the destitute Indians of the state, but not enough to go around. Some lands were reserved for them, but not the vast tracts set forth in the treaties. At the early reservations—one in Tejon valley in the Tehachapis, one at Nome Lackee in the northern Central Valley, one at Round Valley in Mendocino County, one at Covelo in northwestern California, and one at Tule River in the Central Valley—Indian agents went through some of the motions of training Native Americans in agriculture. Although some agents seem to have made an honest effort to provide benefits, they were hampered by inadequate support from the government and the hostility of neighboring settlers, who tended to take over any reservation field that proved fertile, to steal reservation livestock, and to shoot the Native Americans as sport. In all too many instances, the Indian agents themselves were more interested in personal gain than in assisting the Indians to adjust to a changing situation.

The 1850s and 1860s constituted a period when California Indians had no civil rights (they could neither vote nor give testimony in court), and when slavery and indentiture were common. The conditions under which they lived made them more vulnerable than ever to epidemics of disease. A smallpox epidemic in 1863 was particularly deadly, depleting the Native American population so that it was no longer even a source of labor, and reversing the balance of power. The last military conflict between California Indians and non-Indians was the Modoc war in the northern part of the state, which came to an end in 1873.

By the early 1870s, population pressures were threatening to result in the eviction of Native Californians from the settlements on those private ranches where they were tolerated by non-Indians who had secured title to the land, in part because they were a convenient source of labor. In some instances, as at Temecula in southern California, Indians were literally thrown out on the public roads after land fell into new ownership.

At this same period, Indian advocate organizations were springing up, reflecting the fact that Indians were no longer considered a threat (Spicer 1972). Among the most important were the Indian Rights Association of Philadelphia and the annual Mohonk Conferences. As a result of pressure from such groups, President Grant in the 1870s started appointing Protestant ministers as Indian agents, a strategy that produced conflict in southern California, where most Indians had been baptized as Catholic. He also began setting aside land as Indian reservations by Presidential proclamation. These were mainly for "mission Indians" in southern California. Impingement on these lands by settlers seeking land and water and the resulting outcry brought about investigations by Abbott Kinney and Helen Hunt Jackson in the early 1880s, and by the Mission Indian Commission in 1890–1891. The findings of the latter Commission with respect to southern California resulted in an act of Congress passed in 1891 that took land away from some reservations, and established a number of new reservations. Shortly before its passage, in 1887, the Dawes Severalty Act of 1887 mandated an effort to allot reservation lands to family heads. Allotment efforts continued for some thirty years on California reservations.

Land continued to be set aside for Indians under one provision or another for many years. A number of groups were placed on small rancherias rather than reservations. Many

Indians whose descendants still recognize their Indian heritage were never provided a land base.

To be given land was to be placed under the jurisdiction of the Office of Indian Affairs and the agency that superseded it, the Bureau of Indian Affairs—a doubtful benefit. This agency provided help in developing irrigation, farming advice, and sometimes from machinery and tools. It provided some medical care. It also took control of those under its jurisdiction. It forced children to go to school and insisted they learn English; it took measures to eradicate Indian religious, social, and economic traditions—for example, it discouraged groups from spending time on such "time-wasting" endeavors (from the bureau's point of view) as putting on religious events. It appointed tribal leaders, and diminished, when possible, the authority of leaders chosen by the tribes. This paternalistic system encouraged dependency, and attenuated traditional culture, which nonetheless persisted even as it adjusted to changing conditions.

The scholarly study of Native California cultures may be said to have begun in the late 1890s when David P. Barrows was awarded the first Ph.D. in Anthropology at the University of Chicago for his study of the ethnobotany of the Cahuilla. Shortly thereafter, Constance Goddard DuBois began her work with the Luiseño and Diegueño that climaxed with the publication of her *Religion of The Luiseño and Diegueño Indians of Southern California* in 1908. At the same period, Phily E. Goddard was gathering data on the peoples of northwestern California, and Dr. J. W. Hudson began collecting data on tribes in northern and central California as far south as the Tehachapis. Most important of all was the appointment in 1903 of Alfred L. Kroeber as head of a new Department of Anthropology at the University of California in Berkeley. Kroeber, whose interests encompassed language and prehistory as well as ethnography and ethnology, sent out several generations of scholars to gather data on Native California peoples while elders still remembered traditional ways. His *Handbook of The Indians of California,* published by the Smithsonian Institution in 1925, was finished about 1919 and incorporated much of what was known by that time. Kroeber and his students continued to focus on California peoples for another two decades. Kroeber was a principal expert witness on behalf of Native Californians in the Claims Cases of the 1950s, and continued to study and write about California Indians until his death in the early 1960s.

The ethnographic efforts of Kroeber and his associates were supplemented by the work of John Peabody Harrington and C. Hart Merriam, who collected ethnographic and linguistic data from many California groups from the early years of the century until the 1940s and 1950s.

That we described the beginnings of California ethnography as events at the turn of the century does not negate the importance of certain earlier writers who described the ways of California Indians. These included Spanish priests at the missions, fur traders and explorers, military men, collectors of artifacts, ordinary citizens, and journalists. Despite their various biases, they contributed much to our knowledge.

Native Americans served along with other Americans in World War I. In recognition for their services, the United States Congress in 1924 granted citizenship to American Indians born in the United States—a measure in tune with the government's goal of total assimilation.

At the end of World War I, having realized that their counterparts in other parts of the nation had been paid for their land under the provisions of treaties signed with the United States government, California Indians began to organize an effort to get paid for their traditional lands. Non-Indian advocates—especially Frederick Collett in northern California and Jonathan Tibbets of the Mission Indian Federation in southern California—recruited Indians to their respective organizations, and encouraged them to donate to funds that paid for trips to Washington, the publication of a newsletter, and other organizational costs. These and other efforts led to the Claims Cases—suits against the Federal government that led to reimbursement for the lands in California taken from their ancestors. These cases came to trial in the early 1940s and again in the 1950s, and resulted in individual Native Californians receiving about $150 each for the first set of trials, and about $600 each for the second after years of litigation. Certain issues arising from the Claims case, e.g. water rights, their loss, and resultant damages, are still before the courts.

Native Californians, along with other Californians, suffered increased poverty and hardship during the 1930s. A number of measures were undertaken to help them. They were given, lent, or sold livestock and seed, and some were provided employment. At the same time, an effort to reorganize tribal governing bodies was made by the passage of the Indian Reorganization Act of 1934. This act brought the effort to allot tribal lands to an end; it established a revolving loan fund; and it encouraged the reorganization of tribal governments.

Native Californians were fully participant in World War II. Their participation took many of them, with other Americans, to far flung parts of the world. Those who stayed at home were more fully employed than previously, although even in this period of prosperity their standard of living was far below that of other Californians.

By the 1930s, many in the federal government began to favor the termination of the reservation system, and the withdrawal of the federal government from its commitment to provide services to Native Americans. After World War II, this philosophy reached expression in legislation and Bureau of Indian Affairs policy. The Bureau began to push hard for termination by 1952. Public Law 280, passed in 1953, placed reservations under the civil and criminal jurisdiction of the states. Federal health and welfare services began to be denied to reservation Indians, but state and county agencies were unwilling to provide them the services. The Rancheria Act (27 Stat. 619 as amended by 78 Stat. 39) provided a procedure for rancherias and reservations to vote for termination. Medical, educational, and economic conditions were extremely poor at this time.

Many of the reservations and rancherias fought termination, recognizing that the legislation that authorized it was unfair, taking away rights and privileges without compensation, and threatened the destruction of traditional social structure. A number of rancherias, mainly in northern California, voted to terminate. Most of these have in turn gone through a process of "untermination" in the 1980s, even though the trust lands distributed to individuals have often been lost and cannot be retrieved.

The California Culture Area Today

Today's Californian Indians are for the most part rural people who live in small towns and cities in or near traditional areas, or on reservations and rancherias, but some have made their way to the cities. There is a long-standing custom of going to the city to work, but considering the small town, rancheria, or reservation as home. Many may work for many years in an urban area, but return to their home area upon retirement.

Native Californians have adopted the outer trappings of the dominant culture. Neither their clothing, housing, means of transportation, educational status, nor even religious behavior may seem to distinguish them from other Californians. Nonetheless, the attitudes, psychology, belief systems and other aspects of traditional culture prevail. All over rural California, where there are Native American populations, traditional ritual materials are still made, and traditional rituals are carried out in ceremonial houses. Traditional foods are still consumed on occasion, and there is an attempt to preserve traditional language. There are Indian cultural centers and museums that play an important role in maintaining cultural boundaries and thus abetting cultural persistence. In such centers there are often classes teaching basketry and other traditional crafts.

In urban California Indians are outnumbered by Native Americans from other states, who bring with them a wide range of cultural values and attitudes. In urban Indian centers, and at the "Pow-wows" that have become a major manifestation of Native American culture, today's California Indians take part in a Pan-Indian culture, and have a chance to compare the culture of other Indians with their own.

The status of today's Californian Indian owes much to comparatively recent nationwide developments. The Civil Rights movements of the 1960s focused attention on the plight of America's minorities. In California, the occupation of Alcatraz Island in the latter part of that decade called attention to the fact that Indians were more disadvantaged than any other minority group. A number of federal and state measures were thereupon taken that have somewhat ameliorated this situation. These measures have been operative mainly in the fields of health, housing, education, and legal services. A number of rancherias and reservations now have clinics where health care is available. Tribal centers provide seniors with free lunches and send buses to pick them up. Some supplement school programs with information about traditional culture, and some have programs at the schools to encourage Indian students to complete high school educations, and continue into college and university training. Some new housing has been provided. The California Indian Legal Service has successfully pursued legal remedies for Indian problems. Most of these programs are inadequately funded.

The California Indian Education Association, founded in 1967, has pushed for more Indian involvement in educational planning for Native American students. The American Indian Historical Society, founded in 1964 by Rupert Costo, a Cahuilla, has pushed for more accurate treatment of Native Americans in textbooks, an endeavor in which a new generation of enthnographers has shared. The latter have pointed out that earlier scholars, concerned to refute a stereotype of Native Americans as fierce and hostile barbarians, described them as "simple" hunters and gatherers—a stereotype that scholarly research has now shown to be as false and nearly as damaging as the earlier one.

An important new development in Indian affairs has been that the numerous Native American groups who have never been granted a land base have found themselves unable to qualify for state and federal programs that help the landed groups. In the late 1970s, the federal government passed legislation that permitted non-landed groups to petition for federal recognition as Indian groups. Procedures require that such groups establish their identity as American Indians, that they are associated with a specific traditional area, that they have maintained a measure of tribal autonomy over the years, and that their members are not on the rolls of landed groups. In California, the Timbi-Sha Shoshone of Death Valley were among the first to qualify for recognition. A number of other groups, including the Tolowa, the Yosemite Indians, and the Luiseño of San Luis Rey, are in the process of petitioning for recognition. Funds have been available for grants that can be used to retain anthropologists and lawyers to help prepare petitions. The research carried out in the recognition process has revealed much new information about many California Indian groups and their customs.

Laws having to do with environmental protection have brought Native Californians into the cultural resource management program. Their participation was formalized with the mid-1970s establishment of the California Native American Heritage Commission and the federal government's passage of the American Indian Religious Freedom Act, which, among other things, protected places held sacred by Native Americans. These measures make it necessary to consult Native Americans before such proposed projects impact their traditional territory.

The most widespread current religious revitalization movement comprises a series of "sweats" in a network that spreads from the northern Central Valley to the Sierra Miwok to the Shoshone in the Bishop-Lone Pine area to the Kawaiisu on the Kern River. These ceremonies are held in plastic-covered domes heated by hot stones over which water has been poured. Like earlier sweats held in sod-covered domes, they have several functions. They are spiritual rituals, and rites of ritual intensification that define and strengthen the ethnic boundary. They are also curing rites for those who are ill.

From the early years of contact, there have been Native Californians who have been successful in the world of the invading peoples. In the 1830s, for example, two young Luiseño men were sent by the Spanish missionaries to train as priests in Rome. One of them, Pablo Tac, wrote the story of his people in an account that still speaks to us (Tac 1958). Many California Indian women became nurses and teachers in the late nineteenth century, and since. Many men were and are successful in professional careers—one, for example, becoming a police chief in Santa Barbara in the early twentieth century, a number becoming artists or poets, and several becoming university professors and doctors of medicine.

It should be stated here that Native Californians through the years have successfully applied traditional strategies to the problem of surviving, yet retaining important facets of their cultural traditions. Their leaders are as skillful as non-Indian politicians at coping with federal and state governments. They are familiar with the worlds of Washington and Sacramento. Their success must be evaluated not only in terms of their status in the larger society, but also in terms of cultural persistence.

SUGGESTED READINGS

Bean, Lowell John
  1972   Mukat's People. Berkeley: University of California Press.

Bean, Lowell John and Thomas C. Blackburn, eds.
  1976   Native Californians: A Theoretical Retrospective. Menlo Park: Ballena Press.

Bean, Lowell John and Katherine Siva Saubel
  1972   Temalpakh: Cahuilla Indian Knowledge and Usage of Plants. Morongo Indian Reservation: Malki Museum Press.

Blackburn, Thomas C.
  1975   December's Child. Los Angeles: University of California Press.

Chartkoff, Joseph L., and Kerry Kona Chartkoff
  1984   The Archaeology of California. Stanford, California: Stanford University Press.

Heizer, Robert F., vol ed.
  1978   Handbook of North American Indians, Volume 8 (California). William C. Sturtevant, General Editor. Washington, D.C.: Smithsonian Institution.

Hudson, Travis, Thomas Blackburn, Rosario Curletti and Janice Timbrook
  1977   Eye of the Flute: Chumash Traditional History and Ritual as Told by Fernando Librado Kitsepawit to John P. Harrington. Banning, California: Malki Museum Press.

Kroeber, Alfred L.
  1925   Handbook of the Indians of California. Bureau of American Ethnology Bulletin 78. Washington, D.C.: Smithsonian Institution.

Kroeber, Theodora
  1961   Ishi in Two Worlds: A Biography of the Last Wild Indian in North America. Berkeley: University of California Press.

Jewell, Donald P.
  1987   Indians of the Feather River: Tales and Legends of the Concow Maidu. Menlo Park: Ballena Press.

Laird, Carobeth
  1976   The Chemehuevis. Banning, California: Malki Museum Press.

Margolin, Malcolm
  1978   The Ohlone Way: Indian Life in the San Francisco-Monterey Bay Area. Berkeley: Heyday Books.

Moratto, Michael
  1984   California Archaeology. San Francisco: Academic Press.

Miller, Virginia
  1979   Ukomno'm: The Yuki Indians of Northern California. Menlo Park: Ballena Press.

Rawls, James L.
  1984   Indians of California: The Changing Image. Norman, Oklahoma: University of Oklahoma Press.

REFERENCES

Barrett, Samuel A.
  1952   Material Aspects of Pomo Culture. Bulletin of the Public Museum of the City of Milwaukee 20(1–2). Milwaukee, Wis.

Barrows, David P.
  1900   The Ethno-botany of the Coahuilla Indians of Southern California. Chicago: University of Chicago Press.

Baumhoff, Martin A.
  1978   Environmental Background. *In* Handbook of North American Indians, Vol. 8 California). Robert F. Heizer, vol. ed., William C. Sturtevant, Gen. ed. Washington, D.C.: Smithsonian Institution.

Beals, Ralph L., and Joseph A. Hester, Jr.
  1974   California Indians. Vol. I: Indian Land Use and Occupancy in California. New York: Garland Press.

Bean, Lowell John
  1972   Mukat's People. Berkeley: University of California Press.

Bean, Lowell John
  1976a   Social Organization in Native California. *In* Native Californians: A Theoretical Retrospective, edited by Lowell John Bean and Thomas C. Blackburn. Menlo Park: Ballena Press.
  1976b   Power and Its Applications in Native California. *In* Native Californians: A Theoretical Retrospective, edited by Lowell John Bean and Thomas C. Blackburn. Menlo Park: Ballena Press.

Bean, Lowell John, and Harry W. Lawton
  1976   Some Explanations for the Rise of Cultural Complexity in Native California with Comments on Proto-Agriculture and Agriculture. *In* Native Californians: A Theoretical Retrospective, edited by Lowell John Bean and Thomas C. Blackburn. Menlo Park: Ballena Press.

Bean, Lowell John and Katherine Siva Saubel
  1972   Temalpakh: Cahuilla Indian Knowledge and Usage of Plants. Morongo Indian Reservation: Malki Museum Press.

Bean, Lowell John and Sylvia Brakke Vane
  1978   Cults and Their Transformations. *In* Handbook of North American Indians, Vol. 8 (California). Robert F. Heizer, vol. ed., William C. Sturtevant, Gen. ed. Washington, D.C.: Smithsonian Institution.

Blackburn, Thomas C.
  1975   December's Child. Los Angeles: University of California Press.

Chestnut, V. K.
  1902   Plants Used by the Indians of Mendocino County, California. Contributions from the U.S. National Herbarium, Vol. VII. Reprinted by the Mendocino County Historical Society, Fort Bragg, CA (1974).

D'Azevedo, Warren L.
  1986   Handbook of North American Indians, Volume 11 (Great Basin). William C. Sturtevant, General Editor. Washington, D.C.: Smithsonian Institution.

Dobyns, Henry F.
  1966   Estimating Aboriginal American Population: An Appraisal of Techniques with a New Hemispheric Estimate. Current Anthropology 7:395–416 and ''Reply,'' 440–444.

Du Bois, Constance Goddard
  1908   The Religion of the Luiseño Indians. University of California Publications in American Archaeology and Ethnology 8:69–173. Berkeley.

Forbes, Jack D.
  1966   The Tongva of Tujunga to 1801. Annual Reports of the University of California Archaeological Survey 8:137–150. Los Angeles.

Gayton, Anna H.
  1976   Yokuts-Mono Chiefs and Shamans. *In* Native Californians: A Theoretical Retrospective, edited by Lowell John Bean and Thomas C. Blackburn. Menlo Park: Ballena Press.

Goodrich, Jennie, Claudia Lawson, and Vana Parrish Lawson
  1980   Kashia Pomo Plants. Los Angeles: American Indian Study Center, University of California, Los Angeles.

Heizer, Robert F., vol. ed.
  1978   Handbook of North American Indians, Volume 8 (California). William C. Sturtevant, General Editor. Washington, D.C.: Smithsonian Institution.

Hudson, Travis, and Thomas C. Blackburn
  1982   The Material Culture of the Chumash Interaction Sphere, Volume I (Food Procurement and Transportation). Ballena Press Anthropological Papers, No. 25. Thomas C. Blackburn, series ed. Menlo Park, California: Ballena Press.
  1983   The Material Culture of the Chumash Interaction Sphere. Volume II (Food Preparation and Shelter). Ballena Press Anthropological Papers, No. 27. Thomas C. Blackburn, series ed. Menlo Park, California: Ballena Press.
  1985   The Material Culture of the Chumash Interaction Sphere, Volume III (Clothing, Ornamentation, and Grooming). Ballena Press Anthropological Papers, No. 28. Menlo Park, California: Ballena Press.
  1986   The Material Culture of the Chumash Interaction Sphere, Volume IV (Ceremonial Paraphernalia, Games, and Amusements). Ballena Press Anthropological Papers, No. 29. Thomas C. Blackburn, series ed. Menlo Park, California: Ballena Press.
  1987   The Material Culture of the Chumash Interaction Sphere, Volume V (Manufacturing Processes, Metrology, and Trade). Ballena Press Anthropological Papers, No. 31. Menlo Park, California: Ballena Press.

Kearney, Michael
  1984   World View. Novato: Chandler and Sharp Publishers, Inc.

King, Linda B.
  1969   The Medea Creek Cemetery (LAn-243): An Investigation of Social Organization from Mortuary Practices. Annual Reports of the University of California Archaeological Survey 11:23–69. Los Angeles.

Kroeber, Alfred L.
  1925   Handbook of the Indians of California. Bureau of American Ethnology Bulletin 78. Washington, D.C.: Smithsonian Institution.

Kroeber, A.L.
  1954   The Nature of Land Holding Groups in Aboriginal California. University of California Archaeological Reports 56:19–58. Berkeley.

Lawton, Harry W., and Lowell John Bean
  1968   A Preliminary Reconstruction of Aboriginal Argicultural Technology Among the Cahuilla. The Indian Historian I(5):18–24, 29.

Lee, Dorothy
  1950   Notes on the Conception of Self Among the Wintu. Journal of Abnormal and Social Psychology 45:538–543.

Luomala, Katherine
  1963   Flexibility in Sib Affiliation Among the Diegueno. Ethnology 2:282–301.

Moratto, Michael
  1984   California Archaeology. New World Archaeological Record, James Bennett Griffith, ed. San Francisco: Academic Press, Inc.

Ortiz, Alfonso
  1979   Handbook of North American Indians, Volume 9 (Southwest). William C. Sturtevant, General Editor. Washington, D.C.: Smithsonian Institute.
  1983   Handbook of North American Indians, Volume 10 (Southwest). William C. Sturtevant, General Editor. Washington, D.C.: Smithsonian Institution.

Rogers, Richard A.

1985 Wisconsinan Glaciation and the Dispersal of Native Ethnic Groups in North America. *In* Woman, Poet, Scientist: Essays in New World Anthropology Honoring Dr. Emma Louise Davis, compiled and edited by The Great Basin Foundation. Ballena Press Anthropological Papers No. 29, ed. by Thomas C. Blackburn. Menlo Park, CA: Ballena Press.

Strong, William D.

1929 Aboriginal Society in Southern California. University of California Publications in American Archaeology and Ethnology 29(1):1–154. Berkeley.

Spicer, Edward H.

1972 Indigenismo in the United States, 1870–1960. *In* The Emergent Native Americans. Deward E. Walker, Jr., ed. Boston: Little, Brown, & Co. Pp. 159–169.

Tac, Pablo

1958 Indian Life and Customs at Mission San Luis Rey: A Record of California Mission Life [1835]. Minna Hewes, and Gordon Hewes, eds. San Luis Rey, California: Old Mission.

Zigmond, Maurice

1981 Kawaiisu Ethnobotany. Salt Lake City: University of Utah Press.

Chapter 9

The Great Basin Culture Area

Brooke S. Arkush

University of California/Riverside

Introduction

The Great Basin culture area is distinctive in both its geographical and cultural components, comprising about 400,000 square miles of western North America between the Sierra Nevada range and the Rocky Mountains (Fig. 9.1). This vast intermontane area includes all of Nevada and Utah, most of western Colorado, portions of southern Oregon, Idaho, and Wyoming, as well as eastern California, and northern Arizona and New Mexico.

As defined here, the Great Basin culture area is much larger than the hydrographic Great Basin (Fig. 9.1), which was first clearly identified by John C. Frémont in 1845. The hydrographic Great Basin is a province of interior drainage, in which the rivers and streams are deposited into remnant Pleistocene lakes or playas. The absence of external drainage to the sea has resulted in the development of over 150 more or less closed basins (Morrison 1965). These long desert basins are divided by roughly parallel north-to-south trending mountain ranges.

Elevation of the area is relatively high throughout, as the valleys and lesser basins range from 4,000 to 6,000 feet above sea level, and the mountains from 6,000 to 11,000 and in some places, 12,000 feet. The climate of the region is variable, due to the universal fact that temperature declines and precipitation increases with increasing elevation (Daubenmire 1979). This results in low precipitation, high average temperatures, and high evaporative rates in low desert portions of the Great Basin. As a result, vegetation is sparsest in the southwestern portion of the region (Harper 1986:51). Decreased aridity and more diverse climates characterize the high valleys and mountains of the region, resulting in relatively dense vegetational communities prevailing in areas of increased water supplies.

The vegetation of the Great Basin varied widely in the valleys from creosote (*Larrea tridentata*)—dominated low deserts of the Mojave in southern Nevada and California, to saltbush (*Atriplex* spp.) and sagebrush (*Artemisia* spp.) blanketed high deserts located throughout the balance of the region. Additionally, these high desert areas support numerous seed-bearing grasses that were exploited by native populations, such as Indian rice grass (*Oryzopsis hymenoides*) and wheatgrass (*Agropyron* spp.).

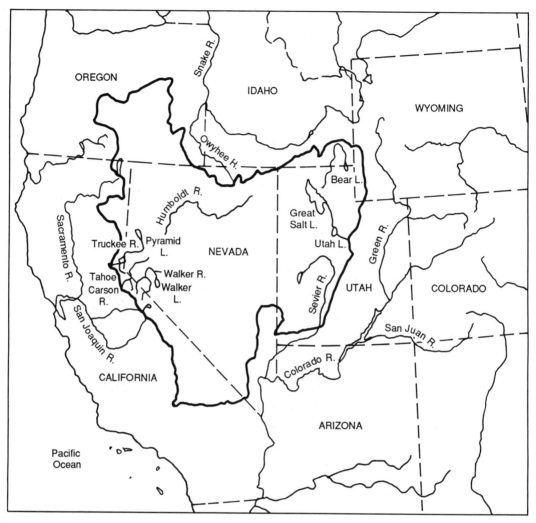

Figure 9.1 Land forms of the Great Basin (darker line indicates boundary of hydrographic Great Basin).

Mountain ranges in the Great Basin tend to support distinct altitudinal zones of vegetation (Harper 1986:53). In general, lower mountain slopes support sagebrush-grasslands, while juniper (*Juniperus* spp.) and pinyon (*Pinus monophylla, P. edulis*) wood-lands occur at successively higher elevations. These in turn are followed by zones of scrub oak (*Quercus gambelii*), ponderosa pine (*Pinus ponderosa*) forest, aspen (*Populus tremuloides*) forest, spruce (*Picea engelmannii*) and fir (*Abies lasiocarpa*) forest, and final-ly open herblands above timberline (Harper 1986:53).

For the purposes of this chapter, 13 major native groups are identified within the Great Basin (Fig. 9.2a,b). These groups are defined by linguistic, geographic, and material

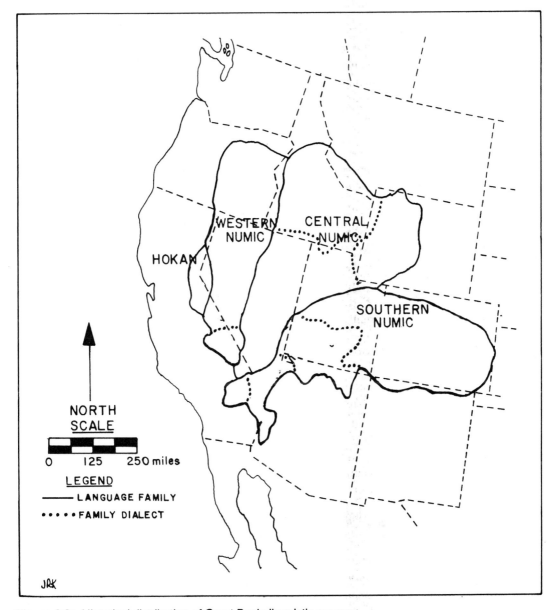

Figure 9.2a Historical distribution of Great Basin linguistic groups.

differences, and are known as the following: Washoe, Northern Paiute, Owens Valley Paiute, Panamint Shoshone, Western Shoshone, Gosiute Shoshone, Northern Shoshone, Bannock, Eastern Shoshone, Kawaiisu, Chemehuevi, Southern Paiute, and Ute.

The earliest reliable estimate for the aboriginal populat of the Great Basin was provided by John W. Powell and George W. Ingalls in 1873 rt of their report to the Commissioner of Indian Affairs. According to estimates therein, about 21,500 natives oc-

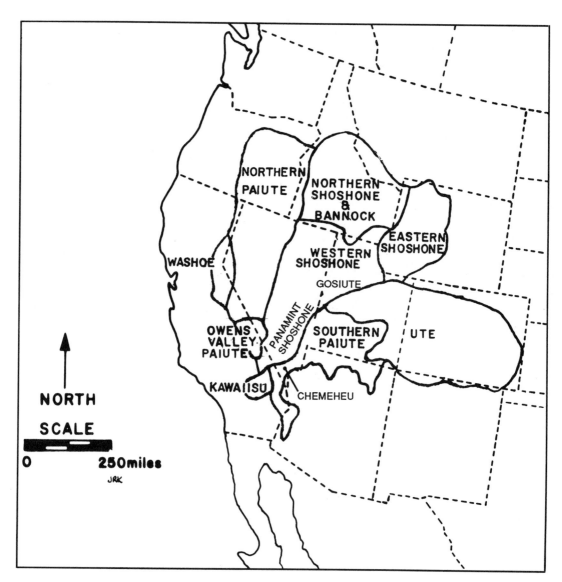

Figure 9.2b Historical distribution of Numic Tribes.

cupied the Great Basin culture area (Leland 1986:Table 1). This estimate should be viewed as an extremely conservative one. Before widespread population decline during historic times, the precontact aboriginal population of the Great Basin probably fell somewhere between 35,000 and 45,000 people. Figures for 1930 reveal that there had been a steady decline to about 12,000 persons (d'Azevedo 1986:4). This reduction in population was a direct result of damage caused by Euroamerican disease and depredations, as well as of the social chaos caused by reservation relocation and the subsequent effects of disillusionment, such as alcoholism and suicide. However, within the next 40 years there was a population increase to about 19,500, and by 1980, the Native American population of the Great Basin stood at 29,000, thereby surpassing the estimates made during the period of early contact (d'Azevedo 1986:4).

Assuming that the figure of 21,500 is indicative of the minimal precontact Great Basin population, it translates to a rough estimate of at most, 18.6 square miles per person. This figure is comparable to that provided by Kroeber (1934:3), who placed the average population density of the Great Basin at 15.6 square miles per person. Of course, there was a great deal of variation from region to region, which was directly related to the productivity of the natural environment. Extremely arid regions with extensive deserts had a relatively low carrying capacity, a situation characteristic of the Gosiute Shoshone home range in eastern Nevada and western Utah, where the population density averaged between 30 and 40 square miles per person. In areas of high mountains and increased precipitation, the native population was much denser. For example, Owens Valley in eastern California averaged 2.1 square miles per person, the Humboldt River region in northern Nevada 3.3 to 5.2 square miles per person, and the Wasatch piedmont in central Utah averaged 4 to 6 square miles per person (Steward 1938:48). For a more comprehensive discussion of regional Great Basin population densities, see Steward (1938:46–49).

Language and Prehistory

The designation of a Great Basin culture area is based upon a synthesis of prehistoric and historic cultural and linguistic traits shared by the different native groups of the region (d'Azevedo 1986:8). With the exception of the Hokan-speaking Washoe, all native peoples of the Great Basin are members of one of the three widespread branches of Numic (Fig. 9.2), a division of the Uto-Aztecan language family which originated in northern Mexico (Miller 1966, 1986). The term Shoshonean has also been used when referring to Numic-speaking groups of the Great Basin (Steward 1938; Fowler 1966; Miller 1966, 1986), and is used here in the same sense.

Linguistic and archaeologic evidence suggests that Numic-speaking groups did not inhabit the Great Basin until after about A.D. 1000, and that they absorbed or replaced earlier occupants of the region (cf. Lamb 1958; Sutton 1987). Based upon linguistic differences and the historically known distribution of Numic groups, it has been proposed that Numic peoples first entered the Great Basin from the south, clustered around the area of the western Mojave Desert and the southern Sierra Nevada in eastern California, and from there spread northward into the interior Great Basin in a fan-shaped movement (Fig. 9.2).

The question of whether or not Shoshonean peoples occupied the Great Basin before A.D. 1000 will probably never be completely answered. Evidence gathered thus far seems to indicate that Numic groups are relatively recent occupants of the region. We have definite archaeological proof that humans have inhabited the Great Basin for the past 10,000 years. Radiocarbon dates pointing to terminal Pleistocene human occupation of the Great Basin have been obtained from cultural deposits at Fort Rock Cave, Oregon (Bedwell 1970), Jaguar Cave, Idaho (Wright and Miller 1976), and Danger Cave, Utah (Jennings 1957).

The prehistoric peoples of the Great Basin were at a cultural level called the Archaic tradition by North American archaeologists. This type of cultural tradition is usually characterized as employing a technology that lacks domesticated animals, horticulture, or permanent villages (Jennings 1986:113). In western North America, including the Great Basin, this technological level is termed the Western Archaic. The ancient way of life established during the Early Archaic period (ca. 8000–2000 B.C.) was maintained with relatively few changes into historic times. Although there was considerable local variation in settlement and subsistence patterns, and many influences from surrounding regions, the precontact Great Basin lifeway has demonstrated a basic cultural unity through time (Spencer and Jennings 1977:188–190; Aikens 1978:131–133).

Subsistence and Technology

The environmental diversity associated with the complex topography of the Great Basin had a profound effect upon the distribution of floral and faunal resources within the region, as well as the economic and sociopolitical organization of aboriginal populations there. The majority of Great Basin native groups were highly mobile during precontact times, following a seasonal cycle of movements designed to exploit available plant and animal resources in the most efficient manner. Hunting and gathering was the basis of subsistence, with plant foods providing between 70 and 80 per cent of the diet, and with animal foods comprising between 20 and 30 per cent of the food base. A limited amount of horticulture did exist, occurring in peripheral Great Basin regions such as Owens Valley, California, where the Owens Valley Paiute diverted the streams descending from the Eastern Sierran escarpment, enhancing the growth of native grasses and tubers (Steward 1933; Lawton et al. 1976). Limited garden horticulture also occurred in portions of Utah, northern Arizona, and southern Nevada, where beans, squash, and maize were grown. Even in areas where horticulture was practiced, these plant species never provided more than about 20 per cent of the diet, as the majority of foods were obtained through hunting and gathering.

Plants

Information concerning aboriginal plant utilization in the Great Basin in relatively complete. Differential distribution of various plant types played a major role in determining which genera and species were exploited from region to region.

The seeds of nut pines, most notably those of pinyons (*Pinus monophylla, P. edulis*), were a major food resource throughout much of the Great Basin. Pine nuts were usually the winter staple, enabling people to establish multi-family encampments near pinyon groves that had been harvested during the late summer and early fall. These nuts were usually cached in rock-lined pits, extracted as needed, parched, processed with mano and metate, and eaten in the form of a mush or gruel (Fowler 1986:65). A certain amount of ceremonialism was associated with pinyon harvests, as Round Dances were held during the harvest, and prayers of thanks were offered.

On the western, southern, and eastern fringes of the Great Basin, acorns were obtained from various species of oaks. In the west, black oak (*Quercus kelloggi*) and blue oak (*Q. douglasii*) were utilized. These species required the lengthy leaching process like that used in California (see Bean, this volume) in order to render the acorns edible. Acorn processing in the southern and eastern Great Basin focussed on scrub oaks (*Quercus turbinella, Q. gambelii*). The preparation involved here was simplified, as no leaching was required. These acorns were pit roasted, shelled, ground into meal with mano and metate, and then made into mush by stone-boiling in large baskets (Fowler 1986:67).

Mesquite (*Prosopis juliflora*) and screwbean (*P. pubescens*) are plants limited to the Mojave and Sonoran deserts, and were therefore exploited primarily by the Panamint Shoshone, Chemehuevi, and various Southern Paiute groups. Mesquite pods were picked in the spring and eaten raw, but in late summer, were processed after the pods had dried. These were placed in either tree stump-, or bedrock mortars, pounded into meal with cylindrical pestles, and usually added to other foods, or made into small cakes (Fowler 1986:67).

Two species of agave (*Agave utahensis, A. deserti*), native to the southern hot deserts, were also exploited by the Panamint Shoshone, Chemehuevi, and Southern Paiute. In spring, the large agave leaves were cut from the plant, placed in earth ovens, and cooked.

In addition to the above plant species, various grass seeds, roots, and berries were also consumed by Great Basin natives. Seed-yielding plants such as Indian ricegrass (*Oryzopsis hymenoides*), blazing star (*Mentzelia* spp.), wheatgrass (*Agropyron spp.*), and wild rye (*Elymus* spp.) were harvested using sticks or basketry seed beaters, as the seeds were collected in conical burden baskets (Fowler 1986:69).

Roots and corms of various species were collected throughout the region using the hardwood digging stick, which usually had a fire-hardened tip. These included camas (*Camassia quamash*), swamp onion (*Alliam validum*), biscuitroots (*Lomatium* spp.), yampa (*Perideridia* spp.), and bitterroot (*Lewisia rediviva*).

Berries and other fruits were also collected. These included buckberry (*Shepherdia argentia*), and wolfberry (*Lycium andersonii*).

Animals

As noted above, animal foods were secondary to plant foods in the native diet. The general aridity of the Great Basin restricted the numbers of all species of large game, and the limited grasslands made it impossible for herd species to predominate (Steward 1983:33). Mule deer (*Odocoileus hemionus*) and bighorn sheep (*Ovis canadensis*) were taken singly or in small herds by one or several hunters in the uplands, as these animals travelled along game trails, watered at springs and streams, or were driven into traps.

Pronghorn antelope (*Antilocapra americana*) were commonly found throughout the open valleys and plains of the Great Basin during precontact times, and formed large herds in winter. For all intents and purposes, the pronghorn was the most important game animal for Shoshonean groups. They were often the objects of communal surrounds and drives, in which part of a herd of 100 or 200 animals might be captured by being driven into wood and brush V-wing traps (Arkush 1986). Both ethnographic and archaeologic data indicate that pronghorn drives usually occurred during fall, winter, and spring. These drives were preceded by a great deal of ceremonialism, in which a shaman would "charm" a nearby herd for three to five nights, in effect, capturing their souls and luring them to the trap.

In light of this, it must be stressed that the capture of large game was not an everyday event. The vast majority of animal meat was provided by small mammals such as black-tailed hares (jackrabbits: *Lepus californicus*), cottontail rabbits (*Sylvilagus* spp.), pocket gophers (*Thomomys* spp.), ground squirrels (*Spermophilus* spp.), prairie dogs (*Cynomys* spp.), chipmunks (*Eutamias* spp.), and woodrats (*Neotoma* spp.).

Reptiles and insects were also important food items, providing additional sources of protein. In areas of lakes, streams, and marshes, various species of fish and waterfowl were major components of the native diet.

Material Culture

The technology utilized by Shoshonean peoples was a relatively simple, but extremely efficient one. This system basically enabled people to obtain and process foods, and to shelter themselves from the environment. Numerous technological elements used by historic Numic groups have been recovered from archaeological contexts dating back some 6000 years. The majority of the aboriginal toolkit can be divided into items that were used almost exclusively by either males or females. This is because a sexual division of labor permeated Great Basin societies, and enabled these resourceful people to survive in a land that was oftentimes harsh and unyielding.

Female-oriented items were usually those used in the harvesting and processing of plant foods. Basketry was a major item in such pursuits, as twined seed beaters, conical burden baskets, winnowing and parching trays, bowls, boilers, and utility baskets were invaluable implements, constructed from local plant species (Fowler and Dawson 1986). Pitch-covered basketry water bottles were also important items that were produced by women. Additionally, woven mats and sandles were important domestic articles. Controlled excavations in numerous dry caves in the Great Basin have recovered basketry collections that span more than 10,000 years of occupation (Adovasio 1986:194).

Another important item related to the storage of food and water is pottery. Both Paiute and Shoshone groups produced various types of plain ceramic vessels by applying successive clay coils, then smoothing and firing the containers. The use of ceramics in the Great Basin is a relatively recent phenomenon, appearing in the southern regions around A.D. 1000, and finally reaching southern Idaho at about A.D. 1300–A.D. 1400 (Madsen 1986).

Various types of ground stone implements were commonly used to process plant foods. Hullers, manos, and metates were used for shelling and milling seeds into meal. Additionally, tree stump-, and bedrock mortars were used with pestles to process hard shelled seeds and nuts, as well as small rodents.

The male toolkit was dominated by various types of hunting and fishing equipment, such as sinew-backed bows and stone-tipped arrows, hafted flaked stone knives, casual flake tools used for cutting and scraping, and nets made of native cordage to capture fish, rabbits, coots (*Fulica americana*), and sage grouse (*Centrocercus urophasianus*). As mentioned above, drive traps were used to secure deer, bighorn sheep, and pronghorn. These large features, which often had drift fences that ran for over a mile, were erected by men, women, and children. Additionally, several types of snares, deadfalls, pits, and traps were used to take small mammals, birds, and occasionally, reptiles.

Pinyon hooks, digging sticks, and hooks for capturing rabbits and reptiles were used by both men and women to secure plant and animal foods.

In terms of shelter, Great Basin natives generally built structures that were designed for different seasons and accompanying weather conditions. During late spring and summer, when warm weather prevailed, most groups simply constructed brush windbreaks about three or four feet high. Open-fronted, gabeled houses were often built when conditions were somewhat colder. The most substantial houses used in the region were winter houses. These were usually conical in form, 8 to 12 feet high, and 10 to 15 feet in diameter. A shallow pit was usually dug before establishing a frame of large pinyon and/or juniper poles around the perimeter. The covering was then completed by adding small branches, sod, bark, grass, and/or tule to the outside. The type of covering used depended largely upon the local resources available. In many areas, woven mats were used exclusively for the covering. An east-facing doorway usually completed the winter house. Some groups in the northern Great Basin used animal skins for house coverings. Each house was capable of sheltering six to twelve or more persons.

Clothing was not necessary in the Great Basin for much of the year, as many people either wore none, or a minimal amount. Animal skins and tule were commonly used to fashion skirts and aprons for women, and breechclouts for men. The most common element of aboriginal clothing throughout the region was the rabbitskin blanket. These were woven on a frame by joining together numerous rolled strips of rabbitskin with a fiber thread. These were worn as capes during the day, and at night, a single rabbitskin blanket could cover a small family. Air was trapped and heated within the fur cylinders, resulting in an extremely warm and durable article of clothing.

Of course, additional warmth was provided by fires, usually made with the aid of fire drills. On trips, an indispensable item usually carried along was a smoldering fire, transported in the form of long, cigar-shaped slow matches, made of tinder wrapped in juniper bark.

From this brief overview, it should be apparent that Shoshonean peoples utilized a simple technology that was perfectly suited to their highly nomadic lifestyle. In pre-horse times, an entire family could pack most of their possessions into one or two burden baskets, and relocate to an area five or ten miles away. Theirs was an extremely utilitarian type of technology, one which had been developed through thousands of years of trial and error.

Social Systems

Throughout the Great Basin, the bilaterally-based nuclear family cluster (Steward 1970), or kin clique (Fowler 1966) was the basis of precontact economic and sociopolitical organization. The typical household, or camp group, consisted of a mother, father, one or two children, one or two grandparents, and maybe an aunt, uncle, or cousin. This group was self-sufficient, self-governing, and basically isolated for most of the year (cf. Shapiro 1986).

Monogamous, cross-cousin marriage was the preferred form of union in Shoshonean society, although sororal polygyny (marriage of a man to two or more sisters) and, less commonly, fraternal polyandry (marriage of a woman to two or more brothers) did occur. These types of marriages functioned to connect families or sibling groups through multiple conjugal bonds (Shapiro 1986:622–623). The existence of cross-cousin marriage in the Great Basin appears to have been related to the maintenance of a widely dispersed support network, in which kinsmen provided each other with information concerning resource availability in different areas (cf. Eggan 1980:178).

Other forms of preferred marriage found in the area included the levirate (marriage of a woman to her deceased husband's brother), and the sororate (marriage of a man to his deceased wife's sister) (Fowler 1966:59; Shapiro 1986:622). As noted by Shapiro (1986), the levirate and sororate have been variously described as obligatory, preferential, or merely optional. A major function of such a system was that it maintained the viability of a family group when one of the parents died. This was extremely important, as both husband and wife were critical economic components of every camp group, allowing each to operate independently of other camp groups.

In Shoshonean society, marriage was an economic alliance "in a very real sense" (Steward 1938:241), where a sexual division of labor dominated daily activities. Men generally hunted large and small game, while women collected seeds, roots, insects, and small animals. This particular type of socioeconomic organization was the inevitable response to areas of widely distributed resources, low population densities, and an annual nomadic cycle.

Increased interaction between family groups before introduction of the horse was due to the availability of more abundant resources within closely spaced microenvironments

310

which could support greater population densities and semi-permanent winter villages (Steward 1970:369). Several related family clusters usually gathered together once or twice a year to carry out rabbit, coot, and pronghorn drives, or to establish winter villages if the local pinyon harvest had been bountiful. These times of increased group interaction were extremely important in both an economic and social sense. During these periods, a great deal of information could be exchanged among camp groups that had covered wide-ranging and diverse areas during previous months. Information regarding the locations of promising pine nut, fishing, and hunting areas, lithic quarries, etc., could be shared. Additionally, potential marriage partners could meet, trade relations could be established and/or maintained, and collective wisdom and mythological tales could be related from elders to the younger generations.

The Shoshonean kin terminologies that have been collected reveal a great amount of similarity in their semantic structures, as well as in the linguistic forms themselves (Shapiro 1986). The most fundamental widespread ordering principles are based on sex, generation, and relative age. In general, descent is traced bilaterally, and the terminological system is strongly generational. Relatives of the same generation are usually distinguished by sex and relative age only. For example, among the Owens Valley Paiute, the term *hama'a* was applied to ego's elder sister as well as ego's elder female cousin, either cross or parallel (Steward 1933). Therefore, there are four generational terms in all: older sister/female cousin, younger sister/female cousin, older brother/male cousin, younger brother/male cousin. Kin terms for adjacent generational relatives usually follow a bifurcate-collateral pattern, in which distinctions are made on the basis of sex, lineality, and the sex of the relative through whom the relationship is traced (Shapiro 1986:625).

Great Basin political systems were highly egalitarian. In many areas, the camp group was the independent unit during much of the year, with the oldest influential male having the greatest amount of input into decisions reached on a consensus basis. Sedentary villages usually had a single headman. His title, *degwani*, means "talker," as this designated his most important function (Steward 1938:247). The major task of the headman was to keep informed about the ripening of plant resources in different areas, and about the location of various game animals. He then related this information to the villagers. As a "talker," the headman delivered long orations, and gave directions to families who cared to cooperate in a particular endeavor. However, his authority was not absolute, and any family could leave the village to pursue independent activities at any time.

From the above description of Great Basin social organization, it should be clear that this system functioned primarily to enable people to adapt to a rigorous environment. Given the simple technology of these native groups, environmental constraints on social groups were a given. Widespread, nomadic camp groups were able to extract necessary resources in the most efficient manner without taxing the carrying capacity of a particular region. The relative sizes and proximity of these groups were determined by the distribution of local resources. Therefore, in areas such as Owens Valley, California, and along the Humboldt River in northern Nevada, people could practice a relatively sedentary lifestyle; whereas in more arid areas, such as eastern Nevada, the Gosiute Shoshone had to maintain

311

relatively small, highly mobile camp groups. These systems were fine-tuned to the various Great Basin ecosystems, and were maintained over a long period of time because they worked. Most Shoshonean groups were probably not living the precarious hand-to-mouth existence that is often portrayed in early historic accounts. It was only after the disruption caused by Euroamerican colonization of the area that Great Basin natives were transformed from independent societies to ones that were almost completely reliant upon white society for material goods, foods, and shelter.

Belief Systems

For the most part, the belief systems of native Great Basin societies are less well known than those of other North American native groups. Early studies by Willard Z. Park (1934, 1938) concentrated upon various aspects of shamanism, particularly among Northern Paiute groups. Park (1941) also collected data concerning the Round Dance. This research established the foundation for subsequent studies that provided overviews of Shoshonean religion (Liljeblad 1969; Fowler and Fowler 1974; Hultkrantz 1976). Other authors have concentrated upon postcontact religious movements in the Great Basin, such as the Ghost Dance (DuBois 1939; Hittman 1973), the Bear Dance (Lowie 1915; Steward 1932), the Sun Dance (Shimkin 1953; Jorgensen 1952), and Peyotism (Stewart 1944, 1948, 1986).

The traditional religious system of Shoshonean culture can be divided into two basic categories: individual, and group ceremonialism. In terms of individual religious activities, guardian-spirit beliefs, shamanism, and life crises rites predominated. Some individuals received power in dreams from spirit protectors that would aid them in certain activities such as doctoring, hunting, gambling, and running. Certain life crises, such as birth, puberty, menstruation, and death, were marked by particular ceremonies such as food restrictions, isolation, and mourning rites (Hultkrantz 1986). Group ceremonialism was mostly limited to the Round Dance, which occurred when larger groups assembled for activities such as pinyon harvests, fish runs, and communal hunts. Round Dances functioned primarily as rites of thanks and fertility, aimed at increasing the food supply and bringing rain (Hultkrantz 1986:634).

A shaman was oftentimes the focus of certain ceremonies. This person (usually a male, although female shamans were quite common) had often received his or her powers from a dream or vision, and could cure the sick. Other shamans had powers that enabled them to capture the souls of pronghorn antelope, and their presence was critical to all successful pronghorn drives. It was the duty of the shaman to serve the community. Shamans who refused to cure the sick, or who had too many patients die under their care, were suspected of witchcraft and oftentimes killed (Hultkrantz 1986:636). Although shamans were influential members of Great Basin native societies, they had no specific authority. They were basically viewed as specialized individuals who had more and stronger powers than other people.

Shoshonean cosmology was highly variable (Liljeblad 1969:51). In many areas, prominent environmental features loomed large in different groups' explanations of the cosmos. As noted by Hultkrantz (1986:632), the Milky Way had a conspicuous place in the cosmology of most Great Basin groups. It was often referred to as the "ghost road," "sky path," or "dusty road," a route travelled by the spirits of the dead to the afterworld. The Milky Way was also seen as the backbone of the sky.

Universal aspects of Shoshonean ideology were concerned with one or several supreme beings, such as the sun. In many areas of the Great Basin, people offered prayers to the rising sun (Hultkrantz 1986:632). Additionally, there were numerous other spirits, some of whom were part of the sky and atmosphere. These entities, such as the moon, thunder and lightning, the winds, and the eagle, were all involved in shaping earthly events. Various natural features also had their rulers. For example, hot springs, lakes, and mountains were all believed to have resident spirits. Water babies inhabited lakes and hot springs, and were fond of capturing naughty children. Most mountains were believed to be inhabited by ogres and giants, both of whom enjoyed hunting and eating people (Hultkrantz 1986:633; Lilijeblad 1986:653–655).

The overall patterns of Great Basin belief systems were directly related to the environmental demands placed on a widely dispersed hunter/gatherer population, as the goals of most religious activities were designed to meet the subsistence needs of the small nomadic groups that constituted the primary socioeconomic unit (Hultkrantz 1976). The supernatural figures that exercised power over humans were manifested in the shapes of local animals and birds. Children learned about traditional mythology and cosmology while at the same time, learned about the habits and characteristics of the animal life around them.

Historical Overview

The Great Basin was the last region of the continental United States to be explored and settled by colonizing Euroamericans. Due to the relative isolation of this vast intermontane area, many of its native occupants were contacted at a much later period than most other North American Indian groups. However, as contact was established with early explorers and trappers (Cline 1963; Ross 1956), Great Basin Shoshoneans were rapidly affected, and their culture permanently altered by the subsequent influx of white immigrants and settlers, as had other indigenous groups who were in the path of expanding European and American interests.

Exploration, settlement, and development of the Great Basin during the eighteenth and nineteenth centuries forced Shoshonean peoples to radically modify their traditional lifeways in order to survive. The most significant factor involved in the historic colonization of the Great Basin which caused Numic-speaking groups to yield to the disruptive pressures of white society was the extensive damage inflicted upon the fragile ecology of the region. Euroamericans exploited resources there in a much more intensive and destructive manner than aboriginal populations of the past (Clemmer 1974:24–26). Trapping, ranching, mining, and farming all resulted in the degradation of important resources in key areas, which permanently altered Shoshonean patterns of subsistence and settlement.

Euroamerican development of the Great Basin was characterized by high-impact activities accompanied by a complex technology that had been developed to extract or utilize resources on a large-scale basis. This practice was a result of the long-standing European philosophy associated with the market economy, where natural resources were seen as entities to be exploited intensively and sold for a profit. Of course, such a philosophy was diametrically opposed to that of Great Basin natives, who had incorporated the land and its resources into their lives and cultures in an intricate fashion that allowed them to utilize a relatively simple, non-intensive technology, and to subsist in a region that was incapable of supporting dense, sedentary native populations. Euroamerican settlement and development of the Great Basin undermined Shoshonean culture, and caused conflict between these two distinct populations.

After initial struggles, Shoshonean peoples were more or less able to adjust to the new situation. Different groups incorporated various aspects of Euroamerican culture into their own systems, while still retaining many traditional practices. Native material culture, subsistence, and settlement patterns were most seriously affected and modified, while traditional aspects of religion and social structure were more successful in remaining intact (Malouf and Findlay 1986:499).

As a documentation of the above pattern of Shoshonean acculturation, this chapter discusses and analyzes the differing types of contact that occurred between elements of white society and Northern and Western Shoshone, and Northern and Southern Paiute peoples, and the accompanying changes in technology, adaptation, and organization of these native cultures.

In a very general sense, the Northern and Western Shoshone, and Northern and Southern Paiute all experienced similar contact situations, but to varying degrees. Each group was first contacted by explorers and/or traders and trappers, with these interactions being relatively brief and narrow in scope. Next, routes of travel such as the Old Spanish Trail and the Overland Trail were established. With the discovery of gold in California in 1848, these routes received increasingly heavy use. After the initial movements of Euroamerican emigrants through the Great Basin, whites began to settle and develop areas of prime land.

In addition to the presence of a rapidly increasing foreign population, Shoshonean peoples saw their streams and springs fenced off and diverted, seed grasses ruined by livestock overgrazing, entire pinyon groves cut down for use as firewood, and game animal populations depleted (Layton 1977:368). White aggression and disease also played a major role in reducing the aboriginal Great Basin population. Toward the end of the early historic era (ca. A.D. 1850–A.D. 1870), even the seasonal movements of natives among important resource areas were first altered and finally prevented by Euroamerican development.

Various sympathetic observers recorded their reactions to the degradation of Great Basin natural resources during the early historic period. Charles Preuss served as cartographer for John C. Frémont, and mentioned the reduction of beaver and other game animals in the northern Shoshone home range in 1843:

> The white people have ruined the country of the Snake Indians and should therefore treat them well. Almost all the natives are obliged to live on roots, game can scarcely be seen anymore [Gudde and Gudde 1958:86].

Another account of the depletion of native resources that occurred historically throughout the Great Basin comes from Indian agent Jacob Lockhart in his report to the Commissioner of Indian Affairs regarding the Western Shoshone on March 1, 1862:

> The wild game is being killed by the whites. The trees from which the Indians gathered nuts (pine nuts) are being cut down, and the grass from which they gathered seeds for the winter is being taken from them . . . [Lockhart 1862].

Throughout much of the Great Basin, the unrestricted grazing of livestock resulted in the permanent alteration in the composition and structure of native plant communities (Young, Evans, and Tueller 1976). Overgrazing during the mid 1800s caused the expansion of big sagebrush (*Artemisia tridentata*) at the expense of perennial grasses (Young, Evans, and Major 1972:195), many of which were important parts of the native diet. Euroamerican livestock also competed with indigenous ruminant game animals, such as mule deer, pronghorn, and bighorn sheep, which had previously enjoyed relatively uncontested access to these grasslands.

Another major development that further degraded Great Basin ranges, and which was directly attributable to Euroamerican settlement, was the prohibition of the aboriginal practice of burning grasslands to enhance growth, improve feed for game, and to prevent the woods and grasslands from being overgrown with brush (Stewart 1952:48–49, 1955:5–9). As a result of white intervention in this practice, meadows turned into sagebrush-covered valleys or were developed into agricultural fields (Malouf and Findlay 1986:510).

Throughout the Great Basin, Shoshonean populations were heavily impacted by European-introduced diseases. New World natives were immunologically defenseless against many Old World diseases, and various epidemics swept through western North America during the eighteenth and nineteenth centuries with deadly results. Diseases such as smallpox, chicken pox, measles, and cholera were first introduced to the Great Basin by fur traders and explorers in the early nineteenth century (Crosby 1972:37; Malouf and Findlay 1986:504–506). The subsequent influx of westward bound immigrant parties in the mid-nineteenth century precipitated a dramatic increase in the occurrence of Old World diseases among Shoshoneans. With few exceptions, fatal diseases were transferred from whites to Native Americans, and not the other way. This puzzling situation, in which the disease vector travelled only one way, can be partially explained by the lack of domesticated herd animals in aboriginal North America. It appears that most and probably all of the distinctive infectious diseases of civilization were originally transferred to Old World human populations from herd animals (McNeil 1976:45).

The vast majority of Shoshonean culture change occurred in five distinct phases, during which each of the following entities dominated native society: aboriginal, trappers, and explorers, early settlers, miners and ranchers, and U.S. government (cf. Malouf 1966).

During these phases of settlement and development, three different types of adaptive strategies were implemented by Shoshonean peoples. One was an attempt to coexist with white populations. This resulted in small groups attaching themselves to ranches, towns, mines, stage stops, and forts (Fig. 9.3); and trading with, working for, or begging from whites in exchange for nontraditional material goods, foodstuffs, and/or wages (Layton 1977:368). Another strategy was to withdraw altogether from contact with Euroamericans, traveling away from established roads and settlements, as certain groups attempted to continue to practice a traditional lifestyle with a minimum of interference (Malouf and Findlay 1986:513). A third strategy implemented by Shoshoneans was to consolidate several or many group camps to form raiding bands. These bands were usually well-mounted and highly organized, and assaulted emigrant wagon trains and ranches, appropriating livestock, foodstuffs, and material goods, including guns and ammunition (Layton 1977:368; Malouf and Findlay 1986:513). These raids caused a marked increase in armed conflict between Indians and Euroamericans, which in turn escalated as U.S. Army troops and volunteer regiments carried out punitive missions against Shoshonean groups, many of whom were innocent, but were attacked nevertheless.

In three of the four native groups discussed here, short lived "Indian Wars" broke out which led to the subjugation of the Great Basin peoples, and insured that Euroamericans would come to dominate this final frontier of the continental United States. These military engagements eventually eliminated armed native resistance, and ushered in a confusing and tragic period of treaty negotiations and reservation allotments.

This chapter provides the reader with a broad examination of Numic ethnohistory and acculturation. The four groups discussed below are representative of Great Basin native culture change as a whole. By becoming familiar with these different ethnohistories, the reader can obtain an understanding of the resourceful strategies implemented by these peoples, and thereby perceive the processes that changed, but did not destroy, Great Basin native society.

Northern Shoshone

Euroamerican settlement of North America had a major effect upon the Northern Shoshone long before they actually encountered white explorers and trappers. This was due to the introduction of the horse to the Snake River region sometime during the late seventeenth century (Murphy and Murphy 1986:300). The horse enabled Northern Shoshone groups to become highly mobile. As a result, they soon acquired a number of Plains Indian cultural traits, such as composite mounted bands (actually incipient bands), intensive bison exploitation, tepees, and warrior societies. Major factors of actual contact with Euroamerican society that caused widespread changes among the Northern Shoshone were the activities of trappers and Mormon settlers, and the establishment of the Oregon Trail.

Figure 9.3 Northern Paiute village., Virginia City, Nevada, with mine tailings in background. This photograph attests to increased native sedentism, as well as their participation in the mining economy of the Comstock Lode region of western Nevada. This encampment was located on the outskirts of town, away from white residences. (Photograph number 704 by William Cann, 1891, courtesy of the Nevada Historical Society.)

Introduction of the Horse.

Horses were reintroduced to North America during the Historic period in a northward fashion from the Spanish settlements of the Southwest (Shimkin 1986:517). This dissemination followed two major routes, one east and the other west of the Rocky Mountains (Haines 1938). The Shoshone of the upper Snake River region received horses primarily by way of the western route, and a substantial number of Northern Shoshone were mounted as early as 1690 (Haines 1938:430; Murphy and Murphy 1960:294; Layton 1978:241).

The Northern Shoshone played an important role in the introduction of the horse to other Indian groups of the greater American Northwest. With the aid of the Shoshone, the horse was established in the western Great Basin, the Columbia River drainage, the Plateau, and the northern Plains (Murphy and Murphy 1960:294). Through use of the horse, the Northern Shoshone were able to rapidly expand their territory beyond the Rockies and onto the northern Plains as far north as Saskatchewan in the early 1700s (Thompson 1916:328). By the mid 1700s, the Blackfoot and other northern Plains tribes were armed with firearms obtained through interactions with various French and English traders, and pushed the Northern Shoshone back to their general home range at the time of contact in 1805 (Murphy and Murphy 1960:295). Acquisition of the horse also resulted in the southward migration of a segment of the Shoshone who later became known as the Commanche (Shimkin 1986:517). This movement occurred at the beginning of the eighteenth century (Murphy and Murphy 1986:302). In addition to the mounted Northern Shoshone bands who relied heavily upon the bison, a substantial number of these people remained in traditional pedestrian economic and sociopolitical units. These groups did not incorporate the horse to the degree that the bison hunting groups had, as they used horses primarily as pack animals and continued to rely mostly upon seasonal runs of salmon, and the harvesting of berries and roots.

Through the use of the horse, some Northern Shoshone groups developed a more complex social organization (Steward 1938:236). The pursuit of bison required highly organized bands with local chiefs and band councils. The institution of chief was not firmly institutionalized anywhere among the Shoshone, and it was quite common for a chief to lose his following to a rising new leader (Lowie 1909:208–209; Murphy and Murphy 1986:291). The high degree of political development of buffalo hunting "bands" diminished rapidly to the west.

In addition to extending their range onto the northern and eastern Plains, the Northern Shoshone were also able to expand westward into the central Great Basin, where they participated in horse trading activities in the Humboldt River region of northern Nevada (Layton 1981:131–132, 135).

The overall effect of the horse was that it induced an incipient type of band organization, facilitated the acquisition of many Plains Indian traits, and brought about the major differences between the Northern and Western Shoshone noted during the historic period.

Explorers and Trappers

The earliest documented Euroamerican contact with Northern Shoshone populations was that of the Lewis and Clark expedition in 1805, when it first met with the Shoshone in southwestern Montana; after crossing the Continental Divide, the party visited a Northern Shoshone village on the Lemhi River in August of that year (Lowie 1909:171). Early exploration parties such as that of Lewis and Clark proved that the far Northwest region has worthy of commercial exploitation, and by 1810, rival British fur companies were pushing southward from Canada to trap the rivers and streams in Northern Shoshone territory. In 1809, David Thompson of the North West Company had established several trading posts on and near Pend Oreille Lake in northern Idaho. At this time, American traders were moving into the region from the east, as Andrew Henry built a post on Henry's Fork of the Snake River in 1810 (Murphy and Murphy 1960:295).

These early developments resulted in the thorough penetration of the Snake River drainage by approximately 1812, and the North West Company had exploited much of the region by 1818 (Murphy and Murphy 1986:302). In the mid 1820s, Peter Skene Ogden of the British Hudson's Bay Company entered the region and systematically trapped the waters of the Snake River (Cline 1963). Competition between trappers of the Rocky Mountain Fur Company, the Hudson's Bay Company, the North West Company, and the American Fur Company spurred the relentless pursuit of beaver for the production of fur hats. The situation became so bad that the Hudson's Bay Company adopted a "scorched stream," or "fur desert" policy, by which they intended to trap out every stream that supported beaver in order to discourage American trappers (Ogden 1910:362; Cline 1974:69; Rusco 1976:159).

Zenas Leonard was a member of the Joseph R. Walker expedition, which travelled through a portion of the northern Great Basin from Green River, Wyoming, to California during the years 1832 and 1833. In his diary, Leonard described the nonmounted Northern Shoshone. His characterizations are colored with derogatory remarks, as he was appalled by the lifestyle of these people. Nevertheless, his accounts are valuable, as they provide some keen insights as to the attitudes of trappers toward Great Basin native culture:

> These Indians subsist principally upon salmon, and such other fish as they can catch, with the assistance of roots, buds, berries, and some small game, which they kill with the bow and arrow. They are generally of a more swarthy nature, small and cowardly, and travel in small gangs of from four to five families—this they are compelled to do in order to keep from starvation. They are always roving from plain to plain, and from valley to valley—never remaining in one place longer than till game gets scarce . . . This tribe, which I believe is called the Bawnack, or Shoshonies, are the most indolent, and have the least ambition of any tribe we have yet discovered. They are lazy and dirty, and only strive to get as much as will keep them from starving . . . Between trapping and trading we had made quite a profitable hunt. To get a beaver skin from these Indians worth eight or ten dollars, never cost more than an awl, a fish-hook, a knife, a string of beads, or something equally as trifling [Leonard 1934:78–79].

The climax of the fur trade came in the mid 1830s, when this commerce collapsed during the height of activity. Competition between the trading companies had been disastrous, as the streams and rivers which only a generation before had supported a large number of beaver, had been thoroughly trapped out (Murphy and Murphy 1960:290). The near extinction of beaver in Northern Shoshone territory eliminated an important source of native clothing and food (Rusco 1976:161). Trappers such as Ogden and Ross noted that the beaver robe was important to the Indians of the lower Snake River drainage where other large game animals were not plentiful (Ogden 1950:114; Ross 1956:249).

In addition to the decimation of beaver, fur trappers and Indians also hunted out the remaining bison herds west of the Rocky Mountains during this period (Steward 1938:200). By 1840, bison were absent from the Bear, Green, and Snake River regions (Frémont 1845:265, 1887:217–218; Roe 1970:259). The rapid depletion of both beaver and bison in historic times throughout Northern Shoshone territory was no doubt facilitated by the use of firearms and steel traps, as these were significant improvements in the efficiency of aboriginal hunting and trapping devices employed during precontact times (Rusco 1976:159, 160).

Trapping activity in Northern Shoshone territory also placed adverse pressures upon other game animals. In many instances, animals were slaughtered for mere entertainment, as the diary entry of Peter Ogden (1910:370) for January 22, 1828, related that "A hunter today killed 22 antelopes by driving them in a bank of snow and knifing them, not allowing one to escape. 200 of antelope [sic] have been killed wantonly in the last week, for not more than 1/4 of the meat has been brought to camp."

The journal of the second expedition of John C. Frémont (1843–1844) provides a gross indication of the rate of depletion of certain game animals in the northern Great Basin, particularly that of bison and pronghorn, after the zenith of trapping activity had passed in the early 1840s. Frémont's entry for August 30, 1843, mentioned this:

> A great portion of the region inhabited by this nation [Northern Shoshone] formerly abounded in game; the buffalo ranging about in herds, as we have found them on the eastern waters, and the plains dotted with scattered herds of antelope; but so rapidly have they disappeared within a few years, that now, as we journey along, an occasional buffalo skull and a few wild antelope were all that remained of the abundance which had covered the country with animal life [Frémont 1887:217].

Early modifications of Northern Shoshone culture also resulted from intensive contact between trappers and natives at the annual summer rendezvous. These meetings were held at various localities within Shoshone territory, such as Cache Valley, Utah, Green River, Wyoming, and Pierre's Hole, Idaho (Murphy and Murphy 1960:295; Brooks 1977:197). Here, Indians traded with white trappers, obtaining firearms, iron utensils such as knives, kettles, axes, awls, and arrowheads, as well as blankets, glass beads, western clothing, and alcohol (Rusco 1976:158). This interaction had a tremendous effect on the traditional economy. In many cases, goods acquired from Euroamerican fur traders and companies replaced elements of aboriginal material culture. Trappers oftentimes married Shoshone women, and lived for various periods with native bands. Trappers were also instrumental in introducing various Old World diseases among the local groups with whom they interacted (Malouf and Findlay 1986:504).

The period of 1810–1840 was one of rapid cultural change for the Northern Shoshone, a time during which they lost the isolation they had previously enjoyed, and came into permanent contact with Euroamericans. Because the trappers did not dispossess the Northern Shoshone of their lands, relations between these two groups were mostly friendly. However, amicable feelings between the Northern Shoshone and whites were soon forgotten, due to Euroamerican emigration to Oregon and California during the 1840s.

The Oregon Trail.

The Oregon Trail followed routes originally established by fur trappers. From South Pass, Wyoming, this popular trail passed through the area of Fort Bridger, then followed the Bear River north to Soda Springs, Idaho, and from there led westward along the Snake and Boise rivers, where it passed through the heartland of the Northern Shoshone (Murphy and Murphy 1960:296, 1986:302).

Initial movements of emigrants across this route during the early 1840s were minimal, but the discovery of gold in California precipitated a flood of migrants along the Oregon Trail to the Pacific Coast which peaked in 1850. Although most of the Northern Shoshone were widely scattered in hunting activities during the summer emigration season, and did not often encounter the white masses, establishment of the Oregon Trail was a major step in the subsequent settlement of central and southern Idaho, and northern Utah.

The movements of emigrant wagon trains along the Oregon Trail also placed additional pressure on local game animals, and native grasses along the route were denuded by cattle and horses (Shimkin 1987:523). It should be stressed that these travellers were trying to pass through this region as quickly as possible, and therefore had no motivation to conserve local resources or to establish friendly terms with local native groups. The relations between the Northern Shoshone and white emigrants were entirely different from those with trappers. Indians benefited very little from the presence of Euroamerican migrants, as the dwindling natural resources along the Oregon Trail were further depleted, and a minimum of material goods were salvaged by natives after the parties had moved through the region.

Mormon Settlement.

In 1847, Mormon settlers had reached the Salt Lake Valley of Utah, and after establishing themselves there, expanded into adjacent areas of Wyoming and Idaho where they began farming large portions of arable land. The Bear River Valley of Utah was settled in 1860, and the Mormons soon thereafter colonized the Boise River Valley and other parts of southern Idaho. Mormon settlement of Northern Shoshone lands brought with it the displacement of native groups from optimal resource areas, and also caused the further spread of European diseases, such as the measles epidemic which decimated native groups north of Salt Lake City in 1848 (Malouf 1966:16).

Various food resources of the Shoshone were further reduced by the Mormon influx. Livestock overgrazing severely impacted entire valleys of native grasses, and haying operations also had adverse effects (Christensen and Johnson 1964). As a result, wild game and other native subsistence resources soon became scarce, and in some areas, Northern Shoshone peoples were on the verge of starvation as early as 1852 (Madsen 1985:48–49).

A Mormon mission was established among the Shoshone at Fort Lemhi in 1857, and a large number of Indians were baptized. Not only had the Mormons seriously impacted Northern Shoshone subsistence systems and settlement patterns, they had also partially altered traditional religious practices as well.

As new settlements continued to deplete the native resource base, the raids of mounted bands became one of the more efficient ways to deal with the Mormon presence. Mormon farms soon became the targets of Northern Shoshone raiders. Continued native aggression was met in turn by Mormon attacks upon small, usually unmounted, Northern Shoshone camp groups. Shoshone raiding activities were finally stopped by the reprisals of military engagement. At a winter encampment near Cache Valley, Utah, approximately 225 Northern Shoshone men, women, and children were killed by a regiment of California volunteers under the command of Colonel Patrick E. Connor (Madsen 1985). This battle resulted in the signing of five treaties in 1863, but sporadic Shoshone uprisings continued well into the 1870s. These so-called "Indian Wars" were usually small incidents, and most Great Basin native resistance terminated with the Bannock War of 1878, which began in southern Idaho when white settlers continued to herd their hogs on Camas Prairie, in spite of treaty forbiddance (Brimlow 1938:43). It appears that settlers were depleting one of the few native food resources (camas roots) that was still relatively intact after nearly 75 years of contact. This drawn out "war" consisted of a series of native uprisings throughout much of the western Great Basin, and finally culminated among the Northern Paiutes of Oregon (Brimlow 1938:210; Forbes 1967:6–7).

Western Shoshone

At the time of Euroamerican contact, the territory occupied by the Western Shoshone encompassed a large portion of present-day Nevada, as well as areas of northwestern Utah and southern Idaho (Fig. 2). The region of central Nevada was one of the last areas of the Great Basin to be penetrated and settled by invading whites, as Jedediah Smith initiated contact with various Western Shoshone groups in 1827 (Brooks 1977; Thomas, Pendleton, and Cappannari 1986:263). Although several trapping and exploring parties travelled widely through the region before 1850 (Jedidiah Smith, 1827; Peter S. Ogden 1828–1829; Joseph R. Walker 1833; John C. Frémont, 1844), little useful ecological and ethnographic information was recorded until the expedition of Captain James H. Simpson in 1859. Howard Egan (1917) had recorded relevant data on the Western Shoshone as early as 1847, but this dealt mostly with the Gosiute Shoshone, a related, but geographically distinct group that lived on the eastern fringe of the greater Western Shoshone region.

Many early accounts focussed on the cultural "poverty" that characterized the Western Shoshone and Gosiute, as well as other Great Basin "Diggers." The relatively small population of the Western Shoshone and Gosiute was widely distributed, in accordance with the carrying capacity of the land. The vast majority of these people did not use the horse for transportation, as these animals would have consumed the same staple seed-producing grasses that the Western Shoshone were heavily dependent upon (Steward 1938:230, 235, 236, 1941:215–216; Shimkin 1986:519). Mules and horses were sometimes stolen from trappers and emigrants, and these were promptly eaten (Harris 1940:75–76).

Euroamerican settlers of the mid-nineteenth century had a far greater impact upon the Western Shoshone than did the earlier groups of trappers and explorers. With the movement of emigrants over the California Trail, the natural resources of the Great Basin were severely affected, and displacement of Nevada Shoshone groups commenced (McKinney 1983:11–16). Gosiute groups in western Utah and eastern Nevada were heavily impacted by Mormon settlers as early as 1847. Pony Express and Overland Stage stations also adversely affected the aboriginal subsistence base, as these systems began operations in 1860 and 1861, respectively (Egan 1917:198–199). These developments helped establish permanent routes of travel through Western Shoshone lands, and ushered in the period of ranching and mining, which most seriously impacted the traditional Western Shoshone lifeway.

Explorers and Trappers.

In 1827, Jedediah Smith became the first Euroamerican to cross the Great Basin from west to east (Brooks 1977). His party of three men passed through the central Great Basin, but they experienced minimal contact with natives of the region. The most extensive interaction between Smith's party and the Western Shoshone and/or Gosiute occurred along the present-day Nevada/Utah border, and in valleys directly east of the border. On June 10, 1827, Smith reported meeting three Indians just east of Monitor Valley, Nevada, where he obtained a piece of buffalo hide robe and one beaver skin from them. Judging from the collective native reactions, it appears that the Smith party was the first non-Indian group to contact Western Shoshone peoples in this portion of the central Great Basin. Smith noted that these natives had already obtained iron arrowheads and glass beads through trade (most likely with other natives), as the following passage provides some interesting data regarding this particular Western Shoshone groups' first experience with firearms:

> Early this morning the Indians that were at the camp last night returned and with them several others. They seemed to have come out of mere curiosity and as I was ready for starting they accompanied me a short distance. Some of them I presume had never before seen a White man and as they were handling and examining almost everything I fired off my gun as one of them was fingering about the double triggers. At the sound some fell flat on the ground and some sought safety in flight. The Indian who had hold of the gun alone stood still although he appeared at first to be thunder struck, yet on finding that he was not hurt he called out to his companions to return. I endeavored to learn from these Indians by signs something in relation to the distance and course to the Salt Lake. But from them I could get no satisfaction whatever for instead of answering my signs they would imitate them as nearly as possible. After vexing myself for sometime with these children of nature I left them and continued on my way. All the Indians I have seen since the Lake [Walker] had been the same unintelligent kind of beings. Nearly naked having at most a scanty robe formed of the skin of the hare peculiar to this plain which is cut into narrow strips and interwoven with a kind of twine or cord made apparently from wild flax or hemp [Brooks 1977:185].

In 1833, Zenas Leonard of the Bonneville-Walker party recorded several instances of contact with natives in Western Shoshone territory. The Walker group followed the Humboldt River to its sink, trapping beaver and trading with natives for pelts. For the most part, Leonard held these Indians in contempt, as he related:

> The natives which we occasionally met with still continued to be the most poor and dejected kind— being entirely naked and very filthy. We came to the hut of one of these Indians who happened to have a considerable quantity of fur collected. At this hut we obtained a large robe composed of beaver skins fastened together, in exchange for two awls and one fish hook. This robe was worth from 30 to 40 dollars [Leonard 1934:110].

In addition to the Walker party further depleting the beaver population of the Humboldt River drainage, they also instigated the process of deteriorating relations between western Great Basin natives and Euroamericans. On at least two occasions on the upper reaches of the Humboldt River, Walker's men had killed "several" Indians in retaliation for stealing their traps (Leonard 1934:111). When the trappers encountered a large group of Western Shoshone and/or Northern Paiute at the Humboldt Sink, they ruthlessly slaughtered at least 39 of them (Leonard 1934:112–117; Scott 1966:12). Walker's group repeated these actions the following year on their return trip through central Nevada, this time killing approximately 15 Western Shoshone.

The military exploring excursion of Captain James H. Simpson in 1859 to establish a direct wagon route from Camp Floyd, Utah, to Carson Valley, Nevada, resulted in a permanent road being established through the heart of the Western Shoshone homeland (Thomas 1982:10–11). Simpson was an extremely observant individual, and he kept a precise journal throughout his trip. In this journal he recorded the most accurate and detailed accounts of Western Shoshone culture and ecology that were known in his time. Simpson described his interactions with Gosiute and Western Shoshone peoples, discussing numerous aspects of their material culture and social organization, as well as their varied subsistence strategies (Simpson 1876). In one passage of his report, he mentioned a meeting with a Western Shoshone group east of Reese River Valley, in central Nevada:

> Some fifteen or twenty Diggers have come into camp. From these I have been enabled to get the names of some of the mountains and streams. They are the most lively, jocose Indians I have seen. Say two rats make a meal. Like rabbits better than rats, and antelope better than either, but cannot get the latter. Have no guns; use bow and arrow. They occasionally amuse us very much in their attempts to ride our mules which are, however, so much frightened at their rabbit-skin dress as to cause them to run off with them [Simpson 1876:75].

In addition to describing various facets of Western Shoshone culture, Simpson also made numerous references to the stands of native grasses that were then relatively unaffected by the grazing of horses and cattle. Captain Simpson also noted that there was a fairly large population of game animals in central Nevada prior to white settlement and development, as he observed that in Ruby Valley "A great deal of game such as antelope and aquatic fowl, is said to abound in this region, and deer and mountain sheep are also seen" (Simpson 1876:64).

It appears that the first two or three decades of Euroamerican contact did not overwhelm the Western Shoshone subsistence base. Certain components of their material culture were modified and/or replaced as a result of them having had access to white trade goods, but natural resources within Western Shoshone territory were not severely impacted until the establishment of Pony Express and Overland Stage stations, and ranches and mines. For all intents and purposes, widespread resource degradation did not affect the Western Shoshone until approximately 1860.

White Emigrants.

During the 1840s, westward-bound groups of Euroamericans travelled across the Overland Trail to Oregon and California. The southern route, popularly known as the California Trail, had a substantial impact upon those Western Shoshone groups that inhabited the Humboldt River region (Stewart 1962). In 1841, John Bidwell organized the first emigrant wagon train to California. Virtually unguided, the Bartleson party eventually reached California in the fall of that year. This particular group had little contact with local Shoshone Indians, as interaction was mostly limited to whites obtaining fish and pine nuts at various points along the route.

The number of emigrants along the California Trail gradually grew until it peaked during the years 1849 and 1850, after gold had been discovered in the foothills of the Sierra Nevada (Stewart 1962:193, 217; Malouf and Findlay 1986:507). Heavy use of the California Trail placed increasing pressure upon aboriginal food resources along the Humboldt River, and it did not take long for the migrant parties to permanently damage the fragile ecology of this region. Emigrant livestock grazed on the lush grasses along the river and compacted the turf. The whites also hunted and drove away important native game species such as pronghorn, deer, mountain sheep, and waterfowl. In 1849, one of the years of heaviest traffic, it has been estimated that 6200 wagons, 21,000 people, and 50,000 head of livestock passed over the California Trail (G. R. Stewart 1962:231–232). In addition to ruining the local grasses, emigrant livestock probably introduced various Old World diseases to local game animals such as rabbits, deer, and mountain sheep, further reducing these populations (Malouf and Findlay 1986:507).

The Western Shoshone responded to this adverse situation in two basic ways: many simply withdrew from their former camps along the Humboldt River, while others remained along the California Trail, and resorted to begging or stealing livestock as well as other material goods and foodstuffs. Most whites interpreted the Indians' attempts to replace lost food resources as acts of aggression, and were quick to shoot first and ask questions later. During the late 1840s, and throughout the 1850s, hordes of overland migrants continued to deplete the aboriginal subsistence base along the Humboldt River, an area that had once supported a relatively dense native population.

Pony Express and Overland Stage Operations.

Establishment of the Pony Express and its various support stations in 1860, and the construction of 22 stations of the Overland Stage system in 1861, affected a large segment of the Western and Gosiute Shoshone. These systems passed through the center of Nevada Shoshone country, following the route established by Simpson in 1859 (Thomas 1982:15). These stations were usually located at the springs that were relied upon by natives, and displaced many local groups. Euroamerican employees of these systems monopolized the water, grasses, and game animals in the vicinity of these stations (Malouf 1966:27). These developments led to Indian raids upon stages and coaches from 1860 to 1863 (Egan 1917:200–201; Allen and Warner 1971:164–165). In response to these native attacks, U. S.

Army units were called into the area, and fought with local Indians. Needless to say, the Shoshone were usually routed by white military units, and the groups that suffered were not always guilty parties. These disputes were eventually settled by the Treaty of Tooele Valley in 1863 (Forbes 1967:5; Allen and Warner 1971:168–169; Malouf 1974:124–134).

In each case of military conflict, Euroamericans had placed increasing pressure upon native subsistence resources and cultural systems, and the Western Shoshone responded by raiding white travelers and settlements. These hostilities resulted in the establishment of American military posts in the central Great Basin, and federal authorities began to implement plans to establish farms and reservations in order to isolate Western Shoshone peoples from white populations.

Euroamerican Settlement and Development.

The close of the 1850s marked the end of an aboriginal and independent lifeway for the Western Shoshone. Mormons had established farms throughout the Gosiute homeland of western Utah and eastern Nevada, the well-watered valleys once occupied by Western Shoshone in central and western Nevada were claimed by ranchers, and as gold and silver were discovered in the Comstock region, miners flocked to Nevada from both the west and east.

Ranching and farming played the most influential role in transforming traditional Western Shoshone culture. These operations occupied optimal aboriginal resource areas, and historic agricultural practices such as open grazing and plowing depleted large stands of native grasses. Important perennial grasses such as Indian ricegrass, Great Basin wild rye, and wheatgrass were severely depleted through overgrazing and haying (Thomas 1971:5–6, 1982:20, 24, 25; Young, Evans, and Tueller 1976).

With increased white settlement in Nevada, there was a corresponding need for construction timber and cordwood. As a result, large amounts of both Utah juniper and pinyon pine were cut to meet these demands (Harris 1940:80; Thomas 1971:6–8). The mass cutting of these woodlands reduced important sources of native food, firewood, and construction material.

With the widespread destruction of various subsistence resources, a large segment of the Shoshone began to work as wage laborers for Euroamerican settlers. One adaptive strategy implemented by the Nevada Shoshone was to either form small settlements on the outskirts of towns, or to attach themselves as family units or individuals to local ranches (Fig. 9.4). (Harris 1940:82; Malouf 1966:26; McKinney 1983:18; Malouf and Findlay 1986:510).

By approximately 1862, Euroamerican settlement and development in much of Nevada had exhausted the Western Shoshone's adaptive strategies within their own cultural system. Participation in a non-native economy became the only viable choice for most Nevada Shoshone groups. This acculturative process involved learning ranching and farming skills, adopting white foods, performing menial tasks for wages and goods, changing settlement patterns from seasonal movements to sedentary residences, and learning a new

Figure 9.4 Western Shoshone camp at Bullfrog, Esmerelda County, Nevada. These people are standing in the middle of a brush windbreak. Such structures were usually built and occupied during warm weather months. The woman at left is wearing a basketry hat over a scarf, the infant appears to be wearing a pair of animal skin moccasins, and the man behind the fire is holding a double barreled shotgun. Note the use of a 5-gallon kerosene can in cooking, as well as a metal coffee pot. Metal utensils quickly replaced aboriginal items used in cooking, such as brown ware pottery. Photographed in 1906. (Photo number 550 courtesy of Nevada Historical Society.)

language (Clemmer 1978:63). The predicament of the Western Shoshone was explained to Indian agent Levi Gheen (1876:117) by Captain Sam, a local Shoshone leader:

> . . . the game was all gone; the trees that bore pine-nuts were cut down and burned in the quartz mills and other places; the grass-seeds, heretofore used by them for food, were no more; the grass-land all claimed by and cultivated by the white people; and that his Indians would soon be compelled to work for the ranchers for two bits (twenty-five cents) a day or starve.

The jobs performed by Shoshone men involved cutting and hauling wood, herding stock, building fences, and hauling water. Shoshone women washed clothes, worked as maids, cooked, and some became involved in prostitution (Harris 1940:82–83; Wells 1983:25; Malouf and Findlay 1986:510). Begging, stealing, and scavenging were also resorted to in order to avoid starvation. Traditional clothing was quickly replaced by Euroamerican garments. Basketry and pottery were replaced by metal containers (Fig. 9.4), and traditional plant materials used for building shelters were superceded by canvas, metal, and milled lumber.

Although a great deal of Euroamerican culture was adopted by the Shoshone, various aspects of aboriginal culture survived and were incorporated into the new Western Shoshone lifeway. Pine nuts were harvested and sold to local whites (Wells 1978:25,

1983:54), and game animals were hunted for the market in exchange for money, or food and goods. Traditional belief systems still flourished, as the institution of shamanism remained important. This particular aboriginal practice may have even been strengthened by the need to cope with the new diseases that had spread unchecked into the native population (Harris 1940:84).

A great deal of data concerning historic resource degradation and native acculturation is available for central Nevada. This is mostly due to the various archaeological and ethnohistorical projects that have been carried out in the Grass Valley, Monitor Valley, and Reese River Valley regions since the early 1970s (Thomas 1971; Ambro 1972; Bettinger 1976; Clewlow and Pastron 1978; Rosen 1978; Wells 1978, 1983; Thomas 1982).

Grass Valley.

The Grass Valley project contributed a large body of data to the area of Great Basin ethnohistory through the implementation of archaeologic, historic, and ethnographic research. In her 1978 study, Wells was able to document aspects of the contact situation involving native peoples of Grass Valley and Reese River Valley by reviewing articles published in the *Reese River Reville,* an early local newspaper of Austin, Nevada, a town located about 25 miles southwest of Grass Valley. The *Reveille* was first published in June of 1863, and provided information regarding the disruption of the hunting and gathering economy and social structure of the Western Shoshone due to white settlement in central Nevada (Wells 1978:13). Changes in traditional settlement patterns, food resources, economic activities, and material culture were documented for the period 1863 to 1878.

Another source of data concerning acculturation among the Grass Valley Shoshone was provided by archaeological investigations (Ambro 1972; Clewlow and Pastron 1972, 1978; Rosen 1978). This research documented changes in aboriginal subsistence and settlement patterns, which began as early as 1860. Archaeological research at several historical Shoshone camps allowed the researchers to document modifications in components of traditional material culture. Flaked stone and ceramic technologies were apparently the first aboriginal traditions to be replaced by Euroamerican counterparts such as metal knives, guns, and metal containers. Changes in aboriginal house construction, clothing, and domestic utensils were also noted.

Several traditional aspects of Nevada Shoshone culture continued to be practiced during historic times in Grass Valley. The processing of grass seeds and pinyon nuts remained an integral part of the postcontact Western Shoshone subsistence system, as a large number of ground stone implements were recovered from historic habitation sites (Clewlow and Pastron 1978:166). Other aboriginal artifacts found in historic contexts included basketry and clay figurines (Ambro 1972:94).

It appears that pine nuts were still an important part of the native diet in Grass Valley, as Ambro (1972) reported that pinyon hulls were widely distributed over the surface of the Ridge Village North site. Subsequent work by Wells (1983) indicated that the traditional fall pine nut harvest in the Grass Valley area was retained in the postcontact native economy. Although the local Shoshone were employed by the whites in Grass Valley, and whites had grown dependent upon the native labor force, the fall pinyon harvest caused the seasonal disappearance of the Indian labor pool from the region (Wells 1983:63). The harvested pine nuts were consumed by the Shoshone, and a portion was sold to local ranchers and the townspeople of Austin.

Changes in the aboriginal diet of the Grass Valley Shoshone has been illustrated by the analysis of faunal materials found in association with Historic period Shoshone campsites (Rosen 1978). Through his study, Rosen demonstrated how ''. . . ecofactual data can be applied to an investigation of culture change to indicate 1) preference in animals exploited as food resources during the acculturation period; and 2) changes in aboriginal butchering, hunting and food preparation practices as effected by the acculturation process'' (1978:37).

Surface faunal remains were recovered from six historic sites in Grass Valley. It was found that cows (*Bos taurus*), jackrabbits, and cottontail rabbits comprised the major portion of native animal food resources during historic times in Grass Valley (Rosen 1978:44). Rosen concluded that the Grass Valley Shoshone shifted from a broad subsistence base to a specialized one, exploiting only a few of the available animal resources. It seems likely that this phenomenon was related to the fact that these people were no longer following a traditional seasonal round, where diverse ecozones were exploited for a wide variety of animal foods. The nomadic seasonal round had been replaced by semisedentary habitation near the ranches of Grass Valley. This change in settlement pattern, along with the excessive pressures placed upon large game animals by white settlers, had effectively reduced the wide range of animal species formerly available for exploitation.

Reese River Valley.

Other historical and archaelogical projects carried out in central Nevada have provided additional information on acculturational processes of Nevada Shoshone populations. In one study, the establishment and growth of Austin, Nevada, was found to be directly related to the rapid destruction of various native resources in the Reese River Valley (Thomas 1971). Heavy cutting of juniper, pinyon, and mountain mahogany in the Toiyabe and Shoshone mountains (Thomas 1971:5; Young and Budy 1971), and overgrazing in the Reese River Valley (Thomas 1971:6), depleted a large segment of the native food base. This caused local native groups to become increasingly dependent upon wage labor, as staples of the aboriginal diet were ruined.

Archaeological data obtained by Bettinger (1976) from an historic Shoshone encampment in Reese River Valley documented changes in native material culture. The Flat Iron Ridge site is a small camp containing "moderate" amounts of flaked stone debitage, several flaked and ground stone artifacts, and a considerable amount of historic refuse, such as tin cans, nails, and glass, in addition to a stone-lined house ring (Bettinger 1976:313–314). Excavation of the house ring exposed a cultural deposit approximately 18 cm. deep, and yielded numerous artifacts of Euroamerican origin.

This research indicated that some aspects of the traditional Shoshonean economy, such as flaked stone and ground stone industries, were still utilized during the Historic period in Reese River Valley. This indicates that not all Western Shoshone groups in Nevada abandoned the use of prehistoric lithic technology, as proposed by Clewlow and Pastron (1978:169).

Monitor Valley.

The historic settlement and development of Monitor Valley, Nevada, and the growth of the nearby mining town of Belmont also displaced local Shoshone peoples and depleted native food resources (Thomas 1982). White settlers homesteaded the lowland springs and drove away local game animals; farms were established to supply Belmont with food; and numerous sheep and cattle grazed throughout the region (Sawyer 1971:7–8; Thomas 1982:24–25). Local stands of pinyon and juniper were rapidly exhausted, as wood was needed for construction, fuel at the stamp mills, mine shoring, fence posts, and firewood (Young and Budy 1979; Thomas 1982:25). All of these developments occurred during the early 1860s.

Euroamerican settlement of central Nevada resulted in widespread degradation of traditional Western Shoshone resources, which in turn caused native peoples to become heavily reliant on the white economic system and material culture. Although the discovery of the Comstock Lode and various other Nevada mining booms precipitated a large influx of Euroamericans to Nevada during the 1860s (Eliott 1973:118–120), the greatest changes in Western Shoshone culture were caused by the ranching industry. Ranchers and their livestock significantly and permanently modified the local environment, and most severely impacted native subsistence systems. In less than three decades, the contact situation in central Nevada had crippled an economic system that had flourished for several thousand years.

Native Resistance.

A relatively small segment of the Western Shoshone became involved in organized raids upon white settlements during the 1860s. Groups that carried out such attacks were usually those who had isolated themselves from direct contact with Euroamericans at an early period. The *tosawi·ccih*, or White Knife Shoshone of the Battle Mountain region of central Nevada was one such predatory band. The White Knives first obtained horses and guns during the early 1850s, and formed mounted bands that attacked emigrant parties, Pony Express and Overland Stage stations, and small settlements (Harris 1940:76–77; Egan 1972:275; Shimkin 1986:519, 523).

As with other Great Basin native groups, the adoption of the horse had radically changed the aboriginal sociopolitical organization of the White Knives, as incipient band organization and increased mobility allowed these people to cover a much wider range and to effectively exploit new resources available along emigrant trails and at white settlements. By 1859, at least seven mounted Western Shoshone bands roamed throughout the Humboldt River drainage, with each band having one principal chief, and at least one sub-chief (Harris 1940:76). However, the existence of these embryonic bands was short-lived, as the discovery of silver and gold in Nevada generated a substantial influx of miners, settlers, and U.S. military troops into the region. Due to the relatively sparse stands of grass in much of central Nevada in early contact times, there had never been many horses among the Western Shoshone. When combined with several harsh winters during the early 1860s, further depletion of the native food base by white expansion, and increased protection of whites against Indian raids, mounted Western Shoshone bands were forced to return to pedestrian hunting and gathering, and supplemental wage labor on white settlements (Harris 1940:79).

By 1865, most Nevada Shoshone raids had ceased. A U. S. Army unit had massacred a large number of Shoshone in Steptoe Valley in 1862, and several treaties signed in 1863 initiated the period of reservation allotments. The contact situation experienced by the Western Shoshone was quite similar to other Great Basin groups during the mid-nineteenth century, as exploration, settlement, and extractive industries impacted subsistence resources, and transformed aboriginal culture. For the Nevada Shoshone, development of the Nevada livestock industry was the critical force which affected and transformed aboriginal subsistence systems, settlement patterns, social organization, language, and material culture. Unchecked grazing of cattle and sheep irreparably damaged native grasslands and water resources, and forced Western Shoshone groups to become economically dependent upon the invading population in order to survive.

Northern Paiute

The Northern Paiute traditionally occupied a large portion of the western Great Basin, as well as southern parts of the Columbia and Snake River drainages (Fig. 9.2). In precontact times, the Northern Paiute consisted of several linguistically uniform, but culturally and politically distinct groups (Fowler and Liljeblad 1986:435). One segment that originally inhabited areas of eastern Oregon, known historically as the Bannock, acquired the horse sometime during the mid-to-late eighteenth century, moved eastward into Northern Shoshone territory, and developed Shoshone-like patterns of subsistence and social structure (Madsen 1980:18–19; Fowler and Liljeblad 1986:455). Cultural changes related to adoption of the horse included the development of fully mounted bands with shifting leadership, eastward and northward expansion onto the Plains to exploit bison, and involvement in a raiding complex for horses and other material goods (Steward 1938:201; Stewart 1970; Steward and Wheeler-Voegelin 1974; Layton 1978).

The vast majority of Northern Paiute groups never adopted the horse to the extent that their Bannock relatives had. Most of these people maintained traditional pedestrian cultural systems, emphasizing a kin clique, or extended family camp group type of social organization, and practiced a wide array of subsistence strategies, based on the specific resources found within their home range (Stewart 1939:130).

Extensive contact between most Northern Paiute groups and Euroamericans did not occur until the 1830s and 1840s, as fur trappers expanded southward along the Humboldt River drainage, and emigrant parties moved along the California Trail. With the discovery of gold and silver in California and Nevada during the mid 1800s, whites quickly penetrated eastern California and western Nevada, and established settlements throughout these areas.

Above all other developments, the mining industry most severely impacted Northern Paiute culture. The feverish search for gold and silver deposits, and the large-scale extraction of these precious metals resulted in mass degradation of natural resources throughout the Northern Paiute homeland, and caused change in Northern Paiute subsistence systems, social organization, and material culture. Prior to the Gold Rush, the fur trade and overland migration had set in motion the processes that eventually overwhelmed Northern Paiute society.

Explorers and Trappers.

In 1827, Peter S. Ogden became the first person to record detailed accounts of the Northern Paiute. His interaction with native groups was largely confined to the unmounted Paiutes of eastern Oregon and northern Nevada. Ogden noted that the native population of the Humboldt River region was relatively dense, and that they relied heavily on roots and waterfowl in the late fall (Ogden 1910:384). The Ogden trapping party apparently was the first white group to contact natives along the Humboldt, as many fled at the trappers' approach. After determining that these strangers were only in the region to trap beaver, the natives became less wary. Ogden's journal entry of November 18, 1828, reported that his party "encamped as usual on the banks of the river lined with deserted Indian villages, no less than 50 tents. 150 Indians paid us a visit, miserable looking wretches, with scarcely any covering, the greater part without bows and arrows without any defense. They were fat and in good condition" (Ogden 1910:385).

The journal of Jedediah Smith also contains data regarding early contact between whites and Northern Paiutes. His party camped at Walker Lake, Nevada, and noted the native fishing industry there. Smith also encountered between 20 and 30 native horsemen at Walker Lake (Brooks 1977:173–175). It seems that these mounted Indians were not Walker Lake Paiute, but possibly Bannock, Northern Shoshone, Ute, or California natives, apparently on friendly terms with the people of Walker Lake, and who were probably using western Nevada as a base of operations for raiding and trading (Layton 1981:134–135).

The accounts of Ogden and Smith indicate that components of Northern Paiute material culture had been modified by European imports as early as 1825. At this time the Northern Paiute possessed glass trade beads, Spanish blankets, and various metal implements, such as arrowheads, awls, and knives.

Just as trappers were the first Euroamericans to contact many Northern Paiute groups, they were also responsible for the beginnings of hostilities between the two populations. This was marked by the misdeeds of the Joseph R. Walker party at the Humboldt Sink in

1833. As mentioned above, this was the incident when Walker and his men killed approximately 40 curious natives in order to "scare the Indians away" (Leonard 1934:112–115).

The penetration of Northern Paiute territory by trappers also initiated the process of ecological degradation. Beaver was trapped out along the Humboldt River, and trapping parties, sometimes with 100 to 200 horses, temporarily decreased the local forage and game supplies (Forbes 1967; Rusco 1976:160).

Early explorers travelling among the Northern Paiute also described aspects of aboriginal social and subsistence systems. Several accounts are available for the Pyramid Lake Paiute from John C. Frémont's 1843 expedition, as he described the thriving fishery of the Truckee River (Frémont 1845:11–12; 218). The journal of Edward M. Kern, a member of the 1845 Frémont party, recorded information on several Northern Paiute groups (Kern 1876). At the east end of the Humboldt River, Kern (1876:478) observed that "The Indians that we first met were better clad than one would suppose; having also a few horses among them . . . they belong to the Bannack tribe of Diggers, and are generally badly disposed towards the whites." Kern apparently saw no significant differences among the Indians during the passage down the Humboldt River. This suggests that at this time, some Northern Paiute groups had obtained horses, but most were still carrying on traditional pedestrian economic and cultural pursuits.

The California Trail.

Heavy emigrant use of the California Trail began in the late 1840s, in response to the California Gold Rush. This development marked the end of an independent Northern Paiute society. During the early 1850s, native use of the horse in western Nevada expanded, and several Paiute bands raided white parties crossing their territory (Steward and Wheeler-Voegelin 1974:97; Fowler and Liljeblad 1986:455). These predatory bands had adopted a successful strategy in adjusting to the depletion of native resources, as mass migration along the Humboldt River had severely impacted native seed-bearing grasses and large game animals. With increased use of the California Trail, supplies of firewood were exhausted, and waterholes fouled (Gould, Fowler, and Fowler 1972:269; Fowler and Liljeblad 1986:456).

In a short period of time, the prehistoric carrying capacity of the Humboldt River drainage was greatly reduced. A significant portion of the natives quickly withdrew from the lowlands and came to occupy mountainous regions, where they avoided contacts with non-natives (Hopkins 1883:10–11). Other groups remained in the valleys along the Humboldt River, exploiting stock animals and wagons, and collecting castaway items (Downs 1963:123; Scott 1966:31).

As in other areas of the Great Basin, emigrant parties introduced several Old World diseases to various Northern Paiute groups. Because New World natives had no immunity to these viruses, these diseases exacted a heavy toll on the aboriginal population. In 1850 alone, a cholera epidemic in western Nevada was responsible for the deaths of several hundred Northern Paiutes (Scott 1966:26–27; Nissen 1982:66–69, 115–116).

Pressures placed upon Northern Paiute society by overland immigrants increased native dependence on Euroamerican society and economy. The depletion of a large portion of the aboriginal food base caused many groups to abandon a hunting and gathering economy. As ranches and farms became established, many Paiutes attached themselves to these settlements and survived by performing odd jobs. By the mid 1850s, practically every component of aboriginal culture had been modified to some extent through prolonged contact with white society.

Euroamerican Settlement and Development.

Discovery of gold and silver between 1857 and 1860 in the eastern Sierra Nevada of California, the Virginia Range in western Nevada, and the Owyhee Basin in Oregon, disrupted Northern Paiute culture far more rapidly and thoroughly than had earlier Euroamerican incursions into their home range.

The goal of the mining industry was to dig as much ore from the earth as rapidly as possible, and to use whatever amounts of local resources that were necessary to obtain this objective. Miners and mining companies really had no long term interests in the area, and consequently saw no need to conserve resources, nor to establish peaceful relations with native groups who resisted their monopolizing tactics.

In many areas, urban mining communities appeared overnight. These boomtowns had a devastating effect on the Northern Paiute subsistence base, a situation amply illustrated by the following passage concerning the Comstock mining district:

> Mountain slopes were deforested as lumbermen felled trees in order to provide wood for mine shafts, railroad tracks, housing, and fuel. Heavy logging increased the extent of erosion, flooding, and fires, depleted the stock of pine nuts, destroyed the habitat of the mountain sheep, and drove away large animals that Indians had hunted. Miners also reduced freshwater resources through the overfishing, damming, diverting, and silting of local streams. As the need to feed miners produced a sizeable market for foodstuffs, farmers and ranchers also came to the Comstock and occupied lands that Indians had once used for gathering food resources. Ranchers' herds trampled and consumed wild grasses until they died off, often to be replaced by sagebrush and non-native weeds [Malouf and Findlay 1986:513].

These changes in the environment elicited three common strategies which had been implemented by other Shoshonean groups: some Northern Paiutes moved away from settled areas, others intensified military assaults on the invading group, and some natives attempted to co-exist with Euroamericans and participated in the new economy (Malouf and Findlay 1986:513–514).

The boomtowns attracted a large segment of the Northern Paiute, as they were drawn to these settlements by curiosity, the desire for white material goods, and the need to replace food resources that had been depleted (Gould, Fowler, and Fowler 1972:169–170). Traditional settlement patterns were quickly modified, as small sedentary camps were established on the fringes of mining towns (Fig. 9.3).

The Paiutes who occupied these camps were quickly absorbed by the white economy. Many of them labored on nearby farms and ranches, cut trees and hauled wood, hunted, fished, and collected plant foods for the market, worked as domestics, and begged, stole, and scavenged to avoid starving (Scott 1966:59–60; Gould, Fowler, and Fowler 1972:273).

The acculturative pressures exerted upon Northern Paiute peoples near mining regions were overwhelming. Two boomtowns that drained local resources were Bodie, California, and Virginia City, Nevada. Both historical and archaeological data are available concerning native reactions to these developments, and are reviewed below.

The Northern Paiute-speaking *kucadïkadï*, 'eaters of brine fly [hydropyrus hians] pupae' historically occupied the Mono Lake basin of eastern California (Steward 1933; Davis 1965; Fowler and Liljeblad 1986:484). This group was heavily affected by the discoveries of gold at Dogtown, Monoville, Aurora, and Bodie (Fig. 9.5) between 1857 and 1859 (Wedertz 1978; Fletcher 1982, 1987). With the establishment of mining operations, farms, and ranches on and near the springs, streams, and meadows that had formerly served as seasonal habitation sites, the *kucadïkadï* Paiute were forced to inhabit the more marginal areas of the Mono Basin that had not been developed by Euroamericans (Davis 1965:7; Fletcher 1982:53–54).

Introduction of cattle and sheep to the Mono Basin had a marked effect upon perennial grasses, as overgrazing greatly reduced their abundance, and allowed sagebrush to become established in many areas (Fletcher 1982:127). The impact of livestock upon native grasslands of the region was observed by both John Muir (1916:96), and Israel C. Russell (1889:278), an early employee of the U.S. Geological Survey.

As in other areas of the Great Basin, a transition slowly took place from an independent, aboriginal lifeway to one that was increasingly dependent upon white employment, foods, and technology (Davis 1965:8). Both Mono Basin Paiute men and women earned wages by working for local ranches, mines, farms, and the Bodie Railway and Lumber Company (Fig. 9.6) (Billeb 1968:128; Cain 1961:115; Calhoun 1984:22; Fletcher 1982:55–57, 1987:77–78). Aspects of the aboriginal economy were incorporated into the new one, as the Mono Basin Paiute sold pine nuts, fish, waterfowl, and gull eggs to the merchants and townspeople of Bodie and Mono Valley (Cain 1961:120–121; Billeb 1968:129; Calhoun 1984:32–33).

Archaeological data that sheds additional light on the acculturative processes of the *kucadïkadï* has recently been obtained from a multi-component encampment (formally recorded as CA-Mno-2122) (Fig. 9.5) located on the east side of Mono Lake (Arkush 1987a, 1987b). By comparing the artifactual assemblages from both pre- and postcontact activity areas, it has been determined that native crafts such as ceramics and beads of shell and bone were quickly replaced by Euroamerican equivalents, such as metal containers and glass beads. Steel implements such as knives, axes, wire, nails, and screws replaced some flaked stone implements and plant materials previously used for cutting and binding activities, respectively. The occurrence of spent shotshells and cartridge cases indicate that the Mono Basin Paiute were using shotguns and rifles, although obsidian projectile points were still being produced in historic times. Additionally, the occurrence of hole-in-cap and

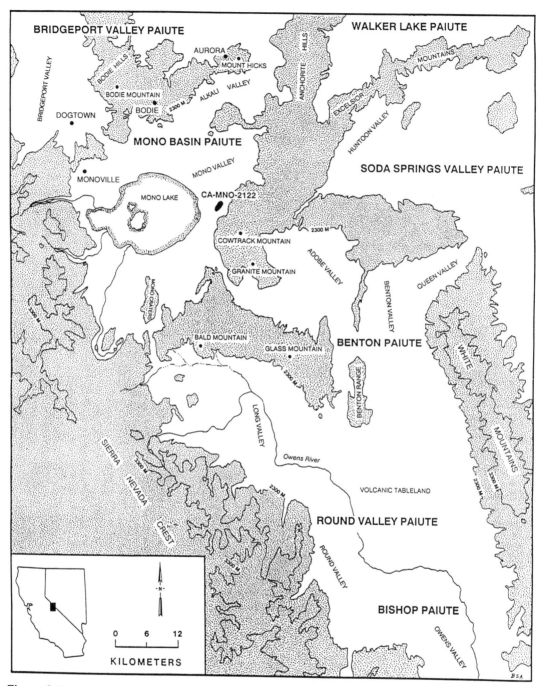

Figure 9.5 Natural and cultural geography of the central eastern Sierra Nevada region, showing locations of nineteenth century mining developments in and around the Mono Basin, as well as the location of archaeological site CA-Mno-2122. (Brooke S. Arkush)

Figure 9.6 "PI-UTE INDIANS 'WASH DAY' AT HOT SPRINGS." Benton Paiute women washing clothes at Benton Hot Springs, Mono County, California. She probably was employed by the Benton Dude Ranch. Note that she is using a large basin metate as a washboard. Photograph number 372 by Burton Frasher, sometime between 1910 and 1915. (Courtesy of Nevada Historical Society.)

slip-top cans, meat tins, pickle jars, bourbon, beer, and soda water bottles, patent medicine bottles, as well as metal clasps and glass and shell buttons from clothing indicate that these people had access to a wide variety of the goods, foods and beverages that were available in Mono Valley and Bodie.

Other data from Mno-2122 also point to aspects of cultural persistence among the *kucadɨdadɨ*. Two traditional winter houses dating between 1880 and 1910 indicate that the Mono Basin Paiute still maintained precontact architectural practices, as these round houses were constructed from juniper posts, had east-facing doorways,and various other features that agree with ethnographic descriptions of prehistoric Northern Paiute winter houses (Steward 1933, 1941; Stewart 1941). There is also evidence of the production of coiled basketry at the site.

The presence of ground stone implements, as well as the remains of carbonized pinyon nuts and hulls at numerous historic activity areas points to the fact that the seed processing economy was still an important aspect of the postcontact Mono Basin Paiute lifeway.

The intensified fall/winter occupation of Mno-2122 seems to verify historic and ethnographic accounts that the *kucadɨkadɨ* Paiute were forced onto the more marginal areas of the Mono Basin after whites claimed the well-watered portions for their own. However, the historic component of Mno-2122 may also reflect a concerted effort by a segment of the Mono Basin Paiute to isolate themselves from whites in order to practice traditional fall/winter activities such as harvesting pine nuts, producing native craftwork, and establishing macroband encampments.

In 1859, gold and silver were discovered in the Virginia Range in western Nevada. Subsequent development of the Comstock Lode resulted in the founding of Virginia City, and the "Rush to Washoe" was on (Eliott 1973:61). This sparked a period of intensive mining which eventually affected the entire state of Nevada, and which, of course, had disastrous consequences for the Northern Paiute groups of the Comstock region. From the map provided by Stewart (1939:Map 1), it appears that the specific Northern Paiute groups that aboriginally occupied the Comstock region were the *tasiget tuviwarai* 'Between Dwellers' of Winnemucca Valley (Stewart 1939:138), and the *kuyuidɨkadɨ* 'cui-ui eaters' of Pyramid Lake (Stewart 1939:138–139).

Settlement of the Comstock region exhausted local native food resources. Entire tracts of pinyon were cut for firewood, and a wide area around Virginia City was denuded of pinyon trees (Lyman 1946:37–38; Young and Budy 1979:114). The cutting of pinyon alone had a severe impact on regional ecology, as Young and Budy (1979:114) reported that:

> In 1864, several thousand American laborers were constantly cutting and hauling firewood from nearby woodlands. Chinese laborers followed the woodcutters, pulling up the brush, stumps and roots from the cut-over hills . . . An estimated 120,000 cords of firewood were used in the district in 1866. The scant supply of pinyon and juniper on the neighboring hills was rapidly exhausted, and woodcutters moved to the eastern slopes of the Sierra Nevada, some twenty miles from the mines.

In addition to destruction of pinyon, white settlement of the Comstock District displaced native groups from optimal resource areas. Livestock ruined native grasses and introduced diseases to local game animals, most notably to mountain sheep. This rapid influx of humanity played a key role in upsetting the native economy and social structure (Forbes 1967:2; Hattori 1975:4). Local Indians were compelled to become part of the Comstock economy, working as cowboys, hired hands, woodcutters, maids, servants, and laundresses. Modifications of traditional subsistence activities involved hunting ducks, geese, and jackrabbits for the market, and selling pine nuts to white settlers (Wright 1947:215; 1963:22; Waldorf 1970:77–78).

The lure of wage labor, new foods, and white material culture led to a small population of Northern Paiute settling on the Comstock (Fig. 9.3). These natives, accustomed to maximum utilization of resources, obtained a number of exotic products that were discarded by whites on the outskirts of Virginia City. The abundance of these foodstuffs and materials replaced depleted aboriginal resources, and played a significant role in the new economy of the Virginia City Paiutes, as shelter, food, and clothing were constantly available within the Comstock District (Hattori 1975:19). Food was purchased, salvaged from restaurant and market refuse, begged from townspeople, or donated by churches and community organizations. During the summer, when fresh fruits and vegetables were available, the Paiutes collected damaged produce which had been discarded (Wright 1947:210, 215; Hattori 1975:20).

In addition to modifications of aboriginal material culture, food resources, and settlement patterns, there were also changes in traditional house structures. Shelters built and occupied by Virginia City Paiutes reflected adaptations to new building materials and designs introduced by Euroamericans (Hattori 1975:20). Changes in the traditional doomed house, or *wickiup*, involved the use of canvas, muslin, burlap, carpet, or sheet metal as covering; steel pipes were commonly used as framing (Waldorf 1970:77; Hattori 1975:21). Another modification of the aboriginal house design was the substitution of a woodburning stove in place of a central fire pit, with a flue passing through the top of the structure (Fig. 9.3).

Archaeological research at an historic Northern Paiute site (formally recorded as NV-St-2009) in Virginia City documented aspects of acculturation among the natives who settled on the outskirts of the mining town (Hattori 1975). A wide array of Euroamerican materials was recovered from three features, as well as from the surface artifact assemblage. These included whole and fragmentary bottles which at one time contained alcohol, patent medicines, and soda water; glass beads, marbles, ironstone ceramic sherds, nails, cartridge cases and bullets and buttons (Hattori 1975:43–64). Flaked stone, ground stone, and shell artifacts recovered from NV-St-2009 indicate that certain components of precontact culture were retained during historic times (Hattori 1975:65, 68–70).

Given the fact that a vast majority of traditional subsistence resources had been depleted in the western Great Basin, native participation in the white economic system was one of the few viable strategies available to the average Northern Paiute. For the most part, it appears that this major shift in lifestyle was successful, as these people relied upon traditional resourcefulness to adapt to a potentially disastrous situation.

Native Resistance.

Several uprisings occurred among the Northern Paiute during the 1860s and 1870s. These confrontations with Euroamerican citizens and soldiers were the end products of three decades of intensive contact, and the corresponding depletion of traditional subsistence resources. These military battles marked the height of native frustrations, as Northern Paiute culture was being overpowered and repressed by a foreign population, most of which was either supportive of, or indifferent to, this obliteration.

The Pyramid Lake War of 1860 primarily involved those Paiutes living in the vicinity of the Comstock mining district. On May 12 of that year, a force composed of various Northern Paiute groups from Oregon and Nevada killed 43 members of a mounted white volunteer unit in a canyon just south of Pyramid Lake (Egan 1972). A regiment of 160 men had set out from Virginia City to avenge a justified native raid on William's Station, along the Carson River. The Williams brothers had kidnapped and raped two young Paiute girls, and had in turn been killed by the girls' relatives. The deeds of the "bloodthirsty savages" could not go unpunished, and the ill-prepared regiment was lured into the confines of a canyon, and soundly defeated (Egan 1972).

Two weeks after this battle, a large military force from California defeated the Paiute warriors in several additional encounters at Big Meadows and Pinnacle Mount, near the Carson River (Egan 1972:203–248). Later that summer, a council was held between a U.S. government representative and two Northern Paiute leaders, Numaga and Winnemucca. This ended hostilities in the Carson and Comstock districts, and the Pyramid Lake War was over.

The Owens Valley ''war'' was actually a series of skirmishes between natives and whites which broke out between 1862 and 1863. The Paiute of Owens Valley were so poorly equipped with horses and firearms that it would be misleading to say that true predatory bands had developed in response to Euroamerican encroachment (Steward and Wheeler-Voegelin 1974:156). Warfare against white settlers produced joint effort rather than well-coordinated military action. These hostilities ultimately resulted in the removal of a number of Owens Valley Paiute and Panamint Shoshone to Fort Tejon in central California.

In 1861, the first white settlers arrived in the Owens Valley of eastern California. For the most part, these settlers were cattlemen from central California and Nevada, intent on securing the well-watered lands of the valley for stock raising purposes (Chalfant 1933:140–43). Conflict quickly arose as natives fought over rights to their irrigated lands. With an increase in white settlement, native food resources such as game animals, pinyon pine, and seed-bearing grasses were depleted, and clashes escalated. The Owens Valley Paiute soon resorted to stealing cattle to replace traditional resources that had been lost, and ranchers responded by killing several Indians (Liljeblad and Fowler 1986:430).

Owens Valley natives were then united under the leadership of Captain George and Joaquin Jim (a Yokuts from the San Joaquin Valley of central California). The Indian force outnumbered that of the whites, and natives were in control of Owens Valley by early 1862 (Chalfant 1933:156). However, native control of the region proved to be temporary, as Camp Independence was established in July of 1862 in order to protect white interests. With the Euroamerican minority now bolstered by a U.S. Army unit, depredations against the Owens Valley Paiute resumed in order to usurp native holdings. Under the command of Captain Moses McLaughlin, the military adopted a disgraceful ''scorched earth'' policy against the Paiute, burning and destroying cached food suppliers, shelters, and equipment (Chalfant 1933:190–191; Wilke and Lawton 1976:7–8).

One of the sergeants under McLaughlin succeeded in holding a conference with Captain George, and convinced him to visit Fort Independence in peace, and a truce was arranged. The destruction of stored supplies, the starved conditions of the natives, and negotiations between the warring factions finally ended hostilities. The Indians of Owens Valley were instructed to assemble at Camp Independence in July of 1863, and approximately 900 men, women, and children were marched to San Sebastian Reservation, near Fort Tejon, California.

Although numerous treaties were signed, and several reservations were established as a result of mid-nineteenth century uprisings in the Great Basin, these actions did not

340

prevent additional outbreaks of violence, as was illustrated by the Bannock War of 1878. The series of battles that comprised the Bannock War began when white settlers continued to herd their hogs on the Camas Prairie of southern Idaho, an area that had been set aside for Northern Shoshone/Bannock peoples (Brimlow 1938:43–45).

A segment of Oregon Northern Paiutes from the Malheur Reservation also participated in the Bannock War. The corrupt agent in charge of the Malheur Agency had repeatedly failed to distribute rations of food and clothing to the natives there, and the staring people revolted (Hopkins 1883:137–146).

The future of the Northern Paiute, as well as other Shoshonean groups of the Great Basin remained highly uncertain as they entered the reservation period. The many influences of Euroamerican culture had seriously compromised the cultural integrity of these Native Americans, as out of necessity, they grew increasingly dependent upon white society. With their aboriginal population severely reduced by war and disease, the Northern Paiute attempted to retain elements of traditional culture while adapting to the disruption caused by Euroamerican settlement and development.

Southern Paiute

The last Great Basin group to be discussed here is the Southern Paiute, a member of the Southern Numic branch of the Uto-Aztecan linguistic family which includes the Chemhuevi, a closely related group (Kelly 1964:1; Euler 1966:2; Kelly and Fowler 1986:368). At the time of contact, the Southern Paiute occupied a crescent-shaped area that extended from the southern California deserts into southern Nevada, and reached the high plateaus of southcentral Utah and northern Arizona (Kelly and Fowler 1986:368).

In precontact times, Southern Paiutes were organized into small extended family camp groups for most of the year. These kin-based social units were economically self-sufficient, as there was no overall "tribal" organization, or individuals who exerted control over large numbers of people. Many Southern Paiute groups practiced a limited type of garden horticulture, based on the cultivation of corn, beans, squash, sunflowers, and other native plant species (Kelly 1964:39–41; Fowler and Fowler 1971:101).

Some incipient band organization did develop among the Southern Paiute in historic times (Euler 1966:100–101), but this phenomenon was mostly a response to interaction with the U. S. government and its various representatives, who wished to communicate and negotiate with a central tribal figure (Manners 1974:33–35; 212–214).

Spanish colonization of the American Southwest, which began in 1540, had little direct impact upon Southern Paiute culture for approximately 250 years. Nevertheless, there were indirect impacts, as the Southern Paiute probably knew of the Spanish presence, and may have obtained a few items of their material culture through trade with other Indian groups. An additional indirect effect of Spanish settlement may have been the introduction of European diseases to various Southern Paiute peoples before actual contact (Fowler and Fowler 1971:150).

The most significant and best documented direct impact of Spanish presence in the southwest was the slave raiding complex of the early nineteenth century. Mounted parties of Utes and Navajos, as well as Spaniards, Mexicans, and white trappers participated in slaving activities, in which Southern Paiutes were abducted and sold in New Mexico and southern California (Fowler and Fowler 1981:150; Kelly and Fowler 1986:386).

Explorers and Trappers.

The earliest Euroamerican contact with the Southern Paiute occurred in 1776, when the Franciscan priest Father Francisco Garcés and Juan de Anza led an exploratory party into the southernmost portion of the Great Basin in California (Cline 1963:35–38; Euler 1966:99). It was during this expedition that Garcés and Anza encountered a number of Chemehuevi Indians in the Mojave River region. Several months after this initial Spanish penetration, another expedition led by Fathers Francis Domínguez and Silvestre Escalante entered the Great Basin from the east (Bolton 1950; Stewart 1952:47), and travelled southward from Utah Lake to the Colorado Plateau of Arizona. The Escalante party was probably the first Euroamerican group to contact the Southern Paiute of Utah and Arizona (Fowler and Fowler 1971:102). In his journal, Escalante described aspects of native ideology, material culture, and subsistence activities, describing what were mostly aboriginal conditions.

Like the Garcés-Anza expedition before them, the Escalante-Domínguez party was searching for an overland route to link the Spanish settlements of Santa Fe, New Mexico, and Monterey, Alta California (Bolton 1950:9; Cline 1963:43–48). Although they failed to accomplish this goal completely, the Escalante-Domínguez expedition did succeed in pioneering a portion of the Old Spanish Trail.

Information concerning early modification of Southern Paiute culture was furnished by Jedediah Smith in 1826, when he met either Chemehuevi or Paiute groups along the Mojave River. At this time, some Southern Paiutes possessed horses, iron, and blue cloth (Brooks 1977:42–43). Smith traded with these natives, obtaining horses, "cane grass candy", and water jugs in exchange for colored cloth, glass beads, and metal knives (Euler 1966:97).

Early use of the Spanish Trail had a substantial impact upon the Southern Paiute. The great demand for horses and mules in the southwest and midwest portions of North America caused Ute, Navajo, Spanish, and American parties to travel over this new route to southern California on both raiding and trading expeditions to obtain livestock (Kelly 1964:87, 89; Malouf 1966:11). By 1830, regular excursions were passing back and forth along the Old Spanish Trail. Various Southern Paiute groups soon had access to horses and other articles of Euroamerican material culture. Early on, most Southern Paiutes ate the horses that they acquired (Frémont 1845:263).

Use of the Old Spanish Trail also depleted resources along the route, and displaced natives that had previously occupied the area (Malouf and Findlay 1986:507). The trade in mules and horses along the trail precipitated the slave trade of the early nineteenth century. Slave raiding had the most profound impact upon the Southern Paiute, causing them to withdraw from optimal resource areas, and to lose a substantial portion of their population. Slavery as a cultural institution was minimally developed in the aboriginal Southwest, but in postcontact times it became a lucrative business among equestrian natives, most notably the Ute and Navajo.

Slave Trade.

The spread of horses to the Ute and Navajo during the eighteenth century increased their mobility and intensified their contact with the Southern Paiute. Equipped with horses, Ute and Navajo raiders were able to exploit neighboring Indian groups for slaves (Snow 1929; Malouf and Malouf 1945:382).

The promotion of slavery as part of the Spanish social system influenced many native groups of the Southwest culture area, as well as those of the eastern Great Basin. In later times, Euroamericans, and Spanish-Mexicans also participated in the slave trade. Slave sources were usually divided into two categories: those acquired in relatively peaceful interactions, such as barter or exchange, and gambling; and those acquired by force, such as through organized raids and warfare (Malouf and Malouf 1945:389).

Hunger was oftentimes a major factor in stimulating the sale of children by the Southern Paiute, as there is documentation of Indians trading children to whites, Mexicans, Utes, and Navajos in exchange for horses, which were usually eaten (Fowler and Fowler 1971:104).

The earliest known documentation of the slave trade in the Great Basin described the encounter in 1813 between mounted natives of Utah Lake (most likely Utes) and the Spanish traders Anza and Garcia. Under sworn testimony, the men had declared that these natives had insisted on selling them slaves, and when the Spaniards refused, had killed at least eight of their horses (Snow 1929:68; Malouf and Malouf 1945:380).

In 1839, T. J. Farnham (1843:248–249) reported that "Piutes" living near the Sevier River were exploited by slave traders:

> These poor creatures are hunted in the spring of the year, when they are weak and helpless, by a certain class of men, and when taken, are fattened, taken to Santa Fe and sold as slaves in their minority. "A likely girl" in her teens brings oftentimes 60 pounds or 80 pounds. The males are valued less.

Children who become captives of slavers were treated cruelly, as they were often starved and beaten. They were also killed if they became a burden to their captors through sickness or inability to travel.

The slave trade had various effects upon the Southern Paiute. Foremost was the reduction of their population, as the young members who were the crucial component of their breeding stock were most sought after by slave raiders (Kelly and Fowler 1986:386). Slave raids among the Southern Paiute forced some groups to become increasingly hostile to mounted strangers, while others became more shy and apprehensive, withdrawing from contact with outsiders. In 1826, Jedediah Smith noted that some Southern Paiutes were afraid of mounted groups, and had hidden their women and children as his party approached (Brooks 1977:49–53).

Fear of slave raiding also resulted in the withdrawal of Southern Paiutes from important resource areas near trails and rivers (Kelly and Fowler 1986:386). Departure from favored ecological settings may also have repressed the expansion of horticulture during the early Historic period (Fowler and Fowler 1981:151).

Although mounted Ute parties often raided Southern Paiute camp groups for slaves, they were also responsible for modifying Paiute material culture. Utes introduced horses, tipis, guns, kettles, knives, and dogs to various Southern Paiute peoples (Fowler and Fowler 1971:105; Manners 1974:200).

Mormon Settlement.

Mormon settlement in Utah in 1847 ushered in a new era of contact and cultural modification for the Southern Paiute. Mormons intended to remain in Utah, and therefore had to develop a stable relationship with local natives. Brigham Young instituted a policy of friendliness towards natives which was designed to minimize tensions between the two groups. This practical Mormon strategy was based on the premise that it was cheaper to clothe and feed the Indians than it was to fight them.

During the early years of their settlement, Mormons became unwilling participants in the slave trade. Mormons were forced to buy Southern Paiute children from Ute bands who killed the youngsters if the Mormons refused to cooperate (Malouf and Malouf 1945:384–386; Kelly and Fowler 1986:386). Actions taken by Brigham Young and the territorial legislature ultimately ended the slave trade in Utah (Fowler and Fowler 1971:106).

In spite of this, the positive effects of Mormon intervention in the native slave trade were soon offset by the various negative effects of their settlement. Mormon farms and towns displaced Southern Paiutes from their best hunting and gathering, and horticultural lands. Traditional food resources were depleted by grazing livestock, plowing, timbering, and other activities.

Another Mormon modification of aboriginal Paiute culture was the halt of the native burning of meadows and grasslands (Stewart 1952:49). Prior to white settlement, both Ute and Southern Paiute had burned brush away from meadows "in order to provide open, clean, grassy pastures to attract wild game and thereby facilitate hunting" (Stewart 1952:49). As the Mormons put an end to this practice, former grasslands turned into sagebrush-covered valleys or were turned into agricultural fields (Malouf and Findlay 1986:510).

The degradation of traditional subsistence resources had reduced a large portion of the Southern Paiute to extreme poverty by 1860 (Forney 1860). The condition of the Southern Paiute in the early 1870s was aptly described by John W. Powell and George W. Ingalls (1874:431):

> They are broken into many small tribes, and their homes so interspersed among the settlements of the white men that their power is entirely broken and no fear should be entertained of a general war with them. The time has passed when it was necessary to buy peace. It only remains to decide what should be done with them for the relief of the white people from their petty depredations and from

the demoralizing influences accompanying the presence of savages in civilized communities, and also for the best interests of the Indians themselves.

The Mormon presence also further modified Southern Paiute material culture. By the 1860s and 1870s, most groups had access to items such as metal arrowheads, iron and brass buckets, canned goods, pans, and cast-off clothing (Euler 1966:98, 115–116). These natives also obtained bottles, from which they produced glass projectile points (Euler 1966:114–115).

There was also a change in traditional social organization. By the early 1870s, some Southern Paiutes had mobilized their loosely organized kin cliques into larger and more complex political and residential units. Some of these "bands" had spokesmen or "chiefs" who served as go-betweens for the entire group (Fowler and Fowler 1971:108).

Traditional religious practices were modified to some extent by the activities of Mormon missionaries who held mass baptisms among local groups (Malouf and Findlay 1986:509–510). The overall impact on traditional belief systems by Mormon missionaries was probably negligible, as native groups most likely accommodated the Mormons in order to minimize tensions. However, the process of linguistic acculturation was substantial, as English loanwords were added to earlier loans from Spanish, and linguistic modification had begun (Fowler and Fowler 1971:152).

Native Resistance and Accommodation.

Not all Southern Paiute and Chemehuevi groups reacted passively to native and Euroamerican exploitation. Some became mounted and formed predatory bands, raiding settlements and travellers during the 1850s and 1860s (Euler 1966:103). Kelly and Fowler (1986:387) have also noted that "Some Chemehuevis, alone or with Mojave allies, raided miners in northern Arizona and travelers along southern California desert trails from the 1860s to the early 1870s."

Although predatory bands did develop among the Southern Paiute, it should be emphasized that normal economic activities during this period were still carried out by extended family camp groups. Ties of allegiance probably were strong only during times of military conflict. According to Euler (1966:103), the Southern Paiute ". . . never amassed large numbers for battle, but resorted to ambushes of small parties or stragglers, and to hit and run tactics."

By the mid 1870s, most Southern Paiute groups had experienced either temporary or continuous contact with Euroamericans for at least a decade. Most natives who did not participate in organized raids settled on lands adjacent to Mormon farms and towns. Mormon settlements offered economic advantages such as food, clothing, and wage labor, as well as some protection from marauding native bands. Here, as elsewhere throughout the Great Basin, Native Americans combined components of aboriginal subsistence systems with unskilled labor, begging, and scavenging in order to sustain themselves.

Euroamerican contact with the Southern Paiute, and the subsequent settlement of their lands, elicited a number of changes in the traditional lifeway of these people. As with the other three Shoshonean groups discussed above, rapid depletion of the aboriginal subsistence base forced Southern Paiutes to implement new adaptive strategies to effectively deal with the contact situation. New levels of social organization were utilized to minimize the adverse effects of historic developments within their home range.

Discussion

The nineteenth century was a time of rapid cultural change for Great Basin Shoshoneans. Euroamerican expansion in this region had seriously impacted native resources, and corresponding aboriginal exploitative strategies that had been practiced for millennia. Numic-speaking peoples usually reacted to the process of white emigration and settlement in one of several ways. During early contact, many camp groups chose to isolate themselves from Euroamericans in an attempt to pursue an aboriginal lifestyle. However, the viability of this strategy diminished rapidly as whites claimed and developed increasing amounts of land. This forced natives onto smaller and more marginal lands, and compelled them to cooperate with each other more extensively. Such was the impetus for the development of new levels of social organization by Shoshoneans in their efforts to adapt to historic conditions (Malouf and Findlay 1986:515).

As Great Basin natives lost most of their traditional subsistence resources, they formed both mounted and unmounted ''bands'' in order to exploit Euroamerican travellers and settlements for food and material goods. ''Band'' organization was short-lived for most Shoshonean peoples, as military defeats of the 1860s further reduced the indigenous population and their will to fight. By the early 1870s, most predatory bands had dispersed, and many groups reverted to the small, extended family units that had been the focal point of social organization prior to introduction of the horse.

As native resistance to white encroachment was gradually eradicated, Great Basin natives became increasingly dependent upon white society. No longer able to move about freely to exploit traditional resources, the majority of Shoshoneans became progressively sedentary, forming small communities on the outskirts of towns, or attaching themselves as families or individuals to farms and ranches. These groups were incorporated into local economies, but still managed to retain aspects of traditional culture, as well as some degree of autonomy (Clemmer 1978:62–63). An example of this was the continued practice of the fall pinyon harvest. This activity temporarily depleted the local native work force of white communities, which had become dependent upon the native workers. During historic pine nut harvests, entire urban Indian populations deserted their ''improved conditions'' and moved en masse to the pinyon groves (Wells 1983). This communal activity, which is still prevalent today, functioned to maintain Shoshonean cultural identity, and allowed these people to feel some sense of independence in spite of being surrounded by adversity. Retention of traditional lifestyles was most successful in areas of the Great Basin where Euroamerican contact and development had been minimal, and in those components of society least influenced by Euroamerican material culture.

In an overall sense, acculturation of Great Basin Shoshoneans into white society was incomplete. Some, but certainly not all aspects of aboriginal culture, such as economic and sociopolitical organization, and material culture, were modified and partially replaced by corresponding Euroamerican elements. However, the establishment of reservations, although in many cases on marginal lands, allowed some Shoshoneans to pursue some aspects of traditional culture and to maintain group identity by being isolated from white society.

The Great Basin Culture Area Today

Establishment of Reservations and Federal Policies

As lands in the Great Basin were organized into United States territories in the mid-nineteenth century, an official Indian policy for the region was developed in Washington. This policy was based on the assumption that most western lands would be claimed and developed by whites, and that Shoshonean groups would be prevented from occupying and/or using those areas that they had previously inhabited (Clemmer and Stewart 1986:525). The government decided that it was best to establish reservations in or near the natives' aboriginal home ranges, where they could be contained, isolated from Euroamerican populations, and taught agricultural and stock-raising skills that would eventually enable them to become self-sufficient.

Toward the end of the nineteenth century, there were 20 Indian reservations in the Great Basin (Clemmer and Stewart 1986:Fig. 4). It was during this time that Ulysses S. Grant initiated what has been termed the "Pan-Reservation Policy" (Clemmer and Stewart 1986:539). This began in 1869, and was an attempt to streamline the administration of Indian affairs and to apply a blanket policy to all United States reservations. As noted by Clemmer and Stewart (1986:539), the purpose of such a policy was:

> . . . to de-Indianize the Indians: to make them into rural farmers of Christian faith, literate in English (and preferably speaking no other language), "unfettered" by ancient traditions and customs, and skilled in blue-collar professions that would turn Indian communities into approximations of rural American towns. The cornerstones of the policy were: a resident agent for each reservation; one or more Christian missions for each community; establishment of farming as the dominant economic strategy, regardless of the pre-existing expertise of their inhabitants; removal of all Indians to reservations or creation of reservations around them; and implementation of behavioral codes meant to encourage acculturation.

This policy was clearly one that promoted a type of bureaucratic genocide, in which Native American culture would be done away with by making it illegal to practice traditional culture. For example, shamanism and native religion were banned, and children were forced to attend government-operated schools where native languages were not allowed to be spoken, and sectarian Christian instruction was the order of the day. This policy was dominant from 1870–1890.

347

The Pan Reservation Policy was followed by the Allotment Period (1890–1933) (Clemmer and Stewart 1986:543–546), in which the government attempted to abolish various Great Basin reservations and either allot all reservation lands to Indians in severalty, or to have the natives moved onto other reservations. As reservations were being divided into allotments, and occupied by white homesteaders, off-reservation natives were being concentrated onto small parcels that became known as "camps" or "colonies."

The "Indian New Deal" (1933–1945) was instituted by then Commissioner of Indian Affairs director John Collier for his efforts to reform the United States government's Indian policy. Collier halted the allotment of native lands, restored former reservation lands, created new reservations for native groups that had none, encouraged the practice of traditional culture, improved health care, and established federal programs of employment, community development, college scholarships, and loans for individuals and tribes (Philp 1977:113–134; Taylor 1980:18–31).

The Indian Reorganization Act of 1934 introduced the tribal council system, which began the process of native self-determination. Following this, the Indian Claims Commission Act of 1946 set into motion the process of adjudicating Indian claims, most of which stemmed from the United States government's securing of native lands through past treaties. The Indian Claims Commission determined the dates that specific parcels of native land were taken, how much was taken, and the value of the land at the time it was taken. These decisions were made in response to legal documents filed by attorneys for various Indian groups and for the government (Clemmer and Stewart 1986:551). These hearings resulted in a total of $137,206,129.00 being made available to Great Basin tribes as compensation for lands and other resources taken without payment (Clemmer and Stewart 1986:553).

The Contemporary Situation

The Self-Determination Era started in 1964, as the Johnson administration implemented social and economic improvement programs on Great Basin reservations and colonies. This policy brought on-the-job training programs for youths and adults, housing developments financed and constructed through the Department of Housing and Urban Development Administration, community action programs, Headstart centers, and various educational and rehabilitational programs (Clemmer and Stewart 1986:553).

On reservations, tribal governments were given priority in bidding to operate various federally funded programs, and local non-Indian businesses were provided with economic incentives to establish operations on reservation lands, and to employ native workers.

By 1972, numerous Great Basin reservations had developed programs in which: the vast majority of employment was provided by federal agencies or tribal governments, seniors had access to improved health care as well as subsidized meal and recreation programs, and annual tribal budgets registered in hundreds of thousands of dollars.

Contemporary Great Basin native economies have grown as the result of federal grants and tribal contracts, which have provided the necessary capital for first time investments and subsequent expansions of tribal business pursuits (Knack 1986). Various groups have successfully marketed agricultural products and native crafts, and have established on-reservation enterprises such as fish hatcheries (i.e., Pyramid Lake), and smoke shops. Additionally, economic growth of Great Basin tribes in the 1980s has resulted from mineral, gas, and oil leases and royalties from large energy corporations.

In recent years, Great Basin groups have continued to encounter difficulties in retaining their lands and resources, as outside forces desire to obtain and/or exploit native lands, water, and minerals. However, with the help of tribal leaders and lawyers, as well as government representatives and agencies, Great Basin Indian peoples have been able to protect their lands and to maintain themselves as separate economic and cultural entities from the dominant Euroamerican society.

Although several reservations and various rancherias have succeeded in developing economic programs, and in interfacing with the dominant white economy and culture, most Great Basin native peoples today are in rather desperate straits. The cattle industry is depressed, and the effects of impoverishment and cultural devastation have resulted in alcoholism, and problems with drugs and crime. The cutting and chaining of pinyon pine over hundreds of thousands of acres in order to provide more cattle range (almost all of it uneconomic), has led to protest movements and much sorrow. Various improvements have been made in the lives of contemporary Great Basin natives, but serious economic and social problems still persist.

Conflicts between traditionalist and progressive intertribal factions are among the most important kinds of contemporary group problems that threaten Great Basin native cultural identity. Although these conflicts raise a certain amount of concern, they do not necessarily mean that traditional orientations are disappearing and that the majority of these people will soon be fully assimilated into the melting pot of American society (cf. Rusco and Rusco 1986:571). Factionalism has always existed in human political systems, and it remains to be seen whether or not this phenomenon will seriously damage native identity. As long as Great Basin peoples retain reservation lands, they will most likely be able to operate as a distinct cultural group, and to continue practicing a semi-traditional lifestyle.

SUGGESTED READINGS

Cline, Gloria G.
    1963   Exploring the Great Basin. Norman: University of Oklahoma Press.

d'Azevedo, Warren L., Wilbur A. Davis, Don D. Fowler, and Wayne Suttles, eds.
    1966   The Current Status of Anthropological Research in the Great Basin: 1964. Desert Research Institute Technical Report Series, Social Sciences and Humanities Publications No. 1. Reno.

d'Azevedo, Warren L., ed.
    1986   Handbook of North American Indians, Vol. 11: Great Basin. Washington, D. C.: Smithsonian Institution.

Hopkins, Sarah Winnemucca
    1883   Life Among the Paiutes: Their Wrongs and Claims. Mrs. Horace Mann, ed. Boston: Cupples Upham. (Reprinted 1969, Chalfant Press, Bishop, California.)

Madsen, David B., and James F. O'Connell, eds.
1982   Man and Environment in the Great Basin. Society for American Archaeology Papers No. 2. Washington, D. C.: Society for American Archaeology.

Simpson, Captain James H.
1876   Report and Journal. In: Report of Explorations Across the Great Basin of the Territory of Utah for a Direct Wagon Route from Camp Floyd to Genoa, in Carson Valley, in 1859. Washington, D. C.: Government Printing Office. (Reprinted 1983, University of Nevada Press, Reno.)

Steward, Julian H.
1938   Basin-Plateau Aboriginal Sociopolitical Groups. Bureau of American Ethnology Bulletin 120. (Reprinted 1970, University of Utah Press, Salt Lake City).
1941   Culture Element Distributions: XIII Nevada Shoshone. University of California Anthropological Records 4(2):209–359. Berkeley.
1943   Culture Element Distributions: XXIII Northern and Gosiute Shoshone. University of California Anthropological Records 8(3):263–392. Berkeley.
1970   The Foundations of Basin-Plateau Shoshonean Society. In: Languages and Cultures of Western North America: Essays in Honor of Sven Liljeblad, Earl Swanson, Jr., ed., pp. 113–151. Pocatello: Idaho State University Press.

Stewart, Omer C.
1941   Culture Element Distributions: XIV Northern Paiute. University of California Anthropological Records 4(3):361–446. Berkeley.
1942   Culture Element Distributions: XVIII Ute-Southern Paiute. University of California Anthropological Records 6(4):231–355. Berkeley.

REFERENCES

Adovasio, James M.
1986   Preshistoric Basketry. In: Handbook of North American Indians, Vol. 11: Great Basin, Warren L. d'Azevedo, ed., pp. 194–205. Washington, D. C.: Smithsonian Institution.

Aikens, C. Melvin
1978   The Far West. In: Ancient Native Americans, Jesse D. Jennings, ed., pp. 131–181. San Francisco: W. H. Freeman.

Allen, James B., and T. J. Warner
1971   The Gosiute Indians in Pioneer Utah. Utah Historical Quarterly 39(2):162–172.

Ambro, Richard D.
1972   Preliminary Observations on the Surface Archaeology of Ridge Village North, an Historic Period Shoshone Village. Nevada Archaeological Survey, Research Paper No. 3, pp. 85–106.

Arkush, Brooke S.
1986   Aboriginal Exploitation of Pronghorn in the Great Basin. Journal of Ethnobiology 6(2):239–255.
1987a   A Summary of Work Completed During the 1986 Field Season at CA-Mno-2122, a Protohistoric/Historic Site in Mono Basin, Mono County, California. (MS on file at the Archaeological Research Unit, Department of Anthropology, University of California, Riverside.)
1987b   A Summary of Work Completed During the 1987 Field Season at CA-Mno-2122. (MS on file at the Archaeological Research Unit, Department of Anthropology, University of California, Riverside.)

Bedwell, Stephen F.
1970   Prehistory and Environment of the Pluvial Fort Rock Area of Southcentral Oregon. Unpublished Ph.D. Dissertation in Anthropology, University of Oregon, Eugene.

Bettinger, Robert L.
1976   Flat Iron Ridge Site, 26-Ny-313. In: Prehistoric Pinyon Ecotone Settlements of the Upper Reese River Valley, Central Nevada, by David H. Thomas and Robert L. Bettinger. Anthropological Papers of the American Museum of Natural History 53(3):313–327.

Billeb, Emil W.
1968   Mining Camp Days. Berkeley: Howell North Books.

Bolton, Herbert E.
1950   Pageant in the Wilderness: The Story of the Escalante Expedition to the Interior Basin, 1776. Utah Historical Quarterly 18(1–4):1–265.

Brimlow, George F.
1938   The Bannock Indian War of 1878. Cadwell, Idaho: Caxton Printers.

Brooks, George R., ed.
1977   The Southwest Expedition of Jedediah S. Smith: His Personal Account of the Journey to California, 1826–1827. Glendale, California: The Arthur H. Clark Co.

Cain, Ella M.
1961   The Story of Early Mono County. San Francisco: Fearon Publishers, Inc.

Calhoun, Margaret
1984   Pioneers of Mono Basin. Lee Vining, California: Artemisia Press.

Chalfant, Willie A.
1933   The Story of Inyo. Bishop, California: Chalfant Press. (Reprinted 1975, Chalfant Press.)

Christensen, E. M., and H. B. Johnson
1964   Presettlement Vegetation and Vegetational Change in Three Valleys in Central Utah. Brigham Young University Science Bulletin, Biology Series 4:1–16.

Clemmer, Richard D.
1974   Land Use Patterns and Aboriginal Rights: Northern and Eastern Nevada, 1858–1971. The Indian Historian 7(1):24–41, 47–49.

Clemmer, Richard O., and Omer C. Stewart
1986   Treaties, Reservations, and Claims. In: Handbook of North American Indians, Vol. 11: Great Basin, Warren L. d'Azevedo, ed., pp. 525–557. Washington, D. C.: Smithsonian Institution.

Clewlow, C. William, Jr., and Allen G. Pastron
1972   Preliminary Archaeological Investigations in Grass Valley. In: The Grass Valley Archaeological Project: Collected Papers, C. William Clewlow, Jr., and Mary Rusco, eds. Nevada Archaeological Survey Research Paper No. 3, pp. 11–32.
1978   Ethnoarchaeology and Acculturation in Grass Valley. In: History and Prehistory at Grass Valley, Nevada, C. William Clewlow, Jr., Helen F. Wells, and Richard D. Ambro, eds., pp. 163–173. Monograph VII, Institute of Archaeology, University of California, Los Angeles.

Clewlow, C. William, Jr., Helen F. Wells, and Richard D. Ambro, eds.
1978   History and Prehistory at Grass Valley, Nevada. Monograph VII, Institute of Archaeology, University of California, Los Angeles.

Cline, Gloria G.
1963   Exploring the Great Basin. Norman: University of Oklahoma Press.
1974   Peter Skene Ogden and the Hudson's Bay Company. Norman: University of Oklahoma Press.

Crosby, Alfred W., Jr.
1976   Virgin Soil Epidemics as a Factor in the Aboriginal Depopulation in America. William and Mary Quarterly 3rd Series, 33(2):289–299.

Daubenmire, Rexford R.
1979   Plants and Environment: A Textbook for Plant Autecology. New York: Wiley.

Davis, Emma Lou
1965   An Ethnography of the Kuzedika Paiute of Mono Lake, Mono County, California. In: Miscellaneous Collected Papers 8–10, No. 8, University of Utah Anthropological Papers No. 75, pp. 1–55.

d'Azevedo, Warren L.
1986   Introduction. In: Handbook of North American Indians, Vol. 11: Great Basin, Warren L. d'Azevedo, ed., pp. 1–14. Washington, D. C.: Smithsonian Institution.

Downs, James F.
1963   Differential Response to White Contact: Paiute and Washo. University of Utah Anthropological Papers No. 67, pp. 115–137.

DuBois, Cora A.
1939   The 1870 Ghost Dance. University of California Publications in American Archaeology and Ethnology 3:1–151.

Egan, Howard R.
1917   Pioneering the West, 1846–1878. Richmond, Utah: Howard R. Egan Estate.

Egan, Ferol
1972   Sand in a Whirlwind: The Paiute Indian War of 1860. New York: Doubleday and Company, Inc.

Eggan, Fred
1980   Shoshone Kinship Structures and Their Significance for Anthropological Theory. Journal of the Steward Anthropological Society 11(2):165–193.

Elliot, R. R.
1973   History of Nevada. Lincoln: University of Nebraska Press.

Euler, Robert C.
1966   Southern Paiute Ethnohistory. Glen Canyon Series No. 28, University of Utah Anthropological Papers No. 78.

Euler, Robert C., and Catherine S. Fowler
1973   Southern Paiute Ethnohistory. University of Utah Anthropological Papers No. 78.

Farnham, Thomas J.
1843   Travels in the Great Western Prairies, The Anahuac and Rocky Mountains, and in the Oregon Territory. New York: Greely and McElrath. (Reprinted: 1906 in vols. 28–29 of Early Western Travels, Reuben G. Thwaites, ed. Cleveland: Arthur H. Clark.)

Fletcher, Thomas C.
1982   The Mono Basin in the Nineteenth Century: Discovery, Settlement, Land Use. Unpublished M. A. Thesis in Geography, University of California, Berkeley.
1987   Paiute, Prospector, Pioneer: A History of the Bodie-Mono Lake Area in the Nineteenth Century. Lee Vining, California: Artemisia Press.

Forbes, Jack D.
1967   Nevada Indians Speak. Reno: University of Nevada Press.

Forney, Jacob
1860   Report of the Utah Superintendency, Great Salt Lake City, September 29, 1859. In: Papers Accompanying the Annual Report of the Commissioner of Indian Affairs, 1859, No. 174. Executive Documents, 36th Congress, 1st Session, Document No. 2, pp. 730–741. Washington, D. C.: Government Printing Office.

Fowler, Catherine S.
1986   Subsistence. In: Handbook of North American Indians, Vol. 11: Great Basin, Warren L. d'Azevedo, ed., pp. 64–97. Washington, D. C.: Smithsonian Institution.

Fowler, Catherine S., and Lawrence E. Dawson
1986   Ethnographic Basketry. In: Handbook of North American Indians, Vol. 11: Great Basin, Warren L. d'Azevedo, ed., pp. 705–737. Washington, D. C.: Smithsonian Institution.

Fowler, Catherine S., and Don D. Fowler
1971   Notes on the History of the Southern Paiutes and Western Shoshonis. Utah Historical Quarterly 39(2): 95–113.

1981   The Southern Paiute: A. D. 1400–1776. In: the Protohistoric Period in the American Southwest, A. D. 1450–1700, David R. Wilcox and Bruce Masse, eds., pp. 129–162. Arizona State University Anthropological Research Papers No. 24.

Fowler, Catherine S., and Sven Liljeblad
1986   Northern Paiute. In: Handbook of North American Indians, Vol. 11: Great Basin, Warren L. d'- Azevedo, ed., pp. 435–465. Washington, D. C.: Smithsonian Institution.

Fowler, Don D.
1966   Great Basin Social Organization. In: The Current Status of Anthropological Research in the Great Basin: 1964, Warren L. d'Azevedo, Wilbur A. Davis, Don D. Fowler, and Wayne Suttles, eds., pp. 57–74. University of Nevada Desert Research Institute Social Sciences and Humanities Publications No. 1.

Frémont, John C.
1845   Narrative of the Exploring Expedition of the Rocky Mountains in the year 1842; and to Oregon and North California in the Years 1843–1844. Washington, D. C.: Gales and Seaton.
1887   Memoirs of My Life, Including in the Narrative Five Journeys of the Western Exploration During the Years 1842 . . . 1849, 1853–54. 2 Vols. Chicago: Belford, Clark and Co.

Gheen, Levi A.
1876   Report of the Commissioner of Indian Affairs for 1876. Washington, D. C.: Government Printing Office.

Gould, Richard A., Don D. Fowler, and Catherine S. Fowler
1972   Diggers and Doggers: Parallel Failures in Economic Acculturation. Southwestern Journal of Anthropology 28(3):265–281.

Gudde, Erwin G., and Elisabeth K. Gudde
1958   Exploring With Fremont: The Private Diaries of Charles Preuss, Cartographer for John C. Fremont on His First, Second, and Fourth Expeditions to the Far West. Norman: University of Oklahoma Press.

Haines, Francis
1938   The Northward Spread of Horses Among the Plains Indians. American Anthropologist 40(3):429–437.

Harper, Kimball T.
1986   Historical Environments. In: Handbook of North American Indians, Vol. 11: Great Basin, Warren L. d'Azevedo, ed., pp. 51–63. Washington, D. C.: Smithsonian Institution.

Harris, Jack S.
1940   The White Knife Shoshoni of Nevada. In: Acculturation of Seven American Indian Tribes, Ralph Linton, ed., pp. 39–118. New York: D. Appleton-Century Company, Inc.

Hattori, Eugene M.
1975   Northern Paiutes on the Comstock: Archaeology and History of an American Indian Population in Virginia City, Nevada. Nevada State Museum Occasional Papers No. 2, pp. iv–82, Donald R. Tuohy and D. L. Rendall, eds. Carson City: Nevada State Museum.

Hittman, Michael
1973   The 1870 Ghost Dance at the Walker River Reservation: A Reconstruction. Ethnohistory 20(3):247–278.

Hopkins, Sarah Winnemucca
1883   Life Among the Paiutes: Their Wrongs and Claims. Boston: Cupples, Upham. (Reprinted 1969, Chalfant Press, Bishop, California.)

Hultkrantz, Åke
1976   Religion and Ecology Among the Great Basin Indians: In the Realm of the Extra-human: Ideas and Actions, A. Bharati, ed., pp. 137–150. The Hague: Mouton.

1986   Mythology and Religious Concepts. In: Handbook of North American Indians, Vol. 11: Great Basin, Warren L. d'Azevedo, ed., pp. 630–640. Washington, D. C.: Smithsonian Institution.

Jennings, Jesse D.
1957   Danger Cave. University of Utah Anthropological Papers No. 27.
1986   Prehistory: Introduction. In: Handbook of North American Indians, Vol. 11: Great Basin, Warren L. d'Azevedo, ed., pp. 113–119. Washington, D. C.: Smithsonian Institution.

Jorgensen, Joseph G.
1972   The Sun Dance Religion: Power for the Powerless. Chicago: The University of Chicago Press.

Kelly, Isabel T.
1964   Southern Paiute Ethnography. Glen Canyon Series No. 21, University of Utah Anthropological Papers No. 69.

Kelly, Isabel T., and Catherine S. Fowler
1986   Southern Paiute. In: Handbook of North American Indians, Vol. 11: Great Basin, Warren L. d'-Azevedo, ed., pp. 368–397. Washington, D. C.: Smithsonian Institution.

Kern, Edward M.
1876   Journal of Mr. Edward M. Kern of an Exploration of the Mary's or Humboldt River, Carson Lake and Owen's River and Lake, in 1845. In: Report of Explorations Across the Great Basin of the Territory of Utah for a Direct Wagon Route from Camp Floyd to Genoa, in Carson Valley, in 1859 by James H. Simpson, pp. 475–486 (Appendix Q). Washington, D. C.: Government Printing Office.

Knack, Martha C.
1986   Indian Economies, 1950–1980. In: Handbook of North American Indians, Vol. 11: Great Basin, Warren L. d'Azevedo, ed., pp. 573–591. Washington, D. C.: Smithsonian Institution.

Kroeber, Alfred L.
1934   Native American Population. American Anthropologist 36(1):1–25.

Lamb, Sydney M.
1958   Linguistic Prehistory in the Great Basin. International Journal of American Linguistics 24(2):95–100.

Lawton, Harry W., Philip J. Wilke, Mary DeDecker, and William M. Mason
1976   Agriculture Among the Paiutes of Owens Valley. Journal of California Anthropology 3(1):13–50.

Layton, Thomas N.
1977   Indian Rustlers of the High Rock. Archaeology 30(6):366–373.
1978   From Pottage to Portage: A Perspective on Aboriginal Horse Use in the Northern Great Basin Prior to 1850. Nevada Historical Society Quarterly 20(4):241–251.
1981   Traders and Raiders: Aspects of Trans-Basin and California Plateau Commerce, 1810–1830. Journal of California and Great Basin Anthropology 3(1):127–137.

Leland, Joy
1986   Population. In: Handbook of North American Indians, Vol. 11: Great Basin, Warren L. d'Azevedo, ed., pp. 608–619. Washington, D. C.: Smithsonian Institution.

Leonard, Zenas
1934   Narrative of the Adventures of Zenas Leonard. Milo M. Quaife, ed. Chicago: The Lakeside Press.

Lewis, Henry T.
1982   Fire Technology and Resource Management in Aboriginal North America and Australia. In: Resource Managers: North American and Australian Hunter-Gatherers, Nancy Williams and E. Hunn, eds., pp. 45–67. American Association for the Advancement of Science Selected Symposium 67. Boulder, Colorado: Western Press, Inc.

Liljeblad, Sven
1969   The Religious Attitude of the Shoshonean Indians. Rendezvous: Idaho State University Journal of Arts and Letters 4(1):47–58.

1986   Oral Tradition: Content and Style of Verbal Arts. In: Handbook of North American Indians, Vol. 11: Great Basin, Warren L. d'Azevedo, ed., pp. 641–659. Washington, D. C.: Smithsonian Institution.

Liljeblad, Sven, and Catherine S. Fowler
1986   Owens Valley Paiute. In: Handbook of North American Indians, Vol. 11: Great Basin, Warren L. d'-Azevedo, ed., pp. 412–434. Washington, D. C.: Smithsonian Institution.

Lockhart, Jacob
1862   Letter from Agent to Commissioner of Indian Affairs, March 1. National Archives, "Letters Received by the Office of Indian Affairs, 1824–1880", M-234, Roll 538.

Lowie, Robert H.
1909   The Northern Shoshone. Anthropological Papers of the American Museum of Natural History 2(2):165–307.
1915   Dances and Societies of the Plains Shoshone. Anthropological Papers of the American Museum of Natural History 11(10):803–835.

Lyman, George D.
1946   The Saga of the Comstock Lode: Boom Days in Virginia City. New York: Charles Scribner's Sons.

McKinney, Whitney
1983   A History of the Shoshone-Paiutes of the Duck Valley Indian Reservation. The Institute of the American West and Howe Brothers.

McNeil, William H.
1976   Plagues and Peoples. Garden City, New York: Anchor Books.

Madsen, Brigham D.
1980   The Northern Shoshone. Caldwell, Idaho: Caxton Printers.
1985   The Shoshone Frontier and the Bear River Massacre. Salt Lake City: University of Utah Press.

Madsen, David B.
1986   Prehistoric Ceramics. In: Handbook of North American Indians, Vol. 11: Great Basin, Warren L. d'-Azevedo, ed., pp. 206–214. Washington, D. C.: Smithsonian Institution.

Malouf, Carling
1966   Ethnohistory in the Great Basin. In: The Current Status of Anthropological Research in the Great Basin: 1964, Warren L. d'Azevedo, Wilbur A. Davis, Don D. Fowler, and Wayne Suttles, eds., pp. 1–38. University of Nevada, Desert Research Institute Social Sciences and Humanities Publications No. 1.
1974   The Gosiute Indians. In: Shoshone Indians, David A. Horr, ed., pp. 25–172. American Indian Ethnohistory: California and Basin-Plateau Indians. New York: Garland Publishing Inc.

Malouf, Carling, and A. A. Malouf
1945   The Effects of Spanish Slavery on the Indians of the Intermountain West. Southwestern Journal of Anthropology 1(3):378–391.

Malouf, Carling, and John M. Findlay
1986   Euro-American Impact Before 1870. In: Handbook of North American Indians, Vol. 11: Great Basin, Warren L. d'Azevedo, ed., pp. 499–516. Washington, D. C.: Smithsonian Institution.

Manners, Robert A.
1974   Southern Paiute and Chemehuevi: An Ethnohistorical Report. In: Paiute Indians I, David A. Horr, ed., pp. 29–300. American Indian Ethnohistory: California and Basin-Plateau Indians. New York: Garland Publishing Inc.

Miller, Wick R.
1966   Anthropological Linguistics in the Great Basin. In: The Current Status of Anthropological Research in the Great Basin: 1964, Warren L. d'Azevedo, Wilbur A. Davis, Don D. Fowler, and Wayne Suttles, eds., pp. 75–112. University of Nevada Desert Research Institute Social Sciences and Humanities Publications No. 1.

1986   Numic Languages. In: Handbook of North American Indians, Vol. 11: Great Basin, Warren L. d'-
        Azevedo, ed., pp. 98–106. Washington, D. C.: Smithsonian Institution.

Morrison, Roger B.
    1965   Quaternary Geology of the Great Basin. In: The Quaternary of the United States, Herbert E. Wright,
            Jr., and David G. Frey, eds., pp. 265–285. Princeton, New Jersey: Princeton University Press.

Muir, John
    1916   The Mountains of California. Boston: Houghton Mifflin Co.

Murphy, Robert F., and Yolanda Murphy
    1960   Shoshone-Bannock Subsistence and Society. University of California Anthropological Records
            16(7):293–338.
    1986   Northern Shoshone and Bannock. In: Handbook of North American Indians, Vol. 11: Great Basin,
            Warren L. d'Azevedo, ed., pp. 284–307. Washington, D. C.: Smithsonian Institution.

Nissen, Karen M.
    1982   Images From the Past: An Analysis of Six Western Great Basin Petroglyph Sites. Unpublished Ph.D.
            Dissertation in Anthropology, University of California, Berkeley.

Ogden, Peter S.
    1910   The Peter Skene Ogden Journals: Second Expedition to Snake Country, 1827–1828, and 1828–1829,
            T. C. Elliot, ed. Oregon Historical Quarterly 11:355–399.
    1950   Peter Skene Ogden's Snake Country Journal, 1826–1827. K. G. Davies and A. M. Johnson, eds.
            Publication XXIII, Hudson's Bay Record Society. London.

Park, Willard Z.
    1934   Paviotso Shamanism. American Anthropologist 36(1): 98–113.
    1938   Shamanism in Western North America: A Study in Cultural Relationships. Northwestern University
            Studies in the Sciences No. 2. Evanston, Illinois.
    1941   Cultural Succession in the Great Basin. In Language, Culture, and Personality: Essays in Memory of
            Edward Sapir, Leslie Spier, A. I. Hallowell, and Stanley S. Newman, eds., pp. 180–203. Menasha,
            Wisconsin: Sapir Memorial Publication Fund.

Philp, Kenneth R.
    1977   John Collier's Crusade for Indian Reform, 1920–1954. Tucson: University of Arizona Press.

Powell, John W., and George W. Ingalls
    1874   Report on the Conditions of the Ute Indians of Utah, the Paiutes of Utah, Northern Arizona, Southern
            Nevada, and Southeastern California; the Western Shoshones of Idaho and Utah; and the Western
            Shoshonies of Nevada; and Report Concerning Claims of Settlers in the Mo-a-pa Valley,
            Southeastern Nevada. In: Annual Report of the Commissioner of Indian Affairs for 1873, pp. 409–
            443. Washington, D. C.: Government Printing Office.

Roe, Frank G.
    1970   The North American Buffalo: A Critical Study of the Species in its Wild State. Toronto: University
            of Toronto Press.

Rosen, Martin D.
    1978   Faunal Remains as Indicators of Acculturation in the Great Basin. In: History and Prehistory at Grass
            Valley, Nevada. C. William Clewlow, Jr., Helen F. Wells, and Richard D. Ambro, eds., pp. 37–81.
            Monograph VII, Institute of Archaeology, University of California, Los Angeles.

Ross, Alexander
    1956   The Fur Hunters of the Far West. The American Exploration and Travel Series 20, Kenneth A.
            Spaulding, ed. Norman: University of Oklahoma Press.

Rusco, Mary K.
    1976   Fur Trappers in the Snake Country: An Ethnohistorical Approach to Recent Environmental Change.
            In: Holocene Environmental Change in the Great Basin, Robert Elston, ed. Nevada Archeological
            Survey Research Paper No. 8, pp. 152–173.

Rusco, Elmer R., and Mary K. Rusco
  1986   Tribal Politics. In: Handbook of North American Indians, Vol. 11: Great Basin, Warren L. d'-
          Azevedo, ed., pp. 558–572. Washington, D. C.: Smithsonian Institution.

Russell, Israel C.
  1889   Quarternary History of the Mono Valley, California. U. S. Geological Survey Eighth Annual Report,
          pp. 267–394.

Sawyer, B. W.
  1971   Nevada Nomads. San Jose, California: Harlan-Young Press.

Scott, Lalla
  1966   Karnee: A Paiute Narrative. Reno: University of Press Press.

Shapiro, Judith
  1986   Kinship. In: Handbook of Northern American Indians, Vol. 11: Great Basin, Warren L. d'Azevedo,
          ed., pp. 620–629. Washington, D. C.: Smithsonian Institution.

Shimkin, Demitri B.
  1953   The Wind River Shoshone Sun Dance. Anthropological Papers 41, Bureau of American Ethnology
          Bulletin 151: 397–484.
  1986   The Introduction of the Horse. In: Handbook of North American Indians, Vol. 11: Great Basin, War-
          ren L. d'Azevedo, ed. , pp. 517–524. Washington, D. C.: Smithsonian Institution.

Simpson, Captain James H.
  1876   Report of Explorations Across the Great Basin of the Territory of Utah for a Direct Wagon Route
          from Camp Floyd to Genoa, Carson Valley, in 1859. Washington, D. C.: Government Printing Of-
          fice.

Snow, William J.
  1929   Utah Indians and Spanish Slave Trade. Utah Historical Quarterly 2(3):67–90.

Spencer, Robert F., and Jesse D. Jennings
  1977   The Native Americans. New York: Harper and Row.

Steward, Julian H.
  1932   A Uintah Ute Bear Dance, March 1931. American Anthropologist 34(2):263–273.
  1933   Ethnography of the Owens Valley Paiute. University of California Publications in American Ar-
          chaeology and Ethnology 33(3):233–350.
  1938   Basin-Plateau Aboriginal Sociopolitical Groups. Bureau of American Ethnology Bulletin 120.
          Washington, D. C.: Government Printing Office. (Reprinted 1970, University of Utah Press, Salt
          Lake City.)
  1941   Culture Element Distributions: XIII, Nevada Shoshone. University of California Anthropological
          Records 4(2):209–259.
  1970   The Foundations of Basin-Plateau Shoshonean Society. In: Languages and Cultures of Western
          North America: Essays in Honor Sven Liljeblad, Earl Swanson, Jr., ed., pp. 113–151. Pocatello:
          Idaho State University Press.

Steward, Julian H., and Erminie Wheeler-Voegelin
  1974   The Northern Paiute Indians. In: Paiute Indians III, David A. Horr, ed., pp. 9–328. American Indian
          Ethnohistory: California and Basin-Plateau Indians. New York: Garland Publishing Inc.

Stewart, George R.
  1962   The California Trail. New York: McGraw-Hill Book Company.

Stewart, Omer C.
  1939   The Northern Paiute Bands. University of California Anthropological Records 2(3):127–149.
  1941   Culture Element Distributions: XIV, Northern Paiute. University of California Anthropological
          Records 4(3):361–446.
  1944   Washo-Northern Paiute Peyotism: A Study in Acculturation. University of California Publications in
          American Archaeology and Ethnology 40(3):63–142. (Reprinted 1984, University of Utah
          Anthropological Papers 108:47–127, Salt Lake City.)

1948   Ute Peyotism: A Study of a Cultural Complex. University of Colorado Studies, Series in Anthropology 1:1–42. Boulder. (Reprinted 1984, University of Utah Anthropological Papers 108:1–46, Salt Lake City.)

1952   Escalante and the Ute. Southwestern Lore 18(3):47–51.

1955   Forest and Grass Burning in the Intermountain West. Southwestern Lore 21(1):5–9.

1970   The Question of Bannock Territory. In: Languages and Cultures of Western North America: Essays in Honor of Sven Liljeblad, Earl Swanson, Jr., ed., pp. 201–231. Pocatello: Idaho State University Press.

1986   The Peyote Religion. In: Handbook of North American Indians, Vol. 11: Great Basin, Warren L. d'Azevedo, ed., pp. 673–681. Washington, D. C.: Smithsonian Institution.

Sutton, Mark Q.
1987   A Consideration of the Numic Spread. Unpublished Ph.D. Dissertation in Anthropology, University of California, Riverside.

Taylor, Graham D.
1980   The New Deal and American Indian Tribalism: The Administration of the Indian Reorganization Act, 1934–45. Lincoln: University of Nebraska Press.

Thomas, David H.
1971   Historic and Prehistoric Land Use Patterns at Reese River. Nevada Historical Society Quarterly 14(4):2–9.

1982   The Colonization of Monitor Valley, Nevada. Nevada Historical Society Quarterly 25(1):2–27.

Thomas, David H., Lorrann, S. A. Pendleton, and Steven C. Cappannari
1986   Western Shoshone. In: Handbook of North American Indians, Vol. 11: Great Basin, Warren L. d'Azevedo, ed., pp. 262–283. Washington, D. C.: Smithsonian Institution.

Thompson, David
1916   David Thompson's Narrative of His Explorations in Western North America, 1784–1812. Joseph B. Tyrell, ed. Publications of the Champlain Society 12. Toronto: The Champlain Society.

Waldorf, John T.
1970   A Kid on the Comstock. Palo Alto: American West Publishing Company.

Wedertz, Frank S.
1978   Mono Diggings. Bishop, California: Chalfant Press, Inc.

Wells, Helen F.
1978   Historical Accounts of Grass Valley, 1863–1872. In: History and Prehistory at Grass Valley, Nevada. C. William Clewlow, Jr., Helen F. Wells, and Richard D. Ambro, eds., pp. 13–33. Monograph VII, Institute of Archaeology, University of California, Los Angeles.

1983   Historic and Prehistoric Pinyon Exploitation in the Grass Valley Region, Central Nevada: A Case Study in Cultural Continuity and Change. Unpublished Ph.D. Dissertation in Anthropology, University of California, Riverside.

Wilke, Philip J., and Harry W. Lawton
1976   The Expedition of Captain J. W. Davidson from Fort Tejon to the Owens Valley in 1859. Ballena Press Publications in Archaeology, Ethnology and History No. 8.

Wright, Gary A., and Susanne J. Miller
1976   Prehistoric Hunting of New World Wild Sheep: Implications for the Study of Sheep Domestication. In: Cultural Change and Continuity: Essays in Honor of James Bennett Griffin, Charles E. Cleland, ed., pp. 293–312. New York: Academic Press.

Wright, William (Dan De Quille)
1947   The Big Bonanza. New York: Alfred K. Knopf.

1963   Washoe Rambles. Los Angeles: Western Lore Press.

Young, James A., Raymond A. Evans, and J. Major
1972   Alien Plants in the Great Basin. Journal of Range Management 25(3):194–201.

Young, James A., Raymond A. Evans, and Paul T. Tueller
  1976   Great Basin Plant Communities—Pristine and Grazed. In: Holocene Environmental Change in the Great Basin, Robert G. Elstron and Patricia Headrich, eds. Nevada Archeological Survey Research Paper No. 6, pp. 187–216.

Young, James A., and James D. Budy
  1979   Historical Use of Nevada's Pinyon-Juniper Woodlands. Journal of Forest History 23:111–121.

Chapter 10

The Plateau Culture Area

Eugene S. Hunn
University of Washington

Introduction

The Plateau culture area is roughly equivalent to the region drained by the Columbia and Fraser Rivers east of the Cascade Mountains in Washington and Oregon and of the Coast Range in British Columbia. The upper Snake River plain is excepted as it is better treated as part of the Great Basin Culture Area. The Plateau is often divided between the Northern or Canadian Plateau and the Southern or Columbia Plateau. This division reflects not only contrasting historical and political contexts of American Indian experience—between United States hegemony, on the one hand, and that of Great Britain and Canada, on the other—but a significant ecological contrast as well. The Northern Plateau is largely forested, while the Southern Plateau cultures adapted to life in a semi-arid steppe environment. Vegetable foods that were critically important in the south—such as camas (*Camassia quamash*), bitterroot (*Lewisia rediviva*), and various species of "desert parsley" or lomatiums (*Lomatium* spp.)—were scarce or absent to the north.

The Columbia River basin east of the Cascade Mountains and exclusive of the upper Snake River encompasses more than 150,000 square miles. (The Fraser River would add nearly 90,000 square miles.) Estimates of native population for the period prior to 1775—when the first historically recorded smallpox epidemic swept through—suggest a total for the Columbia Basin subregion of 57,000 for an average density of 0.37 persons per square mile. Subregional population density estimates vary within the Columbia basin from a low of 0.08 for the Kutenai and 0.10 for the Cayuse to 0.74 for the Sahaptin language area on the mid-Columbia River (Boyd 1985).

These figures are *educated guesses* based on population estimates by early explorers such as Lewis and Clark that have been adjusted to take account of losses due to early epidemics. Overall these densities are several times as great as for the Great Basin, but densities on the Northwest Coast are several times as great as on the Plateau. Average population densities reflect the relative environmental productivity of each of these regions. Average population density—one index of the regional social environment—is in turn a powerful predictor of economic, political, and social patterns, as will be noted below.

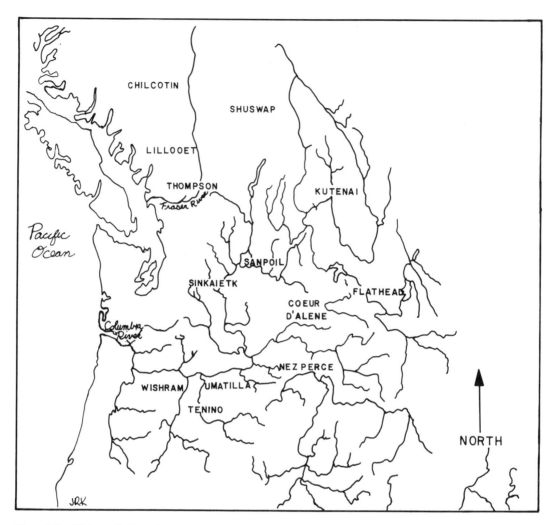

Map of the Plateau Culture Area

Anthropological experts in the early decades of this century argued vehemently over the question whether Plateau culture had unique indigenous characteristics or whether it was entirely derivative of the better known and more dramatic cultures of the Plains to the east or of the Coast to the west (Ray 1939). This issue seems of no great moment today. We would understand Plateau culture rather from the perspective of how Native American peoples used their accumulated knowledge and established values and beliefs to carve a comfortable niche for themselves in the rugged Plateau environment.

Archaeological evidence of humanity's 10,000 year continuous occupation of the Plateau (Cressman 1977) supports the view that Plateau ways of life are ancient (if ever changing) and eminently successful. That Plateau peoples learned from their neighbors proves only that they were not frozen within a rigid traditional pattern of habitual reactions to environmental stimuli. Plateau peoples' responses to the stresses of Euroamerican contact were creative and involved selective incorporation of new techniques and adaptive strategies within a resilient framework of traditional beliefs and values. Among the most dramatic examples of the Plateau cultural response to outside forces is the adoption of the horse and the prophetic religious revival, to be discussed in detail below.

The Plateau is defined by the two great rivers that drain these lands. The rivers were arteries of travel and communication for both Indians and white explorers, traders, and settlers. They also concentrate the vast stocks of salmon that return each year from their Pacific Ocean nurseries to spawn in their natal streams, providing a rich and dependable staple food for many Plateau groups. But Plateau peoples did not live on fish alone: of equal importance were the abundant root foods such as bitterroot, lomatiums, and camas. Camas is a plant of wet meadows; bitterroot and the lomatiums are adapted to the thin, dry soils of ridge crests of the arid steppes and dry forests of the intermountain region of the southern Plateau.

Rainfall in the driest portions of the Columbia Valley is just six inches per year. The moisture-laden Pacific air masses are wrung dry by the Cascade peaks leaving the southern Plateau in a deep *rain shadow*. The Cascade and coastal ranges also cut the Plateau off from the moderating effects of the sea on local temperatures. Thus the Plateau is a land of extremes: temperatures may range from 110° F in late summer to –50° F in winter. This great range of seasonal temperature brings a comparable range in seasonal availability of food: thus the Plateau economy is based on the production of substantial surpluses each spring, summer, and fall for winter storage. Fortunately the dry winds that sweep across the Plateau facilitate the preservation by drying of roots, fish, and berries.

The Plateau heartland was set off somewhat from neighboring culture areas on the south, east, and north by a ring of forested uplands—typical of the northern Plateau—where root and fish resources were more limited. Within the Plateau and between the Plateau and the adjacent coastal regions a web of interpersonal ties was forged of kinship and trade connections. These links crossed language boundaries and were exploited in the formation of regional *task groups* (Anastasio 1973 [1955]) and in the maintenance of a more-or-less effective and enduring peace within the region (Ray 1939).

Language

Two major language families dominated the Plateau culture area at first Euroamerican contact. Speakers of languages of the Sahaptian family—a small family that included *Nez Perce* and the complex of mutually intelligible dialects known to linguists as *Sahaptin* (which includes Yakima, Klikitat, Warm Springs, Umatilla, Walla Walla, Wanapam, and Palus)—occupied winter villages along the Columbia River between the Dalles and Priest Rapids, along the Yakima River, and on the Snake River below Hell's Canyon. North of the Sahaptian area lived speakers of Interior Salishan languages, of which there are seven. Linguistic analysis suggests that the Interior Salishan languages evolved from an ancestral language spoken in the Fraser River canyon some 4500 years ago (Elmendorf 1965). *Lillooet, Thompson,* and *Shuswap* developed from a branch of interior Salish that spread up the Fraser River, while *Okanagan-Colville* (which includes also the Sanpoil-Nespelem and Lakes dialects), *Columbia* (also including Methow, Chelan, and Wenatchee dialects), *Kalispel* (also including Spokane, Pend d'Oreille, and Flathead dialects), and *Coeur d'Alene*.

Wasco-Wishram, a dialect of Upper Chinookan (now better known as *Kiksht*), was spoken at the Dalles and below. A few speakers of this dialect live on the Yakima and Warm Springs reservations today. They are often bilingual in Kiksht and Sahaptin, as was also the case in the past. *Carrier* and *Chilcotin* are two Athapaskan languages spoken on the northwestern edge of the Plateau, bordering the Subarctic Culture Area. *Kutenai* was spoken on the Kootenay River in the northern Rocky Mountains, bordering the Plains Culture Area. Its linguistic affinities are still the subject of debate among the experts.

The dynamic nature of linguistic relationships in the Plateau is exemplified by *Cayuse,* a now-extinct language spoken at first contact in the Blue-Wallowa Mountain area on the headwaters of the Walla Walla, Umatilla, Grand Ronde, and Powder Rivers. This language was reduced to a few bilingual speakers by the early decades of the nineteenth century, apparently through a process of attrition due to intermarriage with Nez Perce, Walla Walla, and Umatilla Sahaptin speakers. Sahaptin has expanded recently on the west also, spilling over the Cascade crest from the upper Yakima basin into that of the upper Cowlitz River. Intermarriage between Cowlitz-speaking men and Sahaptin-speaking women seems responsible (Jacobs 1937).

A recent ambitious attempt to trace the genetic relationships among all New World Indian languages (Greenberg 1987) groups Cayuse and the Sahaptian and Chinookan languages with many other North American Indian languages—including those of the Mayan family of Central America—in a *Penutian phylum.* According to Greenberg, both Penutian and Salishan belong in turn to the great Amerind superphylum, descendants alike of the language of the first Asiatic peoples to cross Bering Straits to the New World more than 10,000 years ago.

A dozen Plateau Indian languages are still spoken today, though most are in danger of extinction in the near future. Most, if not all, native speakers as of 1988 are bilingual in English and the great majority of native speakers of Plateau Indian languages are over 50 years of age. Sahaptin, with several hundred native speakers, constitutes the largest extant native speech community in the Plateau. Kiksht, Columbia, and Coeur D'Alene are represented today by a bare handful of elderly native speakers. The preservation of Plateau Indian languages for future generations is given a high priority by scholars and Indian people alike, as these languages represent a direct link to the rich and enduring conceptual traditions of Plateau Indian peoples and are a powerful means for expressing Indian cultural identity.

There are published or soon to be published grammatical analyses, dictionaries, and native language texts for most Plateau languages. However, large gaps remain to be filled. For example, no comprehensive dictionary exists for Sahaptin, and the diversity of dialects of many Plateau languages is poorly documented. Published textual materials include accurately transcribed and carefully translated collections of Plateau mythology for Sahaptin (e.g., Jacobs 1929), Nez Perce (Phinney 1934), Wishram (Sapir 1909), and Kutenai (Boas 1918).

Prior to the introduction of phonetic alphabets, Indian mythology—the collective creative genius of indigenous cultural expression—was transmitted orally and safeguarded in the memories of the elders. The core of the Plateau mythological tradition consists of dozens of "Coyote stories," powerfully dramatic and often humorous accounts set in the "Myth Age" that preceded the present reality in which the Indian people lived. In this earlier time animals (and sometimes plants, winds, etc.) were cast in leading roles.

Coyote plays a morally complex part, illustrating the best and the worst in human action by his larger than life ambitions. Coyote taught each new generation of Plateau Indians not only by moral pronouncement but also by his own bad example! Coyote did not "create" the present world as did the God of Genesis, but he "prepared" this world for the arrival of (Indian) people who—in the mythic refrain—"are coming soon." Thus Coyote releases the salmon captured by the Swallow Sisters (or, in the Salishan area, by the Spotted Sandpiper Sisters), breaking up their dam (and creating Celilo Falls, in one version). He destroys the great Swallowing Monster that lurks in the deepest pools of the Columbia River (or the Snake, for the Nez Perce), blowing the monster to bits by building a fire beneath its heart—in a story vaguely reminiscent of the Biblical account of Jonah and the Whale. The fragments of the beast fell to earth from which sprang all the known Indian peoples. This mythological tradition is a monument to the power of language to create, educate, entertain, and inspire generation upon generation. Contemporary Indian people speak of this tradition as their "Indian Bible," as well they might.

Subsistence and Technology

Plateau Indian societies were built on an economic foundation of gathering, fishing, and hunting. Agriculture was not practiced prior to Euroamerican contact, with the possible exception of a few small plots of tobacco. The nearest agricultural economies were on the Missouri River and in the Southwest. The same suite of key resources apparently had supported human life on the Plateau for at least 10,000 years, though technological innovations

Figure 10.1 Pounding fish—Wishham (in maple mortar with stone pestle), c. 1909. NAI text v. 8, f.p. 94. (Courtesy of Special Collections Division, University of Washington Libraries. Photo by Edward S. Curtis. Negative No. NA 159.)

such as the adoption of specialized grinding implements (ca. 5000 years ago according to Ames and Marshall 1980–1981), new fishing techniques (ca. 4500 years ago according to Nelson 1973), and the introduction of bows and arrows (sometime before ca. 500 AD according to Cressman 1977:106) may have altered the relative contribution of various types of resources over the time span of prehistoric occupation.

Variation in Plateau subsistence strategies is also attributable to climatically-governed habitat contrasts within the Plateau at a single point in time. We will describe below the subsistence system practiced by Sahaptin-speaking communities of the mid-Columbia at the time of first European contact, but noting contemporary local variants on that theme.

It is first essential to correct a widespread misconception, to wit, that Plateau economies were based primarily on the harvest of salmon. Ecological and ethnohistorical research suggests rather that plant foods, especially the carbohydrate rich tuberous roots and bulbs, contributed over 50% of the total food energy consumed by southern Plateau peoples (Hunn 1981, Hunn and French 1981). Plant foods also contributed key vitamins

Figure 10.2 The fisherman—Wishham, c. 1909. *NAI* folio v. 8, pl. 274. (Courtesy of Special Collections Division, University of Washington Libraries. Photo by Edward S. Curtis. Negative No. NA 207.)

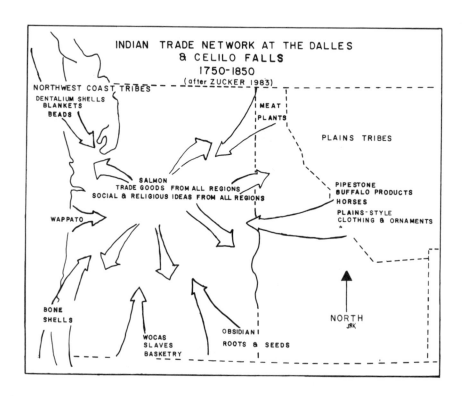

INDIAN TRADE NETWORK AT THE DALLES
& CELILO FALLS
1750-1850
(after ZUCKER 1983)

NORTHWEST COAST TRIBES
DENTALIUM SHELLS
BLANKETS
BEADS

MEAT
PLANTS

PLAINS TRIBES

SALMON
TRADE GOODS FROM ALL REGIONS
SOCIAL & RELIGIOUS IDEAS FROM ALL REGIONS

PIPESTONE
BUFFALO PRODUCTS
HORSES
PLAINS-STYLE
CLOTHING & ORNAMENTS

WAPPATO

BONE
SHELLS

NORTH
JRK

WOCAS
SLAVES
BASKETRY

OBSIDIAN
ROOTS & SEEDS

and minerals, notably Vitamin C from "Indian celeries" (e.g., *Lomatium grayi*, *L. nudicaule*, *Balsamorhiza* spp., and *Heracleum lanatum*) harvested in early spring and eaten raw. Plants collected by women (primarily) also provided medicinal herbs and essential materials for the manufacture of tools. Particularly noteworthy in this regard are "Indian hemp" (*Apocynum cannabinum*)—used to make string and rope for binding, twined baskets and hats, and nets used for fishing and rabbit hunting—and "tules" (*Scirpus acutus*), a bulrush used to make the mats that insulated the walls and covered the floors of Plateau winter lodges and in which Plateau people were wrapped for burial.

Five species of salmon plus the steelhead trout were harvested from the Columbia and Fraser Rivers for an estimated annual average consumption of one pound of fish per person per day (Hewes 1973 [1947]). However, fish consumption varied widely depending upon the relative abundance of anadromous fish available to each group. For example, Fraser River salmon runs exhibit great variation from year to year, while most Flathead speakers lived beyond the limits of salmon migration. Large surpluses were preserved by drying, especially by the Wasco-Wishrams, Columbia River Sahaptins, and the Thompson of the Fraser River canyon; these groups controlled the most productive fisheries. The surpluses were a major trade item in a regional trade network centered in the Dalles-Celilo Falls area at the head of the Columbia gorge. The Wasco-Wishram, in particular, specialized in the salmon trade, trading their surplus dried salmon for foodstuffs and other products brought in by surrounding groups. Salmon for trade were dried, pounded into meal, then packed in cattail bags lined with salmon skin. Each such bag weighted approximately 100 pounds;

they were arranged neatly twelve to a stack. Lewis and Clark have left a dramatic account of this aspect of Plateau life as they witnessed it in 1805 and 1806.

Most Plateau communities were highly mobile (the Wasco-Wishram less so, as noted above), depending for their livelihood on the practice of a *seasonal round*, seeking out resources at the times and places of their greatest annual productivity. Each "winter village" community had access to resources at all elevations from a few hundred feet above sea level on the major rivers to timberline in the adjacent mountain ranges.

Winter villages were occupied at least from November through February and occasionally year round. They were typically located at or near major fisheries, in a sheltered side canyon where driftwood for fuel was abundant. Food supplies were cached here throughout the year, and the winter village was the conceptual "home" for those who were raised there. If a person died at some distance from the village, as at a summer gathering or hunting camp, his or her remains would be reinterred close to the village at a later time.

In March and April resources were sought at no great distance from the winter village: suckers or trout might be harvested by line or trap from an adjacent stream, roots would be dug on the dry ridges above the river, and a rabbit or ground squirrel hunt might be organized on a nearby sagebrush-covered flat. The spring Chinook salmon run on the Columbia River commenced in earnest in late April or early May and was intercepted at progressively later dates as the run moved upriver (e.g., in late May by the Sanpoil-Nespelem and at Kettle Falls near the Canadian border). The spring flood in June made fishing unproductive. At this time people dismantled their winter lodges (storing the timbers nearby but carrying the tule mats with them to use at their summer camps) and moved progressively higher into the mountains, taking advantage of the fact that the roots they sought matured later at higher elevations. By this means, the root harvest was prolonged for three months. Roots were dried (or baked in the case of camas) in camp, which reduced by a factor of three the weight of food supplies that had to be transported back to the village site for winter use.

In July and August a succession of fish runs drew most Plateau people to the river once again, where large numbers of people congregated at favored sites such as Celilo Falls, the Dalles, Priest Rapids, Kettle Falls, and the Fraser River canyon. In late summer and fall many moved again into the mountains to harvest fruits and to escape the oppressive heat. Again the dramatic topography with its sharp elevational contrasts was exploited to prolong the gathering season; chokecherries (*Prunus virginiana*), currants (*Ribes* spp.), and saskatoon berries (*Amelanchier alnifolia*) were harvested in mid-summer near the rivers; huckleberries and blueberries (*Vaccinium* spp.) were harvested in late summer and fall in high mountain meadows. Here also deer and elk were hunted where they sought the protein rich foliage at the edge of mountain meadows and clearings. Indian people used fire systematically to enhance the productivity of their mountain habitat, creating by controlled burning clearings rich in berries and attractive to game.

With the first snowfall these high camps were abandoned and the winter villages rebuilt, now well stocked with dried roots, fish, and berries to last all winter. Winter was a time of intensive social and spiritual activity, when myths were told and guardian spirits

369

honored. Abundant food was needed for feasting and generous chiefs were rewarded by a strengthened following. Villages also had to be supplied with raw materials assembled throughout the year for use during the long winter in the manufacture and repair of the tools on which their lives depended.

Social Systems

Plateau Indian society *must not* be imagined to have been organized as European feudal societies were, i.e., regimented by the powerful rule of warriors or hereditary kings. The low density of human population in the Plateau compared to that of medieval Europe—and of most agriculturally-based societies—precluded the development of authoritarian states. Plateau villages were each politically autonomous, or at most they recognized the superior influence of the chief of a dominant nearby village (Marshall 1977). Village "chiefs" (and there might be more than one person so recognized in a single village) did not rule, rather they *exercised influence* based upon their reputation for generosity, good judgment, and eloquence. "Salmon chiefs," shamans (known locally as "Indian doctors"), and war leaders exercised more specialized authority based on their particular spiritual gifts. The glue that held Plateau society together was not power imposed from above but collateral ties of mutual respect and obligation, ties based on links of kinship, friendship, and/or economic exchange (of gifts or in trade).

People rarely married within their own village due to the blanket prohibition on marriage between recognized blood relatives. Thus marriage ties linked neighboring villages and often bridged language barriers. Chiefs used the marriage of their children to forge wider alliances. This fostered a high degree of multi-lingualism and rather intense social interaction within the Plateau.

Verne Ray has argued that "pacifism" was a characteristic feature at the core of Plateau culture. However, there is evidence that raiding and intergroup violence was not infrequent in the Plateau. At first contact the mid-Columbia River villages lived in fear of Northern Paiute/Shoshone raids from the southeast, while the Flathead were in a state of constant conflict with Blackfoot groups on the Plains for control of access to the high plains bison hunting grounds. Much of this violence is clearly due to the introduction of horses, which provided both means and motive for long-distance raiding. It is still unclear to what extent *intra-Plateau* violent conflict was between individuals—seeking to redress a wrong—rather than between groups. Only in the latter case is the term "warfare" appropriate.

Plateau society has been held up as an example of sexual equality (Ackerman 1982). While a clear-cut division of labor by sex was basic to Plateau socio-economic life—in which women gathered plant products, processed and prepared foods of all kinds, and had primary responsibility for infant care, while men fished, hunted, and had a primary role in village politics and intervillage political and military action—social relations between the sexes could scarcely be construed as reflecting exploitation of one sex by the other or of the existence of a significant power differential between the sexes. The division of economic

Figure 10.3 Nez Perce baby, c. 1900. NAI folio
v.9, pl. 266. (Courtesy of Special Collections
Division, University of Washington Libraries.
Photo by Edward S. Curtis. Negative No. NA
199.)

labor by sex within extended families clearly enhanced the productive efficiency of the
family.

Kinship terminology is bilaterally symmetrical, that is, though relatives on maternal
and paternal sides are differentiated, the distinctions are equivalent on each side. The terminology and associated ideal marriage partners indicate the importance of extended family relations. For example, throughout the Plateau cousins are equated with siblings—a convention known as "Hawaiian cousin terminology." Thus, in Sahaptin **pat** refers not only
to a person's elder sisters but to his or her elder female cousins as well, while ísxáp refers
not only to a man's younger brothers but also to a man's younger male cousins.

The equation of cousins with siblings may have been reinforced by the widespread
practice of the *levirate* and *sororate* and the preference for *sororal polygyny* reported for a
number of Plateau groups. The cultural expectation was that following the death of a
spouse, the deceased spouse's family would replace that spouse with a "sibling" (whether
a "true" sibling or a cousin was immaterial). If a man's wife died, he would be expected
(though not required) to marry one of his wife's sisters or female cousins. If a woman's

husband died, she would be expected to marry one of her husband's brothers or male cousins. In this way the enduring bond established by marriage *between two families* would not be broken by death. A special kinship term, **awít,** is used in Sahaptin to refer to a sibling-in-law of opposite sex, but is used only after the death of the linking spouse.

A corollary of the levirate and sororate is that a person's children might be raised by the parent's same-sex sibling after his or her death. Thus, in Sahaptin, the term for step-father is the same as for "father's brother" and that for step-mother is the same as for "mother's sister." In such cases note also that children would be step-siblings to their father's brother's or mother's sister's children (i.e., their [parallel] "cousins"). Sororal polygyny—the marriage of a man to two or more "sisters"—had a similar effect.

Another revealing feature of Plateau kinship terminology is the fact that grandparents were distinguished not only by sex but also by "side." Thus **four** kinds of grandparents are recognized in many Plateau languages. In some, grandparents and their grandchildren are called by a single reciprocal term. In Sahaptin, for example, a person's mother's father is **tíla** and so is a man's daughter's child. In other words, each calls the other **tíla.** This hints at the strong emotional ties between individuals two generations apart. Grandparents played key roles within the extended family and were instrumental in training and educating their grandchildren, most notably in their role as storytellers. This Plateau nomenclatural system contrasts sharply with that of English, in which greater emphasis is placed on generational seniority and the sex of the kinsman.

Slavery was reported as a hereditary status only among the Wishram and Thompson (Murdock 1967). Both had strong ties to coastal groups for which holding slaves captured in war played a prominent social role. Plateau social ideology stressed the autonomy of the individual and was highly egalitarian. In addition, Plateau mobility and the more dispersed resources of the Plateau did not encourage the institutionalization of social hierarchy, of which slavery is one manifestation. The participation of Plateau groups in slave trading appears to have been promoted by patterns of raid and counter-raid that developed with the introduction of horses in the mid-eighteenth century. In the Plateau, slaves were war captives, usually women and children, and—with the exception of groups with strong coastal ties—were readily adopted into the families and communities of their captors without prejudice.

Belief Systems

Before white contact Plateau religion focused on the spiritual relationships between each individual and the forces of nature on which life so clearly depended. Children were sent on *vision quests* by their elders: a child's grandfather or father might send the boy or girl (normally at puberty or a few years before) to find some lost item (often intentionally left behind). The quest might last one night or several; the destination was most often a prominent summit, an island, or a mountain lake known as a place frequented by spirits. The spirit might appear as a person who would approach the child, offering a song or a dance, then turning into its animal (or plant, or wind, etc.) form before vanishing. Though details vary from group to group, the typical pattern was for the child to be overcome by the experience, ''forgetting'' what had happened until some years later. The identity of the guardian spirit should never be revealed explicitly on penalty of abandonment by the spirit power.

One's powers were revealed only indirectly, expressed first with the aid of a powerful shaman on the occasion of a shamanic winter dance. The identity of a person's guardian spirit was inferred from the character and talent the individual demonstrated in his or her life as well as from the nature of his or her power song and dance, taught by the spirit to the child during the quest and later ''reawakened'' in the winter dance with the shaman-guide's help. A young person who denied his or her spirit's desire for recognition and public expression at the winter dances was expected to sicken and eventually die (Schuster 1975).

Spirit powers were essential for a successful life. Exceptional talents, such as those of salmon chiefs, noted warriors, and shamans were attributed to the strength, nature, and number of that person's guardian spirits. Shamans in particular sought to obtain power from a number of particularly powerful guardians through repeated questing. Illness and its cure were in many cases attributed to imbalances of spirit power, as, for example, due to the intrusion of a shaman's more powerful spirit into the body of the sufferer or as a consequence of the loss or denial of one's own power. The shaman, or ''Indian doctor,'' sought to diagnose these spiritual causes and to effect a cure by overpowering harmful intrusive spirits or by recovering or placating lost or offended spirits.

Plateau religion was not ''nature worship.'' Rather the spirits of animals, plants, wind, water, and rock were recognized as **persons,** that is, as members of an all-inclusive society of interdependent beings, beings with human qualities of intelligence, will, and a sense of *moral* obligation to one another. The most fundamental ethical principle of this *animistic* belief system was that one must treat other ''persons''—human or otherwise—with RESPECT.

The Plateau mythological tradition gives a vivid dramatic reality to these beliefs by recalling a prior myth age in which animals and other natural forces were more fully human. These stories often offer an explicit moral teaching, as when Coyote shows callous disregard for the feelings of the deer he hunts: the deer spirit withdraws her favor from him and he hunts to no avail. Only by affirming the rights of deer to respect and by disavowing waste is Coyote's hunting power restored—and the hunting power of human beings in the present assured (Jacobs 1929:200). These qualities of Plateau belief and the moral teachings based upon them clearly supported the continuing success of the Plateau foraging way of life.

A prominent feature of Plateau religious life since the earliest contact period is the belief in apocalyptic prophecy and the related practice of a communal worship dance. Smohalla—the best known of the many Plateau prophets who lived during the later half of the nineteenth century—established a church at his home village near Priest Rapids in what is now central Washington State. Smohalla's preaching involved a call to his Indian followers to reject white influence, to refuse to plow the earth or to dig for gold as tantamount to "tear[ing] my mother's bosom" and to "dig[ging] under her skin for her bones" (Mooney 1896:721). By leading a strict moral and traditional lifestyle and by intense worship through sacred dancing and singing—inspired by the prophet's experiences at the gate of the afterlife during an earlier "death"—his followers believed they would achieve salvation in the impending apocalypse. They expected the imminent end of the world, the destruction of white society, and the return of the Indian dead, which were, in those days, all too numerous.

Plateau prophecy shares many features with *revitalization movements* in other parts of North America and the world (Wallace 1956). Plateau prophecy was inspired in part at least by the Indians' experience of the devastating effects of introduced epidemic diseases against which they had no genetic or physiological resistance. The ravages of these diseases were seen as evidence of the whites' overwhelming and evil **spiritual** power; the only hope was in forging an Indian community united by the power of common worship of the earth and sun which bring life.

The contemporary Long House or Seven Drums religion (known in Sahaptin as **wáashat** or "sacred dance") faithfully preserves the belief and ritual practice of the Plateau prophetic movement. Today over a dozen Long House congregations count hundreds of adherents. They observe weekly Sunday worship, host semiannual first foods or thanksgiving feasts dedicated to honoring and preserving traditional Indian foods, and honor their people at name-giving ceremonies, funerals and memorials, and at other *rites of passage*.

The Long House religion does not demand exclusive allegiance. In this respect it contrasts sharply with both the Indian Shaker churches (founded on Puget Sound by a prophetic revelation not unlike Smohalla's) and the many fundamentalist Christian congregations popular on Plateau Indian reservations today. Many Seven Drums adherents consider themselves to be Christians and are leery of traditional "Indian doctors"; many also respect the Indian Shakers' power to cure certain maladies, especially alcoholism.

Historical Overview

Archaeological evidence demonstrates that Plateau populations were well established by at least 9000 years ago. These early peoples gathered, fished, and hunted much as did the protohistorical inhabitants of the Plateau, though their technological repertoire and specific adaptive strategies no doubt evolved substantially over that long time span. Historical linguistic analyses suggest furthermore that speakers of ancestral Sahaptian and Interior Salishan languages have occupied the interior Columbia and Fraser River basins for at least several millennia. In short, it is fair to say that Indian cultures of the Plateau at the time of first Euroamerican contact represented a very long, stable cultural adaptation to the Plateau natural and social environment.

Written history on the Plateau begins with the Lewis and Clark journals dating to 1805–1806. However, Lewis and Clark's visit does not represent the point of first Euroamerican *influence* in the Plateau, as they recorded evidence of previous epidemics of smallpox (the first occurring about 1780), observed a number of items of European manufacture including (nonfunctioning) guns and clothing, and remarked frequently upon the obviously well-established Plateau equestrian tradition. Most scholars are convinced that horses first arrived in the Plateau after 1730 AD through exchanges with Shoshone groups of the upper Snake River plain (Haines 1938). These Shoshone had most likely obtained their horses in turn from Indians with direct access to the Spanish herds set free during the Pueblo uprising of 1680. We may surmise that horses greatly enhanced the established patterns of seasonal mobility allowing more effective harvests and the transport of larger quantities of dried foods over greater distances for winter consumption. Bison hunting on the high plains east of the Rocky Mountains no doubt expanded in scope and its social and economic significance increased among Plateau groups living along the mid-Columbia and lower Snake Rivers as a consequence of acquiring horses. Horses also made available a form of movable wealth thereby fostering a heightened contrast between rich and poor within Plateau society. Shoshone-Northern Paiute raiding along the mid-Columbia River—which Lewis and Clark remarked upon—no doubt spurred Plateau peoples to master the horse and to raid in their turn, bringing back not only horses and notoriety but captives as well. Still, the vast majority of Plateau families continued to rely for subsistence on the same wild roots, berries, fish, and game of their Plateau homeland.

The enhanced mobility brought by the horse may also have hastened the arrival of a second biological import: smallpox. The impact of smallpox on New World peoples from Peru and Mexico to Alaska proves its Eurasian origin (Crosby 1972). New World populations were "virgin soil" for the smallpox virus and epidemic mortality is estimated at an average of 30% under such conditions (cf. Boyd 1985). Euroamericans, by contrast, were largely immune. As the Euroamerican influence grew in the Plateau so did the impact of the legion of exotic diseases these immigrants brought with them (however unintentionally). Malaria massacred an estimated 80% to 90% of the Indian people of the Lower Columbia and Willamette Valleys in four short years, 1830–1833 (Cook 1955), while influenza, measles, scarlet fever, whooping cough, and venereal disease added to the toll of the periodically recurring smallpox epidemics.

These epidemics were not simply biological disasters, but social and spiritual catastrophes as well. Prophets called their people home in a desperate effort to salvage their way of life and to resurrect their dead.

Euroamerican occupation of the Plateau proceeded at first gradually. During the fur trade era Plateau Indians dealt with whites on a more or less equal footing. Fur traders had no interest in radically altering the Indian way of life. However, the fur trade era lasted only from 1811 until the mid-1840's, when a tide of settlement swept the Oregon territory (south of the 49th parallel) into the United States. Immigration from the east was encouraged by the well publicized adventures of Christian missionaries. The Presbyterian-Congregationalist mission to the Cayuse and Nez Perce was founded amidst considerable fanfare by Marcus Whitman and Henry Spalding in 1836. The Methodist mission at the Dalles was begun by Daniel Lee and Henry Perkins in 1838, and the itinerant Catholic priests Frances Blanchet and Modest Demers scouted the Plateau territory that same year.

The Catholic fathers received a warm welcome among the largely Catholic *voyageurs* and their Indian friends and relations on the upper Columbia River and inspired their Protestant competition to redoubled efforts.

The so-called Whitman massacre of 1847 brought this first period of missionary activity to an abrupt end. The attack on the Waiilatpu Mission by a group of Cayuse Indians culminated a decade of constantly increasing traffic on the emigrant trails, of parallel increases in exotic diseases, and of a steady diet of criticism from the missionaries of the Indian way of life. The aftermath of this attack was an uneasy military occupation (at least south of the 49th parallel) setting the stage for the treaty councils of 1855.

Governor Isaac Stevens for Washington Territory and Indian Agent Joel Palmer for Oregon signed five treaties that year:with confederations of "tribes and bands" of Yakimas, Warm Springs Indians, Nez Perces, Flatheads and Kutenais, and the Walla Wallas, Umatillas, and Cayuses. Stevens failed only with the Interior Salish groups, as he was forced to cancel a planned council with the Coeur d'Alenes, Spokanes, Colvilles, and Okanagans because of the outbreak of hostilities among the Yakimas. (Colville, Spokane, and Couer d'Alene reservations were later established by executive order.) The treaties were eventually ratified by the U. S. Congress after four years of skirmishing among Indians, marauding gold miners, and feuding territorial militias and the U. S. Army. Stevens and Palmer succeeded in their goal: "the extinguishment of the Indian Claims to the lands . . . so as not to interfere with the settlement of the territories . . ." (in Relander 1962:39). The treaties also *reserved* to the signatory Indian tribes and bands the *exclusive* use of a reservation (carefully selected to be out of the settler's path west), financial and other assistance in adjusting to the new conditions that reservation life would bring, and a grudging acceptance of the Indians' continuing right to harvest traditional resources—such as fish and game—throughout their aboriginal territory *in common with* the settlers.

While it is clear that the Indians' acceded to these treaties *under duress* and with only a very sketchy understanding of the legal meaning of the documents, the treaties nonetheless have established a solid legal foundation on which contemporary Indian rights are built and upon which the continued existence and vitality of Indian cultures depend (Cohen 1986).

The period 1859–1914 was one of constant attrition of Indian population, Indian land, and Indian rights in the Plateau. Symptomatic of this era in Indian-white relations is the infamous Dawes Severalty Act of 1887. This set in motion the privatization of Indian reservations by allotting to each individual tribal member a share of the tribal reserved lands judged sufficient to support that individual by means of farming or stock raising—the only proper, "civilized" ways to make a living, according to the dominant opinion of the time. After a certain trial period those allotments were deeded to the allottees or their heirs *in fee simple.* Such lands could then be freely bought and sold (often as not for back taxes levied by land hungry local governments). The original plan was to then declare all remaining Indian lands "surplus" to be sold at auction by the Federal government.

The allotment process was stopped in 1914, but not before the Yakimas had lost the most productive 10% of their lands and the Umatilla reservation had been whittled down to about one third of its original size. The Nez Perce and Colville reservations had already been reduced to a small fraction of their original size by a series of "renegotiated" boundary settlements.

An *Indian New Deal* was inaugurated in 1934 with passage of the IRA (Indian Reorganization Act) and the Johnson-O'Malley bill. The first defined procedures for establishing tribal self government (on the lines of a basically Euroamerican model of representative government). The second provided funds for Indian education and welfare programs. Contemporary Plateau tribal governments owe their existence to the IRA in large measure. A resurgence of the assimilationist position in Washington, D. C., during the Eisenhower administration led to new efforts to *terminate* Indian tribes and to privatize their reservations. The Klamath Tribe of southern Oregon was terminated by this process in 1961 and the Colvilles narrowly escaped the same fate. Today the pendulum has swung back in the direction of *Indian self-determination.*

North of the 49th parallel similar processes were in motion, first under the British crown and only since 1868 under Canadian control. No large reservations were established in British Columbia. Rather Indian communities were organized in dozens of small bands each established on a small reserve. This fragmentation allowed Indian communities in many cases to stay within their aboriginal homelands, but left them with smaller total land holdings than their counterparts in the United States and tended to favor a greater degree of social and political fragmentation. However, both in the United States and Canada Indian life retains a strong hold on the lives of Indian citizens.

The Plateau Culture Area Today

Plateau Indian cultures have changed far more in the past two centuries than in the previous ten millenia. The transition from the role of *ecological dominant* to that of *social subordinate* has not been easy and is a drama still unfolding. Rapid change coupled with the destruction of much of the ecological and social base upon which Plateau Indian traditions were built has opened a gulf between successive generations. The traditional knowledge that elders possess—knowledge of the Indian languages, of how things were done in generations past, values and beliefs about nature and the world of spirit powers—is of uncertain relevance for confronting the contemporary realities young people must face: succeeding in school, finding wage or professional employment, submitting to modern medicine, and engaging in legal and political disputation about the meanings of treaty language. Yet that traditional knowledge is the Indian peoples' only link to their past, to a tradition they can call their own, a way of life that sets them apart from the mass of the American poor. The vision of America as a great "melting pot" absorbing peoples of diverse cultural and racial backgrounds into a single progressive society has been largely abandoned. The ideal of equal opportunity has proved illusory and the pull of traditional and ethnic roots too strong. Though Indian people do not enjoy being poor, many are unwilling to trade the wealth of their cultural heritage and the comfort of strong family ties for the faint hope of success chasing the American dream.

Poverty is the predominant economic reality for Indian people on Plateau reservations today. Annual income of Yakima Indian families living on reservations was estimated at 47% of the national average in 1965 (Schuster 1975:295), while unemployment was estimated at 51%. Furthermore, only half of those employed had full-time jobs. Many Indian people qualify for state welfare programs based on need. However, the widely held view that Indian people are largely dependent on government handouts is incorrect. Tribal governments operate much as do corporations (though the Bureau of Indian Affairs retains ultimate authority): the costs of tribal self-government—including salaries of tribal employees (and tribal governments are major employers of reservation Indians), of tribal police and courts, and of legal, education, and housing programs are financed by income earned from tribal lands and other capital resources. For most Plateau tribes timber harvests are the major income source (representing 67% of Yakima tribal income in 1962, for example), with smaller amounts derived from mineral development, grazing leases, and hunting and fishing licenses. Tribal members receive a small annual *per capita* payment out of tribal income, analogous to the *dividends* paid by corporations to stockholders. Other services—especially in the areas of health and education—are provided by the federal government to members of federally recognized tribes in accord with requirements of the special *trust* relationship established by treaty between Indian tribes and the United States government.

The most contentious fact of Plateau Indian life today is the issue of *tribal sovereignty*. The U.S. Supreme Court has ruled that Indian tribes are "distinct, independent, political communities" with a right to internal self-government. By treaty these tribes relinquished their external powers, becoming "wards" of the federal government. Today tribes are *in* states but not entirely *of* them, while tribal members have a sort of dual citizenship in their eligibility for both tribal and local government services. The proper relationship between tribes and local governments with respect to such governmental functions as public schools, police protection, criminal and juvenile justice, child welfare and adoption, fishing and hunting regulations, and the taxation that pays for these services is a continuing battle ground. Tribal exemptions from state taxation and business regulations—constantly under attack by the states—have provided a small window of capitalist economic opportunity that Indian entrepreneurs have learned to exploit. This explains the ubiquitous smoke shops, fireworks stands, and bingo parlors that are hallmarks of "Indian country."

Treaty rights to fish off-reservation at "usual and accustomed" places "in common with . . . [other] citizens" has provoked loud and bitter opposition from sports and commercial fishermen. What is not well understood is that Indian off-reservation fishing *is regulated* by tribes, intertribal commissions, cooperative state-tribal compacts, and even international conventions. In accord with the Boldt decision (the key Indian fishing rights case in the Pacific Northwest, handed down in 1973 and extended to cover the Columbia River in 1974), the right of treaty tribes to active participation in the management of the regional fisheries is firmly established. A whole set of new issues is raised by what is known as Boldt Phase II, the adjudication of the tribes' right to protect their fisheries against actions that might diminish or destroy them, such as destructive logging practices, dams for hydropower or irrigation, and water pollution. However these issues are resolved, it is certain that Plateau Indian tribes will play a key role in determining the future of the Intermountain West.

Plateau Language Relationships

Stock	Family	Language	Dialect
Na Dene —— Athapaskan —————		Carrier-Chilcotin	
Isolate ———————— ? —————		Kutenai	
Salishan —— Interior Salish ————		Lillooet	
		Thompson	
		Shuswap	
		Okanagan ————————	Sinkaietk, Sanpoil-Nespelem, Colville, Lakes
		Columbia ———————	Columbia, Wenatchee, Chelan, Methow
		Kalispel ———————	Spokane, Kalispel, Pend d'Oreille, Flathead
		Coeur d'Alene	
Penutian	?—Chinookan	Kiksht (Upper Chinook)	
	Sahaptian —————	Sahaptin	
		NW Sahaptin ———	Kittitas, Yakima, Klikitat, Upper Cowlitz
		CR Sahaptin ———	Tenino-Tygh, Celilo, Rock Creek, John Day River, Umatilla
		NE Sahaptin ———	Walla Walla, Snake River, Palus, Priest Rapids
		Nez Perce	
		Klamath ———————	Klamath, Modoc
	? ———————	Cayuse	
	? ———————	Molala	
Uto-Aztekan — Numic ———————		Northern Paiute	

Adapted from Hunn (1989).

A Sample Traditional Plateau Indian Diet

	Quantity grams	Cal.	Pro. gms	Carb. gms	Fat gms	Calc. mgs	Iron mgs	Vit. C mgs
bitterroot	500	450	4	108	0.5	223	7.0	—
Lomatium canbyi	500	540	4	130	0.6	179	5.5	—
camas	300	339	2	81	0.7	151	20.7	—
roots total	**61%**	**52%**	**6%**	319	**1.8**	553	33.2	—
huckleberries	100	62	1	15	0.5	29	0.3	64.5
plants total	**66%**	**55%**	**6%**	334	**2.3**	582	33.5	64.5
salmon	500	850	107	0	43.5	875	4.5	—
fish total	**23%**	**33%**	**64%**					
venison	240	302	50	0	9.6	24	—	—
animal total	**34%**	**45%**	**94%**	**0**	**53.1**	**899**	**4.5**	—
grand total	**2140**	**2543**	**168**	**334**	**55.4**	**1481**	**38.0**	**64.5**
RDDA		**2267**	**45**			**898**	**14.0**	**45.0**

Notes to Table: Recommended Daily Dietary Allowances (RDDA's) are calculated from age and sex specific values in the *Encyclopedia Americana* (International Edition, 1986, volume 20, pg. 569), averaging age and sex sub-groups, then weighting males, females, and children (<15 years) as equal components of the total population. Sources of data for these estimates are given in Hunn 1989.

Plateau Historical Time Line

ca. 1730	Horses to the Cayuse and Nez Perce
ca. 1775	Smallpox throughout, from coastal contacts?
1805	Lewis and Clark expedition descends the Snake and Columbia Rivers in October; returns up river in April and May, 1806
1811	Astorians of the Pacific Fur Co. establish Astoria at the Columbia River mouth, arriving by sea from Boston
1830–33	Malaria ravages Indians of the lower Columbia and Willamette valleys
1836	Marcus Whitman and Henry Spalding establish missions among Cayuses (Whitman) and Nez Perces (Spalding)
1840–43	Some 250 Nez Perce and Cayuse farming; similar numbers of children in school at Lapwai and The Dalles at height of mission success
1843–45	Heavy use of the Oregon Trail by immigrant wagon trains; 5000 Americans settled in the Willamette valley by 1845
1847–48	Measles epidemic throughout central and southern Plateau

1847	Whitman "massacre" on Nov. 29; 14 whites killed; P. Ogden ransoms 48 captives; beginning of end of mission era
1855	Treaty council convened by I. Stevens at Walla Walla in June; treaties signed that established Yakima, Umatilla, and original Nez Perce Reservations
1855–58	"Indian wars": a series of skirmishes in the Yakima, Walla Walla, and Palouse country; Col. G. Wright defeats resistance of Paluses, Coeur d'Alenes, and Spokanes (1858)
1859	Treaties ratified
1872	Colville Reservation established by executive order
1877–78	The "Nez Perce War"; anti-treaty group led by Joseph eludes three U.S. armies; finally trapped in north-central Montana; taken as POWs to Oklahoma Indian Territory
1883	N. Pacific Railroad begins operating through Yakima valley bringing tide of settlement
1887	Dawes Severalty Act (General Allotment Act) passed
1914	Allotment rolls closed; allotments stopped after 440,000 acres at Yakima allotted, 90,000 of those in fee patent, and 27,000 acres sold
1934	Indian "New Deal" legislation: Johnson-O'Malley Act provides support for education, health, and welfare; Wheeler-Howard Act (Indian Reorganization Act or IRA) provides for local option tribal government
1938	Bonneville Dam completed; Grand Coulee under construction
1953	Termination Act defines Eisenhower policy; Klamath Reservation in Oregon terminated (1961)
1957	The Dalles Dam completed
1974	The Boldt decision defines treaty fishing rights on Puget Sound and the Columbia River
1980	Judge R. Orrick issues first decisions in Boldt Phase II defining rights of Indians to hatchery-reared fish and to protection of habitat

Southern Plateau Indian Reservations

Washington

Yakima c/o Yakima Agency P.O. Box 632 Toppenish, WA 98948	Pop: 7,500 (1980) Area: 1,134,830 acres Groups: Sahaptin, Wishram Govt: tribal council	Treaty: 1855
Colville c/o Colville Agency P.O. Box 111 Nespelem, WA 99155	Pop: 4,500 (2,750 resident) Area: 1,087,271 acres Groups: Okanagan-Colville, Columbia, Nez Perce, Palus Govt: tribal council	Exec. Order: 1872
Spokane c/o Spokane Agency P.O. Box 86 Wellpinit, WA 99040	Pop: 1,500 (500 resident) Area: 138,750 acres Groups: Spokane Govt: tribal council	Exec. Order: 1887

| Kalispel
c/o N. Idaho Agency
P.O. Drawer 277
Lapwai, ID 83540 | Pop: 150
Area: 4,500 acres
Groups: Kalispel | Exec. Order:
1887 |

Oregon

| Warm Springs
Warm Springs Agency
P.O. Box 1239
Warm Springs, OR 97761 | Pop: 1,750
Area: 563,916 acres
Groups: Sahaptin, Wasco, N. Paiute
Govt: tribal council | Treaty: 1855, 1865 |
| Umatilla
Umatilla Agency
P.O. Box 520
Pendleton, OR 97801 | Pop: 500
Area: 92,273 acres
Groups: Umatilla, Walla Walla, Cayuse
Govt: tribal council | Treaty: 1855 |

Idaho

Nez Perce c/o N. Idaho Agency	Pop: 750 Area: 92,685 acres Groups: Nez Perce Govt: tribal council	Treaty: 1855, 1863, 1868 Exec. Order: 1875
Coeur d'Alene c/o N. Idaho Agency	Pop: 600 Area: 69,435 acres Groups: Coeur d'Alene Govt: tribal council	Exec. Order: 1889
Kootenai c/o N. Idaho Agency	Pop: ? Area: 2,680 acres Groups: Kutenai Govt: by Flathead Tribe	Treaty: 1855

Montana

| Flathead
Flathead Agency
Box A
Pablo, MT 59855 | Pop: 3,000
Area: 140,000 acres
Groups: Flathead, Kutenai
Govt: tribal council | Treaty: 1855 |

Adapted From Hunn (1989).

SUGGESTED READINGS

Cohen, Faye G.
　　1986　*Treaties on Trial.* University of Washington Press, Seattle.
　　　　Cohen's book presents a comprehensive discussion of Indian fishing rights in Washington and Oregon today. The key role played by Columbia River Indians in the continuing fight for treaty rights is well documented.

French, David H.
　　1961　"Wasco-Wishram." In *Perspectives in American Indian Culture Change,* E. H. Spicer, ed., pp. 337–430. University of Chicago Press, Chicago, Illinois.
　　　　French's summary is meticulously careful to distinguish established fact from inference. He carefully distinguishes Wasco-Wishram cultural patterns at several historical periods.

Hunn, Eugene S.
　　1989.　*Nch'i Wana (The Big River): Mid-Columbia Indian People and their Land.* University of Washington Press, Seattle. In press.
　　　　Hunn's book is the only up-to-date, comprehensive ethnographic treatment of Plateau Indian culture available. He focuses on Sahaptin-speaking peoples of the mid-Columbia with particular emphasis on traditional cultural ecological relationships.

Josephy, Alvin M., Jr.
　　1965　*The Nez Perce Indians and the Opening of the Northwest.* Yale University Press, New Haven, Connecticut.
　　　　Josephy's history of the Nez Perce is the best of that popular genre.

Kirk, Ruth, and Richard D. Daugherty
　　1978　*Exploring Washington Archaeology.* University of Washington Press, Seattle.
　　　　This popular introduction to the prehistory of Washington State is beautifully illustrated, readable, and current.

Leslie, Craig
　　1984　*Winterkill.* Dell, New York.
　　　　Leslie's prize-winning novel provides a sensitive, intimate account of contemporary Plateau Indian life, recounting the story of a Umatilla Indian sometime rodeo cowboy searching for a meaningful foundation for his life and that of his son.

Phinney, Archie
　　1934　*Nez Perce Texts.* Columbia University Contributions to Anthropology, No. 25.
　　　　Phinney is the first Plateau Indian to earn a Ph.D. in Anthropology (under Franz Boas at Columbia University). This collection of Nez Perce mythology—dictated by his mother in Nez Perce—can't be beat for authenticity.

Miller, Christopher L.
　　1985　*Prophetic Worlds: Indians and Whites on the Columbia Plateau.* Rutgers University Press, New Brunswick, New Jersey.
　　　　Miller's ethnohistorical treatise on Plateau Indian prophecy and the strangely complementary prophetic vision that drove the Protestant missionaries to the Plateau provides fresh insight into the phenomenon of culture contact here in the nineteenth century.

Ramsey, Jarold
　　1977　*Coyote Was Going There: Indian Literature of the Oregon Country.* University of Washington Press, Seattle.
　　　　Ramsey's collection of Indian myths and stories reflects his concern to preserve the authentic meaning and style of the original while communicating the power of the original in translation.

Thwaites, Reuben Gold, ed.
　　1959　*Original Journals of the Lewis and Clark Expedition, 1804–1806.* Antiquarian Press, New York.

Still a gold mine of ethnographic and ethnohistoric information on the Plateau. Lewis and Clark traveled down the Snake River and the Columbia in October 1905, wintered at the Columbia River mouth, then returned over much the same route in April and May 1806.

Turner, Nancy J., Randy Bouchard, and Dorothy I. D. Kennedy
    1980   *Ethnobotany of the Okanagan-Colville Indians of British Columbia.* British Columbia Provincial Museum, Victoria, B.C. Occasional Paper No. 21.
           This compilation of contemporary Indian knowledge of the Plateau botanical environment gives eloquent testimony to the depth of indigenous Plateau empirical culture.

Walker, Deward E., Jr.
    1985   *Conflict and Schism in Nez Perce Acculturation: A Study of Religion and Politics.* Washington State University Press, Pullman.
           Walker's study of Nez Perce religion and politics focuses on the complex interaction of Christian missions and reservation political factions under the demands of adjustment to the overwhelming power of white society.

Zucker, Jeff, Kay Hummel, and Bob Høgfoss
    1983   *Oregon Indians: Culture, History, and Current Affairs: an Atlas and Introduction.* Western Imprints, Oregon Historical Society, Portland.
           This is an encyclopedic compilation of essential information about Oregon Indians, past and, especially, present.

REFERENCES

Ackerman, Lillian Alice
    1982   "Sexual Equality in the Plateau Culture Area." Ph.D. dissertation, Washington State University, Pullman.

Ames, Kenneth M., and Alan G. Marshall
    1980–
    1981   "Villages, Demography and Subsistence Intensification on the Southern Columbia Plateau." *North American Archaeologist* 2:25–52.

Anastasio, Angelo
    1972   "The Southern Plateau: An Ecological Analysis of Intergroup Relations." *Northwest Anthropological Research Notes* 6:109–229. (Ph.D. dissertation, University of Chicago, 1955)

Boas, Franz
    1918   "Kutenai Tales." *Bureau of American Ethnology Bulletin* No. 59.

Boyd, Robert T.
    1985   "The Introduction of Infectious Diseases Among the Indians of the Pacific Northwest, 1774–1874." Ph.D. dissertation, University of Washington, Seattle.

Cook, Sherburne F.
    1955   "The Epidemic of 1830–1833 in California and Oregon." *University of California Publications in American Archaeology and Ethnology* 43:303–326.

Cressman, Luther S.
    1977   *Prehistory of the Far West: Homes of Vanished Peoples.* University of Utah, Salt Lake City.

Crosby, Alfred W., Jr.
    1972   *The Columbian Exchange: Biological and Cultural Consequences of 1492.* Greenwood Press, Westport, Connecticut.

Elmendorf, William
    1965   "Linguistic and Geographic Relations in the Northern Plateau Area." *Southwestern Journal of Anthropology* 21:63–77.

Greenberg, Joseph H.
    1987   *Language in the Americas.* Stanford University Press, Stanford, California.

Haines, Francis
1938 "The Northward Spread of Horses Among the Plains Indians." *American Anthropologist* 40:429–437.

Hewes, Gordon
1973 "Indian Fisheries Productivity in Pre-Contact Times in the Pacific Salmon Area." *Northwest Anthropological Research Notes* 7:133–155. (Ph.D. dissertation, University of California, Berkeley, 1947)

Hunn, Eugene S.
1981 "On the Relative Contribution of Men and Women to Subsistence Among Hunter-Gatherers of the Columbia Plateau: A Comparison with *Ethnographic Atlas* Summaries." *Journal of Ethnobiology* 1:121–134.

Hunn, Eugene S., and David H. French
1981 "*Lomatium:* A Key Resource for Columbia Plateau Native Subsistence." *Northwest Science* 55:87–94.

Jacobs, Melville
1929 "Northwest Sahaptin Texts." *University of Washington Publications in Anthropology* 2:175–244.

Jacobs, Melville
1937 "Historic Perspectives in Indian Languages of Oregon and Washington." *Pacific Northwest Quarterly* 28:55–74.

Marshall, Alan G.
1977 "Nez Perce Social Groups: An Ecological Interpretation." Ph.D. dissertation, Washington State University, Pullman.

Mooney, James
1896 "The Ghost-Dance Religion and the Sioux Outbreak of 1890." *Fourteenth Annual Report of the Bureau of Ethnology* Part 2, pp. 641–1136.

Murdock, George Peter
1967 *Ethnographic Atlas.* University of Pittsburgh Press, Pittsburgh, Pennsylvania.

Nelson, C. M.
1973 "Prehistoric Culture Change in the Intermontane Plateau of Western North America." In *the Exploration of Cultural Change: Models in Prehistory.* C. Renfrew, ed., pp 371–390. Duckworth, London.

Ray, Verne F.
1939 "Cultural Relations in the Plateau of Northwestern America." *Publications of the Frederick Webb Hodge Anniversary Publication Fund* Volume 3. Southwestern Museum, Los Angeles, California.

Relander, Click
1962 *Strangers on the Land.* Franklin Press, Yakima, Washington.

Sapir, Edward
1909 "Wishram Texts." *Publications of the American Ethnological Society* No. 2.

Schuster, Helen H.
1975 "Yakima Indian Traditionalism: A Study in Continuity and Change." Ph.D. dissertation, University of Washington, Seattle.

Wallace, Anthony F. C.
1956 "Revitalization Movements." *American Anthropologist* 58:264–281.

Chapter 11

The Northwest Coast Culture Area

Daniel L. Boxberger
Western Washington University

Introduction

The Northwest Coast has been described as a culture area that is 1,000 miles long and one mile wide. While that description may not be exactly true it nonetheless speaks to some unique facts about the Northwest Coast. Primarily consisting of the coastal areas of Southeast Alaska, British Columbia, Washington and Oregon, the geographical extent of the Northwest Coast is long and narrow in comparison with other culture areas. Also, for the most part, the native inhabitants of the Northwest Coast were oriented towards the sea coasts and rivers and the resources found there. For our purposes we will consider the Northwest Coast area to be that area west of the Cascade and Coast mountain ranges from Yakutat Bay in the north to the central Oregon coast in the south.

The Northwest Coast people have long fascinated anthropologists. For over one hundred years scholars have been drawn to the area to study the extreme diversity in language, kinship and social organization and ceremony. This area has served as a testing ground for theories about human behavior and has long been an area that anthropologists have pointed to as exhibiting "exceptions" to generalities concerning human behavior. Although we speak of the Northwest Coast as a distinct culture area the similarities between the various groups are often shadowed by the differences. Therefore it is difficult to discuss those traits that characterize the Northwest Coast because we almost always have to add "well, except for . . ."

It is also with some difficulty that we speak of the number of tribes in the Northwest Coast culture area. The particular types of social organization that are represented do not necessarily lend themselves to categorization. Some anthropologists have suggested that a better way to talk about cultures in the Northwest Coast is to talk about language groupings, but as with any classificatory scheme this approach too has its limitations. We will limit our discussion to fifteen "tribes", as they have been discussed traditionally in anthropology, understanding that in any one case the appellation could properly refer to a language group (as with the Tlingit), a native political grouping (as with the Bella Coola), or a term that was applied to them by some other people (as with the Nootka).

Beginning in the north, the area of Southeast Alaska is inhabited by the Tlingit. At the time of first European contact, in 1741, the Tlingit numbered approximately 10,000 (these,

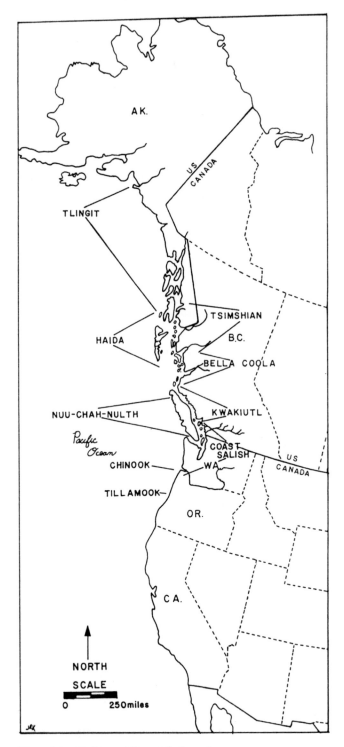

Map of the Northwest Coast Culture Area

and the population figures that follow, are from Kroeber 1939: 135–136). The area of Southeast Alaska is extremely rugged country as the coastal range of mountains extends into the sea. Therefore the Tlingit resided on the many islands just offshore and near the mouths of rivers on the mainland. The entirety of the Northwest Coast is broken up by numerous streams, most of which supported runs of salmon, and near these streams is where the native people usually made their homes.

South of the Tlingit on the Queen Charlotte Islands and the southern portion of Prince of Wales Island reside the Haida. The Haida are especially noted for their huge canoes and elaborate art work. Numbering about 9,800 at the time of first contact the Haida are today primarily concentrated in the villages of Masset and Skidegate on the Queen Charlotte Islands and Hydaburg in Southeast Alaska.

To the south of the Tlingit and west of the Haida we find the Tsimshian. Usually the Tsimshian are divided into three main groups, the Coast Tsimshian residing in the north-central coastal area of British Columbia and the Nishga and Gitksan whose villages are more inland. At the time of European contact these groups probably numbered 8,300.

South of the Tsimshian, along the mainland and northeast coast of Vancouver Island, are located the Wakashan speakers, including the Haisla, Heiltsuk and Kwakwala (Kwakiutl). The Wakashan group also includes the "West Coast People" (Nootka and Nitinat) on the west coast of Vancouver Island and the Makah on the northwest tip of the Olympic Peninsula in Washington State. Usually all six of these groups are treated as different "tribes" but many native people have come to resent the designations that outsiders have applied to them. For example, "Nootka" is said to have been misapplied to the native people in the vicinity of Nootka Sound by Captain Cook in 1778. It is believed that when Cook asked the natives the name of the sound they thought he was asking if it continued around the island, so they answered "notka," which means "to circle around" (Arima 1983:v). Beginning in 1980 the West Coast People have asked that they be referred to as "Nuu-chah-nulth." Similarly the term "Kwakiutl" only properly refers to the village in the vicinity of Fort Rupert on northern Vancouver Island. While the people subsumed under the term have not asked that the misnomer be dropped they have asked that it be properly pronounced, often spelled "Kwawgwelth" or "Kwagulth," there is still no convention as to how the term should be applied. At the time of first European contact the totality of the Wakashan groups was probably about 8,700.

The next major group is the Coast Salish of western Washington State, the mainland of southwest British Columbia and the southeast portion of Vancouver Island. In addition to the Coast Salish there are also two other Salish groups, the Bella Coola of the north-central coast of British Columbia and the Tillamook of the north coast of Oregon State. It is especially among the Coast Salish that our concept of "tribe" really takes a beating as virtually every village was an autonomous group. To further complicate matters there was a great deal of interchange between villages in a local area, so often an individual could change allegiance from one village group to another. As will become clear when we discuss linguistic groups, the language group may be a better way of discussing a "tribe"

Figure 11.1 The inside of a house at Nootka Sound, from the Cook Expedition, 1778. (Courtesy of Special Collections Division, University of Washington Libraries, Negative No. NM 3918.)

among the Salish. At the time of first contact the Coast Salish probably numbered about 32,400, the Bella Coola 1,400 and the Tillamook 1,500.

The final major group of Northwest Coast natives is the Chinook. Located in the area around the mouth of the Columbia River and upriver to the Cascade range, the Chinook figured prominently in the early history of the Northwest. At the time of initial contact the Chinook probably numbered 22,000 but by 1850 their numbers had dwindled to little more than 100 due to introduced disease and other ravages of "civilization." Noted for their shrewd trading and skilled seamanship the Chinook have captivated the imagination of scholars for over a century.

As should be evident the Northwest Coast presents special problems when we begin to discuss social groups beyond the village level. That is part of the fascination these groups have held for anthropology, they defy any attempt to categorize or generalize. Although we are forced at some point to generalize in order to be able to talk about the Northwest Coast cultures we must not lose sight of the fact that these categorizations are arbitrary in that they are applied by outside observers and the native people themselves do not see the same boundaries or well-defined delineations that we may give the impression exist. Let us now examine the languages represented on the Northwest Coast which will present us with further interesting problems.

Language

One of the things about Northwest Coast cultures that has captivated the attention of anthropologists for a long time is the diversity of languages. Of the seven language families found here four have no other known speakers and two have extremely limited distribution beyond the Northwest Coast. The only major language group represented that has wide distribution in North American has only limited distribution in the Northwest, this is the Athabascan language group represented by two isolated groups of Athabascan speakers on the north and south sides of the mouth of the Columbia River, the Kwalhiokwa and Klatskanie. The following chart illustrates the languages represented and their affiliations.

Table 11.1

Languages of the Northwest Coast

Phylum	Family	Northwest Languages	Examples of Related Languages
NaDene	Athabascan	Kwalhiokwa Klatskanie	Chipewyan, Carrier, Navajo, Apache
Penutian (Classification Questionable)	Tsimshian	Nishga Gitksan Tsimshian	Yakima, Nez Perce, Maidu, Klamath
	Chinook	Chinook Cathlamet Kiksht	
Isolates	Tlingit	Tlingit	none
	Haida	Haida	none
	Chemakuan	Chemakum Quileute	none
	Salish	Bella Coola Tillamook Quinalt Chehalis Cowlitz Lushootseed Straits Halkomelem Comox	Okanagan, Shuswap, Kalispel, Flathead, Cour d'Alene

Source: Suttles 1985

By "Isolate" we mean a language that has no known affiliation with any other language group. The relatively large number of language isolates in the Northwest Coast may be a reflection of the comparative lack of linguistic work done in this area. Further research may uncover relationships between these isolates and other language groupings. On the other hand it may be that the Tsimshian family is an isolate too as there is some disagreement among linguists as to whether we can justify including it in the Penutian phylum. Hopefully as further research is carried out many of the confusions will be clarified. One researcher (Greenberg 1987) has attempted to develop a scheme that would demonstrate relatedness between many of the language isolates in North America but his explanations have yet to gain wide acceptance.

Most Northwest languages today are spoken by just a few elderly members of the groups. In many cases when the present elderly generation of speakers is gone so will be the language. Many Native people are attempting to institute language programs through their educational services or through their tribally operated schools.

Subsistence and Technology

If anything characterizes the Northwest Coast in most peoples' minds it is the reliance on two important resources—the salmon and the cedar. While the importance of these two resources cannot be denied we will attempt in this chapter to point out that there was a good deal more involved in the subsistence patterns of the Northwest Coast people.

Perhaps the best way to discuss the subsistence and technology of the Northwest Coast people is to look at a yearly round of activities. Certain resources were used during certain times of the year and all of the different resources had specialized technologies to exploit them.

Table 11.2

Northwest Coast Yearly Round

Jan	Feb	Ma	Apr	May	Jun	Jul	Aug	Sep	Oct	Nov	Dec

-------------------salmon fishing----------------------

---------------other fishing-----   ---------

-----shellfish----------------------   --------------------

--sea mammal hunting------

--land mammal hunting-----

--------------------   ---plant foods------

Plant Resources

Besides cedar the Northwest Coast people utilized a variety of plant resources for food and technological items. It is difficult to characterize plant use for the entire Northwest Coast as the availability of specific plant resources varied so dramatically from the south to the north. Generally speaking all Northwest coast people gathered berries during the summer and fall. At least two dozen different species of berries were used, most of them being smashed and dried into cakes that could be stored for later use. Another important part of the Northwest Coast diet was starchy roots such as camas (Camassia quamash), wapato (Sagittaria latifolia) and bracken fern roots (Pteridium aquilinum). Each of these were used in certain areas, for example wapato was common to the sloughs and back waters of the lower stretches of the Columbia River and there provided an important part of the diet for the Chinookan people.

The majority of other plant resources were gathered in the spring to the fall months. From the first appearance of greens in the spring to the first frosts various plant foods supplemented the diet and provided stored goods for trade and winter use. In addition to berries and the starchy roots already mentioned, the Northwest Coast people used a variety of other plant resources for not only food but for medicines and for technological items. Turner (1975; 1979) notes the use of over two hundred species of plants. To discuss all of these, or even some of them, would be a foolhardy attempt at best. Therefore we will elaborate only on one of the more important plant resources.

Of all the plant resources cedar was undoubtedly of highest importance. Providing clothing, baskets, housing and transportation cedar was literally the backbone of Northwest Coast technology. Cedar bark can be removed from the tree in rather large sheets which can then be shredded for clothing or pulled into strips for weaving of baskets or textiles. The wood from cedar was used in a variety of ways: dug-out canoes of many shapes and sizes; planks for housing or making bent-wood boxes; and for carvings of every imaginable sort. In addition to its technological attributes cedar also had spiritual qualities for most Northwest Coast people.

Salmon

Prior to, and for a considerable period of time after, European contact the native people of the Northwest Coast were engaged in traditional fisheries that adequately met their needs for subsistence. The importance of fisheries resources varied from group to group, but in general it is safe to say that salmon were the most important resource utilized on the Northwest Coast. The techniques employed in the pre-commercial fishery ranged from the simple (dip nets, gaffs, spears) to the technologically sophisticated (seines, reef nets). Beringer (1982) has suggested a typology of twelve methods of salmon fishing and has shown the distribution of each method. From her evidence it would appear that the Coast Salish groups near the United States-Canada border, especially skilled salmon fishers, employed most of the known technologies and, comparatively, had the greatest reliance on salmon as a staple food source.

Figure 11.2 Eulachon racks at Nass River. (Courtesy of Special Collections Division, University of Washington Libraries, negative No. NA 735.)

Table 11.3

Comparative Salmon Use on the Northwest Coast

Native Group	Pounds of Salmon
Tlingit	500
Haida	400
Tsimshian proper	400
Nishga, Gitksan	500
Nuu-chah-nulth (Nootka)	300
Bella Coola	
Kwakiutl	365
Coast Salish	
Fraser River	1,000
North Puget Sound	600
South Puget Sound	365
Washington Coast	365
Chinook	
Tillamook	

Source: Hewes 1973

The only estimates we have of salmon use on the Northwest Coast suggests the following per capita use patterns.

Salmon were not always used fresh and large amounts were wind dried or smoke dried for later use.

Other fisheries resources were also important. Rock fish, halibut, flounder, eulachon, smelt and sturgeon, just to name a few, were also important to the native economies.

Sea Mammal Hunting

Most groups on the Northwest Coast utilized sea mammals, especially seal, but also whale (almost exclusively limited to the Nootkan speakers although other groups would use beached or stranded whales) and porpoise were hunted.

Land Mammal Hunting

The heavy reliance on the water resources greatly overshadowed any land mammal usage but deer, elk, bear, mountain goat and some other species were occasionally hunted

Figure 11.3 Suquamish settlement at Eagle Harbor; fish drying in front of houses, ca. 1900. (Courtesy of Special Collections Division, University of Washington Libraries, Negative No. NA 700.)

for food, hides and horn. Mountain goat was hunted for its wooly hair, used in weaving, and horn, which can be carved into various types of utensils.

Shellfish

Of all the subsistence items used by Northwest Coast people shellfish have been the most overlooked. The huge shell middens at many archaeological sites on the Northwest Coast attest to the importance of this resource. Clams of various sorts, oysters, crab, sea urchins, and other shellfish contributed to the diet and dried clams provided an important trade item with native people east of the mountains.

For many Northwest Coast people shellfish were sometimes seen as "starvation food," that is, a food resource that could be gathered easily at virtually any time of the year. Barnacles and mussels were usually seen as this type of food and usually were not preserved. Clams, however, were taken in quantity to be dried and stored for later use. Other non-fish food resources included such things as crab, sea cucumber and octopus as well as many locally available foodstuffs. Some of the Salish groups have a saying that "when the tide is out the table is set," which certainly speaks to the reliability of and dependence on the inter-tidal areas.

Resource Use

As was common to the more productive salmon fishing locations, often certain plant gathering areas, shellfish grounds and, among some groups, hunting areas were "owned" and controlled by a kin group. We will discuss aspects of Northwest Coast social organization later but for now it is important to note that kinship groups exercised a certain amount of control over certain resource-use areas. Among the Tlingit for example, certain streams were considered the property of clan groups and permission had to be obtained to take fish from that stream. Among some Coast Salish certain fishing sites were considered the "property" of individuals although kin would be recruited to work the sites. What this meant was that certain kin groups exercised control over the more productive resource locations and, as we shall see, this related directly to variations in status and prestige.

Social Systems

The highly complex and intricate set of social relations that existed on the Northwest Coast has been a matter of much scholarly debate and, in the minds of most students, a matter of extreme confusion. Much of the confusion seems to lie in the disruption that occurred during the mid to late 1800s when epidemic diseases were taking their toll and, at the same time, the influx of new sources of riches through trade was breaking down the differences in status and wealth. We may never know the extent to which differences in status existed prior to European contact but we do have some enlightening glimpses into social relations during the early historic period.

One of the most famous of these "glimpses" is the published narrative of John R. Jewitt (Jewitt 1815). Jewitt was a blacksmith on board the American ship the *Boston* when in 1803 the vessel was seized by natives at Nootka Sound and all aboard, save Jewitt and Thompson, a sailmaker, were slain. Because of his metal-working skills Jewitt soon became the prize slave of Maquinna, who appeared to be the head of the village at Nootka Sound. It is possible that because of his uniqueness Jewitt was treated differently than most slaves, but from what we can garner from his narratives it is unlikely. Jewitt describes in great detail the relationships that existed in Maquinna's household. For example, although a slave Jewitt was allowed to dine with Maquinna's family and slept in the same house. In fact, Maquinna's house consisted of a number of people of different social statuses. Typically Northwest Coast societies are described as consisting of a four-level set of relationships. High status ("nobility") consisting of the wealthiest members of a local group who would claim such a position through heredity and the accumulation and distribution of wealth. A secondary status, which consisted of people of some standing in the community who were respected but did not generally accumulate wealth or potlatch. A low status which Suttles (1958) described for the Salish as consisting of former slaves and people "who had lost their history." And finally, slaves. There has been for some time considerable disagreement as to whether the Northwest coast societies were "class" societies or "rank" societies. Indeed some groups, like the Nootka and Kwakiutl, carried ranking to an extreme. But for most groups the distinctions between individuals were not so clearly defined. Certainly, since this is a matter of much debate, we will not attempt to offer a solution here but we must at least point out that social distinctions did exist and the manner in which these distinctions were expressed permeates every aspect of Northwest Coast social life.

Northwest Coast kinship types vary widely. From the matrilineal groups in the north to the bilateral groups with patri-tendencies in the south, the variety of kinship forms is mind boggling. The northern groups (Tlingit, Haida, Tsimshian) are classically matrilineal. The Coast Salish and Nootkan were bilateral. The Chinook were bilateral with strong patri-tendencies (patrilocality, for example). The Kwakiutl, on the other hand, present a complex problem. We might describe them as "ambilineal" (Adams 1981:365) or "bilineal" because it appears that inheritance could succeed through either the mother's or father's line. Perhaps more accurate is to speak of the "numaym," a sort of corporate kin group among the Southern Kwakiutl which controlled access to resources and owned some privileges (masks, songs, and dances), with somewhat fluid membership requirements. In essence then, what we find on the Northwest Coast is a gradation of kinship types from matrilineal in the north to patri-focal in the south. Many suggestions have been put forth to explain this variation in kinship type, most of which relate to variation in the environment and the need for the more northerly groups to exercise stricter control over access to resources (Suttles 1968; Richardson 1982).

Among the northern matrilineal groups access to resources was strictly controlled by the clan. Fishing sites, hunting territories, and various other rights and privileges were in the ownership and control of the matri-clan. One possible explanation might be that resources, like salmon streams, are less productive in the northern areas and therefore stricter control governs their use. In support of this point of view we can point to the fact that further south on the Northwest Coast control is less prohibitive. Among the Straits Salish only certain fishing sites were owned and controlled by individuals or kin groups. Directly corresponding to decreasing control from north to south is increasing abundance, suggesting that as resources become less available the access is controlled more closely.

One must not lose sight, however, of the fact that it is not just natural resources that are within the control of the kin group. Rights, such as certain songs, dances, and performances, as well as other privileges were directly tied to the kinship system. Perhaps the most distinctive aspect of this tie between kinship and economy is the potlatch. The potlatch, the ceremonial distribution of wealth goods, took place on numerous occasions. Naming ceremonies, funerals, weddings, house or totem pole raisings and other functions were usually reasons for a potlatch. While the evidence overwhelmingly supports the contention that potlatching increased in intensity and the amount of goods distributed in the mid to late 1800s there is also good evidence to support the belief that potlatching was an important part of the socio-economic system prior to contact with Europeans.

Typically a potlatch would involve several days and include guests from numerous surrounding villages. The host would usually recruit help from kin and fellow villagers, for to host a potlatch single-handedly would have been a near impossible task. The potlatch festivities often began over a year in advance with invitations being announced and the gathering of wealth goods getting underway. When the actual potlatch began the entire house would be cleared out and hundreds of people would be seated inside. A potlatch could last up to five to seven days with the actual distribution of goods only being a small part. Feasting, performances by masked dancers, pantomimes, and contests would often take place, filling in the time. Today, with many Native people needing to meet the demands of working for a wage, potlatches have been condensed into one day, or over a weekend but the tradition has persisted.

Belief Systems

Common to the belief systems of the people of the Northwest Coast was a complex centered around the guardian spirit. Almost more a part of the natural rather than the supernatural realm the guardian spirit was manifested in various types of animate and inanimate objects. Often these spirits are lumped in gross categories referred to as "lay" spirits and "shamanistic" spirits but in actuality the categories are not so clear cut. Guardian spirits on the Northwest Coast were an interesting mix of individual expression and hereditary rights. Among most native North Americans the guardian spirit was obtained during a period of self-sacrifice, fasting and praying, and this was certainly true of the people of the Northwest Coast, but additionally an individual would often tend to encounter spirit helpers that "ran in their family," that is, that they had a right to by virtue of kinship. Seemingly the guardian spirit complex was a relationship between an individual and a spirit "power" that imparted some skill, such as hunting, warrior, healing, or some special

Figure 11.4 Potlatch at Alert Bay, British Columbia, September 1911. The men are seated behind china plates with money in them and blankets ready to be given away. (Courtesy of Special Collections Division, University of Washington Libraries, Negative No. 2850.)

knowledge. It was a very personal relationship, one that was not divulged but which was expressed during the winter ceremonials with a song and dance. Yet, despite all the secrecy surrounding the complex people knew what spirit a person possessed based on their actions, their skills and abilities, and based on the words and movements of their songs. Usually what is meant by a "lay" spirit is a relationship between an individual and their guardian spirit that imparts some basic skill, such as hunting, fighting, or fishing for men and basketry, weaving, or berry picking for women just to name a few. The "shaman" spirit, on the other hand, meant the ability to heal people (or in some cases to harm people) either spiritually or physically. Spiritual healing involved traveling to the world of the dead to retrieve lost souls or to remove foreign objects that had been placed in the person's body by someone meaning harm. Thus, the major component of the religious belief system of the people of the Northwest Coast was centered around the relationship between an individual and their guardian spirit.

Usually an individual would be sent at about the age of puberty to a place of solitude to seek their spirit encounter. Among most groups both boys and girls would participate. If unsuccessful they would be sent again. Some individuals would seek more than one spirit, although it was said that only the strongest could handle more than one. In addition to obtaining spirits through the quest, guardian spirits also could come announced when the person was ill, in grieving, in a dream, or as a result of a chance encounter. As we have seen the guardian spirit complex is a common aspect of Native American religions and represents a type of religious expression that is highly individualistic. There were, however, some communal rites conducted on behalf of the group as a whole. Perhaps the most common, and the most famous, is that of the "first salmon ceremony." The actual species varied from group to group but generally the first caught fish of the species most important to the local group was the object of this ritual. For example, the Straits Salish depended upon sockeye salmon to a large extent and considered it most important to their livelihood, therefore it was the sockeye salmon that was the species treated with reverence in the Straits Salish version of this ceremony. The belief persisted that the salmon lived in the ocean in longhouses much like those inhabited by humans. But once a year the salmon would don their fish clothing and swim up freshwater streams where they would make themselves available to people. The belief was that if the salmon were treated with respect they would allow themselves to be caught and continue to return year after year. When the first salmon was taken each year the fish would be brought into the village where it would have several rituals conducted over it. It would be sprinkled with eagle down and red ochre and then would be ritually cooked. Then members of the community would all eat a small piece and the bones would all be gathered up and placed back in the water. The fish would then resume its living form and go to inform the rest of the species that it had been treated well. From that point members of the community could commence fishing for food to eat and store.

Other than the first salmon ceremony the numbers of communal rituals were few. Although ceremonies were conducted that included the entire community, and neighboring communities, as participants the activities were usually conducted on behalf of an individual or his family. Of course the best known of these ceremonies is the potlatch. The word "potlatch" literally means "to give" and the word has come to be applied by anthropologists and native people alike to ceremonies that involve the ceremonial redistribution of wealth goods. A potlatch was often conducted during ceremonies marking certain life stages, for example, at a naming, a wedding, or at a funeral. but there were other occasions that may be marked by a potlatch as well. Some groups, like the Tlingit, would give a potlatch to commemorate the raising of a totem pole or the construction of a new clan house. Some groups, like the Kwakiutl, would potlatch for the purpose of enhancing one's status or belittling a rival. For the Salish potlatches were often used to mark one's entry into a secret society or for the purpose of making one's spirit dance public. Although the potlatch has entered into general anthropological parlance as a grandiose ceremony used to enhance an individual's status it must be remembered that potlatches took a variety of forms and served numerous functions.

Historical Overview

In 1778 when Captain James Cook traded several sea otter pelts that he had taken on board quite by chance on the Northwest Coast to Chinese Mandarins, he discovered that the prices they were willing to pay made this commodity made it one of the most valuable natural resources in the world. Although some European explorations—Spanish, English, French and Russian—had visited the Northwest Coast before, it was Cook's accidental discovery of the value of sea otter pelts that started intense and prolonged contact between Europeans and the Native people.

Initially European traders came by ship, anchoring at Nootka Sound and trading along the coast for sea otter and other furs. The Native people found items of European manufacture welcome additions to their technological inventory. However, as the anthropologist Eric Wolf points out, the impact of this trade was minimal.

> As long as the native Americans were able to direct most of the social labor available through kin-ordered relations to the task of guaranteeing their subsistence, the goods attained by part-time fur hunting supplemented rather than replaced their own means of production. (Wolf 1982:193)

Shortly after, however, land-based trade operations began to appear at various places in the Northwest. The Spanish established a post at Nootka Sound in 1789, the Russians at New Archangel (Sitka) in 1799, and the British, after taking possession of the American Fort Astoria during the War of 1812, established numerous posts along the coast.

In general the era of the fur trade, so influential in other culture areas of North America, was relatively short-lived in the Northwest, lasting until approximately 1850. This is not to say that this period of early contact did not have a noticeable impact on the Native cultures.

The impact of infectious diseases occurred before European contact and likely had devastating effects. In 1792 Captain George Vancouver, the first European to explore Puget Sound, noted numbers of deserted villages with ". . . the scull, limbs, ribs, and back bones, or some other vestiges of the human body. . . promiscuously scattered about the beach in great numbers" and numerous adults who bore the scars of smallpox (Vancouver 1798:111). Perhaps the most devastating of epidemics noted in the historic record occurred between 1832 and 1835 along the Lower Columbia River. The Chinook and Cowlitz were especially hard hit by this particular disease. There is some debate over exactly what the cause of this epidemic was. Historical documents identify the disease as "intermittent fever." Some scholars have suggested that it was influenza and others claim that it was malaria. The whites who contracted the disease did not die but the Native people died by the hundreds. Fully 96 percent of the Lower Chinook population succumbed in the three year period the intermittent fever raged and comparable numbers of Cowlitz and other groups were likewise affected. While other Northwest Coast groups were not as severely affected, large population declines from other epidemics were certainly in evidence and continued to effect Northwest Coast people for several generations. The last major smallpox epidemic, for example, occurred as late as 1882. By the time of increasing European settlement in the mid-1800s, the Native population had declined dramatically.

Beginning in the 1850s scores of settlers began to arrive in the Northwest, first settling in the Willamette Valley in Oregon, and shortly after in the Puget Sound area of Washington. Settlement in British Columbia and Alaska also began at this time but proceeded much more slowly.

With the growth of Euro-American society in the Northwest conflict between the Natives and Whites was inevitable. While we do not see the all-out warfare, as was evident in other culture areas, such as the Plains, we do see the implementation of the reservation system (with the exception of Alaska) and increasing economic and political control over the lives of the Native people. We will look briefly at the developments in Alaska, British Columbia and Washington separately.

In 1867 Russia sold the territory of Alaska to the United States. It was just after the Civil War and the United States was in a severe financial situation. In the late 1800s the United States had little use for Alaska and little funds available to institute a political structure. As a result the Native people were left pretty much alone. In 1884 Alaska's status was changed from a "customs district" to a "land district." The unusual position of Alaska Natives was noted at that time.

> That the Indians . . . shall not be disturbed in the possession of any lands actually in their use or occupation or now claimed by them, but the terms under which such persons may acquire title to such lands is reserved for future legislation (United States Government 1976:1).

Until 1884 the only governmental personnel in Southeast Alaska were a customs officer and a detachment of the United States Navy, both stationed in Sitka. From 1884 to the creation of the Territory of Alaska in 1912, the United States Government gradually increased civil authority in Alaska. In the 1890s when the Yukon gold rush began to produce an influx of settlers and transients economic enterprise began to appear in Alaska as well. In Southeast Alaska the most notable development was in the growth of the commercial fishing industry. The number of fish canneries rose from seventeen in 1888 to 135 in 1918. Much of the labor both in fishing and in the canneries was supplied by Native people. It was not until after the turn of the century that the white population of Southeast Alaska outnumbered the Native population but by 1960 the White population was three times larger.

For years the only contact the federal government had with the Alaska Natives was through the territorial court system. It was not until 1931 that the Bureau of Indian Affairs took over administration of the affairs of Alaska Natives when it set up a special office, the Alaska Native Service. Nevertheless, despite the lack of governmental intervention we see significant changes occurring among the Tlingit during the early 1900s.

One of the most influential forces of change among the Tlingit was a "fraternal" organization. In 1912 ten young Tlingit men, mostly from the Sitka area, met to form an organization that has come to be known as the Alaska Native Brotherhood (ANB). The anthropologist Philip Drucker believed that the ANB had its roots in several benevolent societies the missionaries had sponsored in Tlingit villages in the late 1800s (Drucker 1958:20).

From the conception of the ANB until the early 1920s the organization had three major policies on which it concentrated: the recognition of citizenship rights for Natives;

education for Natives; and the abolition of aboriginal customs, or at least those popularly regarded by the Whites as "uncivilized" (Drucker 1958:41).

The early leaders of the ANB were men who had been brought up under the influence of the missionaries at Sitka, and they seemed to believe that if the Tlingit "comported themselves enough like a white American, the white man would eventually become benevolent and give the Indian his long-awaited rights." From the entire range of traditional culture the ANB singled out two targets for their disapproval, the native language and the potlatch (Drucker 1958:43).

During the 1920s the policies of the ANB underwent revision and the ANB began to take an aggressive stand on political issues. Some of these issues were the "two school system" where the Indian children in predominately white communities had to attend government schools rather than public schools; the right of citizenship, and with it the right to vote; discrimination against Indians in theaters, stores, restaurants and other public places; the destruction of salmon runs by commercial fish traps; and the resistance against reservations (Drucker 1958:44, 45, 51, 70). The ANB even gathered enough political backing to place one of their members, William Paul, in the territorial legislature.

The ANB has never been consistent in its stand against traditional customs. The original charter stated that only English speakers could belong, but in fact many of the meetings were conducted in Tlingit for the benefit of the non-English speaking members. The potlatch was discouraged, but became instituted in the ANB as a means to increase the treasury (Drucker 1958:60–61). From its beginning the ANB has been a dominant political force in the territory and, after 1959, the state of Alaska. The policies and actions of the ANB have changed with changing circumstances. The ANB continues, to the present day, as a major player in the relationship between the Tlingit and the dominant society.

In 1973 when the United States implemented the Alaska Native Claims Settlement Act (ANCSA) the Tlingit and Haida of Southeast Alaska were formed into one of thirteen regional corporations. In addition two hundred village corporations were formed. Native people who had been born by 1973 were issued shares in their regional corporation which after 1991 can be sold on the open market. The goal of the ANCSA was to stimulate economic growth and development in the State of Alaska by placing land and capital within the control of the Alaska Native Corporations. However, as one observer has pointed out this action was misguided as control of resources that Native Alaskans are so dependent upon will potentially be taken from them as the shares become available to non-Natives and non-Alaskans.

When British Columbia joined Confederation in 1871 the non-Native population was primarily concentrated in the Lower Fraser River Valley and Southeast Vancouver Island. As in Alaska, those Native people who lived in the more isolated areas were left to make their living much the way they had before. In Canada the responsibility of Native Affairs belongs to the federal government which carries out its duties under a comprehensive law known as the "Indian Act." The first Indian Act was passed in 1884 and it has been revised several times since, the last time in 1985. Two important components of the first Indian Act are of concern here. First, the Indian Act placed into motion the move to establish

Figure 11.5 The village at Metlakatla, Alaska, showing part of the mission, 1908. (Courtesy of Special Collections Division, University of Washington Libraries, Negative No. NA 2452.)

reserves for Native people throughout Canada. Most of Canada is covered by at least one of the eleven treaties that were negotiated between 1871 and 1921 (Frideres 1983:11). However, British Columbia was excluded from the treaty process except for a small portion of the Northeast corner of the province and a few groups on Vancouver Island who signed treaties with the Hudson's Bay Company in the 1850s. Nonetheless, a treaty commission was established and between 1880 and 1912 approximately two hundred reserves were formed in British Columbia. The reserve system in British Columbia differs significantly from the reservation system in the United States. In most of the western states fairly large reservations were established in order to concentrate several groups in one location. In British Columbia, however, many small reserves were set aside for the different bands, especially along the coastal area of the province. A reserve may consist of an area that is a fishing location, a cemetery, or a village site. The idea being that Natives would use these reserves to remain self-sufficient whereas in the United States the purpose of the reservation system was to encourage the Native people to become farmers and to abandon their traditional patterns of subsistence.

The other part of the Indian Act that affected the Native people of British Columbia was the clause that outlawed the potlatch. Initially the ban on the potlatch was impossible to enforce because of the remoteness of the Native villages and the lack of governmental control over their lives. The potlatch law was not strictly enforced until after the turn of the century when Indian agents began to target the abolition of the ceremony as a means of bringing about the "civilization" of the Natives.

The most famous incident occurred in 1921 when dozens of people were arrested for participating in a potlatch in the Nimpkish (Kwakiutl) village at Alert Bay. Not only were the participants arrested, convicted and sent to jail but thousands of dollars worth of pot-latch goods were confiscated. Despite the persecution the potlatch did not stop, instead it went underground and the Native people of British Columbia continued to petition for an end to the ban on the ceremony. In 1954 the potlatch law was repealed and potlatching has since received renewed interest. Many of the items that were confiscated during the pot-latch raids in the 1920s were eventually returned to their rightful owners. In 1979 museums were built at Cape Mudge and Alert Bay to house the potlatch goods and make them available for public view.

In British Columbia today Native people are seeking recognition of their aboriginal rights. One of the most publicized cases is that of the Gitksan (Tsimshian) of the Skeena River area who have demanded legal and political jurisdiction over a large portion of north-central British Columbia. In 1984 forty-eight members of the Gitksan (and their Athabas-can neighbors the Wet'suwet'en) petitioned the Supreme Court of British Columbia to declare that the provincial government had no right of jurisdiction over 22,000 square miles of their territory. An important component of this action was the demand for an al-location of salmon specifically for Native fishers on the Skeena River. While in 1986 the Gitksan-Wet'suwet'en sat in on negotiations to co-manage the Skeena River fishery in order to allow a Native harvest, the Department of Fisheries later refused to recognize a specific Native fishery. The matter is now under consideration by the Supreme Court of British Columbia.

As the Skeena River case has built other Native groups are voicing their desire to ex-ercise jurisdiction over land and resources. In the near future we may see the Native people of British Columbia taking a more forceful role in governmental affairs that directly affect their lives.

The situation in western Washington differs from both Alaska and British Columbia. White settlement in the western Washington area progressed much more rapidly and conse-quently the interaction with Native people necessitated the formation of Indian policy which early formulated Indian reservations and actions that had a dramatic influence on their lives. In 1846 the United States and Great Britain signed a treaty which established the boundary between British North America and United States territory in the Northwest at the 49th Parallel. Soon the influx of settlers obligated the United States government to settle the question of land title with the Native inhabitants. When Washington Territory was established in 1853 Isaac I. Stevens was assigned the governorship and with it the responsibility for Indian Affairs. Over the course of the next few years Stevens negotiated and placed into effect five treaties covering most of the western portion of what is now the State of Washington. During the latter part of the nineteenth century the United States instituted numerous policies designed at assimilating the Native people into the mainstream of American life. Many of the activities of the Indian agents during this period of "assimilationist" policy were aimed at destroying the tribal unit and teaching the Native people the skills of "civilization." In other words, the intent of the federal government was that Indians would become English-speaking, farming land-owners.

The anthropologist Joseph G. Jorgensen has characterized the history of Indian policy in the United States as like a "pendulum," periodically swinging from one extreme to another (Jorgensen 1978). If we visualize these extremes as "individualism" at the one end and "collectivism" at the other we can look at the different policies that have been enacted on behalf of Indian people and begin to understand the confusion that has characterized the place of Native people in American society.

Certainly the assimilationist policies that were enacted after the treaties of western Washington came into effect and the reservations established can be seen as an individualistic swing. Numerous legislative acts and policies could be cited here to demonstrate the intent of the federal government in the latter part of the 1800s but we will just mention one. Perhaps the most important act during this time was the General Allotment Act or Dawes Act of 1884. This act was intended to divide the reservation lands in severalty and encourage Indians to pursue a lifestyle like that of their White neighbors. An Indian agent in charge of several western Washington reservations stated the government's goal most clearly when he said: "The effect of the allotment system, so far as title to a separate tract of land goes, is most beneficial, and incites the Indian to greater industry, gives him more individual independence, and tends greatly to weaken the tribal relation."

Since many of the reservations in western Washington were not in areas that were conducive to agricultural production it made little sense to try and coerce the Native people into becoming farmers. Agriculture never provided a viable alternative to traditional forms of subsistence and the General Allotment Act, rather than encouraging independent self-sufficiency, actually caused the reservations to lose much of their land base. Not only did the General Allotment Act divide the reservations into individually owned parcels but it also allowed the sale of the land to non-tribal members. As a result many reservations lost much of their land base by the 1920s.

By the 1920s it had become clear that the assimilationist policies of the late 1800s were not working. In 1926 the federal government commissioned an investigation into the status of Native people in the United States. It was disclosed in the "Meriam Report" that federal legislation had harmed rather than helped Native people and demonstrated that federal appropriations had been too small, the administrative staff of the Bureau of Indian Affairs had been either incompetent or corrupt, and that housing, health, and education on Indian reservations had fallen far below the national average.

The response of the federal government was to usher in an entirely new set of policies designed to rectify the harm done during the assimilationist period. We then see a swing to the other extreme of our pendulum with an emphasis on collectivism and the attempt to strengthen the tribal unit. In western Washington Indian policies were enacted under the general name of the "Indian New Deal" named after the New Deal policies of the

Roosevelt administration. In general the Indian New Deal policies encouraged tribes to adopt constitutions and tribal governments in order to have a body with which the federal government could establish relations. Tribes were encouraged to develop tribal enterprises but in western Washington there was little the tribes could do with their limited land base, few resources and lack of capital.

After World War II we see Indian policy taking another swing and the focus once again being on individualism. Usually this period of Indian policy is referred to as the era of "Termination" and although a few tribes around the United States were terminated none were in western Washington. Nonetheless termination policy affected the Native people of western Washington, especially the program known as "Relocation." One historian of Indian policy has stated that the intent of the relocation program was to terminate the reservations by attrition (Burt 1982:57). The relocation program encouraged individual tribal members to leave the reservation in pursuit of wage labor in urban areas. Several metropolitan areas in the United States were identified as "relocation centers" including Seattle, San Francisco, Denver, and Minneapolis-St. Paul, cities that still have significantly large urban Indian populations. Relocation had a dramatic impact on many reservations. For example on the Lummi reservation in western Washington it has been estimated that over one-third of the total population was relocated during the 1950s (Boxberger 1989:130). Generally the relocatees were unskilled and undereducated, so the jobs found for them by the Bureau of Indian Affairs were at the lower end of the economic scale. In addition, since housing had to fit within the income level they were located in lower-class neighborhoods.

About the time that the reservation populations were beginning to adapt to the changes brought about by the era of termination we see the policies once again taking a dramatic shift to a return to an emphasis on tribalism. In the latter part of the twentieth century we are in a period of Indian policy referred to as "Indian Self-Determination." Typical of today's policies are acts that encourage economic growth on reservations through the development of reservation resources. Numerous legislative acts and, more importantly, court cases have attempted to clarify what control Native people have over their lands and resources and how development on reservations is to proceed. One of the more famous of these court cases was the 1974 decision in the case United States v. The State of Washington, commonly referred to as the "Boldt Decision" after Judge George Boldt who heard the case. In this case it was determined that the treaty Indians of western Washington were entitled to 50 percent of the allowable harvest of salmon in the state. Each of the five treaties from the mid-1800s contain an article referring to the Indian's right to fish "in common" with the other citizens of Washington. For over 120 years no one bothered to seek an interpretation of exactly what "in common" meant. In 1974 Judge Boldt ruled that "in common" meant to share equally which meant that 50 percent of the harvestable salmon was to be allocated to treaty Indians and 50 percent to non-treaty fishers. As pointed out in Boldt's decision the State of Washington had, over the years, enforced policies and regulations which served to discriminate against treaty Indian fishers. The result in the attempt to rectify this discrepancy by court action was to cut in half the numbers of fish available to the non-treaty fishers and create a potential economic boom for the treaty tribes.

Like most Indian tribes in the United States the tribes of western Washington are attempting to utilize the resources they have to bring economic stability to their tribes. This means that the salmon resource has, in recent years, become a focal point in tribal economic development programs. However, since the economic potential of salmon fishing varies from area to area some tribes are better able to build their fishing fleets than others. As a result we have seen an uneven buildup of fishing potential among the twenty-four western Washington tribes and different approaches taken in pursuit of their goal of self-sufficiency. Some tribes have pursued "spin-off" programs such as fish processing ventures, marinas, or other marine-related industries. Others have pursued a variety of schemes which include salmon fishing but also such activities as other tribes around the United States are following which take advantage of the special status Indian tribes enjoy, such as bingo parlors, tax-free markets, and for at least one tribe, a "foreign trade zone."

The current economic and political status of Native people throughout the Northwest Coast culture area is improving as the tribes continue to strive for self-sufficiency. As the tribal governments clarify their role and as the economic value of Native labor and resources begins to work for the benefit of the tribes we will see stronger, more independent Native communities all along the Northwest Coast.

SUGGESTED READINGS

Adams, John W.
    1981   "Recent Ethnology of the Northwest Coast." *In* Annual Review of Anthropology, Vol. 10, pp. 361–392, Annual Reviews, Inc., Palo Alto.

Arima, Eugene
    1983   The West Coast (Nootka) People. British Columbia Provincial Museum, Special Publication No. 6, Victoria.

Boas, Franz
    1966   Kwakiutl Ethnography. University of Chicago Press, Chicago.

Boxberger, Daniel L.
    1989   To Fish in Common: The Ethnohistory of Lummi Indian Salmon Fishing. University of Nebraska Press, Lincoln.

Carlson, Roy L., ed.
    1976   Indian Art Traditions of the Pacific Northwest. Archaeology Press, Simon Fraser University, Burnaby.

Cole, Douglas
    1985   Captured Heritage: The Scramble for Northwest Coast Artifacts. Douglas and McIntyre, Vancouver.

Drucker, Philip
    1965   Cultures of the North Pacific Coast. Chandler Publishing Company, Scranton.

Gunther, Erna
    1972   Indian Life on the Northwest Coast of North America as seen by the Early Explorers and Fur Traders during the Last Decades of the Eighteenth Century. University of Chicago Press, Chicago.

Krause, Aurel
    1956   The Tlingit Indians. Translated by Erna Gunther. University of Washington Press, Seattle.

MacDonald, George
1983   Ninstints: Haida World Heritage Site. University of British Columbia Press, Vancouver.

Stewart, Hilary
1977   Indian Fishing: Early Methods on the Northwest Coast. University of Washington Press, Seattle.

Suttles, Wayne
1987   Coast Salish Essays. University of Washington Press, Seattle.

REFERENCES

Adams, John W.
1981   "Recent Ethnology of the Northwest Coast." Annual Review of Anthropology, Volume 10, pp. 361–392. Annual Reviews, Inc., Palo Alto.

Arima, Eugene
1983   The West Coast (Nootka) People. British Columbia Provincial Museum Special Publication No. 6. British Columbia Provincial Museum, Victoria.

Boxberger, Daniel L.
1989   To Fish in Common: The Ethnohistory of Lummi Indian Salmon Fishing. University of Nebraska Press, Lincoln.

Beringer, Patricia Ann
1982   Northwest Coast Traditional Salmon Fisheries Systems of Resource Utilization. M.A. Thesis, Department of Anthropology/Sociology, University of British Columbia, Vancouver.

Burt, Larry W.
1982   Tribalism in Crisis: Federal Indian Policy, 1953–1961. University of New Mexico Press, Albuquerque.

Drucker, Philip
1958   The Native Brotherhoods: Modern Intertribal Organizations on the Northwest Coast. Bureau of American Ethnology, Bulletin No. 168. Smithsonian Institution, Washington, D.C.

Frideres, James S.
1983   Native People in Canada: Contemporary Conflicts. Prentice-Hall, Scarborough.

Greenberg, Joseph H.
1987   Language in the Americas. Stanford University Press, Stanford.

Hewes, Gordon
1973   "Indian Fisheries Productivity in Pre-contact Times in the Pacific Salmon Area." Northwest Anthropological Research Notes, Vol. 7, No. 2, pp. 133–155.

Jewitt, John R.
1815   Narrative of the Adventures and Sufferings of John R. Jewitt. Reprinted by Ye Galleon Press (1967), Fairfield.

Jorgensen, Joseph G.
1978   "A Century of Political Economic Effects on American Indian Society." Journal of Ethnic Studies, Vol. 6, No. 3, pp. 1–82.

Kroeber, Alfred L.
1939   Cultural and Natural Areas of Native North America. University of California Press, Berkeley.

Richardson, Allan
1982   "The Control of Productive Resources on the Northwest Coast of North America." In Resource Managers: North American and Australian Hunter-Gatherers. N. Williams and E. Hunn, eds. pp. 93–112.

Suttles, Wayne
1958   "Private Knowledge, Morality and Social Classes Among the Coast Salish." American Anthropologist, Vol. 60, No. 3, pp. 497–507.

1968 "Coping With Abundance: Subsistence on the Northwest Coast." *In* Man the Hunter. R. B. Lee and I. DeVore, eds., pp. 56–69. Aldine Press, Chicago.

1985 Native Languages of the Northwest Coast (Map). Western Imprints, The Press of the Oregon Historical Society, Portland.

Turner, Nancy J.

1975 Food Plants of British Columbia Indians: Part I—Coast Peoples. Handbook No. 34, British Columbia Provincial Museum, Victoria.

1979 Plants in British Columbia Indian Technology. Handbook No. 38, British Columbia Provincial Museum, Victoria.

United States Government

1976 Alaska Native Claims Settlement Act. United States Government Printing Office, Washington, D.C.

Vancouver, George

1798 A Voyage of Discovery to the North Pacific Ocean and Around the World. London.

Wolf, Eric

1982 Europe and the People Without History. University of California Press, Berkeley.

Chapter 12

Native North Americans in Contemporary Society

Daniel L. Boxberger

Western Washington University

Colleen Murray

Washington State University

Introduction

Although Native Americans represent just a small proportion of the populations of Canada and the United States they have, as the previous chapters have pointed out, played an important role in the history of North America and they continue to be of interest because of their unique position in contemporary society. In this chapter we will discuss some of the problems and concerns of Native people today and explore what it means to be a minority in your own land.

It is difficult to arrive at an accurate count of the number of Native people today because there is much disagreement over how that is to be defined. In the United States to be "Indian" or Alaska Native you must be a member of a federally recognized "tribe" and have at least one-fourth degree "Indian blood." Right away many people can see the problem with such a definition. First of all not all Native American tribes have been officially recognized by the United States federal government and secondly blood quantum has nothing whatsoever to do with an individual's socialization and cultural identity. In Canada the problem is even further exacerbated by the fact that there are large numbers of people who are "non-status" Natives and large numbers of people who call themselves "Metis" who, until recently, received no recognition by the Canadian government. Nevertheless some figures will give an idea of the numbers of people we are discussing and where they stand in relation to the general population.

According to the most reliable census data there are approximately 1.5 million Native people in the United States, representing just 3.3 percent of the total population. It has been estimated that the Native population may exceed 2 million in the 1990 census. In Canada the proportion is somewhat higher, 310,000 Native people representing 7.8 per cent of the population. This last figure would be higher if we included the Metis whose numbers are estimated at anywhere from 500,000 to one million. Yet we must ask the question, why do such a small number of people command so much attention?

To date anthropologists and historians have been overly concerned with traditional aspects of Native societies, ignoring the fact that Native cultures, like any culture, are dynamic, that is, change through time is expected. The popular notion that Native people have "lost their culture" is without foundation. Some people harbor the romanticized notion that the only Native cultures worthy of our attention are those that exhibit traditional traits, but the situation is far more complex. Indigenous people throughout the world are faced with problems of modernization and the Native people of North America have, in many ways, set an example of how indigenous cultures may cope with change and how relationships may develop between Native societies and the dominant government.

Everyone knows that most Native communities are economically depressed, but what exactly does that mean? Social scientists use a variety of indicators to determine quality of social life. Such things as demography, economy, community structure, public services and social well-being are examined both quantitatively and qualitatively to arrive at some general conclusions as to the social health of a community.

How do Native communities compare with the general population in terms of these indicators? The answer is, in general, not well. Data from the most recent censuses show that Native Americans are generally of lower economic status, fall below the average for educational levels, and have poorer health than the general populations of the United States and Canada. For example unemployment rates for Natives are nearly five times the national averages, those living below the "poverty level" are four times greater than the general population, educational levels fall about 20 percent below the general population and general health characteristics indicate that Native health problems are of special concern.

While this information alone paints a dismal picture the self-perception of Native people may not be that they are living a depressed lifestyle. For example, a Native family living in the bush of the Canadian Subarctic may have a very low monetary income but through subsistence gathering and the strategic use of other resources they may live a relatively affluent lifestyle by their standards. While this represents one sort of lifestyle it may not be practical or desirable by most. There is a wide variety of attitudes and beliefs as to what constitutes a good standard of living among Native people as there is in the non-Native population. In fact, many Native people are taking steps to bring about change in their lives and their communities both economically and in terms of other aspects of social life.

Economic Development

One cannot assess the current state of Native economies without consideration of the historical factors involved. Once people become incorporated into the Western market economy there is no turning back. Native people of North America and the world have generally not fared well in the age of capitalism. First through the fur trade and later through the extraction of primary resources the Native people of North America have long been incorporated into the dominant economies of Canada and the United States but they remain an underdeveloped segment of those economies—the so-called "Fourth World."

In general Native people placed on reserves have had limited access to resources. When resources are developed, such as coal mining on the Navajo Reservation or the construction of a hydroelectric project in the territory used by the James Bay Cree, these ventures are controlled by outside interests and the Native communities rarely reap the benefits of development. Monetary and other gains are not redistributed through the Native communities, rather, they are enjoyed largely within the non-Native segment of society. These factors create a state of chronic economic hardship demonstrated by the unemployment and underemployment rates in Native communities.

In recent years many Native groups have taken measures to overcome the problems of Fourth World dependency and underdevelopment. Under the Indian Self-Determination Act of 1975 in the United States and the 1985 amendment to the Indian Act in Canada, Native people are beginning to take a stronger role in determining how reservation resources are to be utilized and the direction Native economies are going to take.

In the past many attempts have been made to develop reservation economies but these programs have been largely unsuccessful. One explanation is that many, if not most, of these development schemes have been supported by federal funds allocated for a specific purpose. These were short-term attempts to alleviate problems that require long-term investments.

For example, along the border between Washington State and British Columbia there exists an ideal situation to examine the long-term effect of Native resource control and economic development within these two countries.

In the 1970s and 1980s important changes have occurred along the West Coast of North America in regard to the Native people's use of natural resources—most importantly the salmon resource. The Native Indians of the Northwest Coast Culture Area were, traditionally, engaged in a fishery that met their needs for subsistence and had the potential to develop into a viable economic endeavor. To some extent Native people on both sides of the 49th Parallel participated in the commercial salmon fishery during its developmental period (roughly 1880 to 1900) but this changed dramatically in the subsequent years as extractive and processing technology became more sophisticated and as labor of other ethnicities came to predominate.

The Native people not only had to cope with the changes inherent in the fishery itself but they were also subject to political dominance by their respective countries. Many of the differences between British Columbia and the State of Washington lie in the fact that different ideological bases of policy, enacted in regard to the Native people, have directed social change.

Prior to and for a considerable period of time after white contact, the Native people of the Northwest Coast were engaged in a traditional fishery that adequately met their needs for subsistence. The importance of the salmon resource varied from group to group, but it is safe to say that in general salmon were the most important resource utilized by the Native Northwest Coast people of British Columbia and Washington. The techniques employed in the pre-commercial fishery ranged from the simple (dip nets, gaffs, etc.) to the technologically sophisticated (seines, reef nets).

Coast Salish groups about the mouth of the Fraser River were especially skillful salmon fishers, employing most of the known technologies and, comparatively, having the greatest reliance on salmon as a staple food source. It is no coincidence that early non-Indian efforts in commercial fishing concentrated on the Fraser River and North Puget Sound waters as one of the focal areas of commercial endeavor. The abundant runs of sockeye salmon especially made this area one of special importance.

The reliance on salmon that characterized traditional Northwest Coast culture continued into the late 1800s and, in a few isolated areas, even into the early 1900s. It was only after commercialization of the resource that the Native economies began to shift from a subsistence-based economy to one dependent upon wage labor.

The events which eventually led to the establishment of commercial salmon operations in the Northwest area began in 1864 on the Sacramento River of California. It was there that Hapgood, Hume, and Co. set up the first salmon cannery on the Pacific Coast. In the 1860s the canning industry was still in its infancy. The first year of operation in Sacramento produced only two thousand cases of salmon, and lack of technological sophistication caused the loss of at least half of this first pack. In subsequent years this fledgling company found that due to overfishing and environmental degradation resulting from hydraulic mining, there were not enough salmon in the Sacramento River to allow an increase in pack size. Consequently, in 1866, William Hume moved to the Columbia River, where he created the first commercial salmon operation in what is now the State of Washington.

Before long Hume was followed by dozens of others. Eleven years later, salmon canneries appeared on Puget Sound, the first, at Muckilteo (near Everett) in 1877 and the number of canneries continued to increase from 1891 until peaking at forty-five in 1917.

The earliest canning operations in British Columbia appeared on the Fraser River near New Westminster in 1866 although there had been some minor attempts earlier. The first recorded pack in British Columbia, 8,215 cases in 1873, was entirely Fraser River-caught fish. Subsequent canning operations followed developing all along the British Columbia coast so that by 1901 there were seventy canneries in operation from the Fraser River to Portland Canal.

Indian labor was necessary in the formative years of the industry, as they had the requisite skills as fishers and processors. The earliest commercial operations obtained the majority of their fish from Indian fishers. Very rapidly, during the 1890s, Native people became part of the fishing industry and began fishing for cash as well as subsistence. Although wage labor was an aspect of Native livelihood prior to 1880, it did not become a dominant part of the Native economy until the canneries began to employ Native labor both as fishers and as cannery workers. Some Native people worked as miners, lumberjacks, or migrant farm laborers throughout the period, in order to supplement traditional fishing and gathering, but the integration of a few individuals into the labor force did not mean a shift of the entire society. Specialized labor linked the Native people to the networks of the market system prior to the 1880s, but as occasional subordinate producers not as partners. Subsequent developments in the salmon canning industry were to change all that.

As we have seen the Native people were instrumental in the development of the commercial salmon fishery of the Northwest Coast. As the development of the fishery accelerated around the turn of the century the Natives of British Columbia were a significant force in the industry. By 1919 the British Columbia fishery employed nine thousand people, the "majority of whom were Indians" (Pearse 1982:151). The Native people adjusted remarkably well to the changes in the fishery and continued to participate as part of the labor force. This participation seemed to articulate well with the traditional fishing economy in which the division of labor was between gender. The men did the fishing and the women processed the catch. As the fishery became commercialized the Native people fished and processed for cash instead of subsistence but the traditional division of labor persisted (Knight 1978).

During the 1920s and 1930s the development of larger and more expensive vessels in the fishing industry caused the number of Native fishers to decline. This decline however, was minor compared to the drastic decline after World War II. Pearse believes this displacement was caused by the consolidation of the canning industry and the adoption of still bigger and costlier vessels. From 1954 to 1979 the number of Native-owned vessels dropped by nearly two-thirds. The number of Natives employed as crew and cannery workers also fell precipitously. The decline in participation in the salmon industry was a severe economic blow to the Native communities. Not only did Native people in British Columbia depend upon fishing as a source of income but the vessels were important means of transportation in the more remote communities and Native people depended upon the food fishery for a major portion of their subsistence.

By the late 1970s the Native fishers of British Columbia accounted for just 15 percent of the salmon fleet and over one-third of the Native-operated vessels were leased from the canneries. The Native people perceived the attrition of the fishery as the most serious threat to their future economic well-being. Various organizations developed to halt the decline of Native fishers, such as the Indian Fisherman's Assistance Program, the Northern Native Fishing Corporation, and the Indian Fisherman's Development Board, to name a few. These organizations were designed to assist Natives in participating in an ever more competitive industry.

Since most British Columbia Natives never formally negotiated treaties with the Canadian government relinquishing their aboriginal claim to the land and resources, several groups began to claim aboriginal rights of access to the salmon resource. The Canadian Charter of Rights and Freedoms of 1982 states that "existing aboriginal and treaty rights of the aboriginal peoples of Canada are . . . recognized and affirmed" but what this means in terms of the salmon resource of British Columbia is not clear.

The adoption of the Canadian Constitution coupled with the 1985 amendment to the Indian Act appear to have been the impetus behind many Native people in Canada pushing for recognition of their aboriginal rights. Unlike most of Canada, however, the situation in British Columbia is not clear since the majority of British Columbia Natives have never negotiated treaties with the government of Canada. Although the Native people of Canada, as their counterparts in the United States, began seeking recognition of their rights in the late 1960s/early 1970s, the majority of the political and legal activity has taken place in the 1980s. Various organizations, especially the Union of B. C. Indian Chiefs, have lobbied for Native rights and several bands have made demands and/or negotiated with federal and provincial governments for certain rights, especially rights to land and resources. While we may not see the same type of all-encompassing court decision such as occurred in Washington State, we may see that the Native people of British Columbia are going to exercise some jurisdiction over salmon that run through their traditional grounds. Whether or not this will mean a specific Native allocation or not remains to be seen.

Unlike the majority of Native people of British Columbia, most of the Natives of Washington State have treaties with the federal government. Most of the treaties contain an article affirming the right to resources, especially the salmon resource. Nevertheless, access to those resources was lost over the years (Boxberger 1989). Although essential as fishers and processors during the formative years of the salmon industry, by the early 1900s most Native people in Washington State came to be almost totally excluded from participation in the commercial salmon fishing industry. An important aspect of the Native experience in Washington State was the effect of United States Indian policy in the late 1800s/early 1900s. This period of so-called "assimilationist" policy included efforts by the federal agency overseeing Native people—the Bureau of Indian Affairs—to assimilate Native people into mainstream American society. This policy especially encouraged farming as a "civilized" pursuit. Fishing and other activities seen as "traditional" were actively discouraged.

Other reasons contributing to the exclusion of Native Washington fishers appear to be similar to the experience of Native people in British Columbia. Native people could not continue to compete as the industry became increasingly capitalized and as labor of other ethnicities came to replace Native labor in the processing sector, especially reservation labor (Boxberger 1988:172). In Washington State the Native people held to the belief that their treaties gave them assured rights to an allocation of the resource, but the State of Washington consistently refused to recognize Indian treaty fishing rights.

By the early 1900s treaty Indians in the State of Washington were primarily restricted to on-reservation fisheries, and even this activity was suppressed by the State of Washington and the federal government. By 1935 the total salmon harvest by Native fishers in Washington State was only 2 percent of the total.

For a short period of time during World War II and for a few years thereafter, the Native people enjoyed a temporary reincorporation into the fishing industry. But, again, as increasing sophistication in fishing technology and increasing participation by non-Natives—those primarily with access to capital—the Native people once again found themselves pushed aside.

In the 1960s several Washington tribes began to question the manner in which the fishery had developed and contested the exclusion of Native people from the salmon fishery. Through a series of protests and court cases the Native people slowly gathered support to contest the fact that the commercial fishery had developed to the exclusion of Native fishers. The argument centered around the interpretation of the treaty articles guaran-

416

teeing fishing rights, and it was on the basis of these treaty rights that thirteen Washington tribes entered a suit against the State of Washington. In February of 1974 Federal District Court Judge George Boldt decided that wording in the 1855/6 treaties was to be interpreted to mean that the treaty tribes were entitled to a guaranteed allocation of salmon. He set that allocation at 50 percent.

Commonly referred to as the "Boldt Decision", the Federal Court Decision in United States *v.* State of Washington (384 F. Supp 312 (1974)) received more public attention in the State of Washington than any other court case in history. Ostensibly the Boldt Decision was to clarify, once and for all, the controversy over treaty fishing in Washington State. Nevertheless, the controversies and conflicts that developed as a direct result of the Boldt Decision further complicated the matter of Native fishing many times over.

The Boldt Decision has been maligned, ridiculed, and vastly misunderstood. Based on similar wording in articles contained in the ratified Washington treaties the decision legally defined the phrase "in common", part of the wording of the original treaties, to mean 50 percent.

An important consideration of the courts was the interpretation that fishing rights were *reserved* to the treaty tribes whereas fishing was a *privilege* non-Natives were granted. In other words the interpretation held that the Native people owned the resource aboriginally and through treaties had relinquished a share of it.

The Boldt Decision was the culmination of dozens of state and federal court cases that dealt with isolated aspects of the treaty rights controversy. Among other conflicts it brought to the fore the differences between the State of Washington and the federal government over allocation of the fisheries resource and the control of treaty fishing. The Boldt Decision was, of course, appealed. Throughout the appeal process the State of Washington was in constant conflict with the federal government, especially the federal court system. The federal courts issued orders to various state agencies to implement the Boldt Decision, and the state agencies, necessarily bound to the wishes of the state legislature and the state courts, managed the resource in opposition to federal court directives. This caused the state, the federal government, and the tribes to return to court on over thirty-five separate occasions between 1974 and 1978. In July of 1978 Judge Boldt stepped in and assumed jurisdiction over the fishery and the responsibility for management. This prompted dozens of non-Native commercial fishers to protest and fish in defiance of the law. Several violent altercations ensued. On one occasion a patrol officer, with a shotgun, wounded a fisherman. After this action the United States Coast Guard was called in to enforce the fisheries regulations.

The level of controversy surrounding the Boldt Decision, the publicity it received, and the nature of the state and federal disputes were factors urging the United States Supreme Court to hear the appeal. Although the Supreme Court had declined to hear the case in 1976, in 1979 it reversed its decision—the first example of such a reversal in the Court's history. On 2 July 1979, the Supreme Court upheld the Boldt Decision, in a six to three decision, with a few minor revisions. With no further recourse, the State of Washington was obliged to acknowledge the decision. The state resumed management of the fishery and has made an attempt to cooperate with the tribes to insure that the salmon resource is allocated as the court decreed.

Throughout this period the Native people were steadily increasing their catch of salmon such that by 1984 they had nearly achieved the 50 percent allocation.

In order to compare economic development of the Northwest Coast Natives of British Columbia and Washington State we have to understand that policy enacted by the dominant societies on behalf of the Native people come from two different ideological backgrounds. As we explore the policies toward Native people it becomes apparent that we cannot understand the differences without looking back much further than the earliest economic development in the Northwest.

Despite the fact that both Canada and the United States were once British colonies there are important differences inherent in their respective policies towards Native people. These differences tend to center around different concepts of the relationship between Native people and dominant governments and different beliefs in the role of government agencies in the administration of Native affairs.

Beginning in 1846, when the Northwest boundary between Canada and the United States was continued along the 49th Parallel, governmental dealings with the Native people became necessary. In the United States treaties were negotiated, reservations established and national policy applied, all by the 1860s. In Canada things moved more slowly. The first of several Indian Acts was applied to British Columbia in the 1880s. Some reserves were not established until after the turn of the century. Despite these differences essentially similar policies came to be enforced. In both nations the ideology behind the policy seemed to be guided by the belief that Native people would eventually become assimilated into the dominant society. The differences lie in the manner in which the policies were carried out.

The United States assumed the role of guiding the assimilation process. The United States allotted reservation land to individual tribal members, sent young people away to boarding schools to learn a trade, encouraged missions, and urged Native people to abandon traditional activities, like fishing, in favor of farming. All of these activities were carried out in the belief that the Native people would eventually assimilate into the dominant society and the need for reservations and special governmental agencies would disappear. While the specific policies have changed periodically over the years (Jorgensen 1978) they were (and are) still guided by the belief that the special needs of Native people would disappear. Yet the Native people have not assimilated and while their cultures have changed dramatically we cannot ignore the fact that they are today still dynamic, vibrant cultures that are just as worthy of recognition as were their ancestors of 150 years ago.

While the political ideology inherent in Canadian Native policy was similar to that of the United States the Canadian government exercised a different approach. The Canadian reserve system was set up differently than its counterpart in the United States, setting aside numerous small reserves instead of a few relatively large reservations. The reserve system principally set aside lands that were village sites, fishing stations and gathering locations. The intent was clearly to allow the Native people to continue as many of their traditional subsistence activities as possible in order to remain self-sufficient. Whereas the United

States attempted to encourage Native assimilation by crushing the traditional culture the Canadian government seemed to hold to the belief that assimilation would occur on its own. Although the various Indian Acts discouraged certain Native practices (especially the potlatch) these laws were not enforced across the board nor were all aspects of the Acts adhered to.

These differing policies have contributed to the historical differences between Native fishing in British Columbia and western Washington discussed above. The British Columbia Natives were able to involve themselves in the commercial fishery early on and persist in the fishery until such time that the industry became more competitive. The Native people of western Washington were also able to become involved in commercial fishing early on but were less able to remain a viable part of the industry after 1900. For Native people in both nations the twentieth century was a period of gradual exclusion from the commercial fishery, such that legal action became the only recourse left open to them.

The changes that are occurring in the 1980s in Canada and the United States, while similar in focus, are very different in content. The Native tribes of western Washington have treaty-assured fishing rights, validated and enforced by the federal court system. The Native people of British Columbia are not treaty bands but they do have valid claims to aboriginal rights of access to the salmon resource.

Education

Many Native people see education as a means of overcoming problems related to economic development. A recent trend in Indian country has been the tendency for communities to develop and operate their own educational facilities, primarily at the grade school level but also, to an increasing degree, at the secondary and postsecondary levels as well.

Historically, many Native people in the United States were educated in boarding schools operated by the Bureau of Indian Affairs. Characterized by Grobsmith (1981:15) as "legalized kidnapping" this method of education intended to separate children from their homes, kin and language in order to assimilate them into the dominant culture much more rapidly. Boarding schools continue to operate to this day but with different educational philosophies. In 1934 with the passage of The Johnson O'Mally Act many Indian children started attending "day schools" on their reservation or, if their reservation was close to a non-Indian population, public schools.

Similarly, in Canada, many Native children in remote areas only received formal education if they attended residential schools. In some cases these schools were operated by the Department of Indian Affairs and in others they were operated by religious organizations. The establishment of village schools began in earnest after World War II and continued well into the 1960s and 1970s.

Since the early 1970s many changes have taken place. Many Native communities have taken over responsibility for operating schools and many changes in curricula have been developed. Today we see tribal schools in operation on most reservations and these schools attempt to incorporate culturally relevant curricula into the education of young Native children.

What is an Indian?

As members of a complex society we are all subject to the constraints of certain social institutions. Native Americans, however, are not only subject to the same social constraints as the general population but there are numerous agencies and bureaucracies that additionally touch Native people's lives. For example, most Americans are aware of the existence of the Bureau of Indian Affairs, but few realize that there are almost sixty other agencies and offices that also exercise some control over the lives of Native people. To be Indian is not only to be the member of an identifiable culture group, but for the majority of Native people in the United States and Canada there are also political and legal considerations. Blood quantum is just one of many ways to determine who is an Indian. In the United States most Native groups have a relationship with the federal government that originated with treaties or some other legally binding agreement. There are, however, numerous groups that have never been recognized as political entities. The Lumbee of North Carolina are one such group.

On the surface the Lumbee appear to defy all of the legally sanctioned definitions of what is an Indian (Blu 1980:1). The federal government conceded that the Lumbee were Indian in 1956 for specific reasons, such as education, but has denied them status as a federally recognized tribe. The case of the Lumbee is interesting for several reasons. Having no discernible "traditional" Indian culture or language and phenotypically not resembling the general perception of what is an Indian the Lumbee have struggled to gain acceptance as an Indian people for well over a century. The Lumbee believe their origin to have been from the incorporation of the "lost colony" of Roanoke in the 1500s into neighboring Indian tribes (Blu 1980:136). Within Robeson County of North Carolina there is a distinct Indian town that is recognized as such by neighboring Whites and Blacks. In addition, all of these groups recognize behavior and social attributes that are considered unique to the Lumbee. Perhaps more importantly the Lumbee claim that they are Indian. While researchers have referred to groups like this as "tri-racial isolates," according to Blu (1980) the Lumbee would reject such a designation, acknowledging only White and Indian ancestry.

To be recognized as an Indian tribe by the federal government of the United States (the Federal Acknowledgment Process) certain criteria must be met. These criteria include such things as a continuous political body, a land base, recognition in the past, and a membership roll. In 1977 the American Indian Policy Review Commission listed 133 unacknowledged tribes and estimates suggest that well over 250 groups may eventually petition the government for recognition. Many groups have been denied, primarily on the basis of being unable to demonstrate a continuous political body since contact. In the eyes of the federal government it is not enough for a people to merely identify themselves as Indian. Anyone can identify themselves as anything they please but obviously in the case of Indians something more is going on.

In Canada the situation is even more complex. Until the 1985 amendment to the Indian Act Native people were dealt with on an individual basis. For example there were large numbers of Native people designated as "non-status" that is, people who had lost their status as a Native person either through disenfranchisement or through the marriage of a Native woman to a non-Native man (on the other hand, a non-Native woman marrying a Native man would become a "Native"). In addition there are large numbers of people with a distinct cultural heritage that are not considered either Native or non-Native. They call themselves the "Metis."

The Metis

The Metis are descended from the unions of Indian women and European men which occurred with the arrival of explorers and traders to present-day Canada. Initially the fur trade was the principle basis of European economy in the New World and the children born to Native-White unions grew up to play a unique but crucial role in this economy. Through their Indian mothers they held kinship ties that were of vital importance to the trade activities between Euro-Canadians and Native people. In addition they had the necessary skills for survival in the often harsh Canadian bush, making the men and women invaluable intermediaries.

With the fur trade, the Metis and their descendants moved westward in search of fur-bearing animals and buffalo, the latter which contributed to a portion of their subsistence base. Their trade experience and partial dependency on buffalo meat enabled some to establish a lucrative trade in pemmican with the Hudson's Bay Company, the Northwest Company and the White settlers moving on to the rich, prairie lands. So important were they to the survival of the newcomers that when The Pemmican Proclamation of 1814 was passed, a law that required they only trade with the Hudson's Bay Company, the Metis successfully ignored it (Driben 1985:28–29).

The decline of the fur trade and the rise in the importance of agriculture decreased the importance of the Metis role in the Canadian economy. As more and more Euro-Canadian pioneers moved on to lands occupied by Native peoples the Metis too felt the pressure. This led to an attempt to establish their own country in 1869. Under the leadership of Louis Riel they claimed land in the western portion of Canada calling it "The New Nation." Their efforts failed and Riel was eventually arrested and hung for treason (Redbird 1980:225).

As other Native groups began to settle land claims and move onto reserves, the Metis found themselves to be a people without a land base. In the 1880s the Treaty Commission was established in Canada. Under its auspices some individuals obtained land scrip which could be exchanged for 240 acres. This practice was halted in 1899 and since then Metis claims have been treated on a province by province basis (Driben 1980:37; Frideres 1983:269).

Today the Metis see themselves as "a race apart from both Whites and Indians and the only race indigenous to Canada" (Redbird 1980:55). It is difficult to determine their current population size since they are no longer listed as a separate ethnic group in the Canadian census. Estimates range from 500,000 to over 1,000,000 (Frideres 1983:267). As a group the economic and social hardships they share with other Native people places them firmly within the Fourth World. However for the Metis the situation is even more complex. They do not enjoy the benefits of either side of their ancestry. They have been consistently denied access to the resources enjoyed by the greater population nor do they have the land base and funding granted to status Indians and Natives. Since 1900 their economic position has become increasingly more marginal, leaving them to be at times "the poorest of the poor." Metis legal rights are determined primarily by the provincial governments therefore the situation varies. For example, in Alberta the Metis have had a recognized land base since the establishment of the Ewing Commission in 1935 which set aside eight agricultural colonies for people meeting certain criteria. If an individual migrates from the colony they are not granted any special status. The other extreme is British Columbia where no Metis rights have ever been acknowledged (Frideres 1983:269). The Canadian federal government has maintained a confusing stance that partially grants some recognition in regard to land claims but is more determined to abolish Metis rights and claims (Frideres 1983:270).

The Metis have either been ignored or treated with contempt. They have been accused of having no culture but this claim is without foundation. They have retained group identity through their distinct history, languages, cultural activities, geographical locations and oral traditions. Like the Lumbee, their assertion that they are a Native people has been the least likely point to be considered. It must be regarded because in the face of tremendous social and economic pressure they refuse to give it up. In 1985 the Indian Act was amended to restore legal status to people who had lost it as a result of the marriage of a Native woman to a non-Native man (Indians and Northern Affairs Canada Annual Report 1985/86:8). In addition the federal government has increased funding that will allow Native people to have a greater voice in resource development. It remains to be seen if these measures mark a trend that will benefit Metis people as well.

Health

With the arrival and subsequent movement of Euro-Americans on to lands occupied by Native people there followed ubiquitous decimations of Indian populations that were the result of the arrival of smallpox, influenza, measles and other contagious diseases. The term "virgin soil epidemic" has been designated for these and it refers to diseases that are released on a population who have had no previous exposure (Crosby 1986). Appalling numbers of Native people succumbed to these diseases beginning at the time of initial European contact and continuing into the nineteenth century. For example between 1700 and 1775 the Indians of New England dropped from a population of 70,000 to one of 12,000 (Cronan 1983:88–89). Historic evidence implies similar stories for Native people throughout North America.

Why Native Americans responded so dramatically to the Old World diseases has been the topic of much scientific and historical research. One argument looks to inherent genetic weaknesses, the "racial vulnerability" hypothesis. This contends that due to lack of previous exposure, Indians did not have the biological means to fight the diseases and died in great numbers as a result (Sievers and Fisher 1981:196). Recent speculation has begun to look at explanations that do not exclude the biological but instead combine it with social factors. When a disease or wave of diseases struck a Native community virtually all individuals became ill leaving no one to adequately care for the sick. This lack of care may have caused far more people to die than would have had this not been the case (Crosby 1986:39–46). Furthermore the contagious were usually not isolated from the healthy and some people in panic, fled to other villages, spreading disease to other localities. Last, the illness and death of men and women of childbearing age meant that the individuals most responsible for subsistence, procreation and care of the very young were not able to perform their tasks. Critical phases of subsistent cycles were missed which weakened populations even further. The affect of all this was severe cultural disruption and a historical tradition of greater health risks for Native people than exists in the non-Native population. This section will explore health issues that currently are of concern to Native people throughout the United States and Canada. We will discuss alcoholism and its related ailments, diabetes and some environmental issues faced by Native communities today. In addition some of the significant measures Native people are taking to help individuals and their communities achieve a greater degree of satisfactory emotional and physical health will be examined.

If there is one disease associated with Native Americans it is alcoholism. Traditionally only a handful of groups consumed fermented beverages and there were strict social controls concerning its use. European traders introduced alcohol initially as a gift item and in time it became an object of trade. Very early on it was recognized as a "poison" by many Indian people (Price 1978:189–190). In 1802 the first laws in the United States controlling the sale of alcoholic beverages to Native people were passed and these were not repealed until 1953. Similar laws in Canada were not changed until 1963. Thus legal restraint by the dominant governments became one of the earliest means for solving the problem of Indian alcoholism. Some researchers view these legislative efforts as causes for dysfunctional drinking patterns amongst Native people today. Arguments are given that "Indians never learned to drink" and "prohibition has encouraged binge drinking episodes" (United States Department of Health and Human Services 1986:4). It should be noted, however, that these explanations implicitly assume that non-Indians know how to drink in appropriate ways. The current trend that has led to the identification of alcoholism throughout North American society should deflate these arguments. Drunken behavior is learned and may have cultural connotations as well. What is needed are non-ethnocentric definitions of what constitutes alcoholism that would be useful in cross-cultural studies and treatment programs. The standard of comparison should not be White drinking patterns. Whether the setting is an urban bar or a suburban barbecue, the potential for dysfunctional behavior exists. For example, studies in Alaska communities indicate that Whites consume far more alcohol than Alaska Natives yet it is the latter who have "the problem" since Whites drink at private functions and Natives prefer public settings (Price 1978:195).

Others have argued that there is a "racial" tendency for alcoholism among Native people (Sievers and Fisher 1981:219–221). Again this is the "racial vulnerability" argument and it has enjoyed varying degrees of popularity over the years. The studies that have been conducted comparing ethanol rates of metabolism between different populations are contradictory and inconclusive, making this argument a rather weak reed to lean upon (Sievers and Fisher 1981:222).

Lastly, alcoholism has been recognized in many indigenous societies in association with cultural disruption, economic deprivation and prolonged dependency upon the dominant government (Bill 1981). In this context it is not only a disease but a learned coping strategy for dealing with factors related to chronic poverty and dependency.

The fact remains, however, that illness and death due to alcoholism and its related problems rank tragically high in many Native communities. Alcohol directly contributes to four of the top ten causes of death for Native Americans. These are accidents, cirrhosis of the liver, homicide and suicide. It also is believed to exacerbate other conditions prevalent in Indian communities like heart disease and diabetes. In addition there is the growing problem of Fetal Alcohol Syndrome, a serious continuum of birth defects related to the use of alcohol during pregnancy (United States Department of Health and Human Services 1986:5–15). In 1983, alcohol accounted for 28.9 percent of Native deaths. Although there has been a steady decline in these figures since 1973, they are still way beyond those of the general population.

Lateral to this are the crippling affects of living as, or among, people suffering from alcoholism. While variation exists between communities, overall the suicide rate for Indians is twice that of the general population and Native people commit suicide at younger ages. Primarily it is the population under thirty-five who are at risk (Sievers and Fisher 1981:222). Correlated with high rates of alcoholism are high rates of divorce, domestic violence and single parenthood. For Indians living away from the reservation community the problems are compounded by the stress of adjustment to urban life. In addition they are at risk because Indian Health Service does not always extend treatment to those who are not federally recognized or are living too far away from the reservation to return for treatment.

It may also be said that no one is more concerned with these problems than Native people themselves. Since the 1960s copious amounts of research have been devoted to the topic of Indian alcoholism. There has also been an increased awareness on the part of governments as to the serious nature of the problem and the need for more treatment programs. Despite these facts, Native communities have not enjoyed a high rate of success. In part this may be due to the comparatively little amount of attention given to sobriety amongst Native peoples. In an important article concerning this topic, the anthropologist Bea Medicine demonstrates the need for more comprehensive studies of individual communities and the factors that encourage and support sobriety (Medicine 1982). She argues that "positive nativistic orientations" may begin to provide the social controls necessary for greater abstinence (Medicine 1982:209). Others support this view by encouraging the training and use of Native professionals and culturally relevant strategies for treatment (Trimble 1982:161–162). As a population Native Americans are young, the average age is 23 compared to 30 in the general population (IHS 1985:17). Thus there is also a need for educational programs for teenagers. One such program was started through the Minneapolis school system and met with success during its one year tenure. Wido-Ako-Da-De-Win was designed to assist Indian girls at high risk for alcoholism and teen pregnancy. Rather than use individual therapy, the young women were shown how to organize and use a social network system consisting of their peer group, their families and elder women from the community. This approach helped them to see their families as a source of support and introduced traditional rational for sexual abstinence through the informal teachings of the older women. It also extended the healing process to the family in a way that recognized and utilized Indian cultural values (Redhorse 1982). However in 1984 only 32 programs of this nature existed in the United States (Department of Health and Human Services 1986).

Another innovative approach has been adopted by the State of Minnesota. Since their were no federal guidelines concerning the hiring of traditional healers, Minnesota officials created a job description for "native practitioners" in order to encourage their use in alcohol counseling (United States Department of Health and Human Services 1986:51). Though this is not a practice that is currently being used by Indian Health Services, the agency most responsible for Indian health care.

Natives and non-Natives concerned with the affect of alcoholism invariably point towards treatment designs that are sensitive to Native value systems and promote holistic healing by recognizing that there are many positive aspects to Native cultures that should be seen as aids in the recovery process and prevention training. The most successful program to date was one which started from within the community itself. The Alkaline Lake Band of Shuswap in British Columbia have experienced nearly total sobriety on their reserve because of the efforts of a few individuals who worked from within the social structure of the community.

It has only been in the latter half of the twentieth century that diabetes has become a prevalent health problem for Native Americans. Today it is considered a major health risk. For example, the Pima Indians living on the Gila River Reservation in southern Arizona have the highest rate of diabetes in the world. In the early 1980s nearly half of the adults beyond the age of 35 were diabetic (Sievers and Fisher 1981: 198–199). While diabetes occurs at differing rates in Indian communities, overall it is about two times higher in this population than it is in the general population (IHS 1985:7). In 1981 it was the second greatest reason for the use of adult outpatient services (IHS 1985:7).

The IHS Ambulatory Nursing Service Criteria of Care lists obesity and aging as contributing factors in the development of diabetes. Other significant factors include a family history of the disease and the use of drugs and alcohol. There is also some evidence that there may be a genetic predisposition (Sievers and Fisher 1981:201–202). Historically Native people were not noted for obesity. Changes in diet and lifestyles including an overall reduction in physical activity have led to more overweight people, not unlike the general population. Because of the importance of diet there has been some attempt on the part of the United States federal government to include the health value of native foods in publications concerning maintenance of diabetes (United States Department of Health and Human Services 1985). It is ironic, however, that the commodity foods distributed to low income people by the U.S. government, some of whom are Indians, are not the most appropriate selections for people at high risk for diabetes. These foods promote a diet high in sodium, preservatives, simple carbohydrates and low in fiber. The same government must then turn around and fund treatment and educational programs concerning health and diet in Native communities.

Diabetes is a serious disease. Its presence in Native communities has resulted in an increase of blindness, kidney disease, gangrene, birth defects and spontaneous abortions. While some reservations have developed educational programs to increase awareness, it is still a health problem that remains to be solved.

With the passage of the Indian Self-Determination and Education Assistance Act (P.L. 93–638) there has been an increasing trend towards the number of tribes taking control of activities and services related to health. There are now six hospitals, 70 health centers and 262 clinics and health stations operated by tribes in the United States (United States Department of Health and Human Services 1988:11). In recent years within the Indian Health Service more jobs are being filled by Native people but they are still one of the most under-represented groups in the health care industry (IHS 1985:11). One quarter of all professional nurses employed by Indian Health Services are Natives but according to the 1980 Census Report only 29 Native people were employed in the "health diagnosing occupations". While it is ultimately positive that the trend is towards increased Indian participation in the health care of Native people, this is only the beginning if Indians, non-Indians and the governments of Canada and the United States are to make the strides necessary to ensure that the health of Native Americans takes on the overall characteristics of the general population.

Poor health due to environmental problems is a topic that may span a wide range. When those concerned with Native health problems speak of environmental health they are primarily referring to communicable diseases, availability of potable water and sewage disposal facilities as well as overall sanitary ordinances and codes. In 1959 the Indian Sanitation Facilities Act was passed to alleviate the problems of unclean water and lack of sanitary disposal facilities within reservation communities. By the early 1980s 136,300 residences had been provided with services. Yet according to the 1980 Census Data over 25 percent of all Indian homes were still without proper facilities.

We will now move to another area of environmental concern that is not exclusively a Native problem but the adverse affects of environmental degradation have the potential to be far more devastating to Indian communities where resources of all types are less available. As an example the case of the Grassy Narrows Reserve will be highlighted.

Grassy Narrows is a small Ojibwa community in Northern Ontario with a population of about 500 people. Like many reserves and reservations in Canada and the United States it has problems with alcoholism, suicide, homicide and domestic violence. What separates this community is not the kinds of problems it has but the dramatically higher incidence for these and other social problems, higher than the general population and higher than other Native communities. Another feature to this story is that until the late 1960s this was not the case for this community. The first problem concerned the relocation of the reserve from its traditional grounds to a new reserve on the English-Wabigoon River systems. Down river from the new reserve was a chloro-alkali plant that dumped 40,000 pounds of mercury into the environment between 1962 and 1975. Over 20,000 pounds of mercury found its way into the river system. Despite the eventual discontinuation of this practice, to date many of the people of Grassy Narrows are likely suffering from the physical effects of mercury poisoning and definitely from the emotional devastation of living in a community that has been poisoned. In addition to the lost revenue from the fishing economy, the fear of waiting for the effects of mercury poisoning, which can take years to show up, has created a community "that appears to be bent on its own destruction" (Shkilnyk 1985:231). In Grassy Narrows the likelihood is that three out of every four people will die a violent death, many by their own hand. The Canadian government was painfully slow in its response to the needs of this community. The mercury poisoning was discovered in 1970 and it was not until November 1985 that an agreement between the federal government, Ontario and other participants in the problem and the Islington and Grassy Narrows Bands was researched. It was agreed that $16,667,000 would be paid in compensation and $2 million have been set aside for individual claims (Indian and Northern Affairs Canada 1985–1986). Perhaps in response to the plight of Grassy Narrows, the Canadian government has increased the ability of Native peoples to have authority in the alterations of their environments. In 1984 $2 million was allocated to Native groups around Canada to allow them to "respond to projects with potential or existing socioeconomic and/or environmental impacts" (Indian and Northern Affairs Canada 1985–1986). This was to be a three-year program but what may be needed are permanent programs and effective legislation.

Environmental concerns have been at the forefront in the United States for the last twenty years. Indeed, the environmentalist lobby is one of the most powerful interest groups in Washington D.C. (Borelli 1987). The passage of the National Environmental Policy Act and individual states' environmental legislation has not ensured that pollution and environmental degradation will not occur but it gives people in this country greater control concerning abuses. Included in the National Environmental Policy Act are specific guidelines for Indian tribes and reservations that provide some safety measures for Native people.

In summation we can say that nowhere are the issues centering around Native health, education and economic well-being of more concern than in the Native communities themselves. The great strides that Native people in the United States and Canada have made in recent years are primarily due to the more aggressive role Native people have taken in seeing that effective legislation is passed that adequately addresses the issues that are of concern to Native people. While much has been done there still remains much to do. We will see many of the issues just discussed remain of concern well into the twenty-first century.

SUGGESTED READINGS

Barsh, Russel L. and James Youngblood Henderson
1980   The Road. University of California Press, Berkeley.

Berger, Thomas R.
1985   Village Journey: The Report of the Alaska Native Review Commission. Hill and Wang, New York.

Blu, Karen I.
1980   The Lumbee Problem: The Making of an American Indian Community. Cambridge Studies in Cultural Systems, Cambridge University Press.

Brody, Hugh
1982   Maps and Dreams. Pantheon Books, New York.

Cronan, William
1983   Changes in the Land: Indians, Colonists and the Ecology of New England. Hill and Wang, New York.

Dyck, Noel
1985   Indigenous Peoples and the Nation State: Fourth World Politics in Canada, Australia and Norway. Social and Economic Papers No. 14, Institute of Social and Economic Research, Memorial University of Newfoundland, St. John's.

Frideres, James S.
1983   Native People in Canada: Contemporary Conflicts. Prentice Hall Canada, Inc., Scarborough.

Jorgensen, Joseph G.
1978   A Century of Political Economic Effects on American Indian Society. The Journal of Ethnic Studies, Vol. 6, No. 3, pp. 1–82.

Manson, Spero M., ed.
1982   New Directions in Prevention Among American Indian and Alaska Native Communities. National Center for American Indian and Alaska Native Mental Health Research. Oregon Health Sciences University, Portland.

Shkilnyk, Anastasia M.
1985   A Poison Stronger Than Love: The Destruction of an Ojibwa Community. Yale University Press, New Haven.

White, Richard
1983   The Roots of Dependency: Subsistence, Environment and Social Change Among the Choctaws, Pawnees, and Navajos. University of Nebraska Press, Lincoln.

REFERENCES

Bill, Willard
1981   Curriculum Research for American Indian Education: Alcohol and the American Indian. *In* American Indian Issues in Higher Education. American Indian Studies Center, University of California, Los Angeles.

Blu, Karen I.
1980   The Lumbee Problem: The Making of an American Indian People. Cambridge Studies in Cultural Systems, Cambridge University Press.

Borrelli, Peter
1987   Environmentalism at a Crossroads. The Amicus Journal, Summer.

Boxberger, Daniel L.
1988 "In and Out of the Labor Force: The Lummi Indians and the Development of the Commercial Salmon Fishery of North Puget Sound." Ethnohistory, Vol. 35, No. 2, pp. 161–190.
1989 To Fish in Common: The Ethnohistory of Lummi Indian Salmon Fishing. University of Nebraska Press, Lincoln.

Brown, Anthony D. and Kenneth Hernasy
1983 The Impact of Culture on the Health of American Indian Children. In the Psychosocial Development of Minority Group Children, Gloria Johnson Powell, et al., eds. Brunn/Mazel Inc., New York.

Cronan, William
1983 Changes in the Land: Indians, Colonists and the Ecology of New England. Hill and Wang, New York.

Crosby, Alfred W.
1986 "Virgin Soil Epidemics as a Factor in the Aboriginal Depopulation in America. In The American Indian Past and Present, Roger L. Nichols, ed. Alfred A. Knopf, New York.

Driben, Paul
1985 We are Metis: The Ethnography of a Halfbreed Community in Northern Alberta. AMS Press, New York.

Frideres, James S.
1983 Native People in Canada: Contemporary Conflicts. Prentice-Hall Canada, Inc., Scarborough.

Grobsmith, Elizabeth S.
1981 Lakota of the Rosebud: A Contemporary Ethnography. Holt, Rhinehart and Winston, New York.

Indian and Northern Affairs Canada
1985/6 Annual Report. Department of Indian and Northern Affairs, Ottawa.

Jorgensen, Joseph G.
1978 "A Century of Political Economic Effects on American Indian Society." The Journal of Ethnic Studies, Vol. 6, No. 3, pp. 1–82.

Knight, Rolf
1978 Indians at Work: An Informal History of Native Labour in British Columbia, 1858–1930. New Star Books, Vancouver.

Medicine, Bea
1982 New Roads to Coping: Siouan Sobriety. In New Directions in Prevention Among American Indian and Alaska Native Communities. Spero M. Manson, ed. National Center for American Indian and Alaska Native Mental Health Research, Oregon Health Sciences University, Portland.

Pearse, Peter H.
1982 Turning the Tide: A New Policy for Canada's Pacific Fisheries. Final Report of the Commissioner on Pacific Fisheries Policy, Department of Fisheries and Oceans, Vancouver.

Price, John A.
1978 Native Studies: American and Canadian Indians. McGraw-Hill, New York.

Redbird, Duke
1980 We are Metis: A Metis View of the Development of a Native Canadian People. Ontario Metis and Non-Status Indian Association, Ottawa.

Redhorse, John
1982 American Indian Mental Health: A Primary Prevention Strategy. In New Directions in Prevention Among American Indian and Alaska Native Communities, Spero M. Manson, ed. National Center for American Indian and Alaska Native Mental Health Research, Oregon Health Sciences University, Portland.

Redhorse, Yvonne
1982 A Cultural Network Model: Perspectives for Adolescent Services and Para-Professional Training. In New Directions in Prevention Among American Indian and Alaska Native Communities, Spero M.

Manson, ed. National Center for American Indian and Alaska Native Mental Health Research, Oregon Health Sciences University, Portland.

Shkilnyk, Anastasia M.
1985   A Poison Stronger Than Love: The Destruction of an Ojibwa Community. Yale University Press, New Haven.

Sievers, Maurice L. and Jeffrey R. Fisher
1981   Diseases in North American Indians. *In* Biocultural Aspects of Disease. H. R. Rothschild, ed., Academic Press, New York.

Trimble, Joseph E.
1982   American Indian Mental Health and the Role of Training for Prevention. *In* New Directions in Prevention Among American Indian and Alaska Native Communities, Spero M. Manson, ed., National Center for American Indian and Alaska Native Health Research, Oregon Health Sciences University, Portland.

United States Department of Health and Human Services (Indian Health Service Publications)
1985   A Comprehensive Health Care Program for American Indians and Alaska Natives.
1985   Plains Indian Diet Handbook.
1986   Contract Health Services: A Guide to Utilization.
1986   Indian Health Service/Substance Abuse Prevention Initiative: Background, Plenary Session and Action Plan.
1988   Allocation of Resources in the Indian Health Service: A Handbook on the Resource Allocation Methodology (RAM).